T0215690

Lecture Notes in Business Information Processing 385

More information about this series at http://www.springer.com/series/7911

Fabiano Dalpiaz · Jelena Zdravkovic ·
Pericles Loucopoulos (Eds.)

Research Challenges in Information Science

14th International Conference, RCIS 2020
Limassol, Cyprus, September 23–25, 2020
Proceedings

 Springer

Editors
Fabiano Dalpiaz (iD)
Utrecht University
Utrecht, The Netherlands

Jelena Zdravkovic (iD)
Stockholm University
Kista, Sweden

Pericles Loucopoulos (iD)
The Institute of Digital Innovation
and Research
Dublin, Ireland

ISSN 1865-1348   ISSN 1865-1356 (electronic)
Lecture Notes in Business Information Processing
ISBN 978-3-030-50315-4   ISBN 978-3-030-50316-1 (eBook)
https://doi.org/10.1007/978-3-030-50316-1

This Springer imprint is published by the registered company Springer Nature Switzerland AG
The registered company address is: Gewerbestrasse 11, 6330 Cham, Switzerland

Editors
Fabiano Dalpiaz 🔟
Utrecht University
Utrecht, The Netherlands

Jelena Zdravkovic 🔟
Stockholm University
Kista, Sweden

Pericles Loucopoulos 🔟
The Institute of Digital Innovation
and Research
Dublin, Ireland

ISSN 1865-1348   ISSN 1865-1356   (electronic)
Lecture Notes in Business Information Processing
ISBN 978-3-030-50315-4   ISBN 978-3-030-50316-1   (eBook)
https://doi.org/10.1007/978-3-030-50316-1

This Springer imprint is published by the registered company Springer Nature Switzerland AG
The registered company address is: Gewerbestrasse 11, 6330 Cham, Switzerland

Fabiano Dalpiaz · Jelena Zdravkovic ·
Pericles Loucopoulos (Eds.)

Research Challenges
in Information Science

14th International Conference, RCIS 2020
Limassol, Cyprus, September 23–25, 2020
Proceedings

 Springer

Preface

It is our great pleasure to welcome you to the proceedings of the 14th International Conference on Research Challenges in Information Science (RCIS 2020). RCIS brings together scientists, researchers, engineers, and practitioners from the whole spectrum of information science and provides opportunities for knowledge sharing and dissemination. The first edition of RCIS was held in 2007 in Ouarzazate, Morocco. Over the years, the various instances of RCIS were hosted in Morocco, France, Spain, the UK, Greece, and Belgium.

RCIS 2020 took place in Limassol, Cyprus, during September 23–25, 2020. The conference was originally scheduled for May 2020, but the Organizing Committee was forced to postpone the conference due to the outbreak of the COVID-19 pandemic. The scope of RCIS 2020 is summarized by the following eight thematic areas: (i) information Systems and their engineering, (ii) user-oriented approaches, (iii) data and information management, (iv) business process management, (v) domain-specific information systems engineering, (vi) data science, (vii) information infrastructures, and (viii) reflective research and practice.

Within the variety of information science areas and domains, we are assisting a dramatic boost in the role of artificial intelligence (AI) techniques. Clear examples of AI technologies that are applied to data and information are machine learning (including deep learning with neural networks), autonomous and self-adaptive systems (such as autonomous cars or the automation in Industry 4.0), and natural language processing. To emphasize this undeniable trend, the theme of RCIS 2020 was "Information Science in the Days of Artificial Intelligence."

Our two keynote speakers provided their perspectives on the role of AI in information science. Hajo Reijers (Utrecht University, The Netherlands) gave a keynote entitled "The Future of Work Automation," which focused on how human work can be analyzed and interpreted through AI techniques, in order to assess whether it makes sense to automate human work. Nana Tintarev (Delft University of Technology, The Netherlands), in her keynote entitled "Explainable AI is not yet understandable AI," investigated how advice-giving systems should be able to explain themselves, in order to avoid mismatches between the system representation of the advice and the representation that is assumed by the user. These interesting perspectives have been further elaborated in a plenary panel discussion.

We are pleased to present this volume comprising the RCIS 2020 proceedings. This is the first edition of RCIS that has proceedings published by Springer through their *Lecture Notes in Business Information Processing* (LNBIP) series. These proceedings include the papers in all the tracks of RCIS 2020, and therefore constitute a comprehensive account on the conference.

The main track received 136 abstracts, which materialized into 118 submissions. The program co-chairs desk rejected 12 papers which were out of scope, resulting in 106 papers that were peer reviewed. Each paper was reviewed by at least three Program Committee members; these reviews served to initiate an online discussion moderated by one Program Board member, who concluded the discussion by writing a meta-review and a suggestion for full acceptance, conditional acceptance with gate-keeping, invitation for poster track, or rejection. The program co-chairs discussed each paper and took the final decisions, largely in line with the Program Board advice, leading to 29 accepted papers in the main track. The breakdown by category is as follows:

- Technical solution: 15 accepted out of 58 reviewed
- Scientific evaluation: 5 out of 21
- Industrial experience: 6 out of 10
- Work in progress: 3 out of 17

The Posters & Demos track, chaired by Elena Kornyshova and Marcela Ruiz, attracted 8 submissions, 5 of which were accepted. Furthermore, 7 additional papers were accepted from those papers invited from the main conference track, leading to a total of 12 posters and demos. The Doctoral Consortium track, chaired by Raian Ali and Sergio España, attracted 5 submissions, 4 of which were accepted. The Tutorials track, chaired by Estefanía Serral and José Ignacio Panach, received 5 proposals, 3 of which were accepted.

To foster the discussion about innovative research projects in information science, we launched the Research Projects RCIS track, organized by the Posters & Demos co-chairs, aiming at short communications on projects such as those funded by the EU Commission via H2020 or ERC projects, or by national research councils. The track received 10 submissions, out of which 8 were accepted.

RCIS 2020 would not have been possible without the engagement and support of many individuals. As editors of this volume, we would like to thank the RCIS Steering Committee members for their availability and guidance. We are grateful to the members of the Program Board and of the Program Committee, and to the additional reviewers for their timely and thorough reviews of the submissions and for their efforts in the online discussions. A special thank you goes to those of them who acted as gatekeepers for the conditionally accepted papers. We would like to thank our social media chair Fatma Başak Aydemir, who guaranteed visibility through Twitter. We are deeply indebted to the George A. Papadopoulos, the general co-chair responsible for the local organization, for his continuous logistics and operation efforts, his extensive advertising activities, his decisive role in coping with the rescheduling, and his initial push regarding the Research Projects track. Finally, we would like to thank Christine Reiss, Ralf Gerstner, and Alfred Hofmann from Springer for welcoming RCIS to their LNBIP series and for assisting in the production of these proceedings.

We believe that this volume provides a comprehensive account on the conversations that took place at the RCIS 2020 conference. We hope you will find innovative and surprising research results and research challenges that can be used for the construction of better information systems that serve our society.

September 2020

Fabiano Dalpiaz
Jelena Zdravkovic
Pericles Loucopoulos

Organization

General Chairs

George Papadopoulos   University of Cyprus, Cyprus
Pericles Loucopoulos   Institute of Digital Innovation & Research, Ireland

Program Committee Chairs

Fabiano Dalpiaz   Utrecht University, The Netherlands
Jelena Zdravkovic   Stockholm University, Sweden

Posters and Demos Chairs

Elena Kornyshova   Conservatoire National des Arts et Métiers, France
Marcela Ruiz   Zurich University of Applied Sciences, Switzerland

Doctoral Consortium Chairs

Raian Ali   Hamad Bin Khalifa University, Qatar
Sergio España   Utrecht University, The Netherlands

Tutorial Chairs

Estefanía Serral   Katholieke Universiteit Leuven, Belgium
Ignacio Panach   Universitat de València, Spain

Social Media Chair

Fatma Başak Aydemir   Boğaziçi University, Turkey

Steering Committee

Saïd Assar   Institut Mines-Telecom Business School, France
Marko Bajec   University of Ljubljana, Slovenia
Pericles Loucopoulos   Institute of Digital Innovation & Research, Ireland
Haralambos Mouratidis   University of Brighton, UK
Selmin Nurcan   Université Paris 1 Panthéon-Sorbonne, France
Oscar Pastor   Universitat Politècnica de València, Spain
Jolita Ralyté   University of Geneva, Switzerland
Colette Rolland   Université Paris 1 Panthéon-Sorbonne, France

Program Board

Raian Ali	Hamad Bin Khalifa University, Qatar
Saïd Assar	Institut Mines-Telecom Business School, France
Marko Bajec	University of Ljubljana, Slovenia
Xavier Franch	Polytechnic University of Catalunya, Spain
Jennifer Horkoff	University of Gothenburg, Sweden
Evangelia Kavakli	University of the Aegean, Greece
Haralambos Mouratidis	University of Brighton, UK
Selmin Nurcan	Université Paris 1 Panthéon-Sorbonne, France
Andreas Opdahl	University of Bergen, Norway
Oscar Pastor	Universitat Politènica de València, Spain
Jolita Ralyté	University of Geneva, Switzerland
Colette Rolland	Université Paris 1 Panthéon-Sorbonne, France
Camille Salinesi	Université Paris 1 Panthéon-Sorbonne, France
Monique Snoeks	Katholieke Universiteit Leuven, Belgium

Main Track Program Committee

Tareq Al-Moslmi	University of Bergen, Norway
Nour Ali	Brunel University, UK
Carina Alves	Federal University of Pernambuco, Brazil
Daniel Amyot	University of Ottawa, Canada
Joao Araujo	Universidade NOVA de Lisboa, Portugal
Fatma Başak Aydemir	Boğaziçi University, Turkey
Youcef Baghdadi	Sultan Qaboos University, Oman
Ilia Bider	Stockholm University, Sweden
Dominik Bork	University of Vienna, Austria
Cristina Cabanillas	Vienna University of Economics and Business, Austria
Mario Cortes-Cornax	University of Grenoble Alpes, France
Maya Daneva	University of Twente, The Netherlands
Adela Del Río Ortega	University of Seville, Spain
Rebecca Deneckere	Université Paris 1 Panthéon-Sorbonne, France
Christos Doulkeridis	University of Piraeus, Greece
Sophie Dupuy-Chessa	University of Grenoble Alpes, France
Hans-Georg Fill	University of Fribourg, Switzerland
Andrew Fish	University of Brighton, UK
Agnès Front	University of Grenoble Alpes, France
Mohamad Gharib	University of Florence, Italy
Paolo Giorgini	University of Trento, Italy
Cesar Gonzalez-Perez	Spanish National Research Council, Spain
Truong Ho Quang	Gothenburg University and Chalmers University of Technology, Sweden
Mirjana Ivanovic	University of Novi Sad, Serbia
Amin Jalali	Stockholm University, Sweden
Haruhiko Kaiya	Shinshu University, Japan

Posters and Demos Program Committee

Raian Ali	Hamad Bin Khalifa University, Qatar
Claudia Ayala	Technical University of Catalunya, Spain
Fatma Başak Aydemir	Boğaziçi University, Turkey
Judith Barrios	University Los Andes, Venezuela
Veronica Burriel	Utrecht University, The Netherlands
Cinzia Cappiello	Politecnico di Milano, Italy
Jose Luis De La Vara	Universidad de Castilla la Mancha, Spain
Elena Viorica Epure	Deezer R&D, France
Renata Guizardi	Universidade Federal do Espírito Santo, Brazil
Mohamad Kassab	Pennsylvania State University, USA
Abdelaziz Khadraoui	Geneva University, Switzerland
Manuele Kirsch-Pinheiro	Université Paris 1 Panthéon-Sorbonne, France
Emanuele Laurenzi	Fachhochschule Nordwestschweiz, Switzerland
Dejan Lavbič	University of Ljubljana, Slovenia
Francisca Perez	University of San Jorge, Spain
Iris Reihnartz Berger	University of Haifa, Israel
Patricia Martin Rodilla	Incipit, Spain
Estefanía Serral	Katholieke Universiteit Leuven, Belgium
Jürgen Spielberger	Zurich University of Applied Sciences, Switzerland
Gianluigi Viscusi	École Polytechnique Fédérale de Lausanne, Switzerland

Doctoral Consortium Program Committee

Nour Ali	Brunel University, UK
Dena Al-Thani	Hamad Bin Khalifa University, Qatar
Rami Bahsoon	University of Birmingham, UK
Nelly Condori-Fernandez	Universidade de Coruña, Spain
Karl Cox	Brighton University, UK
Maya Daneva	University of Twente, The Netherlands
Lin Li	Wuhan University of Technology, China
Lin Liu	Tsinghua University, China
John McAlaney	Bournemouth University, UK
Cees J. H. Midden	Eindhoven University of Technology, The Netherlands
Ignacio Panach	Universitat de València, Spain
Marwa Qaraqe	Hamad Bin Khalifa University, Qatar
Xiaohui Tao	University of Southern Queensland, Australia
Guandong Xu	University of Technology Sydney, Australia

Additional Reviewers

Simone Agostinelli
Amal Ahmed Anda
Sybille Caffiau
Davide Dell'Anna
Irene Bedilia Estrada Torres
Abed Alhakim Freihat
Marc Gallofré Ocaña
João Galvão
Mahdi Ghasemi
Enyo Gonçalves
Catarina Gralha
Faruk Hasic
Jameleddine Hassine
Martin Henkel
Felix Härer

Dimitris Kavroudakis
Angeliki Kitsiou
Blagovesta Kostova
Rena Lavranou
Francesco Leotta
Katerina Mavroeidi
Christian Muck
Marc Oriol Hilari
Ioannis Paspatis
Argyri Pattakou
João Pimentel
Carla Silva
Karim Sultan
Jan Martijn van der Werf

Abstracts of Invited Talks

Explainable AI is Not Yet Understandable AI

Nava Tintarev

TU Delft, The Netherlands
n.tintarev@tudelft.nl

Some computer systems operate as artificial advice givers: they propose and evaluate options while involving their human users in the decision making process [8]. For example, a regulator of waterways may use a decision support system to decide which boats to check for legal infringements, a concerned citizen might used a system to find reliable information about a new virus, or an employer might be use an artificial advice giver to chose between potential candidates. This keynote focuses specifically on explanations for *recommender systems*. Recommender systems such as Amazon, offer users recommendations, or suggestions of items to try or buy. Recommender systems can be categorized as filtering and ranking algorithms, which result in the increase in the prominence of some information, and other information (e.g., low rank or low confidence recommendations) not being shown to people.

For explanations of recommender systems to be useful, they need to be able to justify the recommendations in a *human-understandable* way. This creates a necessity for techniques for automatic generation of satisfactory explanations that are *intelligible* for users interacting with the system[1].

"*Interpretability*" has been qualified as the degree to which a human can understand the cause of a decision [4]. However, understanding is rarely an end-goal in itself. Pragmatically, it is more useful to operationalize the effectiveness of explanations in terms of a specific notion of usefulness or **explanatory goals** such as improved decision support or user trust [7]. One aspect of intelligibility of an explainable system (often cited for domains such as health) is the ability for users to accurately identify, or correct, an error made by the system. In that case it may be preferable to generate explanations that induce appropriate levels of reliance (in contrast to over- or under-reliance) [9], supporting the user in discarding recommendations when the system is incorrect, but also accepting correct recommendations. The domain affects not only the overall cost of an error, but the cost of a specific type of error (e.g., a false negative might be more harmful than a false positive for a terminal illness). In a domain such as news, a different goal might be more suitable, such as explanations that facilitate users' epistemic goals (e.g., broadening their knowledge within a topic) [6].

It is sometimes erroneously assumed that explanations need to be completely transparent with regard to the underlying algorithmic mechanisms. However, a transparent explanation is not necessary understandable to an end-user. [1] distinguishes

---

[1] NWO Artificial Intelligence Research Agenda for the Netherlands (AIREA-NL), https://www.nwo.nl/en/news-and-events/news/2019/11/first-national-research-agenda-for-artificial-intelligence.html, released in November 2019.

between explanation and justification in the following way: *"a justification explains why a decision is a good one, without explaining exactly how it was made."* That is, a user-centered explanation may not be fully transparent, but still useful if it fulfills an explanatory goal.

Assessing the effect of explanations on given explanatory goals requires systematic user-centered evaluation. To understand which explanation (e.g., with regard to modality, degree of interactivity, level of detail, and concrete presentational choices) for explanations, it is vital to identify which requirements are placed by *individual characteristics*, the *domain*, as well as the *context* in which the explanations are given. For example, in the music recommender domain, personal characteristics such as domain expertise and visual memory have been found to influence explanation effectiveness [3]. Further, having additional transparency and control for context such as location, activity, weather, and mood has been found to lead to higher perceived quality and did not increase cognitive load for music recommendations [2]. Other contextual factors, such as group dynamics, create additional requirements on explanations, such as balancing privacy and transparency [5].

References

1. Biran, O., Cotton, C.: Explanation and justification in machine learning: a survey. In: IJCAI-17 Workshop on Explainable AI (XAI), vol. 8 (2017)
2. Jin, Y., Htun, N.N., Tintarev, N., Verbert, K.: Contextplay: evaluating user control for context-aware music recommendation. In: Proceedings of the 27th ACM Conference on User Modeling, Adaptation and Personalization, pp. 294–302 (2019)
3. Jin, Y., Tintarev, N., Htun, N.N., Verbert, K.: Effects of personal characteristics in control-oriented user interfaces for music recommender systems. User Modeling and User-Adapted Interaction pp. 1–51 (2019)
4. Miller, T.: Explanation in artificial intelligence: insights from the social sciences. Artif. Intell. **267**, 1–38 (2019)
5. Najafian, S., Inel, O., Tintarev, N.: Someone really wanted that song but it was not me!: evaluating which information to disclose in explanations for group recommendations. In: 25th International Conference on Intelligent User Interfaces Companion, IUI 2020, Cagliari, Italy, 17–20 March 2020, pp. 85–86. ACM (2020)
6. Sullivan, E., et al.: Reading news with a purpose: explaining user profiles for self-actualization. In: Adjunct Publication of the 27th Conference on User Modeling, Adaptation and Personalization, pp. 241–245 (2019)
7. Tintarev, N., Masthoff, J.: Explaining recommendations: design and evaluation. In: Ricci, F., Rokach, L., Shapira, B. (eds.) Recommender Systems Handbook, pp. 353–382. Springer, Boston. Springer (2015). https://doi.org/10.1007/978-1-4899-7637-6_10
8. Tintarev, N., O'Donovan, J., Felfernig, A.: Introduction to the special issue on human interaction with artificial advice givers. ACM Trans.. Interact. Intell. Syst. (TiiS) **6**(4), 1–12 (2016)
9. Yang, F., Huang, Z., Scholtz, J., Arendt, D.L.: How do visual explanations foster end users' appropriate trust in machine learning? In: Proceedings of the 25th International Conference on Intelligent User Interfaces, IUI 2020, pp. 189–201. Association for Computing Machinery, New York (2020)

The Future of Work Automation

Hajo A. Reijers🆔

Utrecht University, Princetonplein 5, 3584 CC Utrecht,
The Netherlands
h.a.reijers@uu.nl

Due to the advent of Information Technology (IT), our perception of what "work" is evolves. Tasks that were until recently considered to be the exclusive domain of humans are now carried out by robots or algorithms. Examples are plentiful: algorithms are more accurate for some medical diagnosis tasks than medical specialists, simple journalistic texts can be automatically generated, and personal financial advice can be provided by robots to a certain extent [1].

There is a rich debate on the question whether humans will become obsolete in the working place. To some, the real question is *when* this will happen [2]. Others emphasize that what we see happening is a long process of the automation of human *tasks*, while there is still an ongoing growth of human *jobs* [3].

There is another perspective on the relationship between IT and work. IT is not only a means to automate work; it can also be an enabler to better *understand* human work itself.

This can be seen in the following way. Increasingly, human work is less about physical labor and more about cognitive action. Cognition centers around the processing of data. Workers receive, retrieve, interpret, enrich, create, send, and store data. The occurrence of such data actions manifest themselves as *human event data* in logs in all types of records. Very often, it is even possible to determine the exact data that was retrieved or stored during such events.

The capabilities of IT to process large amounts of data and the development of a range of data analysis algorithms all of a sudden make human event data of much interest. Through approaches such a process mining [4] and task mining [5], we are able to find out all kinds of properties of human work, such as their volume, timing aspects, repetitive patterns, etc.

A new step, which now lies ahead of us, is to use our understanding of human work to rethink it. Can we identify the parts of human work that are simple and perhaps boring, so that we can automate these to relieve human workers from it? Can we also identify the demanding parts of human work, so that we can think of better ways to enable workers carrying out those parts, for example by providing them with better data? Could we even do this all automatically, so that we embark on a continuous process of work improvement?

Far-fetched as these questions may seem now, signs can be observed that it becomes feasible to start answering them. Those signs can be observed in new technologies, such as Robotic Process Automation [6], and during running research projects that aim at understanding human work. We may very well be entering a new era for work automation where the focus shifts from replacing humans by computers to design work that gracefully combines the skills of humans and computers.

References

1. Frey, C.B., Osborne, M.: The future of employment: How susceptible are jobs to computerisation. Technol. Forecast. Soc. Chang. **114**, 254–280 (2017)
2. "What happens when our computers get smarter than we are?" https://bit.ly/2W9ny8K. Accessed 30 Apr 2020
3. "Machine learning will redesign, not replace, work" https://bit.ly/3bRkDs5. Accessed 30 Apr 2020
4. Van der Aalst, W.M.P.: Process Mining – Data Science in Action, 2nd edn. Springer, Berlin (2016). https://doi.org/10.1007/978-3-662-49851-4
5. Reinkemeyer, L.: Business view: towards a digital enabled organization. In: Reinkemeyer, L. (eds.) Process Mining in Action, pp. 197–206. Springer, Cham (2020). https://doi.org/10.1007/978-3-030-40172-6_22
6. Syed, R., et al.: Robotic process automation: contemporary themes and challenges. Comput. Ind. **115**, 103162 (2020)

Contents

Data Analytics and Business Intelligence

Toward Becoming a Data-Driven Organization: Challenges and Benefits   3
  Richard Berntsson Svensson and Maryam Taghavianfar

A Big Data Conceptual Model to Improve Quality of Business Analytics. . . .   20
  Grace Park, Lawrence Chung, Haan Johng, Vijayan Sugumaran,
  Sooyong Park, Liping Zhao, and Sam Supakkul

How to Measure Influence in Social Networks?   38
  Ana Carolina Ribeiro, Bruno Azevedo, Jorge Oliveira e Sá,
  and Ana Alice Baptista

Developing a Real-Time Traffic Reporting and Forecasting
Back-End System   58
  Theodoros Toliopoulos, Nikodimos Nikolaidis,
  Anna-Valentini Michailidou, Andreas Seitaridis, Anastasios Gounaris,
  Nick Bassiliades, Apostolos Georgiadis, and Fotis Liotopoulos

IoT Analytics Architectures: Challenges, Solution Proposals
and Future Research Directions.   76
  Theo Zschörnig, Robert Wehlitz, and Bogdan Franczyk

Digital Enterprise and Technologies

Structural Coupling, Strategy and Fractal Enterprise Modeling   95
  Ilia Bider

Systems-Thinking Heuristics for the Reconciliation of Methodologies
for Design and Analysis for Information Systems Engineering   112
  Blagovesta Kostova, Irina Rychkova, Andrey Naumenko, Gil Regev,
  and Alain Wegmann

An Ontology of IS Design Science Research Artefacts.   129
  Hans Weigand, Paul Johannesson, and Birger Andersson

Evolution of Enterprise Architecture for Intelligent Digital Systems.   145
  Alfred Zimmermann, Rainer Schmidt, Dierk Jugel, and Michael Möhring

Human Factors in Information Systems

Online Peer Support Groups for Behavior Change:
Moderation Requirements.   157
    Manal Aldhayan, Mohammad Naiseh, John McAlaney, and Raian Ali

User-Experience in Business Intelligence - A Quality Construct
and Model to Design Supportive BI Dashboards.   174
    Corentin Burnay, Sarah Bouraga, Stéphane Faulkner, and Ivan Jureta

FINESSE: Fair Incentives for Enterprise Employees   191
    Soumi Chattopadhyay, Rahul Ghosh, Ansuman Banerjee,
    Avantika Gupta, and Arpit Jain

Explainable Recommendations in Intelligent Systems: Delivery Methods,
Modalities and Risks.   212
    Mohammad Naiseh, Nan Jiang, Jianbing Ma, and Raian Ali

Participation in Hackathons: A Multi-methods View on Motivators,
Demotivators and Citizen Participation.   229
    Anthony Simonofski, Victor Amaral de Sousa, Antoine Clarinval,
    and Benoît Vanderose

Information Systems Development and Testing

A Systematic Literature Review of Blockchain-Enabled Smart Contracts:
Platforms, Languages, Consensus, Applications and Choice Criteria   249
    Samya Dhaiouir and Saïd Assar

Scriptless Testing at the GUI Level in an Industrial Setting   267
    Hatim Chahim, Mehmet Duran, Tanja E. J. Vos, Pekka Aho,
    and Nelly Condori Fernandez

Improving Performance and Scalability of Model-Driven Generated Web
Applications: An Experience Report   285
    Gioele Moretti, Marcela Ruiz, and Jürgen Spielberger

TesCaV: An Approach for Learning Model-Based Testing and Coverage
in Practice   302
    Beatriz Marín, Sofía Alarcón, Giovanni Giachetti, and Monique Snoeck

Machine Learning and Text Processing

Automatic Classification Rules for Anomaly Detection in Time-Series.   321
    Ines Ben Kraiem, Faiza Ghozzi, Andre Peninou,
    Geoffrey Roman-Jimenez, and Olivier Teste

Text Embeddings for Retrieval from a Large Knowledge Base   338
  Tolgahan Cakaloglu, Christian Szegedy, and Xiaowei Xu

Predicting Unemployment with Machine Learning Based on Registry Data . . .   352
  Markus Viljanen and Tapio Pahikkala

Anomaly Detection on Data Streams – A LSTM's Diary   369
  Christoph Augenstein and Bogdan Franczyk

Process Mining, Discovery, and Simulation

Discovering Business Process Simulation Models in the Presence
of Multitasking   381
  Bedilia Estrada-Torres, Manuel Camargo, Marlon Dumas,
  and Maksym Yerokhin

TLKC-Privacy Model for Process Mining   398
  Majid Rafiei, Miriam Wagner, and Wil M. P. van der Aalst

Incremental Discovery of Hierarchical Process Models   417
  Daniel Schuster, Sebastiaan J. van Zelst, and Wil M. P. van der Aalst

Security and Privacy

Ontology Evolution in the Context of Model-Based Secure
Software Engineering   437
  Jens Bürger, Timo Kehrer, and Jan Jürjens

Blockchain-Based Personal Health Records for Patients' Empowerment   455
  Omar El Rifai, Maelle Biotteau, Xavier de Boissezon, Imen Megdiche,
  Franck Ravat, and Olivier Teste

COPri - A Core Ontology for Privacy Requirements Engineering   472
  Mohamad Gharib, John Mylopoulos, and Paolo Giorgini

Privacy Preserving Real-Time Video Stream Change Detection
Based on the Orthogonal Tensor Decomposition Models   490
  Bogusław Cyganek

Posters and Demos

How the Anti-TrustRank Algorithm Can Help to Protect
the Reputation of Financial Institutions   503
  Irina Astrova

Punctuation Restoration System for Slovene Language   509
  Marko Bajec, Marko Janković, Slavko Žitnik, and Iztok Lebar Bajec

Practice and Challenges of (De-)Anonymisation for Data Sharing   515
Alexandros Bampoulidis, Alessandro Bruni, Ioannis Markopoulos,
and Mihai Lupu

A Study of Text Summarization Techniques for Generating
Meeting Minutes.   522
Tu My Doan, Francois Jacquenet, Christine Largeron,
and Marc Bernard

CCOnto: Towards an Ontology-Based Model for Character Computing   529
Alia El Bolock, Cornelia Herbert, and Slim Abdennadher

A Tool for the Verification of Decision Model and Notation
(DMN) Models.   536
Faruk Hasić, Carl Corea, Jonas Blatt, Patrick Delfmann,
and Estefanía Serral

Text as Semantic Fields: Integration of an Enriched Language Conception
in the Text Analysis Tool Evoq   543
Isabelle Linden, Anne Wallemacq, Bruno Dumas, Guy Deville,
Antoine Clarinval, and Maxime Cauz

MERLIN: An Intelligent Tool for Creating Domain Models.   549
Monique Snoeck

Business Intelligence and Analytics: On-demand ETL
over Document Stores   556
Manel Souibgui, Faten Atigui, Sadok Ben Yahia,
and Samira Si-Said Cherfi

Towards an Academic Abstract Sentence Classification System   562
Connor Stead, Stephen Smith, Peter Busch, and Savanid Vatanasakdakul

DiálogoP - A Language and a Graphical Tool for Formally Defining
GDPR Purposes   569
Evangelia Vanezi, Georgia M. Kapitsaki, Dimitrios Kouzapas,
Anna Philippou, and George A. Papadopoulos

Identifying the Challenges and Requirements of Enterprise Architecture
Frameworks for IoT Systems   576
Filip Vanhoorelbeke, Monique Snoeck, and Estefanía Serral

Doctoral Consortium

A Holistic Approach Towards Human Factors in Information
Security and Risk   585
Omolola Fagbule

A Framework for Privacy Policy Compliance in the Internet of Things 595
  Constantinos Ioannou

Social-Based Physical Reconstruction Planning in Case of Natural Disaster:
A Machine Learning Approach. 604
  Ghulam Mudassir

Explainability Design Patterns in Clinical Decision Support Systems 613
  Mohammad Naiseh

Tutorials and Research Projects

Expressing Strategic Variability and Flexibility of Processes:
The Map Process Modeling Approach 623
  Rébecca Deneckère and Jolita Ralyté

Data-Driven Requirements Engineering: Principles,
Methods and Challenges 625
  Xavier Franch

Automated Machine Learning: State-of-The-Art and Open Challenges 627
  Radwa Elshawi and Sherif Sakr

Managing Cyber-Physical Incidents Propagation in Health Services. 630
  Faten Atigui, Fayçal Hamdi, Fatma-Zohra Hannou, Nadira Lammari,
  Nada Mimouni, and Samira Si-Said Cherfi

6.849,32 New Scientific Journal Articles Everyday:
Visualize or Perish! - IViSSEM 632
  Ana A. Baptista, Pedro Branco, Bruno Azevedo, Jorge Oliveira e Sá,
  Ana C. Ribeiro, and Mariana Curado Malta

A Model Driven Engineering Approach to Key Performance Indicators:
Towards Self-service Performance Management (SS-PM Project) 635
  Corentin Burnay

TESTOMAT - Next Level of Test Automation 637
  Sigrid Eldh, Tanja E. J. Vos, Serge Demeyer, Pekka Aho,
  and Machiel van der Bijl

A cyberSecurity Platform for vIrtualiseD 5G cybEr Range
Services (SPIDER) 640
  Neofytos Gerosavva, Manos Athanatos, Christoforos Ntantogian,
  Christos Xenakis, Cristina Costa, Alberto Mozo, Matthias Ghering,
  and Angela Brignone

DECODER - DEveloper COmpanion for Documented
and annotatEd code Reference   643
 Miriam Gil, Fernando Pastor Ricos, Victoria Torres,
 and Tanja E. J. Vos

Eco/Logical Learning and Simulation Environments
in Higher Education - ELSE.   645
 Christos Mettouris, Evangelia Vanezi, Alexandos Yeratziotis,
 Alba Graziano, and George A. Papadopoulos

IV4XR - Intelligent Verification/Validation for Extended Reality
Based Systems   647
 I. S. W. B. Prasetya, Rui Prada, Tanja E. J. Vos, Fitsum Kifetew,
 Frank Dignum, Jason Lander, Jean-Yves Donnart,
 Alexandre Kazmierowski, Joseph Davidson, and Fernando Pastor Rico

Author Index   651

Data Analytics and Business Intelligence

Toward Becoming a Data-Driven Organization: Challenges and Benefits

Richard Berntsson Svensson[1](✉) and Maryam Taghavianfar[2]

[1] Chalmers and University of Gothenburg, Gothenburg, Sweden
richard@cse.gu.se
[2] Gothenburg, Sweden

Abstract. Organizations are looking for ways to harness the power of big data and to incorporate the shift that big data brings into their competitive strategies in order to seek competitive advantage and to improve their decision making by becoming data-driven organizations. Despite the potential benefits to be gained from becoming data-driven, the number of organizations that efficiently use it and successfully transform into data-driven organizations stays low. The emphasis in the literature has mostly been technology oriented with limited attention paid to the organizational challenges it entails. This paper presents an empirical study that investigates the challenges and benefits faced by organizations when moving toward becoming a data-driven organization. Data were collected through semi-structured interviews with 15 practitioners from nine software developing companies. The study identifies 49 challenges an organization may face when implementing a data-driven organization in practice, and it identifies 23 potential benefits of a data-driven organization compared to a non-data-driven organization.

Keywords: Data-Driven Organization · Data-driven culture · Data-driven decision making · Challenges · Benefits

1 Introduction

Organizations are increasingly dependent on, and are using data and information to support, e.g. customer insights, product and service development, future directions, and decision making [14,22]. Hence, the application of Big Data (BD) and Big Data Analytics (BDA) in driving organizational decision-making has attracted much attention over the past few years [20]. Since the potential benefits that are associated with BD are important for organizations in all industries and domains [9], organizations are turning to BDA [15] to seek competitive advantages [6,10] with the aim of becoming a Data-Driven Organization (DDO) [11]. One reason for aiming toward becoming a DDO is because of the influx of data [1] caused by a constant generation of data from, e.g. cars, mobile phones,

---

M. Taghavianfar—Independent Researcher.

F. Dalpiaz et al. (Eds.): RCIS 2020, LNBIP 385, pp. 3–19, 2020.
https://doi.org/10.1007/978-3-030-50316-1_1

Internet of Things, machines, and other applications. Despite the potential of DDOs, few organizations have successfully transformed into DDOs [3,6,17].

In order to become a DDO, a data-driven culture must be established before the full potential can be exploited [1]. When transforming into a DDO, there are several aspects that need to be considered and implemented, e.g. technological, managerial, and organizational aspects, as well as implementing a data-driven culture. Most studies in the literature have focused on infrastructure, intelligence, and analytic tools [6,20], and there has been a significant evolution of techniques and technologies for data storage, analysis and visualization [15]. However, there has been limited attention on managerial and organizational challenges in order to embrace these technological innovations [19].

In order to successfully transform into a DDO, it is important to understand the whole spectrum of aspects that surround BD and BDA [10]. By understanding the challenges faced by an organization that have become data-driven will help increasing the understanding of transforming into a DDO, thus new insights may be gained. This paper presents the results of an empirical study that includes data collected through semi-structured interviews with 15 practitioners from nine different software developing companies. This study investigates challenges and benefits faced by organizations when moving toward becoming a Data-Driven Organization.

The remainder of this paper is organized as follows. In Sect. 2, related work is presented. The research methodology is described in Sect. 3, and Sect. 4 presents the results while Sect. 5 discusses and relates the findings to previous studies. Section 6 gives a summary of the main conclusions.

2   Related Work

There are several definitions of DDOs in the literature. Anderson [1] defines an organization as data-driven when there is a data-driven culture in which data collection, data quality, and analytics are used to make decisions to gain competitive advantages. Another definition is that an organization is data-driven when there is a data-driven culture that is characterized by a decision process where data is used over opinions [4], while, according to [13], an organization is data-driven *"when it uses data and analysis to help drive action – even if that action is a deliberate inaction"*. Looking into these definitions, there is a common process, collect data, use analytics to derive insights, and make decisions based on the derived insights. Hence, data-driven decision-making [19], and creating a data-driven culture [1] are important aspects of a DDO. Analytics is another aspect that is used, and associated with a DDO. In theory, a DDO may use data-driven decisions for all types of analytics (descriptive, predictive, prescriptive) and all types of decisions (operational, tactical, strategical), but in practice organizations use a subset of combinations of analytics and decisions [5].

There are studies in the literature that reports on challenges in relation to becoming a DDO. LaValle et al. [18] published a survey with over 3,000 responses where they concluded that, despite popular opinions, challenges related to data and technology were not among the top challenges. Instead, the most mentioned challenges for organization when transforming into data-driven were related to managerial and cultural challenges. In another survey, Halper and Stodder [13] identified the top three challenges as lack of business executive support/corporate strategy, difficulty accessing relevant data, and lack of skills. Berntsson Svensson et al. [6] conducted a survey to investigated how common the use of data-driven decision-making is in agile software developing companies. The results show that very few of the respondents (out of 84) indicated a wide-spread use. The main reasons for this were, data is not available, too much data is available, and do not know how to use the data [6]. In an empirical study investigating 13 organizations initial journey to become a DDO [5], the authors identified five challenges, difficulty in accessing relevant data, lack of corporate strategy, lack of middle management adoption and understanding, insufficient organizational alignment, and lack of understanding and business resistance.

Culture-related challenges refer to changing the mindset. The main issues that prevent organizations from a successful transformation to data-driven are cultural resistance to change, and the difficulty related to adaptability to change [21]. A key aspect of becoming data-driven may be related to by letting decision makers take decision regardless of what data says [19]. This is in line with another culture-related challenge, the lack of accountability [1], meaning, decision-makers are not held accountable for their decisions.

Several studies have reported on benefits of being a DDO, including gaining a competitive advantage over competitors [10], improved decisions [6,19], improved performance, [19], improved processes and enabled innovative products and business models [25], and to discover and capitalize on new business insights [4]. McAfee and Brynjolfsson [19] report that the more data-driven an organization is, the more productive it is – 5% more productive and 6% more profitable compared to competitors.

Overall there are a few studies [5,6,13,18] looking into challenges and benefits when implementing a DDO in practice. However, these studies differ in their focus and/or in the background of the participants compare to our study. In [13, 18], the focus of the study was not on challenges and/or benefits when becoming a DDO, but challenges and/or benefits emerged as part of the results. In [6,13], a vast majority of the respondents had (no) little experience from implementing or being part of a DDO. Berndtsson et al. [5] used a set of challenges from the literature to investigate the occurrence of these challenges in organizations' attempts to become data-driven.

3   Research Methodology

The purpose of this study is to gain an understanding of the challenges an organization may face when becoming a DDO, and its advantages. The investigation was carried out using a qualitative research approach, namely semi-structured interviews [24]. Semi-structured interviews help to ensure common information on predefined areas is collected, but allow the interviewer to probe deeper where required. Since the concept of data-driven could be treated differently in industry, it was important to have a presence when eliciting data, making it possible to compensate for differences in culture and naming. In addition, the interviewer had a chance to validate the questions and answers with the interviewee, lessening the chances of misunderstandings. The following research questions (RQ) provided a focus for the empirical investigation:

- **RQ1:** What are the challenges of implementing a data-driven organisation in practice?
- **RQ2:** What are the benefits of being a data-driven organisation compared to a non-data-driven organisation?

3.1   Planning/Selection

The sampling strategies for selecting software developing companies and participants in this study were a combination of maximum variation [23] and convenience sampling [23] within our industrial collaboration network. To achieve maximum variation of the included software developing companies, we contacted companies from different domains and type of products being developed, varying in size (number of employees) and for how long they have used data-driven decision making. For each company that agreed to participate in this study, we contacted a "gate-keeper". The purpose of the study was explained to the "gate-keeper" and we asked him/her to identify participants from various roles that had experience of working with data-driven decision making and knowledge about the company's transformation into a DDO. The "gate-keeper" helped in identifying participants that he/she thought were the most suitable and representative of the company to participate in this study. That is, the researchers did not influence the selection of participants. In total, 15 participants from nine software development companies participated.

All nine companies develop software and, according to the participants, use Agile methods. The companies themselves vary in respect to size, type of products, type of application domain, and for how long they have used data-driven decision making, as can be seen in Table 1 (more details are not revealed for confidentiality reasons).

3.2   Data Collection

Semi-structured interviews with open-ended questions [24] were used as the data collection method in this study. One interviewer and one interviewee attended all interviews. The research instrument[1] was designed with respect to the different areas of interest. During the interviews, the purpose of the study was presented to the participants, followed by demographic questions. Then, questions about what is a DDO, and what are the challenges and benefits of being/becoming a DDO were discussed in detail. The participants were asked to talk about their

---

[1] https://gubox.box.com/s/jsa57533pi3l6mo57fwhk8m8gj6czfud.

Table 1. Company Characteristics

Company	Participant/Role	Domain	Number of employees	Number of months using DDDM
A	Senior manager	Software	350	10
B	Enterprise developer Senior manager	Software	1,500	8
C	Senior systems engineer	Software	2,500	6
D	Requirements engineer Senior systems engineer	Telecom	100	2
E	Product owner Innovation leader	Telecom	3,000	14
F	Developer Software engineer	Energy	40	8
G	Developer	Telecom	700	5
H	System developer Data scientist	Control systems	500	12
I	Product owner Business analyst	Transportation	1,000	18

understanding of, and their views on DDOs as well as the challenges and benefits of being/becoming a DDO. For all interviews, varying in length from 30 to 60 min, we took records in the form of written extensive notes in order to facilitate and improve the data analysis. In order to improve the validity of the findings, all written notes were sent to the interviewees to give them the opportunity to review, correct, clarify, and expand the interviews. All interviewees reviewed the notes from their interviews.

3.3 Data Analysis

Thematic analysis [8] was used to analyse the data in this study. We followed the six phases of thematic analysis as presented by Braun and Clarke [8]. The first author took part in all phases - as described below - while the results from the analysis was validated and discussed with the second author.

Familiarize Yourself Your Data. In this study, this phase meant reading through all of the extensive notes from the interviews.

Generating Initial Codes. We used open coding [24] throughout the data analysis phase. In this phase, the extensive notes obtained from the interviews were coded into categories. None of the categories were obtained prior to the coding as this is discouraged when using open coding [24].

Searching for Themes. In this phase, we put the initial codes into a main category based on the research question. Then, the main categories were divided into sub-categories containing sub-themes.

Reviewing Themes. In this phase, the identified themes were refined. The focus was on determining whether the identified themes and categories were appropriate and reflective of the actual data. New codes were created while others were renamed and/or removed.

Defining and Naming Themes. In this phase, all codes in each category were verified in order to make sure that they were consistent with the overall theme of the category. Moreover, once all codes and categories were verified, we went back to the interviewees to validate the codes, categories, and that the sub-challenges/benefits were placed under the correct category. For example, that the interpretation of the category *Organization* was correct and that the associated sub-challenges were related to *Organization* and not any other categories. The final name of each theme was decided in this phase. An example of the coding process in given in Fig. 1.

Producing the Report. The results from the analysis phase are reported in Sect. 4.

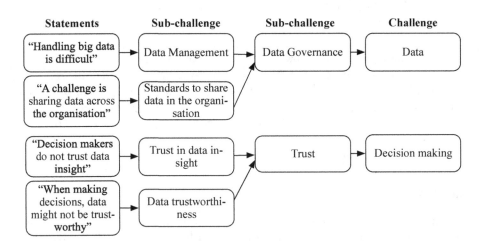

Fig. 1. Example of coding process

4   Results

In order to provide a better understanding of the context in which the challenges and benefits were identified, the participants were asked to define what is a DDO. A general definition among the participants was: *an organization that makes decisions based on a combination of several data sources in order to gain competitive advantages and/or creating value.* The following two sections present the results of one RQ each, corresponding to the RQs in Sect. 3.

4.1   Challenges of Becoming a Data-Driven Organization (RQ1)

In analyzing Research Question 1 (RQ1), this section examines challenges when transforming into a DDO in practice. In total, 49 challenges were identified and divided into four categories, as illustrated in Fig. 2. A description of all challenges is available online[2]. The three most important challenges to address are: *Data vs. opinions* (Decision-Making), *Trust* (Decision-Making), and *Culture* (Organization), which are marked with * in Fig. 2. These three challenges were mentioned by all 15 participants from all nine software developing companies. The participants stated that, if these three challenges are not addressed, it does not matter if everything else is handled, the organization is not data-driven. The identified challenges are discussed below.

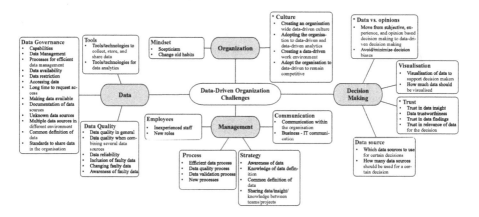

Fig. 2. Data-Driven Organization challenges.

Decision-Making. Four sub-challenges related to Decision-Making were identified, namely: Data vs. opinion, Trust, Data source, and Visualization.

Data vs. Opinion: One of the decision-making challenges, and one of the most important to address, is to move from subjective, experience, and opinion based decisions to data-driven decision-making. Although all nine companies in this study have, according to themselves, transformed into DDOs, some of the decisions are still based on intuition. However, one participant stated that *"it is an ongoing process during which intuition and feelings will progressively decrease over time"*. Making decisions based on facts (i.e. data) also means that the decision makers can understand if their intuition is plausible or not.

Some participants described that the strategical decisions are not made by humans, instead, they are automated. The reason, according to the participants, is to minimize subjective decisions made my decision makers. Other participants stated, in order to move away from subjective decisions, the decision-making

---

process and the decision support systems have changed. Artificial Intelligence and Machine Learning are acting as the basis for decisions, thus relying on facts and evidence instead of subjective decisions.

One challenge was related to the HiPPO concept – the highest-paid person's opinion makes the decisions, regardless of what the data says [19]. However, this concept has started to change since decisions are either automated, or several options (based on facts and evidence) are presented to the decision makers.

Trust: When making decisions based on data, trust in data insights and findings, having trustworthy data, and trust in that the relevant data is presented to the decision makers are of out most importance. Several participants explained that there is a mixed opinion among managers about trusting the presented facts. If there is no trust in the data, either wrong decisions will be made or the decisions makers will ignore the data and base decisions on their experiences and opinions. A related challenge, as explained by one participant, is that *"data behind the presented data could be manipulated"*. In this perspective, the participant explained, when combining different data sources as basis for decisions, a challenge is that the external and internal data may not be secure or trustworthy. Even if, e.g. 75% of the data is internal, the small portion of external data (25%) pose a challenge in trusting the data.

In order to trust the data, it is important for the decision makers to know that the organization has implemented trustworthy tools, techniques, and technologies for data collection and data analytics to guarantee high quality data and high quality reports (when combining data from several sources), and that there are data quality and data validation processes. In addition, the participants also explained, in order to trust the data insights, they need to trust that the right data from the right data sources are collected.

Data Source: A challenge to implement a DDO to improve decisions, is the large amount of available data. The possibility of having quick access to data, to manage the data, and access to data analytics are prominent improvements for becoming a DDO. However, it is challenging, which is partly due to lack of knowledge of using data, and understanding which data sources to use and when to use them. One participant explained, having access to large amount of data does not automatically lead to better decisions, but, if the right data sources are used for the right type of decisions, it has a potential to significantly improve operational, tactical, and strategical decisions.

Visualization: The fourth sub-challenge related to decision-making is visualization of the data in the decision-making process, both in terms of how and how much data should be visualized. The quality of the visualizations (i.e. how) used to support the decision makers have an impact on the decisions. One participant explained, if the data is poorly presented (i.e. visualized) it may lead to wrong decisions since the decision maker may not fully understand the presented data. Moreover, if too much data is presented, it may distract, rather than inform the decision makers.

Organization. Two sub-challenges related to Organization were identified, namely: Culture and Mindset.

Culture: According to all participants, culture is fundamental for transforming into a DDO. Organizations will make changes in order to become data-driven and the changes need to be supported by an organizational culture to enable the process of becoming data-driven. In this sense, as described by one participant, culture *"is reflected on how people behave"* and make decisions. In addition, becoming data-driven is a process where all departments and functions within an organization will have to change based on a common organizational vision.

One of the key ingredients of a data-driven culture is openness. Openness means that the employees should be able to share data and be open to it, and there needs to be a common understanding of why this is done. Another important aspect of creating a data-driven culture is that the change needs to relate to how data is valued within the organization, and that the organization needs to view data as valuable rather than as a cost. However, change does not happen by itself, but starting using different tools, technologies, methodologies, and ways of working that, if turn out to be successful, will lead to a data-driven culture. The participants in this study believe that building a data-driven culture is more difficult for larger organizations compared to smaller ones. However, according to the participants from the larger organizations (B, C, E, and I) in this study, if the employees are self-learning and aware that changes always happens, the process is easier.

Mindset: The results of this study found that challenges related to the employees mindset play an important role when transitioning to a DDO. One respondent clarified, the role played by the employees mindset that needs to change is a matter of modifying the culture. One of the identified mindset challenges is being convinced about the benefits that come from a DDO. The participants reported that they are positive about the concept of data-driven, but they need to experience the benefits that comes with the change. Moreover, the participants explained that employees often get used to working in a certain way and therefore the right mindset is not in place because not all employees share it. In addition, the transition into a DDO, according to several participants, requires new skills and new roles, which challenges how the employees used to work; thus the introduction of a DDO challenges those habits.

Management. The identified sub-challenges related to Management are, Process, Strategy, Communication, and Employees.

Process: Several participants mentioned the need for efficient data processes and establishing new processes in order to become a DDO. Lack of knowledge and understanding of how to integrate BD, BDA, and being data-driven into the organization was a problem. The problem was the need to develop and integrate a data-driven process for the whole organization in order to make decisions based on data. However, the new processes need to focus on data-driven needs where management is fundamental to support the development and integration.

In order to trust the data when making decisions, having a data validation process is important. One participant explained, there is a need to validate the collected data and the performed analytics in order to understand what kind of decisions can be based on data, and to trust the data when making decisions. The initial challenge was the necessity to make assessments on the collected data to ensure that the insights are correct. Another participant clarified, trusting insights from data is a challenge, thus a process for validation is important because a lot of things can be done based on the suggestions from the data, but it can still be wrong if there is no understanding or trust.

Strategy: One challenge related to strategy was the need for everyone having knowledge about, and more importantly, having a common definition of what data is. Several participants explained that the employees were unaware of what data is, which led to confusions of how, and what data to use when making decisions, resulting in the need for informing and asking managers. Since some managers were more inclined to use intuition and experience instead of data when making decisions, there was no consensus among the teams of how to make decisions.

The sharing of data was expressed as a challenge. This relates to the need for accessibility of data across the entire organization. Several participants believe that everyone in the whole organization should have access to all data, otherwise the organization is not data-driven. However, there is a backside to this, data can be manipulated, which can be very dangerous. Especially in large organizations with many systems having control over all data, thus sharing them may be difficult. One organization solved this by giving a few roles full access to all data and everyone else could ask to get access.

Communication: One participant identified communication as a challenge. The participant explained that they experienced a lack of communication between different departments, functions, and teams. It would have been preferable if, e.g., different teams communicated what they are working with since it may be of interest to others, which relates to "openness".

Employees: The challenge of employees refers to the need to establish new roles and the cost of hiring (if needed) skilled staff with regards to analytics, e.g. data scientists, to support the organization in becoming data-driven. Several participants explained that this is an issue to the extent that the management does not perceive this as something necessary. Other participants explained that, there is a need of making investments in new staff as well as training current staff since several may be inexperienced with regards to the new roles and ways of working. Skilled staff in analytics is important for becoming data-driven because without having that capabilities, acquiring data does not make sense.

Data. Challenges related to the Data were divided into three sub-challenges, Data Quality, Data Governance, and Tools.

Data Quality: The better quality of data, the better the outcome will be. Thus, high quality data is important. The high volume of available data can affect the data quality negatively since it may differ in its collection, both for internal and external data. One approach to ensure and verify the quality of the collected data is by combining data using visualization tools. However, for internal data, a challenge is to make sure that the data is well-documented. Otherwise, the decisions can be incorrect. According to one participant, *"the main challenge here relates to human errors"*.

Another challenge is related to maintaining high quality data when combining several data sources. According to one participant, their existing systems that contains all the data are quality based. However, when the data is to be reported into another system, the data from several sources are aggregated. When the data has been aggregated, the users cannot see the details of the aggregation and thus do not know about the quality of the aggregated data. Reliability of the data was also identified as a challenge, which includes data manipulation. One participant highlighted the need of data securitization.

Data Governance: Several challenges related to Data Governance were identified by the participants. However, most of them were only mentioned by one participant. The challenges that were mentioned by at least two participants were: accessing data and data restriction.

Access to external data is limited (in best cases) to a few employees. One reason for this is the needed licence costs. If everyone should have access to all data it would become expensive for the organizations. There is also limited access challenges for internal data, e.g. regarding sensitive and confidential data, which also relates to privacy and GDPR. Therefore, organizations need to adopt to new regulations, especially - according to several participants - within Europe where laws are stricter than in other countries. Moreover, accessing external data - where the organization has no control over the data - is important to take into consideration for organizations that want to become data-driven. If some data cannot be accessed, the insights from the collected data may negatively affect future plans and decisions since the provided insights from incomplete data might be wrong.

Data restriction was identified as a challenge, especially for financial data. This, according to some participants, would affect the prediction analysis for product planning. Other participants mentioned data restriction in relation to not being able to extract real-time data directly from their products. Therefore, plans and decisions are restricted to historical data.

Tools: Regarding tool related challenges, there were two main challenges. First, the need for investments of new tools and technologies for collecting, storing, and sharing data. One participant explained, due to the collection of more data, there was a need to invest in a new Network Inventory System with more capabilities. Moreover, all the large software developing companies in this study (B, C, E, and I) had challenges related to tools and technologies for sharing data across the whole organization. There was a need to invest in standard tools and technologies for data sharing. The second challenge was related to the need to invest in tools and technologies for data analytics.

4.2   Benefits of a Data-Driven Organization (RQ2)

We asked the participants what are the potential benefits of a DDO. In total, 23 potential benefits were identified, divided into six categories, Decisions, Understanding customer/user, Creativity/Innovation, Productivity, Market position, and Growth opportunities, as shown in Fig. 3. A description of all benefits is available online[3].The three most mentioned benefits, which were mentioned by all 15 participants from all nine software developing companies, were: *Decisions*, *Understanding customer/user*, and *Productivity* (marked with * in Fig. 3).

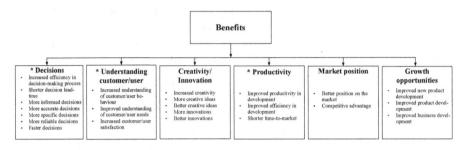

Fig. 3. Benefits of a data-driven organisation compared to a non-data-driven organisation.

All participants stated that their decisions have significantly improved. By combining internal and external data about, e.g. competition and market trends, organizations can make more accurate decisions. Moreover, decisions that are based on insights from data showed to be more reliable, specific and precise, and it made the decision process faster and shorted the decision lead-time, e.g. when targeting business development. One participant explained, *"decisions have turned out to be more precise and quicker, and now it is possible to react to things that happens in your surroundings much earlier"*.

Another benefit of a DDO was identified by all participants in this study, namely improved understanding of the customers/users. Gathering insights from data can help in increasing customer satisfaction since it gives the organization an opportunity to provide better products and services offerings, and an opportunity to obtaining assistance in, *"understanding your organizations target customer/users and how to target them"*, as explained by one participant. Thus, it provides the organizations with an opportunity to understand where the organization is losing customers/users, and understanding customers/users behaviour.

Improved productivity was another potential benefit identified by all participants in this study. Being data-driven enables the organization to increase both efficiency in the development, as well as shorter time-to-market due to automated operations, which also made it easier to identify problems. In addition,

---

[3] https://gubox.box.com/s/w6mw06aa1r4rad4ktbd3zq6z6o9rdoct.

similar to [19], all participants stated that they have improved their productivity and efficiency by doing more with less people since transforming to a DDO.

Five of the nine software developing companies improved their position on the market, and seven of them achieved a competitive advantage over their competitors. Improved growth opportunities, in terms of improved new product development, product development, and business development, were identified by several participants as benefits of DDOs. One participant explained, the business development function has the opportunity to develop strategical plans based on insights from data to enhance new product development.

One software developing company experienced an increase in creative thinking, creativity, and innovations. By using insights from data helps in discovering unexpected factors which were not discovered before, thus it is increasingly becoming an important part of the organizations creativity and innovation processes. By transforming into data-driven, there has been a change of how creativity is defined since it entails curiosity and the ability of re-thinking how things are performed.

5   Discussion

Data-driven culture is considered a key aspect for being a DDO in the literature [1,4,20], therefore it is not surprising that all participants shared that opinion. The mindset leads the organization to embed data-driven aspects and insights into the daily activities. However, some participants explained that the employees had different mindsets because some recognize the value of data while others do not. The difficulties of changing the mindset and ways of working may be due to, e.g. reluctant to change from familiar tools and ways of working, which is supported by the findings in [21]. One possible solution may be to spread the information across the organization in order to enable employees to become knowledgeable about data-driven, and to understand the value it brings to the organization. The presence of human understanding and skills to enhance the implementation DDOs are in line with what theory suggests [20].

Part of the daily activities, which are the other two out of the three most important aspects of being a DDO (third is data-driven culture), includes the fundamental aspect of trusting data insights when moving from subjective and opinion-based decisions to fact-based decisions. According to [18], the most important challenges to get right when transforming into a DDO are managerial and cultural challenges and not related to technologies and data, which supports the findings in this study. However, it contradicts the findings in [6] where the top challenges were related to the data itself. One possible explanation for this difference is that the respondents in [6] had no firsthand experience of challenges when moving toward a DDO.

Moving from opinion-based to fact-based (data) decisions is a challenge. Regarding modifications in mindset when moving to fact-based decisions, the HiPPO concept – the highest-paid person's opinion makes the decisions, regardless of what the data says [19], needs to change. However, the participants in this study believe that the role played by the HiPPO concept and decisions solely based on opinions, intuitions and experiences will decrease due to the role played by evidence from data that will prove, or disprove, a decision makers' gut-feeling. This corresponds to the absence of "instinct-based veto" as suggested in [4]. However, challenges related to making decisions based on data is not new, what is new is that there are many different data sources and the data can be collected faster. Thus, several challenges related to decision-making are the same challenges that existed before, e.g., behavioral aspects of human judgment and decision making [16]. In addition to these biases, algorithmic decisions can be subject to biases too [7]. Thus, not only are the same human decision-making biases present in DDOs, but new ones have been added, which needs to be addressed in order to fully trust the data when making decisions.

In order to trust the data insights when making decisions, several other challenges need to be addressed. One concern is the need for data validation and quality processes for verifying the quality of the data before making decisions based on data. This is in line with theory stating that, due to skepticism on data quality, organizations need to increasingly check its quality [1]. In fact, data may be manipulated, and if an organization does not recognize it, data-driven decisions may be wrong. The lack of trust in data insights that prevents organizations to become data-driven and/or making decisions based on data, might resemble in the skepticism caused by quality concerns [1]. This may be one explanation of why few organizations have successfully transformed into DDOs [3,6,17].

Data quality is a reoccurring challenge. One reason may be related to the amount of collected data where the volume is constantly increasing. Therefore, the extraction of relevant data becomes more difficult. This is partly due to the increased complexity of finding relevant data, and partly because of the focus on maintaining a high quality of the collected data. Another threat to the quality of the data may be related to inactive use of data, which makes it difficult to notice quality concerns.

Several of the identified challenges in this study are in line with challenges reported in the literature. However, there are difference and when looking at the most frequently mentioned challenges when implementing a DDO in practice, the results in this study are not in line with [5,6,13,18]. One possible explanation for this difference may be related to the participants and their roles. For example, in [13,18], a majority of the participants were Business and IT executives, managers, and analysts, while the majority of the participants in this study had more technology-focused roles, e.g. systems engineers and developers. That is, the difference could be explained by the participants' roles and perspectives. Thus, the results in this study complement the results in [13,18]. Moreover, another possible explanation may be that all participants in this study have been part of the transition from a non-DDO to a DDO and have firsthand experience of the identified challenges, which is not the case in [6] where most of the participants had no experience of DDO.

The participants identified several potential benefits of being a DDO compared to a non-data-driven organization. In correspondence with [19,20], all of the 15 participants stated that data-driven decisions are better, more accurate, precis, and informed, and that data-driven decision-making shortens decision lead-time and the time it takes to make decisions. Moreover, several participants believe that the likelihood of having enhanced decisions applies to strategic decisions, e.g. business development, as well as operational decisions due to the automation that increases efficiency. In addition, according to several participants, data insights can help in discovering new opportunities, increase understanding of customers and market trends. The possibility of identifying and discovering unknown paths has been addressed in [12].

5.1   Limitations

Selection bias (*construct validity*) [24], in terms of selecting participants to interview in relation to faced challenges when becoming a DDO, is a threat to this study. Selection bias is always a threat when participants are not fully randomly sampled with the threat that only participants with a negative or positive attitude of a DDO were selected. To reduce this threat, a "gate-keeper" at each software development company selected the participants based on their experiences of data-driven decision making, knowledge of their respective company's transition into a DDO, and their roles. That is, the researchers did not influence the selection of the participants. However, selection bias is not only a threat when selecting participants, it is also a threat when selecting the software development companies. We selected software development companies from various domains, type of products being developed and size (in terms of number of employees) that have transformed into a DDO within our industrial network as it would provide us with the necessary trust. In order to obtain an image of the participants' opinions (*construct validity*), anonymity was guaranteed to all information divulged during the interviews, both within the company and externally. Moreover, the answers was only to be used by the researcher, i.e., not be shown or used by any other participants, software development company, or researchers. Incorrect data (*internal validity*) [24] is a threat to all studies of empirical nature, including this study. To reduce this threat, the written extensive notes from the interviews together with the opportunity to validate the answers and interpretations of the answers with the participants lessening the risks of misunderstandings. In order to improve *reliability* [24], three steps were taken. First, the study was performed by two researchers, which both increases the reliability as well as reduces the risk of single researcher bias. Second, to minimize the threat of internal discussions, the interviews with the participants were conducted at different software development companies where each interview was done in one work session. Third, an interview guideline was created to make sure that all relevant aspects were covered in all interviews. Qualitative studies focus on describing and understanding a phenomenon to enable analytical *generalization*, where the results are generalized to cases which have common characteristics [2]. This means, for the findings in this study to be generalizable, the context and characteristics of the software developing companies in this study needs to be compared with the context of interest. In addition, the background and perspectives of the participants need to be considered. Moreover, since more than one participant and software developing company acknowledged several of the identified challenges and benefits, the results from this study may be generalized to similar contexts when moving toward becoming a DDO.

6   Conclusion

There is a general trend toward data-driven and DDOs, i.e. creating a data-driven culture within the organization and making decisions based on and with data insights. However, there has been a limited focus on how organizations need to change in order to become data-driven. Instead, most studies have focused on infrastructure, intelligence, techniques, and technologies. In this study we thus performed an empirical study and collected data through semi-structured interviews with 15 participants from nine software developing companies to investigate challenges an organization may face when transforming into a DDO in practice, and its potential benefits.

Our main result is that the practitioners see three challenges as the most critical ones to address in order to become a DDO, namely moving from opinion to fact-based (data) decisions, being able to trust the data when making decisions, and implementing a data-driven culture within the organization. Meaning, an organization that have implemented the latest tools, intelligence, and technologies, but have not changed their culture for making decisions, and do not make decisions on facts and evidence (data), is not a DDO.

There are several benefits of transforming into a DDO. The most mentioned benefits was improved and faster decisions. Other common benefits include improved understanding of customers/users, and improved productivity and efficiency in development. Although it is challenging and several decisions and a significant investment in time and cost need to be made, the benefits of DDOs are substantial and may lead to competitive advantages and growth opportunities. Future research should investigate this in more detail.

References

1. Anderson, C.: Creating a Data-Driven Organization. O'Reilly Media, Newton (2015)
2. Baskerville, R., Lee, A.S.: Distinctions among different types of generalizing in information systems research. In: Ngwenyama, O., Introna, L.D., Myers, M.D., DeGross, J.I. (eds.) New Information Technologies in Organizational Processes. ITIFIP, vol. 20, pp. 49–65. Springer, Boston, MA (1999). https://doi.org/10.1007/978-0-387-35566-5_5
3. Bean, R., Davenport, T.: Companies are failing in their efforts to become data-driven. Harvard Bus. Rev. (2019)
4. Berndtsson, M., Forsberg, D., Stein, D., Svahn, T.: Becoming a data-driven organisation. In: Proceedings of the 26th European Conference on Information Systems (2018)

5. Berndtsson, M., Lennerholt, C., Svahn, T., Larsson, P.: 13 organizations' attempts to become data-driven. Int. J. Bus. Intell. Res. **11**(1), 1–21 (2020)
6. Svensson, R.B., Feldt, R., Torkar, R.: The unfulfilled potential of data-driven decision making in agile software development. In: Kruchten, P., Fraser, S., Coallier, F. (eds.) XP 2019. LNBIP, vol. 355, pp. 69–85. Springer, Cham (2019). https://doi.org/10.1007/978-3-030-19034-7_5
7. Boyd, D., Crawford, K.: Critical questions for big data: provocations for a cultural, technological, and scholarly phenomenon. Inf. Commun. Soc. **15**, 662–679 (2012)
8. Braun, V., Clarke, V.: Using thematic analysis in psychology. Qual. Res. Psychol. **3**(2), 77–101 (2006)
9. Bremser, C.: Starting points for big data adoption. In: Proceedings of the 26th European Conference on Information Systems (2018)
10. Constantiou, I., Kallinikos, J.: New games, new rules: big data and the changing context of strategy. J. Inf. Technol. **30**(1), 44–57 (2015)
11. Davenport, T., Bean, R.: Big companies are embracing analytics, but most still don't have a data-driven culture. Harvard Bus. Rev. (2018)
12. Halaweh, M., Massry, A.: Conceptual model for successful implementation of big data in organizations. J. Int. Technol. Inf. Manag. **24**(2), 34 (2015)
13. Halper, F., Stodder, D.: What it takes to be data-driven. TDWI, vol. Q4 (2017)
14. Hannila, H., Silvola, R., Harkonen, J., Haapasalo, H.: Data-driven begins with data; potential of data assets. J. Comput. Inf. Syst. 1–10 (2019)
15. Jensen, M., Nielsen, P., Persson, J.: Managing big data analytics projects: the challenges of realizing value. In: Proceedings of the 27th European Conference on Information Systems (2019)
16. Kahneman, D.: Maps of bounded rationality: psychology for behavioral economics. Am. Econ. Rev. **93**, 1449–1475 (2003)
17. Kart, L.: Big data industry insights. Technical report, Gartner (2015). http://public.brighttalk.com/resource/core/80421/september_29_industry_insights_lkart_118453.pdf
18. LaValle, S., Lesser, E., Shockley, R., Hopkins, M., Kruschwitz, N.: Big data, analytics, and the path from insights to value. MIT Sloan Manag. Rev. **52**(2), 21–32 (2011)
19. McAfee, A., Brynjolfsson, E.: Big data: the management revolution. Harvard Bus. Rev. (2012)
20. Mikalef, P., Pappas, I.O., Krogstie, J., Giannakos, M.: Big data analytics capabilities: a systematic literature review and research agenda. Inf. Syst. e-Bus. Manag. **16**(3), 547–578 (2017). https://doi.org/10.1007/s10257-017-0362-y
21. Partners, N.V.: Big data executive survey 2018 executive summary of findings. Technical report, NewVantage Partners (2018)
22. Patil, D.: Building Data Science Teams. O'Reilly Media, Newton (2011)
23. Patton, M.: Qualitative Research and Evaluation Methods. Sage Publications, New York (2002)
24. Robson, C.: Real World Research. Blackwell, Oxford (2002)
25. Sivarajah, U., Kamal, M., Irani, Z., Weerakkody, V.: Critical analysis of big data challenges and analytical methods. J. Bus. Res. **70**(2), 263–286 (2017)

A Big Data Conceptual Model to Improve Quality of Business Analytics

Grace Park[1]([✉]), Lawrence Chung[2], Haan Johng[2], Vijayan Sugumaran[3],
Sooyong Park[4], Liping Zhao[5], and Sam Supakkul[6]

[1] State Farm, Richardson, USA
g.e.park@ieee.org
[2] University of Texas at Dallas, Richardson, USA
{chung,HaanMo.Johng}@utdallas.edu
[3] Oakland University, Rochester, USA
sugumara@oakland.edu
[4] Sogang University, Seoul, Republic of Korea
sypark@sogang.ac.kr
[5] The University of Manchester, Manchester, UK
liping.zhao@manchester.ac.uk
[6] NCR Corporation, Irving, USA
ssupakkul@ieee.org

Abstract. As big data becomes an important part of business analytics for gaining insights about business practices, the quality of big data is an essential factor impacting the outcomes of business analytics. Although this is quite challenging, conceptual modeling has much potential to solve it since the good quality of data comes from good quality of models. However, existing data models at a conceptual level have limitations to incorporate quality aspects into big data models. In this paper, we focus on the challenges cause by Variety of big data propose IRIS, a conceptual modeling framework for big data models which enables us to define three modeling quality notions – relevance, comprehensiveness, and relative priorities and incorporate such qualities into a big data model in a goal-oriented approach. Explored big data models based on the qualities are integrated with existing data grounded on three conventional organizational dimensions creating a virtual big data model. An empirical study has been conducted using the shipping decision process of a worldwide retail chain, to gain an initial understanding of the applicability of this approach.

Keywords: Big data conceptual model · Big data modeling quality ·
Goal-oriented big data · Business analytics · Goal-orientation

1 Introduction

Big data has quickly been embraced by all walks of life, including businesses, governments, and academia. The big data revolution is unprecedented, due to the promises and hopes built around it. Yet, behind the façade of big data is the simple notion of data – the

© Springer Nature Switzerland AG 2020
F. Dalpiaz et al. (Eds.): RCIS 2020, LNBIP 385, pp. 20–37, 2020.
https://doi.org/10.1007/978-3-030-50316-1_2

data that is characterized by many Vs (Volume, Velocity, Variety, Veracity, Value, and possibly more) that require new technologies to unleash its power.

Business analytics (hereafter, BA) is one of the key areas that can benefit greatly from big data. With new business insights gained by big data from diverse sources and types, BA helps make better business decisions and improve business processes. Yet, the quality of BA can only be as good as the quality of the big data it uses. With good quality big data, BA can accurately identify important business concerns, trends and opportunities, and useful business insights, which, in turn, can lead to good business decisions.

There are many challenges to ensuring the good quality of big data for business analytics. Among them, this paper investigates challenges caused by Variety of big data because the ability to integrate more diverse sources of data drives successful big data outcomes [22]. However, it is crucial for organizations to adequately select external data and incorporate it with internal data fitting for business purposes instead of just blindly adding more data. According to prior research, since the amount of data is huge, it is hard to evaluate big data quality within a reasonable time [1]. If there is irrelevant data, organizations waste more time and money. Additionally, data from diverse sources bring heterogeneous types of data and complex structures causing integration problems with existing data [2]. Furthermore, as current big data analytics focuses too much on data processing itself, it has limitations to support business concerns [3], thus, it is hard for external data to semantically relate to business concerns not knowing the rationales of its selection.

A conceptual model that helps decide project scope at a high-level abstraction and establish a structural organization has great potential to explore many big data entities and relationships for business analytics without collecting or processing concrete data. Some researchers [4, 5] recognize the potential of conceptual modeling for big data, but they are initial stages for business analytics, especially for diversity; there is little work to prescribe how conceptual modeling for big data pursue good quality of business analytics in the perspective of Variety. According to [6], since design decisions positively or negatively affect quality attributes, the process of selection should be rationalized in terms of quality attributes. However, not only existing conceptual models for big data [9] but also traditional data models [8] have limitations to express the process of rational selections on which data entities and relationships are needed for important business considerations resulting in omissions or commissions of big data. Additionally, there is little work to suggest how the new entities of big data from external sources can be incorporated with existing data causing a more complex structure. Moreover, it is hard to identify the origins of the external big data i.e., where a data entity came from, which leads to breaking a balanced view on data diversity and negatively affects reliability.

To address these problems, this paper proposes IRIS, a systematic approach for the quality of Variety of big data in a conceptual level. First, it defines an ontology at which we adopted a goal-orientation approach for rational selections and incorporate concepts such as business problems, solutions on top of Extended Entity-Relationship (EER) model [7]. Second, this approach selects big data modeling quality attributes that are closely related big data quality to support Variety and defines three quality aspects:

relevance, comprehensiveness, and relative priorities, and integrates them into a selection process as selection criteria. These aspects stipulate that the data and relationships between the data should be relevant to their use, comprehensive enough to support balanced views for business decision-making, and prioritized so that their importance is clear. Finally, this paper utilizes conventional three organizational dimensions: Classification/Instantiation, Generalization/Specialization, and Aggregation/Decomposition to integrate existing data entities and the new external entities of big data creating a virtual big data model that helps new or external opportunities.

The key contributions of this paper are as follows: 1) the new ontology including entities and relationships for big data business analytics in which goal-orientation is integrated with big data model enables to explore diverse data entities and select relatively optimal ones into a virtual big data model dealing with good quality of Variety, and eventually, good quality of business analytics; 2) the three attributes to properly resolve challenges caused by Variety provide selection criteria for the selection process of data providing decision rationales both for quality of data and data model; 3) the three organizational dimensions which handle the integration problem with existing data helps reduce complexity.

This paper is organized as follows. Section 2 and 3 describe related work and a running example respectively. Section 4 presents IRIS, a goal-oriented conceptual model for big data models which consists of ontology, the three qualities and organizational dimensions of big data models. Then, Sect. 5 shows an application of the approach to the running example. Section 6 provides a discussion including the limitations of this approach. In the end, a summary of contributions is given, together with future work.

2 Related Work

Conceptual modeling is a key related area. Conventional data models are ER [8] and EER [7], which enable conceptual data modeling. As big data technologies are prevalent, researches on conceptual modeling for big data are increasing. For example, [9] and [10] provides a big data modeling methodology for Apache Cassandra and schema inference for JSON datasets providing an inference algorithm, respectively, and [11] suggests domain ontology as a conceptual model for biomedical informatics to support data partitioning and visualization. Although these works contribute conceptual modeling for big data, they have limitations to build required qualities into big data models. However, our solution is suitable for addressing the problem since it utilizes a goal-oriented approach, combines business concepts, and the collaboration of three dimensions of quality and organization.

In addition, big data quality is another related area. Some researchers have been investigating to improve the quality of big data. For instance, [12] suggests quality in use model for big data providing three data quality dimensions, i.e., Contextual Consistency, Operational Consistency, and Temporal Consistency. Additionally, [13] suggests how to deal with data granularities for data quality evaluation and analyzes data quality dimensions. [14] addresses the quality of big data at the pre-processing phase to support data quality profile selection and adaptation. The key distinctions are 1) this work focus on big data modeling qualities which affect big data quality, and 2) the notion of a virtual repository through a federated approach is applied to our work. A virtual repository is intended to offer easy access to (usually geographically) distributed, and oftentimes independent and heterogeneous, databases, through a single (virtual) database with a single set of mechanisms for accessing the database [15]. Creating a virtual database involves integrating oftentimes incompatible database schemas of a native and a number of foreign database schemas. Our notions of "Internal" and "External" respectively are similar to "native" and "foreign," at least roughly. We also adopt the three abstraction principles of Classification/Instantiation, Generalization/Specialization and Aggregation/Decomposition [16].

Finally, the area of goal-oriented requirements engineering is importantly related to our research. Some research (e.g., [17, 26]) has proposed a conceptual model for business analytics, considering business goals and strategies, although they do not use big data. The former defines three complementary modeling views that help find analytics algorithms and data preparation activities aligned with enterprise strategies. The work is similar to ours from the perspective of using goal-concepts and conceptual models, but our suggestion is more focused on conceptual big data models considering data modeling qualities and organizations. Additionally, our previous work [18, 19] suggests a goal-oriented big data business analytics framework to bridge the gap between big data and business. Although this paper utilizes the basic concepts such as business goals, problems, and solutions, this work is more focused on big data modeling and its quality, exploring diverse data models, and evaluating them using trade-off analysis from the perspective of Variety. Especially, this paper provides guidance on how to quantitatively calculate relevance using structural relevance and semantic relevance.

3   A Running Example: Shipping Decision

We utilize a shipping decision-making process [21] from Zara, Inc. (hereafter, Zara) which is a worldwide fashion retailer as a running example throughout the paper for illustrating the key concepts of IRIS's goal-oriented approach to modeling big data in the perspective of Variety, as well as from the perspective of an empirical study, concerning the applicability of IRIS's approach. Due to the inability to access data inside the company, EER diagrams in this example have been reconstructed based on real case descriptions of [21] and other diagrams are based on our imagination.

For its global distribution, Zara's headquarters sends a weekly offer to each store, with a maximum quantity the store can request for each of the items. Using this data, together with some other data, such as its sales history and local inventory, the manager of the store manually decides the weekly shipment quantity and sends a shipment request to the global warehouse team. This team aggregates all the requests that come from all over the world and reconciles shipment quantities, if there is not enough inventory to fulfill all the requests.

4 IRIS: A Conceptual Modeling Framework for Quality of Big Data Business Analytics

4.1 IRIS Ontology

The main concepts in IRIS and relationships between them that are needed for the purpose of communication and modeling about big data are depicted in Fig. 1 in which thick lines are extended elements from [18].

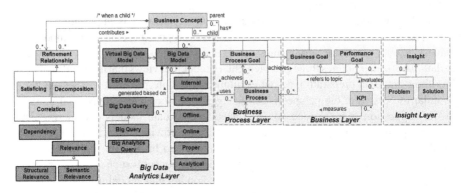

Fig. 1. IRIS ontology for big data modeling.

In IRIS, every concept is treated as a goal which can be refined more specific sub-goals with corresponding relationships. To represent these common characteristics, we define Business Concept as a root element with parent/child relationships. A parent has many children and vice versa. In the case of a child, it has many Refinement Relationships toward its parents but, a Refinement Relationship toward a parent is one since a specific refinement of a child toward a parent is only one. For example, to Increase Global Revenue of Zara *(Business Goal)* as a parent, Effective Shipment Decision *(Business Process Goal)* or Effective Clearance Pricing *(Business Process Goal)* can be explored as children and Weakly Positive of Effective Shipment Decision and Positive of Effective Clearance Pricing are the relationships towards the parent goal respectively. This notion is well explained in [19] about how Big Data Query can evolve from abstract business questions to specific big data analytics query statement using this goal concept. A more specific example of big data models will be shown in Sect. 7.

Additionally, IRIS enables to model both Problem and Solution which are treated as insight on whether a Business Concept respectively makes positive and negative contributions towards achieving a goal. They are validated by the results from Big Data Queries or KPI (Key Performance Indicator). For example, Low Hit Rate on Shipment Decision is identified as a Problem since 15% of Estimation Hit Rate on Shipment Decision (KPI) is lower than 30% of Performance Goal by the result of corresponding big analytics queries.

Concerning the big data part, in particular, Big Data Model is specialized in the three comprehensive dimensions, i.e., Internal-External, Offline-Online, and Proper-Analytical. Any kind of Big Data Model – be it the whole or its parts – can be modeled with EER Ontology. Here, the whole big data model would be a virtual big data model (Sect. 4 will describe details), consisting of both the native and foreign big data models. Since Big Data Model itself is inherited from Business Concept, it has the ability of Refinement Relationship towards Insight that includes Problem and Solution. In this case, Insight is considered as a goal to achieve. This allows modelers to select a relatively best big data model that helps find insights on business problems and solutions. In IRIS, data modeling elements and data insight elements co-exist. A Big Data Query is generated based on Big Data Model and it also helps select Big Data Model. It is specialized in Big Analytics Query and Big Query, and they are distinguished from whether they need analytics such as machine learning or statistical results or not respectively. Additionally, Dependency and Relevance relationships are identified and they play an important role to see diverse views and find the most relevant data elements.

4.2 Quality Definitions of Big Data Model

In improving the quality of business analytics, it is critical to capture important concepts in a specific business domain, their relationships, and constraints on both the concepts and relationships and represent them in a model. Building an ontology as comprehensively as possible helps improve the quality of the data model by reducing omissions and commissions in the model. However, it does not mean we can always collect entire data for the whole of the ontology. Collecting data for some ontology might be too expensive, too time-consuming, or even impossible in the real world. Due to the issues, improving the quality of the data model can help enhance the quality of data.

The key emphasis in IRIS lies in, among other Vs, the notion of Variety, hence the need for accommodating a variety of not only different types of data but also sources of data. This is important, especially in the emergence of social networking sites, online marketplaces, web analytics, sensor networks, etc., that are increasingly becoming part of every walks of life. But then, the growth in the volume of data seems remarkably large and also in their velocity, making the cost and technical feasibility issues become more important than ever before. The availability of more data might mean, the more complete analysis, but at a (possibly prohibitively) increased cost for managing the data.

There are two categories of quality; one for data quality such as accuracy or consistency [20] and the other is data model quality such as understandability or maintainability [25]. Among them, we propose the following three notions of data modeling quality - relevance, comprehensiveness, and relative priorities. The rationales behind the selection are 1) those modeling quality are closely related to data quality, so a given data model can impact data quality [23], 2) they help explore diverse data entities and select ones to achieve good quality of Variety, and 3) this work focuses on data qualities that can be dealt in a conceptual level.

- *Comprehensiveness* of data, for a variety of different types and sources of data.
- *Relevance* of data, for including data that deems potentially relevant to validating problems and solutions and excluding data that does not – this would help avoid a prohibitive increase in cost for collecting, maintaining, processing, transmitting, analyzing, visualizing and understanding the potentially tremendous *v*olume of data.

- *Relative priorities* of data for determining how to allocate a limited amount of resources, for example, when the volume of data is huge or the velocity at which data may arrive needs to be extremely fast.

Comprehensiveness

This aspect is to accommodate a variety of types and sources of data that are increasingly becoming available and useful into a big data model, for better serving BA. This notion is useful to help prevent omissions of potentially important data. For example, for Zara's shipping decision on ladies' apparel, external data in the form of a social network recommendation on popular ladies' apparel products is likely to be useful, hence relevant and included in the big data model.

Besides social networking datasets, there are also other sources of potentially relevant data too, for example, online shopping and advertisement statistics, which could help avoid missing out-trend opportunities due to the consideration of only the historical data that pertains to a particular business. The three comprehensive dimensions of big data, as shown in Fig. 2, are intended to help capture and utilize data from a variety of sources and in many varying types, in carrying out big data analytics.

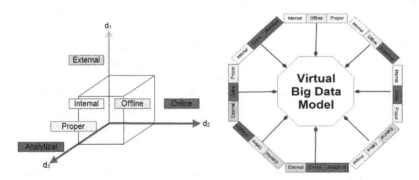

Fig. 2. Three big data comprehensiveness dimensions and the resulting eight squares.

Regarding the perspective of data, there are many dimensions such as structured/unstructured or descriptive/predictive, however, in this paper shows the following three dimensions as an example.

- *Internal/External dimension*: to consider not only data that is *internal* to a business (e.g., in the business's local data center) but also data that is external to the business (e.g., through a national repository or a social networking site);
- *Offline/Online dimension*: to consider not only the traditional offline data but also online data that is increasingly becoming prevalent; and
- *Proper/Analytical dimension*: to consider not only ordinary data (e.g., Sales History or Local Inventory Level – say, of first-order data) but also data that has been generated, through analytics, from such ordinary regular data (e.g., Sales Trend or Local Inventory Level Trend – say, of second-order data and higher).

These three dimensions, then, would yield eight different sources, as the result of the cross product: {Internal, External} X {Offline, Online} X {Proper, Analytical}. Big data entities explored by utilizing this view are selected through the next Relevance and Prioritization quality attributes.

Relevance

This aspect is about the utility of a data element, which can be used as a criterion in determining if the data element should be considered in supporting BA. This notion is useful for helping to prevent commissions. For example, for Zara's shipping decision on ladies' apparel, a social network recommendation on games is unlikely to be useful, hence irrelevant.

A data model element, e, is said to be relevant if there is a link between e and some Problem or Solution. More specifically, a data model (element), e, is said to be structural relevant, if the number of links that lie between e and some nearest Problem or Solution is d. The smaller the distance, the more relevant e is. A data model (element), e, is also said to be semantic relevant if e makes a positive or negative contribution towards validating either a hypothesized Problem or Solution. The more positive the contribution is, the more relevant e is. These two notions of big data relevance are depicted in Fig. 2 (Fig. 3).

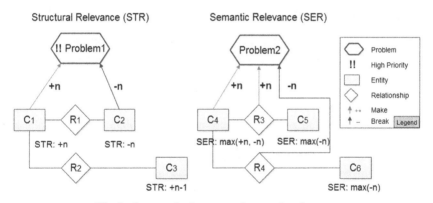

Fig. 3. Structural relevance and semantic relevance.

In Fig. 2, each C_i denotes a class or an entity in EERD (Enhanced Entity Relationship Diagram). For Structural Relevance (STR), C_1's distance to Problem is smaller than C_3's, hence more relevant. Now, C_1's distance is the same as C_2's distance, but C_1's contribution is stronger than C_2's contribution, hence more relevant. Regarding Semantic Relevance (SER), C_4's relevance is the maximum value between R_3's contribution and R_4's one since C_4 is semantically related to Problems2 with R_3 and R_4. More detailed examples will be explained in Sect. 5.

Prioritization

This aspect is useful in determining what data to incorporate into the virtual big data, how much effort should be put on obtaining the data, how much resources to allocate to the data, etc. The priorities of data should reflect the priorities of what the data is intended for. In IRIS, big data is intended for supporting BA, concerning validating potential Problems and Solutions which are hypothesized, then modeled.

The priorities of data are inherited from the priorities of their respective potential Problems and Solutions for the data to be intended to validate. For example, in Fig. 2, there are two Problem1 and 2, and C1 or C4 are the most relevant to validate them respectively. However, C1 can be selected as Virtual Big Data Model since Problem1 has a higher priority which is denoted as !!. While priorities are propagated downward, the priorities of lower-level refinements can change in either direction. In particular, a trade-off analysis can lead to the change in the priorities of those operationalizations that overall make strongly negative contributions to achieving higher-level goals. Section 5 will show more detailed examples.

4.3 Organizational Dimensions

Now, we introduce the three organizational dimensions, which are intended to help structure a large variety of big data, possibly in a huge volume arriving at a fast velocity. All these three dimensions can be used to explore, and relate, data in the same or across different dimensions of big data comprehensiveness.

- *Classification/Instantiation dimension:* This is to relate instances to classes. For example, suppose that Kate's skirt becomes a hot keyword in Internet search (e.g., on Most Read or Trend Now). In this case, Kate's skirt is likely to be an instance of the class of order items that Zara has.
- *Generalization/Specialization dimension:* This is to relate data through superclass-subclass relationships. For example, online shopping is growing as an overall trend in the world, which can be considered to be more general than Zara's own potential online shopping trend. Then, the overall trend may be reflected in Zara's online clothes sales trend, hence consequently affecting shipping decisions on clothes, concerning both offline and online (This is a kind of deductive reasoning, hence likely to be sound). Now let us suppose that the worldwide trend in children's overalls is growing. This is a more special case than Zara's overall sales on all items, and predicting that Zara's overall sales on all items will also go up, hence consequently increase in shipping quantities, will more likely be invalid (This is a kind of abductive reasoning, hence likely to be unsound).
- *Aggregation/Decomposition dimension:* This is to associate data of different classes (in some literature, in the name of attributes or properties). For example, hot keywords from an external search engine can be combined together with internal online feedback. This combined entity may be referred to as a hot fashion trend and could be used in rating Zara's products.

5 IRIS in Action for Quality of Big Data Conceptual Modeling

IRIS's goal-oriented process can help develop a virtual big data model to support the BA for Zara's shipping decision process of the running example in Sect. 2.

Initiate

Let us suppose that Zara's innovation team wants to use big data analytics through a virtual big data model. So, they understand the business process for making shipment decisions, and the current operating data model, as shown in Fig. 4 and Fig. 5. Afterward, the team finds and establishes one or more business goals, here, ☁Increase Global Revenue (the top portion in Fig. 4). There are many ways to increase revenue, including effective marketing and effective shipment decision, which the team considers important, hence treating ☁Effective [Clearance Pricing] and ☁Effective [Shipment Decision] as goals to be achieved.

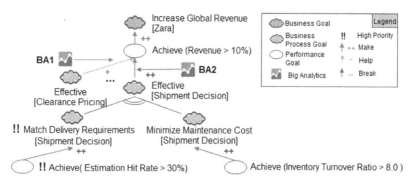

Fig. 4. Diagnostics for shipment decision.

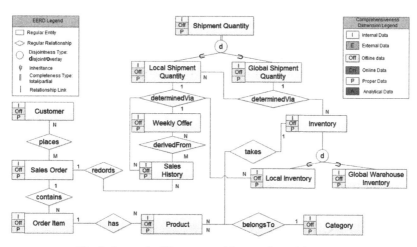

Fig. 5. Internal-offline-proper shipment data with EERD.

Between these two, the team considers Shipment Decision is a more critical factor to increasing revenue, using 📊BA1: correlation between clearance decision and revenue and 📊BA2: correlation between shipment and revenue, so wants to first find out if there is any problem with the current shipment decision making process. So, the team refines ☁Effective [Shipment Decision] in terms of two business process goals, i.e.,

!!Match Delivery Requirements [Shipment Decision], and Minimize Maintenance Cost [Shipment Decision]. Among these two goals, !!Match Delivery Requirements [Shipment Decision] has a higher priority by the team's decision. These two goals are expressed in measurable terms, here, Performance goals – !!Achieve (Estimation Hit Rate > 30%) and Achieve (Inventory Turnover Ratio > 8.0) respectively. As the priority of a child goal is inherited from its parent goal, !!Achieve (Estimation Hit Rate > 30%) is a higher priority than the other.

As in Fig. 5, Local Inventory, Sales History, and Weekly Offer entities are needed for determining Local Shipment Quantity. Likewise, Local Shipment Quantity, Sales History, Global Warehouse Inventory, and Local Inventory are needed for determining Global Shipment Quantity. The data model is represented using EERD, which essentially is ERD augmented with generalization/specialization and aggregation/decomposition. This data model represents only an Internal-Offline-Proper data model from the perspective of a virtual big data model.

Finding Internal Data Entities to Validate Hypothesized Problems/Solutions
The team now hypothesizes potential problems with the current shipment decision process and their sub-problems (root causes) and potential solutions. As Fig. 6 shows, it can be done from the perspective of the Performance goals, here !!Achieve(Estimation Hit Rate > 30%) and Achieve (Inventory Turnover Ratio > 8.0). Zara's team considers two potential problems, High Difference of Demand Estimation [Shipment Decision] and Long Delivery Time [Shipment Decision], as the most likely and important problems because of the results from BQ1: Estimation Hit Rate on Shipment Decision (15%) and BQ2: Inventory Turnover Ratio on Shipment (2.5). As with problems, potential solutions can also be hypothesized - here, !!Reliable Prediction Model on Demand [Decide Quantity Request, Aggregate Reconcile] and Reliable Prediction Model on Delivery [Overseas Delivery]. However, the former solution has more importance since it inherits the priority from !!Match Delivery Requirements [Shipment Decision] through !!Achieve(Estimation Hit Rate > 30%).

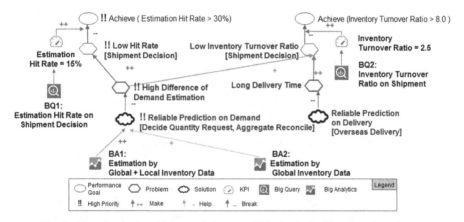

Fig. 6. Hypothesized problems, solutions, and Big Analytics Queries with priority.

If only the Internal-Offline-Proper data model is used, then two queries, ⚙BA1: Estimation Adding Global + Local Inventory Data and ⚙BA2: Estimation Adding Global Inventory Data, might be considered for the purpose of validation in Fig. 6. The team considered not only global but also local inventory affects the accuracy of the estimation model, so the team added ⚙BA1 which uses a superset of the query elements for the estimation model. Then, between the queries, the former would have a stronger contribution (++) than the latter (+) towards validating the potential problem and the solutions they are relevant to, namely, ◯!! High Difference of Demand Estimation [Shipment Decision] and ◯!! Reliable Prediction on Shipment Quantity respectively. More details for finding problems/solutions are in our previous work [18].

To create Big Analytics Query, first of all, they need to include data entities from Internal-Offline-Proper data model. Figure 7 shows an example of which data entities are the most relevant to validate Reliable Prediction on Shipment Quantity using Structural Relevance and Semantic Relevance. For Structural Relevance (STR), Shipment Quantity is the starting point with +3 points and STR will be reduced by 1 whenever a relationship will be passed except for inheritance relationship. The STR of Local Shipment Quantity is still +3 since it inherits from Shipment Quantity, and the STR of Sales Order is +1 since it has two relationship between Local Shipment Quantity. For Semantic Relevance (SER), the relationships of disjoint inheritance, determined Via relationship, and records contribute +3, +3, and −1 respectively to validate Reliable Prediction on Shipment Quantity. The SER of an entity is the maximum of SERs of related relationships. The total Relevance is the sum of STR and SER. Thus, the least related Sales Order $(+1+(-1))$ is not included.

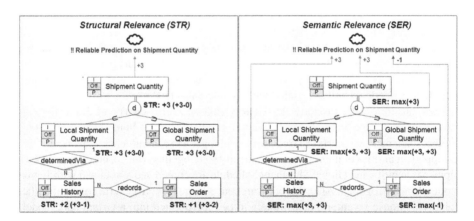

Fig. 7. An example of structural relevance and semantic relevance.

Expanding Existing Data Entities
Let us assume that the innovation team thinks it is important to explore new and external opportunities in validating the potential solutions. By using the Internal-Offline-Proper Dependency Diagram in Fig. 8, the team identifies a variety of other types and sources

of entities in the three comprehensiveness dimensions, here External, Online, and Analytical. The Dependency Diagram in Fig. 8 left box represents the dependent relations between entities which are easily inferred from input-output relationships in BPMN and this is utilized as a reference to explore diverse entities.

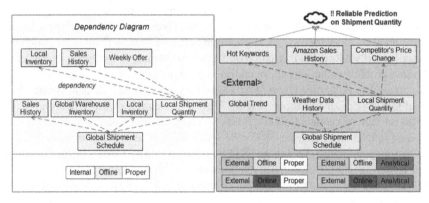

Fig. 8. An example of candidate entities derived from external dimensions.

For example, the team explores the external Amazon Sales History as being relevant to the internal Sales History (this is Zara's own), in Fig. 8 bottom right box. Since these two can be subclasses of some higher-level class, say Sales History, what is applicable to one may also be applicable to the other. So, the chains of entities associated with Sales History, here Local Shipment Quantity and Global Shipment Schedule, are copied and associated with Amazon Sales History.

Similarly, the team considers the offline Sales History (again Zara's own) and the Online Sales History are relevant to each other, since these two can again be subclasses of some class, say Sales History. So, the chain of entities associated with the offline Sales History is copied and associated with Online Sales History.

The team thinks the Proper Sales-History (this is Zara's own) and the analytical Items Frequently Sold Together are relevant to each other, since Items Frequently Sold Together (e.g., hats and scarfs are frequently sold together) can influence Zara's decision on shipping quantities of items that are frequently sold together. Hence, here again, Local Shipment Quantity and Global Shipment Schedule are copied and associated with Items Frequently Sold Together. Also, Global Warehouse Trend is more general concerning the Global Warehouse Inventory, hence likely to be incorporated into a virtual data model later.

Build an Initial Virtual Big Data Model
Zara's team integrates those entities and relationships from every possible dimension, which were derived in the previous step, into Internal-Offline-Proper to produce a virtual big data model. Here, the team utilizes the three organizational dimensions to find relationships between entities-and-relationships of Internal-Offline-Proper and those from other dimensions that might need to be refined during integration. The virtual big data model is represented using EERD, as in Fig. 9.

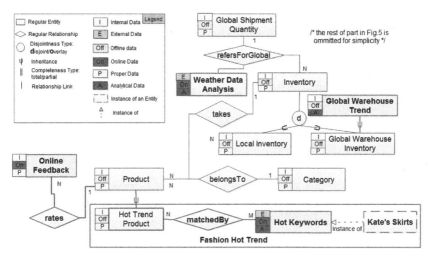

Fig. 9. Virtual big data model, consisting of entities and relationships from multiple sources, for shipment decision.

Figure 9 shows the initial virtual big data model, which consists of existing entities and newly-added entities. In this model, some of the Internal-Offline-Proper entities are integrated with new entities. For example, Global Shipment Quantity in Fig. 9 is related to the Global Warehouse Trend as an inheritance relationship. Global Warehouse Trend is shown as a superclass of Global Warehouse Inventory (Generalization/Specialization dimension). Additionally, Weather Data Analysis is identified as an entity for global shipment quantity (Classification/Instantiation dimension). For another example, Online Feedback and Hot Keywords have some similar traits, so they can be combined together. Then, the resulting composite entity can be used to rate the Product (Aggregation/Decomposition dimension).

The relevance values of entities are able to be evaluated again based on the initial virtual big data model as Fig. 10 shows. Each entity follows the relevance calculation rules.

Evaluate Quality Attributes and Select Entities

Zara's team now checks the Comprehensiveness, Relevance, and Priority of the candidate entities, according to the potential solution that corresponds to the entities, so as to filter the candidate entities to find the most relevant and high priority entities. The team collects, for the potential solution, all the relevant entities - each entity is shown in a row, as in Table 1. Although these tables here are used in validating a potential solution, similar tables can be used in validating other potential solutions and potential problems. Then, for each entity, the team checks the comprehensiveness dimensions the entity or other entities (that it is related to) belong to. For example, Online Feedback has an Internal, Online, Proper attributes. Then, the entity's relevance is indicated, in terms of its STR and SER relevance. In Fig. 8, it has STR:+3 and SER:+3 relevant to the solution with ◇!! *Reliable Prediction on Shipment Quantity.*

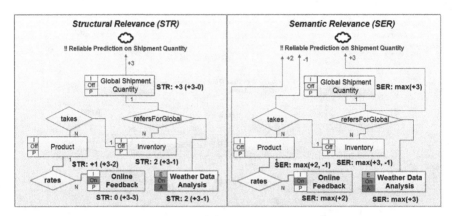

Fig. 10. Virtual big data model, consisting of entities and relationships.

The priority of the entity is related to the priority of parent goals, that is, the business goal, business process goal, and Performance goal. The priority scheme again can be determined, as needed. Here, High, Medium, and Low are used, where their values are 3, 2, and 1 respectively. Zara's innovation team can have a diverse combination of options to be included in the virtual big data model.

Table 1. Selection of entities for shipment prediction their quality characteristics.

Candidate entities	Quality aspects								
	Comprehensiveness						Relevance		Priority
	D1		D2		D3				
	I	E	Off	On	P	A	STR	SER	
Shipment quantity	✓		✓		✓		+3	+3	H (3)
Sales order	✓		✓		✓		+1	−1	L (1)
Online feedback	✓			✓	✓		0	+2	L (1)
Weather data analysis		✓		✓		✓	+2	+3	M (2)

6 Discussion

Zara's decision-making process for its shipping has been used not only for the purpose of illustrating the key concepts of IRIS's goal-oriented approach to modeling for big data but also for the basis of an empirical study. This study shows that IRIS supports the modeling of big data for carrying out business analytics for Zara's shipment decision making. Additionally, a prototype tool is implemented [24].

Additionally, IRIS helps the process of modeling big data conceptually to become mostly traceable, if not all, while helping explore and select among alternatives in problems, solutions, business analytics, and big data models. This would help justify, and boost the level of confidence in, the quality of the resulting big data conceptual model, eventually the quality of business analytics. However, we have not shown that the potential problems and solutions indeed turn out to be real, key problems and solutions. This would require running big data on a real platform using real data, and, afterward, monitoring the various real phenomena that are related to either problems or solutions – this seems difficult, if not infeasible in reality.

IRIS's approach helps hypothesize and validate problems with the business process and solutions which in turn require the use of a big data model. In particular, the three organizational dimensions helped structure and explore data not only in the same but also across different dimensions of comprehensiveness. Additionally, the notion of distance in relevance helped relate data across different dimensions, hence helping avoid omissions or commissions of data.

Despite the above benefits of IRIS's approach, it has some limitations. First, the empirical study was based on publicly available documents, including articles, white papers, and information on websites, but without access to any real (proprietary) documents. Hence, we could not use the real database schema that was being used, which inevitably might have led to biased results and conclusions. Secondly, our empirical study, as the phrase suggests, did not involve real software practitioners or big data scientists who are working for the company, although we did seek some external opinion on our earlier work. Hence, we need to evaluate with regard to the utility of the proposed approach in really complex organization contexts. Thirdly, we investigate only the quality attributes which conceptual data model can deal with, so later we need to further research the relationships between them and extend other qualities. Finally, how to make the automatic measurement of the quality criteria, i.e., relevance, comprehensiveness, and prioritization, and to provide more guides for three organizational dimensions in the context of big data remains a challenge. We need further explorations to resolve this challenge.

7   Conclusion

In this paper, we have proposed a goal-oriented approach for a conceptual model of big data to support business analytics. This goal-oriented approach of IRIS is intended to rationally and systematically help model big data at a conceptual level by exploring alternatives and selecting the appropriate ones to validate potential problems and solutions. Problems and solutions are hypothesized and validated, in consideration of important business goals, using big data analytics. This goal-oriented approach considers three aspects of big data model quality, namely, relevance, comprehensiveness, and prioritization. In particular, three dimensions of comprehensiveness are proposed, for accommodating a variety of types and sources of data, which are related and organized along with the three organizational primitives. More specifically, IRIS's goal-oriented approach to modeling big data includes: 1) an ontology (or essential vocabulary), which explicitly recognizes goals, problems, and solutions, business analytics, big data model; 2) three dimensions of big data model quality; 3) utilization of three organizational dimensions of a data model. Through an empirical study, we have an initial demonstration that the goal-oriented approach can help boost the level of confidence in the quality of the resulting big data model.

There are several lines of future research. One concern offering guidelines and rules for linking a variety of different types and sources of data in different dimensions, towards developing a richer, virtual big data model. We also plan to define rules to automatically measure the three quality attributes, to provide more guidance for three organizational dimensions, to extend the capabilities of IRIS Assistant, concerning the exploration of, and selection among, KPIs and translation into big data queries, and to incorporate the axioms for the comprehensive dimension towards providing some automatic reasoning capability. More studies are needed, be they empirical or case, in a variety of application domains, in order to further determine both the strengths and weaknesses of IRIS.

References

1. Cai, L., Zhu, Y.: The challenges of data quality and data quality assessment in the big data era. Data Sci. J. **14**, 2 (2015). https://doi.org/10.5334/dsj-2015-002
2. Taleb, I., Serhani, M.A., Dssouli, R.: Big data quality: a survey. In: IEEE International Congress on Big Data, pp. 166–173 (2018)
3. Grover, V., Chiang, R.H.L., Liang, T.P., Zhang, D.: Create strategic business value from big data analytics: a research framework. J. Manag. Inf. Syst. **35**, 388–423 (2018)
4. Embley, D.W., Liddle, S.W.: Big data—conceptual modeling to the rescue. In: Ng, W., Storey, V.C., Trujillo, J.C. (eds.) ER 2013. LNCS, vol. 8217, pp. 1–8. Springer, Heidelberg (2013). https://doi.org/10.1007/978-3-642-41924-9_1
5. Storey, V.C., Song, I.Y.: Big data technologies and management: what conceptual modeling can do. Data Knowl. Eng. **108**, 50–67 (2017)
6. Mylopoulos, J., Chung, L., Nixon, B.: Representing and using nonfunctional requirements: a process-oriented approach. IEEE Trans. Softw. Eng. **18**(6), 483–497 (1992)
7. Teorey, T.J., Yang, D., Fry, J.P.: A logical design methodology for relational databases using the extended entity-relationship model. ACM Comput. Surv. **18**(2), 197–222 (1986)
8. Chen, P.: The entity-relationship model – toward a unified view of data. ACM Trans. Database Syst. **1**, 9–36 (1976)
9. Chebotko, A., Kashlev, A., Lu, S.: A big data modeling methodology for apache cassandra. In: Proceedings of IEEE International Congress on Big Data, pp. 238–245 (2015)
10. Baazizi, M.A., Lahmar, H.B., Colazzo, D., Ghelli, G., Sartiani, C.: Schema inference for massive JSON datasets. In: Proceedings of Extending Database Technology (2017)
11. Jayapandian, C., Chen, C.-H., Dabir, A., Lhatoo, S., Zhang, G.-Q., Sahoo, S.S.: Domain ontology as conceptual model for big data management: application in biomedical informatics. In: Yu, E., Dobbie, G., Jarke, M., Purao, S. (eds.) ER 2014. LNCS, vol. 8824, pp. 144–157. Springer, Cham (2014). https://doi.org/10.1007/978-3-319-12206-9_12
12. Caballero, I., Serrano, M., Piattini, M.: A data quality in use model for big data. In: Indulska, M., Purao, S. (eds.) ER 2014. LNCS, vol. 8823, pp. 65–74. Springer, Cham (2014). https://doi.org/10.1007/978-3-319-12256-4_7

13. Cristalli, E., Serra, F., Marotta, A.: Data quality evaluation in document oriented data stores. In: Woo, C., Lu, J., Li, Z., Ling, T.W., Li, G., Lee, M.L. (eds.) ER 2018. LNCS, vol. 11158, pp. 309–318. Springer, Cham (2018). https://doi.org/10.1007/978-3-030-01391-2_35

14. Taleb, I., Dssouli, R., Serhani, M.A.: Big data pre-processing: a quality framework. In: Proceedings of the IEEE International Congress on Big Data, pp. 191–198 (2015)

15. Sheth, A.P., Larson, J.A.: Federated database systems for managing distributed, heterogeneous, and autonomous databases. ACM Comput. Surv. 22(3), 183–236 (1990)

16. Smith, J.M., Smith, D.C.P.: Database abstractions: aggregation and generalization. ACM Trans. Database Syst. (TODS) 2(2), 105–133 (1977)

17. Nalchigar, S., Yu, E.: Business-driven data analytics: a conceptual modeling framework. Data Knowl. Eng. 117, 1–14 (2018)

18. Park, G., Chung, L., Khan, L., Park, S.: A modeling framework for business process reengineering using big data analytics and a goal-orientation. In: Proceedings of the 11th International Conference on Research Challenges in Information Science (RCIS), pp. 21–32 (2017)

19. Park, G., Sugumaran, V., Park, S.: A reference model for big data analytics. In: Proceedings of the 9th IEEE Annual Ubiquitous Computing, Electronics & Mobile Communication, pp. 382–391 (2018)

20. Wang, R.Y., Strong, D.M.: Beyond accuracy: what data quality means to data consumers. Manag. Inf. Syst. (MIS) 12(4), 5–33 (1996)

21. Caro, F., et al.: Zara uses operations research to reengineer its global distribution process. INFORMS J. Appl. Anal. 40(1), 71–84 (2010)

22. https://sloanreview.mit.edu/article/variety-not-volume-is-driving-big-data-initiatives/

23. https://liliendahl.com/2019/06/13/data-modelling-and-data-quality/

24. https://sites.google.com/site/irisforbigdata/

25. Gosain, A.: Literature review of data model quality metrics of data warehouse. Procedia Comput. Sci. 48, 236–243 (2015)

How to Measure Influence in Social Networks?

Ana Carolina Ribeiro$^{(\boxtimes)}$ ⓘ, Bruno Azevedo ⓘ, Jorge Oliveira e Sá ⓘ,
and Ana Alice Baptista ⓘ

Centro ALGORITMI, University of Minho, 4800-058 Guimarães, Portugal
id8730@alunos.uminho.pt, brunomiguelam@engagelab.org,
{jos,analice}@dsi.uminho.pt

Abstract. Today, social networks are a valued resource of social data that can be used to understand the interactions among people and communities. People can influence or be influenced by interactions, shared opinions and emotions. However, in the social network analysis, one of the main problems is to find the most influential people. This work aims to report on the results of literature review whose goal was to identify and analyse the metrics, algorithms and models used to measure the user influence on social networks. The search was carried out in three databases: Scopus, IEEEXplore, and ScienceDirect. We restricted published articles between the years 2014 until 2020, in English, and we used the following keywords: social networks analysis, influence, metrics, measurements, and algorithms. Backward process was applied to complement the search considering inclusion and exclusion criteria. As a result of this process, we obtained 25 articles: 12 in the initial search and 13 in the backward process. The literature review resulted in the collection of 21 influence metrics, 4 influence algorithms, and 8 models of influence analysis. We start by defining influence and presenting its properties and applications. We then proceed by describing, analysing and categorizing all that were found metrics, algorithms, and models to measure influence in social networks. Finally, we present a discussion on these metrics, algorithms, and models. This work helps researchers to quickly gain a broad perspective on metrics, algorithms, and models for influence in social networks and their relative potentialities and limitations.

Keywords: Influence metrics · Influence analysis · Social networks analysis

1 Introduction

Networks are one of the fundamental structures of our complex systems. In the evolution of our cultural information systems, networks are a ubiquitous way to represent the dynamics of economic and social systems [1–4].

The Web allowed simultaneously the exponential production and spreading of digital information. Users are "prosumers", meaning that they are simultaneous interchangeably producers and consumers of information [5]. Social networks exponentially increased the number of social actors that create a wide number of connections forming a vast structure of links between actors and other entities (e.g. documents, messages, posts, recommendations) [6].

© Springer Nature Switzerland AG 2020
F. Dalpiaz et al. (Eds.): RCIS 2020, LNBIP 385, pp. 38–57, 2020.
https://doi.org/10.1007/978-3-030-50316-1_3

The growing use of social networks has attracted many researchers, academics, and organizations to explore social network research topics, including the influence analysis [7]. Influence analysis and its spread on social networks have an important application value [8] by allowing to analyse and explain people's social behaviors. It also provide a theoretical basis for decision making [9]. However, there are still some challenges to work on [8]: there is no mathematical formula of influence; it is difficult to identify the parameters to measure the influence; and, the large amount of data generated by social networks, makes it difficult to analyse and, consequently, to determine the influence.

An influence analysis study covers the study of influence properties such as influence evaluation metrics and algorithms, influence maximization, and social data collection and big data analysis [10].

This paper falls within the scope of the project 6,849.32 New Scientific Journal Articles Everyday: Visualize or Perish! [11] and the main objective of this work is to identify and analyse the most relevant and metrics, algorithms and/or influence models currently available.

The articles' search and selection process was based on the recommendations given by [12] complemented by [13] and was following:

1. Search engines and databases: Scopus, IEEEXplore, and ScienceDirect;
2. Time constraints: January 2014 to January 2020;
3. Keywords: social networks analysis, influence, algorithms, metrics, and measurements;
4. Types of documents: reviews, journals and conference papers;
5. Languages: English;
6. Selection criteria: Iterative process where the titles, abstracts and parts of the articles were reviewed for inclusion/exclusion.

The search resulted in 12 articles. The backward process was applied to these articles, which resulted in an addition of 13 articles, totalling 25 articles.

The main contributions of this work are briefly summarized below:

1. A methodology sufficiently detailed to allow the analysis of this study by other reliable researchers and use this study as a basis for future research into the influence on social networks.
2. An overview of the most relevant and up-to-date metrics, algorithms and/or models in social networks: 21 metrics, 4 algorithms, and 8 models of influence analysis.

The remaining of this article is organized as follows: the section "Methodological Procedure" presents the methodology applied for the selection of articles; the section "Related Work" presents some the related works that analyse the algorithms, metrics, and models of influence; the section "A landscape of influence in social networks" aims to present the overview of the metrics, algorithms, and influence models, the section "Discussion" presents the discussion of the results obtained, and section "Conclusions and Future Work" presents the conclusions, limitations, and some future research directions.

2 Methodological Procedures

This section reports the methodological procedures applied and that were based on [12].
Figure 1 represents all stages of the process.

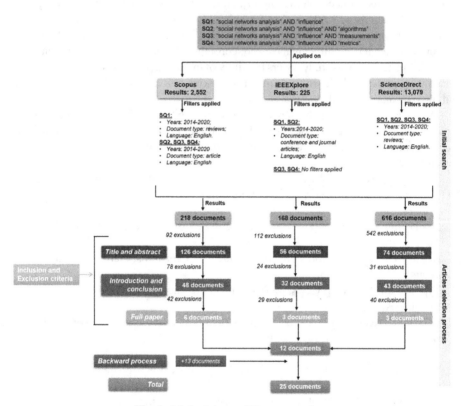

Fig. 1. Methodology of literature review.

2.1 Initial Search

The initial search starts with the selection of three databases: Scopus, IEEEXplore, and
ScienceDirect. These databases have wide coverage of articles related to the topic and
allow to filter the results: according to [14], in the social sciences, the coverage of Scopus
is much higher than that of the Web of Science; The percentage of titles covered only
by Scopus is above 60%, to which is added the almost 40% coverage overlap (Scopus
and WoS), with WoS alone covering a very small percentage of titles; Sources indexed
only by WoS are not necessarily disposable, however, it is safe to use only Scopus.
IEEExplore and Science Direct were used because they are widely used databases in the
area of information systems, as a cross-check measure with Scopus results.

The keywords used were "social networks analysis", "influence", "algorithms",
"measurements", and "metrics". In the initial search, we applied four search queries

(SQ) (Fig. 1) with the following results: Scopus 2,552 articles, IEEEXplore 225 articles, and ScienceDirect 13,079 articles, totalling 15,856 articles.

Considering these values, we used filters to get an acceptable number of results to analyse articles for all search queries: articles published from January 2014 to January 2020, conferences or journals or reviews, and written in English. However, according to the results obtained, it was necessary to adapt these filters for some search queries applied in some digital libraries, namely:

- For search query 1 on Scopus, we applied a different filter concerning the document type: we selected reviews because the values collected in the initial search were very high (2,121 articles). The reviews were selected because this type of articles describe, analyse, and discuss scientific knowledge already published.
- For search queries 3 and 4 applied on IEEEXplore, the values collected were low (6 and 9, respectively), and the application of filters was not necessary.

After applying the filters, all articles collected from Scopus, IEEEXplore, and ScienceDirect will be analysed in the next section.

2.2 Articles Selection Process and Results

After the articles collected in the previous phase, in this phase, all articles will be analysed according to the inclusion and exclusion criteria (Table 1), in parallel with the three phases described below

1. Title and abstract: Articles were selected if the title and abstract were aligned with the research objectives;
2. Introduction and conclusion: The introduction and conclusion of the articles accepted in phase 1 were analysed to proceed to a new selection;
3. Full article: The articles accepted in phase 2 were then fully read and subset was selected to be included in the review.

This process allowed the selection of 12 articles. We then applied a backward process were the references of the twelve previously selected articles were analysed. The implementation of the backward process resulted in the addition of 13 articles. The backward process, which allowed the identification of the most used metrics, algorithms and models to measure the influence on social networks, worked as a complemented the selection process, by allowing to gain a broader perspective on the topic. In total, 25 articles were collected and analysed.

Table 1. Inclusion and Exclusion criteria.

Inclusion criteria	Exclusion criteria
Articles about algorithms or metrics of social networks analysis	Articles not using metrics and/or influence algorithms (mention only metrics used in the social networks analysis, but not oriented to the analysis of influence)
Articles about the algorithms or metrics to computing influence on a social network	Articles focused on the influence that social networks have on people's lives, education, family life and, in general, on society
Articles about the algorithms or metrics to computing influence maximization on a social network	
Articles about the algorithms or metrics to computing influence diffusion on a social network	
Articles about the algorithms or metrics to computing influence applied on a social network	

3 Related Work

In this section, are reviewed the related works that analyse the algorithms, metrics, and models of influence.

The work reported in [15], presents a research on the latest generation of models, methods, and aspects of evaluation associated to influence analysis and provides a comprehensive analysis, helps to understand social behaviours, provides a theoretical basis to influence public opinion and reveal future directions of research and possible applications. The authors distinguish models in two types: microscopic (linear threshold, independent cascade, etc.) and macroscopic (epidemic models are the most common). The authors consider that, in the future, the microscopic models should concentrate on considering human interactions and different mechanisms during the information diffusion, while the macroscopic models consider the same probability of transmission and identical influential power for all users.

Differently, the authors of [8], present the state of the art on the influence analysis on social networks, presenting an overview of social networks, an explanation on the influence analysis at different levels, as a definition, properties, architecture and diffusion models, discuss the assessment metrics for influence and summarize the models for evaluating influence on social networks. In this work, the authors present some of the future trends in this topic that must be taken into account: the integration of cross-disciplinary knowledge due to the complexity of the topic; the development of an effective mechanism for influence analysis (hybrid approaches to improve the efficiency and effectiveness of influence analysis) and an effective model for the efficiency and scalability of influence analysis.

The study [16] is also a relevant work because it focuses on the problem of predicting influential users on social networks. In this work, the authors present a three-level hierarchy that classifies the measures of influence: models, types, and algorithms. The authors also compare, based on empirical analysis, in terms of performance, precision, and correlation the measures of influence using a data set from two different social networks to verify the feasibility of measuring the influence. The results of the study show that the prediction of influential users does not depend only on the measures of influence, but also on the nature of social networks.

In the article [17], the authors study the probability of an individual being an influencer. They grouped the influence measures in some categories: measures derived from the neighbourhood (that is, number of influencers, personal exposure of the network), diversity structural, temporal measures, cascade measures, and metadata. Also, they evaluated how these measures relate to the likelihood that a user will be influenced using actual data from a microblog. Subsequently, the authors evaluated the performance of these measures when used as a resource in a machine learning approach and compared performance in a variety of supervised machine learning approaches. Finally, they evaluated how the proportion of positive to negative samples in training and testing affects the results of predictions - still allowing the practical use of these concepts for applications of influence.

4   A Landscape of Influence in Social Networks

This section starts by presenting the concept of influence on social networks and, some influence analysis applications, and their main properties. Also presented are the various metrics, algorithms and models found in the literature for influence analysis. For each metric, we present its definition and, in some cases, the calculation formula.

4.1   Understanding Influence in Social Networks

In social sciences, the term *influence* is widely used: according to [18], influence is *"The power to change or affect someone or something: the power to cause changes without directly forcing them to happen"*; and [19], *"social influence occurs when an individual's thoughts, feelings or actions are affected by other people"* p. 184.

A social network can be represented as a graph $G = (V, E)$, where V corresponds to the nodes (vertices) in the graph (users), and E corresponds to the edges that indicate the relationship between users [20, 21]. According to [20] the relationship (edges) connects the influencer and influenced node, i.e., who influences whom. The edges' weights correspond to the influence probabilities among the nodes.

Marketing is one of the areas were influence analysis is most frequent. These specialists select a set of influential users and try to influence them to adopt a new behavior, product or service; Later, they expect these users to recommend to others, for example, by spreading word-of-mouth in the social networks [22]. In sentiment analysis, text mining tools and natural language processing to allow extract subjective information from data sets of social networks, for example, users' opinions and attitudes. This makes, it possible to analyse the influence of users [23]. Another interesting application is the influence analysis of academics in their communities. High impact researchers are not necessarily influential [24, 25].

According to [7], influence has the following properties: A user's influence can increase or decrease with new experiences or interactions – dynamic nature. These new experiences or interactions can be more important, and the old ones can become irrelevant over time, i.e., the user can stop being influential at any time; In a social network, information can be propagated from one user to another, allowing the development of chains of influence - propagative nature; Influence has no mathematical definition or measure. Its subjective nature leads to the personalization of the calculation of influence, where the biases and preferences of influencers have a direct impact on its calculation.

To measure the influence on social networks, several metrics, algorithms, and models are known. These are grouped in the following categories:

- **Influence diffusion models** – Influence diffusion models measure the influence of users through their ability to spread information [16].
- **Centrality measures** – Centrality measures classify users according to their position on the network. Centrality measures the central position and importance of a user in a social network [16].
- **Influence measures based on walks between pair of users** – These types of measures provide relative power or status of user in a network by accounting all length paths between pair of nodes [26].
- **Link topological ranking measures** – According to [8], most centrality metrics do not consider the variation of nodes in their calculation: these metrics consider that all nodes contribute equally to their calculation. However, different types of nodes execute an important role in social networks.
- **Types of influence maximization algorithm** – Maximizing influence is a problem widely studied by the community. Influence maximization algorithms should perform fast calculations, high accuracy, and low storage capacity [15].
- **Others** – This category includes measures used by social networks such as Twitter to measure the influence of users [27].

4.2 Metrics and Algorithms Overview

In the category of Influence diffusion models we found the following models: Linear threshold model (LT model), Independent cascade model (IC model), Heat diffusion model (HD model), and Epidemic models (Table 2).

To apply the LT model and IC model, it is necessary to perform the Monte Carlo simulation to determine the influence of a node for a given period. However, the Monte Carlo simulation is time-consuming and inadequate for large-scale social networks [15]. The IC model is used to find highly influential users, find the maximum influence, predict the development of cascades, and understand the diffusion structure in the networks [20, 28]. Similar to the IC model, the LT model is mainly used to maximize the influence of propagation on the network.

Epidemic models are used to find the source of the viral disease and to find the sources of rumours. The epidemic disease in the population is similar to the spread of rumours on a social network [8, 28]. However, these models ignore the topological characteristics of social networks [15].

Table 2. Influence diffusion models.

Influence diffusion models	Description
LT model	In this model, a new idea, or innovation is adopted by a user u, only when a certain number of users influence that user u [8] In a social network $G = (V, E)$, the sum of the influence weights of all neighbouring nodes of node v_i corresponds to: $$\sum_{v_j \in N_{g_i} act} w_{ij} \leq 1,$$ where w_{ij} corresponds to influence weights between node v_i and its neighbour node v_j, and $N_{g_i act}$ corresponds to the neighbouring nodes activated by node v_i [15]
IC model	The IC model describes the procedure of influence propagation in a probabilistic way: a user can influence (activate) his neighbour with a certain probability [8, 16]. The IC model is represented as follows [20]: • The initial seed set creates the active sets S_t for all t $\geq$ 1 using the following rule: at each phase t $\geq$ 1, the first activation step is considered from the set S_t para S_{t-1}; then, for each inactive node u, an activation attempt is performed using the Bernoulli test with a probability of success $p(u, v)$
HD model	There is a similarity between the heat diffusion and the information spread on social networks: a user selecting information acts as a source of heat, which diffuses his influence on the social network [8, 15]
Epidemic models	Epidemic models correspond to models capable of studying the influence of a macroscopic perspective [8]. According to [29], epidemic models are classified into three categories: deterministic models, stochastic models, and space-time models • Deterministic models include the susceptible-infectious model (SI model), the susceptible-infectious-susceptible model (SIS model), and the susceptible-infectious-recovery model (SIR model) • The stochastic epidemic model includes the discrete-time, continuous-time Markov model, and the stochastic differential equation model • The space-time models introduce automated cell phones to model the spread of influence

In the category of Centrality measures we found the following metrics: degree centrality, closeness centrality, betweenness centrality and, eigenvector centrality (Table 3).

Centrality metrics measure a user position in a social network, and the most used tools are graph theory and network analysis [8]. These metrics are used to find the most central and influential node in the network. The centrality metrics for finding the centrality of the node depend on the structural properties of the network and make use of flows to analyse these characteristics [16, 26, 28].

Table 3. Centrality measures.

Centrality measures	Description
Degree centrality	In a social network G = (V, E), degree centrality metric correspond to the number of neighbours of a node, that is, the number of edges that a node has [30–33] It is usually calculated by dividing the degree of a node (k_i) by $N - 1$, restricting the value in the range of [0, 1]. The equation that defines it is as follows: $$C_D(i) = \frac{k_i}{N-1}$$
Closeness centrality	In a social network G = (V, E), closeness centrality corresponds to the average length of the shortest path from one node to all other nodes [30–33]. In the influence analysis, this metric measures the efficiency of each node to disseminate information on the network [8] The equation that defines it is as follows: $$C_C(i) = \frac{N-1}{\sum_{j \neq i}^{N} d_{ij}},$$ Where, N is the number of nodes in the network and d_{ij} is the distance between node i and node j
Betweenness centrality	In a social network G = (V, E), betweenness centrality describes the extent of nodes that need to be crossed to influence other nodes [31–33] The equation that defines it is as follows: $$C_B(i) = \sum_{s \neq i \neq t \in V, s < t} \frac{\sigma_{st}(i)}{\sigma_{st}},$$ Where $\sigma_{st}(i)$ corresponds to the number of shortest paths between nodes s and t through the node i, and σ_{st} corresponds to the number of shortest paths between nodes s and t
Eigenvector centrality	In a social network G = (V, E), eigenvector centrality provides the relative scores for all nodes, according to the nodes connected to the highest scores contribute more to the scores of the nodes than to the lowest scores [32]. Eigenvector centrality use the adjacency matrix, given by: $$C_E(i) = \frac{1}{\lambda} \sum_j A_{ij} C_E(j),$$ Where, A_{ij} corresponds i^{th} eigenvector of the adjacency matrix in the network

In the category of Influence measures based on walks between pair of users we found the following metrics: Katz centrality, Hubbel measure, and Bonacich Power Measure (Table 4).

Table 4. Influence measures based on walks between pair of users.

Influence measures based on walks between pair of users	Description
Katz centrality	Katz centrality allows not only direct links received by a user but also popularity or status of users sending links to him to be included in his score. Further, the status of each, who has link with these users in turn, should also be used for calculating scores in social network [26]. The equation that defines it is as follows: $$\vec{C}_{Katz} = \left(\left(I - \alpha A^T \right)^{-1} - I \right) \vec{I},$$ Where, I is the identity matrix, $\vec{I}$ is a vector of size n (n is the number of nodes) consisting of ones. A^T denotes the transposed matrix of A and $\left(I - \alpha A^T \right)^{-1}$ denotes matrix inversion of the term $\left(I - \alpha A^T \right)$ Through Katz measure, most influential node or individual positive tie network can be found who has connections with most of the other users and can influence or affect other users with his decisions or activities [26]. This measure is similar to PageRank algorithm and eigenvector centrality
Hubbel measure	Hubbel measure corresponds to the flow of influence through interpersonal links in social networks as input and output channels. The Hubbel measure has structural as well as functional significance. The structural significance of index is in identifying cliques and functional significance is in computation of status [26] This measure is similar to Katz centrality, the Katz measure uses an identity matrix (each node is connected to itself) while the Hubble measure does not

(continued)

Table 4. *(continued)*

Influence measures based on walks between pair of users	Description
Bonacich power measure	In social networks, the most central user is not always the most powerful one In order to distinguish between power and centrality, was proposed a set of measures given by $c(\alpha,\beta)$. The parameter β is used to reflect the degree and direction (positive or negative) in which individual user status depends upon status of other users in network [26] Bonacich power measure is useful in valued and signed graphs, negative ties and positive ties networks

The Katz centrality can be used to compute centrality in directed networks (citation networks, WWW, etc.); it can also be used estimate the relative status or influence of user in a social network [8, 20, 34]. Hubbel Measure and Bonacich Power Measure are measures similar to Katz centrality.

In the category of Link topology ranking measures, were found the following metrics: Hyperlink-Induced Topic Search (HITS) algorithm and PageRank Algorithm (Table 5).

Except for eigenvector centrality, most centrality metrics do not consider the variation of the nodes, which means that they consider that all nodes contribute equally to the measures [8]. However, the types of nodes execute an important role in social networks. The HITS algorithm aims to classify web pages based on links, while in PageRank all hyperlinked pages receive numerical weights, used to measure the importance of web pages [27].

The HITS algorithm is used to classify publications in citations networks by Citeseer (search engine). In the context of citation networks, it is natural to identify topical reviews as hubs, as they contain many references to influential articles in the literature [34].

In category of Influence maximization algorithms were found the following algorithms: Greedy-based algorithms and Heuristic-based algorithms (Table 6).

According to the literature, the greedy-based algorithms have higher accuracy compared to the heuristic-based algorithms. This is because greedy-based algorithms have high computational complexity and high execution time, decreasing their efficiency [15]. Concerning the heuristic-based algorithms, these algorithms were proposed to reduce the execution time of the solution and increase efficiency. Also, they present higher values of accuracy [8].

Table 5. Link topology ranking measures.

Link topology ranking measures	Description
HITS algorithm	The HITS algorithm is a popular classification method based on eigenvector to classify web pages [34]. In a network, this algorithm selects two scores to each node: score h – referred to as node hub-centrality score – is large for nodes that point to many authoritative nodes, and score a – referred to as node authority-centrality score – is large for nodes that are pointed by many hubs [8, 34] • Authority-centrality score: In the algorithm it is necessary update each node's authority score to be equal to the sum of the hub scores of each node that point to it. A node is given a high authority score by being linked from pages that are recognized as Hubs for information • Hub-centrality score: A hub is a web page serving as a large directories with no actual authoritative content that it points to. In the HITS algorithm, a directory points to many authorities, and an authority is a page with many incoming links from different hubs. In the algorithm, it is necessary update each node's hub score to be equal to the sum of the authority scores of each node that it points to The corresponding equations for node a and h are [34]: $a = \alpha Ah$ $h = \beta A^T a,$ Where, α and β are parameters of the method
PageRank algorithm	In PageRank algorithm, all hyperlinked pages are given weights, which are used to measure the importance of web pages [35]. PageRank algorithm can be applied to social networks analysis since the relationships of nodes in social networks can be structured like links [36] The PageRank algorithm is defined by the following equation: $PR(r) = \frac{1-\lambda}{N} + \lambda \sum_{i=1}^{k} \frac{PR(r_i)}{K_{out}(r_i)},$ Where N represents the total number of nodes in the network, K_{out} is the out-degree of the node r, r_i denotes th in-degree of node r and λ is the damping factor

In the category of other influence metrics and algorithms were found the following metrics and algorithms: Popularity measures on Twitter (FollowerRank, Popularity, Popularity paradoxical discounted, Network Score, Acquaintance Score, Acquaintance-affinity score, Acquaintance-Affinity-Identification Score), Traditional measure used on Twitter (h-index), Measures based on Twitter metrics and PageRank (Retweet Impact, Mention Impact, Social Networking Potential, ThunkRank, UserRank), Topical influential users (Information diffusion), and Predicting influences (Activity and Willingness

Table 6. Influence maximization algorithms.

Influence maximization algorithms	Description
Greedy-based algorithms	The study of greedy algorithms is based on hill-climbing greedy algorithm, in which each option can provide the highest value of the impact of the node used to the local optimal solution to approximate the global optimal solution [8] Some examples of greedy-based algorithms are present below: 1) Target wise greedy algorithm based on the potential-based node-selection strategy. This algorithm does not have good results in an initial phase, but it can cover more nodes in a later phase of diffusion [37] 2) Community-based greedy algorithm was proposed to reduce the cost in terms of execution time. It is based on the IC model [38] 3) Upper bound-based lazy forward algorithm has been proposed to discover top-k influential nodes. This algorithm sets new limits to significantly reduce the number of Monte Carlo simulations, particularly in the initial phase [39]
Heuristic-based algorithms	According to the computational complexity of the greedy-based algorithms, several heuristic algorithms have been proposed to reduce the solution time and obtain more efficiency of the algorithm. These algorithms select nodes iteratively based on a specific heuristic, instead of computing the marginal gain of the nodes in each iteration. In contrast, its accuracy is relatively low [15] A proposed algorithm was Two-phase Heuristic Algorithm (TPH). This algorithm is composed of two phases: each node has its offline probability of a given product; therefore, the consideration of local-based maximization cannot focus only on the network topology, but also on the offline property of each node [40]

of users (AWI) model, Activeness, centrality, quality of post and reputation (ACQR) Framework, Time Network Influence Model, AuthorRanking) (Table 7).

These metrics were defined to try to combine metrics involving tweets, replies, tweets, and mentions to obtain information about a social network using a numerical value [27]. According to [41], the metrics of retweets are the best quantitative indicators for choosing to read a tweet over the other. Besides this, the most important indicators are qualitative, for example, the friendship between the reader and the author of the tweet.

Table 7. Other influence metrics and algorithms.

Others	Description
Popularity measures on Twitter	**1) FollowerRank** – Corresponds to the standardized version of the in-degree measure. $$FollowerRank(i) = \frac{Number\ of\ followers}{Number\ of\ followers + Number\ of\ followees}$$ **2) Popularity** – This measure was developed to mitigate differences in followers between users $Popularity(i) = 1 - e^{\lambda.Number\ of\ followers}$, Where, λ it is a constant that, by default, is equal to 1 **3) Popularity paradoxical discounted** – Corresponds to the number of reciprocal actors of a user, that is, the number of followers who are also followed $Pradoxixal\ discounted(i) =$ $$\begin{cases} \frac{N^{\Omega}\ of\ followers}{N^{\Omega}\ of\ followees} & if\ N^{\Omega}\ of\ followers > N^{\Omega}\ of\ followees \\ \frac{N^{\Omega}\ of\ followers - reciprocal(i)}{N^{\Omega}\ of\ followees - reciprocal(i)} & otherwise \end{cases}$$ Measuring the value of reciprocal value (i) considerably increases computational costs **4) Network Score (NS)** – Corresponds to a measure of popularity, based on the user's active non-reciprocal followers $$NS(i) = \log(N^{\Omega}\ topically\ active\ followers + 1)$$ $$- \log(N^{\Omega}\ topically\ active\ followees + 1)$$ **5) Acquaintance Score A(i)** – Measures how well-know user i is. Let n be the number of considered user accounts, it is defined as: $$A(i) = \frac{N^{\Omega}\ of\ followers + UMA + URA + UPA}{n}$$ Where, UMA = number of users mentioning the author, URA = number of users who have retweeted author's tweets, and UPA = number of users who have replied author's tweets **6) Acquaintance-Affinity Score AA(j)** – Measures how dear user j is, by considering how well know are those who want him $$AA(j) = \sum_{i \in E_{RP}} A(i).\frac{\#replies\ of\ i\ to\ j}{\#replies\ of\ i} + \sum_{i \in E_M} A(i).\frac{\#mentions\ of\ i\ to\ j}{\#mentions\ of\ i} +$$ $$\sum_{i \in E_{RT}} A(i).\frac{\#retweets\ of\ i\ to\ j}{\#retweets\ of\ i}$$ Where ERP, EM, and ERT are the set of users who reply, mention and retweet the tweets of j, respectively **7) Acquaintance-Affinity-Identification Score AAI(j)** - Measures how identifiable user j is, by considering how dear those who identify him $$AAI(j) = \sum_{i \in F_r} \frac{AA(i)}{\#followees\ of\ i},$$ Where, Fr is the set of followers of j. The AAI Score is well correlated with the number of followers and was used to identify celebrities in the "real world", i.e., outside the Twitter network

(continued)

Table 7. (*continued*)

Others	Description
Traditional measure used on Twitter	**h-index** – In the context of Twitter, it can be defined as the maximum value h such that h tweets of the user have been replied, retweeted, or liked, at least h times
Measures based on Twitter metrics and PageRank	**1) Retweet Impact (RI)** – Estimates the impact of the user tweets, in terms of the mentions received by other users $RI(i) = RT2 * \log(RT3)$, Where RT2 = Number of original tweets posted by the author and retweeted by other users, RT3 = Number of users who have retweeted author's tweets **2) Mention Impact (MI)** – Estimates the impact of the user tweets, in terms of the mentions received by other users $MI(i) = M3 * \log(M4) - M1 * (M2)$, Where M1 = Number of mentions to other users by the author, M2 = Number of users mentioned by the author, M3 = Number of mentions to the author by other users, M4 = Number of users mentioning the author **3) Social Networking Potential (SNP)** – Measure considers all kind of actions on Twitter, except the favorites or likes $SNP(i) = \frac{Ir(i)+RMr(i)}{2}$, Where the Interactor Ratio, Ir(i), and the Retweet and Mention Ratio, RMr(i), are defined as: $Ir(i) = \frac{RT3+M4}{F1}$ and $RMr(i) = \frac{\#tweets\ of\ i\ retweetes + \#tweets\ of\ i\ replied}{\#tweets\ of\ i}$, Where RT3 = Number of users who have retweeted author's tweets, M4 = Number of users mentioning the author, F1 = Number of followers **4) ThunkRank** – Direct adaptation of PageRank algorithm into the context of Twitter $TunkRank(i) = \sum_{j \in followers(i)} \frac{1+p.TunkRank(j)}{\#followees\ of\ j}$, Where $0 \leq p \leq 1$ is the probability that a tweet is retweeted. This probability is assumed to be equal for all users. In the literature, normally use $p = 0.5$, but in fact this value should vary from case to case **5) UserRank** – A variation of ThunkTank, defined to measure the influence of a user according to the relevance of his tweets $UserRank(i) = \sum_{j \in followers(i)} \frac{1 + \frac{\#followers\ of\ i}{\#tweets\ of\ i} * UserRank(j)}{\#followers\ of\ j}$
Topical influential users	**Information diffusion** – Estimates the possible influence of the users's tweets among his followers who are non-followees $ID(i) = \log(N^{\circ}\ of\ followers\ tweeting\ on\ topic\ after\ the\ author + 1)$ $- (N^{\circ}\ of\ followees\ tweeting\ on\ topic\ before\ the\ author + 1)$ The "+1" in the logarithms avoids divisions by zero. This measure only considers follow-up relashionships, but it is independent of the number of followers and followees on the network

(*continued*)

Table 7. (*continued*)

Others	Description
Predicting influences	**1) Activity and Willingness of users (AWI) model** – AWI model is a user interaction model that considers the activity and willingness of users to retweet through time, in order to measure the influence among pairs of users. This model also predicts retweet ratios and influential users **2) Activeness, centrality, quality of post and reputation (ACQR) Framework** – This framework uses data mining to detect activity (original tweets, retweets and replies), centrality, and user reputation (mechanism to distinguish between real users and spammers). It also considers the quality of tweets through the number of replies and retweets, and the reputation of users that reply and retweet. ACQR framework was used to identify and predict the influential users in a relatively small network that was restricted to a specific topic **3) Time Network Influence Model** – Uses a probabilistic generative model to make an offline estimation of the influence power between users. This model considers the time intervals between messages, follow-up relationships, and the relationships of similarity in the content of the tweets **4) AuthorRanking** – Uses the style of the tweets (words, hastags, websites, references to other accounts) and user behavior (profile information, following ratios, number of tweets, and main user activity, previously determined by a text classification task)

5 Discussion

The growing development of social networks has also allowed the production of large amounts of information that can tell who the most influential users are. To try to solve this problem were developed algorithms, metrics, and models to compute the influence of a user on social networks [8]. For this reason, this work presents an extended set of several algorithms, metrics, and models and their applicability found in the literature.

One of the main problems of some metrics, algorithms, and models detected in the literature is the scalability-efficiency capacity [8, 15]. Also, with the continued increase of social networks, most existing methods find the problem of efficiency in runtime, and it becomes difficult to implement them in a large-scale context.

The literature argues that the application of the LT model and the IC model is time-consuming and unsuitable for large-scale networks [20, 28]. Also, greedy-based algorithms present high computational complexity and high execution time, decreasing their efficiency [15]. Other algorithms such as heuristic-based algorithms have been developed to reduce these execution times and, consequently, increase their efficiency [8].

The diversity of metrics, algorithms, and models of influence analysis is due to the need to solve several types of problems: influence maximization [15], the influence diffusion [16], the distinction of the importance of the various nodes in a social network, among others. Centrality measures are the best known and most used in the social networks analysis, but to be used in the analysis of the most influential node, they are dependent on the properties of the networks [15]. The metrics that fall into the Others category are very interesting: the investigators used quantitative measures such as tweets, retweets or mentions to obtain a numerical value and thus be able to classify the user as influential or not [27].

It is important to consider the objectives of the problem and the type of data in hands in order to be able to apply the most appropriate set of metrics to obtain the greatest possible precision of the influence.

6   Conclusions and Future Work

As mentioned at the beginning of the article, influence analysis is one of the biggest problems in social networks analysis. Therefore, the main objective of this literature review was to identify and analyse the most relevant metrics, algorithms, or models to measure the influence on social networks. Also, methodological limitations were recognized and should be refined in future work, namely:

- The article selection process for literature review was performed by only one researcher. This may affect the results because articles were select according to perspective of a single researcher. Recommendation: This phase should be conducted in parallel with other researchers to reduce error and bias in article selection. The usage of social networks (Twitter, Facebook, etc.) may also support the research allowing identify the perspective of other researchers and get new research outputs faster;
- Since Scopus only used reviews, several important studies may have been missed. As future work, a meta-analysis of the reviews must be made. Thus, it will be possible to complement the work with a review of what was produced after the last review analysed.
- Only 3 databases were used – Scopus, IEEEXplore, and ScienceDirect. Recommendation: although these databases have high coverage of scientific articles, other sources (SpringerLink, Web of Science, scientific journals, and social networks) may complement the research.
- The keywords used in search queries can be improved, including new keywords, changing their order and combination to cover more works. For example, "social network", "social networks influence analysis", "models", "social media", "social media platforms", etc.

In this article, was reported a study of influence and respective the metrics, algorithms, and models used for its analysis their challenges and opportunities. Through this search and the analysis of the articles, it was possible to collect 21 metrics, 4 types of algorithms, and 8 models of influence analysis.

The metrics, algorithms, and models of influence found in the literature allowed us to obtain a broad view of this topic: the LT model and the IC model are the most time-consuming and inappropriate models for large-scale networks; the greedy-based algorithms are considered very complex and time-consuming to implement; and the centrality measures are the most well-known measures and the measures based on indicators such as tweets, retweets, and mentions should be deepened to understand how they can contribute when used in conjunction with other types of metrics. Also, as the metrics of Twitter were analysed, metrics from other social networks (for example, Facebook) should be analysed and compare for existing differences; if they can be adapted to other social networks, since it depends on the organization of the social network and the types and numbers of resources it has.

However, it is necessary to consider that, in addition to these metrics, algorithms, and models, other measures should be studied due to their potential in the influence analysis.

Several challenges and opportunities may stimulate, in the future, new theoretical and practical perspectives. This article may serve as a basis for researchers interested in measuring the influence on social networks as they can gain a broad perspective on the topic.

Acknowledgments. This work has been supported by IViSSEM: POCI-01-0145-FEDER-28284, COMPETE: POCI-01-0145-FEDER-007043 and FCT – Fundação para a Ciência e Tecnologia within the R&D Units Project Scope: UIDB/00319/2020.

References

1. Newman, M., Watts, D.J., Barabási, A.-L.: The Structure and Dynamics of Networks. Princeton University Press, Princeton (2006)
2. Wright, A.: Glut: Mastering Information Through the Ages. Cornell University Press, Ithaca (2008)
3. Castellano, C., Fortunato, S., Loreto, V.: Statistical physics of social dynamics. Rev. Mod. Phys. **81**(2), 591–646 (2009)
4. Hidalgo, C.A.: Disconnected, fragmented, or united? A trans-disciplinary review of network science. Appl. Netw. Sci. **1**(1), 6 (2016)
5. Wurman, R.S.: Information Anxiety 2, 2nd edn. QUE (2001)
6. Hansen, D., Shneiderman, B., Smith, M.: Analyzing Social Media Networks with NodeXL: Insights from a Connected World, 1st edn. Morgan Kaufmann (2010)
7. Peng, S., Wang, G., Xie, D.: Social influence analysis in social networking big data: opportunities and challenges. IEEE Netw. **31**(1), 11–17 (2017)
8. Peng, S., Zhou, Y., Cao, L., Yu, S., Niu, J., Jia, W.: Influence analysis in social networks: a survey. J. Netw. Comput. Appl. **106**(January), 17–32 (2018)
9. Yu, S., Liu, M., Dou, W., Liu, X., Zhou, S.: Networking for big data: a survey. IEEE Commun. Surv. Tutor. **19**(1), 531–549 (2017)
10. Kempe, D., Kleinberg, J., Tardos, É.: Maximizing the spread of influence through a social network. In: Proceedings of the Ninth ACM SIGKDD International Conference on Knowledge Discovery and Data Mining, vol. 11, pp. 137–146 (2003)
11. Azevedo, B.M., Oliveira e Sá, J., Baptista, A.A., Branco, P.: Information visualization: conceptualizing new paths for filtering and navigate in scientific knowledge objects. In: 2017 24o Encontro Português de Computação Gráfica e Interação (EPCGI), pp. 1–8 (2017)
12. Webster, J., Watson, R.T.: Analyzing the past to prepare for the future: writing a review. MIS Q. **26**(2), 13 (2002)

13. Kitchenham, B., Pearl Brereton, O., Budgen, D., Turner, M., Bailey, J., Linkman, S.: Systematic literature reviews in software engineering - a systematic literature review. Inf. Softw. Technol. **51**(1), 7–15 (2009)
14. Mongeon, P., Paul-Hus, A.: The journal coverage of Web of Science and Scopus: a comparative analysis. Scientometrics **106**(1), 213–228 (2016)
15. Li, K., Zhang, L., Huang, H.: Social influence analysis: models, methods, and evaluation. Engineering **4**(1), 40–46 (2018)
16. Almgren, K., Lee, J.: An empirical comparison of influence measurements for social network analysis. Soc. Netw. Anal. Min. **6**(52), 1–18 (2016)
17. Kumar, N., Guo, R., Aleali, A., Shakarian, P.: An empirical evaluation of social influence metrics (2016)
18. Merriam, W.: Definition of influence. In: Definition of influence (2011)
19. Li, H., Cui, J.-T., Ma, J.-F.: Social influence study in online networks: a three-level review. J. Comput. Sci. Technol. **30**(1), 184–199 (2015)
20. More, J.S., Lingam, C.: A gradient-based methodology for optimizing time for influence diffusion in social networks. Soc. Netw. Anal. Min. **9**(1), 5 (2019)
21. Jalayer, M., Azheian, M., Agha Mohammad Ali Kermani, M.: A hybrid algorithm based on community detection and multi attribute decision making for influence maximization. Comput. Ind. Eng. **120**, 234–250 (2018)
22. Liqing, Q., Jinfeng, Y., Xin, F., Wei, J., Wenwen, G.: Analysis of Influence Maximization in large-Scale Social Networks. IEEE Access **7**(4), 42052–42062 (2019)
23. Li, D., Shuai, X., Sun, G., Tang, J., Ding, Y., Luo, Z.: Mining topic-level opinion influence in microblog. In: ACM International Conference Proceeding Series, pp. 1562–1566 (2012)
24. Li, N., Gillet, D.: Identifying influential scholars in academic social media platforms. In: Proceedings of the 2013 IEEE/ACM International Conference on Advances in Social Networks Analysis and Mining, pp. 608–614 (2013)
25. Kong, X., Shi, Y., Yu, S., Liu, J., Xia, F.: Academic social networks: modeling, analysis, mining and applications. J. Netw. Comput. Appl. **132**, 86–103 (2019)
26. Kaur, M., Singh, S.: Analyzing negative ties in social networks: a survey. Egypt. Inform. J. **17**(1), 21–43 (2016)
27. Riquelme, F., González-Cantergiani, P.: Measuring user influence on Twitter: a survey. Inf. Process. Manag. **52**(5), 949–975 (2016)
28. Shelke, S., Attar, V.: Source detection of rumor in social network – a review. Online Soc. Netw. Media **9**, 30–42 (2019)
29. Peng, S., Yu, S., Yang, A.: Smartphone malware and its propagation modeling: a survey. IEEE Commun. Surv. Tutor. **16**(2), 925–941 (2014)
30. Russell Bernard, H.: The development of social network analysis: a study in the sociology of science. Soc. Netw. **27**(4), 377–384 (2005)
31. Borgatti, S.P.: Centrality and network flow. Soc. Netw. **27**(1), 55–71 (2005)
32. Frantz, T.L., Cataldo, M., Carley, K.M.: Robustness of centrality measures under uncertainty: examining the role of network topology. Comput. Math. Organ. Theory **15**(4), 303–328 (2009)
33. Kosorukoff, A.: Theory. In: Social Network Analysis - Theory and Applications, pp. 1–4 (2011)
34. Liao, H., Mariani, M.S., Medo, M., Zhang, Y.C., Zhou, M.Y.: Ranking in evolving complex networks. Phys. Rep. **689**, 1–54 (2017)
35. Brin, S., Page, L.: Reprint of: the anatomy of a large-scale hypertextual web search engine. Comput. Netw. **56**(18), 3825–3833 (2012)
36. Liu, Q., et al.: An influence propagation view of PageRank. ACM Trans. Knowl. Discov. Data **11**(3), 2–28 (2017)

37. Wang, Y., Feng, X.: A potential-based node selection strategy for influence maximization in a social network. In: Proceedings of the 5th International Conference on Advanced Data Mining and Applications (ADMA 2009), pp. 350–361 (2009)
38. Wang, Y., Cong, G., Song, G., Xie, K.: Community-based greedy algorithm for mining top-k influential nodes in mobile social networks categories and subject descriptors. In: Proceedings of the 16th ACM SIGKDD International Conference on Knowledge Discovery and Data Mining, pp. 1039–1048 (2010)
39. Leskovec, J., Krause, A., Guestrin, C., Faloutsos, C., Vanbriesen, J.: Cost-effective outbreak detection in networks. In: Proceedings of the 13th ACM SIGKDD International Conference on Knowledge Discovery and Data Mining, pp. 420–429 (2007)
40. Zhou, T., Cao, J., Liu, B., Xu, S., Zhu, Z., Luo, J.: Location-based influence maximization in social networks. In: CIKM 2015, no. 93, pp. 1211–1220 (2015)
41. Chorley, M.J., Colombo, G.B., Allen, S.M., Whitaker, R.M.: Human content filtering in Twitter: the influence of metadata. Int. J. Hum Comput. Stud. **74**, 32–40 (2015)

Developing a Real-Time Traffic Reporting and Forecasting Back-End System

Theodoros Toliopoulos[1], Nikodimos Nikolaidis[1], Anna-Valentini Michailidou[1], Andreas Seitaridis[1], Anastasios Gounaris[1(✉)], Nick Bassiliades[1], Apostolos Georgiadis[2], and Fotis Liotopoulos[2]

[1] Aristotle University of Thessaloniki, Thessaloniki, Greece
{tatoliop,nikniknik,annavalen,sgandreas,gounaria,nbassili}@csd.auth.gr
[2] Sboing, Thessaloniki, Greece
{tolis,liotop}@sboing.net

Abstract. This work describes the architecture of the back-end engine of a real-time traffic data processing and satellite navigation system. The role of the engine is to process real-time feedback, such as speed and travel time, provided by in-vehicle devices and derive real-time reports and traffic predictions through leveraging historical data as well. We present the main building blocks and the versatile set of data sources and processing platforms that need to be combined together to form a working and scalable solution. We also present performance results focusing on meeting system requirements keeping the need for computing resources low. The lessons and results presented are of value to additional real-time applications that rely on both recent and historical data.

1 Introduction

Geographical Information Systems and, more broadly, the development of applications based on or including geo-spatial data is a mature and hot area with several tools, both commercial and open-source, e.g., ArcGIS, PostGIS, GeoSpark [12] and so on. In general, these tools and frameworks are distinguished according to the queries they support [8] and the quality of maps they utilize. For the latter, popular alternatives include Google Maps and OpenStreetMap[1], which can be considered as data-as-a-service. At the same time, urban trips is a big source of data. Developing a system that can process real-time traffic data in order to report and forecast current traffic conditions combines all the elements mentioned above, e.g., modern GIS applications built on top of detailed world maps leveraging real-time big data sources, stores and processing platforms.

The aim of this work is to present architectural details regarding a novel back-end system developed on behalf of Sboing[2]. Sboing is an SME that implements innovative mobile technologies for the collection, processing and exploitation of location and mobility-based data. It offers an app, called UltiNavi, that can be

---

[1] https://www.openstreetmap.org.
[2] www.sboing.net.

© Springer Nature Switzerland AG 2020
F. Dalpiaz et al. (Eds.): RCIS 2020, LNBIP 385, pp. 58–75, 2020.
https://doi.org/10.1007/978-3-030-50316-1_4

installed on in-vehicle consoles and smartphones. Through this app, Internet-connected users share their location information in real-time and contribute to the collection of real-time traffic data. More specifically, Sboing collaborates with academia in order to extend their system with a view to (i) continuously receive feedback regarding traffic conditions from end users and process it on the fly; and (ii) provide real-time and accurate travel time forecasts to users without relying on any other type of sensors to receive data apart from the data reported by the users. In order to achieve these goals, the back-end system needs to be extended to fulfill the following requirements:

R1: provide real-time information about traffic conditions. This boils down to be capable of (i) providing speed and travel time conditions per road segment for the last few minutes and (ii) being capable to report incidents upon the receipt (and validation) of such a feedback.

R2: provide estimates for future traffic conditions. This is important in order to provide accurate estimates regarding predicted travel times, which typically refer to the next couple of hours and are computed using both current and historical data.

R3: manage historical information to train the prediction models needed by R2. This implies the need to store past information at several levels of granularity.

R4: scalability. Traffic forecasting can be inherently parallelised in a geo-distributed manner, i.e., each region to be served by a separate cluster of servers. Therefore, the challenge is not that much in the volume of data to be produced but in the velocity of new update streams to be produced by the system and the need to store historical data.

R5: fault-tolerance. Any modules to be included in the back-end need to be capable of tolerating failures.

There are several other tools that provide this type of information; e.g., Google Maps, Waze[3] and TomTom[4]. However none of these tools that are being developed by big companies have published information about their back-end processing engine. By contrast, we both explain architectural details and employ publicly available open-source tools, so that third parties can rebuild our solution with reasonable effort.

Background. Effective forecasting of traffic can lead to accurate travel time prediction. Due to its practical applications, short-term traffic forecasting is a hot research field with many research works being published. Vlahogianni et al. [11] reviewed the challenges of such forecasting. These challenges refer to making the prediction responsive and adaptive to events (such as, weather incidents or accidents), identifying traffic patterns, selecting the best fitting model and method for predicting traffic and dealing with noisy or missing data. To forecast traffic, data can be collected in two manners, namely either through GPS systems deployed on vehicles or using vehicle detector sensors. The most common data

---

[3] https://www.waze.com.

[4] https://www.tomtom.com/automotive/products-services/real-time-maps/.

features used in traffic prediction models are speed and travel time of vehicles along with the vehicle volume per time unit and occupancy of the roads. Djuric et al. [1] analysed travel speed data from sensors capturing the volume and occupancy every 30 s. and advocated combining multiple predictors. Gao et al. [2] also used data from sensors but the main unit was vehicles per hour. Traffic may also be affected from other incidents and conditions that need to be taken into consideration during prediction. E.g., an accident may lead to traffic congestion that cannot be predicted in advance. Also, weather conditions play a key role. Qiao et al. [9] presented a data classification approach, where the data categories include information like wind speed, visibility, type of day, incident etc., all of which can affect the traffic. Li et al. [6] conclude that a model that includes historical travel time data, speed data, the days of the week, 5-min cumulative rainfall data and time encoded as either AM or PM can lead to an accurate prediction. Based on the above proposals, we also consider the presence of an incident, rain or snow, the visibility, the wind speed and the temperature.

It is important to note that forecasting can be more accurate when there are large amounts of historical traffic data available [6]. The drawback is that this information can be very expensive to store due to its large size. Thus, suitable storage technologies must be used. In this work, we resort to a scalable data warehousing solution.

Contributions and Structure. This work makes the following contributions in relation to the requirements and the setting already described: (i) It presents an end-to-end solution for supporting real-time traffic reporting and forecasting as far as the back-end system engine is concerned. The architecture consists of several modules and integrates different tools and data stores. (ii) It discusses several alternatives regarding design choices in a manner that lessons can be transferred to other similar settings. (iii) It includes indicative performance results that provide strong insights into the performance of each individual module in the architecture so that design choices can be evaluated, the efficiency in which requirements are met can be assessed, and bottlenecks can be identified.

From a system's point of view, the novelty of our work lies in (i) presenting a non-intuitive non-monolithic architecture encompassing three different data store types and two different stream processing platforms with complementary roles in order to meet the requirements; (ii) to the best of our knowledge, it is the first work that compares the two specific main alternatives regarding back-end analytics databases examined; and (iii) the results presented are meaningful for software architects in different domains with similar requirements.

The remainder of this paper is structured as follows. Section 2 presents the overall architecture. In the next section, we discuss the pre-processing of source data. In Sect. 4, we describe the underlying data warehouse and the queries that run over it. Indicative experiments are in Sect. 5. We conclude in Sect. 6.

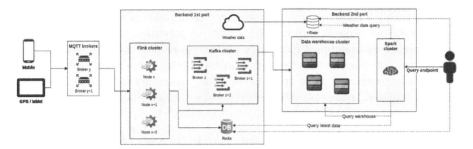

Fig. 1. The diagram of the advocated architecture

2   System Architecture

This section consists of two parts. The first part gives the necessary background regarding the data incoming to the back-end system and the connection mechanisms of the back-end to their sources. The second part provides the overview of the back-end pipeline that will be explained in detail in Sects. 3 and 4.

The raw data are transmitted from the users through user devices, such as GPS tracking devices and mobile navigation apps in a continuous stream. Every device periodically sends its current condition in a specific time interval; if there is no internet connectivity, the device may optionally send all the gathered data when connectivity is restored for historic analysis. The data sent through the messaging system contain information about the latitude and longitude of the device along with the timestamp that the measurements were taken and the speed of the user. Additional metadata about the position of the user such as elevation, course, road/segment id and direction are transmitted as well. That is, the device has the capability to automatically map co-ordinates to road segments ids; explaining the details about how clients are developed are out of the scope of this paper. Finally, tailored techniques for encryption and anonymization along with customized maps based on OpenStreetMap ones that allow for efficient road segment matching have been developed; these issues are not further analyzed in this work. The connection between the user devices and the back-end pipeline is materialized through the use of the MQTT[5] protocol.

The main responsibility of the back-end pipeline is to receive the raw data, clean and process them, derive statistics for the last 5 min tumbling window, and finally store the results in persistent storage for querying. This splits the pipeline into two conceptual parts. The first one handles the data cleaning and processing. The second part consists of the persistent data storage system and the querying engine. The main challenge regarding the first part of the solution is to handle a continuous intense data stream. This implies that the constituent modules need to share the following main characteristics: to be capable of fast continuous processing (to support R1 and R2 in Sect. 1) and to be scalable (which relates to R4) and fault tolerant (which relates to R5).

---

[5] http://mqtt.org/.

The streaming component comprises three main pieces of software, namely a streaming engine, a module to transfer results to persistent storage and a main memory database to support extremely fast access to intermediate results. The streaming engine handles the cleaning, transformation and processing of the raw data. It is implemented using the Apache Flink[6] framework. Flink is an open-source distributed continuous stream processing framework that provides real-time processing with fault-tolerant mechanisms called checkpoints. As such, R5 is supported by default. Flink can also easily scale up when the need arises to meet R4. As shown later, it can support efficiently R1 and R2. The second module that handles the transfer of the processed data to the persistent storage is built using Apache Kafka.[7]. Kafka is the most popular open-source streaming platform that handles data in real-time and stores them in a fault-tolerant durable way. Kafka uses topics to which other systems can publish data and/or subscribe to get access to those data. Kafka inherently meets R5 and does not become a bottleneck. Finally, the first part of the pipeline contains the main-memory database Redis.[8] This is due to the need for querying the latest time window of the stream (R1). Flink and Kafka can run on a small cluster serving a region or a complete country. Redis is a distributed database; in our solution it stores as many entries as the number of the road segments, which is in the order of millions that can very easily fit into the main memory of a single machine. Therefore, it need not be parallelized across all cluster nodes.

The second part of the pipeline is responsible for storing the processed data in a fault-tolerant way (which relates to R5) while supporting queries about the saved data at arbitrary levels of granularity regarding time periods, e.g., average speeds for the last day, for the last month, for all Tuesdays in a year, and so on, to support R2 and R3. For this reason, an OLAP (online analytical processing) data warehouse solution is required, which is tailored to supporting aggregate building and processing through operators such as drill-down and roll-up. To also meet the scalability requirement (R4), two alternatives have been investigated. The first is Apache Kylin[9] and the second is Apache Druid.[10] Both these systems are distributed warehouses that can ingest continuous streaming data. They also support high-availability and fault-tolerance. The main difference between the two systems is that Druid supports continuous ingestion of data, whilst Kylin needs to re-build the cube based on the new data at time intervals set by the user. To the best of our knowledge, no comparison of these two options in real applications, either in academic publications or in unofficial technical reports exists, and this work, apart from presenting a whole back-end system, fills this gap. Finally, Apache Spark[11] is the engine that is used for query processing as an alternative to standalone Java programs. Figure 1 presents the complete back-end architecture.

---

[6] https://flink.apache.org/.
[7] https://kafka.apache.org/.
[8] https://redis.io/.
[9] http://kylin.apache.org/.
[10] https://druid.apache.org/.
[11] https://spark.apache.org/.

3   The Stream Processing Component

In this section, we present in detail the first part of the pipeline that includes the stream processing module, materialized by Flink, through which the raw data pass to be further processed, Kafka, which is the stream controller module that transfers the processed data to the storage, and Redis, which is a temporary main-memory database. We also present a fourth module that gathers weather data to complement the data reported by user devices.

The Stream Processing Module. The data coming from the user devices create a continuous stream that goes through the MQTT brokers. The size of the data can quickly grow up in size due to the nature of the sources. For example, 800K of vehicles in a metropolitan area equipped with clients reporting once every 10 s, still generate 80K new sets of measurements per sec, which amounts to approximately 7 billion measurements per day. Overall, the pre-processing module needs to be able to handle an intense continuous stream without delays. Flink provides low-latency, high-throughput and fault-tolerance via checkpoints. It incorporates the *exactly-once* semantics, which means that, even in the case of node failures, each data point will be processed only once. In addition, scaling up can easily be completed through adding more worker machines (nodes).

In order to get the data that come from the user devices, Flink needs to connect with all of the MQTT brokers, which can adapt their number according to the current workload. Loss of information is not acceptable; this implies that Flink must dynamically connect to all new brokers without suspending data processing. Each Flink machine has a list of all available MQTT brokers along with their IP addresses. Each machine is responsible for one of those brokers in order to ingest its data. This implies that the solution needs to have at least the same number of Flink machines as the MQTT brokers. All of the Flink nodes that do not get matched with a broker remain available and keep checking the pool of brokers for updates. Note that all of the Flink nodes keep working on the data processing even if they do not get connected with a MQTT broker. When a new broker is inserted in the pool, one of the available nodes initiates the connection in order to start the ingestion. This process does not slow down or stop the job even if there are no available nodes. Flink can increase or decrease the number of its worker nodes without shutting down due to its built-in mechanisms.

After Flink starts ingesting the stream, it creates a tumbling (i.e., a non-overlapping) moving time window to process the data points. The measurements are aggregated according to the road segment they refer to. The size of the tumbling window is set to 5 min, since it is considered that the traffic conditions in the last 5 min are adequate for real-time reporting, and the traffic volume in each road segment in the last 5 min is high enough to allow for dependable statistics. The data points that fall into the window's time range are cleaned and several statistics, such as median speed, quartiles and travel time are computed. The results of every window are further sent downstream the pipeline to Kafka. In parallel, the data from the most recent time window are also saved to Redis overwriting the previous window. Continuously reporting real-time changes is plausible, but it is rather distracting than informative.

Flink can also be used for more complex processing that involves data streams. One such example is continuous outlier detection on the streaming data from clients. Detecting an outlier can either indicate an anomaly in a certain road segment, i.e. an accident, or simply noisy data, i.e. a faulty device or a stopped vehicle. Especially in traffic forecasting, quickly detecting an accident can result in a decrease of congestion in the specific road.

Weather Data Acquisition. In order to provide the user with more information about the road conditions as well as make more precise predictions of the future traffic and trip times, we gather weather data by using weather APIs. No more details are provided due to space constraints.

The Stream Controller and Temporary Storage Modules. As depicted in the overall architecture, the processed data are forwarded to Apache Kafka. Kafka is one of the most popular distributed streaming platforms and is used in many commercial pipelines. It can easily handle data on a big scale and it is capable of scaling out by adding extra brokers; therefore it is suitable for meeting the R4 requirement. It uses the notion of topics to transfer data between systems or applications in a fault-tolerant way; thus it also satisfies R5. Topics have a partitioning and replication parameter. The first one is used in order to partition the workload of the brokers for the specific topic whilst the second one is used to provide the fault-tolerant guarantees. An additional useful feature is that it provides a retention policy for temporarily saving the transferred data for a chosen time period before permanently deleting them. We will explain later how we can leverage this feature to avoid system instability. In our work, Kafka is used as the intermediate between the stream processing framework and the data warehouse. In our case, apart from receiving the output of Flink, it is also used for alerts received, such as an accident detection, by passing them through specific topics.

The final module in this part of the pipeline is Redis. One of the data warehouse alternatives used in this work is Apache Kylin. Kylin does not have the capability to ingest a stream continuously and convert it into a cube but it needs to update the cube periodically (according to a user-defined time interval) with the new data of the stream. Thus, by relying on a data warehouse, such as Kylin solely, R1 cannot be satisfied despite the fact that Flink can produce statistics for the most recent time window very efficiently. Redis solves this problem by saving the latest processed data from Flink. Druid does not have the limitations of Kylin, but still, imposes an unnecessary overhead to produce statistics almost immediately after the finish of each 5-min window. Overall, the statistics aggregated by Flink are passed on both to Kafka for permanent storage and to Redis for live traffic conditions update. In addition, as explained in the next section, Redis holds the predicted travel time for each segment id, and, when combined with Kylin, it may need to store the two last 5-min sets of statistics.

Redis is a main-memory data structure store that can quickly save and retrieve data with a key-value format. It is fault-tolerant and can also scale up by adding more machines; i.e., it is suitable for meeting R1, R4 and R5. More specifically, each road segment forms a key and the statistics needed for real-time reporting (typically, mean speed) is stored as a value. Predicted travel times are stored in a similar manner. The table size is inherently small, in the order of hundreds of MBs, even if a complete big country such as France is served. For this reason, the Redis table need not be parallelised.

4   Data Storage and Querying

Here, we describe the OLAP solutions and the type of queries over such solutions and Redis to support R1, R2, and R3 in a scalable manner.

Scalable OLAP. OLAP techniques form the main data management solution to aggregate data for analysis and offer statistics across multiple dimensions and at different levels of granularity. From a physical design point of view, they are classified as ROLAP (relational OLAP), MOLAP (Multidimensional OLAP) and HOLAP (hybrid OLAP) [3]. Scalable OLAP solutions are offered by the Apache Kylin engine. An alternative is to leverage the Druid analytics database. We have explored both solutions.

Kylin is deployed on top of a Hadoop[12] cluster and goes beyond simple Hive[13], which is the main data warehousing solution offered by Apache. Hive allows for better scalability but does not support fast response time of aggregation queries efficiently [3]. To mitigate this limitation, Kylin encapsulates the HBase[14] NoSQL solution to materialize the underlying data cube according to the MOLAP paradigm. The overall result is a HOLAP solution, which can answer very quickly statistics that have been pre-computed, but relies on more traditional database technology to answer queries not covered by the materialized cube.

The important design steps are the definition of dimensions and measures (along with the appropriate aggregate functions). For the measures, we consider all Flink output, which is stored in Kafka, using several aggregation functions. For the dimensions, we employ two hierarchies, namely the map one consisting of road segments and roads, and the time one at the following levels of granularity: 5 min window, hour, day, week, month, quarter, year. Note that the time hierarchy is partially ordered, given that aggregating the values of weeks cannot produce the statistics per month. Overall, precomputed aggregates grouped by time or complete roads or individual road segments or combinations of road and time are available through Kylin. The cube, as defined above, does not consider external condition metadata (i.e., weather information and accidents). There are two options in order to include them, namely either to add metadata conditions

---

[12] https://hadoop.apache.org/.
[13] http://hive.apache.org/.
[14] http://hbase.apache.org/.

as dimensions or to consider them as another type of measure. Both options suffer from severe drawbacks. Thus, we have opted to employ a third type of storage apart from Kylin and Redis, namely HBase. HBase is already used internally by Kylin; here we explain how we employ it directly. More specifically, we store all external condition metadata in a single column family in a HBase table. The key is a road and hour pair, i.e., weather conditions for a specific region are mapped to a set of roads (rather than road segments) and are updated every hour.

An alternative to Kylin is Druid. Druid can connect to Kafka and may be used to replace even Flink aggregation preprocessing to automatically summarize data splitting them in 5-min windows. In our solution, we keep using Flink for preprocessing (since this can also be enhanced with outlier detection) and we test Druid as an alternative to Kylin only. Contrary to Kylin, Druid has no HOLAP features and does not explicitly precompute aggregate statistics across dimensions (which relates to the issue of cuboid materialization selection [4]). However, it is more tailored to a real-time environment from an engineering point of view. Druid data store engine is columnar-based coupled with bitmap indices on the base cuboid, which is physically partitioned across the time dimension.

Query Processing. Supporting the real-time reports according to R1 relies on accessing the Redis database. R2 and R3 involve forecasts, and in order to forecast traffic an appropriate model needs to be implemented. This model acquires two main types of data; real-time statistics of the last 5 min and historical ones. The model analyses data like travel time, mean speed and so on, by assigning a weight to each of the two types mentioned above. The model can also incorporate information about weather or any occurred incidents.

Regarding real-time querying, the results include information for the last 5 min for all the road segments and are stored in a Redis database. We can retrieve them through Spark using Scala and Jedis[15], a Java-Redis library. In order to use this information, that is in JSON string format, there is a need to transform it to a Spark datatype, for example DataSet. Overall, as will be shown in the next section, this is a simple process and can be implemented very efficiently thanks to Redis, whereas solely relying on Kylin or Druid would be problematic. Historical data can grow very large in space as they can contain information about traffic from over a year ago and still be useful for forecasting. Thus, historical querying is submitted to Kylin or Druid. To meet R2 and R3, we need to train a model and then apply it every 5 min. Developing and discussing accurate prediction models for traffic is out of the scope of this work. In general, both sophisticated and simpler models are efficient in several workload forecasting problems with small differences in their performance, e.g., [5]. But, as explained in the beginning, the important issue in vehicle traffic forecasting is to take seasonality and past conditions into account. Without loss of generality, an example function we try to build adheres to a generic template:

$$\tilde{X}_{i,t} = w_{i,1} * X_{i,t-1} + w_{i,2} * X_{i,t-2} + w_{i,3} * (X_{i,t-1week+1} - X_{i,t-1week}), \quad (1)$$

---

[15] https://github.com/xetorthio/jedis.

Table 1. Cluster information

CPU	Cores/Threads	RAM	Storage
Cluster A			
Intel(R) Xeon(R) CPU E5-2620 v2 @ 2.10 GHz	6/12	64G	SSD
Intel(R) Core(TM) i7-3770K CPU @ 3.50 GHz	4/8	32G	SSD
AMD FX(tm)-9370	8/8	32G	SSD
Intel(R) Xeon(R) CPU E5-2640 v2 @ 2.00 GHz	8/16	64G	SSD
Cluster B			
Intel(R) Core(TM) i7-8700 CPU @ 3.20 GHz	6/12	64G	2 SSD & 2 HDD
Intel(R) Core(TM) i7-8700 CPU @ 3.20 GHz	6/12	64G	2 SSD & 2 HDD

where $\tilde{X}_{i,t}$ is the next 5-min metric, either expected speed or travel time of the ith segment at time slot t, that we want to predict based on the values of the last two 5-min windows and the difference in the values exactly 1 week ago. 1 week corresponds to $7*24*12 = 2016$ 5-min windows. Using Spark jobs, we periodically retrain the model, which boils down to computing the weights $w_{i,1}$, $w_{i,2}$ and $w_{i,3}$. To provide the training data, we need to retrieve the non-aggregated base cube contents. We can train coarser models that are shared between road segments or train a different model for each segment. Obviously, the latter leads to more accurate predictions. In the next section, we provide detailed evaluation results regarding the times to retrieve cube contents. Here, using the same setting as in Sect. 5, we give summary information about model building times for Eq. (1): a Spark job that retrieves the historical data of a specific segment from the last month, transforms the data to a set of tuples with 5 fields: $(X_{i,t}, X_{i,t-1}, X_{i,t-2}, X_{i,t-1week+1}, X_{i,t-1week})$ and applies linear regression takes approximately 3 min. Different models for multiple segments can be computed in parallel at no expense on the running time. If the last 6 months are considered in training, the training takes 17 min. The coefficients are cached; Redis can be used to this end. Upon the completion of each 5-min window, based on the precomputed co-efficients, predicted statistics are computed for each road segment for the next time window.

5   Performance Evaluation

Experimental Setting. All of our experiments, unless explicitly stated, are performed on two clusters, the technical characteristics of which are presented in Table 1. The first cluster, denoted as Cluster A, is deployed in private premises and comprises 4 heterogeneous machines both in CPU and RAM resources while the second one, denoted as Cluster B, has two identical powerful machines, rented from an established cloud provider. Both clusters are small in size and are meant to serve a limited geographic region, since it is expected each important municipality or region to have its own small cluster.

For storage, both clusters run HDFS. In the second cluster that has both SSD and HDD storage types, the first one is used for persistent storage of the data

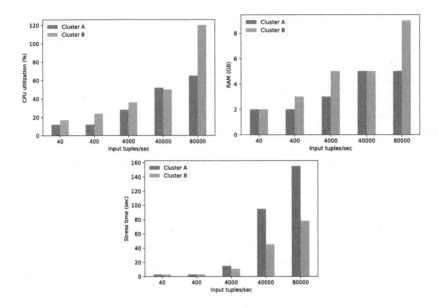

Fig. 2. Flink's average CPU utilization per YARN node (top left), memory consumption (top right) and stress time (bottom) during stream data processing

warehouses' cubes while the HDD are used for temporary data with the help of HDFS's Heterogeneous Storage. The input stream is artificially generated in order to be continuous and intense reaching up to 80000 raw data tuples per second and 10 million total road segments, e.g., serving 800K vehicles reporting once every 10 s simultaneously in a region larger than half of Greece. This yields a stream of 288 million MQTT messages per hour.

Stream Processing Experiments. The objective of this experiment is to reveal the resources Flink consumes for the data processing step while meeting the real-time requirement R1 and the scalability requirement R4. The processing job is tested on both clusters using the YARN cluster-mode. For Cluster A, the YARN configuration comprises 4 nodes with 1 core and 8 GB RAM per node. The job's total parallelism level is 4. For Cluster B, YARN uses 2 nodes with 2 cores and 16 GB RAM per node with a total parallelism level of 4. Note that we aim not to occupy the full cluster resources, so that the components downstream run efficiently as well.

In the experiments, we keep the total road segments to 10 millions, while increasing the input rate of the stream starting from 40 tuples per second (so that each Flink node is allocated on average 10 records in Cluster A) and reaching up to 80000 tuples (i.e., 20000 per Flink node in Cluster A) per second. The reason for the constant number of road segments is to show the scalability of Flink in accordance to the R4 requirement regarding the volume of data produced per time unit keeping the underlying maps at the appropriate level for real world applications. For stress test purposes, the number of distinct devices that send data is also set to 1000 and kept as a constant. This means that each device sends multiple raw tuples, and thus the process is more intense due to the computation of the travel time for each device (i.e., if the same traffic is shared across 100K devices, then the computation would be less intensive). The process window is always a 5 min tumbling one. This implies that the Flink job gathers data during the 5 min of the window while computing temporary meta-data. When the window's time-life reaches its end point, Flink completes the computations and outputs the final processed data that are sent through the pipeline to Kafka and Redis. The time between the window termination and the output of the statistics of the last segment is referred to as Flink stress time.

Figure 2 shows the results of the Flink process job on both clusters by varying the input stream rate. The measurements are the average of 5 runs. The top-left plot shows the average CPU utilization per YARN node for each cluster during the whole 5-min tumbling window. Note that the 100% mark means that the job takes over a whole CPU thread. From this experiment, we can safely assume that Flink's CPU consumption scales up in a sublinear manner, but the current allocation of resources for Cluster B seems to suffer from resource contention for the highest workload. 120% utilization for Cluster B means that on average, 1.2 cores are fully utilized out of the 2 cores available, but the utilization increase compared to 40K tuples per second is 2.5X. In Cluster A, increasing the workload by three orders of magnitude results in a 5-fold increase in Flink demand for CPU resources. Cluster B exhibits lower utilization if we consider that each machine allocates two threads to Flink instead of one, up to 10000 records/sec per Flink node. Overall, the main conclusion is that Flink is lightweight and the example allocation of resources to Flink (a portion of the complete cluster capacity) is adequate to manage the workload.

The top-right plot shows the average memory used by each machine during the 5-min tumbling window. In the first cluster, even though the input tuples per second are increased 2 thousand-fold, the memory is increased by approximately 2.5 times only. Cluster B consumes up to 9 GB of memory taking into account each machine has to process twice the amount of data compared to the physical machines in Cluster A. This further supports the conclusion that the homogeneous cluster exhibits better resource utilization than the heterogeneous, but both clusters can handle the workload.

Finally, the bottom plot deals with meeting R1 and shows the average stress time for the cluster upon the completion of the 5-min window. As mentioned above, Flink computes meta-data and temporary data during the whole window in order to start building up to the final aggregations needed for the process. When the window expires after it has ingested all the data tuples that belong to the specified time period, the computations are increased in order to combine temporary meta-data and complete any aggregations needed in order to output the results. The stress time presented in the figure shows the running time of this process for each cluster in order to output the complete final results for a window to Kafka and Redis. As the rate of the input data increases, so does the stress time due to the increased number of complex computations. In cluster A,

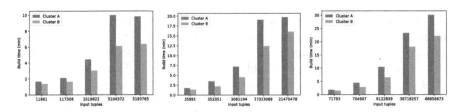

Fig. 3. Kylin's average cube build time after ingesting 1 (left), 3 (middle) and 6 (right) 5-min windows

the stress time starts from 3 s for the lowest input rate and reaches up to 155 s during the maximum rate. On the other hand, the homogeneous cluster exhibits even better results, and its stress time duration does not exceed 80 s even for the highest workload. This means that after 80 s, the complete statistics of the last 5-min are available to Redis even for the last segment; since the whole process is incremental, many thousand segments have updated 5-min statistics even a few seconds after the window slide. After the results are in Redis, they can be immediately pushed or queried to update online maps.

The process stage ends when the results are passed to Kafka and Redis. Due to Kafka's distributed nature and the fact that each Kafka broker is on the same machine as each Flink node, the data transfer between the two systems is negligible. On the other hand, Redis is used on a single machine as a centralized main-memory store according to the discussion previously. This incurs some overhead when transferring data from a remote machine, which is already included in the stress times presented.

Persistent Storage Experiments. Persistent storage is the key component of the whole architecture. We have experimented with Kylin 2.6.1 and Druid 0.15.1. We used the output of the previous experiments to test the ingestion rate of both warehouses that indirectly affects the efficiency regarding R2 and R3. The total number of distinct road segments is kept at 10 million. Since Druid supports continuous ingestion while Kylin needs to update the cube at user-defined intervals, the two solutions are not directly comparable and thus their experimental settings differ. Nevertheless, the results are sufficient to provide strong insights in the advantages and drawbacks of each solution.

The following experiments present the total time that Kylin needs in order to update the cube at 3 different time intervals, namely every 5, 15 and 30 min. The first interval (5-min) means that Kylin rebuilds the cube after every window output from Flink, while 15 and 30 min intervals imply that the cube is updated after 3 and 6 window outputs from Flink, respectively. As more windows are accumulated in Kafka before rebuilding, more data need to be processed by Kylin's cube building tool and incorporated into the cube itself. Based on the previous experiments, different input tuple rates in Flink provide a different number of processed output rows, which in turn are ingested into Kylin. For example, at the lowest rate of 40 tuples/sec arriving to Flink, on average 11961,

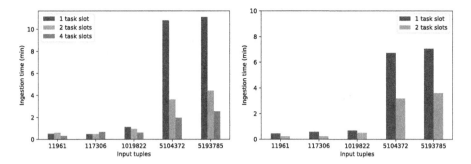

Fig. 4. Druid's average ingestion time in minutes for cluster A (left) and B (right)

35891 and 71793 road segments are updated in 1,3 and 6 windows, respectively. On the contrary, at the highest rate of 80K tuples/sec, the amount of updated segments is 5.19M, 21.47M and 48.86M, respectively. 5.19M implies that more than half of the map is updated every 5 min. Figure 3 shows the results for the two clusters employed. An initial observation is that the homogeneous cluster (Cluster B) consistently outperforms the heterogeneous one. This provides evidence that Kylin is sensitive to heterogeneity. The left plot from Fig. 3 shows the build times when the input tuples vary from approximately 11K to 5M, all referring to the same 5-min window. The two rightmost pairs of bars are similar because the number of updated segments does not differ significantly. The main observation is twofold. First, when the input data increases in size, the build time increases as well but in a sublinear manner. Second, for more than 5M segment to be inserted in the cube (corresponding to more than 40K tuples/sec from client devices), the cube build time is close to 6 min for Cluster B, and even higher for Cluster A. In other words, in this case, Kylin takes 6 min to update the cube according to the preprocessed statistics from a 5-min window. This in turn creates a bottleneck and instability in the system, since Kafka keeps accumulating statistics from Flink at a higher rate that Kylin can consume them. The middle and right plot have similar results regarding the scalability. While the input data increases in size, the time needed to update the cube is also increased but in a sublinear manner. Regarding the time Kylin takes to consume the results from 3 5-min windows, from the middle plot, we can observe that Cluster A suffers from instability when the client devices send more than 40K tuples/sec, whereas Cluster B suffer from instability when the device rate is 80K tuples/sec. In the right figure, which corresponds to the statistics in the last 30 min split in 5-min slots, Kylin does not create a bottleneck using either Cluster A or Cluster B.

What is the impact of the above observations regarding the efficiency in supporting R2? The main answer is that we cannot rely on Kylin to retrieve the statistics of the penultimate 5-min window. But to support real-time forecasts based on the already devised prediction models, such as the one in Eq. (1), Redis should store statistics from the two last 5-min windows rather than the last

Table 2. Querying times to Redis using Spark

Rows	Retrieval (sec)	Transformation (sec)
1	0.012	3.3
10	0.013	3.35
100	0.016	3.39
1000	0.052	3.45
20000	0.78	4.27

one only. Otherwise, R2 cannot be met efficiently, or requires more computing resources than the ones employed in these experiments.

Unlike Kylin, Druid can continuously ingest streams and provides access to the latest data rows. To assess Druid's efficiency and compare against Kylin in a meaningful manner, we proceed to slight changes in the experimental setting. More specifically, we test Druid with exactly the same input rows that Kylin has been tested in the left plot of Fig. 3. Also, Druid can have a different number of ingestion task slots with each one being on a different cluster machine. We experimented with the task slot number in order to detect the difference when choosing different levels of parallelism in each cluster. Figure 4 presents the results of the experiments. As expected the ingestion time increases as the input data size is increased in both clusters. But even for the bigger inputs, Druid can perform the ingestion before the statistics of the new 5-min window become available in Kafka. In any case, Druid still needs Redis for efficiently supporting R1; otherwise the real-time traffic from the last 5-min would be available only after 2–3 min rather than a few seconds.

Another important remark is the difference in the ingestion time when the task slot number changes. In the homogeneous cluster, when the number of tasks increases, the ingestion time decreases. There are exceptions of this in the heterogeneous cluster. As the left plot shows, when the input stream is small in size, the difference between the task slots is negligible, whilst, in some cases, when the task slots increase, the ingestion time increases as well. This is due to the fact that each machine is different and the size is small, which incurs communication and computation overheads that, along with imbalance, outweigh parallelism benefits. Also, when using 1 slot in Cluster A for high client device data rates, there is severe resource contention.

Query Experiments. In the following experiments, Spark is used as a standalone engine on a single machine outside the cluster where the warehouses and Redis are installed. Testing the scalability of Spark on more machines is out of our scope. Also, the warehouse contents refer to more than 1 year of data in an area consisting of 20K segments (overall more than 2 billions of entries).

Table 2 presents the results of the experiments when Spark pulls data from Redis. Because Redis returns data in Json format, Spark needs to transform them into a dataframe in order to process them and return its results. The second column represents the time that Spark needed to fetch data from the cluster machine in seconds, whilst the third column displays the time needed to transform from Json to a dataframe. The results show that fetching data is very fast and even if Spark is used in the front-end to create new maps ready to be asked by clients (R1), the whole process is ready a few seconds after the 5-min window terminates. Also, fetching the results to update the predicted speed/travel times per segment (R2) every five minutes, takes only a few seconds.

For the data warehouses, two different queries were used. The first one, called *Aggregation Query*, asks for the aggregated minimum speed of X road segments over a time period Y returning X rows of data. The second one, called *Stress Query*, asks for the speed of all of the rows of X road segments over a time period Y and may be used for more elaborate prediction models. The objective is to show that such queries take up to a few seconds and thus are appropriate to update segment information every 5 min; this is confirmed by our experiments even for the most intensive queries.

No exact numbers are provided due to space constraints. In summary, for the *Aggregation Query* Druid times seem constant regardless of the number of groups and the number of values that need to be aggregated. On the other hand, Kylin takes more time when the query needs to aggregate values over increased numbers of segments, while the aggregation cost does not seem to be increasing when the number of rows for each road segment increases due to a larger time window benefiting from pre-computations. Finally, the Java standalone program is significant faster for retrieval; however Spark can be easier parallelised and perform sophisticated computations after the retrieval to fulfill R2 and R3.

Regarding the *Stress Query*, the results are mixed. In most of the cases, Druid has the slowest retrieval times whilst the Java program has the fastest. Druid's retrieval performance is greatly affected by the number of rows that it returns. Kylin is also affected but less.

End-to-End Performance. Previously, we investigated the performance of individuals components in a manner that no end-to-end processing evaluation results are explicitly presented. However, in fact, the time taken by the streaming processing engine, which outputs its temporary results into both Redis and Kafka, as shown in Fig. 2 (right), is totally hidden by the time taken to build the Kylin cube (see Fig. 3) or ingest data into Druid (see Fig. 4). The times to query Redis and the persistent storage for each window update are also fully hidden.

6   Lessons Learned and Conclusions

The main lessons learned can be summarized as follows: (1) To support our requirements, we need two big-data processing platform instantiations, one for streaming data and one for batch analytics, that should not interfere with each other in order not to compromise real-time requirements. In our system, we have chosen to employ Flink and Spark, respectively, instead of two instances of either Flink or Spark. (2) We require three types of storage: a main-memory storage for quick access to recently produced results, a persistent data warehousing storage supporting aggregates at arbitrary granularity of grouping (e.g., per road, per weekday, per week, and so on), and a scalable key-value store. We have chosen Redis, Kylin or Druid, and HBase, respectively. (3) Kafka can act as an efficient interface between the stream processing and permanent storage. In addition, Flink is the main option for the stream processing platform. (4) Redis, used as a cache with advanced querying capabilities, is a key component to meet real-time constraints. Solely relying on back-end analytics platforms such as Kylin or Druid, can compromise real-time requirements. (5) Druid is more effective than Kylin regarding ingestion. However, this comes at the expense of less aggregates being pre-computed. (6) Using HBase for metadata not changing frequently and shared across multiple segments can reduce the cube size significantly; otherwise cube size may become an issue.

Developing a back-end system for real-time navigation systems involves several research issues. In our context, we have focused on three areas: outlier detection, quality assessment and geo-distributed analytics. No details are presented due to lack of space, but the relevant publications include [7,10].

Conclusions. Our work is on developing a back-end engine capable of supporting online applications that rely on both real-time sensor measurement and combinations with historical data. This gives rise to several requirements that can be addressed by a non-monolithic modular architecture, which encapsulates several platforms and data store types. We have shown how to efficiently integrate Flink, Spark, Kafka, Kylin (or Druid), Hbase and Redis to yield a working and scalable solution. The lessons learned are explicitly summarized and are of value to third parties with similar system requirements for real-time applications.

Acknowledgements. This research has been co-financed by the European Union and Greek national funds through the Operational Program Competitiveness, Entrepreneurship and Innovation, under the call RESEARCH - CREATE - INNOVATE (project code: T1EDK-01944).

References

1. Djuric, N., Radosavljevic, V., Coric, V., Vucetic, S.: Travel speed forecasting by means of continuous conditional random fields. Transp. Res. Rec. **2263**, 131–139 (2011)
2. Gao, Y., Sun, S., Shi, D.: Network-scale traffic modeling and forecasting with graphical lasso. In: Liu, D., Zhang, H., Polycarpou, M., Alippi, C., He, H. (eds.) ISNN 2011. LNCS, vol. 6676, pp. 151–158. Springer, Heidelberg (2011). https://doi.org/10.1007/978-3-642-21090-7_18
3. Han, J., Kamber, M., Pei, J.: Data Mining: Concepts and Techniques, 3rd edn. Morgan Kaufmann, Burlington (2011)
4. Harinarayan, V., Rajaraman, A., Ullman, J.D.: Implementing data cubes efficiently. In: Proceedings of the 1996 ACM SIGMOD, pp. 205–216 (1996)
5. Kim, I.K., Wang, W., Qi, Y., Humphrey, M.: Empirical evaluation of workload forecasting techniques for predictive cloud resource scaling. In: 9th IEEE International Conference on Cloud Computing, CLOUD, pp. 1–10 (2016)

6. Li, C.S., Chen, M.C.: Identifying important variables for predicting travel time of freeway with non-recurrent congestion with neural networks. Neural Comput. Appl. **23**, 1611–1629 (2013). https://doi.org/10.1007/s00521-012-1114-z
7. Michailidou, A., Gounaris, A.: Bi-objective traffic optimization in geo-distributed data flows. Big Data Res. **16**, 36–48 (2019)
8. Pandey, V., Kipf, A., Neumann, T., Kemper, A.: How good are modern spatial analytics systems? PVLDB **11**(11), 1661–1673 (2018)
9. Qiao, W., Haghani, A., Hamedi, M.: Short-term travel time prediction considering the effects of weather. Transp. Res. Rec. J. Transp. Res. Board **2308**, 61–72 (2012)
10. Toliopoulos, T., Gounaris, A., Tsichlas, K., Papadopoulos, A., Sampaio, S.: Parallel continuous outlier mining in streaming data. In: 5th IEEE International Conference on Data Science and Advanced Analytics, DSAA, pp. 227–236 (2018)
11. Vlahogianni, E.I., Karlaftis, M.G., Golias, J.C.: Short-term traffic forecasting: where we are and where we're going. Transp. Res. Part C Emerg. Technol. **43**, 3–19 (2014)
12. Yu, J., Wu, J., Sarwat, M.: Geospark: a cluster computing framework for processing large-scale spatial data. In: Proceedings of the 23rd SIGSPATIAL, pp. 70:1–70:4 (2015)

IoT Analytics Architectures: Challenges, Solution Proposals and Future Research Directions

Theo Zschörnig[1]([⊠]), Robert Wehlitz[1], and Bogdan Franczyk[2,3]

[1] Institute for Applied Informatics (InfAI), Goerdelerring 9, 04109 Leipzig, Germany
`{zschoernig,wehlitz}@infai.org`
[2] Information Systems Institute, Leipzig University,
Grimmaische Str. 12, 04109 Leipzig, Germany
`franczyk@wifa.uni-leipzig.de`
[3] Business Informatics Institute, Wrocław University of Economics,
ul. Komandorska 118-120, 53-345 Wrocław, Poland

Abstract. The Internet of Things (IoT) presents an extensive area for research, based on its growing importance in a multitude of different domains of everyday life, business and industry. In this context, different aspects of data analytics, e.g. algorithms or system architectures, as well as their scientific investigation play a pivotal role in the advancement of the IoT. Therefore, past research has presented a multitude of architectural approaches to enable data processing and analytics in various IoT domains, addressing different architectural challenges. In this paper, we identify and present an overview of these challenges as well as existing architectural proposals. Furthermore, we categorize found architectural proposals along various dimensions in order to highlight the evolution of research in this field and pinpoint architectural shortcomings. The results of this paper show that several challenges have been addressed by a large number of IoT system architectures for data analytics while others are either not relevant for certain domains or need further investigation. Finally, we offer points of reference for future research based on the findings of this paper.

Keywords: Internet of Things · IoT analytics · Data analytics · Analytics architectures

1 Introduction

The growing number of sensors, actuators and tags utilized in various domains of everyday life, business and industry underlines the importance of the Internet of Things (IoT). On this subject, business analysts predict that the size of the global IoT market will increase to 800 billion U.S. dollars in the year 2023 [1]. Smart devices already play a pivotal role in a multitude of different domains, which are identified by umbrella terms such as "Industry 4.0", "Smart City", "Smart Home", etc. These describe complex fields

© Springer Nature Switzerland AG 2020
F. Dalpiaz et al. (Eds.): RCIS 2020, LNBIP 385, pp. 76–92, 2020.
https://doi.org/10.1007/978-3-030-50316-1_5

of application, which try to digitalize and optimize existing business and industrial processes using smart devices, but also introduce completely new business and consumer application scenarios.

In this regard, data analytics of IoT data play an essential role in current IoT domains and will become even more important in the future [2]. Specifically, *IoT analytics* include the generation of insights and context from smart device data in order to enable IoT applications [2]. *IoT analytics* are based on the ability to process, analyze and understand IoT data [3], which originate from huge numbers of heterogeneous smart devices and are emitted as data streams. Consequently, appropriate analytics algorithms and system architectures need to be utilized.

In this context, *IoT analytics architectures* provide the means to capture, process and integrate these smart device data efficiently. They enable *IoT analytics* by offering tools to process data using various data mining or machine learning algorithms. Additionally, they provide interfaces for the use of the results by external applications and data visualization. Therefore, *IoT analytics architectures* are usually based on different platforms, frameworks and computing paradigms.

While past Big Data research already offers a multitude of architectural solutions for data processing, analytics in IoT domains also expose issues, which are new or different, therefore requiring new approaches. For example, *IoT analytics* include scenarios, which are rapidly changing, in terms of their requirements, data sources and desired insights, etc. Furthermore, IoT data are often times directly linked to the behavior or the immediate surroundings of people and are used to gain insights and make decisions in vitally important areas of everyday life such as healthcare or transportation. For this reason, a number of challenges have to be met by processing architectures, some of which are contradictory.

From a technical standpoint, recent advances in stream data processing as well as relatively new computing concepts such as fog or edge computing offer interesting new approaches to address these challenges. Against this background, we investigate the current state of the art and try to assess existing *IoT analytics architectures* research. Specifically, in this paper, we identify challenges for IoT analytics architectures, portray the current landscape of existing *IoT analytics architectures* proposals and validate to what extent these solutions address the found challenges. This leads to the following research questions:

- RQ_1: Which challenges have to be addressed when designing *IoT analytics architectures*?
- RQ_2: What *IoT analytics architecture* proposals exist in scientific literature?
- RQ_3: To what extend do the found *IoT analytics architecture* proposals of RQ_2 address identified challenges of RQ_1?

The remainder of this paper is structured as follows: In Sect. 2, we describe the research methodology we applied in order to answer the research questions. Found challenges are presented in Sect. 3, therefore offering an answer to RQ_1. Section 4 provides an overview of existing *IoT analytics architectures* and a mapping against the results of Sect. 3. Following, we discuss our findings and offer reference points for future research (Sect. 5). Finally, we provide an overview of this paper (Sect. 7).

2 Research Methodology

The process of comprehensively reviewing literature in order to gain insights into the state of the art of a research topic is an integral part of any scientific work. A literature review should be concept-centric and ensure that all relevant publications are included, thus allowing an overview of major topics and concepts of the field [4]. Various research methods have been designed in order to ensure a systematic approach for reviewing a multitude of different research publications. Consequently, the literature review in this paper was conducted using the framework outlined by *vom Brocke et al.* in [5] and [6], which has been the foundation of many similar works in information systems research before.

2.1 Scope Definition

As a first step, we defined the scope of the literature search based on the research questions in Sect. 1 and the taxonomy provided by *Cooper* in [7]. The *focus* of our research lies on the challenges for designing IoT analytics architectures and on existing IoT analytics architecture proposals. The *goal* of this paper is to integrate these findings to give a comprehensive overview about the state of the art of IoT analytics architectures and future research challenges. The *coverage* was aimed to be exhaustive, but could only be conducted as a representation of the overall literature corpus as not all publications were accessible by the authors. All publications included in this paper were found utilizing a keyword-based search in several scientific search engines and databases as well as a subsequent forward search using all relevant publications and a backward search starting with review and overview papers found in the keyword search. The *perspective* of this overview is supposed to be neutral although the integration of the results of RQ_1 and RQ_2 is subjective concerning the authors' classification. The target *audience* of this overview are specialized scholars in the field of IoT analytics research. Finally, the *organization* of this work is done conceptually.

2.2 Conceptualization

In order to conceptualize the research topic, we used established classification schemes from previous scientific literature and adapted these according to the found publications. For example, if a relevant publication introduced a new characteristic of a category, it was extended. This conceptualization was done in order to categorize the results of RQ_2. Important categories of this paper are: *year, deployment layer* and *application domain*. Answering RQ_3, we additionally used the found challenges of RQ_1 to classify the results of RQ_2.

Significant *years* in this paper range from 2009 to 2019. The different *deployment layers* of analytics architectures are based on [8] and include "cloud", "fog" and "edge". We also use the category "hybrid", which includes approaches that use at least two of the aforementioned deployment layers.

The *application domain* categorization of a paper is based on [9]. It includes the values "Smart Home", "Smart Healthcare", "Smart Industry" and "Smart City". The term "Smart City" encapsulates the terms "Smart Transportation", "Smart Grid" and

"Smart Government" since most of the found publications, which were assigned to the "Smart City" domain, address at least two of these application areas. In addition, we are using the category "generic" for analytics architectures, which do not address a particular application domain.

2.3 Search

The search for relevant literature was conducted in the December of 2019 using the scientific search engines and databases IEEE Explore, Science Direct, Web of Science, SpringerLink, ACM, EBSCO Host and Google Scholar. Following [6], we tested different search terms and did a title search using the term (*"IoT" OR "Internet of Things" OR "Internet of Everything" OR "IoE") AND Analytics*. The time period was not limited. After screening and classifying the found papers, we conducted a forward and backward search in order to identify additional relevant publications to answer the research questions listed in Sect. 1. The number of papers found, screened and filtered at different stages of the search are shown in Table 1.

Table 1. Amount of papers found and included per database using the search term ("IoT" OR "Internet of Things" OR "Internet of Everything" OR "IoE") AND analytics.

Journal	Title Search	Accessible	Duplicate Removal	Inclusion/ Exclusion criteria	Forward/ Backward Search
IEEE Explore	168	168	168	28	3
Science Direct	40	9	9	1	0
Web of Science	238	235	115	10	1
Springerlink	8	0	0	0	0
ACM	49	49	40	4	0
EBSCO Host	25	25	3	0	0
Google Scholar	569	389	163	54	8
	1097	875	498	97	12
				Total	**109**

Overall, 1,097 papers were found. From these, 875 were accessible to the authors and 377 were duplicates, leaving 498 papers for screening. After applying inclusion and exclusion criteria (c.f. Sect. 2.4), 99 relevant papers were left. We also excluded our own research in this field to reduce bias. The resulting corpus of 97 publications was the basis for a forward search. In addition, review and overview papers were also used for a backward search. Combined, both search methods yielded an additional 12 papers, resulting in 109 relevant publications[1].

---

[1] The full list of publications can be found at https://github.com/zsco/IoT-Analytics-Architectures-Challenges/blob/master/publications.md.

2.4 Screen and Classify

The screening process for each paper started with removing publications, which were not accessible to the authors or duplicates of searches with different search engines. Afterwards, the authors screened the title, abstract and, if necessary, other parts of the paper to in- and exclude papers. Inclusion criteria were:

- The paper deals with challenges to be addressed by IoT analytics architectures
- The paper deals with the conceptualization or implementation of IoT analytics architectures
- The paper is either a peer reviewed full paper, short paper, a book or a book chapter
- The paper is written in English

Exclusion criteria were:

- The paper does not deal with challenges to be addressed by IoT analytics architectures
- The paper does not deal with the conceptualization or implementation of IoT analytics architectures

The next step was to identify publications, which describe challenges for IoT analytics architectures and extract them (c.f. Sect. 2.5). Afterwards, all papers, which present IoT analytics architectures, were classified according to the schema of Sect. 2.2 and the schema, which was created using the extracted architectural challenges of Sect. 3. If multiple papers described the same architectural approach, we counted them as a single publication in Sects. 4.1, 4.2 and 4.3 as long as core concepts of the approach did not change over time. The screening and classifying process was iterative. If the classification of a paper was ambiguous, it was marked and discussed among the authors until a consensus was reached. Each author used the reference management software Citavi in order to screen and classify all papers.

2.5 Data Extraction

The extraction process of the challenges for IoT analytics architectures was iterative and followed a bottom-up approach. We conducted a detailed analysis of the found papers, especially sections which describe concepts and implementations. Found challenges were highlighted in the reference management software as well as added to a category by an author and validated by another. If the highlighted text passage was ambiguous, it was discussed among all authors until a consensus was reached. As a result, its reference was either added to an existing category, excluded or introduced under a new category.

3 Challenges

During the screening of all 109 publications, 32 papers were found that describe challenges, which need to be addressed by IoT analytics architectures. As shown in Fig. 1, we identified 16 different challenges for IoT analytics architectures and determined their absolute frequency of occurrence over all 32 publications[2]. In order to answer RQ_1, we describe each challenge in the following:

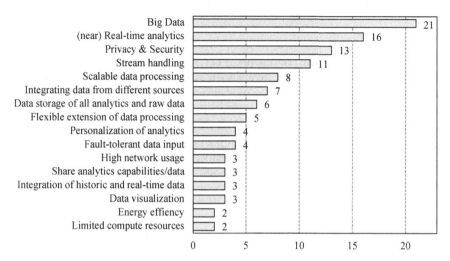

Fig. 1. Absolute frequency of mentioned challenges.

- **Big Data (65.6%):** IoT analytics architectures need to be able to process and analyze the inherently huge amounts of data [10–13], which arrive at high velocity [11, 13, 14] and originate from a multitude of different sources [11, 13, 15, 16], thus exposing heterogeneous data structures [11, 13] and semantics.
- **(near) Real-time analytics (50%):** The dynamic nature of the IoT and smart devices, which emit data that include temporal aspects [12], creates the need to handle data streams in real-time [2, 17–19]. Moreover, as a result of the challenges that arise from their Big Data character, processing IoT data in an adequate amount of time poses a challenge for analytics architectures [20]. Additionally, IoT analytics use cases may be of urgent nature, thus creating the need for prioritization of data processing [21].
- **Privacy & Security (40.6%):** IoT data and subsequent applications and services directly derive from the lives of consumers, but also companies [10]. In this regard, IoT analytics architectures need to be secure and resilient to external penetration attempts. Still, security has to be bearable and low-cost [22] in light of the huge numbers of potential smart devices [23]. In addition, the integrity of all data and consumers' privacy have to maintained at all times [24].
- **Stream handling (34.4%):** As most of the IoT data is generated as time series data, analytics architectures have to be able to process data streams [2, 18, 25]. This includes discovery, access and the combination of data streams from different data sources [26].
- **Scalable data processing (25%):** Based on the huge number of potential data sources, IoT analytics architectures need to be able "to process an arbitrarily large number

---

[2] The data collection form of the challenges can be found at: https://github.com/zsco/IoT-Analytics-Architectures-Challenges/blob/master/challenges.md.

of streams, with only marginal upgrades to the underlying hardware infrastructure" [18]. Additionally, computational tasks will become more complex, thus requiring new concepts to ensure the scalability of IoT analytics architectures [27]. With the emergence of new computing paradigms such as fog and edge computing the scalability of an analytics architecture will also rely on resource discovery, data offloading and management [19].

- **Integrating data from different sources (21.9%):** IoT analytics use cases require the combination of data from different sources, which arrive as streams [26]. The integration of these streams is still an ongoing research topic [28, 29] and needs to be supported by an IoT analytics architecture.
- **Data storage of all analytics and raw data (18.8%):** The volume of the data, which is generated by smart devices is huge [30]. Appropriate IoT analytics architectures need to store these unstructured data efficiently [12]. This may be achieved using low cost commodity storage [31]. In order to enable the usage of different tools to visualize data and analytics results, all data need to be stored at each phase of the processing task [32]. Another important aspect of this challenge is that data which are important for analytics processing have to be stored in-memory for low latency processing [25].
- **Flexible extension of data processing (15.6%):** The fast-paced and quickly changing nature of IoT applications, e.g. in terms of data sources, creates the need for IoT analytics architectures to be able to quickly update the configuration of analytics functions [18]. In addition, these may have to be flexible extended [10], which is also needed for the general data processing capabilities of analytics architectures [15].
- **Personalization of analytics (12.5%):** IoT analytics scenarios, especially in user-centric domains, such as Smart Home, are usually unique in terms of used data sources, expected result sets and available resources. In this regard, IoT analytics architectures have to mirror these preferences and requirements [33]. Furthermore, "they may analyze, process and transform received observations according to different consumer needs" [34]. Moreover, different "business and service logics, data warehouse scheme, template of data and service model[s]" [21] have to be supported.
- **Fault-tolerant data input (12.5%):** Many smart devices are not stationary and therefore enter and leave networks dynamically [11]. In addition, connectivity issues may occur at different network levels [10]. The resulting challenge for IoT analytics architectures is to be fault-tolerant in terms of their data input and to provide resilient analytics pipelines.
- **High network usage (9.4%):** The huge numbers of IoT devices use an equally high amount of network bandwidth to send sensor data to analytics architectures to be processed. This causes increased latency and degraded service availability [17]. Therefore, IoT analytics architectures need to provide solutions in order to decrease network pressure [21, 23].
- **Share analytics capabilities/data (9.4%):** Using different interfaces, IoT analytics architectures have to offer raw and processed data as well as their processing and analytics capabilities to IoT applications [15, 31, 35]. These may be external third-party tools, but also the different layers of an integrated IoT platform.
- **Integration of historic and real-time data (9.4%):** IoT analytics scenarios are manifold and range from real-time analysis to the training of machine learning models and the historical evaluation of error patterns. Moreover, IoT applications may even

need a mixture of outputs with different requirements regarding temporal granularity [25]. For this reason, analytics architecture in the IoT have to address the integration of historic and real-time data [15].

- **Data visualization (9.4%):** The visualization of analytics results, but also of raw data is important, as it allows for insights into and interaction with IoT applications [32]. Consequently, IoT analytics architectures need to provide data visualization tools for users or interfaces, which allow to access raw and processed data for visualization.
- **Energy efficiency (6.3%):** Energy efficiency is a challenge, which is linked to the Big Data characteristics of IoT data [27], but also to the high network usage of smart devices and their communication with each other and analytics architectures [23]. Therefore, analytics architectures need to support deployments, which offer processing in a "network/power/energy aware manner" [23].
- **Limited compute resources (6.3%):** Taking into account the aforementioned challenges, many IoT analytics architectures aim to move compute tasks closer to the edge of the network and closer to the point of origin of the data [25]. This may lead to problems since smart devices, which generate these data, are constrained regarding the availability of processing resources [11]. As a result, analytics architectures have to manage individual analytics scenarios resource requirements against available resources at computing nodes [25].

4   Analytics Architectures

In this section, we present the results of our literature search concerning found IoT analytics architecture proposals. Figure 2 shows the evolution of the amount of publications regarding IoT analytics architectures from 2009 until 2019. Overall, we found 87 papers, which describe architectural approaches for IoT analytics, with only a few (5.1%) published before 2015. The majority (94.9%) of papers were published after 2014. The most papers were published in the years 2016 (23.1%) and 2018 (25.6%). Since some of the papers describe the same architectural approach, we only counted the latest publication to calculate the results presented in the following sections as explained in Sect. 2.4. Answering RQ$_2$, this reduced the total amount of distinct architectural approaches to 78^3.

4.1   Deployment Layer

The analyzed papers describe IoT analytics architectures, which are designed to be deployed at the cloud (37.2%) or at the fog (2.6%) layer. Hybrid approaches were identified in 38.5% of all publications and 21.8% of the found solutions could not be assigned or did not mention a particular deployment layer (Fig. 2).

The number of cloud-based IoT analytics architectures grew from one in 2013 to ten in 2016. In 2017 this number decreased to four, only to increase again in 2018 to seven. In 2019, only one paper describing a cloud-based approach was found. Over time, the

---

^{3} The data collection form of the classification can be found at: https://github.com/zsco/IoT-Ana lytics-Architectures-Challenges/blob/master/classification.md.

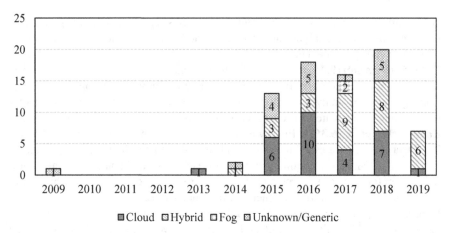

Fig. 2. Total amount of found publications, which describe an IoT analytics architecture, grouped by year and deployment layer.

number of papers describing hybrid approaches increased from one in 2014 to nine in 2017, which was higher as the number of cloud-based architectures (four publications) in the same year. In the following two years, this number was at eight in 2018 and six in 2019 making up the majority of papers of the respective years. Two fog-based approaches were published in 2017.

4.2 Application Domains

The total amount of found publications grouped by their deployment layer (y-axis) and application domain (x-axis) is shown in Fig. 3, with the size of a bubble representing the relative usage of a specific deployment layer in a domain. The distribution between cloud deployments and hybrid deployments was even or almost even for all domains with eight Smart City publications presenting cloud-based and nine hybrid deployment approaches. Furthermore, we found four cloud-based Smart Home deployments and five hybrid approaches. Smart Industry analytics architectures are mostly cloud-based (five) and hybrid (three) deployments. Smart Healthcare analytics architectures are cloud-based (two) and utilize hybrid approaches (two). One of the proposed Smart Healthcare solutions is fog-based. Generic IoT analytics architectures use cloud (ten) and hybrid deployments (eleven) with one approach being fog-based. The rest of the screened publications does not offer sufficient indications to categorize them in this regard.

The total percentage of analytics architectures for Smart City applications is 25.6%. Furthermore, 12.8% of the analyzed literature presented architectural solutions for Smart Home, 12.8% for Smart Healthcare, 11.6% for Smart Industry applications. A total of 37,2% could not be categorized.

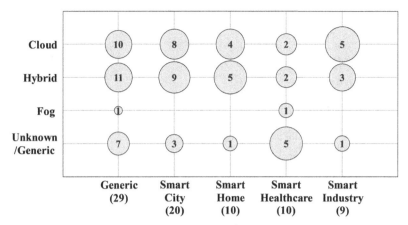

Fig. 3. Found publications, which describe an IoT analytics architecture, grouped by deployment layer and application domain.

4.3 Architectures vs. Challenges

With respect to RQ_3, we mapped the found architectural publications of RQ_2 against the presented challenges of Sect. 3, which are the result of RQ_1. We therefore conducted a more detailed analysis of the 78 relevant architectural proposals. This included studying sections describing architectural concepts and figures. Figure 4 shows the mapping of all architectural papers, grouped by their application domain (x-axis), with respect to the challenges found in Sect. 3 (y-axis)[4].

Overall, the majority of analyzed publications address the challenge of *Big Data* (69.2%) with the highest coverage in Smart City (85%) and the lowest in generic proposals (58.6%). *Real-time analytics* are covered by 56.4% of all found papers. The Smart Home domain has the highest architectural consideration for the topic with 70%, Smart City the least (50%). *Privacy and security* are dealt with in 12.8% of the papers. We found the highest coverage in the Smart Home domain (30%) and the lowest in generic proposals (6.9%). *Stream handling* is considered in 56.4% of the analyzed literature. Again, the highest coverage is in the Smart Home domain with 70% and the lowest in Smart City papers with 50%. *Scalable data processing* as a challenge is addressed by 70.5% of all publications. Most Smart Industry (88.9%) research works tackle this issue. In contrast, only 40% of Smart Healthcare analytics architectural proposals do.

The integration of data from different sources is considered in 74.4% of all papers. We found the highest coverage in generic (82.8%) and the least in Smart Healthcare (60%) architectures. *The storage of data and all analytics and raw data* is an issue, which is tackled by 69.2% of all publications. The highest coverage of this challenge is found in Smart Industry (88.9%) and the lowest in Smart Healthcare proposals (60%). *The flexible extension of data processing* is considered in 9% of the found literature. Generic solutions (17.2%) address this issue most often, Smart Home and Smart City

---

[4] The data collection form of the mapping of architectures versus challenges can be found at: https://github.com/zsco/IoT-Analytics-Architectures-Challenges/blob/master/architecturesVsChallenges.md.

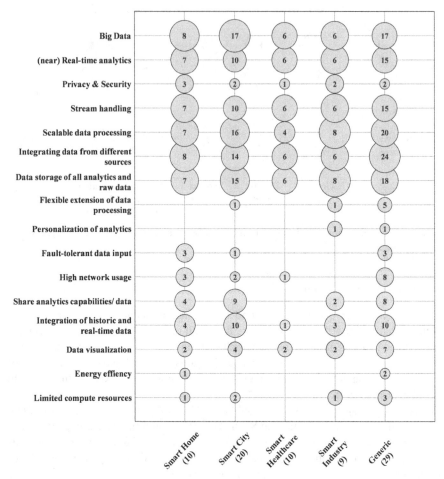

Fig. 4. IoT analytics architecture challenges vs. application domains. Bubble sizes represent the relative amount of publications of a domain dealing with a particular challenge. The number in a bubble is the total amount.

not at all. Only two architectural proposals address *personalization of analytics* (2.3%), one being generic the other one from the Smart Industry domain. The capabilities to offer *fault-tolerant data input* are described in 9% of the overall corpus, including 30% of the relevant Smart Home papers, but none in Smart Healthcare and industry.

The challenge of *high network usage* is addressed by 18% of the publications. Most coverage of this issue is present in Smart Home (30%), but none in Smart Industry papers. *Sharing analytics capabilities and data across IoT applications* is a challenge, which is addressed by 29.5% of all papers. The highest percentage of solutions tackling this issue is in the Smart City domain (45%). The Smart Healthcare domain does not cover it. Regarding the *integration of historic and real-time data*, 35.9% of the analyzed research works present an approach to handle this issue. The highest coverage was found in works in the Smart City domain (50%), the lowest in the Smart Healthcare domain

(10%). The relative coverage of the challenge of *data visualization* is very close in every domain and overall, at 21.8%. We found that 24.1% of generic architecture papers deal with this issue. *Energy efficiency* is addressed by only 3.9% of all publications with no coverage in Smart City, healthcare and industry settings. Finally, the challenge of *limited compute resources* is approached by 9% of architectural proposals almost evenly distributed among all domains with the exception of smart health with no publications addressing this issue.

5   Discussion and Future Research Areas

5.1   Findings

Most papers dealing with IoT analytics architectures were published beginning in 2015, use a cloud-based or hybrid deployment approach, but cannot be assigned to a specific application domain, followed by the Smart City, home, healthcare and industry domains. The amount of relevant published papers was almost identical in the years 2016–2018 and dropped in 2019. Although speculation, the lack of accessibility of the authors, but also missing indexation of relevant papers at the time of the literature search might be reasons for this. Based on the results of our analysis, we conclude that hybrid deployment approaches have become more popular over time, replacing pure cloud-based deployments as the most utilized deployment strategy. In addition, our overview indicates that Smart Home analytics architectures have gained heightened research interest in the year 2019, shifting from the Smart City domain in 2018. The focus on Smart Healthcare and analytics architectures in industry has remained at a steady level since 2015. Furthermore, the number of solutions, which do not have a particular application domain, has decreased since 2016. Most of the concerned papers are rather technical as opposed to those, which we affiliated with a particular IoT domain. This development suggests a shift in the focus of researchers. Application-centric research in real-world settings seems to become more important than purely technical solutions.

In terms of addressed challenges, a majority of publications of all domains focus on Big Data and related challenges such as scalable data processing, the integration of data from different sources and data storage. Another major aspect of past research in all application domains is stream handling of IoT data and their (near) real-time processing. Additionally, the integration of historic and real-time data as well as the ability to share analytics capabilities and data across IoT applications and infrastructures are challenges, which have been addressed by multitude of analytics architectures of different IoT domains. Less prominent are solutions that tackle the challenges regarding data visualization along with privacy and security. Challenges, which are unique to the IoT or play a superordinate role, namely limited compute resources, energy efficiency as well as high network usage, have only been researched by a small number of scientific publications. The same applies to the personalization and flexible extension of analytics.

Looking at the distribution of the number of proposals, which address particular challenges, it becomes evident that some of them are more relevant to individual domains than others. For example, a majority of the analyzed Smart Healthcare papers focus on real-time data processing (60%) which is crucial for up-to-date health monitoring and timely alerting (e.g. [36–38]). In contrast, this aspect is less prominent (50%) in Smart

City analytics architectures as these solutions are also used for planning decisions, thus requiring the integration of historic and current data [39]. Moreover, Smart City domain papers (50%) firmly address this issue, as opposed to smart health analytics architectures (10%). Furthermore, analytics architectures in controlled environments, e.g. factories or hospitals, address challenges such as fault-tolerant data input, high network usage, energy efficiency and limited compute resources almost not or not at all. On the other side, a user-centric IoT domain such as Smart Home has yielded several publications dealing with these topics. Therefore, when designing analytics architectures for the IoT, the supposed application domain of the aspired solution plays a crucial role concerning architectural challenges to be solved.

5.2 Future Research Areas

Comparing the numbers of mentions of challenges in scientific literature and publications, which actually address them, privacy and security as well as personalization of analytics and energy efficiency of data processing, are research areas for future work in all domains of the IoT. In this regard, privacy and security are topics, which are not new in information systems research, but need to be adapted to IoT environments on the basis of the volume, variation and dynamicity of IoT data [29]. Furthermore, a major concern is the transmission and processing of data without interference [13]. This results in the need for security policies [22] as well as new security and privacy mechanisms [29], but also secure system design with focus on the special characteristics of the IoT [28].

The challenge of energy efficiency in IoT analytics architectures is linked to huge number of smart devices, which are potentially sources for data analytics and processing. Leveraging already available computing resources at the edge of the network may lead to reduced cloud computing resource needs synonymous with reduced energy usage [40]. Therefore, future IoT analytics architectures research in all application domains needs to integrate the concepts of fog and edge computing and offer concrete solutions concerning this issue.

In terms of personalization of analytics, current IoT analytics architectures do not provide sufficient solutions. The two publications, which address this challenge use predefined and custom analytics operators in order to build configurable, flow-based analytics pipelines [41, 42]. Considering the rising number of IoT devices and the resulting complexity and dynamics of analytics scenario requirements, future research needs to investigate how to conceptualize and implement technical solutions to address this challenge, especially in user-centric application domains, such as Smart Home.

6 Threats to Validity

We have detailly described the applied research methods for this review to be repeatable. A threat to validity may be the utilization of the wrong search term. Therefore, we tested different search terms before the actual review as described in Sect. 2.3. Although we did not limit the time span of the search, previous research in this field, using a different terminology may not be in the scope of this review. We increased the representative quality of this overview by utilizing multiple search providers and scientific databases. Additionally, we deployed established research methods.

Regarding the objectivity of this work, it should be noted that the selection and classification of the publications as well as the extraction and validation of challenges is influenced by the bias of the researchers. Therefore, every extracted challenge and classified paper was validated by another author. Extracted challenges and papers with an ambiguous classification were marked by the reviewer and discussed by all authors.

The internal validity of this overview was addressed by using a top-down approach to develop the categorization dimensions. In order to increase the external validity of this review, we tried to broaden the sample size as described in Sect. 2.3.

7 Conclusion

In this paper, we provide an overview on the current state of the art of IoT analytics architectures in different application domains. In this regard, we utilized a structured approach to search, filter and categorize relevant literature. Based on the results of this review, we identified and described challenges, which IoT analytics architectures have to address. Furthermore, we identified IoT analytics architectural proposals, which were developed in past research. We categorized these solution proposals using the dimensions *year*, *deployment layer* and *application*. Relevant publications were published beginning in 2009, use cloud-, fog-based and hybrid deployment approaches and are affiliated with Smart City, home, healthcare or industry applications. A number of publications could not be assigned to any category in any of the latter dimensions. Additionally, we mapped the found architectures, grouped by their respective application domains, against the challenges we identified before. The results show that several challenges have been addressed by a large number of IoT analytics architectures while others are either not relevant for certain domains or need further investigation. Based on this, we provide insights into open challenges and future research directions in this field.

Acknowledgements. The work presented in this paper is partly funded by the European Regional Development Fund (ERDF) and the Free State of Saxony (Sächsische Aufbaubank - SAB).

References

1. Statista: Size of the Internet of Things (IoT) market worldwide from 2017 to 2025 (2019). https://www.statista.com/statistics/976313/global-iot-market-size/. Accessed 27 Jan 2020
2. Siow, E., Tiropanis, T., Hall, W.: Analytics for the Internet of Things. ACM Comput. Surv. **51**(4), 1–35 (2018)
3. Simmhan, Y., Perera, S.: Big data analytics platforms for real-time applications in IoT. In: Pyne, S., Rao, B., Rao, S. (eds.) Big Data Analytics, pp. 115–135. Springer, New Delhi (2016). https://doi.org/10.1007/978-81-322-3628-3_7
4. Webster, J., Watson, R.T.: Analyzing the past to prepare for the future: writing a literature review. MIS Q. **26**, xiii–xxiii (2002)
5. vom Brocke, J., Simons, A., Niehaves, B., Riemer, K., Plattfaut, R., Cleven, A.: Reconstructing the giant: on the importance of rigour in documenting the literature search process. In: Proceedings of the 17th European Conference on Information Systems, Verona, Italy (2009)

6. Vom Brocke, J., Simons, A., Riemer, K., Niehaves, B., Plattfaut, R., Cleven, A.: Standing on the shoulders of giants: challenges and recommendations of literature search in information systems research. Commun. Assoc. Inf. Syst. **37**, 205–224 (2015)
7. Cooper, H.M.: Organizing knowledge syntheses: a taxonomy of literature reviews. Knowl. Soc. **1**, 104–126 (1988)
8. Mouradian, C., Naboulsi, D., Yangui, S., Glitho, R.H., Morrow, M.J., Polakos, P.A.: A comprehensive survey on fog computing state-of-the-art and research challenges. IEEE Commun. Surv. Tutor. **20**(1), 416–464 (2018)
9. Saleem, T.J., Chishti, M.A.: Data analytics in the Internet of Things: a survey. Scalable Comput. Pract. Exp. **20**(4), 607–630 (2019)
10. Hasan, T., Kikiras, P., Leonardi, A., Ziekow, H., Daubert, J.: Cloud-based IoT analytics for the smart grid: experiences from a 3-year pilot. In: Michelson, D.G., Garcia, A.L., Zhang, W.-B., Cappos, J., Darieby, M.E. (eds.) Proceedings of the 10th International Conference on Testbeds and Research Infrastructures for the Development of Networks & Communities (TRIDENTCOM), Vancouver, Canada (2015)
11. Stolpe, M.: The Internet of Things: opportunities and challenges for distributed data analysis. SIGKDD Explor. Newsl. **18**(1), 15–34 (2016)
12. Ahmed, E., et al.: The role of big data analytics in Internet of Things. Comput. Netw. **129**, 459–471 (2017)
13. Kaur, M., Aslam, A.M.: Big data analytics on IOT challenges open research issues and tools. IJSRCSE **6**(3), 81–85 (2018)
14. Batool, S., Saqib, N.A., Khan, M.A.: Internet of Things data analytics for user authentication and activity recognition. In: 2017 Second International Conference on Fog and Mobile Edge Computing (FMEC), 8–11 May 2017, Valencia, Spain, pp. 183–187. IEEE (2017)
15. Cheng, B., Longo, S., Cirillo, F., Bauer, M., Kovacs, E.: Building a big data platform for smart cities: experience and lessons from santander. In: Carminati, B. (ed.) 2015 IEEE International Congress on Big Data (BigData Congress), 27 June–2 July 2015, New York, USA, pp. 592–599. IEEE, Piscataway (2015)
16. Ding, G., Wang, L., Wu, Q.: Big data analytics in future Internet of Things (2013)
17. Sharma, S.K., Wang, X.: Live data analytics with collaborative edge and cloud processing in wireless IoT networks. IEEE Access **5**, 4621–4635 (2017)
18. Kefalakis, N., Roukounaki, A., Soldatos, J.: A configurable distributed data analytics infrastructure for the industrial Internet of Things. In: 2019 15th International Conference on Distributed Computing in Sensor Systems (DCOSS), pp. 179–181 (2019)
19. ur Rehman, M.H., Yaqoob, I., Salah, K., Imran, M., Jayaraman, P.P., Perera, C.: The role of big data analytics in industrial Internet of Things. Future Gener. Comput. Syst. **99**, 247–259 (2019)
20. Verma, S., Kawamoto, Y., Fadlullah, Z., Nishiyama, H., Kato, N.: A survey on network methodologies for real-time analytics of massive IoT data and open research issues. IEEE Commun. Surv. **19**(3), 1457–1477 (2017)
21. Biswas, A.R., Dupont, C., Pham, C.: IoT, cloud and bigdata integration for IoT analytics. Build. Blocks IoT Anal. **11**, 11–38 (2016)
22. Stojkoska, B.L.R., Trivodaliev, K.V.: A review of Internet of Things for smart home. Challenges and solutions. J. Clean. Prod. **143**(3), 1454–1464 (2017)
23. Schooler, E.M., Zage, D., Sedayao, J., Moustafa, H., Brown, A., Ambrosin, M.: An architectural vision for a data-centric IoT. Rethinking things, trust and clouds. In: 2017 IEEE 37th International Conference on Distributed Computing Systems (ICDCS), 05–08 June 2017, Atlanta, GA, USA, pp. 1717–1728. IEEE (2017)

24. Kumarage, H., Khalil, I., Alabdulatif, A., Tari, Z., Yi, X.: Secure data analytics for cloud-integrated Internet of Things applications. IEEE Cloud Comput. **3**(2), 46–56 (2016)
25. Cao, H., Wachowicz, M.: Analytics everywhere for streaming IoT data. In: 2019 Sixth International Conference on Internet of Things: Systems, Management and Security (IOTSMS), pp. 18–25 (2019)
26. Tönjes, R., et al.: Real time IoT stream processing and large-scale data analytics for smart city applications. In: Poster Session, European Conference on Networks and Communications (2014)
27. Wich, M., Kramer, T.: Enrichment of smart home services by integrating social network services and big data analytics. In: Bui, T.X., Sprague, R.H. (eds.) Proceedings of the 49th Annual Hawaii International Conference on System Sciences, 5–8 January 2016, Kauai, Hawaii, USA, pp. 425–434. IEEE, Piscataway (2016)
28. Tsai, C.-W., Tsai, P.-W., Chiang, M.-C., Yang, C.-S.: Data analytics for Internet of Things: a review. WIREs Data Min. Knowl. Discov. **8**(5), e1261 (2018)
29. ur Rehman, M.H., Ahmed, E., Yaqoob, I., Hashem, I.A.T., Imran, M., Ahmad, S.: Big data analytics in industrial IoT using a concentric computing model. IEEE Commun. Mag. **56**(2), 37–43 (2018)
30. Anand, P.: Towards evolution of M2M into Internet of Things for analytics. In: 2015 IEEE Recent Advances in Intelligent Computational Systems (RAICS), Trivandrum, Kerala, India, pp. 388–393 (2015)
31. Marjani, M., Nasaruddin, F., Gani, A.: Big IoT data analytics. Architecture opportunities, and open research challenges. IEEE Access **5**, 5247–5261 (2017)
32. Rozik, A.S., Tolba, A.S., El-Dosuky, M.A.: Design and implementation of the sense Egypt platform for real-time analysis of IoT data streams. AIT **6**(4), 65–91 (2016)
33. Biswas, A.R., Giaffreda, R.: IoT and cloud convergence. Opportunities and challenges. In: 2014 IEEE World Forum on Internet of Things (WF-IoT), 06–08 March 2014, Seoul, Korea (South), pp. 375–376. IEEE (2014)
34. Auger, A., Exposito, E., Lochin, E.: Sensor observation streams within cloud-based IoT platforms. Challenges and directions. In: 2017 20th Conference on Innovations in Clouds, Internet and Networks (ICIN), 07–09 March 2017, Paris, pp. 177–184. IEEE (2017)
35. Xu, Q., Aung, K.M.M., Zhu, Y., Yong, K.L.: Building a large-scale object-based active storage platform for data analytics in the Internet of Things. J. Supercomput. **72**(7), 2796–2814 (2016)
36. Din, S., Paul, A.: Smart health monitoring and management system: toward autonomous wearable sensing for Internet of Things using big data analytics. Future Gener. Comput. Syst. **91**, 611–619 (2018)
37. Almeida, A., Mulero, R., Rametta, P., Urošević, V., Andrić, M., Patrono, L.: A critical analysis of an IoT-aware AAL system for elderly monitoring. Future Gener. Comput. Syst. **97**, 598–619 (2019)
38. Manogaran, G., Varatharajan, R., Lopez, D., Kumar, P.M., Sundarasekar, R., Thota, C.: A new architecture of Internet of Things and big data ecosystem for secured smart healthcare monitoring and alerting system. Future Gener. Comput. Syst. **82**, 375–387 (2018)
39. Al-Jaroodi, J., Mohamed, N.: Service-oriented architecture for big data analytics in smart cities. In: Proceedings of the 18th IEEE/ACM International Symposium on Cluster, Cloud and Grid Computing (CCGRID), 1–4 May 2018, Washington, DC, pp. 633–640. IEEE, Piscataway (2018)
40. Taneja, M., Jalodia, N., Davy, A.: Distributed decomposed data analytics in fog enabled IoT deployments. IEEE Access **7**, 40969–40981 (2019)

41. Ge, Y., Liang, X., Zhou, Y.C., Pan, Z., Zhao, G.T., Zheng, Y.L.: Adaptive analytic service for real-time Internet of Things applications. In: 2016 IEEE International Conference on Web Services (ICWS), San Francisco, CA, USA, pp. 484–491 (2016)
42. Hochreiner, C., Vogler, M., Waibel, P., Dustdar, S.: VISP: an ecosystem for elastic data stream processing for the Internet of Things. In: Matthes, F., Mendling, J., Rinderle-Ma, S. (eds.) Proceedings of the 2016 IEEE 20th International Enterprise Distributed Object Computing Conference (EDOC), 5–9 September 2016, Vienna, Austria, pp. 1–11. IEEE, Piscataway (2016)

Digital Enterprise and Technologies

Structural Coupling, Strategy and Fractal Enterprise Modeling

Ilia Bider[(⊠)]

DSV, Stockholm University, Stockholm, Sweden
`ilia@dsv.su.se`

Abstract. The concept of structural coupling, which comes from the biological cybernetics, has been found useful for organizational decision making on the higher level, such as management of organizational identity and strategy development. However, currently, there is no systematic procedure for finding all elements (other organizations, markets, etc.) of the environment to which a given organization is structurally coupled, or will be coupled after redesign. The paper tries to fill the gap by employing enterprise modeling to identify structural couplings. More specifically, an extended Fractal Enterprise Model (FEM) is used for this end. FEM connects enterprise processes with assets that are used in and are managed by these processes. The extended FEM adds concepts to represent external elements and their connections to the enterprise. The paper drafts rules for identifying structural couplings in the model by analyzing FEMs that represent different phases of the development of a company which the author co-founded and worked for over 20 years.

Keywords: Strategy · Organizational identity · Enterprise modeling · Structural coupling · Socio-technical · Fractal Enterprise Model · FEM · Enterprise engineering

1 Introduction

The concept of structural coupling comes from biological cybernetics, more specifically, from the works of Maturana and Varela, see, for example, [1]. The idea of structural coupling is relatively simple; it suggests that a complex system adjusts its structure to the structure of the environment in which it operates. The adjustment comes from the constant interaction between the system and its environment. Moreover, during the system evolution in the given environment, some elements of the environment and interaction with them become more important than others. The latter leads to the system choosing to adjust to a limited number of environmental elements with which it becomes structurally coupled. According to Luhmann [2], a system deliberately chooses to limit its couplings to few elements, as a strategy of dealing with the complexity. These elements, in turn, function as information channels to other parts of the environment.

An element of the environment to which a system becomes coupled, being a system on its own, may, in turn, adjust its structures to the given system, which creates interdependency between the two structurally coupled systems. The process of emergence of the

© Springer Nature Switzerland AG 2020
F. Dalpiaz et al. (Eds.): RCIS 2020, LNBIP 385, pp. 95–111, 2020.
https://doi.org/10.1007/978-3-030-50316-1_6

structural coupling during the co-evolution of two interacting systems is represented in Fig. 1. As the result of mutual interdependency, the structurally coupled systems change together, one changing itself as a reaction on changes in the other. The coupling might not be symmetrical, i.e. one system may dominate the other, making it more likely that the latter would change as a reaction on changes in the former, than vice versa.

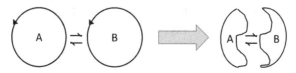

Fig. 1. Emergence of structural coupling. Adapted from [3].

The concept of structural coupling along with other concepts developed by Maturana and Varela, such as autopoiesis, was adopted by other fields that use system theoretical concepts. A typical example is Social Science, to which this term was brought by N. Luchmann, see, for example, [2]. However, in the domain of organizational systems, which are socio-technical systems, the usage of the concept of structural coupling is not widely spread. Actually, we have found only two works that apply the concept of structural coupling to the organizational/business world [4, 5].

The first work [4] suggests using the concept of structural coupling for the purpose of defining the notions of organizational identity and identity management. According to Hoverstadt [4], the identity is defined as a set of structural couplings an organization/enterprise has to other systems/agents in the organizational/business world, such as markets, customers, partners, vendors, regulators. The identity management is defined as activities aimed at maintaining the structural couplings in the dynamic environment, i.e. reacting on changes in the structurally coupled systems, or inducing changes in them when making changes in their own structures.

The second work [5] defines the strategy as a goal of reaching a certain position in relation to the structurally coupled elements of the environment, such as customers, partners, competitors, supplies etc. As an example, consider a segment of market where there is a "herd" of similar companies. Then a position in relation to the herd can be defined as a "leader", "in the middle", "independent", etc. [5] presents around 80 patterns of strategy to choose from, alongside with the requirements on what is needed to implement each pattern.

As far as applying the concept of structural coupling to identity management, we have followed up this idea in own research [6]. Here, we have achieved some success by explaining a number of changes completed in our department under a couple of decennia as reactions on the changes in the structurally coupled elements of the environment. As far as using structural coupling in strategic decision making, though we have not followed it up in any finished research, the idea seems promising.

In connection to the application of the concept of structural coupling to the organizational/business world, a question arises on how to find all structural couplings of a given organization/enterprise. This is important for both identity management and strategic decision-making, including situations when a change in the structural couplings of the organization is planned. As the idea of using the concept of structural coupling is not spread in the Management, IT or Information Systems research fields, we could not find any answer on the question above in the research literature.

Hoversadt and Loh [5] suggest a practically-oriented way of looking for structural couplings that is based on the structure of the business/organizational world. More specifically, dependent on the desired strategy, they suggest looking for main competitors, regulators, key partners, key customers, and key market segments. Our work [6] suggests another approach for finding structural couplings, which is based on finding who is producing inputs for the organizational activities, and who is consuming outputs of the organizational activities. In addition to the input/output approach, a position of the organization in a larger system is determined in accordance to the Viable System Model [7]. The latter gives a hint to find out structural couplings that are connected to the management level of the larger system. Also, a geographical position of the organization is considered to see whether there is a structural coupling to the location.

Both approaches - from [5] and from [6] - can be used in practice, but both have their drawbacks. The approach presented in [5] is pragmatic, but it requires good understanding of organizational/business world. While it can be successfully used by experienced people, e.g. expert management consultants, it might be not as good for less experience people, for example, new entrepreneurs. There is a risk that some important structural couplings would remain outside the consideration when discussing the strategy. The approach from [6] is more formal, i.e. defined on a more abstract level. It does not employ such notions as supplier, partner, market, etc., but rely on formal notions of input, output, position in the larger system, and geographical location. However, using this approach alone, though it worked well in a case of an institution of higher education, may result in missing some important structural connections, like partners. It also does not guarantee that all important inputs and outputs will be taken into the consideration.

The question arises whether it is possible to develop a more systematic and comprehensive method for identifying if not all, than the major part of structural couplings of an organization. A possible way of designing such a method is via using an enterprise model of some sort that depicts not only internal components of the organization, but also components of the environment. Having such a model, it might be possible to add a set of rules that determine which components of the environment constitute structural couplings. The goal of this paper is to investigate whether a particular enterprise modeling technique could be useful for this end. The technique in question is called extended Fractal Enterprise Model (FEM) [8].

FEM has a form of a directed graph with two types of nodes *processes* and *assets*, where the arrows (edges) from assets to processes show which assets are used in which processes and arrows from processes to assets show which processes help to have specific assets in "healthy" and working order. The arrows are labeled with meta-tags that show in what way a given asset is used, e.g. as *workforce, reputation, infrastructure*, etc., or in what way a given process helps to have the given assets "in order", i.e. *acquire, maintain* or *retire*.

Choosing the FEM technique as the first one to try has two reasons. Firstly, the author belongs to the team that has developed and is continue developing FEM. Thus, there is a personal interest to start the trial with FEM. Secondly, recently, we tried to apply

FEM to explain autopoiesis [1] and homeostasis [9] in socio-technical (organizational) systems [10]. This research has resulted in an extension of FEM that allows to represent in the model, at least, some part of the organizational context. This is done with the help of two new notions added to FEM – an external pool and an external actor. With this extension, FEM seems enough equipped to be tested as a means for finding structural couplings of an organization.

Our approach to conducting a trial is pragmatic, we take a real case, build relevant fragments of FEM for this case and see whether we can identify structural couplings in the model. Then, the findings are generalized as a set of rules on how to determine structural couplings more formally.

The rest of the paper is structured in the following way. In Sect. 2, we give an overview of FEM with the extension suggested in [11]. In Sect. 3, we discuss our research approach and business case to be used. In Sect. 4, we build a FEM model for our business case and analyze structural couplings of the company in the center of the business case. In Sect. 5, we draft rules of identifying structural couplings through generalizing what has been discovered in the previous section. In Sect. 6, we summarize our contribution and draft plans for the future.

2   Extended Fractal Enterprise Model - An Overview

2.1   Basic Fractal Enterprise Model

The original version of Fractal Enterprise Model (FEM) from [8] includes three types of elements: business processes (more exactly, business process types), assets, and relationships between them, see Fig. 2 in which a fragment of a model is presented. The fragment is related to the business case analyzed in this paper, and it represents the model of initial business design of a Swedish consulting company called *IbisSoft* [12]. Graphically, a process is represented by an oval, an asset is represented by a rectangle (box), while a relationship between a process and an asset is represented by an arrow. We differentiate two types of relationships in the fractal model. One type represents a relationship of a process "using" an asset; in this case, the arrow points from the asset to the process and has a solid line. The other type represents a relationship of a process changing the asset; in this case, the arrow points from the process to the asset and has a dashed line. These two types of relationships allow tying up processes and assets in a directed graph.

In FEM, a label inside an oval names the given process, and a label inside a rectangle names the given asset. Arrows are also labeled to show the type of relationships between the processes and assets. A label on an arrow pointing from an asset to a process identifies the role the given asset plays in the process, for example, *workforce*, and *infrastructure*. A label on an arrow pointing from a process to an asset identifies the way in which the process affects (i.e. changes) the asset. In FEM, an asset is considered as a pool of entities capable of playing a given role in a given process. Labels leading into assets from processes reflect the way the pool is affected, for example, the label *acquire* identifies that the process can/should increase the pool size.

Note that the same asset can be used in two different processes playing the same or different roles in them, which is reflected by labels on the corresponding arrows. It is

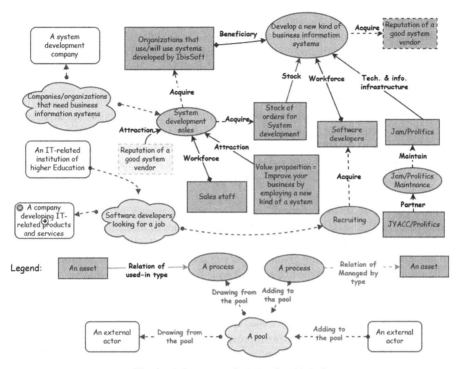

Fig. 2. A fragment of a FEM for IbisSoft

also possible that the same asset can be used for more than one role in the same process. In this case, there can be more than one arrow between the asset and the process, but with different labels. Similarly, the same process could affect different assets, each in the same or in different ways, which is represented by the corresponding labels on the arrows. Moreover, it is possible that the same process affects the same asset in different ways, which is represented by having two or more arrows from the process to the asset, each with its own label. When there are too many arrows leading to the same process or asset, several copies can be created for this process or asset in the diagram. In this case, the shapes for copies have a bleaker color than the original, see asset *Reputation as a good system vendor* in Fig. 2 that appears in two places.

In FEM, different styles can be used for shapes to group together different kinds of processes, assets, and/or relationships between them. Such styles can include dashed or double lines, or lines of different thickness, or colored lines and/or shapes. For example, a diamond start of an arrow from an asset to a process means that the asset is a stakeholder of the process (see the arrows *Workforce* in Fig. 2).

Labels inside ovals (which represent processes) and rectangles (which represent assets) are not standardized. They can be set according to the terminology accepted in the given domain, or be specific for a given organization. Labels on arrows (which represent the relationships between processes and assets) are standardized. This is done by using a relatively abstract set of relationships, such as, *workforce* or *acquire*, which are clarified by the domain- and context-specific labels inside ovals and rectangles. Standardization improves the understandability of the models.

While there are a number of types of relationships that show how an asset is used in a process (see example in Fig. 2), there are only three types of relationships that show how an asset is managed by a process – *Acquire*, *Maintain* and *Retire*.

To make the work of building a fractal model more systematic, FEM uses archetypes (or patterns) for fragments from which a particular model can be built. An archetype is a template defined as a fragment of a model where labels inside ovals (processes) and rectangles (assets) are omitted, but arrows are labelled. Instantiating an archetype means putting the fragment inside the model and labelling ovals and rectangles; it is also possible to add elements absent in the archetype, or omit some elements that are present in the archetype.

FEM has two types of archetypes, process-assets archetypes and an asset-processes archetype. A process-assets archetype represents the kinds of assets that can be used in a given category of processes. The asset-processes archetype shows the kinds of processes that are aimed at changing the given category of assets. The whole FEM graph is built by alternative application of the two types of archetypes in a recursive manner. Actually, the term *fractal* in the name of our modeling technique points to the *recursive* nature of the model, for more detailed explanation, see [8].

Note that in FEM, each process node represents a socio-technical system, while the assets connected to it with solid arrows represent different sides of this system, e.g. people (workforce), technology (technical and informational infrastructure). However, there is no explicit graphical representation of these assets being aligned between themselves. Implicitly, such alignment is presumed, however, as it is necessary for a process being able to function properly. Moreover, changes in any of the assets connected to a particular process node, e.g. people or technology, require readjustment of other assets connected to the node. This issue is covered in more details in [13].

Hereby, we finish a short overview of the standard FEM. The reader who wants to know more about the model and why it is called fractal are referred to [8] (which is in Open Access), and the later works related to FEM.

2.2 Extensions to FEM for Representing the Context

Two new concepts were introduced to FEM in order to represent the business context of the organization and connect it to specific processes [11]. These are as follows:

- *External pool*, which is represented by a cloud shape, see Fig. 2. An external pool is a set of things or agents of a certain type. As an example, in Fig. 2, there are two such pools: (1) pool of organizations that needs an information system, (2) pool of software developers looking for a job. The label inside the external pool describes its content.
- *External actor*, which is represented by a rectangle with rounded corners. An external actor is an agent, like a company or person, acting outside the boundary of the organization. The label inside the external actor describes its nature. If a label starts with indefinite article "a" or "any", the box represents a set of agents of the given type, see Fig. 2, which have three external actors of this kind.

External pools and external actors may be related to each other and to other elements of the FEM diagram. Such a relation is shown by a dashed arrow that has a round dot start. More exactly:

- A business process may be connected to an external pool with an arrow directed from the pool to the process. In this case, the process needs to be an *acquire* process to one or more assets. The arrow shows that the process uses the external pool to create new elements in the asset for which this process serves as an acquire process, see two examples of such relations in Fig. 2.
- An external actor may be connected to an external pool with an arrow directed from the pool to the external actor. In this case, the arrow shows that the external actor uses the external pool as bases for one of its own acquire processes, see two examples of such relations in Fig. 2.
- A business process may be connected to an external pool with an arrow directed from the process to the pool. In this case the arrow shows that the process provides entities to the external pool (there are no examples of such relations in Fig. 2, but an example of this type will be introduced later).
- An external actor may be connected to an external pool with an arrow directed from the actor to the pool. In this case the arrow shows that one of the actor's processes provides entities to the external pool (there are no examples of such relations in Fig. 2, but an example of this type will be introduced later).

External pools and actors represent the context in which an organization operates. External pools can be roughly associated with markets, e.g. a labor market, etc. External actors represent other organizations that are connected to the external pools. Dependent on the nature of the external pool, an external actor connected to it can be a competitor, provider, or collaborator. Note that an external organization can be an *asset*, e.g. partner or customer, or an *external actor*. The difference reveal itself in how the organization is connected to the internal processes; an external actor is always connected via an external pool.

3 Research Approach

The research presented in this paper belongs to the Design Science (DS) paradigm [14, 15], which focuses on looking for generic solutions for problems, known, as well as unknown. The result of a DS research project can be a solution of a problem in terminology of [15], or artifact in terminology of [14]; alternatively, the result can be in form of "negative knowledge" stating that a certain approach is not appropriate for solving certain kind of problems [15].

This research is part of a broader undertaking connected to FEM. Initially, FEM has been developed as a means for finding all or majority of the processes that exist in an organization. The result of this research produced more than a solution to the original problem, as FEM includes not only relations between the processes, but produces a map of assets usage and management in the organization. Therefore, we continue our work on FEM looking for other problems/challenges that can be solved using FEM and enhancing

FEM when necessary. One example of a specific application of FEM, beyond already mentioned work on autopoiesis [11], is using FEM for business model innovation, see, for example, [16]. From the point of view of classification of DS opportunities introduced in [17] and adopted in [15], we use exaptation (in terminology of [17]) or transfer (in terminology of [15]), which amounts to extending the known solutions to new problems, including adapting solutions from the other fields/domains. According to both [15] and [17], exaptation provides a research opportunity.

From the pragmatic point of view, our research is directed from a specific case to a generic solution through the generalization of the specific case. More exactly, we take a real business case, build relevant fragments of FEM for it, and then review them in order to mark FEM components that represent structural couplings of the organization. After that, we specify properties of these components that can serve as generic indicators for a component being a structural coupling. To be able to fulfill the plan, we need a case for which we can gather enough information to be able to determine structural couplings. Identification of structural couplings requires observation of the system in the environment for some period of time, as only in this case, we can see whether the system adjusts its structures to some elements of the environment and/or affects (indirectly) the structure of these elements.

To satisfy the requirements on the case, we have chosen a case from own practice. More specifically, the case used in this research is a small Swedish IT consultancy called IbisSoft [12], which was cofounded by the author of this paper and for which he worked for more than 20 years in the period from 1989 to 2011, as a technical leader, as well as a business and IT consultant and software developer. Due to my position in the company, I have intimate knowledge on the strategic and tactical decisions made during this period, and was partly responsible for successes and failures that resulted from these decisions. The eight years have passed after my leaving IbisSoft, which creates enough distance for analysis and reflection to be independent from the feelings of the days of personal engagement in the everyday business activities of the company.

Note that as the business case has been taken from the practical experience of the author, we can regard, at least partly, our research approach as reflective theory building [18]. The latter does not change the fact of our research belonging to the DS paradigm.

4   Building and Analyzing IbisSoft's FEMs

4.1   Initial Strategy Design

Ibissoft [12] was started as small consultancy with four partners in April 1989. The primary process was envision as developing a new kind of business information systems. The latter was reflected in the company's name *IbisSoft*, where *Ibis*, besides being a bird with connotation to the Egyptian god of wisdom Thoth that had an Ibis head, served as an abbreviation to *Integrated Business Information Systems*. The primary business design in FEM terms is represented in Fig. 2. *IbisSoft* was to develop a new kind of business information systems to the customers. Getting the first relatively small order, *IbiSoft* started system development of a new kind.

As the company had very small staff - two full time employees and some partners that could be engaged, the company needed a high-level system development tool (of the

4th GL kind) to achieve the necessary productivity level. After thorough investigation of the tools market, a particular tool from an US company *JYACC* (Just Your Average Consulting Company), called *JAM* (JYCC's Application Development) was chosen. Later, the company, as well as the tool were renamed to *Prolifics* [19], which is reflected in Fig. 2. After some more time, the product was once more renamed to *Panther* [20], which will not be used in any figures in this paper.

4.2 Strategy for Growth

While the first system was under development, the *IfbiSoft*'s board needed to design a strategy for continuing and expanding the company's operations. As the tool acquired for own system development showed to be quite good, the following strategy had been decided on and implemented. *IbisSoft* becomes a reseller of JYACC's tools in Sweden. This would require setting a business of selling JAM licenses, and at the same time setting a consulting business to help the customers that have bought JAM licenses to start using JAM and successfully complete their system development projects. The idea was (a) to get cash flowing in the company from reselling, and, in a higher degree, from consulting, and (b) get in touch with organizations, some of which could become customers for the main business activity depicted in Fig. 2.

The strategy was fully implemented as shown in Fig. 3, which depicts two interconnected primary processes. One is related to selling licenses, the other is technical consultancy for the companies that already have the JAM/Prolifics licenses. Actually, the first process could be split into two, the second concerns providing support on the subscription bases, but we will not go into this level of details here.

As we see from Fig. 3, the two processes are synergetic. Selling JAM/Prolifics adds new actors to the pool of companies/organizations who use the tools in their system development processes. This pool is used to recruit new customers for the consulting services. For our Swedish market, the major part of this pool was created by our own sales, however, sometimes we got a request from a potential customer that had acquire a license in a different way. Another synergy consists in our efforts to demonstrate the consulting customers how to use JAM/Prolifics in the best possible way, thus helping to create a reputation of it being an excellent tool. This, in turn, helped to conduct the license sales, as there were enough happy customers to whom we could refer.

The design in Fig. 3 worked well enough for arranging a cash flow and ensuring some basis for expansion. As far as the second purpose was concerned, i.e. getting customers to the business depicted in Fig. 2, it does not work well. In retrospective, the design error is quite clear, as depicted in Fig. 4. Namely, the pools from which JAM/Prolifics consulting sales and system development sales acquired customers did not have much intersection. Therefore, most of the customers acquired for JAM/Prolifics consulting were not interested in purchasing development of a new system. The only synergy between the consulting and system development processes that really worked was the JAM/Prolifics consulting served as a maintaining process for the software developers, as it increased their expertise in the use of the tool, which was also used in own system development.

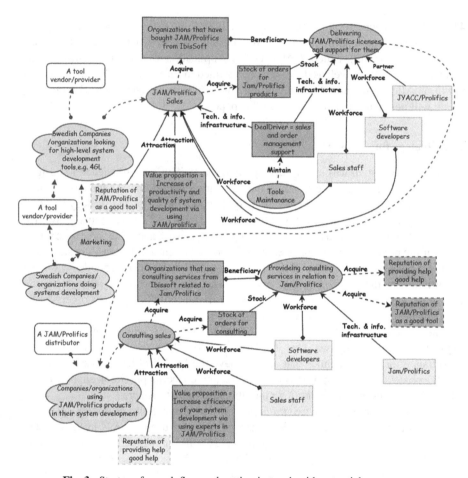

Fig. 3. Strategy for cash flow and getting in touch with potential customers

4.3 Back to System Development

Implementing the strategy described in the previous strategy resulted in *IbiSoft* being stuck with the business activities depicted in Fig. 3 for many years. Actually, they were expanded by recruiting additional staff to deal with JAM/Prolifics consulting projects, but they took all resources that were at *IbiSoft*'s disposal at the time. As the original business activity in Fig. 2 had no synergy with the expanded business, the sporadic ad-hock attempts to get orders for the system development activity were unsuccessful.

The business situation changed by the end of 1990ths in two aspects, one external and one internal:

1. The market for high-level system development tools (4th GL and similar) crashed due to appearing WEB, Java and Java script, i.e. system development went back to using low-level programming. Measures taken by *Prolifics* to adjust to the new deployment platform (WEB), i.e. creating a module for the WEB deployment, did

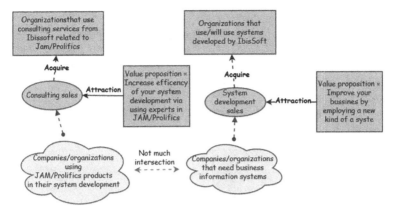

Fig. 4. Comparison between two sales processes

not help much against aggressive marketing for JAVA development. This affected the size of the pool "Swedish companies/organizations looking for high-level system development tools, e.g. 4GL" in Fig. 3, which, in turn, led to substantial decrease in sales of the tools licenses. However, support and consulting continue to give revenues due to the existent customer base. The crash of the market for the old school high-level development tools was substantial all over the world. In the end, this resulted in *Prolifics* ceasing to exist as a tool vendor and transforming itself into a consulting company, see [16].

2. The principles of the new kind of information systems to be produced by the business activity in Fig. 2 were re-conceptualized as principles of building a new kind of business process support systems. Based on the reconceptualization, a new way of looking at, modeling and supporting business processes was developed, which was later dubbed as a state-oriented view on business processes (see [21] for a historic overview). The state-oriented modeling of business processes has been tested in practice and got positive feedback from the customers, see [22].

New business situation required changes in the strategy. Reselling JAM/Prolifics was put on hold. No active marketing and selling was done, though we continued providing technical support to the existing customers. Tool consulting was continued for the existing customer base for quite some time. New activity was designed to deliver process models for the customers' processes. The thinking behind it was that some of the customer could decide to purchase a system from *IbisSoft* to support their process(es). The new strategy, which has been successfully implemented, is presented as a FEM diagram in Fig. 5.

The FEM fragment at the bottom of Fig. 5 represents a revised version of the diagram in Fig. 2. The upper part represents a new business activity - providing the customers with models of their business processes. The difference between the new design and the original one, as in Fig. 2, is as follows.

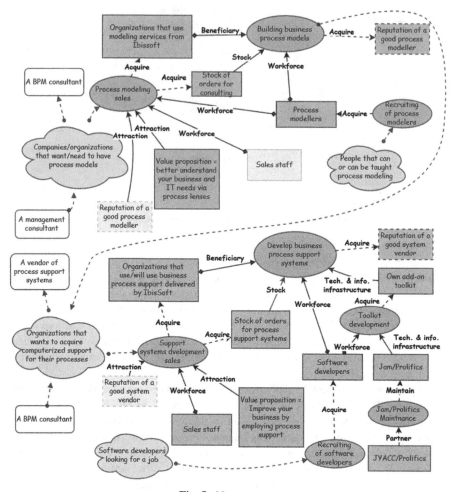

Fig. 5. New strategy

- The system development activity is supported by process modeling activity. Organizations that have completed their process modeling and redesign projects might be more willing to take the next step and introduce a computerize support for their processes. This is represented by a pool of companies that want/are ready to introduce computerized support for their process, and two arrows that connect it to the IbisSoft's activities. The first arrow goes from the process modeling activity to the pool; it shows that this activity adds new organizations to the pool. The second arrow shows that the sales process for system development uses the pool to fill the customer asset for the system development activity. Note that other companies, e.g. management consultants that design process models, can also add to this pool.
- The pool from which the system development sales acquires new customer is much more strictly defined than it is in Fig. 2. Namely, it consists of organizations that want to acquire support for their business processes. As the concept of business process

management had been already established by the time the new strategy was put to implementation, it was much easier to conduct the sales activities.

4.4 Identifying IbisSoft's Structural Couplings

Analyzing FEMs for different phases of IbisSoft's evolution, we can identify the following three main components that represent the company's structural couplings:

1. Asset *JYACC/Prolifics*. This asset is present in all FEM fragments depicted in Fig. 2, 3 and 5, but the nature and the strength of the coupling differ from fragment till fragment. In Fig. 2 and 5, the coupling is due to JAM/Prolifics is used as an internal tool for system development. JYACC/Proifics was the partner who ensured that the tool worked by producing bug fixes and new releases that allowed to move our own applications to new platforms, e.g. Windows. As the tool was chosen based on specifics of the systems being developed and we invested much time in learning to use it, the tool was an essential part of the business, and it was not easy to substitute it by any other tool. In the beginning, JYACC/Prolfics was the only agent that could maintain the tool, due to it being a proprietary software. At the end of our usage of the tool, the dependence on JYACC/Prolifics had been substantially lowered, due to the source code was published at some point of time, and we were able to fix or enhance the tool ourselves.

   For the first business process in Fig. 3 – selling licenses – JYACC/Prolifics was a partner without which it could not function. We could not substitute this partner without stopping selling the JAM/Prolifics licenses. For the second process, we were as dependent on JYACC/Prolifics as in the activities depicted in Fig. 2 and 5.

2. Asset *Swedish companies/organizations looking for high-level system development tools, e.g. 4GL*. This external pool from Fig. 3 represents the market for the process of selling tools licenses. The structural coupling to this market caused the process removal when the market crashed. The second business activity in Fig. 3 – consulting – continued after the crash, as the pool of companies/organizations that had JAM/Prolifics in their development processes continued to exist for quite a time.

   Indirectly, through the pool/market of tool seekers, *IbisSoft* was also connected to all external actors whose efforts were directed to fill the pool. Here belong all our competitors that advertised and promote their tools, thus inspiring customers to look wider and compare different tools before buying a license.

3. Asset *Companies/organizations that want/need to have process models*. This external pool from Fig. 5 represents the process modeling market. The whole strategy presented in Fig. 5 was dependent on the existence of this market. Indirectly, *IbisSoft* was also coupled to all actors that were "boosting" this market, e.g. management consultants establishing the needs to have processes modeled.

5 Rules for Identifying Structural Couplings

Suppose we have built a FEM for an essential part of the business activities of an organization that includes the important external elements – pools and actors. Then, we can use the model to identify structural couplings based on the rules presented in the sub-sections that follows. These rules are obtained through generalization of findings from Sect. 4.4, while taking into consideration suggestions from [5] and [6].

5.1 A Partner Asset as a Structural Coupling

This rule is based on generalization of the first structural coupling from Sect. 4.4 and ideas on looking for key partners, vendors, customers from [5]. The rule is formulated as follows. *If in a FEM of an organization*:

1. there is an essential asset, which is impossible or difficult to substitute for some other (e.g. similar) asset, and
2. one or several processes that are used to manage this asset, i.e. *Acquire*, *Maintain* or *Retire*, have a *Partner* asset that is difficult or impossible to remove or substitute,

then the organization is structurally coupled to the Partner asset.

A partner that constitutes a structural coupling can be a vendor of essential infrastructure component, as in case of JYACC/Prolifics in Fig. 2 and 5. It can, also, be a vendor that delivers important spare parts, formally, it will be a partner in an *Acquire process* that manages the stock of spare parts. It can also be a key customer, if the company relies on a small number of existing customers. In this case, the customer will be a partner of an *Acquire* process for the stock of orders for products or services. *IbisSoft* had some such customers, but for simplicity, we have not placed them in Fig. 3 and 5.

5.2 An External Pool as a Structural Coupling

This rule is based on generalization of the second and third structural couplings from Sect. 4.4 and ideas on looking to key markets from [5]. The rule is formulated as follows. *If in a FEM of an organization*:

1. there is an essential process, which is not easy to remove, and
2. this process has an essential asset with high rate of depletion, which needs to be constantly filled, and which is not possible or not easy to remove or substitute, and
3. an *Acquire* process for this asset is connected to an external pool from which it is getting new elements to fill the asset

then the organization is structurally coupled to the pool.

As an example, a pool of seekers of the high-level tools in Fig. 3 satisfies this rule. As most licenses were sold to new customers, the sales process needed to get both a new customer and a new order at the same time to fill the stock of orders and get new customers to provide support to. Note that the essential asset in the rule needs not to be of the stock type; for example, it can be a pool of work seekers, in case the turnover of workforce for an essential process is high.

Besides being coupled to an external pool as an input, an organization can be structurally coupled to a pool where one of its outputs, e.g. waste, goes, as discussed in [4]. A typical example of such coupling is an institution of higher education that provides new entities to a work seekers pool, see Fig. 2, as an overflow of this pool (not enough job for the graduates) will substantially affect the business. Due to the space limitation, we do not express this rule formally here.

5.3 External Actors as Structural Couplings

The external actor rule is based on formalization of the input/output approach presented in [6], and we do not have examples of this rule in the business case of Sect. 4. The coupling is indirect – through an external pool. This rule is formulated as follows:

If an organization is structurally coupled to an external pool, it may also be structurally coupled to the actors that fill this pool, or draw from the pool (e.g. competitors).

Note that the coupling can be quite strong if there are only few actors filling or drawing from the pool. For example, only few educational institution preparing people for a certain profession (filling the pool), only few companies dealing with the waste produced (drawing from the pool) or only few companies that employs the graduates from the educational institution (drawing from the pool).

6   Concluding Remarks and Plans for the Future

We started the paper with identifying the gap of absence of a systematic procedure that helps to identify structural couplings of an organization. This gap, though not much important for experienced management consultants, might be a barrier to use the concept of structural coupling in strategy development by less experience people, e.g. new entrepreneurs. To fill the gap, we suggested to use enterprise modeling for the purpose of creating a systematic procedure. As a starting point, we used FEM for this end. We drafted a set of formalized rules for identifying structural couplings based on the analysis of a business case that depicts the strategy evolution of a small company. In addition to analysis of the business case, ideas from [5] and [6] have been used.

Our work on the set of rules for identifying structural couplings is in progress, and our current results have a number of limitations. Firstly, while it covers most of the pragmatic rules from [5], it does not cover the one that concerns regulators. The same is true in connection to [6], our rules cover structural couplings based on input/output relationships, but they do not cover couplings related to the position in a bigger system, and geographical location. The question whether the excluded couplings can be detected via FEM remains open, and may have a negative answer. Getting a clearer answer on this question is included in our plans for the future research.

Secondly, the rules we created require more thorough validation, as the business case that we have used for their design can be considered only as a limited validation/demonstration of their practical usefulness. The existence of this case is an important factor for showing that the rules are not arbitrary, but are rooted in practice. However, this might not be enough to convince other practitioners on the solidness of the approach and its usefulness for practice.

From the point of view of Design Science Research (DSR), we can interpret this work using an approach suggested in [15] that describes a DS project as movement inside and between two worlds: (a) the real world of specific problems and solutions in local practices, and (b) the abstract world of generic problems and solutions. Each of the two worlds can be represented by a state space with three coordinates: (1) *situation*, (2) *problem*, and (3) *solution*.

In the state space of the abstract world, we have reached a point, called a hypothesis, with coordinates: (1) *generic situation*: an organization, (2) *generic problem*: need to find structural couplings of the organization, (3) *generic solution*: build FEM for this organization and apply rules from Sect. 5. For this hypothesis, we determined one point in the state space of the real world, called a test case, that instantiates the hypothesis. This point has the flowing coordinates: (1) *concrete situation*: *IbisSoft*, (2) *concrete problem*: finding structural coupling of *IbiSoft* (3) *concrete solution*: build FEM for IbiSSoft and get structural couplings according to rules from Sect. 5. This test case, can be assigned weight +1 (the instantiation supports the hypothesis), as the application of the instantiated solution results in a right set of structural couplings for *IbisSoft*.

From the two worlds point of view, it does not matter whether we (a) first created a generic solution based on previous works in the area and some logical analysis, and then applied it to *IbisSoft*, or (b) first worked on the level of a concrete company *ibiSoft*, and then generalized it to obtain a set of generic rules. In this paper, we have chosen to show the actual way of how the research has been conducted; however, the direction does not matter for the end result. Note also that the result achieved has an additional validation that consists of the rules suggested in this work, at least partially, covering empirical/pragmatic rules from [5] and [6].

Two direction are planned for farther validation. Firstly, conduct case studies that (a) start with building FEMs and (b) end with the stakeholders agreeing on the identified structural couplings really being important elements of their business context. Secondly, we plan to present the approach to the experienced management consultants and ask their opinion on the suggested procedure.

Besides helping to create a set of rules for identifying structural couplings, our business case has shown other ways of using FEM in strategy development. Namely, FEM could be used for identifying the presence or absence of the synergy between different organizational activities. We plan exploring this new opportunity to extend the area of FEM application in practice.

Acknowledgements. The author expresses his gratitude to the anonymous reviewers whose comments helped to improve the text.

References

1. Maturana, H.: Autopoiesis, structural coupling and cognition. Cybern. Hum. Knowing **9**(3–4), 5–34 (2002)
2. Luhmann, N.: Introduction to Systems Theory. Polity Press, Cambridge (2013)
3. Fell, L., Russell, D.: An introduction to Maturana's biology. In: Seized by Agreement, Swamped by Understanding. Hawkesbury, Sydney (1994)
4. Hoverstadt, P.: Defining identity by structural coupling in VSM practice. In: UK Systems Society, Oxford (2010)

5. Hoverstadt, P., Loh, L.: Patterns of Strategy. Taylor & Francis, Abingdon (2017)
6. Bider, I., Perjons, E.: Using structural coupling approach for defining and maintaining identity of an educational institution. Experience report. In: STPIS 2018, vol. 2107, pp. 24–39. CEUR (2018)
7. Beer, S.: The Heart of Enterprise. Wiley, Hoboken (1979)
8. Bider, I., Perjons, E., Elias, M., Johannesson, P.: A fractal enterprise model and its application for business development. Softw. Syst. Model. **16**(3), 663–689 (2016). https://doi.org/10.1007/s10270-016-0554-9
9. Cannon, W.B.: The Wisdom of the Body. Norton & Company, New York (1939)
10. Bider, I., Regev, G., Perjons, E.: Linking autopoiesis to homeostasis in socio-technical systems. In: STPIS 2019, Stockholm, vol. 2398, pp. 160–170. CEUR (2019)
11. Bider, I., Regev, G., Perjons, E.: Using enterprise models to explain and discuss autopoiesis and homeostasis in socio-technical systems. Complex Syst. Inf. Model. Q. (22), 21–38 (2020). https://doi.org/10.7250/csimq.2020-22.02
12. Ibissoft AB: Ibissoft. http://www.ibissoft.se/
13. Bider, I., Perjons, E.: Using fractal enterprise model to assist complexity management. In: BIR Workshops 2018, Stockholm, vol. 2218, pp. 233–238. CEUR (2018)
14. Hevner, A., March, S.T., Park, J.: Design science in information systems research. MIS Q. **28**(1), 75–105 (2004)
15. Bider, I., Johannesson, P., Perjons, E.: Design science research as movement between individual and generic situation-problem–solution spaces. In: Baskerville, R., De Marco, M., Spagnoletti, P. (eds.) Designing Organizational Systems. LNISO, vol. 1, pp. 35–61. Springer, Heidelberg (2013). https://doi.org/10.1007/978-3-642-33371-2_3
16. Bider, I., Perjons, E.: Defining transformational patterns for business model innovation. In: Zdravkovic, J., Grabis, J., Nurcan, S., Stirna, J. (eds.) BIR 2018. LNBIP, vol. 330, pp. 81–95. Springer, Cham (2018). https://doi.org/10.1007/978-3-319-99951-7_6
17. Anderson, J., Donnellan, B., Hevner, A.R.: Exploring the relationship between design science research and innovation: a case study of innovation at chevron. In: Helfert, M., Donnellan, B. (eds.) EDSS 2011. CCIS, vol. 286, pp. 116–131. Springer, Heidelberg (2012). https://doi.org/10.1007/978-3-642-33681-2_10
18. Mott, V.: Knowledge comes from practice: reflective theory building in practice. In: Rowden, R.W. (ed.) Workplace Learning: Debating Five Critical Questions of Theory and Practice, pp. 57–63. Jossey-Bass, San Francisco (1996)
19. Prolifics: Prolifics. https://www.prolifics.com/
20. Prolifics: JAM/Panther Tools: Prolifics. https://www.prolifics.com/jampanther-tools
21. Bider, I.: In search for a good theory: commuting between research and practice in business process domain. In: Halpin, T., et al. (eds.) BPMDS/EMMSAD 2011. LNBIP, vol. 81, pp. 16–30. Springer, Heidelberg (2011). https://doi.org/10.1007/978-3-642-21759-3_2
22. Andersson, T., Andersson-Ceder, A., Bider, I.: State flow as a way of analyzing business processes - case studies. Logist. Inf. Manag. **15**(1), 34–45 (2002)

Systems-Thinking Heuristics for the Reconciliation of Methodologies for Design and Analysis for Information Systems Engineering

Blagovesta Kostova[1]([✉]), Irina Rychkova[2], Andrey Naumenko[3], Gil Regev[1], and Alain Wegmann[1]

[1] LAMS, EPFL, Lausanne, Switzerland
{blagovesta.pirelli,gil.regev,alain.wegmann}@epfl.ch
[2] Université Paris 1, Panthéon-Sorbonne, Paris, France
irina.rychkova@univ-paris1.fr
[3] Triune Continuum Enterprise, Lausanne, Switzerland
naumenko@triunecontinuum.com

Abstract. Many competing, complementary, generic, or specific methodologies for design and analysis co-exist in the field of Information System Engineering. The idea of reconciling these methodologies and their underlying theories has crossed the minds of researchers many times. In this paper, we inquire into the nature of such reconciliation using the interpretivist research paradigm. This paradigm acknowledges the existence of diverse points of view as ways of seeing and experiencing the world through different contexts. We examine why it might be impossible to reconcile these methodologies that each represents a point of view. Instead of searching for the one (overarching, universal, global, ultimate) methodology that reconciles all others, we explain why we should think about reconciliation as an ongoing practice. We propose to the community a set of heuristics for this practice. The heuristics are a result of our experience in reconciling a number of methods that we created as part of our research during the past 20 years. We illustrate the use of the heuristics with an example of use cases and user stories. We believe these heuristics to be of interest to the Information Systems Engineering community.

Keywords: Heuristics · Methodology · Reconciliation · System thinking

1 Introduction

Research in Information Systems (IS) Engineering has resulted in so many methods, ontologies, theories, models, or languages, that much effort has been expended in trying to reconcile them. The trend is somewhat to try to reach *a single true correct ultimate view* over a socio-technical system. Inescapably,

© Springer Nature Switzerland AG 2020
F. Dalpiaz et al. (Eds.): RCIS 2020, LNBIP 385, pp. 112–128, 2020.
https://doi.org/10.1007/978-3-030-50316-1_7

though, every attempt at reconciliation creates yet another artifact (e.g., method, ontology, language). IS engineering researchers are schooled mostly in the predominant positivist tradition where a method's ontology must represent reality as closely as possible. This is similar to the way the law of gravity is a true representation of reality on earth, and to the way its value must be defined as closely as possible to match observations that are the same regardless of the observers' culture and context. This objective observation of reality applies poorly to the socio-technical organizations where IS research is or should be conducted [6]. In a field where an objective reality is not shared among the researchers, the quest for a common ontology is futile. As engineers, we perceive complexity as a phenomenon that has to be broken down into smaller pieces that then have to be weaved back together, or as Jackson points out; "Having divided to conquer, we must then reunite to rule" [27]. This engineering tradition has made its way into IS research, for example, through design with viewpoints [32,44], hierarchies of ontologies with domain, upper, core, and foundational ontologies [5,18], model-driven system design (with UML, for instance), and business and IT alignment with the help of Enterprise Architecture methods [65]. These efforts point in the same direction: that we should analyze a system from many points of view but then synthesize a single one that represents the single true comprehensive view of the system under consideration. Some researchers trace these tendencies to the days when the models of computer systems ultimately had to be represented in machine code as a single source of truth [27].

We challenge the assumption that in the context of IS Engineering for sociotechnical systems it is necessary, or even possible, to reach a single representational format (methodology) that can unite all perspectives. Agreeing to disagree seems to be a better path. The basic assumption of the interpretivists is that all ontologies, methods, and theories are valid and useful in their given context because they are the product of a point of view of an individual or a group of people. From an interpretivist perspective, it is impossible to introduce a point of view that will invalidate, disprove, generalize, replace, or subjugate the others, as it will be *yet another* point of view that has no more (and no less) value than any other, *except for the individual or the interpretation context from which it originates.* Instead of describing how to map, merge, and reconcile to a single point of view, we analyze these efforts through the interpretivist research paradigm to show a different perspective as to why we, as method designers and method users, do so.

We define reconciliation as an agreement and a shared understanding that might only exist momentarily then disappears as the people's world views, uniquely shaped by their experiences, begin to diverge again. Once an agreement is achieved, it is likely to dissolve as time goes by unless it is maintained, just like any system subject to external and internal change. This maintenance is important because in organizations (i.e., socio-technical systems) a lack of any agreement will lead to chaos and to the eventual demise of the organization as a single entity maintaining its identity. Therefore, organizations strive to prevent major disagreements from happening, by repeated and frequent exercises of reconciliation, explicit or implicit.

We propose a set of heuristics inspired by our experience in reconciling the modeling and design methodologies created by our own research group and other methods [54]. These heuristics are based on systems-thinking principles and are independent of our methods. The main take-away is that to reconcile different points of view, it is useful to go beyond the immediate ontology and to understand the differences in all epistemology, axiology, and ontology, thus forming a trilogy that together forms a world view.

The structure of the paper is the following. In Sect. 2, we review existing literature to understand better the reconciliation domain. Then, we present the set of heuristics in Sect. 3. We illustrate the use of the heuristics in Sect. 4 with an example. In Sect. 5, we discuss our findings; and in Sect. 6, we reflect on the limitations of our research findings. We conclude in Sect. 7.

2   Problem Statement

We inquire into different fields of study that propose their points of view about what is to be conceptualized, hence, modeled conceptually within the process of analysis and design of IS. The term point of view refers to different concepts (e.g., ontology, methodology, framework, model, language) in the different fields. We use the term *point of view* to avoid terminology confusion due to overloading constructs that are already in use in the literature. As a result, we reconcile our point of view with others by introducing yet one more point of view.

First, we look into the early work on ontology from the field of artificial intelligence for knowledge representation and sharing that defines ontology as "a specification of a "conceptualization"" [15,16]. Later Guarino and Giaretta clarified the definition of ontology for it to also be a "synonym of conceptualization" [17]. Most attempts to reconcile ontologies, however, assume the former definition by Gruber because of the implicit assumption that there is just one possible conceptualization [24]. The single-conceptualization assumption leads to the goal of explicitly reaching a single specification/ontology.

There are two main approaches to reconciliation: (1) refinement and abstraction and (2) alignment (sometimes called matching [12]). With the help of refinement and abstraction, models of different levels of detail can be (de)composed into more or less detailed ones, with the help of formally defined semantics [1]. Refinement has been used in multiple studies and is one of the main principles in computer science: for example, going between high-level specifications and formally verifiable specifications [28], value models to business process models [26], and user stories and backlog items [40]. The refinement relationship is a semantic one and can rarely be fully automated. Alignment is used, for example, in ontology mapping for web services and semantic web data representations [11,43]. Alignment deals with semantic heterogeneity and with semantically related entities in ontologies [12], recently extended towards the term semantic interoperability [19].

For an illustrative example of reconciliation in ontology-based IS research (without it being called reconciliation), we take the work by Nardi et al. [42] who propose an ontological solution for the service domain. The ontology they propose, UFO-S, is a reference ontology for services [42]. UFO-S is based on the Unified Foundational Ontology (UFO) [18, 20–22]. UFO has three modules: (1) UFO-A that covers endurants (objects) [18], (2) UFO-B that covers events (perdurants) [20, 21], and (3) UFO-C that covers social entities [20, 22]. UFO-S, on its own, is built in multiple parts for the different phases of a service life-cycle: service offer, service negotiation, and service delivery. UFO-S is a reference ontology. It is not as general as a foundational ontology and not as specific as a domain ontology. Hence, even using UFO-S means that for a domain of application (or an interpretation context), a modeler would have to introduce another conceptualization for their particular case.

Ontological work is not the only example where the phenomenon of reconciliation between methodologies, theories, ontologies, conceptualizations on different abstraction levels exists. Zachman and later Sowa and Zachman proposed an overarching framework (in essence, a matrix model) that describes an IS architecture in terms of the fundamental questions (what, how, where, who, when, and why) and discipline-dependent views [49, 65]. The Zachman framework was initially thought of as representing everything there is to represent about an organization and its IS. In the subsequent 30 years, we saw the development of numerous enterprise methods and frameworks (e.g., TOGAF [25]) that led to a "jungle of enterprise architecture frameworks" [48]. The creators of these later methods and frameworks introduce points of view that, in their intended context, are as valid and useful as Zachman's. This shows that whatever framework that is supposed to describe everything will be superseded by others.

We believe that the assumed problem that research communities might be trying to solve is the lack of a single methodology. There is an implicit belief among researchers that there must exist such a single point of view and that it is the ultimate one. Here, we put forward the idea that having all these points of view is not a problem to be solved per se. On the contrary, it shows that there is no established status quo rather mostly disparate schools of thought. These different opinions are valid and valuable for us to be able to express the nearly unlimited points of view that exist when we design an IS. In his seminal work on the nature of scientific revolutions, Kuhn observed that in the preface of a "scientific status quo" before everyone in a domain agrees on something (shared understanding), everyone has to define their own universe and to start from the beginning because there is no common ground to be building upon [34]. We strongly believe that method designers and method users will always strive to reach an agreement. Hence, we propose some heuristics for guiding the inevitable reconciliation efforts that will continue to occur in the academic and the industry domains of IS Engineering.

3   Systems-Thinking Heuristics for Reconciliation

The point of departure for our heuristics is interpretivism. Interpretivism is a philosophical paradigm that regards meaning as an emergent property of the relationship between an observer and their reality [6,39]. The use of interpretivist methods in the IS research domain has been usually used and discussed in juxtaposition to the positivism paradigm with its core belief in an objective, observer-independent reality [6,50]. The relationship of the observer with a *reality* out there helps interpretivists avoid the trap of solipsism, where every observer has their own reality with no connection with other observers [39]. The shared *reality* between observers helps them to create a shared meaning, which is a social construction. According to Weick, in a socially constructed world, the conceptualizations we hold ("the map") creates the reality we see ("the territory") [59]. Hence, co-constructing their conceptualizations makes sense to a group of people who share a similar experience.

In our conceptualization (which is simply another point of view), ontology is the most visible part of the observer's worldview that is called systems philosophy in [46,54]. The other parts are epistemology and axiology. Epistemology roots the knowledge held by the observer about their reality, the hidden part of the conceptualization. Axiology is the choices the observer makes (explicitly or implicitly) about which entities to observe in their reality and those that will be included in their ontology. To attempt to reconcile ontologies at the ontological level is like trying to mix sugar and tea at room temperature. They do not merge well. One needs to heat the tea first. To reconcile ontologies, we need to understand the epistemology and axiology of the people who define the ontologies and try to understand their similarities and differences: what they agree and what they disagree on. This is usually called social construction.

Heuristic 1. Reconciliation as a Process of Accepting Change. To reconcile points of view is to change their creators' minds at the epistemological and axiological levels. We believe that one of the most difficult endeavors is to change people's minds about deeply held beliefs. If it is possible at all, it usually takes time. For example, according to Haldane, there are four stages of acceptance (of a scientific theory): "(1) this is worthless nonsense, (2) this is an interesting, but perverse, point of view, (3) this is true, but quite unimportant, (4) I always said so" [23].

Heuristic 2. Just Enough Change. A corollary of the previous heuristic is that change must come in at just the right amount, not too little and not too much. If there is too little change, nobody will notice that a reconciliation has taken place. If there is too much change, the identity of the reconciled points of view will be lost for the observers. In some cases, the best course of action is to take a moderate approach to change. Or it can be best to take the most conservative option with an absolute resistance to change. And in some other cases for a system it can be best to reach out to high entropy states that disintegrates the identity. The latter option should not be neglected in consideration. In practice it happens as frequently as the former two.

Heuristic 3. Requisite Variety. Requisite variety is a heuristic for studying the responses of a system to existing or future threats [2,41,47,62]. Weick [60] shows that, for effective action in a situation with high ambiguity, it is necessary to maintain as many different points of view as necessary in order to "to grasp the variations in an ongoing flow of events." All of them are valid for a context and all of them are necessary to maintain a requisite variety. For reconciliation, this means that researchers need to suspend their willingness to reduce the variety in the points of view they seek to reconcile, until they have made sure that this variety is not needed in the domain they describe.

Heuristic 4. Understanding the Philosophy of Each Ontology Creator. As ontology is only the visible part of the world view of its creator, it is useful to instantiate a process of social construction in order to explore each creator's epistemology and axiology. Going to the philosophical foundations, epistemology and axiology, enables us to see the source of our differences and to potentially reach a consensus. Staying on the level of only ontology lacks semantics and prevents us from understanding what it actually means to agree or disagree. Staying on the level of only epistemology lacks syntax and a concrete form that we can act upon.

Let us take an example and ask ourselves, "Is a tomato a fruit or a vegetable?" The tomato, as a sign, can be related to either depending on the classification we use. A way to understand which classification to use, with the use of epistemology, a representation can be connected to the contexts → "I'm at home, mom told me tomatoes are a vegetable", "I'm at school, the teacher told us that tomatoes are a fruit." With the use of axiology, the observer can chose the "right or good" context, once this context is identified → "For dinner, we don't put tomatoes in the fruit salad.", "On the test, I should mark tomatoes as a fruit."

Hence, in our work, ontology is used in the broad sense to signify the multiple ways with which we can represent the given concepts (tomato and pomodoro[1] are two ways of naming a round red plant). Epistemology enables us to relate the conceptualization to contexts. And axiology enables us to reason about ethical choices (e.g., about good and bad, beautiful and ugly) as well as about moral values. These definitions are inline with the systemic paradigm as proposed by [4] and used in our own work [46,54].

Heuristic 5. Practicality. In practice, there are reconciliation techniques (alignment, refinement) that have their trade-offs, we can understand each and apply whichever makes sense. Both refinement and alignment are well-recognized ways to reconcile ontologies and models. We can achieve alignment through introducing a new entity (fruit) that a "reconciled" point of view includes because it has some basic properties (attributes) that two or more other entities from different models (e.g., apple, tomato) have in common. With the help of generalization, this alignment will give us one more point of view that departs from the

---

[1] We could interpret pomodoro as pomo d'oro, meaning a golden apple. Thus, the tomato becomes a golden apple, if we only look at the representation (ontology) of methods. We anecdotally call this heuristic the "Golden Tomato" heuristic.

specific context of the other points of view. The resulting models will not contradict in the cases where they do not share interpretation contexts. In the cases where these models share interpretation contexts, conflicts of interpretations are possible. In case of conflicts, generalizations of this sort will resolve the conflicts on a more generic level of interpretation, but on the specific levels the conflicts will remain. For example, if we use an algorithm to use an instance of a type *Fruit* in our fruit salad, yet a tomato is treated as a fruit at home, there might be a conflict as the generalization abstracted away the context of interpretation (tomato is a fruit in class but not a fruit at home.).

Heuristic 6. Duration of an Agreement. Nothing lasts forever, but some things last longer than others. We need to make sure to know what is being institutionalized/cemented in our systems through automation. Some reconciliations persist longer than others. For example, an agreement to map the *ID* field from *Database 1* to the field *PersonalID* from *Database 2* could be done on a white board and could be stable only for a few hours while the discussion continues. Or it could be a longer-lasting reconciliation that has been institutionalized by scripting the mapping between these fields. In both cases, there is a reconciliation, yet the level of automation is different. For implementing an IT system, we need to be able to come up with long-lasting agreements that we could codify in a specification, and then in code, thus, we could express in a formal verifiable form what is to be built (*verification*). Still, to ensure the *validation* of the system, we should not forget that the agreement is not final, and that the process is continuous.

4   Illustrative Example

To develop a specification of what an information system (in a typical project, for example) would do, we can investigate the settings in which the system will operate and can reach an agreement from various stakeholders about the operations that the system should support [66]. The views of people and what the as-is situation in the initial steps of the requirements process are usually a subject of analysis and design, with methods that apply to motivation, goals, sociology, psychology, etc. To express the IT specification, these views are taken as input in a requirements process that, at the end, yields a more precise description of the functionality of the IT system. The format of this specification is varied and of varying degrees of formalism: informal, semi-formal (UML diagrams, semi-structured specifications, user stories), formal e.g., (design-by-contract, formally verifiable specifications). To conduct a (socio-technical) system analysis and design, IS practitioners use different methods and tools.

We use, for an example, a conference submission information system. We scope the example to only highlight certain specificities of the methods in use. We illustrate the use of our heuristics for relating a UML use case diagram (UCD) and user stories. The choice of these two methods is dictated by their widespread use, hence, by the fact our readers are likely to be familiar with the methods. The two models can be used in many methodologies to communicate between different stakeholders hence are versatile and applicable in many contexts.

We also select these two because of the nature of their differences to also emphasize the variety of mediums in IS methods: a UCD is pictorial and a user story is text-based.

A **UML UCD** models the functionalities of a system and the actors who use these functionalities [13]. We use the basic version of a UCD. We explore how to relate a UCD with a user story. A **user story** is a semi-structured way of expressing system requirements that originated in the practice of agile methods. A user story usually follows the following format: "As a `<<type of user>>`, I `<<action>>` so that `<<reason>>`" [9]. User stories employ the vocabulary of the system's users/customers and have to be further refined into concrete technical specifications (known as Backlog Items).

Figure 1 depicts a UCD that includes three actors: (1) reviewers, (2) authors, and (3) PC chairs. These three actors have a common ancestor actor: a user. The conference system has three functionalities (download a paper, assign papers to reviewers, upload a paper) that the actors use and two functionalities that the user has (register, login). The PC chairs and the reviewers share the 'paper assignment' functionality, whereas the authors use only the 'upload a paper' functionality. To construct a user story that is aligned or based on the UCD, we can relate only the ontology elements and create a user story such as: "As an author, I can upload a paper in the conference system."

However, without any interpretation and context, the first two discrepancies become apparent. (1) The author is related to a user. Does this mean that a user can upload a paper as well? It is not possible to show inheritance of an object in user stories. (2) In the UCD, there is no mention of why the author, or any other actor, would like to use any functionality. It is not possible to show the intentions of actors in use cases. If we are to meaningfully relate the two or to use them as complementary to each other, then the need for *Heuristic 4 to use the epistemology, axiology, ontology* of methods is in place. Some authors have proposed ways to map the two models with the use of alignment and refinement *Heuristic 5* [51] or annotated and extended one of the two [8,52]. To illustrate *Heuristic 6*, the duration of the reconciliation proposed by our basic example is short-lived, whereas the rules coded in a computer-aided tool could last longer [51]. These works do not invalidate the original models, they give one more point of view (*Heuristic 3*) that can be used when we deem it to be more appropriate for the context of interpretation (for example, Dalpiaz and Sturm found user stories to

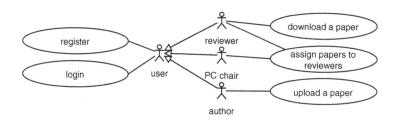

Fig. 1. Use case diagram of a conference management information system

be better fit for deriving conceptual models than use cases [10]). Moreover, this continuous generation of knowledge around UCDs and user stories is the process of reconciliation, which continues to occur (*Heuristic 1*).

To illustrate our heuristics, we also reflect on a meta-level about our choice of points of view. The heuristic that we can highlight here is *heuristic 3 on requisite variety* that there are many points of view, many methods and models, that we could have used in our analysis. For example, only under the name UML are there various diagrams such as use case, sequence, class, responsibility, state diagrams [13]. All of them have their use and can complement others, or can be used by themselves. This can also be said for the other methods that we could have selected to "reconcile" the UML UCD with, for example a value-based method [14]. The other heuristic we would like to exemplify here is *heuristic 1 on reconciliation being a process*. In the initial iterations of our work, we (the authors) selected to relate methods that we created in our research. Yet, we decided to use better-known methods for the design and analysis of IS in order to introduce less changes (*heuristic 2 on just enough change*) and to focus mainly on the change that our heuristics could represent as a new point of view that the reader could potentially find easier to reconcile with.

5 Discussion

Why these Heuristics? The heuristics we describe here are tightly coupled with our experience of reconciling the methods we, as a research group, have created for the past 20 years and with our quests to relate to others [31,36,55,56] and to connect different perspectives within our own methods [30,46,57]. However, throughout the literature search and given our understanding of the field of IS Engineering, we have seen the efforts of connecting different points of view being repeated as patterns. The reformulation of the problem of reconciliation as an ongoing practice is a new idea we put forward. Yet, much academic work has already mentioned their different methods being valid only in particular cases. Moreover, true to intepretivism, we believe we are also offering a point of view with our set of heuristics and not simply *the* set. We have seen other such heuristics, or principles (cf. [29,64]). A future avenue for exploration is to consider the different sets of heuristics that exist in other contexts in the domain of IS and to reconcile the reconciliation heuristics. And even though no one set is exhaustive or all of its constituent principles are valid in every context, we subscribe to the view expressed by Klein and Myers that the "systematic consideration [of the set of principles] is likely to improve the quality of future interpretive field research in IS (especially that of a hermeneutic nature)" [29].

"Technology is Neither Good nor Bad, nor is it Neutral" [33]. One more method, with its corresponding ontology, epistemology, and axiology, is neither good nor bad, nor is it neutral. It is created **for a context**: as an academic endeavor, with an objective to *communicate* or to *share* one's experience with the others (i.e., researchers, students), or as a more pragmatic attempt *to create a common ground* with a group of people (experts from various domains) for discussion and analysis of a situation, or *to find an agreement* on a particular problem/solution. Ontology reconciliation will continue to take place. The question is, Are we, as researchers, cognizant that, by introducing more conceptual work, we are reconciling our point of view with the points of view of others thus creating a new point of view by interpreting through our own philosophy and our context of interpretation?

Are All Points of View Valid, Yet Some Just a Bit More[2]? Any methodology, with its corresponding methods, models, theories, and artifacts may (but, being subjected to fallacies, not necessarily has to) be valid and useful within a particular context where it is defined and used. Outside of that context everything is possible: its validity and usefulness can theoretically be anywhere within the range "absolute–limited–nil". Let us use Boltzmann's entropy as an analogy: $S = k \cdot ln(W)$, where W is statistical weight, and k is the number of possible state configurations within a statistically described thermodynamic system. If we now apply this analogy to methodologies, then we can say that within a social system we can find a set of these. Any of the methods defines a set of conceptual configurations that rely on valid conceptual states within the social system. Hence, any one from the set contributes to the statistical weight. A conceptually rich method will define a rich set of states and a conceptually poor method will define a poor set of states. Every state contributes to the system's statistical weight. However, the contributions of each to the overall social system's entropy might be unequal. The contributions are probabilistic.

Applying the analogy of Boltzmann's entropy, we might say that a particular methodology, or a point of view, regardless of how conceptually rich/poor and probabilistically frequent/rare it is, contributes to the statistical weight of conceptualizations of the social system where it belongs. A contribution of a particular methodology to the social system's entropy depends on the probability of reaching the states of its conceptualizations within interpretation contexts of this social system. The more frequent the states are, the lesser the contribution to the system's entropy is.

A Word on the Context of Interpretation. A particular interpretation context defines its corresponding particular state of the system's conceptual configuration. Any methodology that describes or models the system can be evaluated with regard to how useful/useless it is for a description of this particular conceptual configuration. A richer ontology (with a higher language expressiveness [27]) has a larger probability of being useful. An ideal ontology would cover all conceptual states of the system, even the high-entropy states. All ontologies are equally valid, as there is no one point of view which is superior or inferior to the other (for this there needs to be an objective observer of observers, or the so-called super observer, who does not exist [61]). If "all ontologies" is an unlimited set, then it is logically impossible to define a context where all of them will have the same degree of validity and usefulness. Hence, reconciliation or any effort to make an overarching ontology within a methodology is yet another point of

---

[2] "All animals are equal, but some animals are more equal than others." from *Animal Farm: A Fairy Story*, 1945 by George Orwell.

view. Although it tends to reduce disorder (conflicts, variety, inconsistencies) by enabling actors to express their current beliefs regarding the state of the observed system, it cannot cancel, improve, or rule on the rest.

An ontology can be perceived as independent of context. In this case, an ontology has (1) no dependency on a context to which it could be potentially applied in an attempt to describe the context, and (2) no dependency on an observer who could try to apply the ontology in order to describe some context. An interpretation context is a conceptualizable state perceived as existing or designed to exist within a system that is being modeled by someone (by an observer, by a modeler, by a group of people, etc.). Multiple contexts can exist for a given system. Interpretation contexts are (1) dependent on observers/modelers, and (2) contain conceptualizable representations of some entities within the system, these representations can be attempted to be described by one or several ontologies. Different ontologies can be either more or less useful in their attempts to describe some representations within a particular interpretation context. The potential for a success or a failure of a methodology within a given interpretation context does not depend on a modeler who applies it rather on only the conceptual richness or poorness of this methodology, with regard to the representation needs required by the context. If we seek to represent the state of a system, a data-flow diagram might not be the most informative [27].

Knowledge Representation for AI/ML: The Wave of Automation. There is a trend to connect data that have been generated independently by different sources to enable interoperability and uniformization of formats to ease data sharing [63]. Our set of heuristics could be classified towards the wave of semantic interoperability efforts [19]. Here we pause to pose the question, Should we aim for interoperability and all this uniformization of data formats? Enabling more analytics to be done on the data that we can connect, given that we have shown that irreversibly some of the context of generation of these data is lost in the (model-to-model) translation, might lead to unpredictable consequences. The advancement in semantic interoperability enables data from different sources to be cross-referenced hence to build representations of individuals and groups that could be seemingly labeled as context-rich, even though the context in which the data were generated is decoupled from any information system.

There is an implicit assumption that it is better to allow these uses and to enable more automation through the use of AI/ML-powered systems that use these rich data sets, because humans are perceived to be the weak link in any system [3]. Yet, before we understand the technologies labeled as AI and ML, we should "tread softly because we tread on"[3] uncharted territory of technology than can be employed for the automation of decision making that optimizes predominantly profitability of enterprises [35]. And even if we succeed with automating the human out of the process of translating between models and methods in the context of IS Engineering, the next question is, How and who will handle the mistakes that such automation would eventually lead to?

---

[3] "Tread softly because you tread on my dreams." from *Aedh Wishes for the Cloths of Heaven*, 1899 by William Butler Yeats.

According to Bainbridge, the human who would have to take control over the failure would have to be specialized and highly trained even more than the people whose tasks are being automated [3].

6 Limitations

Reusability of our Findings. Positivist research aims to create objective, generalizable knowledge (e.g., laws of physics) that is absolute and can be reused independently from the context. In this work, we propose a set of heuristics that stem from the interpretivistic research paradigm. In other words, they are a product of our interpretation of our own experience in reconciling methodologies for design and analysis of IS. We reflect on the limitations of the interpretivistic research paradigm and pose the question, Is the validity of our findings in general an oxymoron [45].

We argue that the whole idea of IS research results as being general (or context-independent) should be taken with caution. Once the results are presented as general, the researchers, who rely on the results or implement them in the context of their particular socio-technical system, can be absolved of any responsibility. Interpretivism, in contrast, makes the researchers and their view an integrated part of the research and its findings. Thus, it is the responsibility of a researcher to choose and reuse all or part of our heuristics in their context. Therefore, our findings are reusable, but not absolutely or objectively, they are subjectively reusable.

Generalizability and Reliability of our Findings. One could argue that, if responsibility is in researcher's hands, then what about the reliability or generalizability of the results they produce? They would be inevitably biased. According to the positivist research paradigm, the researcher is independent from the research; they provide objective observations/measures that guarantee the objectiveness of results. Any researcher, by reproducing the same experiment, should obtain the same results. This implies reliability. According to the interpretivistic methods, the researcher is a social actor, a part of a socio-technical system they study, and it is through their observations that the system to be studied emerges and its identity is created. Although, the observations are obviously biased. We argue that the socio-technical system is a product of the biases of its actors. They are not a threat rather a part of the system's identity and hence have to be explicitly taken into consideration [53].

A possible contradiction that could be found is between our interpretivistic approach and the very nature of Systems Thinking. Interpretivism shies away from generalizability, whereas Systems Thinking is an inter-discipline that connects other disciplines through general principles [61]. However, any general Systems Thinking principle (or, in our vocabulary, *heuristic*) is a subject of interpretation and contextualization. Hence, we see the interplay between generally applicable principles and their context of application as being integral to constructing a Systems Thinking body of knowledge, and that it can be applied throughout.

Validity of Our Findings. In positivism, the created knowledge is absolute and can be validated (or invalidated) analytically (by deduction) or through experiments with the use of falsifiable hypothesis. For example, the laws of physics are absolute. In qualitative interpretivistic research, the validity of knowledge can be demonstrated only within a given *frame of reference* [7]. This frame of reference labeled by some transactional validity defines "research as an interactive process between the researcher, the researched, and the collected data that is aimed at achieving a relatively higher level of accuracy and the consensus by means of revisiting facts, feelings, experiences, and values or beliefs collected and interpreted" [7]. Once the frame of reference changes, the knowledge can be invalidated. In the positivist paradigm, such a frame of reference is taken for granted by researchers as "something everyone agrees upon" hence is often omitted (implicit). This creates an illusion of an absolute or objective validity. In interpretivism, the frame of reference, the context or the socio-technical system, is a part of the research, a variable of the equation. It cannot be omitted, as we cannot claim that "everyone shares it". Interpretivism leaves a researcher no choice but to explicitly mention their frame of reference (and to identify a community that shares this frame of reference). Only within this frame of reference and for this community will the produced knowledge be valid.

Bottom line: For some researchers, our findings could potentially be valid, but not "absolutely"; they are valid only within a given frame of reference. In the grand scheme of research pursuits, studies such as ours are natural precursors to a potentially better understanding of the field, that then through the accumulation of a critical mass of knowledge in the domain of systems design, these studies can be re-used in practice [37,58]. Any academic pursuit that investigates a new or understudied phenomenon goes through stages of understanding: from chaos to heuristics to algorithms [38].

7   Conclusion and Future Work

In this paper, we have presented a set of heuristics for the reconciliation of methodologies for design and analysis in the domain of IS Engineering. We have presented some current literature on conceptual and ontological work as well as Enterprise Architecture to illustrate how different domains already accommodate various methods and models. We have put forward the idea of reconciliation as a recurrent practice in the context of IS scholarly and industry works in order to find place for the knowledge we generate. Our heuristics build on the notions of interpretivism, entropy, and well-known principles of computer systems design such as abstraction, refinement and alignment. We have explored the futility of reconciliation solely on the level of ontology and have proposed a way to look at differences on a philosophical level that includes epistemology, axiology, and ontology; but never only one. We have illustrated the use of our heuristics with the help of an example modeled with a use case diagram and user stories. We plan to explore and categorize further the epistemological principles that help us understand differences and points of intersection better, as well as to extend the reconciliation towards research artifacts. For the future, we will inquire into the reconciliation process and heuristics on the level of method users, as opposed to the level of method designers, whose perspective we explored in the current paper.

References

1. Antoniou, G., Kehagias, A.: A note on the refinement of ontologies. Int. J. Intell. Syst. **15**(7), 623–632 (2000)
2. Ashby, W.R.: An Introduction to Cybernetics. Chapman & Hall Ltd., Boca Raton (1957)
3. Bainbridge, L.: Ironies of automation. In: Automatica (1983)
4. Banathy, B.H., Jenlink, P.M.: Systems inquiry and its application in education. In: Handbook of Research for Educational Communications and Technology (2003)
5. Borgo, S., Masolo, C.: Foundational choices in DOLCE. In: Handbook on Ontologies (2009)
6. Checkland, P., Holwell, S.: Information, Systems and Information Systems: Making Sense of the Field. John Wiley, Hoboken (1998)
7. Cho, J., Trent, A.: Validity in qualitative research revisited. Qual. Res. **6**(3), 319–340 (2006)
8. Cockburn, A.: Structuring use cases with goals. J. Object-Oriented Program. **10**(5), 56–62 (1997)
9. Cohn, M.: Succeeding with Agile: Software Development using Scrum. Pearson Education, London (2010)
10. Dalpiaz, F., Sturm, A.: Conceptualizing requirements using user stories and use cases: a controlled experiment. In: International Working Conference on Requirements Engineering: Foundation for Software Quality, REFSQ (2020)
11. Euzenat, J.: An API for ontology alignment. In: International Semantic Web Conference (2004)
12. Euzenat, J., Shvaiko, P.: Ontology Matching. Springer, Heidelberg (2007). https://doi.org/10.1007/978-3-540-49612-0
13. Fowler, M., Distilled, U.: A Brief Guide to the Standard Object Modeling Language. Addison-Wesley, Boston (2003)
14. Gordijn, J., Akkermans, J.: Value-based requirements engineering: : exploring innovative e-commerce ideas. Requirements Eng. **8**, 114–134 (2003)
15. Gruber, T.R.: A translation approach to portable ontology specifications. Knowl. Acquis. **5**(2), 199–221 (1993)
16. Gruber, T.R.: Toward principles for the design of ontologies used for knowledge sharing. Int. J. Hum.-Comput. stud. **43**(5–6), 907–928 (1995)
17. Guarino, N., Giaretta, P.: Ontologies and knowledge bases. towards a terminological clarification. Towards very large knowledge bases (1995)
18. Guizzardi, G.: Ontological foundations for structural conceptual models (2005)
19. Guizzardi, G.: Ontology, ontologies and the "i" of fair. Data Intell. **2**, 181–191 (2020)
20. Guizzardi, G., de Almeida Falbo, R., Guizzardi, R.S.S.: Grounding software domain ontologies in the unified foundational ontology (UFO): the case of the ODE software process ontology. In: Conferencia Iberoamericana de Software Engineering, CIbSE (2008)

21. Guizzardi, G., Wagner, G., de Almeida Falbo, R., Guizzardi, R.S.S., Almeida, J.P.A.: Towards ontological foundations for the conceptual modeling of events. In: Ng, W., Storey, V.C., Trujillo, J.C. (eds.) ER 2013. LNCS, vol. 8217, pp. 327–341. Springer, Heidelberg (2013). https://doi.org/10.1007/978-3-642-41924-9_27
22. Guizzardi, R.S.S.: Agent-oriented Constructivist Knowledge Management. Ph.D. thesis (2006)
23. Haldane, J.B.S.: The truth about death. J. Genet. (1963)
24. Hameed, A., Preece, A.D., Sleeman, D.H.: Ontology reconciliation. In: Handbook on Ontologies (2004). https://doi.org/10.1007/978-3-540-24750-0_12
25. Haren, V.: TOGAF Version 9.1 A Pocket Guide (2011)
26. Hotie, F., Gordijn, J.: Value-based process model design. Bus. Inf. Syst. Eng. **61**(2), 163–180 (2017). https://doi.org/10.1007/s12599-017-0496-y
27. Jackson, M.: Some complexities in computer-based systems and their implications for system development. In: International Conference on Computer Systems and Software Engineering (1990)
28. Klein, G., et al.: seL4: formal verification of an OS kernel. In: ACM Symposium on Operating Systems Principles, SOSP (2009)
29. Klein, H.K., Myers, M.D.: A set of principles for conducting and evaluating interpretive field studies in information systems. MIS Q. **23**, 67–93 (1999)
30. Kostova, B., Etzlinger, L., Derrier, D., Regev, G., Wegmann, A.: Requirements elicitation with a service canvas for packaged enterprise systems. In: International Requirements Engineering Conference, RE (2019)
31. Kostova, B., Gordijn, J., Regev, G., Wegmann, A.: Comparison of two value modeling methods: e^3 value and SEAM. In: International Conference on Research Challenges in Information Science, RCIS (2019)
32. Kotonya, G., Sommerville, I.: Requirements engineering with viewpoints. Softw. Eng. J. **11**(1), 5–18 (1996)
33. Kranzberg, M.: Technology and history: "Kranzberg's laws". Technol. Cult. **27**(3), 544–560 (1986)
34. Kuhn, T.S.: The Structure of Scientific Revolutions. University of Chicago press, Chicago (2012)
35. Kulynych, B., Overdorf, R., Troncoso, C., Gürses, S.F.: POTs: protective optimization technologies. In: Conference on Fairness, Accountability, and Transparency (2020)
36. Lê, L.S., Wegmann, A.: An RM-ODP based ontology and a CAD tool for modeling hierarchical systems in enterprise architecture. In: Workshop on ODP for Enterprise Computing (2005)
37. Le Goues, C., Jaspan, C., Ozkaya, I., Shaw, M., Stolee, K.T.: Bridging the gap: from research to practical advice. IEEE Softw. **35**(5), 50–57 (2018)
38. Martin, R.: The Design of Business: Why Design Thinking is the Next Competitive Advantage. Harvard Business Press, Boston (2009)
39. Maturana, H.R., Varela, F.: Autopoiesis. A theory of living organization, Autopoiesis (1981)
40. Müter, L., Deoskar, T., Mathijssen, M., Brinkkemper, S., Dalpiaz, F.: Refinement of user stories into backlog items: linguistic structure and action verbs. In: Knauss, E., Goedicke, M. (eds.) REFSQ 2019. LNCS, vol. 11412, pp. 109–116. Springer, Cham (2019). https://doi.org/10.1007/978-3-030-15538-4_7
41. Narasipuram, M.M., Regev, G., Kumar, K., Wegmann, A.: Business process flexibility through the exploration of stimuli. Int. J. Bus. Process Integr. Manage. IJBPIM **3**(1), 36–46 (2008)

42. Nardi, J.C., et al.: A commitment-based reference ontology for services. Inf. Syst. **54**, 263–288 (2015)
43. Noy, N.F., Musen, M.A.: PROMPT: algorithm and tool for automated ontology merging and alignment. In: National Conference on Artificial Intelligence and Conference on Innovative Applications of Artificial Intelligence (2000)
44. Nuseibeh, B., Kramer, J., Finkelstein, A.: A framework for expressing the relationships between multiple views in requirements specification. IEEE Trans. Softw. Eng. **20**(10), 760–773 (1994)
45. Onwuegbuzie, A.J., Leech, N.L.: Validity and qualitative research: an oxymoron? Qual. Quant. **41**, 233–249 (2007). https://doi.org/10.1007/s11135-006-9000-3
46. Regev, G., Bajic-Bizumic, B., Golnam, A., Popescu, G., Tapandjieva, G., Saxena, A.B., Wegmann, A.: A philosophical foundation for business and IT alignment in enterprise architecture with the example of SEAM. In: International Symposium on Business Modeling and Software Design (2013)
47. Regev, G., Wegmann, A.: Business process flexibility: Weick's organizational theory to the rescue. In: Workshop on Business Process Modelling (2006)
48. Schekkerman, J.: How to Survive in the Jungle of Enterprise Architecture Frameworks: Creating or Choosing an Enterprise Architecture Framework. Trafford Publishing, Bloomington (2004)
49. Sowa, J.F.: Conceptual graphs as a universal knowledge representation. Comput. Math. Appl. **23**(2–5), 75–93 (1992)
50. Walsham, G.: The emergence of interpretivism in IS research. Inf. Syst. Res. **6**(4), 376–394 (1995)
51. Wautelet, Y., Heng, S., Hintea, D., Kolp, M., Poelmans, S.: Bridging user story sets with the use case model. In: Link, S., Trujillo, J.C. (eds.) ER 2016. LNCS, vol. 9975, pp. 127–138. Springer, Cham (2016). https://doi.org/10.1007/978-3-319-47717-6_11
52. Wautelet, Y., Heng, S., Kolp, M., Mirbel, I.: Unifying and extending user story models. In: Jarke, M., et al. (eds.) CAiSE 2014. LNCS, vol. 8484, pp. 211–225. Springer, Cham (2014). https://doi.org/10.1007/978-3-319-07881-6_15
53. Weber, R.: Editor's comments: the reflexive researcher. MIS Q. (2003)
54. Wegmann, A.: On the systemic enterprise architecture methodology (SEAM). In: International Conference on Enterprise Information Systems (2003)
55. Wegmann, A., Kotsalainen, A., Matthey, L., Regev, G., Giannattasio, A.: Augmenting the Zachman enterprise architecture framework with a systemic conceptualization. In: International Enterprise Distributed Object Computing Conference, EDOC (2008)
56. Wegmann, A., Naumenko, A.: Conceptual modeling of complex systems using an RM-ODP based ontology. In: International Enterprise Distributed Object Computing Conference, EDOC (2001)
57. Wegmann, A., Regev, G., Rychkova, I., Julia, P., Perroud, O.: Early requirements and business-IT alignment with SEAM for business. In: International Conference on Requirements Engineering, RE (2007)
58. Weick, K.E.: Theory construction as disciplined imagination. Acad. Manage. Rev. **14**(4), 516–531 (1989)
59. Weick, K.E.: Cartographic Myths in Organizations. Mapping Strategic Thought. Wiley, New York (1990)
60. Weick, K.E.: Sensemaking in Organizations. Sage, Thousand Oaks (1995)
61. Weinberg, G.: An Introduction to General Systems Thinking. Wiley, Hoboken (1975)

62. Weinberg, G.M.: Rethinking Systems Analysis and Design. Little, Brown, Boston (1982)
63. Wilkinson, M.D., Dumontier, M., Aalbersberg, I.J., Appleton, G., Axton, M., Baak, A., Blomberg, N., Boiten, J.W., da Silva Santos, L.B., Bourne, P.E., et al.: The fair guiding principles for scientific data management and stewardship. Sci. Data (2016)
64. Winograd, T., Flores, F.: Understanding Computers and Cognition: A New Foundation for Design. Intellect Books, Chicago (1986)
65. Zachman, J.A.: A framework for information systems architecture. IBM Syst. J. **26**(3), 276–292 (1987)
66. Zave, P., Jackson, M.: Four dark corners of requirements engineering. ACM Trans. Softw. Eng. Methodol. **6**(1), 1–30 (1997)

An Ontology of IS Design Science Research Artefacts

Hans Weigand[1]([⊠]) [iD], Paul Johannesson[1] [iD], and Birger Andersson[2]

[1] Tilburg University, P.O. Box 90153, 5000 LE Tilburg, The Netherlands
H.Weigand@uvt.nl, pajo@dsv.su.se
[2] Department of Computer and Systems Sciences, Stockholm University, Stockholm, Sweden
ba@dsv.su.se

Abstract. From a design science perspective, information systems and their components are viewed as artefacts. However, not much has been written yet on the ontological status of artefacts or their structure. After March & Smith's (1995) initial classification of artefacts in terms of models, constructs, procedures and instantiations, there have been only a few attempts to come up with a more systematic approach. After reviewing previous work, this conceptual paper introduces an ontology of IS artefacts. It starts with an ontological characterization of artefacts and technical objects in general and proceeds to introduce a systematic classification of IS artefacts and compare it with existing work. We end with some practical implications for design research.

Keywords: Design science · IT artefact · Ontology

1 Introduction

Design Science Research [16] has grown in popularity in the Information Systems field. Whereas empirical sciences acquire knowledge about the natural world (physics) or human behavior (social sciences), Design Science Research (DSR) is interested in IT artefacts, such as algorithms, methods and modeling languages, and the effectiveness of their use. Because of its focus on artificial objects, DSR has similarities with traditional engineering sciences and medicine. Building artefacts and evaluating artefacts in context is often seen as the core of DSR. But what is an artefact. Is artefact the same as "artificial object" [30]? Can we call any solution an artefact? What exactly do we say when we call something an IT artefact? Although by now there is quite a substantial literature about design science, in the form of research articles and textbooks, a systematic investigation of the design artefact concept is still missing. Building on our general ontology of artefacts (in progress), the goal of this conceptual paper is to introduce an ontology of IS artefacts and analyze the practical implications for Design Science Research.

The structure of this paper is as follows. In Sect. 2, we recapitulate what has been written on the artefact concept in the (broad) DSR literature. Section 3 is a short overview of our general artefact ontology. On this basis of this ontology, we analyze the main IS artefacts and their interrelationships in Sect. 4, compare the results with the existing literature and discuss practical implications for DSR researchers.

© Springer Nature Switzerland AG 2020
F. Dalpiaz et al. (Eds.): RCIS 2020, LNBIP 385, pp. 129–144, 2020.
https://doi.org/10.1007/978-3-030-50316-1_8

2 Background

A general understanding of artefact in Design Science is that is an object made by humans with the intention that it is used to address a practical problem [3, 18]. Design Science arose in the 1990's within the field of Information Systems and although its idea of artefacts included physical artefacts like hammers or medical drugs, its interest went mainly in the direction of symbolic artefacts such as encountered in the Information System domain. Simon's *The Sciences of the Artificial* [30] focused on computers and artificial intelligence software viewed as artificial objects. Although Simon is not very explicit, he seems to regard a design object as more specific than an artificial object, witness the fact that he views markets being the result of a social evolution process as artificial objects but without a designer. An also very broad but different definition is expressed by Gregor and Hevner [14:4]: 'We argue toward a more expansive view of the IT artefact to include any designed solution that solves a problem in context'. Wieringa's [37:29] definition is similar ('an artefact is something created by people for some practical purpose'. He prefers to talk about treatments. What the design researcher designs is a treatment, that is, 'a desired interaction between the artefact and the problem context' and he defines design as 'a decision about what to do'. There is a risk that the artefact concept loses its meaning if it includes any decision or any solution. To keep the connection with both common sense and the technical sciences and to able to give substance to the design aspect, an artefact must have something of "an object made by humans". At the same time, we think a proper definition should do justice to the intuitions of Gregor and Wieringa and this is one of the challenges for an ontology of artefacts.

2.1 Design Research Outcome: Artefacts vs Theory

According to Purao [28], characteristic for design research is the situated implementation of an invention (artefact) as software or system. Apart from that, he argues that design research should produce knowledge and understanding, which sometimes he also calls artefacts. Pursuing this second suggestion, Winter [38] proposes "theory" to be a relevant artefact type. What we see as problematic here is that the artefact is identified with (design) research outcome. Although the authors are right in stressing that design research should not just produce an instantiated artefact but contribute to theory [13], it is confusing to take this scientific theory to be the design artefact. That would make all sciences design sciences.

Goldkuhl and Lind [11] make a distinction between artefacts as objects of empirical design practices and abstract design knowledge (see also more recently [9]). This is a useful distinction to start with, as long as we do not conflate again the "meta-artefacts" (their terminology) on the abstract design level with design knowledge *about* these artefacts. This knowledge requires an identification of the meta-artefact but goes beyond the identification by developing, for instance, mathematical models of the artefact or by accumulating experimental results about its performance.

As science in general abstracts from the concrete, so design knowledge abstracts from specific application contexts. This holds in particular for design knowledge as pursued in Design Science Research. However, the level of abstraction is usually not as high as e.g. in physics. Wieringa [37:10] uses the term "middle-range generalization". In the opposition concrete vs. abstract it is often overlooked that there is also an *aggregation* dimension [31]. For instance, in the IT field, there are infinitely many possible programs, with all kinds of variations. These are not all interesting DSR artefacts. IT researchers are typically more focused on developing *components*, e.g. in the form of a method library, than end products. The components are not necessarily more *abstract* than integrated systems, but more *elementary*. It makes sense to see these components as tangible DSR outcomes, and the knowledge thereof as design knowledge. In contrast, evaluation studies in the domain of Information Management typically look at the end product (as blackbox) in some use context. The intended outcome of this type of research does not consist of new artefacts, but of knowledge on the use properties and the effectiveness of some artefact type (e.g. the type ERP system). In our view, the IT and IM perspective complement each other. Sometimes, it is the case that the IT research provides knowledge about the technical feasibility and performance of the artefact and the IM research extends the design knowledge by studying its effects in context. In other cases, the two work on different aggregation levels: the IT research studying the effects of some component in the use context of the integrated IT system, and the IM research looking at the effects of the integrated system in the use context of an enterprise.

2.2   Socio-Technical Systems

We consider IS artefacts to be research objects or units of analysis – what the design knowledge is about. From a Computer Science perspective, the Information System is the information technology that does data processing. The management view on Information Systems sees the object as much broader, including the business processes that use the IT, the humans involved and the organizational structure around it. The Information System, defined in this way, can be called a socio-technical system as it includes a technical component but also people. Sometimes the IT is called a socio-technical system. According to Silver and Markus [29:82-83] IT artefacts 'have both technical and social design features and are therefore better regarded as SocioTechnical (ST) artefacts'....'We define the IT artefact as a sociotechnical assemblage.' As pointed out, among others, by Alter [2], we should be cautious with terms like socio-technical artefacts or ensemble artefacts, as if there are also other artefacts that do not have social design features. Arguably, (cf. [36]) a software application, as any design artefacts, exist in the historical reality in which technical aspects and social aspects (in a broad sense) are intertwined in many ways. The application has been designed by humans, driven consciously or unconsciously by social values. Once implemented it fall under legal rules, has an economic value, has an effect on social relationships etc. However, that does not make these applications socio-technical in the original sense [34].

Alter [2] provocatively suggests avoiding the vague term IT artefact completely, especially when it is applied just to something containing IT, like an airplane, or related to IT, like user training. In the following, we will keep using the terms IT and IS artefact. A precise characterization of the artefact concept and the exploration of all meaningful artefacts in the IS domain is the subject of this paper. We do not need a special category of socio-technical artefacts. A socio-technical system is a *system* that includes people.

2.3 Artefact vs System

Both in Simon [30] and in more recent publications [22] the words artefact and system are sometimes used as synonyms. However, this is problematic. A system is defined as a composite of elements with attributes and relationships between them that makes a meaningful whole. 'The idea of holism which assumes that particular parts can be described only by the knowledge of their meaning and position in the whole, is the basis of the conception of the perception of reality as complex systems' [12]. From its early beginnings, system theory embraces both natural and artificial (man-made) systems. System theory is not so much about a particular class of objects, but is a particular view: the holistic view, in contrast to a reductionist view. The market can be seen as a complex system, or a family. So clearly not every system is an artefact or even an artificial object. One could say that an artefact is a system, as indeed the elements of a composite artefact have a function in the whole, so cannot be characterized exhaustively on their own. A system view on the artefact deemphasizes the role of the designer intention and focuses on understanding how the overall behavior derives or emerges from its parts. In our view, it makes sense to include somehow the system view to the Design Science artefact definition. However, if the Information System is conceived as including humans, then the system is not the output of intentional design. Many elements of the system, not only the IT but also e.g. an authorization scheme or a business process structure, can be designed, and may be viewed as artefacts (or part of the IT artefact).

That we must be cautious to equate system and artefact is supported, be it in other wordings, by management researchers. Pandza and Thorpe [27] expressed skepticism about the work of Van Aken [1] and others who advocate a design research approach to management. If design is taken in the traditional engineering sense, then it only has a limited applicability in management. They describe organizations as social artefacts that evolve over time in unpredictable ways. This evolution could be called *path-creation design*. In our wordings, what is meant here is that the evolution of the organization is not determined by physical laws mobilized by intentional design but includes human creative intervention. We agree. We support a worldview that acknowledges human creativity [36]. The question is whether the word (path-creation) design is appropriate and in what sense the organization is a social artefact (cf. [19] for a discussion of different interpretations of the term "design thinking").

2.4 Typology of IS Artefacts

Some work has been done on a typology of IS artefacts, but surprisingly little. [16, 23] describe artefacts as the outcome of design research, distinguishing four typical types: constructs, models, methods and instantiations. The motivation is brief, but it seems that for March and Smith, *models* are at the core. Constructs provide the language to build models. Methods are described as ways to implement models, and instantiations as the integrated result. The March and Smith proposal has been broadly accepted. Alternatively, based on a literature review of actual design research projects, Offermann et al. [26] identified eight relevant artefact types: notation, requirement, metric, system design, method, algorithm, guideline and pattern. The paper does not try to analyze ontologically how these types are related. It should also be noted that the scope of the literature review was mainly on design research conferences, and not the IS literature as a whole.

A different way of classifying IS artefacts is by means of their function. Iivari [17] distinguished seven functions: to automate, to augment, to mediate, to inform, to entertain, to create art, to accompany. Each function characterizes an archetypical IT application. In contrast to March & Smith's general design science approach, Iivari's classification is more specific to the IS domain, but it also lacks ontological analysis. It can be used to classify IT artefacts on the basis of their use.

2.5   Ontology of IT Artefacts

Wang, et al. [35] provided a detailed ontological analysis of *software*. They follow Osterweil in describing software as something non-physical and intangible. They do not agree with proposals that identify the program with the code. The reason given for the distinction is that software can be updated, so can have different codes at different times, while a code becomes different by each change (the paper talks about a change in the syntactic structure that includes variable renaming and inclusion of a comment, so apparently any change apart from layout). This latter claim is disputable. As in the famous Ship of Theseus example, it is possible to change a part (replace a plank) while the ship keeps its identity.

According to [35] 'when a code is in the circumstance that somebody, with a kind of *act of baptism*, intends to produce certain effects on a computer, a new entity emerges … a computer program'. Again, we have some remarks. First, it feels odd that the code is presented to be there *before* the program emerges. Usually, there is a program design first. Secondly, the paper continues to write that the program is not a physical object as it lacks a location in space – but why is code inside space and the baptized code suddenly outside space? In our view, the issues are caused by a lack of attention to the design itself. We have a problem with calling a program instance non-physical and at the same time saying that it is constituted by (physical) code. However, we do agree that code and program must be distinguished, and also that a program can be distinguished from a software system (where the former has an effect in the computer internally and the latter externally, in the interface).

Coming from outside the IS domain, the Information Artefact Ontology (IAO, [7]) provides an ontological account of information content entities (ICE) such as document, databases and digital images. An ICE is defined as an entity that is 'generically dependent on some material entity and which stands in a relation of aboutness to some [other] entity'. The material entity can be the paper, the other entity can be the person depicted in the digital image ICE. An ICE can be concretized in an information carrier (e.g. a copy of the image). In [8], a distinction is made between the information artefact (a material entity) and the information carrier, now called information quality entity. The information artefact is the disk or paper itself – viewed purely physically, that is used to *bear* information. Although our ontology will be structured differently, with more emphasis on the design, we concur with IAO with respect to the material basis of information artefacts. [8] is a detailed analysis of the "aboutness" relation, and how to deal with cases where the entity that the information content entity is about does not exist. In our view, this analysis is useful when we are talking about language and mental states. However, we regard that as belonging to language ontology, which is different from–although presupposed in–an information object/text ontology.

3   Ontology of Artefacts

Although the focus of this paper is on *IS artefacts*, we start with a short summary of our general ontology of artefacts (in progress) which builds on and extends the work of Borgo [5] as well as Lawson [21] and Kroes [20]. Our aim is to integrate their work with the Design Science Research perspective, such as described in Sect. 2, and ground it in the foundational ontology UFO [15]. In this Section, we first summarize the artefact ontology and illustrate it with some small examples. In 3.4, we focus on text artefacts, and in 3.5 we define DSR artefacts.

3.1   Basic Definitions

An **artificial object** is a physical object intentionally or unintentionally created, modified or adopted by humans. A **natural** object is a physical object that is not an artificial object. For the definition of physical object we follow the UFO definition of a *substance individual*, that is 'an endurant that consists of matter (i.e., is "tangible" or concrete), possesses spatio-temporal properties, and can exist by itself; that is, it does not existentially depend on other endurants, except possibly on some of its parts)' [15]. The distinction artificial object/natural object does not necessarily exhaust the complete set of endurants. For instance, mathematical objects and social entities are endurants but not physical objects. UFO does not split up the world of substantials into artificial and natural, but into agents and objects; and distinguishes social objects from physical objects.

Instrument is a role of an object in an event or activity. The instrument is *used* in the event. This corresponds partially to the UFO definition of resource as 'an object participating in an action'. However, some resources are consumed in the use (e.g. a medicine), and cease to exist, while others are not. We use the role instrument for the latter persisting participating objects only. Note that instruments are not necessarily artificial objects: a shell can be used for drinking water, stars can be used to navigate on sea.

A **technical object** is an *artificial object* (individual) that is made by humans for some purpose (intentionally) whose capacities are (in principle) exhaustively described by the physical laws *and* the intentional design. A technical object has *attributed capacities*[1] that are *realized* in the use.

An **artefact** like "the Diesel engine" is a universal (1stOT in MLT [6] – with artefact a 2ndOT category) that has a design specification consisting of a (at least one) *make plan*, a (at least one) *use plan* and a *capacity specification*. An individual object is said to *conform* to the artefact if it its composition is according to the make plan, it shows the specified capacities, and its use intention corresponds to the use plan (for convenience, we also talk about **artefact instances** for these conforming individuals). We talk about **technical artefacts** when the objects conforming to the artefact are *technical objects*,

---

[1] "capability", "potential" may be better terms but the literature uses the word "capacity".

and non-technical artefacts when there are objects conforming to the artefact but not technical. The *make plan* basically expresses the composition of the object in terms of **components** and allows reproducing individuals conforming to the artefact. The *use plan* specifies at least in which events and under which use conditions the object can be used to achieve which intended effect. To delimit the scope of artefacts to those products that have "a practical purpose", we require the use plan to refer to a *use practice* (this can be an end user practice but also a production system like a plant). The make plan makes it possible that (sooner or later) there is more than one instance (so if an inventor construes a technical object but there is no make plan and it cannot be reproduced, it is not an artefact instance).

3.2 Examples

Examples of artificial objects are not only hammers, cars and software, but also a footprint in the sand, or production waste. However, the latter two are not technical objects, as they are not intentionally made, and have no use plan. A pebble at the beach is a natural object but when cleaned and moved by a human to serve as doorstep, it becomes a technical object.

Seedless bananas [33] are not technical objects, but there is a design for them, so "the seedless banana" is a non-technical artefact. A software program like MS-Word is a technical artefact. An organizational system that includes humans (for instance, a defense system) is not a technical object. Whether it can be seen as conforming to a (non-technical) artefact "defense system type Y" requires in the first place that there is a design specification. So some systems are artefact instances, while others, for instance, a family, are not.

3.3 Conceptual Model of the Artefact and Artefact Network

We posit a *form* event behind any artefact instance, alternatively called making, producing, assembling, reproducing. The form event has a physical input and output, and an intentional input and output. The physical input consists of the components of the artefact, whereas the intentional input corresponds to the make plan (as part of the artefact design). The intentional output corresponds to the attributed capacity, the physical output is the thing made.

The main elements of the (technical) artefact are rendered in the conceptual model of Fig. 1 (grounding in UFO is not in this paper). Design specifies an artefact and consists of three parts (specifications). The design takes place in a conversation between user and designer – as such, it can be requested, proposed, accepted etc. It is also the designer and user who jointly and sometimes after a process of negotiation attribute capacities to the technical object. Note that user is a role. Not all individual users participate in the conversation. The conversation can be organized in different ways.

The make plan *is not* a complete manufacturing plan. At the minimum, it specifies the critical components and their relationships (the artefact composition – system view). The make plan can take different forms, for instance, as a blueprint or a recipe. There

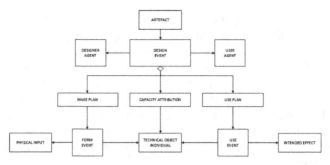

Fig. 1. Artefact ontology (technical artefact; conceptual overview).

is no absolute measure for the level of detail required. It should be sufficient for distinguishing the artefact from siblings (for instance, to distinguish the Diesel engine from the combustion engine).

The use plan consists of several parts. One important element is the intended effect. This effect can be specified more precisely if we consider a subset of technical artefacts that transform some input to some output – for instance, a coffee machine, a 3D printer, but also an application that transforms input data into output data. In that case, the intended effect can be described in the form of the required input and the intended output. We call these the use input and use output of the artefact, to avoid confusion with the make input and make output in the make plan.

In some sense, the artefact is a bridge between the make context and the use context. It is therefore not inappropriate to characterize an artefact as an interface [30].

An *artefact network* is a network of imbricating artefacts. The imbrication is a result of the make plan of one artefact being part of the use plan of another artefact. For instance, we can start with a mathematical Python library used in developing a Python program. The library is part of the make plan of the program, while at the same time should comply with the use plan of the library. The software program can be part of an IS application that is used in a work system – the use plan of the program refers to the work practice, including resources and norms. The goal of the work system may be to build a robot. The use condition of the IS application may be that there is a running computer network that builds on Internet; etc. The implication for artefact design is that it always involves integrating a new artefact into the existing network, and this integration is an ongoing process as the network evolves continuously.

3.4 Text Objects

A **text object** such as the blue book on my desk is a *technical object* where the attributed capacity (the written content) can be recaptured in the use (the reading). Text is to be understood in a wide sense, i.e. a variety of information encoding modes. Any text object has a physical basis (e.g. paper, disk block), a content (the attributed capacity) and an intended use. The intended effect of using the text object (in the case of human reading) is typically a change in the mental state of the human agent corresponding to the attributed capacity (the text meaning). A software program at binary level is to be read by a processor, and the intended effect is a change in the internal memory of the computer.

We need to say something about the relationship between text and language. Although human language is not a technical object, text is. More in general, we can talk about writing technology that started with clay tablets and papyrus and nowadays is evolving into digital technology. Writing is a form event by which a technical (physical) object is created (the individual piece of paper, blank before the writing, and filled with signs after the writing). As for any technical object [32], the intended use must be grasped by the user. In line with the pragmatist slogan "meaning is use", we consider the intended use (behavior) as the meaning of the text/sign. The intended behavior can be, for instance, to run away (in the case of a danger sign). The reading of the text for changing the mental state of the listeners is a special but of course very important use (Fig. 2). Its effectiveness depends (use condition) on the shared language and shared education in reading/writing. The meaning of the sign DOG in English is the evocation of the concept of dog shared by English-speaking people. This concept *is about* a certain kind of animals [8] but this is a property of natural language, not of the signs as such. When we go from the level of signs to the level of texts, then some texts are again closely related to behavior. For example, an IKEA manual that helps the customer to assemble a cabinet (the manual instantiates a make plan).

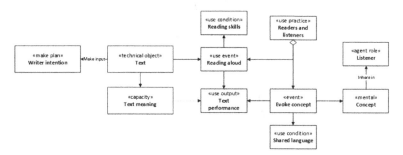

Fig. 2. Text for human reading (conceptual model)

Examples of text objects are Mary's book, and Paul's computer chess game. Text objects may also be called symbolic objects. If the text object is not unique but conforming to an artefact, then the latter is a symbolic artefact. This artefact may survive when individual copies have been destroyed. The traditional distinction between data and information can be interpreted as a distinction between a technical object (the data item, as it may be written on multiple locations), and the artefact to which these data items conform and that specifies the attributed capacity and use plan of the data.

3.5 DSR Artefact

A (domain) **Design Science Research (DSR) artefact** is an artefact with a well-described design specification (formal rigor) that is not only directly or indirectly used in a (domain – e.g. information system) practice for practical purposes but also in the research practice (the scientific community) for the purpose of building up knowledge. As science aims at abstract knowledge, not knowledge of the particular, the DSR artefact should generalize over multiple use contexts. So not every artefact is a DSR artefact. Not every software program is a IS design artefact. Not all design is design research (cf. [24]). DSR artefacts must have at least a certain level of *rigor* and *generalizability*, as well as practical and scientific *relevance*. Moreover, it must have instantiations so that evaluation knowledge can be acquired.

When rigor is required for the design, the specification must be explicit in the form of a text object. Ontologically, the relationship between artefact and design specification is one of inherence (the former cannot exist independently from the latter). The specification is usually a composite object, consisting of several text objects. For instance, in the case of software design, one text object could be an object model.

4   An Overview of IT/IS Artefacts

Whereas some proposals have identified a shortlist of IT/IS artefacts and others have refrained from any characterization, our proposal is to identify a few core IT/IS artefacts and a generative mechanism by which secondary artefacts can be derived. It is possible, for instance, to focus on the design conversation and turn it into an (text) artefact; or to design a tool to support the conversation; or to make the use plan the focus of design research, in the form of a use method. March & Smith [23] mention constructs, models, methods and instantiations as IS design research artefacts, where "method" includes algorithms. Starting with this shortlist, in this section we identify IT/IS core artefacts.

4.1   Algorithms, Programs and IS Applications

According to Offerman et al. [26] an algorithm, like a method, describes a sequence of activities that are executed by a computer. They define, it as 'an executable description of a system behavior'. Examples given are sorting algorithm, data mining algorithm, and protocol. From the ontological perspective, the sorting algorithm, in one of its variants, e.g. quicksort (Fig. 3), is an artefact that is instantiated in all its executable representations (text objects conforming to the algorithm artefact).

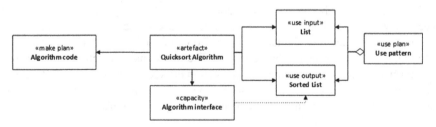

Fig. 3.   The quicksort algorithm as an artefact.

In the pre-computer age, these executable representations had to be executed (on paper) by humans. The sorted list is created so it is a textual technical object. It has an attributed capacity (that the elements in the list are ordered) related to the use output.

In the computer age, the algorithm, in the form of software program, is executed by a computer processor. The use plan of this IT application requires there to be a processor and a database/storage. When the program is executed according to the use plan, a new database state is created. Just like using a manual means that the manual is executed step by step, so the use of the algorithm means that the make plan/algorithm code is executed.

We regard the algorithm as an artefact (*possibly* a DSR artefact) and a software program as a kind of algorithm. Apart from the difference in use plan (and related formal rigor required in the make plan), the structure of a software program is more complex than a sequence of computational steps. Nowadays, its composition is described in terms of objects or services. The way that the components are assembled by the make plan, has become a design object itself. Concrete approaches such as SOA are a DSR artefact.

A software program is used to change the internal state of the computer [35]. To make the bridge to the organizational context, we need I/O devices that are able to create text objects outside the machine. How the I/O device, software program and processor interact exactly is not in the scope of our analysis, but one way of viewing it is that the three are assembled into a new artefact, the IS application. This *IS application* is what is used by the human agent according to its use plan (the prescribed user interaction) to generate and transform data objects in the organization. This typically takes place as part of a work system or business process practice. When an IS application is assembled together with a machine or robot into a *cyberphysical system*, a new category of artefacts arises.

One ontological question is whether the code that is the make plan of the software artefact is an artefact itself. In principle, we prefer make plan and use plan of an artefact to be characterized as *artefact parts* – so that they are not evaluated in isolation. However, the form event governed by the make plan is an activity that is open to optimization and tool support, as any activity. Consider first a non-textual artefact like the Diesel engine. The make plan of the metal object is a textual artefact, e.g. a blueprint. This text object can become the subject of design (of a text writer, addressing the construction workers), meeting user requirements of being easy to read, complete etc., and so becomes an artefact itself. For symbolic artefacts like a software program, the make plan (the blueprint) and made object (the code) *can* be one and the same. However, this is not necessary, and, as we know, it is possible to describe software programs on various levels of abstraction, e.g. in terms of design models, like an UML object model. "The UML object model" is a DSR artefact (see below for more discussion about models).

4.2 Supporting Artefacts – Formal Languages, Constructs and Patterns

Supporting all text objects and in particular the software specification dimensions are formal language artefacts, like programming languages. A programming language provides the constructs (basic components) from which the source code can be assembled according to certain rules (use plan), that is, the syntax. [26] also mention the "pattern" as artefact, but the pattern has multiple levels. It often represents design knowledge about some artefact (and so not a design science artefact itself), but it can also be a semi-component design object and then it is indeed (on the type level) a genuine DSR artefact.

4.3 Models

In traditional system sciences, models are made of social, material, or socio-material situations, conceptualized as systems (cf. 2.1). Examples are models of the economic market, of a missile launch, or of (a part or aspect of) a business organization. The model can be analyzed mathematically or by simulation [30]. Based on the analysis, the manager of the organization can make decisions that influence the system, for instance, by introducing an IT system. In this case, we call the models analysis/design models. Whether the intervention will have the foreseen effect is not guaranteed: what is built is not the system as a whole, but certain elements of it. In the field of Information Systems, the manager can introduce new IT, and new methods (structuring the business processes), and in that way enhance the Information System in the broader sense. In terms of the ontology of artefacts, these systems are non-technical artefacts, if there is a design specification, with a make plan and use plan, and these plans may take the form of a "design model" or "use model". In the near future, we expect these kind of analysis/design models to play a role in autonomous intelligent systems (robots). Not only for building these systems, but also for these systems themselves to reason about their environment.

In many situations, such as a meteorological system, there is no design specification, but we can have a model for analysis and prediction purposes.

Let us consider the example of an Entity Relationship diagram. It has a dual nature. On the one hand, it can be used as an analysis model of a non-technical system, for instance, a household. In most cases, it is an analysis/design model of a non-technical artefact, for instance, a university domain consisting of students, enrollments etc., that wants to build an IS. On the other hand, it is used to build a database system, a technical artefact. This design takes place in the conversation between system designer and user (that is why the graphical representation is useful) and the ER model is the make plan of the IT application. So: database systems are artefacts. "The ER model" as introduced by Chen is an artefact. The use plan of the ER model imbricates with the make plan of the database, while the use plan of the IT application (with database) is imbricates with the make plan of the IS (the analysis/design model of the IS).

We can go one step further and consider the purpose of the model. According to Boon and Knuuttila [4:693], 'the models developed in the engineering sciences should be distinguished from the models produced in engineering [in technological practice]. Whereas the latter usually represent the design of a device or its mechanical workings, models in the engineering sciences aim for scientific understanding of the behavior of different devices or the properties of diverse materials' (cf. [10, 25]).

The intended use of the model for scientific understanding resonates with the design *science* perspective, although the distinction between practical and scientific can be diffuse. It is fair to say that the scientific rigor of the current DSR models is often lower than in the exact sciences with their long mathematical tradition. However, this does not invalidate the DSR ambition. In Transformational Design Research, the conversation for design between designer and user is distinguished from the conversation between the designer-researcher and the scientific community. Once a model is part of the latter conversation, it may be called a techno-scientific object. At the type level we talk about

DSR artefacts: the model in the form of a design text conforms to a DSR artefact at type level, with make plan, use plan and attributed capacities of the model.

Summarizing, we have to distinguish different kinds of models. They are all technical objects, but they have different relationships to artefacts.

- *Analysis models of (socio-technical or other) system.* Some of these are IS artefacts. Examples are domain models that aim to analyze the behavior, for instance, system-dynamics simulations. The model instantiates "the system-dynamics" artefact.
- *Analysis/design models of non-technical artefacts.* Examples are BPMN business process models used in IS design (part of use plan). Another example can be an environment model that intelligent agents use for internal reasoning.
- *Design models of technical artefacts.* For instance, ER model. The model is both a make-plan for the technical artefact database, and instantiates "the ER model" artefact.
- *Scientific models as DSR artefacts.* Example is the use of Petri Net models for analyzing processes within technical or non-technical systems; or Codd's relational database model grounded in set theory.

4.4 Summary

Our claim is that *software program* and *IS application* are the core domain artefact types in Computer Science and Information Systems. The specification of these artefacts can include *models* and *formal languages/constructs.* Instantiated systems [23] are *not* artefacts in our ontology, but evaluation studies of these technical objects (or systems) contribute to the design knowledge accumulated in the artefact to which the individual conforms. From a Design Science perspective, *techno-scientific models* of the domain artefacts and the related systems are artefacts on a second level that typically focus on some aspect of the domain artefact. Our ontological analysis confirms the centrality of most artefact types mentioned by March & Smith, but with several nuances. We have made a key distinction between software program and IS application. We also claim that always some element of a design can be isolated and give rise to new artefact types. Furthermore, we have argued for a holistic view, that is, to see artefacts always in context of the artefact network.

4.5 Practical Implications

Based on our ontological analysis, we can give some practical implications for the designer and design researcher in the form of a preliminary set of guidelines.

- Keep the difference between technical objects and non-technical objects.
- Focus not on building an artefact, but on designing an artefact (where designing includes the evolution of the design). Evaluate the artefact on the basis of its built instances in their use context to accumulate design knowledge.
- Include in the artefact design some make plan that specifies the composition.
- Include in the artefact design one or more use plans that specify use conditions, intended effect and relate to a use practice.

- Perform the design always in conversation with actual or potential users. Identify attributed capacities together and analyze the relationship between inherent and attributed capacities.
- Integrate the designed artefact in the artefact network (aggregation dimension) and in the artefact classification (identify type and distinguish it from siblings)
- (for the design researcher) Aim at developing techno-scientific models of domain artefacts.

5 Conclusion

Artefacts are said to be the object of Design Science Research, but their ontological status is often taken for granted. This has led to discussions and confusion about the artefact status of information systems. In this paper, we have proposed some important distinctions, in particular the distinction between a technical object (individual) and the artefact (universal) and the distinction between technical artefacts and non-technical artefacts. Whereas the literature often isolates either the designer intention or the artefact use, our ontology keeps the two in balance. We have founded IS artefacts on writing technology.

A new element in our ontology is to let the design specification inhere in a conversation between designers and users, a conversation that has several phases, in fact, an ongoing conversation as long as the artefact persists. Another aspect that we emphasize is the imbrication structure of the artefact network. A general conclusion of our analysis is that design research should broaden its narrow scope from building/evaluating an isolated technical object in some delineated time span, at some place towards a holistic view on technology development.

We are currently working on a formal presentation of our artefact ontology grounded in UFO. We are also working on how to represent social artefacts such as laws in the ontology.

References

1. van Aken, J.: Management research as design science: articulating the research products of mode 2 knowledge production in management. Brit. J. Manage. **16**, 19–36 (2005)
2. Alter, S.: The concept of 'IT artifact' has outlived its usefulness and should be retired now. Inf. Syst. J. **25**(1), 47–60 (2015)
3. Baker, L.R.: The ontology of artefacts. Philos. Explor. **7**(2), 99–111 (2004)
4. Boon, M., Knuuttila, T.: Models as epistemic tools in engineering sciences. In: Meijers, A. (ed.) Philosophy of Technology and Engineering Sciences, pp. 693–726 (2009)
5. Borgo, S., Vieu, L.: Artefacts in formal ontology. In: Philosophy of Technology and Engineering Sciences, pp. 273–307 (2009)
6. Carvalho, Victorio A., Almeida, João Paulo A., Fonseca, Claudenir M., Guizzardi, G.: Extending the foundations of ontology-based conceptual modeling with a multi-level theory. In: Johannesson, P., Lee, M.L., Liddle, Stephen W., Opdahl, Andreas L., López, Ó.P. (eds.) ER 2015. LNCS, vol. 9381, pp. 119–133. Springer, Cham (2015). https://doi.org/10.1007/978-3-319-25264-3_9

7. Ceusters, W.: An information artifact ontology perspective on data collections and associated representational artifacts. Stud. Health Technol. Inf. **180**, 68–72 (2012)
8. Ceusters, W., Smith, B.: Aboutness: towards foundations for the information artifact ontology. In: Proceedings 6th International Conference on Biomedical Ontology, CEUR, vol. 1515, pp. 1–5 (2015)
9. Drechsler, A., Hevner, Alan R.: Utilizing, producing, and contributing design knowledge in DSR projects. In: Chatterjee, S., Dutta, K., Sundarraj, Rangaraja P. (eds.) DESRIST 2018. LNCS, vol. 10844, pp. 82–97. Springer, Cham (2018). https://doi.org/10.1007/978-3-319-91800-6_6
10. France, B., Compton, V.J., Gilbert, J.K.: Understanding modelling in technology and science: the potential of stories from the field. Int. J. Technol. Des. Educ. **21**(3), 381–394 (2010). https://doi.org/10.1007/s10798-010-9126-4
11. Goldkuhl, G., Lind, M.: A multi-grounded design research process. In: Winter, R., Zhao, J.Leon, Aier, S. (eds.) DESRIST 2010. LNCS, vol. 6105, pp. 45–60. Springer, Heidelberg (2010). https://doi.org/10.1007/978-3-642-13335-0_4
12. Grabowski, F., Strzalka, D.: Simple, complicated and complex systems—the brief introduction. In: 2008 Conference on Human System Interactions, pp. 570–573 (2008)
13. Jones, D., Gregor, S.: The anatomy of a design theory. J. AIS **8**, 19 (2007)
14. Gregor, S., Hevner, A.: Positioning and presenting design science research for maximum impact. MIS Q. **37**(2), 337–356 (2013)
15. Guizzardi, G., de Almeida Falbo, R., Guizzardi, R.S.: Grounding software domain ontologies in the unified foundational ontology (UFO): the case of the ODE software process ontology. In: Proceedings of CIbSE, pp. 127–140 (2008)
16. Hevner, A., March, S., Park, J., Ram, S.: Design science in information systems research'. MIS Q. **28**(1), 75–105 (2004)
17. Iivari, J.: A paradigmatic analysis of information systems as a design science. Scand. J. Inf. Syst. **19**, 39–64 (2007)
18. Johannesson, P., Perjons, E.: An Introduction to Design Science. Springer, Heidelberg (2014). https://doi.org/10.1007/978-3-319-10632-8
19. Kimbell, L.: Rethinking design thinking: part I. Des. Cult. **3**(3), 285–306 (2011)
20. Kroes, P., Meijers, A.: The dual nature of technical artifacts. Stud. Hist. Philos. Sci. **37**(1), 1–4 (2006)
21. Lawson, C.: An ontology of technology: artefacts. Relat. Functions Technol. **12**(1), 48–64 (2008)
22. Lee, A., Thomas, M., Baskerville, R.: Going back to the basics in design science: from the information technology artefact to the information system artefact. Inf. Syst. **25**, 5–21 (2014)
23. March, S., Smith, G.: Design and natural science research on information technology. Decis. Support Syst. **15**, 251–266 (1995)
24. McPhee, K.: Design Theory and Software Design. Technical report TR 96–26. Univ of Alberta (1997)
25. Nia, M., de Vries, M.: Models as artefacts of a dual nature: a philosophical contribution to teaching about models designed and used in engineering practice. Int. J. Technol. Des. Educ. **27**(4), 627–653 (2017)
26. Offermann, P., Blom, S., Schönherr, M., Bub, U.: Artifact types in information systems design science – a literature review. In: Winter, R., Zhao, J.Leon, Aier, S. (eds.) DESRIST 2010. LNCS, vol. 6105, pp. 77–92. Springer, Heidelberg (2010). https://doi.org/10.1007/978-3-642-13335-0_6
27. Pandza, K., Thorpe, R.: Management as design, but what kind of design? An appraisal of the design science analogy for management. Brit. J. Manage. **21**, 171–186 (2010)
28. Purao, S.: Design Research in the Technology of Information Systems: Truth or Dare. GSU Dept of CIS Working Paper, Atlanta: Georgia State University (2002)

29. Silver, M., Markus, L.: Conceptualizing the sociotechnical (ST) artifact. Syst. Signs Actions **7**(1), 82–89 (2013)
30. Simon, H.: The Sciences of the Artificial, 3rd edn. MIT Press, Cambridge (1996)
31. Simondon, G.: On the Mode of Existence of Technical Objects Minneapolis. Univocal Publishing (1958/2016)
32. Sinha, Ch.: Language and other artifacts. Front. Psychol. **6**, 1601 (2015)
33. Sperber, D.: Seedless grapes: nature and culture. In: Margolis, E., Laurence, S. (eds.) Creations of the Mind: Theories of Artifacts and Their Representation, pp. 124–137. Oxford University Press, Oxford (2007)
34. Vermaas, P., Kroes, P., Poel, van de, I., Franssen, M., Houkes, W.: A philosophy of technology: from technical artefacts to sociotechnical systems. In: Synthesis Lectures on Engineers, Technology and Society, vol. 6, no. 1. Morgan & Claypool Publishers, San Rafael (2011)
35. Wang, X., Guarino, N., Guizzardi, G., Mylopoulos, J.: Towards an ontology of software: a requirements engineering perspective. In: Proceedings of FOIS 2014, pp. 317–329. IOS Press (2014)
36. Weigand, H.: Value expression in design science research. IEEE RCIS **2019**, 1–11 (2019)
37. Wieringa, R.: Design Science Methodology. Springer, Heidelberg (2013)
38. Winter, R.: Design science research in Europe European. J. Inf. Syst. **17**, 470–474 (2008)

Evolution of Enterprise Architecture
for Intelligent Digital Systems

Alfred Zimmermann[1], Rainer Schmidt[2]([✉]), Dierk Jugel[1], and Michael Möhring[2]

[1] Herman-Hollerith-Center, Reutlingen University, Boeblingen, Germany
{alfred.zimmermann,dierk.jugel}@reutlingen-university.de
[2] Munich University of Applies Sciences, Munich, Germany
{rainer.schmidt,michael.moehring}@hm.edu

Abstract. Intelligent systems and services are the strategic targets of many current digitalization efforts and part of massive digital transformations based on digital technologies with artificial intelligence. Digital platform architectures and ecosystems provide an essential base for intelligent digital systems. The paper raises an important question: Which development paths are induced by current innovations in the field of artificial intelligence and digitalization for enterprise architectures? Digitalization disrupts existing enterprises, technologies, and economies and promotes the architecture of cognitive and open intelligent environments. This has a strong impact on new opportunities for value creation and the development of intelligent digital systems and services. Digital technologies such as artificial intelligence, the Internet of Things, service computing, cloud computing, blockchains, big data with analysis, mobile systems, and social business network systems are essential drivers of digitalization. We investigate the development of intelligent digital systems supported by a suitable digital enterprise architecture. We present methodological advances and an evolutionary path for architectures with an integral service and value perspective to enable intelligent systems and services that effectively combine digital strategies and digital architectures with artificial intelligence.

Keywords: Digitalization and digital transformation · Intelligent digital systems · Digital enterprise architecture · Architecture and systems evolution

1 Introduction

Influenced by the transition to digitalization, many companies are in the process of converting their strategy, culture, processes and information systems to digitalization and artificial intelligence. Today, the digital transformation [1] profoundly disrupts existing companies and economies. The potential of the Internet and related digital technologies such as the Internet of Things, cognition and artificial intelligence, data analysis, service computing, cloud computing, blockchain, mobile systems, collaboration networks, cyber-physical systems, and Industry 4.0 are strategic drivers and enable digital platforms with rapidly evolving ecosystems of intelligent systems and services based on service-dominant logic [2].

© Springer Nature Switzerland AG 2020
F. Dalpiaz et al. (Eds.): RCIS 2020, LNBIP 385, pp. 145–153, 2020.
https://doi.org/10.1007/978-3-030-50316-1_9

Digitalization [3] promotes the development of IT systems with many, globally available and diverse, rather small and distributed structures, such as the Internet of Things or mobile systems, which have a strong influence on the architecture of intelligent digital systems and services. Data, information, and knowledge are fundamental concepts of daily activities and drive the digital transformation [4] of today's global society. New services and intelligent, connected digital systems extend physical components by providing additional information and connectivity services using the Internet. Intelligent digital systems are information systems that use artificial intelligence (AI) [5, 6] to support and relieve people, and that interact with people. Advances in artificial intelligence have led to a growing number of intelligent systems and services.

The current work in progress paper focuses on the main research question: *What are key drivers and conceptual models of an advanced digital enterprise architecture that supports intelligent digital systems and services?*

We will proceed as follows. First, we establish the architectural context for digitalization and digital transformation to intelligent digital systems. Then we will introduce basic mechanisms of artificial intelligence and provide insights into our current work on a platform for intelligent digital systems. We present our view of a suitable multi-perspective digital enterprise architecture. We outline fundamental aspects of an architectural evolution path for intelligent digital systems. Finally, in the last section, we conclude our research results and mention our future work.

2 Digitalization and Digital Transformation

In the beginning, digitization was considered a primarily technical term [1]. Therefore, a number of technologies are often associated with digitalization [3]: cloud computing, big data combined with advanced analytics, social software, and the Intranet of Things. New technologies, such as deep learning, are strategic enablers and strongly linked to the progress of digitalization. They enable the use of computers for activities that were previously considered exclusively for humans. Therefore, the current emphasis on intelligent digitalization is becoming an essential research area. Digital services and related products are software-intensive and, therefore, malleable and usually service-oriented [7]. Digital products are able to enhance their capabilities by accessing cloud services and to change their current behavior.

We are at a turning point in the development and application of intelligent digital systems. We see great prospects for digital systems with artificial intelligence (AI) [5, 6], with the potential to contribute to improvements in many areas of work and society through digital technologies. We understand digitization based on new methods and technologies of artificial intelligence as a complex integration of digital services, products, and related systems. For years we have been experiencing a hype about digitalization, in which the terms digitization, digitalization, and digital transformation are often used in a confusing way. The origin of the term digitalization is the concept of digitization. According to [8], Fig. 1, we distinguish levels of digitalization.

When we use the term digitalization, we mean more than just digital technologies. Digitalization [1, 8] bundles the more mature phase of a digital transformation from analog over digital to fully digital. Through digital substitution (digitization), initially, only analog media are replaced by digital media, taking into account the same existing business values, while augmentation enriches related transformed analog media functionally. In a further step of the digital transformation, new activity patterns or processes are made possible by a digitally supported modification of the basic concepts.

Digitalization Level	Description	Transformation Type	Example
1. Substitution	Tool substitute, no functional change	Digital Enhancement (1)	Scientific paper as pdf file
2. Augmentation	Tool substitute, functional improvements	Digital Enhancement (2)	Enhanced pdf file with direct connectors to processes / tools
3. Modification	Significant operation redesign	Digital Transformation (1)	Paper submission automatically triggers the subsequent review process
4. Redefinition	Creation of new operations, previously inconceivable	Digital Transformation (2)	Digital platform and ecosystem of living scientific conferences, journals, and other assets with co-creating people and intelligent services

Fig. 1. Digitalization and digital transformation.

Finally, the digital redefinition (digitalization) of processes, services, and systems results in completely new forms of value propositions [1, 2] for changing businesses, services, products, processes, and systems. Digitalization is thus more about shifting processes to attractive, highly automated digital business processes and not just about communication via the Internet. The digital redefinition usually leads to disruptive effects on business. Beyond the value-oriented perspective of digitalization, intelligent digital business requires a careful adoption of human, ethical, and social principles.

3   Intelligent Digital Systems

The combination of hardware and software product components with intelligent services from the cloud enables new ways of intelligent interaction with customers, as described in [9]. The life cycle of digitized products is extended by intelligent services. One example is Amazon Alexa, which combines a physical device with a microphone and loudspeaker with services, the so-called Alexa skills. Users can extend the capabilities of Alexa with capabilities similar to apps. The set of Alexa capabilities is dynamic and can be adapted to the customer's requirements during runtime. Alexa enables voice interaction, music playback, to-do lists, setting alarms, streaming podcasts, playing audio books, and providing weather, traffic, sports, and other real-time information such as news. Alexa can also connect and control intelligent products and devices.

From today's perspective, probably no digital technology is more exciting than artificial intelligence, which offers massive automation possibilities for intelligent digital systems and services. Most companies expect to gain a competitive advantage from AI.

Artificial intelligence (AI) [5, 6] is often used in conjunction with other digital technologies [10] such as cloud computing, analytics, ubiquitous data, the Internet of Things, and unlimited connectivity. Basic capabilities of AI concern automatically generated solutions from previous useful cases and solution elements derived by causal inference structures such as rules and ontologies, as well as learned solutions based on data analytics with machine learning and deep learning with neural networks.

Artificial intelligence receives a high degree of attention due to recent progress [11] in several areas, such as image detection, translation, and decision support. It enables interesting new business applications such as predictive maintenance, logistics optimization, and automatically added customer service management. Artificial intelligence supports decision-making in many business areas. Today's advances in the field of artificial intelligence [10–12] have led to a rapidly growing number of intelligent services and applications. The development of competencies via intelligent digital systems promises great value for science, economy, and society. It is driven by data, calculations, advances in algorithms for machine learning, perception and cognition, planning, decision support, and natural language processing.

The symbolic AI [5], which predominated until the 1990s, uses a deductive, expert-based approach. By interviewing one or more experts, knowledge is collected in the form of rules and other explicit representations of knowledge, such as horn clauses. These rules are applied to facts that describe the problem to be solved. The solution of a problem is found by successively applying one or more rules using the mechanisms of an inference engine [5]. An inference path can usually be followed backwards and offers transparency and rationality over instantiated inference processes by "how" and "why" explanations. The symbolic AI proved to be very effective for highly formalized problem spaces like dedicated expert systems. After the last wave of enthusiasm in the late 1980s, the focus of research shifted to other areas [10–12]. Ontologies [5] represent the second wave of semantic technologies to support knowledge representations.

Unlike symbolic AI, machine learning [10] uses an inductive approach based on a large amount of analyzed data. We distinguish three basic approaches to machine learning: supervised, unsupervised, and reinforcement learning [12]. In supervised approaches to machine learning, the target value is part of the training data and is based on sample inputs. Typically, unsupervised learning is used to discover new hidden patterns within the analyzed data. Reinforcement Learning (RL) is an area of machine learning where software agents work to cooperatively maximize cumulative rewards. The exploration environment is specified in terms of a Markov decision process, as many reinforcement learning algorithms use dynamic programming techniques. Reinforcement learning does not require marked input/output pairs, and suboptimal actions do not need to be explicitly corrected.

Digital technologies are changing the way we communicate and collaborate with customers and other stakeholders, even competitors, to create value [1, 2]. Digital technologies have changed the way we look at how to analyze and understand a wide range of real-time data from different perspectives. The digital transformation has also changed our understanding of how to innovate in global processes, to archive and develop intelligent digital products and services faster than ever before, to achieve the best available digital technology and quality. We are currently researching a cognitive co-creation platform that enhances key intelligent digital systems. We consider the evolutionary dynamics of an integrated architecture lifecycle management for intelligent artifacts, such as digital strategy, digital operating model, intelligent models for service composition, digital enterprise architecture, and intelligent services and products.

4 Digital Enterprise Architecture

A targeted digital business architecture [1, 3], should be part of an enterprise architecture [13] that provides a comprehensive view of integrated business and IT elements. More specifically, we integrate configurations of stakeholders (roles, responsibilities, structures, knowledge, skills), business and technical processes (workflows, procedures, programs), and technology (infrastructure, platforms, applications) to implement digital strategies and compose value-producing digital products and services. The digital business design does not only include simple business restructuring or just a focus on IT architecture. Above all, digital business is an aspect that is currently in use and constantly changing. Therefore, the digital business design is not an end state.

We start by revisiting and modeling the digital strategy [14], as shown in Fig. 2, which sets the digital modeling direction and establishes the basis and value framework for the business definition models, with the business model canvas [15] and the value proposition canvas [16]. With the basic models for a value-based business [2], we assign these basic digital business models [15, 16] to a business operating model [1]. The value perspective of the business model canvas [15] leads to appropriate mappings to the value models of the enterprise architecture supported by ArchiMate [17, 18]. Finally, we set the framework for the systematic definition of digital services and associated products by modelling digital services and product compositions.

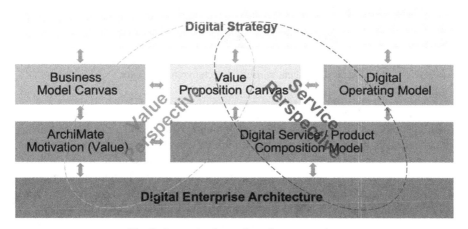

Fig. 2. Integral value and service perspective.

We have extended our service-oriented enterprise architecture reference model [19] for the evolving context of digital transformation by microgranular structures and the consideration of related multi-perspective architectural decision models, supported by viewpoints and functions of an architecture management cockpit. DEA - Digital Enterprise Architecture Reference Cube provides a holistic architectural reference model for the bottom-up integration of dynamically composed microgranular architectural services [7, 20], and their models (Fig. 3).

Enterprise Architecture Management [13], as defined today by various standards such as [18], uses a fairly large number of different views and perspectives to manage current IT. An effective and agile architecture management approach for digital enterprises should also support the intelligent digitalization of products and services and be both holistic and easily adaptable [19]. A successful digital architecture should use a service platform [3] that supports a network of actors-to-actors and hosts a set of loosely coupled services as part of a rapidly growing digital ecosystem [2, 3]. A service platform is a modular structure that connects and integrates resources and actors sharing institutional logics [19] and promotes the value co-creation [1] through the exchange of services according to the service-dominant logic [2].

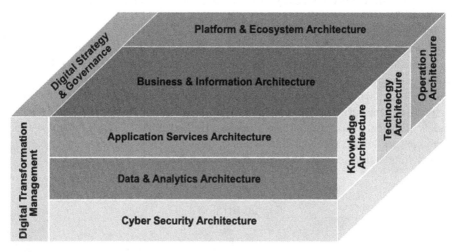

Fig. 3. Digital enterprise architecture reference cube.

The traditional operational backbone of core IT services [1] does not provide the transition speed and flexibility required for continuous, rapid, and agile digital innovation because it is designed for stability, reliability, and efficiency. As a result, digital enterprises are designing a second backbone for the use and hosting of digital services. The digital services backbone [14] brings together business and technology competencies that enable rapid development and deployment of digital innovation. The backbone of digital services includes: digital components as a set of business and technical services; platform as service: a technology environment that hosts large amounts of loosely coupled software as a service, such as microservices; repositories for the continuous collection of large amounts of human and sensor data; analytics to transform data insights into meaningful recommendations and links to data, systems, and processes from the operational backbone.

The ability of a platform to grow rapidly is based on the principle of network effects [1] and smooth entry points for a large number of new participants. Mature platforms often evolve towards greater openness. The value of platforms is derived from the community they serve. The design of a platform should first support its core interaction, which is easily accessible and inevitable. Therefore, a digital platform [2] should provide three core functions: Pull, facilitation, and matching. As the participants and resource base of the platform grows, participants will find new ways to interact to expand the core interaction. Digital platforms are superior to traditional fixed value chains because of the value generated by network effects, which often enable essential disruptive changes in business operations.

5   Evolution Path

Intelligent or smart service systems [21] bring together people, technology, organization, and information. Intelligent or cognitive digital systems [10] are instrumented by sensors and actors [20], store data in the cloud and are accessible from multiple devices. These systems are able to learn, adapt dynamically, and make decisions. Therefore, the design of intelligent service systems requires a clear understanding of human interaction with technology and a human-centric design [21].

Decision analytics offers increasingly complex support, especially in the development and evolution of sustainable digital architectures [19]. We can identify two far-reaching perspectives of software evolution: First, software can be designed to anticipate changes by the original software developer to facilitate evolution by predicting possible change perspectives of new software. The main mechanism of proactive change is based on the modularity of service structures. Secondly, software evolution can be managed during the maintenance phase by using specific tools and methods.

An important prerequisite for building and analyzing solid digital service systems and enterprise architectures [13, 19] is a formal understanding of the nature of services [7] and their model-based relationships. We currently have to consider a major shift from the traditional software engineering approaches of the closed world to open service systems with autonomous parts [20].

The main challenges of service computing for the next ten years lead to a redefinition of service computing, as postulated by [22]. The Service Computing Manifesto sets out a strategy that positions new concepts and technologies to support the service paradigm. The Service Computing Manifesto shows the development path of four main artifacts: Data, Information, Knowledge, and Service. The Service Computing Manifesto recommends focusing on four main research directions by specifying both challenges and a research roadmap: Service Design, Service Composition, Crowdsourcing Based Reputation, and the Internet of Things.

6   Conclusion and Future Research

Starting from our basic research question, we first set the context from digitalization and digital transformation to a systematic value-based digital service design according to the service-dominant logic. We identified suitable AI mechanisms to enable intelligent digital systems and services. To support the dynamics of digital transformation with intelligent digital systems, we have developed an adaptive architecture approach for digital enterprise architecture and a deeper understanding of an evolutionary path for both intelligent digital systems and their architecture. The strengths of our research result from our integral approach of an essential model mapping of digital strategies to value-based digital operating models for intelligent digital systems and services on a closely related digital platform, supported by a unified digital architecture reference model. The limitations of our work result from an ongoing validation of our research and open questions in the investigation of extended AI approaches and the management of inconsistencies and semantic dependencies. We are working on a platform to extend human-controlled dashboard-based architectural decision making with AI support.

References

1. Ross, J.W., Beath, C.M., Mocker, M.: Designed for Digital: How to Architect Your Business for Sustained Success. The MIT Press, Cambridge (2019)
2. Vargo, S.L., Akaka, M.A., Vaughan, C.M.: Conceptualizing value: a service-ecosystem view. J. Creating Value **3**(2), 1–8 (2017)
3. McAfee, A., Brynjolfsson, E.: Machine, Platform, Crowd: Harnessing Our Digital Future. W. W. Norton and Company, New York (2017)
4. Rogers, D.L.: The Digital Transformation Playbook. Columbia University Press, New York (2016)
5. Russel, S., Norvig, P.: Artificial Intelligence: A Modern Approach. Pearson, London (2015)
6. Poole, D.L., Mackworth, A.K.: Artificial Intelligence: Foundations of Computational Agents. Cambridge University Press, Cambridge (2018)
7. Newman, S.: Building Microservices Designing Fine-Grained Systems. O'Reilly Media, Sebastopol (2015)
8. Hamilton, E.R., Rosenberg, J.M., Akcaoglu, M.: Examining the substitution augmentation modification redefinition (SAMR) model for technology integration. Tech Trends **60**(5), 433–441 (2016)
9. Warren, A.: Amazon Echo: The Ultimate Amazon Echo User Guide 2016 Become an Alexa and Echo Expert Now!. CreateSpace Independent Publishing, Scotts Valley (2016)
10. Hwang, K.: Cloud Computing for Machine Learning and Cognitive Applications. The MIT Press, Cambridge (2017)
11. Munakata, T.: Fundamentals of the New Artificial Intelligence: Neural, Evolutionary, Fuzzy and More. Springer, Berlin (2008)
12. Skansi, S.: Introduction to Deep Learning. Springer, Berlin (2018)
13. Lankhorst, M.: Enterprise Architecture at Work: Modelling, Communication and Analysis, 4th edn. Springer, Berlin (2017)
14. Ross, J.W., Sebastian, I.M., Beath, C., Mocker, M., Moloney, K.G., Fonstad, N.O.: Designing and executing digital strategies. In: Proceedings of ICIS, Dublin (2016)
15. Osterwalder, A., Pigneur, Y.: Business Model Generation. Wiley, Hoboken (2010)
16. Osterwalder, A., Pigneur, Y., Bernarda, G., Smith, A., Papadokos, T.: Value Proposition Design. Wiley, Hoboken (2014)
17. Meertens, L.O., Iacob, M.E., Nieuwenhuis, L.J.M., van Sinderen, M.J., Jonkers, H., Quertel, D.: Mapping the Business Model canvas to ArchiMate. In: Proceedings of SAC 2012, pp. 1694–1701. ACM (2012)
18. Open Group: ArchiMate 3.0 Specification. The Open Group (2016)

19. Zimmermann, A., Schmidt, R., Sandkuhl, K., Jugel, D., Bogner, J., Möhring, M.: Architecting service-dominant digital products. In: Damiani, E., Spanoudakis, G., Maciaszek, L.A. (eds.) ENASE 2018. CCIS, vol. 1023, pp. 45–67. Springer, Cham (2019). https://doi.org/10.1007/978-3-030-22559-9_3
20. Atzori, L., Iera, A., Morabito, G.: The Internet of Things: a survey. J. Comput. Netw. **54**, 2787–2805 (2010)
21. Spohrer, J., Siddike, M.A.K., Kohda, Y.: Rebuilding evolution: a service science perspective. In: Proceedings of HICSS 2017, pp. 1663–1672 (2017)
22. Bouguettaya, A., et al.: A service computing manifesto: the next 10 years. Commun. ACM **60**(4), 64–72 (2017)

Human Factors in Information Systems

Online Peer Support Groups for Behavior Change: Moderation Requirements

Manal Aldhayan[1(✉)], Mohammad Naiseh[1], John McAlaney[1], and Raian Ali[2]

[1] Bournemouth University, Poole, UK
{maldhayan,mnaiseh,jmcalaney}@bournemouth.ac.uk
[2] College of Science and Engineering, Hamad Bin Khalifa University, Doha, Qatar
raali2@hbku.edu.qa

Abstract. Technology-assisted behaviour awareness and change is on the rise. Examples include apps and sites for fitness, healthy eating, mental health and smoking cessation. These information systems recreated principles of influence and persuasion in a digital form allowing real-time observation, interactivity and intervention. Peer support groups are one of the behavioural influence techniques which showed various benefits, including hope installation and relapse prevention. However, unmoderated groups may become a vehicle for comparisons and unmanaged interactions leading to digression, normalising the negative behaviour and lowering self-esteem. A typical requirement of such groups is to be of a social and supportive nature whereas moderation, through humans or artificial agents, may face a risk of being seen as centralised and overly managed governance approach. In this paper, we explore the requirements and different preferences about moderators as seen by members. We follow a mixed-method approach consisting of a qualitative phase that included two focus groups and 16 interviews, followed by a quantitative phase, including a survey with 215 participants who declared having well-being issues. We report on the qualitative phase findings achieved through thematic analysis. We also report and discuss the survey results studying the role of gender, self-control, personality traits, culture, the perception of usefulness and willingness to join the group as predictors of the members' expectations from moderators, resulted from the qualitative phase.

Keywords: Human factors in information systems · Peer support groups · Behaviour change system

1 Introduction

There is a growing number of studies on the use of technology to combat problematic behaviour and enhance wellbeing. Examples include the use of mobile apps for smoking cessation, improving mental health, fitness, diet and physical activities [21]. The advances in sensing technology and handheld devices combined with the ubiquitous connectivity to internet created opportunities for utilising technology to assist behavioural change and self-regulation systems in a more intelligent, contextualised and situation-aware style. Such solutions have been applied both in work environments, e.g.

© Springer Nature Switzerland AG 2020
F. Dalpiaz et al. (Eds.): RCIS 2020, LNBIP 385, pp. 157–173, 2020.
https://doi.org/10.1007/978-3-030-50316-1_10

gamifying task performance [29], and in a personal context such as enhancing wellbeing and combatting problematic behaviour [19, 20].

Most technology-assisted behaviour awareness applications available in the market and discussed in the literature are meant for a single user where the communication is between the software and the user and where exploitation of social techniques, such as peer learning and support, is limited. The main challenge of these information systems was typically to engage users with such solutions and increase their retention [33]. For example, Ciocarlan et al. [28] studied and designed an application around happiness where user engagement was maximised by sending different persuasive messages for activities to do. Feedback messages about individual performance are the main techniques utilised in health applications to motivate users and keep them engaged [24].

The strategies and techniques used to motivate, and influence behaviour can differ according to the personal and environmental context. Factors such as age, personality traits, gender and culture have been studied, and such differences were identified. Orji and Mandryk [25] studied the effect of culture on the persuasive intervention in the context of healthy eating behaviour change applications, as well as the role of gender and age groups as moderating factors. Also, Orji et al. [26] studied the effect of gender and age on the six principles of influence proposed by Cialdini [30] and showed significant differences. Mainly, it showed that females are more responsive to most of the influence strategies than males. Alkis and Temizel [27] studied the relationship between personality traits and the effectiveness of Cialdini strategies and showed significant differences. For example, people with high agreeableness (as one of the Big Five personality traits model [31]) are more likely to be affected by the opinions of others whether peer, i.e. social proof, or authority (two of Cialdini strategies [30]).

Online peer groups are a type of technology-assisted behaviour awareness software that is meant to provide peer support, counselling, motivational and learning environment, and ambivalence reduction through sharing and hope installation. Online peer groups are a synthesis of various influence strategies, including peer pressure, commitment and goal setting, surveillance, and authority through moderator or caregiver. This means that online peer groups, in their governance, design, acceptance and rejection can similarly be affected by variables like gender, personality traits, culture and self-control. Peer groups are typically moderated to prevent unintended harmful interactions within them. They may become a forum for learning or boosting negative behaviours and normalising the problematic behaviour and reducing the sense of culpability of committing it due to excessive peer emotional support [22]. However, the moderator role is delicate as the spirit of groups is social and authority can be seen as overly restrictive and deter members from joining, entice reactance, conformity and dishonesty.

In this paper, we explore the peer groups members perception of the moderator role and how their personal and cultural characteristics can affect that perception. This is to help the engineering of online peer groups platforms so that moderators are assisted by tools and access needed to play their role and also to help the governance strategies and configuration of such online platforms. As a method, we adopted a mixed-method approach exploring in its qualitative phase the members' perception of the role of the moderator and in its quantitative face, the effect of gender, self-control, personality traits, culture and the perception of usefulness and willingness to join the group on that perception. Such users' studies yield important knowledge for health and social information systems design and increasing users' acceptance [34, 35].

2 Research Method

We adopted a mixed-methods approach which consisted of an initial qualitative phase followed by a quantitative phase. The participants in both phases self-declared to have problematic behaviour, mainly online behaviour, that has been affecting their wellbeing issues.

2.1 Qualitative Phase: Exploring Participants Perception of the Moderator Role

We first conducted a focus group study consisting of two sessions. The first session aimed at getting insights into how online peer groups are perceived by people who self-declared to have problematic online behaviour and what they needed to see in it. The second focus group aimed at identifying the design of online peer groups platforms where mock interfaces were made available to the participants. The interfaces were based on the results of the first focus group, and the participants were able to amend and comment on them. The two focus group sessions were conducted with the same six university students; three male and three females, aged between 20 and 26. The participants were a social group in real life, and this was beneficial as it removed concerns regarding trust and privacy during the discussion process. We performed a thematic analysis [23] on the data collected through the sessions and analysed the annotations on the interfaces. The analysis revealed main factors concerning the (i) acceptance and (ii) rejection factors of this approach as well as (iii) governance styles and (iv) moderator profile and role.

Then we performed in-depth interviews to delve into the details of these themes. For example, we explored the role of feedback and monitoring, membership and exit protocol within the governance theme and the skills expected, allocation strategy and authority within the moderator role. We conducted 16 interviews with students who self-declared to have a wellbeing issue around their digital behaviour, e.g., obsessive or compulsive use. The sample consisted of 8 males and 8 females, aged between 18 and 35. Each interview lasted between 30 and 40 min. The interviews were transcribed and analysed via thematic analysis [23].

2.2 Quantitative Stage: Members' Profile Effect on Perception of Moderator

We designed a survey around the interview findings, which included the perception of moderator and their role. The survey was disseminated both online and in person. A £5 incentive was offered to respondents given the lengthy nature of the survey. We collected 215 completed responses; 105 (49%) male and 109 (50%) Female and one participant preferred not to answer on the gender question. The participants were 17 to 55 years old. The survey started with a validation question of whether a participant has wellbeing issues as a precondition to take part.

To study the effect of personal and environmental factors on the perception of moderator, the survey included questions around six factors which were gender (male/female);

country; perceived usefulness of peer support groups; willingness to join a peer support group; the five personality traits [31] (extraversion, agreeableness, conscientiousness, neuroticism and openness); and self-control [32]. The survey included 29 questions around the six themes of moderator roles which were the findings from the qualitative study, summarised in Table 1 and Table 2. The moderator roles Likert scale questions are based on "agreeing" or "disagreeing" with five rating scale. We disseminated the survey mainly in the UK, the Kingdom of Saudi Arabia (KSA) and Syria. We collected 104 completed surveys from KSA and Syria (55 male/49 female, mean age = 26.7, SD = 6.39), and 85 from the UK (35 male/50 female, mean age = 24.07, SD = 6.39) while the rest were from other countries, mainly in Europe. This allowed us to study statistically whether there was a difference between Middle Eastern culture (KSA and Syria) and Western culture (UK). As such, the total sample size used within the analysis reported here was 189.

3   Moderation Requirements: Members Perspective

The qualitative phase analysis revealed six main themes are summarised in Fig. 1 and Fig. 2. Table 1 and Table 2 include the phrasing in survey questions which was used to reflect the qualitative findings. In the survey, we aggregated codes further to reduce the number of survey options.

3.1   Moderator Nature

The analysis indicated various requirements of the group moderator's traits, especially of the sentient nature of the moderator. Participants have three viewpoints regarding the

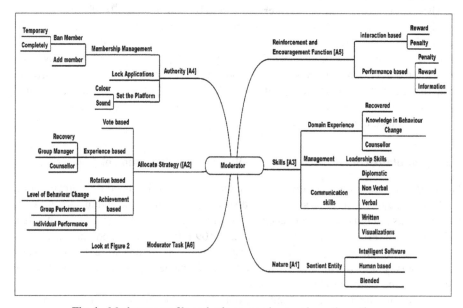

Fig. 1. Moderator profile and role as seen by members: thematic map

Table 1. Moderator profile and role as seen by members: a table view

Theme	Sub-theme
[A1] Moderator nature	[A1.1] Software, e.g. automatic target calculation and advice-giving [A1.2] Human [A1.3] Blended, i.e. human and software together
[A2] Moderator allocation strategy	[A2.1] Voting by members [A2.2] Experience-based, e.g. experience in group management, counselling, previous success, etc. [A2.3] Rota-based, i.e. each member becomes a moderator for sometime [A2.4] Performance, e.g. those who prove to be a helper to others, enhancing personal wellbeing score, etc.
[A3] Moderator skills	[A3.1] Had the well-being issue in the past and recovered from it [A3.2] High communication skills [A3.3] Management and leadership skills
[A4] Moderator authority	[A4.1] To manage membership, e.g. adding new members and banning members who violate the rules [A4.2] To ban members from doing certain activities, e.g. banning video games and social media at night hours [A4.3] To set up the online environment, e.g. the colours, the forum topics, the sounds, the reminders
[A5] Moderator reinforcement role	[A5.1] Reward members based on the improvement of their performance [A5.2] Issue penalty based on the poor performance [A5.3] Reward members based on interactions, e.g. help others and adherence to chat rules [A5.4] Issue penalty based on interactions within the online group

moderator's nature. The first viewpoint [A1.1] was that the platform should be managed by intelligent software which would provide "*24-h help, and advice and members will get a response immediately from the moderator*". The second viewpoint [A1.2] was that the moderator should be human and that "*would help to understand members feelings and provide support based on a human experience*". The last viewpoint [A1.3] recommended that the platform is designed to have blended management which has both human and software management. The participants argued that the platform should be assisted by intelligent software and administered and configured by a human moderator for tailoring, scheduling and sending notifications and feedback messages. Participants emphasised that human moderator is more credible for providing emotional support and personalised dialogue.

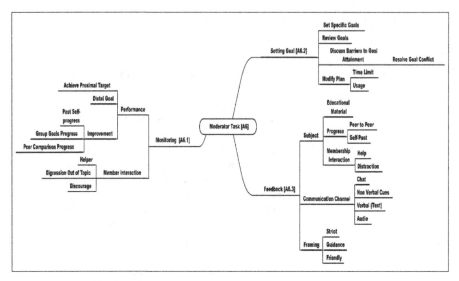

Fig. 2. Moderator tasks as seen by members: thematic map

3.2 Moderator Allocation Strategy

There has not been a consensus on the strategy to allocate moderator and different viewpoints were expressed. The first opinion [A2.1] was that moderator allocation is done based on voting technique and *"group members should vote for the group moderator, the moderator could be a group member, or persons offer themselves to be moderator"*. The second opinion [A2.2] is that moderator allocation should be based on personal experiences such as having the same problem as the members in the past or skills in group management and counselling. The third opinion [A2.3] is that the moderator allocation should be a rota-based and everyone is given a chance to play it as this *"would help members to learn how to be moderator"* and also increase their belongingness and relatedness to others. The last opinion [A2.4] is that group moderators should be one of the group members and allocated based on the past performance and goals achieved. A participant commented that *"the member who has achieved most of the group goals or collected more points could become the moderator of the group"* and act as a role model.

3.3 Moderator Skills

The facet of moderator knowledge and experience was highlighted as one of the most important factors which would motivate members to join a group and engage in its interactions. Different requirements were expressed. The first [A3.1] was domain experience, such as having had the same issue in the pasting and overcoming it so that their advice and support are more influential. The second [A3.2] related to having communication skills including verbal, non-verbal, written, visualizations and diplomatic skills. The participants justified the need for diplomatic skills believing that this would help members epically when they set collective goals requiring all of them to work together and also help to manage the members' interactions and potential tensions. The third [A3.3]

Table 2. Moderator tasks as seen by members: a table view

Theme	[A6] Moderator tasks
[A6.x] Sub-theme	[A6.x.y] Sub-Sub-theme
[A6.1] Monitor group members	[A6.1.1] Access the data about members' performance, e.g. achievement of goals and progress made towards them [A6.1.2] Access data around the style of communication of members, e.g. reports indicating members to be helpful, distractor, digression, etc.
[A6.2] Manage performance goals	[A6.2.1] Specify performance goals for members [A6.2.2] Modify goals for members, e.g. grant an extension [A6.2.3] Review goal achievement with members frequently [A6.2.4] Discuss barriers to goals achievement with members, e.g. resolving conflicting goals [A6.2.5] Send personalised best practices and advice on how to achieve goals to members
[A6.3] Provide feedback	[A6.3.1] Send feedback about how the group is performing as a whole, i.e. collectively [A6.3.2] Send feedback about self-progress to members, e.g. their self-improvement [A6.3.3] Send feedback to members about their interaction, e.g. being seen as a helper or distractor [A6.3.4] Choose the communication channel to use with members, e.g. text, audio, non-verbal such as emoji, chat, etc. [A6.3.5] Choose the framing and the tone of the feedback, e.g. guidance, assertive, strict, friendly, etc.

related to leadership and management skills. The participants felt that the moderator who has leadership skills would be able *"to explain in clear steps how to achieve the goals"* and what is expected for them to do so and be able to follow up.

3.4 Moderator Authority

It was generally agreed that moderators should have the power to manage group membership, restrict some interactions and actions and change the platform interface. The first authority aspect [A4.1] related to managing membership, such as adding members and keeping groups live so that *"if a member leaves the group the group moderator should have the ability to replace them with a new member"*. The second [A4.2] related to the ability to ban members based on progress or unhealthy and negative interactions with others. A participant commented that *"any member who doesn't interact with other group members could be banned for a period of time by the moderator"* as this is against the spirit of being in a group. Others suggested that *"any member who distracts other members could be banned"*. The third moderator authority aspect [A4.3] related to the manager ability to change the online platform settings such as the colours, available emoji and notification sounds. Participants mentioned that this could be for cosmetics purposes but also to reflect progress, e.g. the use of colours to indicate group member performance and collective performance.

3.5 Reinforcement and Encouragement Functions

Participants felt that the online peer groups should provide tools for the moderator to apply reinforcement and encouragement functions around both the performance towards achieving goals and the interactions with other members. The moderator shall be able to reward [A5.1] and issue penalty [A5.2] based on tracking and comparing member performance in relation to achieving goals. Similarly, the moderator shall be able to give rewards [A5.3] and issue penalty [A5.4] based on the characteristics of the interactions of a member within the group, e.g. being helpful, adhering to the chat rules, and avoiding distraction and private messaging outside the group. A user who becomes a helper, for example, by helping other group members with advice and moral support should *"get points and a member who has high points could become group admin as a reward"*. Penalty, such as reducing points or banning members, temporarily or completely should be related to when *"violating the group norms and disturbing others"*. The participants appreciated that the group moderator should be able to monitor the group members' progress and performance toward their goals and interactions. Also, the participants thought members performance and interaction shall not be measured in a uniform style as members roles and stage of behaviour change can be different.

3.6 Moderator Tasks

The group moderator is considered central to running and managing the online peer groups. The participants suggested various preferences and opinions around the set of activities and tasks for moderators which are [A6.1] Monitor group members, [A6.2] Manage performance goals and [A6.3] Provide feedback.

Monitor Group Members. The participants recommended that two requirements should be considered when designing the group monitoring system administered by the moderator. The first design requirement is that the moderator is able to monitor group members' performances [A6.1.1] and require the moderator should be able to *"monitor group member's progress and achievement and compare it with other group members"*. The second requirement is that the moderator should have the ability to monitor the group's communication style and interactions, such as being a distraction or helper [A6.1.2]. Monitoring members' interactions such as *"monitor messages and feedback send between members"*, the interaction could be positive or annoying messages.

Manage Performance Goals. The participants highlighted the importance of setting goals and considered it as one of the moderator's tasks and they suggested various opinions to the moderator when managing performance goals. The first opinion recommended moderator should specify performance goals for members [A6.2.1] and the participants suggested the online peer group platforms should be designed to "*allow moderators to set goals specifically for new members*". Some of the participants mentioned that some of the group members had difficulty controlling their behaviour and they required "*more help and support from moderators, specifically in setting their own goals*".

The second viewpoint was that the moderator should be able to modify goals for members [A6.2.2]. The participants suggested two various ways of modifying the goals. The first viewpoint is that the moderator should be able to stop the tracking system for specific users for a period. For example, a participant said that "*I am a student and sometimes I use digital media for study purposes, so it is useful if the moderator enables me to stop the tracking system, after contacting the moderator and clarifying a reasonable reason*". The second viewpoint is the platform should be designed to enable the moderator to change the time-plan for a specific user. For example, a participant mentioned that "*sometimes I am doing something important or I am travelling so I need extra time on specific days' the moderator should be able to change the time plan*".

The third requirement is that the moderator should be able to review individual and collective goals [A6.2.3] and have the ability to modify the goals to become achievable goals that would motivate users to commit to the group goals. The fourth opinion is that the moderator should have the ability to discuss with members the "*barriers to goal attainment*" [A6.2.4]. The last opinion is moderator should be able to send personalised best practices and advice on how to achieve goals to members [A6.2.5].

Provide Feedback. The participants suggested various design requirements of the moderator feedback; also, they recommended several features to moderator feedback which included reason and subject of the feedback, communication channel and feedback framing. The interview analysis indicated that participants required various requirements about the feedback's reasons and subject, the first requirement is to send feedback about how the group is performing [A6.3.1]. The moderator feedback should be based on "*compare peer progress with a specific peer*" that has a similar profile or demography. Participants argue that peer-to-peer progress feedback would help them to know their progress level and identify if their progress is good, or if they or need to work more to achieve the group goals.

The second requirements suggested moderator provide feedback about self-progress to members [A6.3.2]. The participants recommended that the moderator feedback should be based on "*compare current performance and past-performance which would help to know the progress and would encourage achieving the usage goals*". Moreover, participants felt that the moderator feedback is not only about user performance and progress; they recommended that the feedback should involve member's interaction within the group [A6.3.3].

The fourth requirement is that the moderator should choose the communication channel to use with members [A6.3.4]. Participants suggested different communication preferences and moderator feedback, such as receiving feedback as writing, non-verbal cues such as emoji's, pop-up text messages or in chatrooms, whether audio or text. The last requirement is that the moderator should choose the framing and the tone of the feedback [A6.3.5]. Participants mentioned two types of framing in which is a positive frame or frame the feedback to have "*an order and gaudiness*". Also, the participants mentioned the importance of feedback tone; they suggested that the feedback tone should be "*strict and more formal*". In their opinion, strict feedback should be more effective and forced to follow the moderator guide and advice.

4   Moderation Requirements: Personal and Cultural Effects

A series of linear multiple regressions using the enter method were conducted on the survey results. In each model the predictors were *gender* (male/female); *country* (UK/Middle East); *perceived usefulness* of peer support groups; *willingness to join* a peer support group; the *five personality trait* scores of extraversion, agreeableness, conscientiousness, neuroticism and openness; and finally, the *self-control* score. For each model, the outcome measure was the individual questions used to measure attitudes relating to the moderator role and tasks, as identified within the description of each model result in the section below. Multicollinearity diagnostic was conducted prior to the analysis to determine the suitability of conducting multiple regressions.

4.1   Moderator Nature [A1]

In term of the nature of the moderator models, we found that none of the models was significant for the three outcome measures relating to this topic were significant, which were [A1.1] *Software, e.g. automatic target calculation and advice-giving;* [A1.2] *Human;* or [A1.3] *Blended, i.e. human and software together.*

4.2   The Strategy for Allocating Human Moderators [A2]

The strategy for allocating group moderator has four models; the regression analysis indicated that one of the models tested within this section was significant. The findings showed that [A2.1] *voting by group members* is a significant model for allocating the group moderator. Voting by members significantly predicted 12% of the variance (R^2 = .12, $F (10,160) = 2.12$, $p < .05$), with the significant predictors being perceived usefulness of online peer support groups ($\beta = -.21$), willingness to join online peer support groups ($\beta = .25$), openness ($\beta = -.09$) and self-control ($\beta = -.03$). As such as perceived usefulness of online peer support groups increased if the agreement with the strategy of voting by members increased; however conversely willingness to join online peer support groups decreased as an agreement with this strategy increased. As both openness and self-control increase is a decrease as acceptance of the strategy decreases. The models for the three remaining strategies ([A2.2], [A2.3] and [A2.4]) within this section were non-significant.

4.3   Moderator Skills [A3]

In term of the moderator skills models, we found that none of the models was significant for the three outcome measures relating to this topic, which were [A3.1] Had the wellbeing issue themselves in the past and recovered from it; [A3.2] High communication skills (verbal and non-verbal, diplomacy, motivating language, etc.); [A3.3] Knowledge, e.g. behavioural change, management and leadership skills.

4.4 Moderator Authority [A4]

In term of the moderator authority in the peer group, the analysis found that one of the models within the section was significant. The model for [A4.1] Manage membership, e.g. adding new members and banning members who violate the rules, etc. ($R^2 = .15$, $F(10,160) = 2.74$, p < .01) accounted for 15% of the variance was significantly predicted by the single predictor of conscientiousness ($\beta = .19$). As such acceptance of this strategy increased as conscientiousness increased. The other two models ([A4.2] and [A4.3]) were not significant.

4.5 Ability and Responsibility to Apply Reinforcement Functions [A5]

The responsibility of the moderator to issue rewards and penalties has four models. The regression analysis finding showed that two of the models in this section were significant. The outcome of [A5.1] Rewards to members based on the improvement of their performance model ($R^2 = .15$, F $(10,160) = 2.19$, p < .05) accounted for 15% of the variance and was significantly predicted by agreeableness ($\beta = .09$), conscientiousness ($\beta = .12$) and self-control ($\beta -.03$). As such acceptance of this strategy increases as does agreeableness and conscientiousness; however, as self-control increases acceptance of the strategy decreases. The outcome of [A5.3] Rewards based on the member's interactions within the online group, e.g. helping others, etc. model ($R^2 = .11$, F $(10,160) = 1.98$, p < .05) accounted for 11% of the variance and was significantly predicted equally by agreeableness ($\beta = .10$) and conscientiousness ($\beta = .10$). The other two models within this section ([A5.2] and [A5.4]) were not significant.

4.6 Moderator Tasks [A6]

[A6.1] Moderator Ability and Responsibility to Monitor the Group Members.
One of the moderator tasks is to monitor the group members, which was analysed with two models. The regression analysis findings show that one model in this section was significant. The finding showed that [A6.1.2] *Access data around the style of communication of members, e.g. reports indicating members to be helpful, distractor, digression, etc.* model ($R^2 = .12$, (F $(10.160) = 2.222$, p < .05) accounted for 12% of the variance, with two predictors significantly contributing to the model: conscientiousness ($\beta = .13$), and self-control ($\beta = -.03$). As such acceptance of this strategy increased as conscientiousness increased; however, as self-control increases acceptance of the strategy decreases. The other model in this section [A6.1.1] was not significant.

[A6.2] Moderator Ability and Responsibility to Manage Performance Goals.
The responsibility of the moderator to manage performance goals has five models. The regression analysis showed that three models in this section were significant. The model [A6.2.1] *specify performance goals for members* ($R^2 = .12$, F $(10,160) = 2.317$, p < .05) accounted for 12% of the variance and was significantly predicted by conscientiousness ($\beta = .08$), and self-control ($\beta = -.02$). As such acceptance of strategy increased as conscientiousness increased, however, as self-control increases acceptance of the strategy decreases. The outcome of [A6.2.3] *The strategy of Review goal achievement with*

members frequently ($R^2 = .12$, F (2.233), p < .01) accounted for 12% of the variance and was significantly predicted by the willingness to join online peer support groups ($\beta = .19$), conscientiousness ($\beta = .09$) and neuroticism ($\beta = .07$). As such as acceptance of strategy increased as the willingness to join online peer support groups and neuroticism increased; however, respondents from the Middle East were significantly less likely to demonstrate acceptance of this strategy. The other three models within this section were not significant, which had the outcomes of [A6.2.2], [A6.2.4] and [A6.2.5].

[A6.3] Moderator Responsibility and Permission to Provide Feedback to Members. In term of the moderator provide feedback, the analysis found that two models within section were significant. The model for [A6.3.2] *Send feedback about self-progress to members, e.g. their self-improvement* ($R^2 = .12$, F (10, 160), p < .05) accounted for 12% of the variance was significantly predicted by the single predictor of self-control ($\beta = -0.025$). As such acceptance of this strategy increased as does self-control decreased. The model for [A6.3.4] *Choose the communication channel to use with members, e.g. text, audio, non-verbal such as emoji, chat, etc.* was significant ($R^2 = .15$, F (10,160) = 2.712), p < 0.05), accounting for 15% of the variance, significantly predicted by the three predictors. These were culture, extraversion and openness ($\beta = -.49$), ($\beta = -.13$), ($\beta = -.11$). As such, both extraversion and openness increased, acceptance of the strategy decreases. There was significantly greater acceptance of this strategy in the UK than in the Middle East.

The model for [A6.3.5] *Choose the framing and the tone of the feedback, e.g. guidance, assertive, strict, friendly, etc.* was significant ($R^2 = .14$, F (10,160), p < .01), accounting for 14% of the variance of the model. This was predicted by culture and self-control ($\beta = -.29$) and ($\beta = -.31$). As such acceptance of this strategy increased as self-control decreased, and the strategy was significantly more likely to be accepted in the UK than the Middle East. Both models for [A6.3.1] and [A6.3.3] were not significant.

5 Discussion

The regressions that were found to be significant accounted for approximately 12 – 15% of the variance in each outcome measure. As such, they in part, explain the reported attitudes and opinions, albeit it to a relatively small degree. The two personality traits of agreeableness and conscientiousness, along with self-control, were consistently amongst the significant predictors. This is perhaps as would be expected, as each of these predictors can feasibly relate to how accepting an individual is to be part of a group and to have their actions shaped and monitored by members in that group.

It is interesting to note which predictors were not found to be significant. The model for a preference towards the moderator being human, software or a combination of both was not significant. This is in contrast to various models of technology acceptance, from which it could be expected that individuals may not respond to technology-based agents in the same way as human group members [1]. In addition, it has been found consistently throughout social psychological research that individuals exhibit biases when comparing their own knowledge and skills against those of their peers (for example [2]). In relation to the results of the current study, this may suggest that people do not distinguish between a moderator who is human and one who is software-based. Research into the leader-member exchange theory in a range of domains, including health information management [3], has demonstrated that the relationship between a leader and a group is complex, with expectations on the part of the group members on how the group should be managed. Despite this, the regression models for moderators' skills (knowledge, leadership communication) were also not significant. Given this, it is of interest that none of the predictors appeared to differentiate between human and software-based group moderators.

The model for moderator allocation occurring through a voting system was significant, although it is notable that whilst the perception of the usefulness of this strategy was a positive predictor, the willingness to join such a group was a negative predictor. This may suggest that individuals recognise the benefits of the democratic process of choosing the moderator through an election, without necessarily wishing to be subject to the consequences of this voting process. This could relate to the need to *assert uniqueness*, which refers to the drive individuals have to demonstrate that they are not bound by social rules [4]. This could reflect an awareness of the part of the respondents of the phenomena of *groupthink*, in which groups are observed to make more risky, extreme and often objectively worse decision than individuals do alone [5]. Avoiding unintended consequences such as these are of course one of the underlying reasons why the group would have a moderator in the first instance; however, given the relative novelty of moderator facilitated online peer support groups it is possible that when asked about this respondents struggled to conceptualised what was meant.

Social facilitation occurs when the presence of an audience improves performance, as explained by drive theory [6]. This may result in part account for the significant regression model which found that the personality traits of agreeableness and conscientiousness positively predicted the acceptance of rewards within the group, although it was also noted that increased self-control appeared to reduce the acceptance of this strategy. This suggests that there is a trade-off between the willingness to engage in this strategy and the desire to maintain personal independence and control. Related to this is evaluation apprehension, in which performance is negatively impacted by the presence of others [7]. This may account for the non-significant regressions models relating to applying penalties to members for poor performance, i.e. individuals may be receptive of the concept of group monitoring provided that this is not associated with evaluation or punishment. This is in keeping with previous research, which suggests that whilst group membership typically decreases *evaluation apprehension,* this only occurs when the individual knows they will not be scrutinised individually [8]. In the case of online peer support groups individuals may perceive that their actions are highly quantifiable and traceable, leading to an increase in evaluation apprehension.

There is limited research on the relationship between personality and preferred group moderation characteristics in either online or offline settings. There is though some research on personality and management styles within organisation that are of relevance to this study, such as for example [9], which found that openness and conscientiousness contributed towards group performance, when managed appropriately. Both personality traits were significant predictors in several of the regression models conducted within this study. However, several other personality traits were not significant predictors in any of the models. This includes neuroticism, which refers to the tendency to experience emotions such as anxiety, fear, frustration and loneliness. Given the nature of the proposed online peer support groups, and the aforementioned possibility of phenomena such as apprehension evaluation occurring, it is odd that this personality trait was not a significant predictor.

The overall pattern of results was reflected in relation to the tasks, responsibilities and powers of the group moderator, with the significant predictors with the significant models typically including self-control and the personality trait of conscientiousness. These results can be considered in relation to research into power and group dynamics in groups. It has been noted, for example, that group members expect those with a leadership role within a group to adhere to the social norms of that group [10]. This reflects the comments made by participants that they would accept rules and permissions determined by the moderator, provided that these are transparent and fair. It was found that participants from the UK were more likely to wish to have control over how these tasks and permissions were controlled. This is consistent with research from Hofstede Insights, which suggests that the UK scores are higher on individualism and power distance as compared to the KSA and Syria [11]. This relationship between culture and power within-group leadership roles has, however, been found to be a complex one, with for example, leaders who violate norms in individualistic cultures being viewed as more powerful. Similarly, identification with the group has been found to be associated with a greater sense of responsibility for the wellbeing of the group [12]. This highlights the importance of those individuals who have the power within the group having an investment in that group. Finally, it was noted that some participants stated a preference for direct and authoritarian styles of communication from the moderator provided that, as noted previously, this did not violate the expectations and social norms of the group. It has been observed within sports psychology research that whilst prescriptive and authoritarian approaches to behaviour change are increasingly seen as outdated they can in some contexts nevertheless still be effective, particularly in relation to deviation from desired behaviour [13].

Previous research into gender would suggest the males and females make different use of social support networks to manage behaviour change [14]; including within internet support groups [15]. This was not found to be the case in this study, as gender was not a significant predictor in any of the significant regression models. Similarly, culture was not a significant predictor in the majority of models. These are both factors which could be expected to impact on attitudes towards peer group hierarchies and purposes, and so it is of interest that they appeared to be of relatively little importance with regards to online behaviour change peer support groups in this study. Again there is a lack of research on this particular topic, with little understanding of how group dynamics are influenced by cultural factors [16]. This may reflect a criticism that has been made of psychological research, which it relies too heavily upon samples from Western countries [17]. The research reported in this study contributes to reducing this gap.

Overall several predictors within the regression models reported in this study should, as based on previous psychological research, be reasonably expected to significantly predict attitudes towards the moderation of online peer groups. The fact that they did not is important, both for our theoretical understanding and for the practical implementation of such systems. As identified by [18] with reference to the online disinhibition effect, there is a question over whether the internet enhances or transforms; that is whether it causes people to behave in fundamentally different ways when online, or if it enhances pre-existing traits and processes. This is not a question that has been definitively addressed within the research literature and, as this study illustrates, is something we must investigate further if effective and appropriate behaviour change systems are to be developed.

6 Conclusion

In this paper, we extended our work in [36], where we studied the acceptance and rejection factors of online peer support groups and investigated the role and tasks of the moderator of such groups. Such groups are purpose-driven social networks which are meant to encourage and boost positive behaviour and prevent relapse. We did the investigation qualitatively and quantitatively with people who self-declared to have wellbeing issues. The understanding of their views is meant to help the design of the online platforms that host peer support groups in Human-Centered Design (HCD) approach. For example, it helps in the decision of the tools to make available to moderators to manage the groups in facets like memberships and rewards. It also helps governance processes and common grounds formation, e.g. in the allocation of moderators and their management style. Tailoring the group moderation settings correctly can help to prevent negative side effects such as members' reactance and lowering their self-esteem and to increase commitment to groups and their mission. Finally, this study contributes to the literature by helping the elicitation and customisation of the requirements and design of social behaviour change tools, mainly on what moderation aspects to be studied and analysed and fitted to the application domain. In the wider context, this study is meant towards an interdisciplinary systems analysis and design where social sciences and psychology support software engineering processes, especially where mistakes in the design can lead to negative behaviour and cause harm to users. Most commercial apps around behaviour change seem to lack theory-informed design. They are mainly focused on usability and attractiveness and seem to apply engagement elements, such as gamification, in ad-hoc style instead of robust evidence and established theories.

References

1. Taherdoost, H.: A review of technology acceptance and adoption models and theories. Proc. Manuf. **22**, 960–967 (2018)
2. Olson, J.M., Ross, M.: False feedback about placebo effectiveness - consequences for the misattribution of speech anxiety. J. Exp. Soc. Psychol. **24**(4), 275–291 (1988)
3. Hunt, T.J.: Leader-member exchange relationships in health information management. Perspect Health Inf. Manag. **11**(Spring) (2014)
4. Imhoff, R., Erb, H.P.: What motivates nonconformity? Uniqueness seeking blocks majority influence. Pers. Soc. Psychol. Bull. **35**(3), 309–320 (2009)
5. Schafer, M., Crichlow, S.: Antecedents of groupthink: a quantitative study. J. Conflict Resolut. **40**(3), 415–435 (1996)

6. Zajonc, R.B.: Social facilitation. Science **149**, 269–274 (1965)
7. Platania, J., Moran, G.P.: Social facilitation as a function of the mere presence of others. J. Soc. Psychol. **141**(2), 190–197 (2001)
8. Crisp, R.J., Turner, R.N.: Essential Social Psychology, vol. 4th. SAGE Publications India Pvt. Ltd., Thousand Oaks (2017). pages cm
9. Dai, S.L., Li, Y.C., Zhang, W.: Personality traits of entrepreneurial top management team members and new venture performance. Soc. Behav. Pers. **47**(7), 15 (2019)
10. Stamkou, E., van Kleef, G.A., Homan, A.C.: Feeling entitled to rules: entitled individuals prevent norm violators from rising up the ranks. J. Exp. Soc. Psychol. **84**(1), 10 (2019)
11. Hofstede Insights. Compare countries (2019). https://www.hofstede-insights.com/product/compare-countries/. Accessed 28 April 2019
12. Scholl, A., Sassenberg, K., Ellemers, N., Scheepers, D., De Wit, F.: Highly identified power-holders feel responsible: the interplay between social identification and social power within groups. Brit. J. Soc. Psychol. **57**(1), 112–129 (2018)
13. Delrue, J., Soenens, B., Morbée, S., Vansteenkiste, M., Haerens, L.: Do athletes' responses to coach autonomy support and control depend on the situation and athletes' personal motivation? Psychol. Sport Exerc. **43**, 321–332 (2019)
14. Matud, M.a.P., Ibañez, I., Bethencourt, J.M., Marrero, R., Carballeira, M.: Structural gender differences in perceived social support. Pers. Individ. Differ. **35**(8), 1919–1929 (2003)
15. Strom, J., Høybye, M.T., Laursen, M., Jørgensen, L.B., Nielsen, C.V.: Lumbar spine fusion patients' use of an internet support group: mixed methods study. J. Med. Internet Res. **21**(7), 17 (2019)
16. van Zomeren, M., Louis, W.R.: Culture meets collective action: exciting synergies and some lessons to learn for the future. Group Process. Intergroup Relat. **20**(3), 277–284 (2017)
17. Henrich, J., Heine, S.J., Norenzayan, A.: The weirdest people in the world? Behav. Brain Sci. **33**(2–3), 61–83 (2010)
18. Suler, J.: The online disinhibition effect. Cyberpsychol. Behav. **7**(3), 321–326 (2004)
19. Ciocarlan, A., Masthoff, J., Oren, N.: Kindness is contagious: study into exploring engagement and adapting persuasive games for wellbeing. In: Proceedings of the 26th Conference on User Modeling, Adaptation and Personalization, pp. 311–319. ACM, July 2018
20. Rajani, N.B., Weth, D., Mastellos, N., Filippidis, F.T.: Use of gamification strategies and tactics in mobile applications for smoking cessation: a review of the UK mobile app market. BMJ Open **9**(6), e027883 (2019)
21. McKay, F.H., Wright, A., Shill, J., Stephens, H., Uccellini, M.: Using health and well-being apps for behavior change: a systematic search and rating of apps. JMIR mHealth uHealth **7**(7), e11926 (2019)
22. Alrobai, A., Algashami, A., Dogan, H., Corner, T., Phalp, K., Ali, R.: COPE.er method: combating digital addiction via online peer support groups. Int. J. Environ. Res. Publ. Health **16**(7), 1162 (2019)
23. Braun, V., Clarke, V., Terry, G.: Thematic analysis. Qual. Res. Clin. Health Psychol. **24**, 95–114 (2014)
24. Matthews, J., Win, K.T., Oinas-Kukkonen, H., Freeman, M.: Persuasive technology in mobile applications promoting physical activity: a systematic review. J. Med. Syst. **40**(3), 72 (2016)
25. Orji, R., Mandryk, R.L.: culturally relevant design guidelines for encouraging healthy eating behavior. Int. J. Hum.-Comput. Stud. **72**(2), 207–223 (2014)
26. Orji, R., Mandryk, R.L., Vassileva, J.: Gender, age, and responsiveness to Cialdini's persuasion strategies. In: MacTavish, T., Basapur, S. (eds.) PERSUASIVE 2015. LNCS, vol. 9072, pp. 147–159. Springer, Cham (2015). https://doi.org/10.1007/978-3-319-20306-5_14
27. Alkış, N., Temizel, T.T.: The impact of individual differences on influence strategies. Pers. Individ. Differ. **87**, 147–152 (2015)

28. Ciocarlan, A., Masthoff, J., Oren, N.: Kindness is contagious: exploring engagement in a gamified persuasive intervention for wellbeing. In: PGW@ CHI PLAY (2017)
29. Lowensteyn, I., Berberian, V., Berger, C., Da Costa, D., Joseph, L., Grover, S.A.: The Sustainability of a workplace wellness program that incorporates gamification principles: participant engagement and health benefits after 2 years. Am. J. Health Promot. **33**(6), 850–858 (2019)
30. Cialdini, R.: Influence: The Psychology of Persuasion
31. Rammstedt, B., John, O.P.: Measuring personality in one minute or less: a 10-item short version of the big five inventory in English and German. J. Res. Pers. **1**(41), 203–212 (2007)
32. Tangney, J.P., Baumeister, R.F., Boone, A.L.: High self-control predicts good adjustment, less pathology, better grades, and interpersonal success. J. Pers. **2**(72), 271–324 (2004)
33. Maro, S., Sundklev, E., Persson, C.-O., Liebel, G., Steghöfer, J.-P.: Impact of gamification on trace link vetting: a controlled experiment. In: Knauss, E., Goedicke, M. (eds.) REFSQ 2019. LNCS, vol. 11412, pp. 90–105. Springer, Cham (2019). https://doi.org/10.1007/978-3-030-15538-4_6
34. Barn, Balbir S., Barn, R.: Human and value sensitive aspects of mobile app design: a foucauldian perspective. In: Krogstie, J., Reijers, Hajo A. (eds.) CAiSE 2018. LNCS, vol. 10816, pp. 103–118. Springer, Cham (2018). https://doi.org/10.1007/978-3-319-91563-0_7
35. Haake, P., et al.: Configurations of user involvement and participation in relation to information system project success. In: Krogstie, J., Reijers, Hajo A. (eds.) CAiSE 2018. LNCS, vol. 10816, pp. 87–102. Springer, Cham (2018). https://doi.org/10.1007/978-3-319-91563-0_6
36. Aldhayan, M., Cham, S., Kostoulas, T., Almourad, M.B., Ali, R.: Online peer support groups to combat digital addiction: user acceptance and rejection factors. In: Rocha, Á., Adeli, H., Reis, L.P., Costanzo, S. (eds.) WorldCIST'19 2019. AISC, vol. 932, pp. 139–150. Springer, Cham (2019). https://doi.org/10.1007/978-3-030-16187-3_14

User-Experience in Business Intelligence - A Quality Construct and Model to Design Supportive BI Dashboards

Corentin Burnay[1(✉)], Sarah Bouraga[1], Stéphane Faulkner[1], and Ivan Jureta[1,2]

[1] Department of Business Administration, PReCISE Research Center,
NaDI Research Institute, University of Namur, Namur, Belgium
`corentin.burnay@unamur.be`
[2] Fonds National de la Recherche Scientifique (FNRS), Brussels, Belgium

Abstract. Business Intelligence (BI) intends to provide business managers with timely information about their company. Considerable research effort has been devoted to the modeling and specification of BI systems, with the objective to improve the quality of resulting BI output and decrease the risk of BI projects failure. In this paper, we focus on the specification and modeling of one component of the BI architecture: the dashboards. These are the interface between the whole BI system and end-users, and received smaller attention from the scientific community. We report preliminary results from an Action-Research project conducted since February 2019 with three Belgian companies. Our contribution is threefold: (i) we introduce BIXM, an extension of the existing Business Intelligence Model (BIM) that accounts for BI user-experience aspects, (ii) we propose a quality framework for BI dashboards and (iii) we review existing BI modeling notations and map them to our quality framework as a way to identify existing gaps in the literature.

Keywords: Business Intelligence · Dashboards · Requirements Engineering · Non-functional requirements · Business Intelligence Model (BIM)

1 Introduction

Business Intelligence (BI) refers to the architecture in a company consisting of tools and softwares used to extract valuable information from operational data. The goal is to provide managers with a timely and consistent view on the performance of their business, i.e., how well the business is doing in terms of operations and value-adding activities. The ultimate objective of any BI system is to use and control past performance of the company as a way to better inform managers about the state of the company, and help them drive business planning [6]. Implementing an effective BI system is an increasingly common yet critical requirement for companies.

© Springer Nature Switzerland AG 2020
F. Dalpiaz et al. (Eds.): RCIS 2020, LNBIP 385, pp. 174–190, 2020.
https://doi.org/10.1007/978-3-030-50316-1_11

Researchers addressed this problem in various ways, by defining methodologies and models to specify the different components inside the BI architecture such as the Extract-Transform-Load (ETL) process, the data warehouse or even the OLAP applications. Surprisingly however, we find little research focusing specifically on the specification of dashboards. This is particularly surprising considering that dashboards are the interface between the entire BI architecture and end-users; a poorly specified dashboard may be a threat to the success of the entire BI system if it leads end-users to turn away and use alternative sources of information. The few scientific contributions we found on the topic (e.g. [20, 27, 30]) all seem to focus on the same question: *how to detect as much as possible of the information that is relevant to decision makers?* In other words, how to ensure dashboard *completeness.*

Focusing on completeness only, however, is not always desirable. Imagine a manager who has access to a large quantity of highly *relevant* information. The manager has a *complete* view on his business and can use the dashboard to make decisions. But what if that information is *not presented properly* and is *hard to interpret?* What if the information is relevant given the corporate strategy, but does not *bring anything new* in terms of perspective on the problems the business is confronted to? What if there is *too much information*, so that the manager is simply overwhelmed and cannot treat the information correctly? The previous intends to illustrate the existence of a trade-off when designing a BI dashboard between (i) the necessity to provide *complete* and relevant information to support decision-makers and (ii) the necessity to provide information in a way that actually supports the decision maker. To the best of our knowledge, most scientific approaches focus on the first part of the trade-off and tend to overlook the second one. This may result in very rich BI outputs, with which managers may however be struggling, because too complex to leverage.

Our claim in this paper is therefore that *supportiveness* matters, as much as *completeness.* This brings us to the following research questions:

1. What are the different qualities a dashboard should satisfy to be supportive?
2. How to ensure these qualities actually operationalize in the dashboards?
3. Which of the existing BI models supports which qualities of our framework?

To the best of our knowledge, these questions have received little attention from information management research community in general. The problem has been addressed by some practitioners (e.g.,[12]) but without any real scientific insight. In [1,4], methods for the automated generation of engaging dashboards are reported. While our conclusions are partly aligned, the central place that human designers occupy in our research project stresses out some specific dashboard qualities that are not/can hardly be handled in such automated approaches (Efficiency or Relevance for instance). Other pieces of work focus on the definition of KPIs included in a dashboard [8,9]. While our questions could also be treated on such thinner granularity level, this is outside the scope of this paper. Starting from this gap, this paper reports the result of the first ten months of Action-Research we conducted to answer those questions. When writing this paper, we are still collaborating with one company and expect additional improvements and results. The length of the action-research process, combined with the necessity to somehow formalize our results and obtain an intermediate validation/discussion of those results with the research community motivates the present paper, despite the data collection process not being totally completed.

2   Methodology - Action Research

Studying qualities related to supportiveness of dashboard is challenging, because the topic is rather subjective and tacit. We therefore opted for *Action Research* (AR), as a way to actually experience the problems of dashboard design, rather than simply questioning practitioners about it. AR can be defined as *"a systematic form of inquiry undertaken by practitioners into their attempts to improve the quality of they own practice"* [40]. It is a qualitative approach that is considered as *"systematic and orientated around analysis of questions whose answers require the gathering and analysis of data and the generation of interpretations directly tested in the field of action"* [16]. According to Coghlan and Brannick [5], it is *"appropriate when the research topic is an unfolding series of actions over time in a given group, community or organization, and the members wish to study their own action in order to change or improve the working of some aspects of the system, and study the process in order to learn from it"*. AR specifics fit well with the engineering approach adopted in this paper, in which we focus on the maximization of a hard-to-measure concept, i.e., supportiveness. We see in AR a great opportunity to bring changes to an existing – but theoretical – model (i.e., BIM) based on practically informed experience and opinions collected from practitioners. Those improvements could not be made based solely on interviews or focus groups, isolated from a clear application area.

Companies: We worked with companies that are all located in Belgium and are in the process of implementing BI solutions. There are 3 of them, active in the airspace, health and banking industry. In each company, the authors were invited to participate to meetings, calls, etc. Involvement was moderate to keep a distance between the research project and the BI project. The disclosure of practical information about the projects is constrained by non-disclosure agreements; the only content to be disclosed in this paper is related to the methodology and the models used to produce specifications of the dashboards.

Procedures: In order to collect data, we applied the same procedure in all three projects, following the AR iterative process as prescribed by Susman and Evered [36]:

1. *Diagnosing*: identifying or defining a problem;
2. *Action planning*: find alternative courses of action for solving the problem;
3. *Action taking*: applying a course of action;
4. *Evaluating*: studying the consequences of the action;
5. *Specifying learning*: identifying general findings.

All companies entered the process at the same time. Up to now, we conducted a total of 4 such iterations, and are currently working on a fifth one. We group those iterations in 3 rounds, as described in Table 1 (a round is a set of iterations focusing on a same dashboard quality, see below). Not all companies were involved in all iterations; company A and C for instance joined the project later and did not participate in iteration 1.

Validity: The question of validity is a central question, especially in AR. Each iteration relied on the combination of standard qualitative data collection methods like focus groups, interviews, fields notes and observations. We applied those methods under an ethnographic perspective as a way to uncover people practices and issues in real-world setting [10]; especially, we made use of the data triangulation technique by combining interviews, workshops and participatory observation to ensure validity of our conclusions [29]. Most interviews were conversational [31], taking place as new issues were discovered or specific actions were taken and tested. Using structured interviews was not feasible, given the practical constraints in projects and the necessity to interfere as least as possible with people practices. Interviews were useful to capture ideas or identify possible action planning. This approach made the audio recording of the interviews impossible, leading instead the author to produce systematic summary notes after each exchange with members of the project. Finally, we also organized a series of conclusion workshops/focus groups, necessary to the "evaluation" step. We ran those sessions as Delphi sessions [33], a type of focus group were stakeholders are invited to provide feedback anonymously and iteratively, in order to reach a consensus within the group. This technique was useful to uncover strengths and weaknesses of our solutions, and to define new potential action planning.

3   Results

We completed four iterations grouped in three rounds which are summarized in Table 1. For each round, we discuss (i) the diagnosing step and related dashboard quality, (ii) the literature related to that quality, (iii) the change proposed in the dashboard design process and (iv) the evaluation and formalization of learning.

3.1   Round 1 - Dashboard Relevance in BIXM

Diagnosis - Relevance of Information. Discussions with stakeholders from company A quickly lead to a first diagnosis: *dashboards presented to users do not always include the necessary information, and some aspects that are key for the evaluation of business operations are in fact not monitored in the dashboard.* Several stakeholders pointed out that they "*could indeed produce dashboards aligned with their strategy, but that it would require several iterations before achieving a satisfying content*". This was negatively perceived by stakeholders, because costly and very time consuming. We call this a need for *relevance.*

Table 1. Summary of research action iterations

Round 1	Round 2	Round 3
1 iteration	2 iterations	1 iteration
Companies		
A	A, B, C	A, B, C
Duration		
1,5 month	3,5 months	3 months
Diagnosing		
Dashboards are not in line with user's perception of business strategy; indicators are missing or unnecessary and do not clearly relate to actual business goals	Dashboards are hard to read, and users experience difficulties when trying to retrieve the information from the dashboard	Dashboards are large, difficult to grasp fully for end users because too rich, too detailed, too heavy
Action planning		
A. Use BIM to identify relevant indicators. (adopted)	**A.** Let users create their dashboards themselves with self-service software (rejected). **B.** Model indicators with their respective visualization and balance between expressiveness and efficiency. (adopted)	**A.** Establish a system of weights for each elements in the dashboard
Action taking for selected planning		
1. Model business goal model 2. Brainstorm indicators for each elements of the model 3. Prioritize (rank) indicators 4. Implement most important indicators, as long as budget is available	1. Elicit visual requirements of stakeholders 2. Find a balance between expressiveness and efficiency 3. Model resulting dashboard specification in BIXM	1. Assign weights to each type of visuals 2. Compute weights of each dashboard 3. Detect outliers in terms of weight 4. Split or merge dashboard to balance the load across the dashboards
Evaluating		
Stakeholders recognize information included in the dashboard was necessary and sufficient. They acclaim the rapidity at which we obtained a validated dashboard, without several iterations between the business and the IT	Action plan A was strongly rejected by stakeholders, because too time-consuming. Action plan B was positively received. The Delphi validation session did not emphasize any problem in the resulting dashboards, and stakeholders of the different projects gave credits to the proposed solutions of plan B	The definition of a clear procedure to compute the actual load of a dashboard was the central issue in this round, and took a large portion of the time dedicated to this iteration. During validation, two of the Delphi sessions requested to re-evaluate the initial load associated with each visual, switching from an initial 1/1/1 to the current 1/3/6 key
Research learnings		
1. application of BIM for the specification of BI solution 2. application of BIM for BI Dashboards specification	1. definition of an expressiveness/efficiency matrix 2. BIXM notation to model type of visuals of indicators	1. BIXM notation for dashboards 2. Definition of weights for indicators 3. Procedure of dashboard load computation
Suggested Dashboard Qualities		
Relevance	Efficiency	Balanced load

Planning and Theory - Relevance in the Literature. Sperber & Wilson define relevance as follows: "An input is relevant to an individual when it connects with available contextual assumptions to yield positive cognitive effects: for example, true contextual implications, or warranted strengthening or revisions of existing assumptions" [34]. Applied to a BI context, a piece of information in a given context will be relevant if it helps the decision maker to confirm some intuition she has in that context, or if it helps her getting more (or less) confident about an assumption she made in that same context. Theory therefore suggests the following criteria to discuss the concept of relevance:

– Dashboard is sufficiently context-related
– Dashboard generates cognitive effects (cause-effect links, comparisons, ...)

Action Taking - Modeling Indicators Using BIM (1 Iteration). We suggested to company A that the problem could be anticipated for future dashboards by using an indicators modeling notation such as BIM. We therefore decided to model a segment of the business strategy under the form of a goal model using the concepts of goals, soft-goals and decomposition links. This process was intuitive to most business stakeholders. We then used the resulting model to brainstorm with the different stakeholders about all candidate indicators. The resulting list was then prioritized to select most relevant ones using a simple Must-Should-Could-Would priority scale [19]. Indicators were finally implemented in dashboards by people in charge of the dashboard implementation.

Evaluation of Relevance and Learnings. It took two weeks to document the goal model of the dashboard and validating it. The brainstorming and prioritizing sessions were conducted directly after, and it took two additional weeks to implement the identified KPIs. The result was presented during a conclusion session to members of the project in charge of the performance management. As expected, stakeholders agreed on the fact that the information included in the dashboard was necessary and sufficient. They also acclaimed the rapidity at which we obtained a validated dashboard, without several iterations between the business and the IT. Scientific learning in this first round are minor; we simply obtained additional evidences that BIM actually helps implementing strategy-aligned BI solutions, and that it can also be used to inform the specification of BI Dashboards. Improvements for the company were significant, decreasing to a large extent the time-to-release of new dashboards.

3.2   Round 2 - Dashboard Efficiency in BIXM

Diagnosis - Efficiency of Information. Additional interviews in company A lead to the identification of a new problem: *the dashboard produced in round 1 was relevant, but turned out to be relatively hard to read.* Stakeholders in company A claimed that *"the information is there but it's presented strangely and I can't* *extract what I need to decide about [...]"*. Similarly, a stakeholder from company B commented about another dashboard of their own that *"everything is there, but it is all numbers and commas and I had a hard time reading it"*. Clearly, the problem is not related to the relevance of the information proposed in the dashboard, but rather to the way that information is displayed and to the way it can be "extracted" from the dashboard. The problem here was that managers needed to obtain the relevant information quickly, and did not wish to spend time interpreting and capturing the information. We call this a need for *efficiency*.

Planning and Theory - Efficiency in the Literature. Efficiency of a dashboard deals with the acquisition of information, not its interpretation. We find a similar idea in the Information Context (IC) framework of Lurie et al. [22]. In this framework, the concept of Vividness is used to refer to how salient a piece of information is simply by displaying data *"in a form that uses preattentive graphic features, such as line orientation, width, length, and color, which are readily processed with little effort"* [22]. Research on Visual Analytics also confirms the importance of dashboard efficiency [38]; information must be present, and easy to read and extract from the dashboard. To identify underlying factors of dashboard efficiency, we use the operationalization of information accessibility as proposed by Teo et al. [37] and the factors for the accessibility of information source by O'Reilly [25]. The following criteria have been used during round 2 to discuss the concept of efficiency:

- Dashboard must ensure vividness of information [22]
- Dashboard facilitates interactions with data [37]
- Dashboard has a clearly delimited scope [25,37]
- Dashboard simplifies access the information [25]
- Dashboard reduces costs of information access [25]
- Dashboard displays information in a well organized and structured way [37]

Action Taking - Types of Indicators in BIXM (2 Iterations). Firstly, we investigated the adoption of self-service BI as a way to solve the problem of efficiency. The goal was to let managers define the presentation of data by themselves instead of relying on IT, because they are the ones who know best how they want to visualize their data. This idea was rejected by managers, who found it too technical and too time consuming. As an alternative, we initiated a second iteration in this round in which we opted for a notation specifying the visualization to be used for each indicator. Our intuition was that indicators represented in different forms (graphs, tables, etc.) would differ in terms of efficiency, e.g., a table with volume of sales per month will make the information harder to extract than a line chart with the evolution of sales per months. This brought us to the definition of three different types of visualization following Tory and Möller's high-level taxonomy of visualization [39]. This also corresponds to what is available in most existing BI softwares. The BIXM notation for visualization is depicted in Fig. 1, together with a fictive illustration adapted from [18]:

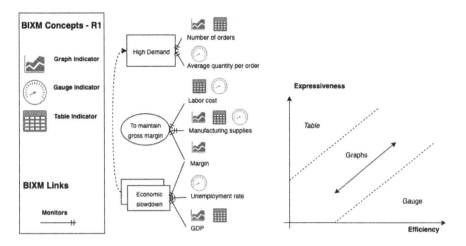

Fig. 1. Visualisation notation in BIXM   **Fig. 2.** Expressiveness vs. efficiency

- *Tables*: report discrete variables, showing any item details, supporting filtering, drill-down and item exclusion;
- *Graphs*: report continuous variables, showing trends over time, geographical distribution. They support filtering but drill-down is not always possible;
- *Gauges*: report an aggregated indicator together with target and limit values.

After additional discussion with stakeholders, it turned out quickly that efficiency alone was a poor criteria to design dashboards. Some stakeholders pointed out that *"it doesn't make sense [to use only efficiency]; we would only include Gauges to have efficient dashboards then, and would never resort to Tables or Graphs, which is clearly not the case in our habits"*. Another one pointed out that *"graphs are nice, but they do not hold sufficient information, or when they do they become quickly messy"*. This led to the identification of a trade-off between *efficiency* and *expressiveness*, understood as the property of a visualization that effectively conveys meaning or feeling [24]. A visual can be highly efficient (information can be extracted quickly, at small cost) but poorly expressive (it conveys little information). We see those two qualities as orthogonal. We consider Gauges are highly efficient but poorly expressive (they show only one number with some targets and thresholds), tables are on the contrary poorly effective but highly expressive. Graphs finally can be poorly, reasonably or highly efficient and expressive, depending on how they are designed and aligned with reporting objectives (see Fig. 2). Ultimately, the objective for the dashboard designer is therefore to select one or more visualization to deal with the trade-off, depending on the importance of the indicator and how it relates to the business strategy.

Evaluation of Efficiency and Learnings. Two weeks were dedicated to investigating self-service BI approach. The proposition of BIXM notation and matrix took three weeks, under the form of interviews and discussion with stakeholders. We then applied the notation in all three companies. The discussion was focused on the identification of most relevant visuals for each indicator, and on the necessity or not to duplicate visuals. The Delphi validation session did not emphasize any problem in the resulting dashboards, and stakeholders of the different projects gave credits to the proposed solutions. Learnings for the companies are in the management of visuals and their relative efficiency/expressiveness, decreasing the risk of unsupportiveness. Stakeholders also recognized that discussing the alignment between visuals and the strategic goal they enable to control is a good way to anticipate multiple iterations with the IT; although relatively trivial, this type of discussion was not systematic before the introduction of BIXM. Scientific learnings are in the definition of BIXM visuals notation and in the proposition of the efficiency vs. expressiveness matrix.

3.3   Round 3 - Dashboard Load in BIXM

Diagnosis - Load of Information. After round 2, companies began to produce dashboards including various representations of a same indicator as a way to balance efficiency and expressiveness. This brought up a new problem; *the duplication of indicators led companies to the definition of heavier dashboards, which in turn generated several negative feedback from end-users.* Despite stakeholders' enthusiasm to include several visuals for one single indicator (for multiple perspectives on a same data), authors' field notes report that *"stakeholders observe the apparition of heavier dashboards, which are too loaded and hence harder to leverage for decision making"*. We call this new quality *balanced load*.

Planning and Theory - Load in the Literature. *Balanced load* means that dashboards should not contain a quantity of information that cannot be correctly treated by managers in reasonable delays. This echoes research in psychology about information overloads during decision making. Information overload occurs when information received becomes a hindrance rather than a help, even though the information is potentially useful [2]. Shields [32] observes a link between supplied information and the accuracy of judgment in the form of an inverted U-shaped curve; too little or too much information decreases decision accuracy. A sweet spot seems to exist where the quantity of information maximizes the accuracy of judgments, but we find no agreement on the optimal quantity of information, usually quantified in terms of the number of alternative offered to the decision maker. Prudential studies report optimal number of alternatives around 4 [17], some suggest to not exceed 6 alternatives [41], others still report decreases in performance above 10 alternatives [23]. Shields' U-shaped curve, on the other hand, positions the optimal quantity of information – expressed in terms of performance parameters, and not alternatives – around 45 information items [32]. The following criteria have been used during round 3 to discuss the concept of balanced load:

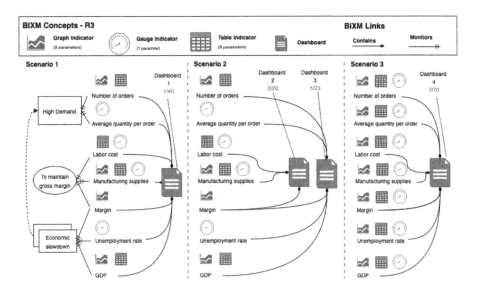

Fig. 3. BIXM with dashboard and load notation

- Dashboard displays reasonable number of alternatives, i.e., the number of indicators on one page, regardless of the visuals (from 4 to 10 alternatives)
- Dashboard displays reasonable number of parameters, i.e., the total number of dimensions (not distinct) reported in the dashboard (up to 45 parameters)

Action Taking - Weights of Visuals in BIXM. After discussion with stakeholders, we agreed on two important assumptions related to the load of a dashboard: (1) different loads can be assigned to the different indicators in a dashboard and (2) loads can be used to compute a general score for the dashboard. If applied properly, those two ideas make it possible to detect dashboards which are not balanced. The previous ideas raised two practical issues.

First, BIM does not include any modeling mechanism to associate explicitly an indicator to a dashboard, making it practically unfeasible to compute the weight of that dashboard. We solved this with the introduction of a "dashboard" concept in the BIXM notation, together with a "contains" relationship to relate indicators to dashboard. A dashboard is understood as "an interaction board containing a set of consistent information about one specific aspect of the business, i.e., a scope". This new notation is illustrated in Fig. 3 and enables to define and visualize more formally the content of a dashboard in relation to business strategy. For instance, we observe that all the indicators used to control the goal model could be gathered in a single "Dashboard 1" as in Scenario 1 or split in two different dashboards as depicted in Scenario 2. Alternative visuals for the very same indicators could also be used, as depicted in scenario 3.

The second problem was methodological; how to proceed in order to compute the measure of load for a dashboard? After several attempts, we converged to the procedure depicted in Fig. 4. The process makes use of the two load metrics discussed in our review of the literature; *number of alternatives* and the *number of parameters*. The number of alternatives in a dashboard is easy to compute, e.g., in Fig. 3, there are 7 different indicators (one per indicator title). This metric reflects the width of a dashboard; how many different business indicators does it include. *Number of parameters* on the other hand is used to reflect the depth of a dashboard; how detailed is the dashboard? It directly gives an indication of the size of the dashboard. Note that the values assigned to compute the number of parameters (1, 3 and 6) were defined based on discussions with stakeholders. We did not conduct any empirical evaluation of these numbers beside the one on the three projects. The number of parameters reflects the number of dimensions used in a visual. As Gauges are non-dimensional by nature, we assigned 1 parameter to it. Graphs usually have a X and Y axis on which a measure is reported, leading to a number of 3 parameters. Tables (and especially Pivot Tables) can include a number of nested levels and drill-down options, leading stakeholders to assign 6 parameters. We acknowledge the necessity to investigate this in more details, but keep it as future work. Using this procedure, we observe that Dashboard 1 in Fig. 3 has a 7/40 weight score in Scenario 1, that we consider as balanced. In Scenario 2 however, Dashboard 2 contains too few alternatives to cover effectively the scope (3/20, below the 4 alternative threshold). Dashboard 4 on the contrary has an acceptable number of alternatives, but has too many parameters (70, way above the 45 limit). Remember that the limits we used (max 10 alternatives and max 45 parameters) follows from our review of the literature in Round 3, but could evolve as our AR project advances. Note also how the concept of load complements the solution proposed in round 2; users could be tempted to include all three kinds of visualization for all indicators in order to solve the efficiency/expressiveness tension (Scenario 3). But doing so would generate high loading score and would imply to split the indicators in several dashboards focusing on very specific elements of the goal model, which is not desirable for decision makers, i.e., efficiency is somehow counter-balanced by load issues. Similarly, they could be tempted to specify one dashboard per element in the goal model, then resulting in too poor dashboards which will not be balanced either (Scenario 2).

Evaluation of Balanced Load and Learnings. It took three months to conclude round 3. The definition of a clear procedure to compute the actual load of a dashboard was the central issue in this round, and took a large portion of the time dedicated to this iteration. During validation, two of the Delphi sessions requested to re-evaluate the initial load associated with each visual, switching from an initial 1/1/1 to the current 1/3/6 key. Learnings for the companies were threefold; (i) more in a dashboard is not always better, and managers and dashboard designers gain in balancing the quantity of information to be shown in a dashboard, (ii) the distribution of various indicators to dashboards based on

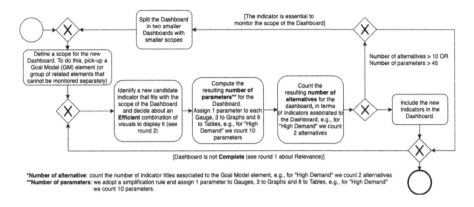

Fig. 4. Dashboard load measurement procedure

underlying Goal Model elements is essential; related elements should be grouped, when feasible, in a same dashboard and not allocated to dashboards randomly or based on intuition and (iii) dashboards should focus on two or three business goal elements at most. Research Learnings are twofold: (i) additional notation elements for BIXM, namely the dashboard concept and the "contains" link and (ii) the definition of a standard procedure to measure the load of a dashboard.

4   Dashboard Quality Framework and BI Models

We summarize in Fig. 5 the essential qualities of dashboard identified throughout our AR project. The figure takes the form of a checklist, that we believe should be accounted for when implementing new dashboards. As a reminder, the AR process is still ongoing, and additional qualities may enrich this framework in the future. As a last step in this paper, we review some existing BI modeling notations and try to explain which of the qualities of our framework they support. The problem at hand in this paper is a Requirements Engineering (RE) one, and various models have been proposed in RE to support the design of BI systems. GRAnD [14] for instance is a goal-oriented approach building on Tropos which permits to relate BI measures and dimensions to strategic business intentions. Although the focus is on the data warehouse, it offers a perspective on the *relevance* of information to include in BI dashboards. Similarly, models in [13,15,26] focus on data warehouse content and could help determine which information is *relevant* or not in a dashboard, although they were not designed for this specific purpose. Pourshahid et al. [28] extends the so-called Goal-oriented Requirement Language (GRL) with decision-making concepts such as indicators. Both BIM [18] (on which we build BIXM) and extended GRL enable to define *relevant* indicators and to reason on them. Beside, soft-goal concepts used in GRL and BIM could also be used to ensure Balanced dashboard, despite the absence of

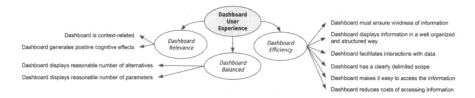

Fig. 5. BIXM essential dashboards quality construct

formal mechanisms to handle the load of a dashboard. Stefanov et al. [35] propose an alternative formalism where BI concepts (e.g. indicators, reports, ...) are included in UML activity diagrams to facilitate the identification of pertinent indicators in a process-oriented mood. Information is also related to goals, processes and role concepts, further ensuring its *relevance* in case of inclusion in a dashboard. We note that the model is expected to *"provide BI objects on different aggregation levels and thus permits to the modeler to choose the right level of detail for different purposes or target audiences"* [35], which may help designers to produce *efficient* dashboards, and maybe to help ensuring the quantity of information displayed in a dashboard is *Balanced*.

Other models have been proposed outside RE. While not all specifically designed for BI purposes, most of them offer a perspective on the information to include in dashboards. The Balanced Scorecard (BSC) identifies four business dimensions for monitoring a company [21]. The BSC can also be linked to the business strategy via a Strategy Map [21], thereby contributing to the definition of *relevant* indicators. GRAI grid [3,11] models organizations and complex systems; it identifies where important decisions are made in the business, and most importantly the information relationships that exist among these decisions, so that the model can also be used to identify *relevant* information for a BI dashboard. ARIS [7] is another framework to model all the dimensions of a business repository, from the business processes, the softwares and the technical aspects of a company to the data and information used in that company. We see in ARIS another possible approach to prove the *relevance* of information used in a dashboard, e.g., an indicator is *relevant* if it relates to a business process.

Both in RE and in Performance Management literature, it seems clear that existing models and methods are numerous, but tend to focus on the relevance of information only. It is striking however that most of these models simply overlook other essential qualities of dashboards identified in our Dashboard Quality Framework. We did not manage to find a formal support to specify dashboards that are, at the same time, *relevant*, *efficient* and *balanced*. Table 2 summarizes our observations.

Table 2. Mapping of existing approaches in our BI dashboard qualities construct

BI approach	Dashboard relevance	Dashboard efficiency	Dashboard balance
Balanced scorecard [21]	X		
GRAI grid [3,11]	X		
ARIS [7]	X		
BI: activity diagram [35]	X	?	?
GRAnD [14]	X		
DWH notations [13,15,26]	?		
BIM [18]	X		?
GRL [28]	X		?

5 Limitations

The contribution in this paper builds on Action Research, and therefore starts from practice to suggest a theory in an inductive way. The work presented in this paper is the result of extensive data collection and observation over a long period of time, following the guidelines for rigorous Action Research [5]. It is grounded in practice and reflects actual people thoughts and perceptions of issues related to the design of BI dashboards. Nevertheless, it builds on a limited sample of three cases with a limited number of person involved. The suggested problems and solutions inevitably reflect part of the corporate cultures and values, and adapts to the processes of the selected companies. BIXM, as is, therefore presents a risk of not being neutral. It was critical for the authors to remain detached from those values and stay critic in any case; several times on the projects, there were opportunities to discuss with members of the project on whether or not the solution would be different in another company, or in another context. Doing so, we tried to isolate the problem from the specifics of the organization. The author also paid attention to ground all solutions on scientific literature; improvements on BIM are therefore not simply informed by action research, but also build on well established theories in psychology, management and data sciences as well as requirements engineering. Previous limitations make it difficult to generalize our conclusions to other projects and other fields without further investigation of the model. Still, we believe those limitations do not hold us back from drawing relevant conclusions about the design of dashboard, and we wish to pursue in the future with more applications of the present framework to other industries and other projects.

6 Conclusions

This paper presents preliminary results of an Action-Research project that took place between February and October 2019 in three Belgian companies, active in the Airspace, Healthcare and Banking industries. The paper investigates various qualities of Business Intelligence dashboards that stakeholders perceive as essential in order for the dashboard to be supportive. BIXM, a new notation for the specification of BI dashboard, is proposed. It extends the BIM model and adds a number of BI-related concepts such as visualization, dashboards and loads. Each addition to BIM was carefully discussed and evaluated with practitioners. To the best of our knowledge, no existing BI modeling framework exist that supports the engineering of dashboard as BIXM does. At the moment of writing this paper, we are still involved in two companies and keep identifying new qualities.

References

1. Aksu, Ü., del-Río-Ortega, A., Resinas, M., Reijers, H.A.: An approach for the automated generation of engaging dashboards. In: Panetto, H., Debruyne, C., Hepp, M., Lewis, D., Ardagna, C.A., Meersman, R. (eds.) OTM 2019. LNCS, vol. 11877, pp. 363–384. Springer, Cham (2019). https://doi.org/10.1007/978-3-030-33246-4_24
2. Bawden, D., Robinson, L.: The dark side of information: overload, anxiety and other paradoxes and pathologies. J. Inf. Sci. **35**(2), 180–191 (2009)
3. Chen, D., Vallespir, B., Doumeingts, G.: GRAI integrated methodology and its mapping onto generic enterprise reference architecture and methodology. Comput. Ind. **33**(2), 387–394 (1997)
4. Chowdhary, P., Palpanas, T., Pinel, F., Chen, S.K., Wu, F.: Model-driven dashboards for business performance reporting. In: Proceedings of 10th IEEE International Enterprise Distributed Object Computing Conference (EDOC 2006), pp. 374–386. IEEE, October 2006. https://doi.org/10.1109/EDOC.2006.34
5. Coghlan, D., Brannick, T.: Doing Action in Your Own Organization (2005)
6. Davenport, T.H., Harris, J.G.: Competing on Analytics : The New Science of Winning. Harvard Business School Press, Boston (2007)
7. Davis, R., Brabänder, E.: ARIS Design Platform: Getting Started with BPM. Springer, London (2007). https://doi.org/10.1007/978-1-84628-613-1
8. Del-Río-Ortega, A., Resinas, M., Cabanillas, C., Ruiz-CortéS, A.: On the definition and design-time analysis of process performance indicators. Inf. Syst. **38**(4), 470–490 (2013)
9. Del-Río-Ortega, A., Resinas, M., Durán, A., Bernárdez, B., Ruiz-Cortés, A., Toro, M.: Visual ppinot: a graphical notation for process performance indicators. Bus. Inf. Syst. Eng. **61**(2), 137–161 (2019)
10. Denzin, N.K., Lincoln, Y.S.: Handbook of Qualitative Research. Sage Publications, Inc. (1994)
11. Doumeingts, G., Vallespir, B., Chen, D.: GRAI grid decisional modelling. In: Bernus, P., Mertins, K., Schmidt, G. (eds.) Handbook on Architectures of Information Systems, pp. 321–346. Springer, Heidelberg (2006). https://doi.org/10.1007/978-3-662-03526-9_14
12. Few, S.: Information Dashboard Design: The Effective Visual Communication of Data. O'Reilly (2006)
13. Gam, I., Salinesi, C.: A requirement-driven approach for designing data warehouses. In: Requirements Engineering: Foundation for Software Quality (2006)
14. Giorgini, P., Rizzi, S., Garzetti, M.: GRAnD: a goal-oriented approach to requirement analysis in data warehouses. Decis. Support Syst. **45**(1), 4–21 (2008)

15. Golfarelli, M., Maio, D., Rizzi, S.: The dimensional fact model: a conceptual model for data warehouses. Int. J. Coop. Inf. Syst. **7**(02n03), 215–247 (1998)
16. Greenwood, D.J., Levin, M.: Introduction to Action Research: Social Research for Social Change. SAGE Publications (2006)
17. Hayes, J.R.: Human data processing limits in decision making. Technical report, (No. ESD-TDR-62-48). Electronic Systems DIV Hanscom AFB MA (1962)
18. Horkoff, J., et al.: Strategic business modeling: representation and reasoning. Softw. Syst. Model. **13**, 1015–1041 (2012)
19. IIBA: Guide to the Business Analysis Body of Knowledge. No. Version 1.6, International Institute of Business Analysis (2006)
20. Isik, O., Jones, M.C., Sidorova, A.: Business Intelligence (BI) success and the role of BI capabilities. Intell. Syst. Account. Finance Manag. **18**(4), 161–176 (2011)
21. Kaplan, R.S., Norton, D.P.: Linking the balanced scorecard to strategy. Calif. Manag. Rev. **39**(1), 53–80 (1996)
22. Lurie, N.H., Mason, C.H., Glazer, R., Hamilton, R., Hearst, M., Hoffman, D.: Visual representation: implications for decision making. J. Mark. **71**, 160–177 (2007)
23. Malhotra, N.K.: Information load and consumer decision making. J. Consum. Res. **8**(4), 419–430 (1982)
24. Merriam Webster: Effectiveness (2019). https://www.merriam-webster.com/dictionary/effectiveness
25. O'Reilly, C.: Variations in decision makers' use of information sources: the impact of quality and accessibility of information. Acad. Manag. J. **25**(4), 756–771 (1982)
26. Paim, F.R.S., de Castro, J.F.B.: DWARF: an approach for requirements definition and management of data warehouse systems. In: Proceedings of 11th IEEE International Conference on Requirements Engineering, pp. 75–84. IEEE Computer Society (2003)
27. Palpanas, T., Chowdhary, P., Mihaila, G., Pinel, F.: Integrated model-driven dashboard development. Inf. Syst. Front. **9**(2–3), 195–208 (2007)
28. Pourshahid, A., Richards, G., Amyot, D.: Toward a goal-oriented, business intelligence decision-making framework. In: Babin, G., Stanoevska-Slabeva, K., Kropf, P. (eds.) MCETECH 2011. LNBIP, vol. 78, pp. 100–115. Springer, Heidelberg (2011). https://doi.org/10.1007/978-3-642-20862-1_7
29. Reeves, S., Kuper, A., Hodges, B.D.: Qualitative research methodologies: ethnography. Br. Med. J. **337**(7668), 512–514 (2013)
30. Roest, P.: The golden rules for implementing the balanced business scorecard. Inf. Manag. Comput. Secur. **5**(5), 163–165 (1997)
31. Rubin, H.J., Rubin, I.S.: Qualitative Interviewing: The Art of Hearing Data. Sage (2011)
32. Shields, M.D.: Effects of information supply and demand on judgment accuracy: evidence from corporate managers. Account. Rev. **58**(2), 284–303 (1983)
33. Skulmoski, G.J., Hartman, F.T., Krahn, J.: The Delphi method for graduate research gregory. J. Inf. Technol. Educ. **6**, 93–105 (2007)
34. Sperber, D., Wilson, D.: Pragmatics. In: Oxford Handbook of Contemporary Analytic Philosophy, pp. 468–501. Oxford University Press, Oxford (2005)
35. Stefanov, V., List, B., Korherr, B.: Extending UML 2 activity diagrams with business intelligence objects. In: Tjoa, A.M., Trujillo, J. (eds.) DaWaK 2005. LNCS, vol. 3589, pp. 53–63. Springer, Heidelberg (2005). https://doi.org/10.1007/11546849_6
36. Susman, G.I., Evered, R.D.: An assessment of the scientific merits of action research. Adm. Sci. Q. **23**(4), 582 (1978)

37. Teo, H.H., Chan, H.C., Wei, K.K., Zhang, Z.: Evaluating information accessibility and community adaptivity features for sustaining virtual learning communities. Int. J. Hum.-Comput. Stud. **59**, 671–697 (2003)

38. Thomas, J.J., Cook, K.A.: The science of visual analytics. IEEE Comput. Graph. Appl. **26**, 10–13 (2006)

39. Tory, M., Möller, T.: Rethinking visualization: a high-level taxonomy. In: Proceedings - IEEE Symposium on Information Visualization, pp. 151–158 (2004)

40. Whitehead, J.: How do I improve the quality of my management? Manag. Learn. **25**, 137–153 (1994)

41. Wright, P.: Consumer choice strategies: simplifying vs. optimizing. J. Mark. Res. **12**(1), 60 (1975)

FINESSE: Fair Incentives for Enterprise Employees

Soumi Chattopadhyay[1(✉)], Rahul Ghosh[2(✉)], Ansuman Banerjee[3],
Avantika Gupta[4], and Arpit Jain[5]

[1] Indian Institute of Information Technology Guwahati, Guwahati, India
soumi@iiitg.ac.in
[2] American Express AI Labs, Bengaluru, India
rahul.ghosh@aexp.com
[3] Indian Statistical Institute, Kolkata, India
[4] Play Games24×7 AI Labs, Bengaluru, India
[5] Xerox Research Centre, Bengaluru, India

Abstract. Service enterprises typically motivate their employees by providing incentives in addition to their basic salary. Generally speaking, an incentive scheme should reflect the enterprise wide objectives, e.g., maximize productivity, ensure fairness etc. Often times, after an incentive scheme is rolled out, non-intuitive outcomes (e.g., low performers getting high incentives) may become visible, which are undesired for an organization. A poorly designed incentive mechanism can hurt the operations of a service business in many ways including: (a) de-motivating the top performers from delivering high volume and high quality of work, (b) allowing the mid-performers not to push themselves to the limit that they can deliver, and (c) potentially increasing the number of low performers and thereby, reducing the profit of the organization. This paper describes *FINESSE*, a systematic framework to evaluate the fairness of a given incentive scheme. Such fairness is quantified in terms of the employee ordering with respect to a notion of employee utility, as captured through disparate key performance indicators (KPIs, e.g., work duration, work quality). Our approach uses a multi-objective formulation via Pareto optimal front generation followed by front refinement with domain specific constraints. We evaluate *FINESSE* by comparing two candidate incentive schemes: (a) an operational scheme that is known for non-intuitive disbursements, and (b) a contender scheme that is aimed at filling the gaps of the operational scheme. Using real anonymized dataset from a BPO services business, we show that *FINESSE* is effectively able to distinguish between the fairness (or lack thereof) of the two schemes across a set of metrics. Finally, we build and demonstrate a prototype dashboard that implements *FINESSE* and can be used by the business leaders in practice.

S. Chattopadhyay, R. Ghosh, A. Banerjee, A. Gupta, and A. Jain—This work was done when all the authors were at Xerox Research Centre, India.

F. Dalpiaz et al. (Eds.): RCIS 2020, LNBIP 385, pp. 191–211, 2020.
https://doi.org/10.1007/978-3-030-50316-1_12

1   Introduction

Incentive schemes are critical to any service enterprise (e.g., BPO) to motivate its employees for delivering high performance, and to ensure that organizational processes and objectives are met. A well-designed incentive scheme is a critical instrument for a service enterprise to remain competitive in the market. Employees in the enterprise are evaluated based on the efforts they put in. Such efforts are quantified in terms of some observable parameters known as Key Performance Indicators (KPI)s. Examples of such KPIs are work duration, quality of work, complexity of projects handled etc. Employees are ranked based on their KPI values and rewarded with suitable incentives for social and economic wellness of the organization.

The problem of incentive scheme design [15,29] is replete with an arsenal of challenges, and the area of research [13] has deep roots in the science of socio-economic theory [13], computational finance and in the theory of social choice [21]. On one hand, an ill-designed incentive scheme can often de-motivate the high performers of an enterprise and thereby, affect the organizational well being and performance. On the other hand, a well designed incentive policy can not only motivate the high performers to strive to deliver more, but also boost the performances of the middle and low performers, to motivate them to perform better. There exists a number of research articles [8,9,14,22,28,29] in literature that address the problem of effective incentive scheme design.

While most of the existing literature describe the design of effective incentive schemes, this paper takes a different perspective. We propose *FINESSE*, a framework that evaluates the fairness of a given incentive scheme. As defined later in this paper, such fairness is quantified with respect to a notion of employee utility. Specifically, we present a data driven approach to analyze a given incentive disbursement record of an organization. *FINESSE* quantifies the deviation demonstrated by a given scheme with respect to a fair incentive scheme that honors the relative ranking of the employees based on their KPI values.

Do Operational Incentive Schemes Exhibit Non-intuitive Disbursement? Figure 1 presents an instance of an operational incentive scheme where we collect real incentive data over a period of one month from a large services business. Here, the incentive is a function of two KPIs, namely work duration (measured in minutes) and quality of the work (measured in a scale of 0 to 100). Quality of the work is a measure of accuracy and is computed by the fraction of error-free work items with respect to the total number of work items. Every employee has an incentive target. In Fig. 1, we show the percentage of incentive (with respect to a target incentive) received by an employee compared to her work duration and work quality. Nature of the incentive scheme allows employees to receive incentive more than 100% of their targets. Such dataset reveals several interesting facets, as marked in Fig. 1 as well: (1) top performer in the organization (in terms of number of work duration and work quality) may not receive the highest incentive percentage, (2) employees may get incentive even without any significant work duration, (3) small difference in work duration may

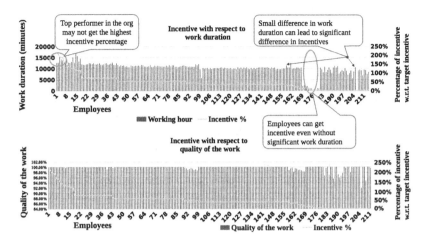

Fig. 1. Incentive in a services business. Bars represent the KPI values (work duration and quality) while the line represents the incentive received.

lead to large difference in the incentive received even when the quality of the work is not compromised.

Motivated by these non-intuitive outcomes of an operational incentive scheme, this paper scientifically addresses two key questions: *(1) how do we evaluate the fairness of an incentive scheme?* and *(2) when there are different KPIs affecting the incentive decision, what would be the desired ranking of the employees if they are eligible for receiving incentives?* We argue that proposing an alternate incentive scheme does not necessarily solve the core problems unless the above two questions are addressed. Specifically, our contributions are:

- We describe *FINESSE*, a systematic framework that takes a data driven approach to evaluate the fairness of an incentive scheme. Fairness is quantified in terms of the employee ordering with respect to a notion of employee utility, as captured through disparate KPIs.
- Unlike similar evaluation approaches, which, to the best of our knowledge, mostly use empirical techniques [26, 28], we use a multi-objective formulation via Pareto optimal front generation [17] to capture the impact of one or more KPIs that control an existing incentive scheme. Based on business domain constraints, we propose a Pareto front refinement process that generates an employee ranking in terms of their incentive eligibility.
- We evaluate *FINESSE* by comparing two candidate incentive schemes: (a) an operational scheme that is known for non-intuitive disbursements, and (b) a contender scheme proposed by us aimed at filling the gaps of the operational scheme. Using real dataset from a BPO services business, we show that *FINESSE* is effectively able to distinguish the fairness (or lack thereof) of the two schemes across a set of metrics. Finally, we build and demonstrate a prototype dashboard that implements *FINESSE* and can be used by the business leaders in practice.

2   Background and Notion of Fairness

In this section, we present a few formalisms that are needed to describe the *FINESSE* framework. A KPI for which a higher value is desirable for getting more incentives is termed as a *positive KPI*, while a KPI for which a lower value is desirable is called a *negative KPI*. As an example, the work duration of an employee is a positive KPI, whereas the number of errors committed is a negative KPI. The value of a KPI k for an employee e_1 is considered better than the corresponding one for another employee e_2, in either of the following cases: (a) if k is a positive KPI, the value of k for e_1 is more than that of e_2, or (b) the value of k for e_1 is less than that of e_2 where k is a negative KPI. We assume that the actual value achieved by an employee for a KPI is always non-negative.

KPIs and Incentives. Every employee has a *target incentive* that depends on the gross salary of the employee. Due to gross salary variation across all employees, the target incentive amount varies across employees. The *incentive* function takes as input a vector of KPI values for an employee and her target incentive to produce an incentive value that the employee is eligible for. Therefore if the employees are compared based on their absolute eligible incentive amount, it is not a fair comparison. Hence, for comparison purpose, the incentive amount for each employee is normalized. The normalized incentive value *(NIV)* of an employee is the ratio of the incentive amount received by the employee with respect to her target incentive amount.

Fairness in Incentives. We now introduce the notion of *utility* using which we define fairness in the context of incentive disbursement. A KPI vector of an employee is mapped to a scalar quantity, called utility. The notion of utility helps us define the notion of fairness in the context of an incentive scheme. Given a set of employees, we can define a total order of the employees based on their utility values, with ties being resolved randomly.

Definition 1. *An incentive scheme is* fair *if it orders the employees in agreement with the utility order.* ∎

Let $\mathcal{R}(e)$ denote the rank of an employee e. An employee with better KPI values should have a lower rank in the rank ordering. Additionally, employees to be rewarded more are the ones who hold lower ranks in the incentive ordering.

The specification of the utility function is domain specific. We now present some properties of the utility function. We begin by defining two important notions, that of *strict dominance* and *majority dominance*. Consider u_1 and u_2 are the utilities of two employees with KPI vectors $\mathcal{P}_1 = (v_{11}, v_{12}, \ldots, v_{1k})$ and $\mathcal{P}_2 = (v_{21}, v_{22}, \ldots, v_{2k})$ corresponding to two employees e_1 and e_2.
The properties of the utility function are:

- If v_{1i} is *better* than v_{2i} for all $p_i \in \mathcal{P}$, u_1 has an utility value more than u_2. This is known as *strict* dominance and we say, u_1 dominates u_2 in a strict sense.

– If v_{1i} is *better* than v_{2i} for majority (more than 50%) of $p_i \in \mathcal{P}$, u_1 has an utility value more than u_2. This is known as *majority* dominance and we say, u_1 dominates u_2 in a majority sense.

Challenges in Fairness Evaluation. An employee e_1 with a better KPI vector compared to another employee e_2 is expected to receive higher incentive than that of e_2. However, in an enterprise, disparate KPIs are used to measure employee performance. Some of these KPIs are combinable and some are not. For example, the work duration of an employee and the quality of her work are two disparate KPIs that are non-combinable. On the other hand, the employee may be involved in different types of work. The work duration for each type of work are combinable in an additive sense, and the total work duration of the employee is the addition of these individual work durations. In cases where the importance of each type of work is not equal, the combination may not be a simple sum, rather it can be a weighted sum. On the other side, the non-combinable parameters can be completely independent or they may have some relationship between them with respect to the incentive function. For example, the work duration of an employee has an indirect impact with the quality of her work with respect to the incentive function, since an employee having a significantly long work duration but very low quality of work should not be eligible for high incentives. Such KPIs cannot be combined to create a single objective based on which the incentive ordering can be decided.

3 Detailed Description of FINESSE

To generalize our approach, we assume that all KPIs are non-combinable. Even if there are some combinable KPIs, we assume that they are combined to a single parameter in $\mathcal{P}$. Figure 2 summarizes the major building blocks of *FINESSE*. The inputs to *FINESSE* are a set of KPIs and their importance. The objective of *FINESSE* is to come up with a fair ranking. As the KPIs are non-combinable, this gives rise to a multi-criteria optimization problem [25] involving more than one objective (work duration/quality/complexity etc.) to be optimized simultaneously. We begin by defining a non-dominated vector.

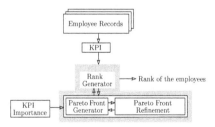

Fig. 2. Internals of the *FINESSE* framework.

Definition 2. [Non dominated vector]: *A vector $t_1 = (v_{i1}, v_{i2}, \ldots, v_{ik})$ is called non-dominated, iff there does not exist any other vector t_2, such that at least one element of t_2 has more value than it has in t_1 without degrading the values for the rest of the elements.* ∎

Example 1. Consider 3 employees e_1, e_2 and e_3 with two KPIs: work duration and work quality. The KPI values for e_1, e_2 and e_3 are (17650 min, 99%), (16892 min, 98%) and (13621 min, 100%) respectively. Clearly the vectors (17650 min, 99%) and (13621 min, 100%) are non-dominated, since the former has the largest value of the first element of the vector (work duration) and the latter has the largest value on the second element (work quality). On the other hand, (16892 min, 98%) is strictly dominated by (17650 min, 99%) on both the elements. ∎

3.1 Pareto Front Generator

The set of non-dominated vectors constitute the Pareto optimal front [25]. We first construct such a front for incentive rank ordering as a first cut solution to the problem. Successive levels of the Pareto optimal front give us sets of non-dominated vectors at that level.

ALGORITHM 1: *RankGeneration*

Input: A set of employees $\mathcal{E}$ with KPI values
Output: The desired ranking $\mathcal{R}_D$
Initialize i to 1;
repeat
  Find the Pareto optimal front using the KPI values;
  $\mathcal{E}_1 \longleftarrow$ Set of employees in the Pareto optimal front;
  Include employees in $\mathcal{R}_D$ with rank i;
  $\mathcal{E} \longleftarrow \mathcal{E} \setminus \mathcal{E}_1$;
  Increase the value of i by 1;
until $\mathcal{E}$ *is not empty*;

Algorithm 1 presents an iterative algorithm for successive level construction of the Pareto front for rank generation. The front construction in each step is done by comparing the KPI vectors pair wise. In each iteration, we construct a front containing a set of non-dominated vectors, in other words, the employees who hold the non-dominated KPI values. We begin with the set of non-dominated vectors in the entire set of employees and report them as the first tier of candidates eligible for the highest rank order in the organization, and in turn, the highest proportion of the incentive. We remove these elements from the set and construct the next Pareto front with the remaining set of employees. This gives us the next rank order. The algorithm proceeds likewise and terminates when all employees are done with. Employees in the same level of the Pareto optimal front have the same rank in the overall rank ordering. We illustrate the working of our algorithm on the example below.

Example 2. Consider 5 employees $e_1, e_2, ..., e_5$ with work duration and quality values (12647 min, 100%), (16771 min, 100%), (12685 min, 99%), (11559 min, 100%), and (11600 min, 50%) respectively. In the first iteration, the front consists of e_2. In the second iteration, the front consists of e_1, e_3 and in the third iteration, the front produces e_4, e_5. The ranking generated by the algorithm is $<e_2, 1>, <(e_1, e_3), 2>, <(e_4, e_5), 3>$, wherein $<e, r>$, represents the employee and its corresponding rank in $\mathcal{R}_D$. ∎

3.2   Pareto Front Refinement

In the above discussion, we consider the KPIs of an employee as completely independent. This may not always be the case. Though the KPIs are non-combinable, they cannot be considered in isolation while creating the incentive ordering. Consider an employee who has the highest value of work duration and a very low value of work quality. A classical Pareto front analysis will place her in the top tier of the solution frontier due to the dominance analysis step. However, this is completely undesirable considering the fact that she has not delivered quality.

Example 3. In Example 2, work quality of e_4 is much greater than the work quality of e_5 but the work durations of e_5 and e_4 are comparable. Therefore, it is not desirable that e_4 and e_5 have the same rank. ∎

A classical Pareto front analysis, therefore, needs to be refined to incorporate such domain specific constraints. To perform such *Pareto front refinement*, we use a thresholded dominance analysis, whereby we do not allow any solution vector to enter the dominating frontier if it has a very low value on any element of the vector. In such a condition, we still resort to a Pareto front generation step, wherein, all vectors in the Pareto optimal front are not accepted for the current rank and adjusted to a suitably later rank. If the Pareto optimal front in an iteration consists of only one vector, no refinement is required. A Pareto optimal front with multiple vectors may consist of vectors which are not desired as discussed above. The challenge is to find and reposition such vectors. Algorithm 2 describes the steps for choosing the most promising vector from the Pareto optimal front in any iteration. The main motivation is driven by the fact that we do not wish to compromise on the value of any of the elements in a vector in the Pareto optimal front beyond a threshold. As the values of the KPIs may come from different contexts and domains, we normalize the KPIs as:

$$N\_V(v_{ij}) = \frac{(v_{ij} - Min_{pj})}{(Max_{pj} - Min_{pj})}$$

where $N\_V(v_{ij})$ is the normalized value of v_{ij}. The terms Min_{pj}, Max_{pj} are the minimum and maximum values of the KPI p_j across all employees respectively. We then multiply $N\_V(v_{ij})$ by a constant, this is done to avoid precision problems. The constant depends on the size of the data set.

Once we have the most promising vector, we choose the other vectors from the Pareto optimal front based on threshold values $(t_1, t_2, \ldots, t_k)$, where t_i is the

---

ALGORITHM 2: *ChooseMostPromisingVector*

Input: KPI values $\{(v_{i1}, v_{i2}, \ldots, v_{ik})\}$ for $i = 1$ to n
Output: The most promising vector $\mathcal{P}_y$
Normalize KPI Values;
$(v_{y1}, v_{y2}, \ldots, v_{yk}) = (v_{11}, v_{12}, \ldots, v_{1k})$;
$MinD = MAX_j\{(MAX_i\{N\_V(v_{ij})\} - N\_V(v_{1j}))\}$;
for $x = 2$ *to* n **do**
    $d = MAX_j\{(MAX_i\{N\_V(v_{ij})\} - N\_V(v_{xj}))\}$;
    if $d < MinD$ **then**
        $MinD = d$;
        $(v_{y1}, v_{y2}, \ldots, v_{yk}) = (v_{x1}, v_{x2}, \ldots, v_{xk})$;
    end
end
return $\mathcal{P}_y = (v_{y1}, v_{y2}, \ldots, v_{yk})$;

---

threshold for the ith KPI. Algorithm 3 shows how we calculate the threshold limit for each KPI. The values of the threshold change in every iteration. We do not accept any vector for the current rank position which has a value lower than the threshold. Employees in the original Pareto optimal front but not considered for the current rank position, are stored in a set $\mathcal{X}$. In the subsequent iterations, these vectors are examined and the ones which satisfy the threshold criterion are included in the rank list and removed from $\mathcal{X}$.

ALGORITHM 3: *GetThresholdLimit*

Input: The value set $\mathcal{V}_i$ for each KPI p_i
Output: Threshold limit (T_i) of p_i
$\mathcal{N}_i \leftarrow$ Normalized value of $v \in \mathcal{P}_i$;
Sort $\mathcal{N}_i$ in descending order;
$T_i \leftarrow$ average of the difference between two consecutive elements in $\mathcal{N}_i$;
return T_i;

Is choosing the Most Promising Vector Sufficient for Complete Rank Generation?
Consider the following example.

Example 4. Consider the records of 3 employees, e_1 : (12560 min, 99.8%), e_2 : (11648 min, 100%), e_3 : (11648 min, 99.9%). e_2 dominates e_3 and hence, e_3 does not appear in the same Pareto optimal front. Assume, e_1 and e_2 are chosen for a rank position r. Why should we not choose e_3 for the rank r as e_3 and e_1 are mutually non-dominated? ∎

Algorithm 4 shows the formal steps to address this issue. Although this algorithm chooses the most promising element for the current rank position, the element actually belongs to the Pareto optimal front of the data set. We pass the entire employee data set as input. While choosing the most promising solution, if there exists multiple vectors with the same representative value, we choose the one which dominates others. If there are multiple non-dominated vectors, we choose all in the considered set and randomly designate one as the most promising solution.

It may be noted that all the algorithms proposed above are polynomial both in the size of the employee and KPI sets.

4   Evaluation and Discussions

In this section, we use *FINESSE* to evaluate two candidate incentive schemes across a set of comparison metrics. Both schemes are designed in the context of a real service enterprise. First, we describe the dataset that contains the employee and KPI details of this business. Subsequently, we define the comparison metrics, discuss the results and present the dashboard view of the prototype that implements *FINESSE*.

ALGORITHM 4: *FinalRankGenerationAlgorithm*

Input: A set of employees $\mathcal{E}$
Output: The desired ranking $\mathcal{R}_D$
$T_i \leftarrow GetThresholdLimit()$ for p_i, $\forall p_i \in \mathcal{P}$;
Normalize KPI Values; Initialize r by 1;
repeat
 $\quad$ $\mathcal{P}_y \leftarrow ChooseMostPromisingVector()$ from $\mathcal{E}$; $\mathcal{E}_1 \longleftarrow e_y$ corresponding to $\mathcal{P}_y$;
 $\quad$ $\forall i = 1, 2, \ldots, k; t_i \leftarrow v_{pi} - T_i$;
 $\quad$ **for** $e_i \in \mathcal{E}$ **do**
 $\quad\quad$ **if** *the value of at least one KPI of e_i is above that of e_y and rest of the values*
 $\quad\quad$ *are above threshold* **then**
 $\quad\quad\quad$ | $\quad$ Add e_i in $\mathcal{E}_1$;
 $\quad\quad$ **end**
 $\quad$ **end**
 $\quad$ Include employees in $\mathcal{R}_D$ with rank r;
 $\quad$ $\mathcal{E} \longleftarrow \mathcal{E} \setminus \mathcal{E}_1$; $r = r + 1$;
until $\mathcal{E}$ *is not empty*;
return $\mathcal{R}_D$;

4.1   Dataset Description

We collect data from a specific department of a BPO service business. Four KPIs are used within this department to measure employee performance: (1) *Duration of work type 1 (WT1)* which measures the time to process a business transaction (e.g., manual processing of payment), (2) *Duration of work type 2 (WT2)* which measures the time to audit a processed transaction (e.g., check the quality of work), (3) *Duration of work type 3 (WT3)* which measures the time spent in special tasks (e.g., on-boarding a new client) and (4) *work quality (QW)* which measures the percentage of transactions that are processed correctly. All durations are measured in minutes. The dataset contains 214 employee records in terms of their target incentive and the values of these four KPIs.

4.2   Scheme 1: An Operational Incentive Scheme

This scheme, adopted in the concerned department of the BPO business, additively combines the 3 work types. The total work duration WD_i of an employee

e_i is the sum total of individual work types. Productivity score (Pr_i) of an employee is defined as: $Pr_i = WD_i/C$, where C is the total work duration in the business over a period of time. A monotonically increasing function $g(.)$ takes a continuous range of productivity score values and then maps it to a discrete fraction between $[0, 1]$. For each employee e_i, this discrete fraction is called productivity multiplier (PM_i). Similarly, another monotonically increasing function $h(.)$ takes a continuous range of QW values and then maps it to a discrete fraction between $[0, 1]$. For each employee e_i, the latter discrete fraction is called quality multiplier (QM_i). The incentive received by an employee e_i, with target incentive B_i, is then given by: $\mathcal{I}^{(1)}(e_i) = B_i * PM_i * QM_i$.

Incentive for High Performers. In Scheme 1, a set ($\mathcal{E}'$) of employees is called high performers, if for each $e_i \in \mathcal{E}'$, $PM_i = 1$ and $QM_i = 1$. These high performers are eligible for additional incentives. Scheme 1 computes a score θ_i for each employee $e_i \in \mathcal{E}'$ as: $\theta_i = (WT1_i + WT2_i)/(\sum_{i\in\mathcal{E}'}(WT1_i + WT2_i))$, where $WT1_i$ and $WT2_i$ are the values for $WT1$ and $WT2$ for employee e_i. If $\mathcal{B}'$ is the additional incentive budget, additional incentive for e_i in $\mathcal{E}'$ is given by: $\mathcal{I}^{(2)}(e_i) = \mathcal{B}' * \theta_i$. The final incentive amount $\mathcal{I}(e_i)$ for employee e_i is the sum of $\mathcal{I}^{(1)}(e_i)$ and $\mathcal{I}^{(2)}(e_i)$.

Notice the key characteristics of Scheme 1: (a) it constructs a naive single objective function based on disparate set of measures (i.e., PM_i, QM_i), (b) it unnecessarily transforms a continuous quantity (i.e., Pr_i) into a discrete value, and (c) high performers are selected based on the discrete multipliers but their additional incentives are determined only by considering $WT1$ and $WT2$. Motivated by these observations, we design another incentive scheme that considers the same dataset but removes the mentioned features of Scheme 1.

4.3   Scheme 2: A Contender Incentive Scheme

Our proposed scheme categorizes KPIs into two broad classes: regular KPIs and special KPIs. Further, regular KPIs are divided into two types: combinable KPIs and outcome influencing KPIs. If $\mathcal{K} = \{k_1, k_2, \ldots, k_r\}$ is a set of combinable KPIs, each $k_i \in \mathcal{K}$ has the same dimension and the organization is interested in the combined value. Hence, for each $\mathcal{K}$, scheme 1 defines a $\mathcal{K}' = \sum_{i=1}^r \alpha_i * k_i$, where $\alpha_i \in (\alpha_1, \alpha_2, \ldots, \alpha_r)$ is the priority of $k_i \in \mathcal{K}$. Incentive of an employee depends on the value of $\mathcal{K}'$. Once the combinable KPIs are transformed into a single KPI, scheme 2 introduces the notion of outcome influencing KPIs. For a given outcome influencing set of KPIs, it is not really possible to increase the incentive amount significantly by compromising one KPI value and improving the other KPI values. Hence, the impact of all the outcome influencing KPIs are considered together. Let, $\mathcal{K}_1 = \{k_1, k_2, \ldots, k_d\}$ be a set of outcome influencing KPIs. For employees belonging to a specific *role* (e.g., manager, senior manager), for each KPI, an upper limit and lower limit is calculated. The key motivation behind setting such limits is to identify the employees that are high (low) performers, i.e., KPI values are above (below) the upper (lower) limit. The normalized value $NoV(v_{ij})$ for an employee e_i within a role and a KPI

$k_j \in \mathcal{K}_1$ is computed as: $NoV(v_{ij}) = (v_{ij} - \mathcal{L}_j)/(\mathcal{U}_j - \mathcal{L}_j)$. where v_{ij} is value of k_j of employee e_i and $\mathcal{L}_j$ is an acceptable lower limit for k_j and $\mathcal{U}_j$ is the desirable upper limit for k_j as specified by the organization. Notice that, Scheme 1 is agnostic about the roles of the employees as different measures (e.g, productivity score) do not take into account employee roles.

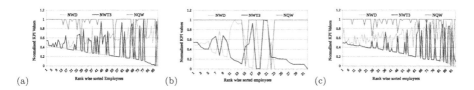

(a)   (b)   (c)

Fig. 3. Rank-wise sorted employees (as per FINESSE) vs normalized KPIs (a) $Role_1$, (b) $Role_2$, (c) $Role_3$

To limit $NoV(v_{ij})$ between $[0, 1]$, another parameter ϕ_{ij} for an employee e_i and a KPI k_j is defined. The value of ϕ_{ij} is: (a) 1 when $NoV(v_{ij}) \geq 1$, (b) 0 when $NoV(v_{ij}) \leq 0$, and (c) $NoV(v_{ij})$ otherwise. Though the outcome influencing KPIs may not be semantically comparable, we can always compare their normalized values. Assume that, in the set of outcome influencing KPIs $\mathcal{K}_1$, the priority (between $[0,1]$) of the KPIs are $\beta_1, \beta_2, \ldots, \beta_d$. Then, for an employee e_i, two quantities are defined - (i) the average KPI value: $\mu_i = \sum_{j=1}^{d} (\phi_{ij} * \beta_j)$ and (ii) the average deviation: $\sigma_i = \sum_{j=1}^{d} (\sigma_{ij} * \beta_j)$, where, $\sigma_{ij} = 0$, if $\mu_i \leq \phi_{ij}$ and $\sigma_{ij} = \mu_i - \phi_{ij}$, otherwise. For an employee, a parameter λ_i is defined for the outcome influencing set of KPIs as: $\lambda_i = \mu_i - \sigma_i$. The performance of an employee in terms of the KPI values and their overall spread are both aptly captured by λ. Let, B_i be the target incentive of an employee e_i. The amount of incentive received by an employee considering only combinable and outcome influencing KPIs is $\lambda_i * B_i$. If $\mathcal{B}$ is the sum total target (i.e., incentive budget) for all employees, the left-over budget (B_1) is given by: $B_1 = \mathcal{B} - \lambda_i * B_i$. A fraction $(f_s \in (0, 1))$ of this left-over budget is distributed to the employees based on their performance in special KPIs. Such distribution is done in a proportional fair manner within a given employee role. Let DT be the total duration spent by the employees in a given role for special KPIs and DS_i be the time spent by employee e_i. Then, the incentive received due to special KPI is: $f_s * (DS_i/DT) * B_1$. Finally, an employee receives the incentive amount $\mathcal{I}^{(1)}(e_i) = \lambda_i * B_i + f_s * (DS_i/DT) * B_1$. At this point, the remaining budget (B_2) is given by: $B_2 = B_1 - f_s * (DS_i/DT) * B_1$. In the context of the dataset, regular KPIs are WT1, WT2 and QW and the special KPI is WT3. The KPIs WT1 and WT2 are combinable and lead to a new KPI denoted by WD. Further, QW and WD are classified as outcome influencing KPIs.

Incentive for the High Performers. An employee is called high performer within her role, if her performance is above the upper limit for at least one regular KPI and not below the lower limits for no regular KPIs. Let $\mathcal{E}'$ denote the set

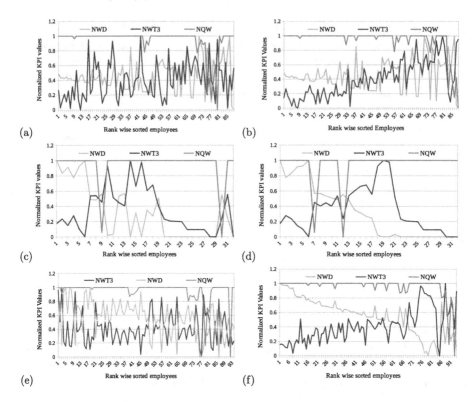

Fig. 4. Rank wise sorted employees versus normalized KPIs; Rank obtained by (a) $Role_1$:, Scheme 1, (b) $Role_1$:, Scheme 2, (c) $Role_2$:, Scheme 1 (d) $Role_2$:, Scheme 2, (e) $Role_3$:, Scheme 1 (f) $Role_3$:, Scheme 2

of high performers within a role. For a high performer e_i, $\phi_{ij} = NoV(v_{ij})$ and hence, μ_i or λ_i can now be higher than one. Scheme 2 computes a score η_i for each employee $e_i \in \mathcal{E}'$ within a role as: $\eta_i = \lambda_i / \sum_i \lambda_i$. The high performance incentive budget (B_h) is a fraction ($f_h \in (0,1)$) of remaining budget B_2, i.e., $B_h = f_h * B_2$. Thus, the high performance bonus received by an employee e_i is: $\mathcal{I}^{(2)}(e_i) = \eta_i * B_h$. Then the final incentive amount $\mathcal{I}(e_i)$ for an employee is sum of $\mathcal{I}^{(1)}(e_i)$ and $\mathcal{I}^{(2)}(e_i)$.

4.4   Comparison Metrics

In this subsection, we define a few metrics for comparing the two candidate incentive schemes. We begin by defining the distance function.

Distance Based Metrics

Using the distance functions, we compare the rank orderings obtained by *FINESSE* with the ranks obtained by Scheme 1 and 2. We infer a scheme is better than another, if the distance between the ordering obtained by the former with the ordering obtained by *FINESSE* is less than the same for the latter for the same employee record set. We now define two different distance functions.

Definition 3 [Kendall Tau Distance (KTD)]: *Kendall Tau distance [6]* δ_k *between two rank orderings* $\mathcal{R}_E, \mathcal{R}_D$ *is mathematically defined as follows:*
$\delta_k = |\{(t_1, t_2) : (\mathcal{R}_E(t_1) > \mathcal{R}_E(t_2) \text{ and } \mathcal{R}_D(t_1) \leq \mathcal{R}_D(t_2)) \text{ or } (\mathcal{R}_E(t_1) < \mathcal{R}_E(t_2)$
and $\mathcal{R}_D(t_1) \geq \mathcal{R}_D(t_2)) \text{ or } (\mathcal{R}_E(t_1) = \mathcal{R}_E(t_2) \text{ and } \mathcal{R}_D(t_1) \neq \mathcal{R}_D(t_2))\}|,$
$t_1, t_2 \in \mathcal{R}_E, \mathcal{R}_D.$ ∎

Definition 4 [Spearman FootRule Distance (SFRD)]: *Footrule distance [12]* δ_s *between two rank orderings* $\mathcal{R}_E, \mathcal{R}_D$ *is mathematically defined as follows:* ∎

$$\delta_s = \sum\nolimits_{t \in \mathcal{R}_E} |\mathcal{R}_E(t) - \mathcal{R}_D(t)|$$

The Kendall Tau distance basically counts the number of pairwise inversions between two ranks, whereas the Spearman footrule distance measures the displacement of each element. The classical Kendall Tau distance does not consider the equality in ranking. Therefore we redefine these functions for the sake of our purpose.

Property Based Metrics

Here we define two comparison metrics derived from the fairness property of an incentive scheme $\mathcal{I}$, namely the strict dominance and the majority dominance. If the utility u_1 of an employee e_1 dominates the utility u_2 of another employee e_2, the incentive of e_1 should be greater than the incentive of e_2. Using this concept, we now define two metrics.

Definition 5 [Strict Dominance Metric (SDM)]: *The strict dominance metric is defined as the ratio of the total number of employee pairs* e_i, e_j *for which* u_i *dominates* u_j *in the strict sense and* $\mathcal{I}(e_i) \geq \mathcal{I}(e_j)$, *to the total number of employee pairs* e_k, e_l *for which* u_k *dominates* u_l *in strict sense.* ∎

Definition 6 [Majority Dominance metric (MDM)]: *The majority dominance metric is defined as the ratio of the total number of employee pairs* e_i, e_j *for which* u_i *dominates* u_j *in majority sense and* $\mathcal{I}(e_i) \geq \mathcal{I}(e_j)$, *to the total number of employee pairs* e_k, e_l *for which* u_k *majority dominates* u_l. ∎

Rank Wise Sorted Employee Versus Normalized KPI Values

Finally, we plot the normalized KPI values for rank wise sorted employees and show the fairness of an incentive scheme. Instead of plotting WT1 and WT2 separately, we plot their combined normalized value denoted by NWD. Similarly, the normalized values of WT3 and QW are denoted by NWT3 and NQW respectively.

4.5   Results

FINESSE is implemented in JAVA. We start with the data set, interact with the business leaders in the organization who developed Scheme 1, and generate the ranking of the employees using the Pareto optimal front refinement approach. The employees of the organization are divided into three different roles based on their designation and we have shown our results on these three sets of employees. For each set, we compare the employee rankings generated by Scheme 1 and Scheme 2 with the ranking obtained by *FINESSE*. Since Scheme 1 is agnostic of employee roles, for all three sets, the employee ranking remains same for Scheme 1.

Table 1. Comparison among the ranks using MDM

Methods	MDM		
	Role 1	Role 2	Role 3
Scheme 1	76.10%	91.63%	77.50%
Scheme 2	61.02%	99.03%	65.20%
FINESSE	62.80%	92.93%	76.87%

Table 2. Comparison among three ranks using SDM

Methods	SDM		
	Role 1	Role 2	Role 3
Scheme 1	97.92%	93.30%	94.97%
Scheme 2	100%	100%	100 %
FINESS	100%	100%	100 %

Table 3. Distance measures for the two schemes

Distance function	KTD			SFRD		
	Role 1	Role 2	Role 3	Role 1	Role 2	Role 3
Scheme 1	2197	237	2292	2793	299	3888
Scheme 2	2039	187	2263	3007	226	3031

Figures. 3(a), (b) and (c) show the normalized KPI values of the rank wise sorted employees using *FINESSE* for $Role_1$, $Role_2$, and $Role_3$ respectively. From Fig. 3(a), we observe a decreasing trend of the lower bound of the KPI values for the rank wise sorted $Role_1$ employees using the Pareto optimal front refinement. This demonstrates that the ranking generated by *FINESSE* honors the aggregated KPI ordering. Similar trend is visible for the employees in $Role_2$ and $Role_3$ as shown in Figs. 3(b) and (c) respectively. Notice that, *FINESSE* also reflects the negative correlations among the KPIs while determining the employee rank. This is quite evident from Fig. 3(b), i.e., for the employees in $Role_2$. Observe the employee ranks from 23 and upwards. For this set of employees, NQW is quite high and NWD is quite low. Hence, the ordering is predominantly due to the value of NWT3. Similar trends can be observed in Fig. 3(a) and (c), where high performance in one KPI tries to compensate the low performance in another KPI to determine an employee rank.

These trends are hard to perceive in Figs. 4(a) to (e) that show the normalized KPI values of the rank wise sorted employees for $Role_1$, $Role_2$, and $Role_3$ respectively using both Scheme 1 and Scheme 2. While both schemes demonstrate imperfections in terms of fairness behavior, the aspect of negatively correlated KPIs and their impact on the rank ordering is better visible for Scheme 2. For example, Fig. 4(f), shows such negative correlations among the rank ordering of the $Role_3$ employees. For employees, ranked between 1 to 68, the higher value of NWD is compensated by the lower value of NWT3 which is reversed for the employees ranked between 68 to 86. Such visualization reveals the fact that Scheme 2 is more closer to a fair ranking compared to Scheme 1. To quantify this visual aspect, we resort to distance based and property based metrics.

Table 1 shows the value of MDM in *FINESSE*, Scheme 1, and Scheme 2. Notice that, MDM can not decisively tell whether one scheme is more fair than the other. This is primarily due to the fact that, MDM is reliant on the majority KPIs (in this case two out of three KPIs) and does not take into account how the KPIs are combined to generate the final incentive amount. This concludes that MDM is perhaps not the best metric to evaluate the fairness of incentive schemes in a comparative manner. We then resort to SDM which, by virtue of strict dominance, looks at all the KPIs at once. Table 2 shows the value of SDM in *FINESSE*, Scheme 1, and Scheme 2. Observe, both *FINESSE* and Scheme 2, achieves the maximum value of SDM (i.e., 100%) across all the employee roles. However, this is not true for Scheme 1. For $Role_1$, $Role_2$, and $Role_3$, the values of SDM are 97.92%, 93.30%, and 94.97% respectively. Hence, we can quantitatively conclude that, w.r.t. SDM, Scheme 2 is more fair than the Scheme 1. Still, neither MDM nor SDM reveals the individual employee level granularity while quantifying the fairness. To address this issue, we use the distance based metrics, i.e., KTD and SFRD. Table 3 shows the KTD and SFRD distance of the ranks generated by Scheme 1 and Scheme 2 w.r.t. the rank generated by *FINESSE*. Across all roles, the value of KTD for Scheme 2 is less than that of Scheme 1 when compared against *FINESSE*. This shows that Scheme 2 is more close to *FINESSE* compared to Scheme 1, and hence, more fair w.r.t. KTD metric. Using SFRD as the metric, we notice that, Scheme 2 is closer to *FINESSE* for $Role_2$ and $Role_3$, while Scheme 1 is closer to *FINESSE* w.r.t. $Role_1$. The lack of fairness w.r.t. $Role_1$ could be due to improper selection of upper and lower limits in Scheme 2. Thus, by jointly considering SDM and distance metrics, we can quantitatively conclude that Scheme 2 is more fair than Scheme 1, although the proposed approach and metrics also reveal some of the fairness gaps in Scheme 2 which can be further optimized. In fact, after sharing these results with the internal business groups, we receive positive feedback about our conclusions.

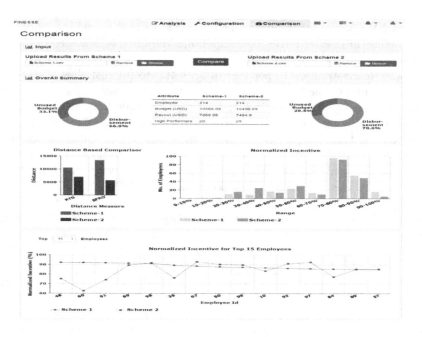

Fig. 5. Dashboard screenshot of the prototype that implements.

4.6 Prototype Dashboard

Figure 5 shows the screenshot of the prototype that implements *FINESSE* in the back-end. We use a model view controller (MVC) architecture [4] to build such a prototype. There are three major components: (a) database server (model), (b) application server (controller), and (c) user interface (views). The database server is implemented via a MySQL database for data persistence. The application layer includes the implementation of the algorithms, incentive scheme and defines the RESTful interface for the presentation layer to consume. This is written in JAVA and it uses Hibernate object-relational mapping [3] and Spring framework [5]. The UI is the presentation layer. UI includes the `html` pages and the supporting scripts which call the REST APIs of the application layer to get the data for visualization. The UI is developed using HTML, CSS, Javascript making use of external visualization libraries, such as D3 [1] and DataTables [2]. There are three key navigation tabs as shown on the top: (a) *Analysis*, (b) *Configuration*, and (c) *Comparison*. *Analysis* page lets the user understand the details of a candidate incentive scheme after it is analyzed via *FINESSE*. *Configuration* page allows the user to modify the inputs (e.g., KPIs, their importance) to *FINESSE*. *Comparison* page demonstrates a head-on comparison between two incentive schemes. We show only the partial screenshot of the *Comparison* page due to space limitation. On the *Comparison* page, after taking in the data derived from the two incentive schemes, an overview is shown in terms of: (i) total disbursement, (ii) total incentive budget, (iii) number of high performers etc. The other components include the distance based metrics, histogram of normalized incentive w.r.t. target and top k employees sorted w.r.t. one of the schemes.

We run a pilot study with a set of enterprise employees to evaluate the efficacy of such dashboard. As part of the study, the dashboard takes in employees' performance data and runs both Scheme-1 and Scheme-2 to get a comparative insights on employee incentives.

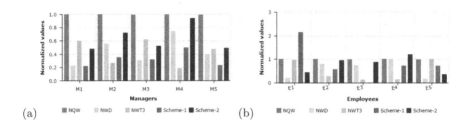

(a)   (b)

Fig. 6. Comparison of (a) peer managers, (b) employees w.r.t. their performance and incentive

One of the purposes of such pilot study is to understand the difference in incentive recommendations for the two competing schemes. The dashboard is primarily used by first level or second level managers to understand the employee performance and incentives. Figure 6(a) shows the comparison of selected peer first level managers w.r.t. their employee performance and incentive. Note that, for a given manager, it is possible to have employees of three different roles. Thus, for a comparison, we normalize the record of every employee w.r.t. their role and then compute the average values of the KPIs. As shown in Fig. 6(a), Scheme-2 consistently recommends a higher payout when compared with Scheme-1. This can be easily explained by carefully analyzing Scheme-1. Within Scheme-1, while computing the incentive amount, few steps involved discretization of employee performance via measures like productivity multipliers or quality multipliers. We observe that, due to such discretization, small difference in employee performance, leads to large difference in employee incentive. Unlike Scheme-1, such discretization is absent in Scheme-2 and hence, normalized incentive in Scheme-2 is more aligned with the normalized employee performance.

Although, Fig. 6(a) shows first-level manager wise information, it does not provide the granularity at the level of individual employees. Figure 6(b) shows the comparison among a set of sample employees. Let us first compare the employees $E1$ and $E5$. Even though, these two employees have comparable values of KPIs, $E1$ receives a significantly higher normalized incentive compared to $E2$ via Scheme-1. Such imperfections of Scheme-1 are corrected in Scheme-2. In fact, such unfair behavior is quite prominent, when we compare employees $E2$ and $E3$. Even with a comparable performance w.r.t. $E2$, Scheme-1 provides a negligible (close to zero) incentive to $E3$. The fairness of Scheme-2 becomes quite evident as it offers a significantly higher incentive to $E3$ compared to Scheme-1. Finally, the employee $E4$ stands out as a high performer in Scheme-2 because of a very high value of NWD and NQW. Hence, she is recognized and receives an incentive amount that is beyond her target incentive. Scheme-1 fails to recognize such high performers and falls short of driving an organizational objective of rewarding high performers.

4.7   Discussions

In light of the evaluation, results, and our experience from a pilot study we discuss few aspects of *FINESSE* that may clarify the positioning of this research.

(1) Can the proposed approach be used as a benchmark? We never claim that the proposed approach of evaluating the fairness of an incentive scheme should be treated as a benchmark. This is primarily because of the fact that the notion of fairness may vary from one enterprise to another. However, when a total ordering of employees needs to be established, non-dominance coupled with enterprise specific refinement can serve as a good measure of fairness. In that context, based on the evaluation results, we believe that *FINESSE* can be used as a good yardstick for fairness quantification.

(2) Dealing with outliers. The notion of outliers may creep in when an employee has too high or too low values of a KPI. Notice that, few employees in $Role_1$ in our dataset exhibit such features. We argue that such outliers should not be discarded from the data set as they represent the segment of employees who perform substantially different (i.e., extreme high or low performers) from rest of the population. However, the organization needs to pay attention for understanding such behavior. If several data driven approaches tag the employees as outliers, it may indicate that the employees may no longer fit within the designated role, leading to promotion or severance.

(3) Relationship with Taylor's scientific management. Taylor's principles of scientific management include determining the most efficient way to perform specific tasks and performing employee allocations such that it maximizes efficiency. Although, productivity can be used as a KPI in our approach, we do not focus on task allocation. The key problem addressed in this paper is the fairness evaluation of a given incentive scheme and to provide some actionable insights. How such actions might be implemented to increase the efficiency, is beyond the scope of this paper.

5   Related Research

Within an enterprise, there are different approaches to provide incentives to employees. One such approach is known as tournament style incentive scheme [16,18]. The main idea of a tournament style incentive scheme is to conduct a contest among the employees belonging to an enterprise. Following such a contest, the employees with expected values of KPIs are declared as winners. The winners receive a prize (e.g., promotion for executives, bonus for sales persons) that is typically pre-determined. A tournament based incentive scheme is appropriate when monitoring and measuring the KPI values are costly for an employer. There are few important shortcomings for an incentive motivated from a tournament style. First, such a scheme can potentially increase the level of risk that an employee would take to perform certain tasks. Second, tournament based approaches are suitable for employees who perform same kinds of tasks and they are skilled in a homogeneous manner [19]. The problem of disparate KPIs, as discussed in our paper, is thus not addressable by a tournament based strategy. Another alternate approach for designing incentive scheme is via piece-rate or variable pay mechanism [20]. An incentive scheme motivated via piece-rate approach typically rewards an employee with an amount that is proportional to the corresponding value of KPI. Evidently, such a scheme is more appropriate when employees are inherently heterogeneous is terms of their skills [20]. Piece-rate incentive schemes also suffer from certain disadvantages as it lacks the relative comparison of employee KPIs. Clearly, in an ideal scenario, an incentive scheme should maintain a balance between tournament-style and piece-rate based approaches. This is to ensure that the employees do not stay idle and at the same time, reduce the level risk required to perform the daily tasks [7]. All of these incentive schemes are around the idea of principal-agent model, where a principal computes the salary for agents. Observe, none of the prior research addresses the problem of quantifying fairness within an incentive scheme, which is the focus of our work.

There are several other areas where efficient incentive scheme have been designed in the past. Examples include market manipulation [9], business process outsourcing [22], health-care operation [11], participatory sensing [15,27], organizational work [8] etc. However, our formal setting is different from the existing approaches and to the best of our knowledge, no incentive evaluation technique exists that scientifically evaluates an existing incentive scheme based on quantified distance measures with respect to a fair ranking. The issue of fairness in incentive scheme design has been addressed in other domains [23,24], but not in the context of services organization incentives, to the best of our knowledge. For addressing the fairness issue, we leverage on the power of multi objective optimization [10] by systematically characterizing the KPIs and converting the KPI values to employee incentive.

6   Conclusions and Future Work

In this paper, we describe an approach to quantitatively evaluate the fairness of an enterprise incentive scheme. While we never claim that the approach should be used as a benchmark, we believe that it promotes a systematic mindset for incentive scheme evaluation and design. During the course of evaluation, to reflect the enterprise specific objectives, we propose a novel Pareto front refinement process that creates the ordering of employees and quantifies the fairness gap. We evaluate our approach with an incentive data set collected from a large business. In future, we plan on extending the proposed research from regular enterprise tasks to special projects, which lack well-defined KPIs.

References

1. D3.js - Data-Driven Documents, March 2016. https://d3js.org/
2. DataTables - Table plug-in for jQuery (2017). https://datatables.net/
3. Hibernate ORM - Idiomatic persistence for Java and relational databases (2017). http://hibernate.org/orm/
4. Model View Controller (2017). http://heim.ifi.uio.no/trygver/themes/mvc/mvc-index.html
5. Spring Framework (2017). https://projects.spring.io/spring-framework/
6. Betzler, N., Fellows, M.R., Guo, J., Niedermeier, R., Rosamond, F.A.: Fixed-parameter algorithms for Kemeny rankings. Theor. Comput. Sci. **410**(45), 4554–4570 (2009)
7. Bonner, S.E., Sprinkle, G.B.: The effects of monetary incentives on effort and task performance: theories, evidence, and a framework for research. Acc. Organ. Soc. **27**(4), 303–345 (2002)
8. Chen, T., Klastorin, T., Wagner, M.R.: Incentive contracts in serial stochastic projects. Manuf. Serv. Oper. Mgmt. **17**(3), 290–301 (2015)
9. Chen, Y., Gao, X.A., Goldstein, R., Kash, I.A.: Market manipulation with outside incentives. AAMAS **29**(2), 230–265 (2015)
10. Coello, C.A.C., et al.: Evolutionary Algorithms for Solving Multi-Objective Problems, vol. 242. Springer, Heidelberg (2002). https://doi.org/10.1007/978-0-387-36797-2
11. Dai, T.: Incentives in U.S. healthcare operations. Decis. Sci. **46**(2), 455–463 (2015)
12. Diaconis, P., Graham, R.L.: Spearman's footrule as a measure of disarray. J. R. Stat. Soc. **39**, 262–268 (1977)
13. Dubina, I.N., Oskorbin, N.M.: Game-theoretic models of incentive and control strategies in social and economic systems. Cybern. Syst. **46**(5), 303–319 (2015)
14. Francis, B., et al.: Impact of compensation structure and managerial incentives on bank risk taking. Eur. J. Oper. Res. **242**(2), 651–676 (2015)
15. Gao, H., et al.: A survey of incentive mechanisms for participatory sensing. IEEE Commun. Surv. Tutor. **17**(2), 918–943 (2015)
16. Gibbs, M.: Testing tournaments? An appraisal of the theory and evidence. Labor Law J. **45**(8), 493 (1994)
17. Horn, J., et al.: A Niched Pareto genetic algorithm for multiobjective optimization. In: World Congress on Computational Intelligence, pp. 82–87. IEEE (1994)
18. Hvide, H.K.: Tournament rewards and risk taking. J. Labor Econ. **20**(4), 877–898 (2002)
19. Lazear, E., Rosen, S.: Rank-order tournaments as optimum labor contracts. J. Polit. Econ. **89**(5), 841–64 (1981)
20. Lazear, E.P.: The power of incentives. Am. Econ. Rev. **90**(2), 410–414 (2000)
21. LeBaron, B.: Agent-based computational finance. Handb. Comput. Econ. **2**, 1187–1233 (2006)
22. Liu, Y., Aron, R.: Organizational control, incentive contracts, and knowledge transfer in offshore business process outsourcing. Inf. Syst. Res. **26**(1), 81–99 (2015)

23. Lv, Y., Moscibroda, T.: Fair and resilient incentive tree mechanisms. In: ACM-PODC, pp. 230–239 (2013)
24. Mahmoud, M.E., Shen, X.S.: FESCIM: fair, efficient, and secure cooperation incentive mechanism for multihop cellular networks. IEEE Trans. Mob. Comput. **11**(5), 753–766 (2012)
25. Marler, R.T., Arora, J.S.: Survey of multi-objective optimization methods for engineering. Struct. Multidiscip. Optim. **26**(6), 369–395 (2004)
26. Matsumura, E.M., et al.: An empirical analysis of a relative performance-based incentive plan: evidence from a postal service. Soc. Sci. Res. Netw. **556153** (2004)
27. Radanovic, G., Faltings, B.: Incentives for truthful information elicitation of continuous signals. In: AAAI, pp. 770–776 (2014)
28. Santos, D.O., Xavier, E.C.: Taxi and ride sharing: a dynamic dial-a-ride problem with money as an incentive. Expert Syst. Appl. **42**, 6728–6737 (2015)
29. Xie, H., Lui, J.C.S.: Modeling crowdsourcing systems: design and analysis of incentive mechanism and rating system. SIGMETRICS **42**(2), 52–54 (2014)

Explainable Recommendations in Intelligent Systems: Delivery Methods, Modalities and Risks

Mohammad Naiseh[1]([✉]), Nan Jiang[1], Jianbing Ma[2], and Raian Ali[3]

[1] Faculty of Science and Technology, Bournemouth University, Poole, UK
{mnaiseh,njiang}@bournemouth.ac.uk
[2] Chengdu University of Information Technology, Chengdu, China
mjb@cuit.edu.cn
[3] College of Science and Engineering, Hamad Bin Khalifa University, Doha, Qatar
raali2@hbku.edu.qa

Abstract. With the increase in data volume, velocity and types, intelligent human-agent systems have become popular and adopted in different application domains, including critical and sensitive areas such as health and security. Humans' trust, their consent and receptiveness to recommendations are the main requirement for the success of such services. Recently, the demand on explaining the recommendations to humans has increased both from humans interacting with these systems so that they make an informed decision and, also, owners and systems managers to increase transparency and consequently trust and users' retention. Existing systematic reviews in the area of explainable recommendations focused on the goal of providing explanations, their presentation and informational content. In this paper, we review the literature with a focus on two user experience facets of explanations; delivery methods and modalities. We then focus on the risks of explanation both on user experience and their decision making. Our review revealed that explanations delivery to end-users is mostly designed to be along with the recommendation in a push and pull styles while archiving explanations for later accountability and traceability is still limited. We also found that the emphasis was mainly on the benefits of recommendations while risks and potential concerns, such as over-reliance on machines, is still a new area to explore.

Keywords: Explainable recommendations · Human factors in information systems · User-centred design · Explainable artificial intelligence

1 Introduction

The fast development in the fields of artificial intelligence and machine learning introduced more complexity in human-agent systems where humans and the algorithms interact with each other [31] (e.g. recommender systems, social robots

© Springer Nature Switzerland AG 2020
F. Dalpiaz et al. (Eds.): RCIS 2020, LNBIP 385, pp. 212–228, 2020.
https://doi.org/10.1007/978-3-030-50316-1_13

and decision support systems). It is becoming increasingly important to offer explanations on how algorithms decisions and recommendations are made so that humans stay informed and make better decisions whether or not to follow them and to which extent. The need for explanations is reinforced by the demand on openness culture around artificial intelligence applications and the adoption of good practices around accountability [44,53], ethics [65] and compliance with the new regulations such as the General Data Protection Regulation in Europe (GDPR) [28].

An explanation is an information that communicates the underlying reasons for an event [58]. Explanation in artificial intelligence is a multi-faceted concept embracing elements from transparency, causality, bias, fairness and safety [31]. End-users need explanations for various reasons such as the verification of the output, learning from the system and improving its future operation [71]. Recent studies and surveys in this field explored the user experience facets of explanations such as the explanation goals, content and the different forms of presenting and communicating these explanations including natural language and charts [1,64,69]. However, an understanding of the existing research on the delivery methods and modalities is becoming also needed. Recent studies showed that the development of explaining the intelligent human-agent recommendations often faces problems and raises questions that must be addressed [79] (e.g. users ask for more functionalities in the explainable interface to satisfy their needs [23]). Failing in accommodating these facets and coping with the increasing complexity in the explanation interface and content leads to failure in meeting user needs and goals [11,23]. Moreover, explanations could lead to undesirable effects on end-users and introduce new errors such as over-trust [20], when the end-users fail to recognise the absence of the correct recommendations.

Given the above research challenges and the increasing number of papers in the field of explaining intelligent human-agent recommendations is evidence that user experience facets had been an open research challenge recently. Hence, we conduct a systematic review around two design facets of explanations in intelligent human-agent systems: delivery methods and modalities types. These facets have not been explored in previous surveys and this, together with the increasing demand for usable explanations, motivated us to do this work. Also, we identify and present several risks of explanation both on user experience and their decision making with the purpose of informing the design process and help to detect explanation risks and to mitigate them proactively. The main goals of this study are to (i) identify classes of current explanation delivery methods and explainable interface modalities and their design considerations; (ii) identify potential risks while users are interacting with the explainable interface along with the potential design solutions; (iii) assist researchers in positioning the research challenges and problems to be resolved in this domain appropriately.

The remainder of this paper is structured as follows. Section 2 summarises the methodology and defines research questions. Section 3 outlines the results of the review organised according to each research question defined in Sect. 2. Section 4 discusses the results and future research challenges.

2 Research Method

We carry out a systematic review to classify, describe, and analyse existing literature around explainability in intelligent human-agent systems. A systematic review is a valuable tool to provide a holistic picture of the research in a particular area. It can also help in providing facets to consider when designing software systems and its results can be seen as a reference model. For example, Hosseini et al. performed a systematic review of crowdsourcing [34] to inform engineers on what to consider in their analysis and design processes in crowdsourcing projects. We follow PRISMA [59] rationale and method and conduct a systematic study for explanations with a focus on two design facets: delivery methods and modalities types. Also, and through the analysis of the literature, we extract several design challenges considering the explanation risks and present them as a road-map of future research for researchers and practitioners in the field. This systematic study will focus on addressing the following questions to get a clear depiction of the concept and the distribution of the research about it:

1. Delivery - What are the methods proposed to deliver the explanations to end-users and their design implications?
2. Modalities - What are the proposed modalities to be used by end-users to provide input to the explanation interface?
3. Reported risks with explanations - What are the main risks while users are interacting with the explanation interface?

Search String and Relevant Data Sources. In our search for literature, we relied on four popular search engines that contain a large number of Journals and conferences of information systems which are: Google Scholar, IEEEXplore, ACM Digital Library, and Science Direct. We started the formation of the search string intending to cover the literature that combines intelligent systems, explainability and HCI. We select ("explanation" OR "Justification" OR "explainable" OR "Explainability") AND ("Intelligent" OR "Smart") AND ("System" OR "Agent") AND ("HCI" OR "User experience" OR "Human-Centred" OR "User-centred") as the search string. In order to address our research questions in the initial filtering phase, we choose to filter the papers through their title, abstract, and keywords. If there were some doubts about the relation between a paper and our scope, an additional reading through the introduction and the key parts of the paper was required to decide on the relevance. Based on the initial filtering search, we came up with 460 papers. We present our search results in Table 1.

Content Scanning. For each of the papers which we retrieved based on the initial filtering, we conducted a full-text content scanning to assess the relevance of the papers to our research questions ensuring that the paper was within the scope of this systematic study. The number reduced to 66 papers after the content scanning phase. The full set of Inclusion Criteria (IC) and Exclusion Criteria (EC) used in this reduction included:

– Recency (IC-1): Since the aim of the study is to identify the emerging research trends, challenges and gaps, we chose to focus on papers published in the last decade (2009- December 2019).

Table 1. Data sources and results from literature search.

Data source	Total results	Initial filtering	Content scanning
IEEEXplore	35	20	7
Google Scholar	443	218	29
ACM Digital Library	552	152	18
ScienceDirect	322	90	12

- Relevance (IC-2): The paper has to relate to one or more of our research questions. The reviewed papers should define explicitly one or more of our user experience facets (delivery methods, modalities and reported risks with the explanations).
- Full Access(IC-3): To include the paper, the content of the paper should be accessible in full-text.
- Duplicated papers (EC-1): We excluded repeated papers which have been published in an extended or complete version and considered the more inclusive version.
- Language and peer review (EC-2): We restricted our selected papers on papers that are written in English and published in recognised peer-reviewed journals and conferences.
- Domain-related (EC-3): The paper must be centred around the intelligent human-agent systems domain. For example, our search results introduced us with papers addressing the explanations from psychology, social science and theoretical computing perspective without direct relation to the user-experience aspect; these papers were excluded.

Data Extraction and Synthesis Process. Considering the aforementioned criteria, 66 papers were selected for the data extraction and synthesis phase. After the content scanning phase, we formed data extraction forms to record the extracted data needed to answer our research question. The data extraction process was performed by the first author. However, an inter-rater reliability test was performed in which the other authors confirmed the first author results by a randomly selected set of papers. Then, we used an iterative process between the research team to formulate, combine and conceptualise the emerged concepts.

3   Results

This section summarises the results of our analysis of the reviewed papers and answers our three research questions. Later in Sect. 4, we comment on the overall picture of the research in this area and the challenges to address in future work. Also, Table 2 lists our reviewed papers with their corresponding aspects of explanations.

3.1   Delivery Methods

In this section, we answer RQ1 around the different delivery methods of explanations with a particular focus on how the delivery methods inter-relate with other design considerations. Delivery methods are not mutually exclusive, and multiple delivery options can be used in the same interface based on the context, the recipient of the explanation and the nature of the application. Our results revealed four delivery methods which have been studied in our reviewed papers and comment on their motivations and goals in the next sub-sections.

Persistent-Specific: Explanations are delivered to the users for along with the recommendation in a straightforward and accessible way and without waiting for the user to request the explanation. The lifetime of the explanation in this method is specific to the user interaction time with the recommendation. In other words, the user is unable to consume the explanation after finishing the task. The main goal is to inform the user decides whether to accept the recommendation. This method used in the literature to foster trust [27], transparency [27], persuasiveness [72], user acceptance [39] and prevent errors and bias [73]. The cost-benefit analysis is challenging design consideration [11,47], as users may perceive the cost of reading explanations to exceed their benefits [11].

Ad-Hoc: The explanation in this category is designed to be delivered to the end-users when it is necessary and needed. This method is used in the literature in two ways:

On-demand: This method enables the users to request the explanation where the explanation is embedded in a separate view, and the users can ask for it. This is meant to reduce information overload in the interface [5,57] when explanations are not always beneficial or crucial for the performing task [11,84]. Also, this delivery method could blend well with the persistent-specific method, e.g. when users ask for further details in order to reveal the full set of explanation features [60]. On-demand method is useful where explanations contain a high level of information so users may get distracted and need more time to consume it [27,76]. Also, it is argued to be more effective to reduce users cognitive effort and avoid overwhelming end-users with unnecessary information [67]. On the other hand, embedding explanations in a separate view argued in the literature that it might not fulfill the goal of presenting the explanation and become an additional burden on user-experience. Eslami et al. [25] and Leon et al. [52] found that users might not benefit from this method as end-users may hardly notice the on-demand button due to factors like their main focus and flow state.

Exploration: The users in this method are able to explore the nature of the explanation and the agent process and increasing the understanding of the reasoning behind the recommendation [9,83]. This exploration could be: (a) feature-based exploration, where user can investigate how individual feature contributes to the recommendation and explanation output [49], (b) subset-based where input features specified by users are leveraged [46,77] and (c) global exploration where the nature of the data and its distribution are exploited [74]. Exploration techniques help users to build useful mental models and provide the user with the ability to discover more knowledge and about the agent in an interactive and engaging way [45]. Examples of such tools help the users in some problems like detecting bias in data [43], combat the filter-bubble effect in social media [38].

Persistent-Generic: Explanations are stored as a report for later investigation, and the explanation is persistent without time limit. The report may include more information compared to persistent-specific and ad-hoc methods. For instance, information about the underlying processes of the algorithm decision making on each step of the process and the reasons for selecting each decision point [50]. This is essential in some application domains, such as clinical decision support systems where the explanation is a crucial factor for accountability, traceability and ethics [6,17]. Most of our reviewed studies did not focus on developing approaches with the ability to access the explanation after finishing the task. Main approaches provided in the literature to apply this method include i) embedding the explanation in the "help page" [22] and ii) providing a dialogue interface to navigate the archive interactively [87].

Autonomous: This method appeared twice in our reviewed studies. The system in this method is responsible for deriving users' needs for an explanation based on the context. In other words, it is about the autonomy of the system to choose the time and the context to deliver the explanation. In contrary to the ad-hoc approach, which is a user-based delivery method, autonomous approaches are a systems-based method. Lim et al. [55] argued that this method could be used to provide privacy-sensitive information when the recommendation could provoke privacy violation so that it acts as a precautionary measure. Understanding the nature of the application and the different users' personas is essential to lunch this approach in human-agent systems. The papers that studied this method appeared in the domains of ubiquitous computing [55] and robots [36]. For instance, Huang et al. [36] develop an approach to explain the intelligent agent behaviour only in the critical situations, e.g. there is no need to explain why the autonomous vehicles slow down when the road is empty. This method was helpful to calibrate user trust and avoid over-trust and under-trust states.

3.2 Modalities Types

Explanations in common applications are presented either as text or graphical representations in a static way [64]. However, explanations can be designed as interactive systems where the initial explanation represents a starting point for further user interactions, e.g. asking the user for correct parts of the explanation. Designers use such modalities to streamline user functionalities to explore more details about the underlying algorithm and put the user into control the output. Providing such interactive explainable interfaces can fulfil both persuasion and over-trust reduction requirements by demonstrating the algorithmic reasoning in a thoroughness and experimental way to the end-users [73]. Research in this area is still limited, and it is unclear how to design interactive explanation interfaces in a way that is tailored and fit to users in standardised or personalised ways. Kulesza et al. [46] mentioned that supporting users with interactive explanation could lead to more complexity, as it needs a level of knowledge in software engineering and machine learning and also burden on the user experience. In this section, we focus on discovering common input modalities in the literature that typical explanation not only conveys information but also might trigger an interactive approach. We highlight these types and their potential usage scenarios.

Control: Users are enabled to play, change, regenerate or elicit some preferences about the agent in order to enhance their understanding of the underlying system [51]. The main principles behind this interaction style include boosting transparency and interpretability of the system processes and giving users control on their output [49,56]. Studies found that the control functionalities can enhance the user experience as well as enriching mental models. The research in this area focused on providing dynamic explanations more than static approaches when users need to observe the inter-relation between different factors that influence the output - e.g. Tsai et al. [81] presented an approach based on a user-controlled function that include different explanation components, which allows tuning recommendation parameters for exploring social contacts at academic conferences.

Configure: This modality gives end-users the ability to choose what information, presentation, colours, order and size are suitable to reflect the importance, relevance and focus of certain parts of the explanation. This method is rarely studied in the literature as it appeared twice in our selected studies and without elaborating on the design considerations [16].

Dialogue: It indicates the explanations provided to the end-users in an interactive bi-directional style. The user can ask for specific information about the recommendations [87]. This approach is argued to be beneficial for the design of explanation interfaces and balance between the amount of information presented to the end-users and their cognitive efforts to process that information [68]. Our findings show that users have specific information requirements before they are willing to use recommendation such as system capability, the algorithmic reasoning and detailed information about the recommended item. For instance, Eiband et al. [23] revealed that users called for more accurate information about the recommended item rather than relying on the item-based and user-based explanations. These requirements could be fulfilled by using a dialogue interaction, as the user will be assured asking specific questions about the recommendation.

Debug: In this approach, the system presents its explanation to the end-users, where, on the other hand, users are enabled to provide corrections and feedback about the explanation to the systems in order to improve output in the future recommendations [37,45,47]. User debugging can occur by different types of inputs, such as providing ratings to the explanation [24] and correcting parts of the explanations explicitly [45]. Providing the debug modality is argued to increase the algorithm accuracy by putting the Human-In-The-Loop.

3.3   Reported Risks

In this section, we present the main risks and side effects while users are receiving the explanations from the human-agent systems. In the following, we compile a list of potential risks and side-effects of explanations which are likely to arise when the design process overlooks the user experience aspect.

Over-Trust. In the situations where the cost of adopting the recommendations is high such as diagnosis and medical recommendations, it is risky to follow a recommendation rashly i.e. over-reliance. This effect could be enhanced through explanations [12,20]. Research on how to reduce over-trust effect suggested different solutions, but it needs more investigation to measure and adjust the relationship between different variable including trust, certainty level, cognitive styles, personality and liability. Existing proposals revolve around comparative explanations [13], argumentation [20], personalised explanation based on user personality [75], uncertainty and error presentation [76]. Research is still needed to investigate how to embed these solutions in the interfaces considering other usability and user experience factors such as the timing, the level of details, the feedback to collect from end-users and the evolution of explanation to reflect it. It is worth noting that over-trust can be seen as a merging property which requires observing throughout the life-cycle of the intelligent human-agent systems. For example, users may over-trust a system due to cognitive anchoring and overconfidence biased, when it proves to be correct in a number of previous occasions.

Under-Trust. As explanations could promote over-trust, it also could lead to under-trust issues [73], when the explanation is perceived to have a limited quality or fitness to the user intentions and context. Research of explanation quality discussed that improving the quality of the explanation is not about increasing transparency and recommendation rationale only. Springer et al. [76] showed that increasing the level of explanation details in an intelligent system may not necessarily lead to trust and it can lead to confusing users and harming their experience with the system. Another study showed that users could have an algorithm disillusionment when the algorithm use information derived about users as part of the explanation [25]. Explanations should be designed to simulate natural human interaction patterns so trust can be taken in a way similar to what a user would do in real life [73]. Another research linked under-trust with end-user personality. Millecamp et al. [57] found that explainable recommendations have under-trust issues to users with a high need for cognition e.g. the need to interpret and understand how the situation is composed. On the other hand, the explanations increased the trust to the users with a low need for cognition.

Suspicious Motivations. The motivation behind the explanation could be perceived as an attempt to manipulate the users. For example, marketing companies may try to explain with the purpose of enhancing the chance of purchasing the item recommended rather than informing the decision of the customer. This case is discussed by Chromik et al. [14] as a dark pattern of explainability. They discuss the problem in terms of explanation style, which is the phrasing of explanations and the modality type. The correction of the perception of a motivation to be suspicious could be conveyed to the user through the explanation itself. Eiband et al. [21] found that placebic explanations which do not supply the user with enough information about the algorithm decision-making process invoke a perception of a suspicious motivation behind the explanation.

Information Overload. Explanations could cause information overload and overwhelm the end-users. They can become confusing and complicated [47]. Bunt et al. [11] argued that robust system design should help the users to derive its underling reasoning without much need for explanations and must avoid overwhelming users with unnecessary information. More transparency in the explanation affects users ability to detect the errors in the recommendations themselves [67] and increase users response time [62] and this may lead to losing timeliness, e.g. in taking an offer available for a limited time. Hence, approaches for balancing between the soundness and completeness of the explanations need to be developed [45].

Perceived Loss of Control. Users may perceive a loss of control when the system presents static explanations rather than dynamic and interactive explanations allowing them to query and investigate further. Holliday et al. [33] studied this effect when they examined the perceived control as a factor in two conditions (with and without explanations). They concluded that users in the absence of explanations showed more control-exerting behaviour of intelligent systems. Andreou et al. [2] and Eiband et al. [23] also found that static explanations are going to be seen incomplete for some users and sometimes misleading. This calls for personalised and more dynamic interfaces for explanations.

Refusal. Refusing the explanations may happen when users feel that putting cognitive efforts to read the explanations does not lead to better recommendations or better understanding. Moreover, users cab be typically focused on completing their tasks more than reading the explanations and improving their mental models [11]. The conflict between the explanations and prior beliefs, cultural backgrounds, the nature of the application, level of knowledge and interests could be other reasons for refusing the explanations. For example, Eiband et al. [23] found that some users were more interested to know information about the specific recommendation rather than the recommendation process itself in the everyday intelligent systems (e.g. social media), whereas, this kind of explanations could be critical for other users in other application domains. This calls again for user-centred approaches to meet users' explainability needs that take users personality and contextual variables into account.

Table 2. The categorisation of the reviewed papers.

Delivery methods	Persistent-specific	$[4, 6-8, 15, 17, 18, 21, 35, 37, 49, 50, 60, 70, 85, 86]$
	Ad-hoc	$[43, 49, 66, 74, 80]$ $[4, 5, 30, 40, 52, 60, 68, 83]$
	Persistent-geniric	$[8, 22, 50]$
	Autonomous	$[36, 55]$
Modalities types	Control	$[9, 38, 43, 66, 74, 80]$ $[29, 51, 56, 57, 81, 82, 82]$
	Configure	$[16, 78]$
	Dialogue	$[3, 63, 68, 87]$
	Debug	$[10, 24, 46, 49, 54, 78]$ $[37, 45]$
Reported risks	Over-trust	$[12, 13, 20, 48, 75]$ $[76]$
	Under-trust	$[13, 25, 42, 57, 73, 76]$
	Refusal	$[11, 23, 25, 32]$
	Perceived loss of control	$[2, 23, 33, 82]$
	Information overload	$[41, 47, 55, 62, 67, 76]$
	Suspicious motivations	$[14, 21]$

4 Discussion and Research Challenges

Our systematic review study investigated two design facets of explainable recommendations and we reported on the results and synthesised main dimensions and facets and focus areas in each of these facets in the previous section. In this section, we reflect on the status of the research in them and present a set of research challenges as open issues for future research.

Delivery Methods. The popular methods in the literature focused on delivering the explanations to end-user while performing the task and while looking for recommendations. We still lack studies and the long term retrieval of such explanations, e.g. through a digital archive, and the effect of that on the accountability and traceability of these systems and users trust and adoption of them. Such approaches are important with the increasing adoption of intelligent human-agent systems in sensitive areas such as security and health. Also, it remains a challenge to design autonomous delivery which is able to consider the context and the situation when and where the users need explanations from the system. A cost-benefit analysis would then need to integrate explanations well with the good practice of user experience. Personal factors are various and they can affect that autonomous-based delivery method (e.g. users with a low level of curiosity need less frequent and simple explanations). Techniques such as UI adaptation [26] can be used to adapt the delivery method based on users' personal factors. The perceived cost of the decision is another factor (e.g. recommending changing password v.s buying security device). Privacy can also determine how recommendations and their explanation are derived and delivered. For example, some recommendations can be based on simple demographic information about the user while others utilise usage and real-time data of the user.

Modalities. Explanations can be required to provide functionalities to allow users to navigate through them and query them in an interactive style rather than being only passive recipients of static information content. For instance, Bostandjiev et al. [9] studied whether adding additional interaction functionalities (e.g. supporting a "what-if" scenario) affects the user experience and they concluded that it increases the recommendation accuracy and enhances user experience. The integration of specific modalities could lead to different experiences during the interaction [46] i.e. some modalities cannot be utilised by end users without a high-level of understanding of the agent algorithm. Hence, modalities should be used with the consideration of the automatic usability evaluation (AUE). Also, user-friendliness and intelligent modalities would need to learn the explanation that best fit users goals and needs. For instance, simple feedback such as "explain more", "redundant explanation" or "different explanation" can support users who wish to involve with the explanations and improve the explanations in future interactions. In a previous paper [61], we reported on the results related to input modalities meant for tailoring the explanations for a specific user or group of users i.e. personalisation.

Reported Risks. The researchers in our systematic review reported several challenges for HCI researchers and practitioners to develop explainability solutions and avoid the potential risks. Explaining recommendations can offer benefits for users trust and acceptance. Additionally, the emphasis on the benefits and overlooking the side effects can lead to less critical consequences in low-cost recommendation services, e.g., movies. In high-cost recommendations, e.g. prescription recommendations, users may over-trust, or under-trust the advice provided by the system and this may lead to critical consequences. Hence, the design of the explanations needs to consider the potential risks of presenting the explanations as a first-class issue. Also, the research needs to design explanations to evolve during the time considering what has been explained before to work for long-term interaction with the end-users and consider techniques from learning (e.g. constructive feedback [19]) that could mitigate these risks.

We would need to develop evaluation metrics and questionnaires that cover the user-centred aspects of explanations and evaluate error-proneness and potential risks.

5   Conclusion and Future Work

Driven by a growing need for, and interest in, intelligent human-agent systems, this paper presented a systematic review to clarify, map and analyse the relevant literature in the last ten years. The findings present the results regarding two main explanation design facets which are the delivery methods and the modalities. Also, we reflected on our systematic review and presented several challenges considering the risks while users are receiving the explanations. We elaborated on the status of the field and where research is lacking to aid future research in the area. We made the argument that explanations should be engineered using user-centred approaches and be evolved and adapted iteratively as their acceptance and trust are not only reliant on the information content and correctness but rather require consideration of a wider set of factors around users and their usage context and experience.

Acknowledgments. This work is partially funded by iQ HealthTech and Bournemouth university PGR development fund.

References

1. Al-Taie, M.Z., Kadry, S.: Visualization of explanations in recommender systems. J. Adv. Manag. Sci. **2**(2), 140–144 (2014)
2. Andreou, A., Venkatadri, G., Goga, O., Gummadi, K., Loiseau, P., Mislove, A.: Investigating ad transparency mechanisms in social media: a case study of Facebook's explanations (2018)
3. Arioua, A., Buche, P., Croitoru, M.: Explanatory dialogues with argumentative faculties over inconsistent knowledge bases. Expert Syst. Appl. **80**, 244–262 (2017)
4. Bader, R., Woerndl, W., Karitnig, A., Leitner, G.: Designing an explanation interface for proactive recommendations in automotive scenarios. In: Ardissono, L., Kuflik, T. (eds.) UMAP 2011. LNCS, vol. 7138, pp. 92–104. Springer, Heidelberg (2012). https://doi.org/10.1007/978-3-642-28509-7_10
5. Barria-Pineda, J., Akhuseyinoglu, K., Brusilovsky, P.: Explaining need-based educational recommendations using interactive open learner models. In: Adjunct Publication of the 27th Conference on User Modeling, Adaptation and Personalization, pp. 273–277. ACM (2019)
6. Binns, R., Van Kleek, M., Veale, M., Lyngs, U., Zhao, J., Shadbolt, N.: 'It's reducing a human being to a percentage': perceptions of justice in algorithmic decisions. In: Proceedings of the 2018 CHI Conference on Human Factors in Computing Systems, p. 377. ACM (2018)

7. Biran, O., McKeown, K.R.: Human-centric justification of machine learning predictions. In: IJCAI, pp. 1461–1467 (2017)
8. Blake, J.N., Kerr, D.V., Gammack, J.G.: Streamlining patient consultations for sleep disorders with a knowledge-based cdss. Inf. Syst. **56**, 109–119 (2016)
9. Bostandjiev, S., O'Donovan, J., Höllerer, T.: TasteWeights: a visual interactive hybrid recommender system. In: Proceedings of the sixth ACM Conference on Recommender systems, pp. 35–42. ACM (2012)
10. Brooks, M., Amershi, S., Lee, B., Drucker, S.M., Kapoor, A., Simard, P.: FeatureInsight: visual support for error-driven feature ideation in text classification. In: 2015 IEEE Conference on Visual Analytics Science and Technology (VAST), pp. 105–112. IEEE (2015)
11. Bunt, A., Lount, M., Lauzon, C.: Are explanations always important?: A study of deployed, low-cost intelligent interactive systems. In: Proceedings of the 2012 ACM International Conference on Intelligent User Interfaces, pp. 169–178. ACM (2012)
12. Bussone, A., Stumpf, S., O'Sullivan, D.: The role of explanations on trust and reliance in clinical decision support systems. In: 2015 International Conference on Healthcare Informatics, pp. 160–169. IEEE (2015)
13. Cai, C.J., Jongejan, J., Holbrook, J.: The effects of example-based explanations in a machine learning interface. In: Proceedings of the 24th International Conference on Intelligent User Interfaces, pp. 258–262. ACM (2019)
14. Chromik, M., Eiband, M., Völkel, S.T., Buschek, D.: Dark patterns of explainability, transparency, and user control for intelligent systems. In: IUI Workshops (2019)
15. Coba, L., Zanker, M., Rook, L., Symeonidis, P.: Exploring users' perception of collaborative explanation styles. In: 2018 IEEE 20th Conference on Business Informatics (CBI), vol. 1, pp. 70–78. IEEE (2018)
16. Díaz-Agudo, B., Recio-Garcia, J.A., Jimenez-Díaz, G.: Data explanation with CBR. In: ICCBR 2018, p. 64 (2018)
17. Dodge, J., Liao, Q.V., Zhang, Y., Bellamy, R.K., Dugan, C.: Explaining models: an empirical study of how explanations impact fairness judgment. In: Proceedings of the 24th International Conference on Intelligent User Interfaces, pp. 275–285. ACM (2019)
18. Dominguez, V., Messina, P., Donoso-Guzmán, I., Parra, D.: The effect of explanations and algorithmic accuracy on visual recommender systems of artistic images. In: Proceedings of the 24th International Conference on Intelligent User Interfaces, pp. 408–416. ACM (2019)
19. Du Toit, E.: Constructive feedback as a learning tool to enhance students' self-regulation and performance in higher education. Perspect. Educ. **30**(2), 32–40 (2012)
20. Ehrlich, K., Kirk, S.E., Patterson, J., Rasmussen, J.C., Ross, S.I., Gruen, D.M.: Taking advice from intelligent systems: the double-edged sword of explanations. In: Proceedings of the 16th International Conference on Intelligent User Interfaces, pp. 125–134. ACM (2011)
21. Eiband, M., Buschek, D., Kremer, A., Hussmann, H.: The impact of placebic explanations on trust in intelligent systems. In: Extended Abstracts of the 2019 CHI Conference on Human Factors in Computing Systems, p. LBW0243. ACM (2019)
22. Eiband, M., Schneider, H., Buschek, D.: Normative vs. pragmatic: two perspectives on the design of explanations in intelligent systems. In: IUI Workshops (2018)

23. Eiband, M., Völkel, S.T., Buschek, D., Cook, S., Hussmann, H.: When people and algorithms meet: user-reported problems in intelligent everyday applications. In: Proceedings of the 24th International Conference on Intelligent User Interfaces, pp. 96–106. ACM (2019)

24. Elahi, M., Ge, M., Ricci, F., Fernández-Tobías, I., Berkovsky, S., David, M.: Interaction design in a mobile food recommender system. In: CEUR Workshop Proceedings, CEUR-WS (2015)

25. Eslami, M., Krishna Kumaran, S.R., Sandvig, C., Karahalios, K.: Communicating algorithmic process in online behavioral advertising. In: Proceedings of the 2018 CHI Conference on Human Factors in Computing Systems, p. 432. ACM (2018)

26. Galindo, J.A., Dupuy-Chessa, S., Mandran, N., Céret, E.: Using user emotions to trigger UI adaptation. In: 2018 12th International Conference on Research Challenges in Information Science (RCIS), pp. 1–11. IEEE (2018)

27. Gedikli, F., Jannach, D., Ge, M.: How should I explain? A comparison of different explanation types for recommender systems. Int. J. Hum Comput. Stud. **72**(4), 367–382 (2014)

28. Goodman, B., Flaxman, S.: Eu regulations on algorithmic decision-making and a 'right to explanation'. In: ICML Workshop on Human Interpretability in Machine Learning (WHI 2016), New York (2016)

29. Gretarsson, B., O'Donovan, J., Bostandjiev, S., Hall, C., Höllerer, T.: SmallWorlds: visualizing social recommendations. In: Computer Graphics Forum, vol. 29, pp. 833–842. Wiley Online Library (2010)

30. Gutiérrez, F., Charleer, S., De Croon, R., Htun, N.N., Goetschalckx, G., Verbert, K.: Explaining and exploring job recommendations: a user-driven approach for interacting with knowledge-based job recommender systems. In: Proceedings of the 13th ACM Conference on Recommender Systems, pp. 60–68 (2019)

31. Hagras, H.: Toward human-understandable, explainable AI. Computer **51**(9), 28–36 (2018)

32. ter Hoeve, M., Heruer, M., Odijk, D., Schuth, A., de Rijke, M.: Do news consumers want explanations for personalized news rankings. In: FATREC Workshop on Responsible Recommendation Proceedings (2017)

33. Holliday, D., Wilson, S., Stumpf, S.: The effect of explanations on perceived control and behaviors in intelligent systems. In: CHI 2013 Extended Abstracts on Human Factors in Computing Systems, pp. 181–186. ACM (2013)

34. Hosseini, M., Shahri, A., Phalp, K., Taylor, J., Ali, R.: Crowdsourcing: a taxonomy and systematic mapping study. Comput. Sci. Rev. **17**, 43–69 (2015)

35. Hu, J., Zhang, Z., Liu, J., Shi, C., Yu, P.S., Wang, B.: RecExp: a semantic recommender system with explanation based on heterogeneous information network. In: Proceedings of the 10th ACM Conference on Recommender Systems, pp. 401–402. ACM (2016)

36. Huang, S.H., Bhatia, K., Abbeel, P., Dragan, A.D.: Establishing appropriate trust via critical states. In: 2018 IEEE/RSJ International Conference on Intelligent Robots and Systems (IROS), pp. 3929–3936. IEEE (2018)

37. Hussein, T., Neuhaus, S.: Explanation of spreading activation based recommendations. In: Proceedings of the 1st International Workshop on Semantic Models for Adaptive Interactive Systems, SEMAIS, vol. 10, pp. 24–28. Citeseer (2010)

38. Kang, B., Tintarev, N., Höllerer, T., O'Donovan, J.: What am I not seeing? An interactive approach to social content discovery in microblogs. In: Spiro, E., Ahn, Y.-Y. (eds.) SocInfo 2016. LNCS, vol. 10047, pp. 279–294. Springer, Cham (2016). https://doi.org/10.1007/978-3-319-47874-6_20

39. Karga, S., Satratzemi, M.: Using explanations for recommender systems in learning design settings to enhance teachers' acceptance and perceived experience. Educ. Inf. Technol. **24**, 1–22 (2019)
40. Katarya, R., Jain, I., Hasija, H.: An interactive interface for instilling trust and providing diverse recommendations. In: 2014 International Conference on Computer and Communication Technology (ICCCT), pp. 17–22. IEEE (2014)
41. Kleinerman, A., Rosenfeld, A., Kraus, S.: Providing explanations for recommendations in reciprocal environments. In: Proceedings of the 12th ACM Conference on Recommender Systems, pp. 22–30. ACM (2018)
42. Knijnenburg, B.P., Kobsa, A.: Making decisions about privacy: information disclosure in context-aware recommender systems. ACM Trans. Interact. Intell. Syst. (TiiS) **3**(3), 20 (2013)
43. Krause, J., Perer, A., Bertini, E.: A user study on the effect of aggregating explanations for interpreting machine learning models. In: ACM KDD Workshop on Interactive Data Exploration and Analytics (2018)
44. Kroll, J.A., Barocas, S., Felten, E.W., Reidenberg, J.R., Robinson, D.G., Yu, H.: Accountable algorithms. U. Pa. L. Rev. **165**, 633 (2016)
45. Kulesza, T., Burnett, M., Wong, W.K., Stumpf, S.: Principles of explanatory debugging to personalize interactive machine learning. In: Proceedings of the 20th International Conference on Intelligent User Interfaces, pp. 126–137. ACM (2015)
46. Kulesza, T., Stumpf, S., Burnett, M., Kwan, I.: Tell me more?: The effects of mental model soundness on personalizing an intelligent agent. In: Proceedings of the SIGCHI Conference on Human Factors in Computing Systems, pp. 1–10. ACM (2012)
47. Kulesza, T., Stumpf, S., Burnett, M., Yang, S., Kwan, I., Wong, W.K.: Too much, too little, or just right? Ways explanations impact end users' mental models. In: 2013 IEEE Symposium on Visual Languages and Human Centric Computing, pp. 3–10. IEEE (2013)
48. Lai, V., Tan, C.: On human predictions with explanations and predictions of machine learning models: a case study on deception detection, pp. 29–38 (2019)
49. Lamche, B., Adıgüzel, U., Wörndl, W.: Interactive explanations in mobile shopping recommender systems. In: Joint Workshop on Interfaces and Human Decision Making in Recommender Systems, p. 14 (2014)
50. Langley, P., Meadows, B., Sridharan, M., Choi, D.: Explainable agency for intelligent autonomous systems. In: Twenty-Ninth IAAI Conference (2017)
51. Le Bras, P., Robb, D.A., Methven, T.S., Padilla, S., Chantler, M.J.: Improving user confidence in concept maps: exploring data driven explanations. In: Proceedings of the 2018 CHI Conference on Human Factors in Computing Systems, p. 404. ACM (2018)
52. Leon, P.G., Cranshaw, J., Cranor, L.F., Graves, J., Hastak, M., Xu, G.: What do online behavioral advertising disclosures communicate to users? (cmu-cylab-12-008) (2012)
53. Lepri, B., Oliver, N., Letouzé, E., Pentland, A., Vinck, P.: Fair, transparent, and accountable algorithmic decision-making processes. Philos. Technol. **31**(4), 611–627 (2018)
54. Li, T., Convertino, G., Tayi, R.K., Kazerooni, S.: What data should I protect?: Recommender and planning support for data security analysts. In: IUI, pp. 286–297 (2019)
55. Lim, B.Y., Dey, A.K.: Assessing demand for intelligibility in context-aware applications. In: Proceedings of the 11th International Conference on Ubiquitous Computing, pp. 195–204. ACM (2009)

56. Loepp, B., Herrmanny, K., Ziegler, J.: Blended recommending: integrating interactive information filtering and algorithmic recommender techniques. In: Proceedings of the 33rd Annual ACM Conference on Human Factors in Computing Systems, pp. 975–984. ACM (2015)

57. Millecamp, M., Htun, N.N., Conati, C., Verbert, K.: To explain or not to explain: the effects of personal characteristics when explaining music recommendations. In: IUI, pp. 397–407 (2019)

58. Miller, T.: Explanation in artificial intelligence: insights from the social sciences. Artif. Intell. **267**, 1–38 (2018)

59. Moher, D., Liberati, A., Tetzlaff, J., Altman, D.G.: Preferred reporting items for systematic reviews and meta-analyses: the PRISMA statement. Ann. Int. Med. **151**(4), 264–269 (2009)

60. Muhammad, K., Lawlor, A., Rafter, R., Smyth, B.: Great explanations: opinionated explanations for recommendations. In: Hüllermeier, E., Minor, M. (eds.) ICCBR 2015. LNCS (LNAI), vol. 9343, pp. 244–258. Springer, Cham (2015). https://doi.org/10.1007/978-3-319-24586-7_17

61. Naiseh, M., Jiang, N., Ma, J., Ali, R.: Personalising explainable recommendations: literature and conceptualisation. In: WorldCist 2020 - 8th World Conference on Information Systems and Technologies. Springer, Heidelberg (2020)

62. Narayanan, M., Chen, E., He, J., Kim, B., Gershman, S., Doshi-Velez, F.: How do humans understand explanations from machine learning systems? An evaluation of the human-interpretability of explanation (2018)

63. Nguyen, T.N., Ricci, F.: A chat-based group recommender system for tourism. In: Schegg, R., Stangl, B. (eds.) Information and Communication Technologies in Tourism 2017, pp. 17–30. Springer, Cham (2017). https://doi.org/10.1007/978-3-319-51168-9_2

64. Nunes, I., Jannach, D.: A systematic review and taxonomy of explanations in decision support and recommender systems. User Model. User-Adap. Inter. **27**(3–5), 393–444 (2017)

65. Paraschakis, D.: Towards an ethical recommendation framework. In: 2017 11th International Conference on Research Challenges in Information Science (RCIS), pp. 211–220. IEEE (2017)

66. Parra, D., Brusilovsky, P., Trattner, C.: See what you want to see: visual user-driven approach for hybrid recommendation. In: Proceedings of the 19th International Conference on Intelligent User Interfaces, pp. 235–240. ACM (2014)

67. Poursabzi-Sangdeh, F., Goldstein, D.G., Hofman, J.M., Vaughan, J.W., Wallach, H.: Manipulating and measuring model interpretability (2018)

68. Ramachandran, D., et al.: A TV program discovery dialog system using recommendations. In: Proceedings of the 16th Annual Meeting of the Special Interest Group on Discourse and Dialogue, pp. 435–437 (2015)

69. Rosenfeld, A., Richardson, A.: Explainability in human-agent systems. Auton. Agent. Multi-Agent Syst. **33**(6), 673–705 (2019)

70. Ruiz-Iniesta, A., Melgar, L., Baldominos, A., Quintana, D.: Improving childrens' experience on a mobile EdTech platform through a recommender system. Mob. Inf. Syst. **2018** (2018)

71. Samek, W., Wiegand, T., Müller, K.R.: Explainable artificial intelligence: understanding, visualizing and interpreting deep learning models (2017)

72. Sato, M., Ahsan, B., Nagatani, K., Sonoda, T., Zhang, Q., Ohkuma, T.: Explaining recommendations using contexts. In: 23rd International Conference on Intelligent User Interfaces, pp. 659–664. ACM (2018)

73. Schäfer, H., et al.: Towards health (aware) recommender systems. In: Proceedings of the 2017 International Conference on Digital Health, pp. 157–161. ACM (2017)
74. Schaffer, J., Giridhar, P., Jones, D., Höllerer, T., Abdelzaher, T., O'donovan, J.: Getting the message?: A study of explanation interfaces for microblog data analysis. In: Proceedings of the 20th International Conference on Intelligent User Interfaces, pp. 345–356. ACM (2015)
75. Schaffer, J., O'Donovan, J., Michaelis, J., Raglin, A., Höllerer, T.: I can do better than your AI: expertise and explanations. In: IUI, pp. 240–251 (2019)
76. Springer, A., Whittaker, S.: Progressive disclosure: empirically motivated approaches to designing effective transparency, pp. 107–120 (2019)
77. Stumpf, S., et al.: Interacting meaningfully with machine learning systems: three experiments. Int. J. Hum. Comput. Stud. **67**(8), 639–662 (2009)
78. Stumpf, S., Skrebe, S., Aymer, G., Hobson, J.: Explaining smart heating systems to discourage fiddling with optimized behavior. In: CEUR Workshop Proceedings, vol. 2068 (2018)
79. Svrcek, M., Kompan, M., Bielikova, M.: Towards understandable personalized recommendations: hybrid explanations. Comput. Sci. Inf. Syst. **16**(1), 179–203 (2019)
80. Tamagnini, P., Krause, J., Dasgupta, A., Bertini, E.: Interpreting black-box classifiers using instance-level visual explanations. In: Proceedings of the 2nd Workshop on Human-In-the-Loop Data Analytics, p. 6. ACM (2017)
81. Tsai, C.H., Brusilovsky, P.: Providing control and transparency in a social recommender system for academic conferences. In: Proceedings of the 25th Conference on User Modeling, Adaptation and Personalization, pp. 313–317. ACM (2017)
82. Tsai, C.H., Brusilovsky, P.: Explaining recommendations in an interactive hybrid social recommender. In: Proceedings of the 24th International Conference on Intelligent User Interfaces, pp. 391–396. ACM (2019)
83. Verbert, K., Parra, D., Brusilovsky, P., Duval, E.: Visualizing recommendations to support exploration, transparency and controllability. In: Proceedings of the 2013 International Conference on Intelligent User Interfaces, pp. 351–362. ACM (2013)
84. Wiebe, M., Geiskkovitch, D.Y., Bunt, A.: Exploring user attitudes towards different approaches to command recommendation in feature-rich software. In: Proceedings of the 21st International Conference on Intelligent User Interfaces, pp. 43–47. ACM (2016)
85. Zanker, M., Ninaus, D.: Knowledgeable explanations for recommender systems. In: 2010 IEEE/WIC/ACM International Conference on Web Intelligence and Intelligent Agent Technology, vol. 1, pp. 657–660. IEEE (2010)
86. Zanker, M., Schoberegger, M.: An empirical study on the persuasiveness of fact-based explanations for recommender systems. In: Joint Workshop on Interfaces and Human Decision Making in Recommender Systems, vol. 1253, pp. 33–36 (2014)
87. Zhao, G., et al.: Personalized reason generation for explainable song recommendation. ACM Trans. Intell. Syst. Technol. (TIST) **10**(4), 41 (2019)

Participation in Hackathons: A Multi-methods View on Motivators, Demotivators and Citizen Participation

Anthony Simonofski[1,2]($\boxtimes$), Victor Amaral de Sousa[1], Antoine Clarinval[1], and Benoît Vanderose[1]

[1] Namur Digital Institute, University of Namur, Namur, Belgium
{anthony.simonofski,victor.amaral,antoine.clarinval,
benoit.vanderose}@unamur.be
[2] Faculty of Economics and Business, Katholieke Universiteit Leuven,
Leuven, Belgium
anthony.simonofski@kuleuven.be

Abstract. Hackathons are problem-focused programming events that allow conceiving, implementing, and presenting digital innovations. The number of participants is one of the key success factors of hackathons. In order to maximize that number, it is essential to understand what motivates people to participate. Previous work on the matter focused on quantitative studies and addressed neither the topic of demotivators nor the relationship between participation in hackathons and citizen participation, although hackathons constitute a promising participation method where citizens can build their own project, amongst other methods such as meetings or online platforms. Therefore, in this study, we examined a specific hackathon organized in Belgium and collected data about the motivators and demotivators of the participants through a questionnaire and in-depth interviews, thereby following a multi-methods approach. This study contributes to the scarce theoretical discussion on the topic by defining precisely the motivators and demotivators and provides recommendations for hackathon organizers to help them bring in more participants. Furthermore, from our exploration of the relationship between participation in hackathons and citizen participation, we suggest a citizen participation ecosystem embedding hackathons to provide benefits for the society.

Keywords: Hackathon · Motivator · Citizen participation · Multi-methods

1 Introduction

A hackathon can be defined as a "problem-focused computer programming event, as well as a contest to pitch, program, and present instances of prototype digital

Electronic supplementary material The online version of this chapter (https://doi.org/10.1007/978-3-030-50316-1_14) contains supplementary material, which is available to authorized users.

© Springer Nature Switzerland AG 2020
F. Dalpiaz et al. (Eds.): RCIS 2020, LNBIP 385, pp. 229–246, 2020.
https://doi.org/10.1007/978-3-030-50316-1_14

innovations [...]. It brings together programmers and others [...] to collaborate intensively over a short period of time on software projects [...]" [3]. There are different types of hackathons [3], which can serve different purposes. As mentioned in [5], hackathons can be used by organizations looking for a way to innovate within their line of business (company-internal hackathons). Hackathons are also more and more organized in the academic world and in the public domain (civic hackathons) as a solution to develop new ideas and improve the skills of the participants. In the latter case, hackathons are considered as a way for citizens to participate and to contribute to the improvement of services delivered by governments, for example by exploring public data repositories [4,7]. For focus-specific hackathons to which anyone can participate (e.g. hackathons about climate, finance, etc.), one critical success factor is the number of participants. Therefore, it is key to understand the factors impacting people's motivation to participate.

While research on the hackathon phenomenon is still scarce, several studies have been conducted on the factors impacting the willingness of people to participate to such events [3,6,7,10,13]. However, most of the motivators are presented in a vague way and without detailed information. As a result, it is difficult for organizers to leverage these motivators to take concrete actions aiming to increase people's willingness to participate in hackathons. Also, the factors demotivating participation are left aside by the related studies. Finally, the relationship between the participation in a hackathon and citizen participation remains unexplored. A wide variety of citizen participation methods exist (e.g. workshops, participation in town hall meetings, etc.) and hackathons represent one of them where citizens can build their own projects and have a concrete impact on society if the project is implemented [17].

In order to bridge these gaps, this paper presents a study conducted during a focus-specific hackathon organized by a junior enterprise of computer science students in Belgium. We followed a multi-methods approach combining a questionnaire and in-depth interviews to collect insights on motivators, demotivators and on the relationship between hackathons and citizen participation. Then, we compared our findings to previous studies and provided recommendations for hackathon organizers based on the gathered insights. Finally, our findings allowed us to propose a citizen participation ecosystem aiming at generating benefits for society through hackathons.

The remaining of this paper is structured as follows. First, Sect. 2 presents related studies and the theoretical model used as a basis for the research. Then, the methodology applied to collect and analyze the data is detailed in Sect. 3. Section 4 presents the findings on motivators, demotivators, and the relationship between participation in hackathons and participation as a citizen. The implications of these findings for research and practice are discussed in Sect. 5. Section 6 discusses the limitations of the study and provides leads for further research. Finally, Sect. 7 closes the paper with a summary of its contributions.

2 Previous Studies and Theoretical Model

Previous work has studied the motivators to participate in hackathons. We must here note that we restricted this background evaluation to papers explicitly studying the motivations to participate in hackathons. Indeed, other studies related to motivation to engage in crowdsourcing (e.g. [15,18]) and in Open Source Communities (e.g. [1]) were not considered as their focus is different. Table 1 summarizes the previous studies within the scope of the present research and presents the most important elements they identified.

Table 1. Overview of previous work studying motivators to participate in hackathons

Code	Reference	Methodology	Studied motivators
P1	[3]	Questionnaire	Learning, Networking, Social change, Prizes
P2	[7]	Questionnaire	Learning, Networking, Solving civic issues, Performing teamwork
P3	[10]	Questionnaire, interviews (not for motivators)	Fun, Intellectual challenge, Reputation, User need, Career
P4	[13]	Documents, questionnaire, interviews, observations	Professional networking, Fun, Intellectual challenge
P5	[6]	Questionnaire	Recognition, Fun, Financial rewards, Learning

Building up on these sources, we designed a theoretical model represented in Fig. 1. First, the model includes the motivators identified in previous work. In order to extract these factors, we listed several individual motivators from the studies and grouped them into overarching categories that can be found in the model. Three additional factors, namely logistics, coaching, and influence from others, have been added following preliminary discussions with 8 hackathon participants. These discussions were open-ended in nature where we first asked the participants about what motivates them to participate to have more fine-grained information about their motivation. We then showed them the theoretical model and asked them if it was complete in their opinion. We also added a general "demotivating factors" element impacting the willingness to participate. Finally, we added the relationship between the willingness to participate in hackathons and the willingness to participate as a citizen, in the broader sense. For each element of the theoretical model, Fig. 1 specifies the past studies in which the element was found (see Table 1). The elements that were not found in past studies are indicated as "NEW".

This model constitutes the basis to develop the questionnaire as well as the interview guide we used to collect data for this research. These are also based on previously developed instruments such as [6], authors of which called for the use in other regions of the world than Brazil to compare the significance of the motivators they identified.

3   Methodology

3.1   Context of the Study

In order to collect data for this study, we examined the "Hope For Climate" hackathon that took place in Namur (Belgium) from the 18th to the 20th of October 2019. It is a focus-specific hackathon that did not have requirements in terms of participants profiles, data, or technology to use. This event drew 65 participants. As Namur is a city with one university and several colleges, participants were, to a large extent, students coming from different institutions. They had to form groups of 4–5 to build their solutions. The goal of this hackathon was to envision and implement innovative solutions to address the phenomenon of climate change, with different sub-themes such as agriculture, waste management and green mobility. The ideas and their implementation were, on the last day, evaluated by a jury of professors and domain experts. After that, a number of non-financial rewards were given to the winning teams.

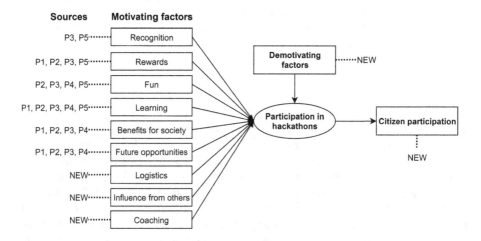

Fig. 1. Theoretical model based on previous studies

3.2   Data Collection and Analysis

In the present study, both quantitative (through a questionnaire) and qualitative (through in-depth interviews) data were collected. According to Jonhnson et al. [9], a combination of both quantitative and qualitative methods contributes to the identification of informative, complete, balanced, and useful research results.

Furthermore, this multi-methods approach combining a questionnaire and interviews was also followed in a study on eliciting participants' motivation to participate in Google's Summer of Code [15] and it allowed the authors to provide a rich view of the motivators.

The quantitative insights helped us understand the importance of particular motivators for the participants and compare the results with related studies. These insights also helped us rework the interview guide to emphasize elements that seemed particularly important as well as elements identified as important in other studies, that however received less interest from the people in our sample. Through the interviews, we were able to gain a detailed understanding of the motivators and demotivators, which was lacking in most related studies.

Quantitative Data. The questionnaire is made of four parts. First, general questions are asked about previous experience with hackathons. In the second part, we refined the nine motivating factors in Fig. 1 into 26 individual motivators, each relating to only one higher-level factor. We did this in order to gather information at a more granular level, which is key to have a better understanding of the higher-level motivators. Respondents were invited to indicate to which extent they were motivated by each motivator on a 5-point Likert scale going from "Totally disagree" to "Totally agree". To develop this part of the questionnaire, inspiration was drawn from the one used in [6]. An open-ended question was then asked about what could demotivate participation in a hackathon. Since no previous work details demotivators, an open-ended question appeared as the best option to leave room for creativity in respondents' answers [2]. The third part is dedicated to the relationship between participation in hackathons and citizen participation. Respondents were asked to what extent they participate in hackathons because they feel engaged with the theme and whether participating in hackathons increases their willingness to give their opinion on public matters as citizens. Respondents were also asked on the effect of participating in hackathons on their willingness to exercise citizen participation through the participation methods listed in [17] or through a civic hackathon. All the questions in this part are presented on a 5-point Likert scale. The last part of the questionnaire contains demographic questions and allowed collecting data on respondents' gender, age, education, and background. The full questionnaire is available as supplementary material[1].

A pre-test of the questionnaire was conducted with 8 people, including 4 with experience in organizing and participating in hackathons. These 8 people were the ones interviewed for the preliminary discussions. Feedback was collected on the completeness of the motivators list, on the clarity of the questions, and on the layout of the questionnaire. No issues were raised about the completeness of the questionnaire, and no unclear statement or question was mentioned in the feedback. However, some aspects related to the layout/structure were criticized and the questionnaire was adapted accordingly.

---

[1] https://www.researchgate.net/publication/338885008_Participation_in_Hackathons_External_Report_Questionnaire_and_Interview_Guide.

Qualitative Data. In order to complement the results obtained in the quantitative analysis, we conducted in-depth interviews with hackathon participants. We relied on the results of the qualitative study to select people to interview according to a diversity criterion. We focused on the participants that had opinions differing from was is typically observed in related studies, as well as participants conforming well to what was observed in these studies.

To define the themes to cover during the interviews, we established an interview guide. It includes questions related to the motivators and demotivators of our theoretical model as well as citizen participation. The interview guide has been refined several times thanks to the feedback received from an expert in qualitative studies and the pre-test conducted with 8 people not being part of the study. We are aware that presenting a list of motivators to respondents might drive their choice. However, the preliminary discussions and the choice to answer open-ended questions about overall motivations mitigate that risk. The interview guide is available in the supplementary material.

To analyze the data gathered through interviews, we used a coding approach as described in [14]. First, we summarized the interviews by keeping only the interesting parts of the transcripts and we recorded the summaries in a data memo, interview per interview. Afterwards, the coding of the summarized interviews was split between the researchers involved in the present paper. Each researcher coded the data about the factors assigned to him, through all the interviews. To do so, the first step consisted in skimming through all the interviews to get an overall view on participant's answers. After that, important sentences were highlighted and coded using short sentences. The codes were then inserted in a table, allowing to perform analysis for a given theme across all the interviews. As the analysis was progressing, the researchers could write memos to record insights and thoughts. The whole coding phase was conducted in a cloud-based document shared among the researchers who could therefore follow the coding process as applied by the others. This was useful to reach agreement on the codes that were used and to make adjustments as needed.

4   Results

4.1   Sample Description

In total, 50 of the hackathon participants (40 males and 10 females) completed the questionnaire. They are aged between 18 and 25, with an average age of 21. The young age of the participants is a result of the fact that the hackathon attracted mostly students. Whereas the examined hackathon was a first experience for most of the respondents, 14 (all males) reported having participated in hackathons in the past. 9 of them participated in one previous hackathon, the 5 remaining having participated in two or more. Table 2 describes the respondents sample by education level (i.e. highest degree obtained) and background. The larger part of the sample consists of males enrolled in computer science studies.

Table 2. Respondents sample description by education level and background.

Education/Background	Computer science	E-business	Other	Total
Secondary	25	1	3	**29**
Bachelor	11	4	–	**15**
Master	4	–	1	**5**
Other	1	–	–	**1**
Total	**41**	**5**	**4**	**50**

In total, we were able to interview 11 of the 50 respondents. Due to space restrictions, a summarized view of the sample's distribution is provided. The detailed information is available in the supplementary material of this paper.

4.2 Quantitative Analysis

Motivators. Figure 2 shows, for each of the 26 individual motivators, the number of respondents who considered it as such. These are the ones who answered "agree" or "totally agree" when asked if their participation in a hackathon was motivated by the motivator at hand. The motivators colored in dark blue motivate at least 75% of the respondents. They mainly cover aspects related to fun, learning, and influence from other people. The motivators colored in light blue motivate at least half of the respondents but less than 75%. They mainly concern the benefits of the hackathon for the society, the logistics, and the opportunity to learn about a domain. Finally, the motivators colored in red motivate a minority of the respondents. They cover recognition and rewards for the main part.

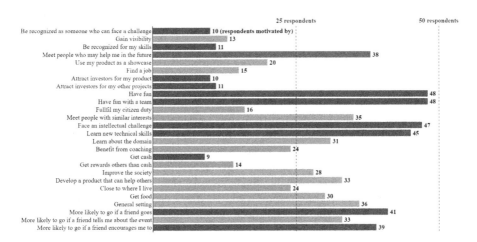

Fig. 2. Number of respondents who are motivated by each motivator. Individual motivators are colored from dark red to dark blue accordingly. (Color figure online)

Table 3. Demotivators for participation listed in the questionnaire.

Demotivating factor	Occurrences
Financial aspects (participation fee, no free food)	11
Theme (not interesting, not inspiring)	11
Personal schedule (not enough free time to participate, inconvenient date, already something else planned, laziness)	9
Location (accessibility)	7
Organization (lack of commitment from staff, bad organization)	5
Too high requirements (expectations for the output to produce, level of skill required, fear of lacking skills)	5
Setting (general setting, sleeping conditions, not enough food, not enough activities during breaks)	5
Social aspects (no friends attending, not enough participants)	5
Constraints (not enough freedom, mandatory attendance to talks, mandatory technology)	4
Too much competition	3
No reward	2
Business (no sponsor, too strong emphasis on business)	2

Demotivators. Concerning the demotivators, the question was asked in an open-ended way. Although it was not mandatory to answer, 44 of the 50 respondents did provide an answer. In total, 27 distinct demotivators were extracted from the answers. They were aggregated into 12 categories listed in Table 3 and ordered by number of respondents having mentioned them.

Link with Citizen Participation. As for the questions related to citizen participation, 25 respondents reported that they participate in hackathons because they feel engaged in the theme addressed during the event. Also, 22 respondents indicated that participating in a hackathon increases their willingness to give their opinion as citizens. Pearson's correlation coefficient between the answers to these two questions reaches 0.54. This suggests that participants whose participation is motivated by the theme could be good candidates for citizen participation initiatives on the same subject. Regarding the questions on whether participating in a hackathon increases respondents' willingness to exercise citizen participation through various methods, no striking finding could be extracted. For each method, approximately half of the respondents gave a neutral answer. Nonetheless, a slight preference toward offline methods can be observed. Figure 3

Fig. 3. Answers distribution for the questions on whether participating in a hackathon increases respondents' willingness to exercise citizen participation through various methods, going from "Totally disagree" in dark red (left) to "Totally agree" in dark blue (right). (Color figure online)

shows the answers distribution, going from "Totally disagree" in dark red to "Totally agree" in dark blue. It can be observed that the workshop and the civic hackathon received more positive answers than the others. Another interesting observation is the high correlation between the answers for the "learn about the domain" motivator and those for the questions on participation methods (ranging from 0.38 to 0.48 for most methods). This suggests that participants attending talks on the domain at the hackathon may be interested to extend their engagement on the theme through citizen participation.

4.3   Qualitative Analysis

Overall Motivators. As introductory question, interviewees were asked about their motivators to attend hackathons in general. The most important motivator is fun, mentioned by 9 out of 11 informants. The motivators that came next are the opportunity to learn (8), the influence from others (7), the theme (4), the proximity of the hackathon location (3), the opportunity to test one's development skills (3), the conviviality (2), the rewards (2), the opportunity to work on new projects (1), the prestige (1), the convincing communication by the organizers (1), the opportunity to meet sponsors (1), and the professional recognition (1). The two interviewees who had participated in hackathons in the past indicated that their motivations evolved since their first hackathon.

Rewards. The rewards were not considered as a major motivation by the interviewees. This finding is consistent with the quantitative insights. Depending on the interest of the interviewees, the preference was set on non-financial rewards (for the pleasure of receiving a "gift" and part of the fun experience) or on financial ones. This latter interest on financial reward was revealed by an interviewee with a high number of participation in hackathons. He now makes a balance between the efforts necessary to win the hackathon and the amount of money to be won. One interviewee mentioned he would like hackathons to offer a more diverse set of prizes to soften competition during the event.

Recognition. Most of the interviewees do not participate in hackathons hoping to get some recognition. Rather, they view recognition as a nice side-effect. Those who are looking for recognition want to be recognized for their technical skills, but not only. They also want to be recognized for their way of thinking, their determination, their engagement in societal issues, etc. For other interviewees, participating in hackathons is a way of feeling proud of themselves and building up self-confidence, thus as a form of self-recognition.

Future Opportunities. This motivator was elicited as heavily linked with recognition. Indeed, recognition is sought either from peers (e.g. other participants, fellow students) or from companies. Some participants have a prior interest in specific companies. In this case, the presence of these during the event can be a motivator as the hackathon represents an opportunity to be recognized by these companies. Those participants would seek recognition by getting in touch with the companies, demonstrating their abilities during the event, or promoting their participation in a hackathon on their resume.

Fun. One of the elements that was mentioned multiple times is the general atmosphere of the hackathon and the fun associated with it. There are a number of elements contributing to the creation of the atmosphere, making the fun a complex yet essential motivator to define. A first element is the freedom left to the participants. Besides the final deadline, participants of the examined hackathon had no obligations and had complete freedom around what they were doing and how to manage their time. A number of training sessions and conferences where organized but attendance was not mandatory. Participants seemed to like this ability to walk freely and "do whatever they want". Another element contributing to the atmosphere is the fact that participants were barely sleeping and had the possibility to sleep on premises, which was fun for some of the interviewees.

Besides this, a number of elements related to the social context created in the hackathon were identified as contributors to the fun. These include the fact that people are programming with friends, interacting and meeting with other people with similar interests, being among "geeks" to code for fun and finally, engaging in distracting activities such as playing cards during breaks.

Another recurrent element is the competition spirit of the participants. The examined hackathon was centered around conviviality rather than competition. While it was mentioned as a positive aspect by some, others would have liked more competition.

In addition to these elements, the ability to learn and to challenge oneself to create something concrete in a short time frame to solve issues faced in a problem domain was also mentioned as part of the fun. The social dimension of the hackathon came to reinforce the fun that participants found in these aspects.

Learning. Learning was one of the motivating factors identified by past studies which applied also in our case. Through the interviews, we gained insights about the elements participants expected to learn. They can be grouped into three categories. First, there are technical skills such as programming languages and libraries. Second, there are skills related to project management and particular soft skills such as time management, the ability to work under pressure, the efficient coordination and collaboration with freshly met people, and communication about a project idea and about a product. Finally, there is knowledge about the theme of the hackathon (e.g. climate change). Based on the interviews, it appears that hackathons could be a good way to raise awareness on particular problems. Most of the interviewees were interested in more than one of the learning categories previously mentioned, to a different extent. Some expected learning more about technical elements while others had more interest for soft skills.

Interestingly, one interviewee mentioned he was participating in hackathons to put his prior knowledge into practice rather then learn new skills. For him, the hackathon contributed to the learning of previously acquired skills, thereby building up experience rather than acquiring new knowledge.

Coaching. In the examined hackathon there were coaches with limited technical knowledge but able to help participants with soft skills, project management, idea development, and communication. Overall, the presence of coaches was well received by the interviewees and considered useful. We found that coaches should help participants mostly regarding soft skills and idea development. Technical assistance is nice to have but less important and it should not be the main aspect of coaching. Coaches should be present without disturbing the participants. According to the interviewees, coaches should provide short trainings on specific soft skills and come to check on them 1–2 times a day.

The quantitative findings show that coaching is not a motivator. However, some interviewees mentioned that the presence of coaches to support them and to challenge their ideas was a source of motivation and stimulation. We believe that the discrepancy between the quantitative and the qualitative findings is due to the fact that we discussed coaching in detail during the interviews and defined with the interviewees what would be an appropriate coaching. The questionnaire did not provide any detail about how the coaching would be done.

Benefits for Society. The quantitative analysis showed that improving the society and developing a product that can help others are important motivators. However, the findings from the qualitative analysis temper this result as most interviewees do not think hackathons can have a concrete impact on society. They believe that the ideas are not innovative enough as they have probably been tested elsewhere already. Another criticism linked to the theme is that the problem to address is complex and will not be impacted by simple solutions. One interviewee mentioned that if he wanted to help with climate (theme of the examined hackathon), he would "go out and clean the streets". A possible solution proposed by two interviewees is to invite investors at the beginning of the hackathon so that they can express their needs and later invest in the projects with high potential or provide them incubators to develop their idea.

Another solution is to develop a wiki where all ideas developed in the hackathon can be gathered for others to build upon them.

Providing benefits to society is considered as a nice side-effect of hackathons but the majority of the informants do not view it as a part of their civic duty to participate in such events. However, four interviewees mentioned that it is the responsibility of students to suggest ideas, learn about different topics through hackathons, and that it was a way for a different audience to "bring something on the table" without being interested in politics. These interviewees underlined that the positive impact of hackathons on society does not reside in the ideas themselves but rather in the brainstorming exercise, the raising of awareness about a theme, and the sensitivity it could raise in people about a specific issue.

Logistics. The interviewees mentioned that wifi, food, tables, and working rooms are must haves. Showers and beds are considered as nice to have. Furthermore, several interviewees noted that the pizza they received was a motivator.

Influence from Others. The influence from the social environment was considered as a key motivating factor by the interviewees. Out of the 11 interviewees, 7 stated they would never have participated without friends coming with them. This reluctance to go alone is due to the additional difficulties it induces (working with freshly met people, getting out of one's comfort zone). However, one interviewee mentioned that this could constitute a nice challenge as well.

Demotivators. When asking the interviewees which elements would drive their decision not to participate in a hackathon, several elements were cited. The most important demotivating factor is the theme, mentioned by 6 of the 11 interviewees. Other demotivators include a high fee to join the hackathon (5), a too basic setting (3), a too strong competition spirit (3), the location and bad accessibility (3), the technical skills of the team (1), the lack of reward (1), the jury evaluating only the idea (1), the lack of learning opportunities (1), the lack of networking opportunities (1), and vagueness in the information published by the organizers when advertising the hackathon (1). These demotivators and their importance are consistent with the results of the quantitative analysis.

Link with Citizen Participation. Among the interviewees, 4 mentioned that they were not interested in being involved in a citizen participation activity whereas 7 stated they would like to. The reasons for non-participation mentioned by the interviewees were a lack of interest, a lack of experience, a lack of skills, the distance to the participation activity, shyness, and a selfish personality. Among the reasons to participate in public life, the most important driver was that the political representatives should not be in charge of everything (4), that every citizen has something to add in the discussion, that some groups such as students can be underrepresented in political discussions (2), and the possibility of getting out of one's comfort zone and suggest ideas (1).

Regarding the preferred participation methods, the quantitative analysis showed a slight preference for offline methods (workshops and civic hackathons). This is consistent with the insights obtained from the interviews. Participating through social media and online platforms was dismissed by the interviewees because it is not a real-life setting and it could foster extreme or non-constructive opinions. Furthermore, social media force participants to share their opinion publicly. Interviewees' opinion toward offline methods was more favorable. Through a workshop, the direct communication with officials and the consequent possible impact on political decisions was considered as a good benefit. However, the time-consuming nature of this method still remains a barrier. The civic hackathon method was the most preferred by the interviewees. According to them, it allows solving concrete societal issues if they are not too complex, delivering practical and usable ideas, meeting real-life stakeholders, and submitting semi-anonymous ideas as they emerge from a team and not from a person.

5   Discussion

5.1   Implications for Theory

Based on previous studies, we devised a theoretical model structuring motivators, demotivators, and the link between participation in hackathons and citizen participation. Compared to previous literature, we included additional motivators and we added the concepts of demotivators and citizen participation. Also, motivators were studied on a finer-grained level. This allowed having a more complete understanding of the meaning of motivating factors. In most related studies, the factors are reported as such, without further explanation of what they actually meant (e.g. what is meant when mentioning the fun experienced by participants). By splitting each motivating factor into individual motivators, we were able to understand which aspects of learning, fun, and the other factors were motivating for participants.

The results we observed are, to some extent, similar to those reported by previous studies. For instance, the fun and the learning opportunities were identified as the most important motivators in our study. For other motivators, however, our findings differ. Whereas recognition and networking were identified as prominent motivators by several previous studies, they did not appear as such in our case. We believe this may be due to contextual and cultural differences between our study and previous ones. However, we did not consider these factors in our work, and further research is required to measure their impact.

Regarding the aspects unexplored by other studies, the interviews revealed that coaching was well-perceived by the participants and that, in an appropriate form, it can be a motivator. Second, the influence from others and the logistics were revealed to play an important role, respectively as motivator and demotivator. Our study uncovered several demotivators, some of which are direct counterparts of motivators. However, as a first attempt, their identification remained exploratory. A valuable research work would be the design of a detailed survey instrument for demotivators, that could be completed by non-participants as well. As for citizen participation, we noted that the questionnaire was not sufficient for our research question. Answers to the questions were mostly neutral, and it was thus difficult to formulate insights. We believe this is due to the fact that citizen participation is an unfamiliar topic for many respondents, which were therefore not sure what to answer. The complementary qualitative approach was thus necessary. It showed that the civic hackathon is the preferred participation method of hackathon participants. This opens the way for further research on this method with this audience.

5.2   Implications for Practice

Hackathons Within a Citizen Participation Ecosystem. Hackathons can be considered as a participation method allowing citizens to give ideas and concretely build solutions to improve society. These hackathons are referred to as civic hackathons [8]. However, as highlighted by the qualitative insights, hackathons do not necessarily lead to increased benefits for society even though they are the favored participation method for the hackathon audience. Therefore, based on the insights gathered from the interviews and on previous literature [8,16], we propose to embed hackathons within a participation ecosystem with complementary methods, as illustrated in Fig. 4.

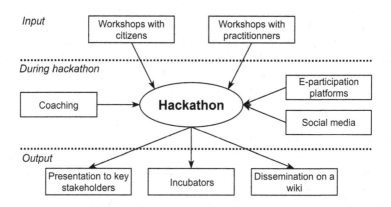

Fig. 4. Hackathons within a citizen participation ecosystem

As input for the ecosystem, workshops with practitioners and citizens can be conducted in order to elicit concrete needs from the population. Then, during the hackathon, other methods could be used to fuel the idea generation. Social media and e-participation platforms could be analyzed using opinion mining algorithms (see [11] for an overview of methods). Furthermore, a strong coaching by knowledgeable experts should be performed to challenge ideas and help refine them. As output of this ecosystem, we recommend the ideas to be put on a wiki to facilitate dissemination. Furthermore, we recommend the invitation of public agents, political representatives or investors to witness the presentations of the top ideas to increase their chance of implementation. Finally, the ideas and the respective teams behind them could be supported by an incubator to help the team going from a prototype to a fully-functional solution.

Recommendations for Organizers. Based on the insights collected in the in-depth interviews, we list nine recommendations for potential hackathon organizers in order to maximize the number of participants.

1. Provide activities to develop the fun experience (playful activities or interaction between participants).
2. As the main demotivator to attend a hackathon is the theme, find a balance between the relevance and the feasibility of the theme.
3. Since a lot of interviewees would not go alone, especially as first-time participants, provide an ice-breaking activity to encourage people to come alone without fear. Furthermore, organizers should clearly communicate about these activities before the hackathon to encourage the prospective participants to come (even alone if none of their friends is participating).
4. As competition is not a main motivator, plan different rewards to keep a sense of competition but give everyone a chance to win by focusing on different aspects of their solution.
5. Develop the technical training if the focus is on technology and the thematic training to raise awareness on the topic if the hackathon has a specific theme. In both cases, provide training for soft skills such as pitching and ideation.
6. Enroll coaches to support participants in the development of their idea. Coaches should remain non-intrusive and intervene at appropriate times.
7. As the participation fee is an important demotivator, find sponsors or apply for funding instead of charging participants.
8. Be clear on the objectives of the hackathon and provide development opportunities for the ideas (incubators, investors, wiki, etc.) after the event.
9. Plan the basic hackathon requirements (beds, showers, wifi, etc.) and do not underestimate the importance of pizzas.

6   Limitations and Future Work

The study presented in this paper has several limitations. These are discussed below, along with further research leads resulting from them.

As discussed in Sect. 5, some of our findings differ from what has been reported by related studies. This may be due to differences in contextual (e.g. type of hackathon, characteristics of participants) and cultural factors. Thus, the extent to which our findings can be generalized is limited. However, we developed a new survey instrument which we believe can be applied in other hackathon contexts as well. Conducting different studies with our survey instrument would allow measuring the impact of those contextual and cultural factors. For further studies, we recommend to study a larger hackathon with a more diverse set of participants. Then, by applying random sampling to select respondents, the risk of bias can decrease. Furthermore, we also recommend to interested future researchers to collect data from people that considered going to hackathons and that decided not to go in the end. This would allow a richer analysis of the demotivating factors.

The second limitation stems from the audience of this hackathon, which mostly consists of first-time participants enrolled in computer science studies. This sample was interesting as the previous experience did not influence their motivations. However, the qualitative analysis hinted that the factors impacting a potential participant's motivation evolve as they attend hackathons. Due to its focus on one hackathon and the nature of its participants, our study could not yield detailed insights on this phenomenon. Therefore, we recommend to conduct a longitudinal study to better understand this evolution.

Third, even though we suggest actionable recommendations for organizers as well as a participation ecosystem for hackathons, these are not tested in practice. Therefore, we recommend to follow action research [12] to test these elements in practical cases and validate them over time.

7   Conclusion

One critical success factor of hackathons is a sufficient number of participants. In order to maximize it, it is key to understand what motivates participants to attend hackathons. With this purpose, we conducted a study following a multi-methods approach, involving the collection and analysis of both quantitative and qualitative data, respectively through a questionnaire and in-depth interviews. In total, we collected 50 answers to our questionnaire and interviewed 11 of the respondents. Data was collected from participants of a focus-specific hackathon organized by computer science students on the theme of climate change.

The contribution of this paper is threefold. First, based on existing work on motivations to participate in hackathons, we built a new survey instrument measuring 26 individual fine-grained motivators. The quantitative data collected from the questionnaire allowed us to identify the most important motivators and to compare our findings with previous studies. The fun, the intellectual challenge, the opportunity to learn technical skills, and the influence from others appeared as the main motivators. Through the interviews, further insights were collected to define them more precisely. Second, we studied the demotivators to cast some light on the factors that can deter people from going to hackathons. We observed that the theme and the entry price are the most important ones. Third, as hackathons constitute a citizen participation method, we investigated the relationship between participating in a hackathon and the willingness to engage in various citizen participation methods. We found that participating in hackathons would increase the willingness of participants to engage in offline participation methods, and especially in civic hackathons.

Based on the collected insights, we were able to provide actionable recommendations to hackathon organizers and to propose a model embedding hackathons within a citizen participation ecosystem. These outputs constitute a promising basis for further research.

Acknowledgments. We would like to thank the European Regional Development Fund (ERDF) and the Belgian Federal Science Policy Office (BELSPO) for their support. The research pertaining to these results received financial aid from the ERDF for the Wal-e-Cities project with award number [ETR121200003138] and the Federal Science Policy according to the agreement of subsidy [BR/154/A4/FLEXPUB]. We also thank the members of CSLabs who agreed to integrate our research in the event they organized. Finally, we thank the participants of the hackathon who, despite the tight schedule, dedicated time to our research.

References

1. Alexander Hars, S.O.: Working for free? Motivations for participating in open-source projects. Int. J. Electron. Commer. **6**(3), 25–39 (2002)
2. Boynton, P.M., Greenhalgh, T.: Selecting, designing, and developing your questionnaire. Br. Med. J. **328**(7451), 1312–1315 (2004)
3. Briscoe, G., Mulligan, C.: Digital innovation: the hackathon phenomenon. Technical report, Arts Research Centre, Queen Mary University London (2014)
4. Crusoe, J., Simonofski, A., Clarinval, A., Gebka, E.: The impact of impediments on open government data use: insights from users. In: Proceedings of the 13th IEEE International Conference on Research Challenges in Information Science (2019)
5. Decker, A., Eiselt, K., Voll, K.: Understanding and improving the culture of hackathons: think global hack local. In: 2015 IEEE Frontiers in Education Conference (FIE), pp. 1–8. IEEE (2015)
6. de Deus Ferreira, G., Farias, J.S.: The motivation to participate in citizen-sourcing and hackathons in the public sector. Braz. Adm. Rev. **15**(3), 15–37 (2018)
7. Gama, K.: Crowdsourced software development in civic apps-motivations of civic hackathons participants. In: ICEIS, vol. 2, pp. 550–555 (2017)
8. Johnson, P., Robinson, P.: Civic hackathons: innovation, procurement, or civic engagement? Rev. Policy Res. **31**(4), 349–357 (2014)
9. Johnson, R.B., Onwuegbuzie, A.J., Turner, L.A.: Toward a definition of mixed methods research. J. Mixed Methods Res. **1**(2), 112–133 (2007)
10. Juell-Skielse, G., Hjalmarsson, A., Johannesson, P., Rudmark, D.: Is the public motivated to engage in open data innovation? In: Janssen, M., Scholl, H.J., Wimmer, M.A., Bannister, F. (eds.) EGOV 2014. LNCS, vol. 8653, pp. 277–288. Springer, Heidelberg (2014). https://doi.org/10.1007/978-3-662-44426-9_23
11. Maragoudakis, M., Loukis, E., Charalabidis, Y.: A review of opinion mining methods for analyzing citizens' contributions in public policy debate. In: Tambouris, E., Macintosh, A., de Bruijn, H. (eds.) ePart 2011. LNCS, vol. 6847, pp. 298–313. Springer, Heidelberg (2011). https://doi.org/10.1007/978-3-642-23333-3_26
12. Mills, G.E.: Action research: a guide for the teacher researcher. ERIC (2000)
13. Purwanto, A., Zuiderwijk, A., Janssen, M.: Citizens' motivations for engaging in open data hackathons. In: Panagiotopoulos, P., et al. (eds.) ePart 2019. LNCS, vol. 11686, pp. 130–141. Springer, Cham (2019). https://doi.org/10.1007/978-3-030-27397-2_11
14. Saldaña, J.: The Coding Manual for Qualitative Researchers. Sage, Thousand Oaks (2015)
15. Silva, J.O., Wiese, I., German, D.M., Treude, C., Gerosa, M.A., Steinmacher, I.: Google summer of code: student motivations and contributions. J. Syst. Softw. **162**, 110487 (2019)

16. Simonofski, A., Asensio, E.S., De Smedt, J., Snoeck, M.: Hearing the voice of citizens in smart city design: the citivoice framework. Bus. Inf. Syst. Eng. **61**(6), 665–678 (2018). https://doi.org/10.1007/s12599-018-0547-z
17. Simonofski, A., Snoeck, M., Vanderose, B.: Co-creating e-government services: an empirical analysis of participation methods in Belgium. In: Rodriguez Bolivar, M.P. (ed.) Setting Foundations for the Creation of Public Value in Smart Cities. PAIT, vol. 35, pp. 225–245. Springer, Cham (2019). https://doi.org/10.1007/978-3-319-98953-2_9
18. Zheng, H., Li, D., Hou, W.: Task design, motivation, and participation in crowd-sourcing contests. Int. J. Electron. Commer. **15**(4), 57–88 (2011)

Information Systems Development and Testing

A Systematic Literature Review
of Blockchain-Enabled Smart Contracts:
Platforms, Languages, Consensus, Applications
and Choice Criteria

Samya Dhaiouir$^{(\boxtimes)}$ and Saïd Assar🆔

Université Paris-Saclay, Univ Evry, IMT-BS, LITEM, 91025 Evry, France
{samya.dhaiouir,said.assar}@imt-bs.eu

Abstract. Blockchain technology is touted to revolutionize the financial sector at the beginning of its emergence. However, its area of application has expanded to include: Supply Chain Management (SCM), healthcare, e-commerce, IoT, etc. Moreover, Smart contracts are now used by different industries not only for their high transparency and accuracy but also for their capability to exclude the third parties' involvement. Blockchain-enabled smart contracts are being adopted in different kinds of projects but still face many challenges and technical issues. This gap stems mostly from the lack of standards in smart contracts despite the Ethereum Foundation's efforts. When seeking to use this technology, it is a challenge for companies to find their way in this multiplicity. This paper is a tentative response to this problem; we conduct a systematic review of the literature and propose a preliminary guidance framework. This framework is applied to three illustrative cases to demonstrate feasibility and relevance.

Keywords: Blockchain-enabled smart contracts · Ethereum · Systematic review

1 Introduction

Blockchain, the underlying technology of cryptocurrencies, was intended to replace banks with the creation of bitcoin. However, with time, it was proven that it could even replace any other third party or intermediary [1]. The need for greater transparency, enhanced security, and improved traceability makes blockchain the most convenient technology for overseeing the different transactions of an organization [2]. Blockchain-enabled smart contracts have excellent potential for remedying the existing difficulties in different application areas due to high customizability [3, 4]. However, several limitations are identified, mainly technical issues that are related to privacy, performance, security, and codifying standards [3, 5].

The two most known and common blockchain platforms that develop smart contracts are Ethereum and Hyperledger Fabric, since 50% of projects are hosted in these networks [6]. Moreover, the most prominent blockchain networks that adopt smart contracts implement and run these computer programs written in the Solidity programming

© Springer Nature Switzerland AG 2020
F. Dalpiaz et al. (Eds.): RCIS 2020, LNBIP 385, pp. 249–266, 2020.
https://doi.org/10.1007/978-3-030-50316-1_15

language [7], more notably for Ethereum. However, it is hard to state if it is the best programming language to build a smart contract because of its infancy [4]. Many blockchain developers still opt for more mature languages such as C++, JavaScript and Java due to their high ability to scale resource-intensive applications in terms of running time and storage.

As long as we deal with decentralized systems, a general agreement between the whole nodes of a network should be reached. For this purpose, consensus algorithms are needed to approve transactions like Proof-of-Work (PoW) and Proof-of-Stake (PoS). However, these two consensus protocols still face some big issues. On the one hand, PoW algorithm consumes considerable computing power and electricity. Therefore, commitment becomes very expensive, which is unnecessary for businesses that are using private blockchains where all participants are known. On the other hand, we face another type of phenomenon with PoS, which is "the rich get richer" [8].

Moreover, businesses need to understand blockchain-enabled smart contracts, their application areas, their promises, and their limitations. Organizations should weigh their options wisely before starting a blockchain project as it is recently developed and relatively untested in all its use cases. Indeed, there are several application domains where smart contracts could be applied; according to [6], more than 70% of smart contract projects are in fields such as SCM, healthcare, finance, information security, IoT, and smart city. Smart contracts seek to establish trust and transparency for immutable transactions, stored and executed within a network, whatever their application area.

In this paper, we raise the following research question: How does the choice of the appropriate smart contract-enabled platform enable companies to fulfill their domain application requirements? To help us tackle this question, we defined three research sub-questions: *1) What are the current studies in blockchain enabled smart contracts in terms of platforms and consensus protocols? 2) What are the main application areas and their requirements for using smart contracts? 3) What are the critical requirements to fulfill and the main criteria that help organizations while choosing their blockchain platform?*

To answer these questions, we conducted a Systematic Literature Review. We rely on the obtained results to discuss critical requirements for blockchain applications and present three brief illustrative examples of application areas.

The sections of the study are structured as follows; Sect. 2 presents necessary background and related researches. Section 3 handles the Systematic Review Process. Section 4 analyses the findings and results and answers the three research questions. Section 5 carries out a discussion of the findings by giving different illustrations of real cases. Section 6 concludes the results of the SLR and defines some best practices for future research.

2 Background and Related Work

Blockchain can be regarded as a decentralized distributed ledger database [9]. It records transactions in multiple blocks chained together to compose a chain that grows autonomously. A block may contain data about one or more transactions and holds a timestamp and the hash function of the preceding block. Blocks are thus cryptographically linked using unique hash code to avoid any modification of the records once they are completed and committed. Because it is decentralized and distributed, a copy of the entire chain of blocks, i.e., the block-chain, is stored at each participating node.

The consensus mechanism ensures information consistency between all the servers in a distributed system. The consensus mechanism makes sure that every server of the distributed system has the same information replica, and each replica must have the same data in the same chronological order.

A contract is a legal document that binds two or more parties who agree to execute a transaction immediately or in the future. A smart contract can be considered as the digitization of a legal contract, i.e., a software component encompassing business logic and transactions that run on a blockchain [10]. A smart contract is also known as self-executing contracts or digital contracts [11, 12]. It embeds contractual clauses for facilitating, verifying, or enforcing contractual obligations; such a protocol is executable and provides an automatic realization of the contract. Consequently, smart contracts allow general-purpose computations to occur on the chain [11].

There are many literature reviews about blockchain, consensus mechanisms, and smart contracts. We briefly mention some of them here, according to their relevance to the aim of our research questions and their popularity (i.e., citations).

In [5], the authors analyze 24 papers and seek to identify current research topics and open challenges. Four critical issues related to smart contracts are identified: codifying, security, privacy, and performance issues. The study in [4] is more extensive. The authors selected 64 papers that seek to analyze available knowledge and evidence about blockchain challenges and solutions. Findings indicate that most current research work consists in proposing new solutions (47 out of 64); nevertheless, evaluation research is of a significant amount (34). The authors further investigate smart contract related problems. They identify 16 known issues and discuss potential solutions. In a similar endeavor, Leka et al. in [13], conducted a systematic literature review and selected 28 publications. They seek to classify current research topics in blockchain and identify security vulnerabilities of smart contracts.

From this brief overview of the literature, we observe that blockchain development is very dynamic with a multiplicity of initiatives, experimentations, and evaluations. Thus, when seeking to leverage this technology for its specific uses, it is challenging for a company to find its way. This paper is a tentative response to this problem; we systematically analyze the literature according to our perspective and elaborate on this a preliminary guidance framework that is applied to three illustrative cases.

3 Systematic Review Process

This study carries out a Systematic Literature Review (SLR). SLR method is known for its ability to rigorously and systematically assess the findings and outcomes of a specific research problem statement [14]. It also determines the poorly defined or documented research domains [15]. We conducted the review process in four steps.

First, after reviewing the literature and according to our main research question, we defined three research sub-questions:

RQ1: *What are the current studies in blockchain-enabled smart contracts in terms of platforms and consensus protocols?*

RQ2: *What are the main application areas and their requirements for using smart contracts?*
RQ3: *What are the critical requirements to fulfill and the main criteria that help organizations while choosing their blockchain platform?*

Next, we defined search terms. In addition to reviewing related works in Sect. 2, we also studied and analyzed one of the most cited articles (according to Google Scholar) on smart contracts [11] to define the search terms and possible keywords combinations. Here are the main steps of the search protocol; a more detailed description is available in an online appendix[1]:

- Search strings:

  - To find papers with a focus on the existing blockchain-enabled smart contracts' platforms, languages, and consensus protocols, we used the following combination of keywords: Smart contract AND (platform OR language OR consensus OR algorithm).
  - To find articles with a focus on smart contracts application domains: Smart contract AND (application OR domain OR area).
  - To find articles with a focus on benefits and advantages: Smart contract AND (benefit OR advantage OR purpose OR opportunity OR challenge).

- We restricted the search to years from 2013 to 2020.
- We used three well known digital libraries (IEEE, ScienceDirect, Web of Science) together with Google Scholar.
- We conducted the search queries using the field TITLE (i.e., publication or document title) exclusively.
- For Science Direct digital library, the search included only articles of type "Research articles" or type "Book chapter", and for Google Scholar, search excluded "citations" and "patents".
- We applied inclusion, exclusion, and quality criteria (detail description available in online appendix (see footnote 1)).

The search protocol led to the identification of 173 publications and the final selection of 30 papers (cf. Fig. 1). The reason behind the high number of excluded papers was that they were not relevant or with not various and good enough findings for our study as well as they do not bring appropriate answers to our initial research questions. The list of the 30 selected papers is available in the online appendix.

Finally, we extracted and mapped entirely the information that will be used in the finding and analysis section, in the form of tables.

---

[1] Appendix available online on ResearchGate at https://doi.org/10.13140/RG.2.2.26799.28328.

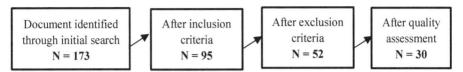

Fig. 1. Document selection process (for more details, see online appendix (Appendix available online on ResearchGate at https://doi.org/10.13140/RG.2.2.26799.28328))

4 Findings and Results Analysis

This section carries out the first outcomes of our research regarding our research questions. We analyzed the 30 reviewed papers according to the three research questions that have been defined. The reviewed articles are cited using the notation [sl<nn>] where <nn> refers to the reference number in the online appendix (see footnote 2).

4.1 RQ1 - What Are the Current Studies in Blockchain Enabled Smart Contracts in Terms of Platforms and Consensus Protocols?

Status of Smart Contract Research
Satoshi Nakamoto invented the bitcoin blockchain in January 2009. He introduced in his experiment both the decentralized peer-to-peer virtual cryptocurrency Bitcoin and the proof-of-work consensus mechanism [sl03]. These two fundamental concepts have significantly contributed to the emergence of blockchain technology and constitute the solid ground on which most of the SLR findings below are based. Since then, the focus of attention has shifted to different application areas other than finance as it offers the ability to ensure transparency, increase productivity, and reduce inefficiencies in organizations [sl18, sl24]. Smart contracts can be very complex to implement, especially for non-computer specialists [sl28]. Therefore, it is crucial to understand smart contract features and their limitations in terms of performance and scalability.

Smart Contracts Platforms
Smart contracts can be developed and processed in different blockchain platforms, depending on several criteria and characteristics [sl25]. In this section, we pinpointed some essential technical features of the top five most-cited platforms in the 30 reviewed articles. We highlighted the key differences between these platforms in terms of the industry type, the ledger type, the smart contract functionality, the transaction fees, the supported languages, the consensus protocol, and the governance.

A. Bitcoin
Bitcoin is a decentralized digital cryptocurrency platform. It relies on a permissionless blockchain network to record the whole transactions currency's history in an immutable and open way [sl02]. Bitcoin uses a cryptographic hash function, namely SHA256, that enables the creation of 256 bits long hash for digital documents, which could be used to verify their authenticity [sl22]. Bitcoin relies on a proof-of-work consensus mechanism, which presents a significant limitation of its usability. Nodes work in completion within a bitcoin platform to generate the new chain's block by solving an algorithmic problem.

B. Ethereum

Ethereum is a decentralized open-source platform of money and other application areas created in July 2015. Unlike many other blockchains, Ethereum is a programmable platform in which smart contracts are compiled and executed in different languages [sl29]. Indeed, Ethereum provides a Turing-complete machine called Ethereum Virtual Machine (EVM), which supports the execution of several programming languages. The most known ones are Solidity and Vyper, mainly used in complex smart contracts' development [sl30]. Following the example of Bitcoin, Ethereum has adopted the Proof-of-Work consensus mechanism as well to validate its computations.

C. Hyperledger Fabric

Hyperledger Fabric is a decentralized open-source consortium distributed ledger that was established by the Linux Foundation. Fabric is one of the most modular and configurable platforms due to high customizability in terms of programming language and consensus protocol [sl26]. Hyperledger Fabric was the first blockchain platform that supports general-purpose programming languages such as Python, Go, Java, JavaScript, and Node.js and uses pluggable consensus frameworks to adapt to particular use cases. Fabric is also known to solve scalability and performance issues.

D. R3 Corda

Corda is a decentralized open-source platform in which digital-assets could be exchanged privately [sl29]. Corda is known for its capability to help businesses reach efficiency and transparency as it supports a point-to-point messaging and a pluggable consensus protocol. Unlike Ethereum, Corda supports very high-quality programming languages like JavaScript and C++ but remains "Turning-incomplete" to verify contracts.

E. NXT

NXT is a permissionless decentralized platform released in November 2013 to support the cryptocurrencies' environment. NXT provides built-in smart contracts' templates [sl16] with several features that include asset trading and encrypted messaging [sl17].

Smart Contracts Programming Languages

Blockchain-enabled smart contracts technology is still in its nascent stage. For this reason, new programming languages are being introduced according to each platform's structure. Indeed, in this subsection, we highlighted the most known smart contracts' programming languages, as it is crucial to know which one is supported by which blockchain platform before to initiate any project. We choose to focus on these four languages according to their contract's complexity level.

A. Solidity

Solidity is the most known object-oriented and Turing-complete programming language for developing smart contracts [sl18], which is inspired by Javascript. Ethereum first supported this contract-oriented language and then was adopted by other platforms such as Quorum [sl18] and MONAX [sl16] due to high convenience and an extensive array of features. However, many researchers have reported Solidity's vulnerabilities against security attacks [sl09, sl18, sl25, sl26].

B. Vyper

Vyper is a programming language that was created to prevent bugs and attacks [sl09]. It stems from Python and is very similar to Serpent language. Unlike Solidity, Vyper provides more productivity and reliable results due to Python's high-level syntax.

C. Rholang

Rholang is a behaviorally typed, concurrent programming language formally modeled by Rho-calculus. This programming language was first used by Rchain blockchain [sl09].

D. Kotlin

Kotlin is an object-oriented and functional programming language with static typing that allows compiling several other programming languages of high-level such Java and JavaScript in the virtual machine [sl10, sl18].

Consensus Mechanisms in Blockchain-Enabled Smart Contracts

The correct and successful implementation and execution of a smart contract is strengthened by the consensus protocols. In fact, all the transactions of a network should be tracked, and all concerned smart contracts should be executed. These two operations are carried out by the same network's nodes in a single and consistent way [sl17]. To attain this state, nodes should first reach consensus.

Many consensus protocols were introduced recently. However, the most common ones are Proof-of-Work (PoW) and Proof-of-Stake (PoS).

A. Proof-of-Work (PoW)

In blockchains, every block contains data that is securely recorded. Trust is established using cryptography. To generate and validate a block by a network's participants, miners should achieve a proof-of-work by solving a mathematical problem [sl14]. Figure 2 shows the flow of the PoW protocol.

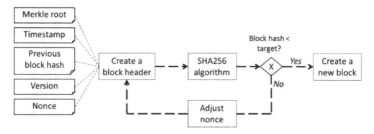

Fig. 2. Flow of PoW (source Zhang and Lee, 2019 (Zhang, S., Lee, J.-H.: Analysis of the main consensus protocols of blockchain. *ICT Express.* Online first (2019). https://doi.org/10.1016/j.icte. 2019.08.001))

B. Proof-of-Stake (PoS)

To avoid PoW's energy waste, the PoS algorithm can be used by a network to achieve distributed consensus. Unlike PoW's rewarding system for miners, which is based on solving complex puzzles and algorithms, PoS chooses the participants that will create the next block based on how rich they are [sl24]. Figure 3 shows the flow of the PoS protocol.

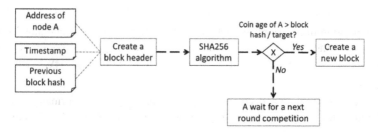

Fig. 3. Flow of PoS (source Zhang and Lee, 2019 (Zhang, S., Lee, J.-H.: Analysis of the main consensus protocols of blockchain. *ICT Express*. Online first (2019). https://doi.org/10.1016/j.icte. 2019.08.001))

C. Other consensus protocols

There are many other consensus algorithms such as Delegated Proof of Stake (DPoS) and Practical Byzantine Fault Tolerance (PBFT):

- DPoS: is low computational power consumption and high-efficiency consensus protocol [16]. DPoS is known to be the most democratic consensus protocol as it allows nodes, who are stakeholders, to elect and chose the delegates that will create the blocks [sl16].
- PBFT: While PoW, PoS, and DPoS are probabilistic-finality protocols with a fault tolerance of 50%, PBFT is considered as an absolute-finality protocol with 33% of fault tolerance [sl16]. Currently, Hyperledger Fabric adopts the PBFT mechanism [sl25]. It is an excellent protocol for networks where parties are partially trusted. However, it is known that the main limitation of PBFT is bad scalability [16].

Table 1. A comparison of the most common consensus mechanisms.

Consensus Algorithms	Energy consumption	Scalability-time/Storage	Transaction fees	Papers #
Proof of Work **PoW**	High	7–30 transactions/second	High	[sl03, sl04, sl14, sl16, sl17, sl18, sl25]
Proof of Stake **PoS**	Low	30–173 transactions/second	Low	[sl01, sl14, sl16, sl18, sl25]
Proof of Importance **PoI**	Low	N/A	Low	[sl16, sl18]

(*continued*)

Table 1. (*continued*)

Consensus Algorithms	Energy consumption	Scalability-time/Storage	Transaction fees	Papers #
Delegated Proof of Stake **DPoS**	Very low	2.5–2500 transactions/second	Low	[sl16, sl18, sl25]
Practical Byzantine Fault Tolerance **PBFT**	Very low	100–2500 transactions/second	Very low	[sl04, sl16, sl18, sl25]
Zero Knowledge Proof **ZKP**	Very low	N/A	Very low	[sl07]
Raft	Very low	N/A	Very low	[sl18]
Istanbul BFT **IBFT**	Very low	N/A	Very low	[sl18]

4.2 RQ2 - What Are the Main Application Areas and Their Requirements for Using Smart Contracts?

To measure and evaluate the extent of blockchain-enabled smart contracts' business value, we focused our research analysis based on the application area of smart contracts and their purpose.

Blockchain-enabled smart contract usage has extended to reach many fields. The main reasons for adopting this technology revolves around data security, trust, and traceability [sl24]. However, some areas might have additional purposes for using it.

Indeed, critical application fields such as healthcare, voting, pharmaceutical Industry, and the educational system have adopted the blockchain-enabled smart contracts to ensure not only privacy and data security but also traceability and tamper-proof information [sl11]. IoT and Information security use smart contracts for the same purposes [sl01, sl11, sl26].

The need for trust-based transactions has resulted in the implementation of the blockchain enabled smart contracts in Smart Cities [sl12, sl24], business process management [sl18] as well as land administration and real estate [sl22]. Data relevance is also a sought quality that the marketplace prediction [sl11, sl25] found within the blockchain-enabled smart contracts.

Other fields of applications are looking for optimization, security and efficiency. Industrial production [sl01], energy resources [sl26], supply chain management [sl18] and finance [sl01, sl11, sl14, sl24, sl26] are relevant examples of such fields.

Based on the results of Table 2, we propose some relevant examples of platforms for every application area. The choice of the platform was made after matching the main characteristics of the blockchain platform and the domain requirements. Although Ethereum remains the most used platform due to high data immutability [sl13], it still faces many challenges in terms of speed and scalability, which makes it more likely to be substituted by other platforms.

For instance, NXT [sl16] aims to implement security and ensures efficiency in terms of avoiding end to end delays in the finance domain. WAVES [sl18] also improves scalability and speed and can be adopted by application areas that aim to reach excellent performance in terms of time and cost reduction (Table 3).

Table 2. Summary of blockchain platforms' technical features

Platform	Permission	Cons. mech.	Smart contracts languages	Application domain	Other Characteristics	Paper #
Ethereum	Both	PoW	Solidity, Vyper LLL, Serpent, Mutan, Bamboo, Flint, Mandala, SCILLA	Cross-industry	*Smart contract feature Slow speed/scalability issues*	[sl01, sl02, sl05, sl08, sl09, sl10, sl14, sl16, sl17, sl18, sl19, sl20, sl21, sl25, sl27, sl28, sl29, sl30]
Bitcoin	Both	PoW	IVY for Bitcoin, RSK and BitML	Cryptocurrencies	*Decentralized Transparent and secure Simple to put in place*	[sl01, sl02, sl10, sl14, sl16, sl17, sl18, sl20, sl25]
Hyperledger Fabric	Yes	PoS Pluggable framework	Go, JavaScript, Java, Node.js, Python	Cross-industry	*Expensive Efficient and scalable Quality code Optimized performance Protection of sensitive data*	[sl01, sl10, sl13, sl16, sl18, sl20, sl25, sl29]
R3 Corda	No	Raft, ABFT	Kotlin, Java	Cross-industry	*Open source Smart contract functionality Transparent*	[sl13, sl17, sl18, sl25, sl29, sl30]

(continued)

Table 2. (*continued*)

Platform	Permission	Cons. mech.	Smart contracts languages	Application domain	Other Characteristics	Paper #
NXT	No	PoS	TC Script	Cryptocurrencies and payment	*Smart contract feature Efficient Secure*	[sl14, sl16, sl17, sl18]
Counterparty	No	Proof-of-Burn	Same languages used by Ethereum	Cryptocurrencies	*Open source*	[sl02]
RootStock	No	Hybrid merge-mining	N/A	Cross-industry	*Hosted on Bitcoin platform Deploys complex SC as sidechains*	[sl13, sl29]
RChain	No	PoS	Rholang	N/A	*In development*	[sl09]
Exergy	N/A	N/A	N/A	Energy	*N/A*	[sl26]
Tezos	No	DPoS	Liquidity	Digital assets	*Open source*	[sl15, sl17, sl20, sl23]
Kadena	Both	N/A	Pact	Cross-industry	*N/A*	[sl15, sl20]
EOS	Both	DPoS	C ++, WASM	Cross-industry	*N/A*	[sl10, sl27, sl29]
BigChain DB	Both	BFT	N/A	Digital asset	*Open Source Customizable*	[sl25]
Iota	N/A	POS	N/A	IoT	*Free transactions No smart contracts feature*	[sl01]
NEM	No	PoI	Java Node.js	Cryptocurrencies	*Based on an OO programming language Can combine several distributed ledgers*	[sl16, sl18]
STELLAR	No	BFT	Stellar SDK & Go	Payment	*Open-source payment protocol*	[sl02, sl16, sl29]
WAVES	No	N/A	RIDE	Digital assets	*Open, secure Simple*	[sl16, sl18]

(*continued*)

Table 2. (*continued*)

Platform	Permission	Cons. mech.	Smart contracts languages	Application domain	Other Characteristics	Paper #
LISK	No	DPoS	Lisk JScript	Cryptocurrencies	*Decentralized platform of sidechains*	[sl02, sl16]
MONAX	Yes	PoS	Monax SDK, Solidity	Contract Lifecycle management	*Open source Smart contract-based applications for processes*	[sl02, sl16]
QTUM	No	PoS	QSCL, Solidity	Cross-industry	*Bitcoin-Ethereum hybrid Secure and scalable*	[sl16]
Neo	Both	DBFT	Python, Java, JavaScript, Go, VB.Net, C#, F#, Kotlin	Smart economy	*Non-profit blockchain project that aims at developing a "smart economy" and digitize assets*	[sl10, sl17, sl18]
Hyperledger Sawtooth	No	PBFT Pluggable	N/A	Cross-industry	*Dynamic consensus*	[sl10]
Tendermint	Yes	BFT	Python, C++, Go, Java, JavaScript, Rust	Cross-industry	*Any language*	[sl18]
Cardano	No	PoS	Plutus	Cryptocurrencies	*Very scalable*	[sl17, sl18]
QUORUM	Yes	Raft Istanbul BFT	Solidity	Cross-industry	*No Smart Contract features Confidentiality of records*	[sl18]

R3 Corda [sl30], EOS [sl27] are cross-industrial platforms that ensure transparency and establish trust between the different participants of the network. These qualities make them the adequate platforms for Supply Chain Management application domain.

Quorum [sl18] and Hyperledger Fabric [sl20] platforms focus on the privacy and confidentiality of records. They deal with applications that necessitate high speed of private transactions, which is important for patients and healthcare users.

4.3   RQ3 – What Are the Criteria that Help Organizations While Choosing Their Blockchain Platform?

On a practical level, we propose a criteria grid that can be used by organizations to help them decide the appropriate blockchain platform for their business (Table 5). Based on the literature, we identified five essential platform's technical features and criteria that should be supported by the organization to fulfill its requirements.

1. *Scalability*
   Scalability is a significant issue of smart contracts application [sl24]. Indeed, some application areas like IoT require high robustness and scalability because of their

Table 3.   Applications of blockchain enabled smart contracts in enterprises.

Application area	SC's Purpose/benefit	Examples of relevant platforms	Papers #
Supply Chain Management	Data immutability, tracking and monitoring, quality control, integrity and trust, transparency	R3 Corda [sl30]	[sl18, sl24]
Finance	Accountability, Eliminates delays, security	NXT [sl16], WAVES [sl18]	[sl01, sl11, sl14, sl24, sl26]
Healthcare	Data consistency, interoperability, Privacy, record management	Quorum [sl18]	[sl11, sl14, sl18, sl24, sl26]
Information security	Resource management, Tamper-proof	Hyperledger Fabric [sl20]	[sl24]
Smart Cities	Cost reduction	R3 Corda [sl30]	[sl01, sl12, sl24]
Internet of Things (IoT)	Data security, privacy, verifiability, auditability, transparency, cost-cutting	Hyperledger Fabric [sl20]	[sl01, sl11, sl16, sl18, sl24, sl26]
Pharmaceutical Industry	Data security, auditability, traceability	Rootstock [sl29]	[sl11]
Marketplace predictions	Market forecast, decentralization, data relevance,	Quorum [sl18]	[sl11, sl25]
Voting	Security and privacy, trust, Tamper-proof, immutability	LISK	[sl01, sl11, sl14, sl18]
Educational systems	Record keeping, efficiency	Quorum [sl18]	[sl11]
Energy resources	Optimization, resiliency, efficiency, security	Exergy [sl26]	[sl14]
Business process Management	Trust, record keeping, tamper-proof	R3 Corda [sl30]	[sl18, sl24]
Land administration and real estate	Data correctness, transparency, stakeholders' trust,	NEO [sl10]	[sl22]
Industrial production	Automation, equipment unification, optimization, reliability, fault tolerance, security	EOS [sl27]	[sl01]

transaction-intensive nature [sl16]. Storing data in the blockchain may result in critical scalability issues [sl06]. For this purpose, an organization must choose a blockchain platform that can scale to adapt to growth.

2. *Ledger Type*

As an emerging technology, blockchain provides three categories of ledgers: public, consortium and private [sl13]. The choice of the ledger category depends on the network scope. For instance, in public networks, everyone can be a node. In consortium networks, authorizations are controlled, and nodes are designated. In private networks, permissions are more restricted, resulting in very low decentralization. Because blockchain comes in many different types, not all its platforms support fully open networks or less decentralized ledgers such as R3 Corda [sl29], which is entirely permissioned.

3. *Consensus mechanism*

A non-adaptable consensus protocol limits the usage of some platforms [sl24], and a proper consensus protocol must ensure security and provide fault tolerance [sl29]. It is known that PoW consumes a lot of power, and transaction throughput is only 3-7 per second, which is very limited. To solve this scalability issue for platforms that only support PoW, e.g., Ethereum [sl23], there are some other protocols and techniques to use to mitigate the limitation of this mechanism, such as Merkle tree [17]. PoS and DPoS based platforms could also be a good alternative [sl19].

4. *Programming language*

Several programming languages have been introduced after the blockchain emergence. The most common one is Solidity [sl18], which is a language designed explicitly for blockchains, but mainly inspired by JavaScript. Thus, an organization must inquire about the programming languages that are supported by a blockchain platform. We identified four other languages types: object-oriented languages (C++, Python …), functional languages, procedural languages, and declarative languages.

5. *Smart contracts support*

Some blockchain platforms may not have the smart contract functionality that is responsible for executing operations that are done by a general programming language in a blockchain network [sl13]. A typical example of these platforms is Quorum [sl18].

This list of criteria is not exhaustive. Many other factors can help determine the choice of the adequate distributed platform such as ease of use, toolchain maturity, human resources' skills. However, this research paper focuses only on the five criteria previously defined.

5   Discussion

Three Illustrative Examples

In this part, we present three blockchain-enabled smart contracts projects to illustrate and apply the findings of RQ3. The details of these projects were gathered from an ongoing empirical investigation that we are conducting for our research project. Data was collected from blockchain project stakeholders during semi-structured interviews in autumn 2019. The primary purpose of this illustration is to highlight that the use of the criteria grid will enable us to choose the same platforms that the firms implemented in the respective projects. Here is the description of the three selected projects with their requirements. These requirements are part of the main findings of the empirical research (Table 4).

Table 4. The three projects' requirements and chosen platforms

Project	Application area	Description	Requirements	Platform
P1	SCM	P1 aims to use blockchain to ensure food safety by tracking and monitoring the provenance of the products sold in stores	-Trust -Traceability -Transparency	Hyperledger Fabric
P2	Healthcare	P2 aims to use the blockchain technology to ensure the liability of the medical records for cancer patients	-Tamper-Proof -Privacy -Integrity	Hyperledger Fabric
P3	Automotive	P3 aims to use blockchain to optimize interactions between the car manufacturers and automotive suppliers to increase responsiveness and efficiency	-Real-time data sharing -Efficiency -Transparency, -Decentralization	Corda

The information that we have already collected regarding the previous three projects enabled us to fill in the grid criteria previously introduced. The results are presented in Table 5.

After filtering on the five criteria mentioned above based on the information of Table 1, we succeeded in reducing the number of platform choices and reached the following results:

- Hyperledger Fabric [sl20], Corda [sl30], EOS [sl27] and NEO [sl10]

As noticed earlier, projects P1 and P2 are hosted in Hyperledger Fabric, and project P3 is hosted in Corda. This information fits with the findings of the platform criteria grid (Table 5).

Table 5. Platform criteria grid: application to the selected three projects

Technical features		P1	P2	P3
Scalability	Transaction intensive	x		
	Time		x	x
Ledger type	Permissioned	x	x	x
	Pretensionless			
Supported consensus mechanism	PoW			
	PoS	x		x
	DPoS			
	Pluggable framework		x	
Supported Programming language	Object-oriented language	x	x	x
	Functional language			
	Specifically designed language			
	Procedural language			
	Declarative language			
Smart contracts functionality	Yes	x	x	x
	No			

After comparing the results of the SLR and the findings of the illustration, we conclude that the criteria grid can indeed be used to enable organizations to choose the suitable blockchain platform. Following these steps will allow the institutions to leverage the full potential of the selected technology and reduce any potential risk of not fulfilling its domain requirements.

Nevertheless, there are certainly other criteria that must be considered. Undoubtedly, the most fundamental question is whether a blockchain is needed in the first place. We acknowledge the analysis made by some studies, e.g., Wüst and Gervais in [18], that considers that in some situations, when scrutinized, blockchain technology is unnecessary, and conventional technologies, e.g., centralized databases, can perfectly do the required job.

6   Conclusion

This paper carried out a systematic literature review that expressed the essential features of blockchain-enabled smart contracts and the existing knowledge in its different application areas. We highlighted an extensive set of distributed platforms and compared them in terms of several technical specificities and protocols, namely the supported programming languages and the consensus mechanisms.

We tend to believe that this study will help businesses to understand their requirements and needs regarding the development of their blockchain-based applications. Indeed, not every blockchain platform is suitable for every network. We concluded that the most critical points that an organization should first know about its target platform are: (i) verify if the platform deals with smart contracts, (ii) check the consensus mechanism supported by this platform, (iii) know what programming languages the Software Developments Kits (SDKs) of the platform support, and finally, (iv) what kind of scalability does the solution need. This preliminary diagnosis will not only enable the organization to choose the right blockchain platform but also will help to mitigate the significant technical issues that could occur after a smart contract's implementation in terms of performance and scalability. The limited empirical illustration that was presented in the discussion section highlighted the contribution of our research regarding smart contracts platforms. Further research can expand the scope of this study and explore more determinant criteria to enrich the platform grid and thus keep up with the application areas' evolving requirements.

References[2]

1. Nofer, M., Gomber, P., Hinz, O., Schiereck, D.: Blockchain. Bus. Inf. Syst. Eng. **59**, 183–187 (2017). https://doi.org/10.1007/s12599-017-0467-3
2. Swan, M.: Blockchain: Blueprint for a New Economy. O'Reilly Media Inc, Sebastopol (2015)
3. Zheng, Z., Xie, S., Dai, H.-N., Chen, X., Wang, H.: Blockchain challenges and opportunities: a survey. Int. J. Web Grid Serv. **14**, 352–375 (2018). https://doi.org/10.1504/IJWGS.2018. 095647
4. Macrinici, D., Cartofeanu, C., Gao, S.: Smart contract applications within blockchain technology: a systematic mapping study. Telematics Inform. **35**, 2337–2354 (2018). https://doi. org/10.1016/j.tele.2018.10.004
5. Alharby, M., van Moorsel, A.: Blockchain-based smart contracts: a systematic mapping study. In: Fourth International Conference on Computer Science and Information Technology (CSIT-2017) (2017). https://doi.org/10.5121/csit.2017.71011
6. Udokwu, C., Kormiltsyn, A., Thangalimodzi, K., Norta, A.: The state of the art for blockchain-enabled smart-contract applications in the organization. In: 2018 Ivannikov ISPRAS Open Conference (ISPRAS), pp. 137–144. IEEE, Moscow (2018). https://doi.org/10.1109/ISPRAS. 2018.00029
7. Buterin, V.: A next-generation smart contract and decentralized application platform. Ethereum White Pap. **3**, 37 (2014)
8. Vukolić, M.: The quest for scalable blockchain fabric: proof-of-work vs. BFT replication. In: Camenisch, J., Kesdoğan, D. (eds.) iNetSec 2015. LNCS, vol. 9591, pp. 112–125. Springer, Cham (2016). https://doi.org/10.1007/978-3-319-39028-4_9
9. Yli-Huumo, J., Ko, D., Choi, S., Park, S., Smolander, K.: Where is current research on blockchain technology?—a systematic review. PLoS One **11**, e0163477 (2016). https://doi. org/10.1371/journal.pone.0163477
10. Liao, C.-F., Cheng, C.-J., Chen, K., Lai, C.-H., Chiu, T., Wu-Lee, C.: Toward a service platform for developing smart contracts on blockchain in BDD and TDD styles. In: 2017 IEEE 10th Conference on Service-Oriented Computing and Applications (SOCA), pp. 133–140 (2017). https://doi.org/10.1109/SOCA.2017.26
11. Christidis, K., Devetsikiotis, M.: Blockchains and smart contracts for the internet of things. IEEE Access **4**, 2292–2303 (2016). https://doi.org/10.1109/ACCESS.2016.2566339

---

[2] The references of the 30 articles selected for the Systematic Literature Review can be found in the online appendix at ResearchGate: https://doi.org/10.13140/RG.2.2.26799.28328.

12. Giancaspro, M.: Is a 'smart contract' really a smart idea? Insights from a legal perspective. Comput. Law Secur. Rev. **33**, 825–835 (2017)
13. Leka, E., Selimi, B., Lamani, L.: Systematic literature review of blockchain applications: smart contracts. In: International Conference on Information Technologies (InfoTech), pp. 1–3 (2019). https://doi.org/10.1109/InfoTech.2019.8860872
14. Okoli, C., Schabram, K.: A guide to conducting a systematic literature review of information systems research. Sprouts: Working Papers on Information Systems, vol. 10 (2010)
15. Brereton, O.P., Kitchenham, B.A., Budgen, D., Turner, M., Khalil, M.: Lessons from applying the systematic literature review process within the software engineering domain. J. Syst. Softw. **80**, 571–583 (2007)
16. Zhang, S., Lee, J.-H.: Analysis of the main consensus protocols of blockchain. ICT Express (2019). https://doi.org/10.1016/j.icte.2019.08.001
17. Kim, S., Kwon, Y., Cho, S.: A survey of scalability solutions on blockchain. In: 2018 International Conference on Information and Communication Technology Convergence (ICTC), pp. 1204–1207. IEEE (2018). https://doi.org/10.1109/ICTC.2018.8539529
18. Wüst, K., Gervais, A.: Do you need a blockchain? In: Crypto Valley Conference on Blockchain Technology (CVCBT), pp. 45–54. IEEE (2018)

Scriptless Testing at the GUI Level in an Industrial Setting

Hatim Chahim[1], Mehmet Duran[2], Tanja E. J. Vos[3,4]($\boxtimes$), Pekka Aho[3],
and Nelly Condori Fernandez[5]

[1] ProRail, Utrecht, The Netherlands
[2] Capgemini, Utrecht, The Netherlands
[3] Open Universiteit, Heerlen, The Netherlands
[4] Universidad Politecnica de Valencia, Valencia, Spain
tvos@dsic.upv.es
[5] University of A Coruña/Vrije Universiteit, Amsterdam, The Netherlands

Abstract. TESTAR is a traversal-based and scriptless tool for test automation at the Graphical User Interface (GUI) level. It is different from existing test approaches because no test cases need to be defined before testing. Instead, the tests are generated during the execution, on-the-fly. This paper presents an empirical case study in a realistic industrial context where we compare TESTAR to a manual test approach of a web-based application in the rail sector. Both qualitative and quantitative research methods are used to investigate learnability, effectiveness, efficiency, and satisfaction. The results show that TESTAR was able to detect more faults and higher functional test coverage than the used manual test approach. As far as efficiency is concerned, the preparation time of both test approaches is identical, but TESTAR can realize test execution without the use of human resources. Finally, TESTAR turns out to be a learnable test approach. As a result of the study described in this paper, TESTAR technology was successfully transferred and the company will use both test approaches in a complementary way in the future.

Keywords: GUI test automation tools · TESTAR · Compare test approaches · Industrial case study · Technology transfer · Railway sector

1 Introduction

Testing software at the Graphical User Interface (GUI) level is an important part of realistic testing [1]. The GUI represents a central juncture to the Software Under Test (SUT) from where all the functionality is accessed. Consequently, testing at the GUI level means operating the application as a whole, i.e., the system's components are tested in conjunction. However, automated testing at the GUI level is difficult because GUIs are designed to be operated by humans. Moreover, they are inherently non-static interfaces, subject to constant change caused by functionality updates, usability enhancements, changing requirements or altered contexts. This makes it very hard to develop and maintain automated test scripts. And today, most companies still resort to time-consuming and expensive manual testing [2, 3].

© Springer Nature Switzerland AG 2020
F. Dalpiaz et al. (Eds.): RCIS 2020, LNBIP 385, pp. 267–284, 2020.
https://doi.org/10.1007/978-3-030-50316-1_16

The state of the practise tools for automated testing at the GUI level used in the industry are **script-based**. Capture and Replay (CR) tools [4–6], for example, enable the tester to record (or capture) the test scripts automating the sequences of actions (like clicks, keystrokes, drag and drop operations) that compose the use case. These scripts are then replayed on the UI to serve as regression tests for new product releases. However, since GUIs change all the time, recorded scripts break and need to be captured again or manually maintained. Consequently, the maintenance cost can get real high, and if the scripts are repaired instead of capturing the whole sequence again, the competence required can become an obstacle [7]. Due to this maintenance problem, companies return to manual regression testing which results in less testing being done and faults that still appear to the users.

Other script-based tools for automated testing at the GUI level are Visual GUI Testing (VGT) tools [8]. These tools take advantage of image processing algorithms to simulate the operations carried out manually by testers on the GUI. These visual testing approaches simplify the work of testers as other test automation tools. However, they also rely on the stability of the graphical appearance of the GUI. Although better than the CR approach, VGT tools also suffer from high scripts maintenance costs [9].

A different and **scriptless** approach to automate testing at the GUI level has been introduced with a tool called TEST Automation at the user inteRface level (TESTAR) tool [1]. TESTAR does not only automate test *execution*, it also automates the *design* of test cases. It does this without the need of test scripts, i.e., TESTAR is a scriptless test approach. And when there are no scripts, these do not need to be maintained. However, TESTAR has SUT-specific configuration that sometimes requires some maintenance effort.

The value of TESTAR in industrial context has been previously investigated and compared, to our knowledge, in four studies (discussed in Sect. 2). Such "which is better" case studies in realistic environments are powerful [10] even if there are a limited number of subjects involved. Although they cannot achieve the scientific rigor of formal experiments and they will never provide generalizable conclusions with statistical significance, the results can provide sufficient information to help companies judge if a specific technology being evaluated will benefit their organization. As Briand et al. [11] clearly, generalizability is overrated. We need more of this type of context-driven software engineering research to reach effective technology transfer of the academic results to the industry. According to Wieringa and Daneva [28] the variability of the context is reduced by decomposing a single case into elements with interactions, such as, for example experience of people involved in a project, defects present in a project, etc. Given that the generalizability might be enhanced due to that these elements may be recurrent across a large set of different cases, we conducted -another study but in a different context (i.e. problem domain, type of software).

The study in this paper has been carried out in the context of an industrial collaboration with a rail infrastructure company in the Netherlands and an IT services company which is global leader in information technology and outsourcing services. The rail infrastructure company is a Dutch company that has mission-critical software applications that ensure the daily train traffic control. Railway tracks are controlled by train traffic controllers using complex real-time systems. Any failure in one of these systems may cause millions of passengers to be stranded in the stations and instantaneously the Railway Companies become breaking news in bad performance. This company has a real need to automate testing at the GUI level in their context. To this end, the rail company already tried to adopt a commercial Capture & Replay tool. However, this test automation tool was abandoned because of the high maintenance costs due to changes in the GUI. The test coverage reached by the commercial tool got lower and lower, while the company needs high coverage because of the mission critical application. Motivated by this real need, TESTAR was challenged to test a mission-critical web application called "Basis Gegevens Service" (BGS), which is in charge of carefully saving train and rail data. Given the complexity of this application and its IT landscape, the IT services company that developed BGS was committed to support the implementation and research described in this paper.

The structure of this paper is as follows. Section 2 describes related work. Then, Sect. 3 presents the methodology of the case study and provides further explanation of the context of this study. In Sect. 4, the results are presented. Section 5 reflects on the methodological issues, and Sect. 6 discusses the results and implications for practice and further research. Finally, the conclusions of this study are drawn.

2   Related Work

As indicated before, there are currently four case studies that have been conducted to evaluate TESTAR in different industrial contexts [12–14]. In these studies, mainly the efficiency and effectiveness of TESTAR were investigated. The results of these case studies showed that in some contexts, TESTAR could improve the fault-finding effectiveness of current test suites. For example, TESTAR detected 10 previously unknown faults that were classified as critical by the company Clavei[1] in [13]. In case of efficiency, we see that the preparation time of TESTAR is almost similar in all studies compared to the other test automation approach. In the study at SOFTEAM, learnability was also measured. Learnability seemed good to the subjects. However, during the hands-on learning process, they found out that developing test oracles was not well understood. The need to do Java programming caused some initial resistance, but this resistance disappeared after explaining the need of test oracles and turned into some enthusiasm to program them. Eventually, they were able to deliver a working version of TESTAR with test oracles far more sophisticated than the implicit oracles that are present in TESTAR by default.

Based on these case studies and contexts, no general conclusions are possible. More research is needed in different contexts. In this paper, we investigate TESTAR in another context in yet another "which is better" case study and compare it to the manual test approach used in an industrial context of the rail sector with real application and subjects. It would have been desirable to be able to compare TESTAR to another automation approach used in the company, but unfortunately this context did not allow for that [10, 15].

---

[1] www.clavei.es/.

3 Methodology

3.1 Case Study Design

Similar to the other studies [1, 12–14, 17], we use the methodological framework from the existing literature [16], this framework is based on well-known general case study design guidelines, e.g., by Runeson and Höst [15]. The following sections describe the design of our study.

3.2 Objectives

The research questions are formulated below:

- RQ1: How does TESTAR contribute to the *effectiveness* of testing when it is used in the described industrial context and compared to the current test approach?
- RQ2: What is the *learnability* of TESTAR for the test practitioners in the described industrial context?
- RQ3: How does TESTAR contribute to the *efficiency* of testing when it is used in the described industrial context and compared to the current test approach?
- RQ4: How *satisfied* are the testing practitioners with TESTAR when it is used in the described industrial context and compared to their satisfaction with the current test approach?

3.3 Objects of the Case Study

3.3.1 The Context: Rail Sector

This case study has been carried out in a rail infrastructure company within the Dutch rail sector. The company has approximately 4,000 employees and is responsible for controlling rail traffic all over the Netherlands. The core business of this company is controlling the traffic management, which is achieved through a chain of IT systems.

At the company, continuity of service is very important. Therefore, the applications should operate without faults. To assure a high level of quality, the web application BGS is manually tested in the current situation. This will give the company the ability to evaluate their own current test approach with the TESTAR tool.

3.3.2 The SUT

The BGS application records basic information about trains, which is required for the traffic controllers to control the traffic in the traffic support system. The application is developed by one of the biggest IT companies in Europe tailor-made for the railway company. The basic data can be read, modified, created, deleted, released, and withdrawn. The SUT is tested after each release. The web application is Java based (JEE6) and has 12,263 lines of code (LOC). This SUT has more LOC than in the previous case study of SOFTEAM.

The web application consists of three layers: the interface layer, the service layer, and the persistence layer. The interface layer contains the GUI and a Java Message

Service (JMS) receiver. It is set up with PrimeFaces[2] and Java Server Frames (JSF[3]). The service layer is the layer between the interface and the persistence layer. Finally, from the persistence layer, communication takes place with an Oracle database. Sending data to other applications takes place through JMS from the service layer. Tibco EMS[4] is used as a JMS provider. Through the JMS receiver from the interface layer, the web application can receive data from other applications.

3.3.3 Manual Test Approach

The existing test approach used for the described SUT was manual and contained a test plan with a corresponding test suite of 100 test cases. After a change in the application, the SUT had to be re-tested and all the 100 test cases were executed as regression tests. The test cases were structured as follows: precondition, action, and expected results. To have an indication of the quality of the test suite, the company has defined a functional test coverage criterion to provide the business (customer) information about the coverage. The functional coverage is clearly preferred by the business instead of code coverage.

This functional test coverage is measured by logging the executions of the SUT. The web application BGS has 251 explicit functionalities. When executing any of these functionalities through the GUI level of the web application, this is logged. In this way, it is possible to calculate functional test coverage after executing the test suite. After execution of each test approach, the logs are inspected and the functional test coverage is determined. The test suite consisting of the abovementioned 100 test cases covered 73% of the defined functional test coverage.

The test suite is maintained in a quality management system. In this system, the test cases are grouped based on functionalities from the use case. As indicated, the test cases are performed manually. If a fault is found, it is registered in the issue tracking part of the quality management system.

Within the company, the testing process consists of preparing, specifying, executing, and evaluating. It took 43 h to prepare the test cases. Subsequently, manual testing of the test cases takes 6 h and the evaluation of the results another 2 h.

3.3.4 TESTAR: A GUI-Level Test Approach

TESTAR[5] is an open source tool for traversal-based scriptless test automation at the GUI level. It carries out automated testing following the test cycle depicted in Fig. 1. The cycle consists of the following steps: (A) TESTAR starts the SUT. Thereafter it will (B) scan the GUI using the accessibility API of the operating system. The latest version of TESTAR also supports Selenium WebDriver, but during this case study, it was not available yet. This API provides information about all the widgets that are available in the state that the GUI is in. TESTAR uses this information to (C) derive a set of possible GUI actions that a user can execute in the current state s of the SUT. Subsequently, TESTAR randomly selects an action from this set (D) and executes it (E). This makes

---

[2] www.primefaces.org.

[3] JSF is a Java-based component to build a GUI.

[4] https://www.tibco.com/products/tibco-enterprise-message-service.

[5] www.testar.org.

the SUT go into a new GUI state s'. This new state s' is evaluated with the available oracles (F). If no fault is found, again the set of possible GUI actions for the new state s' is derived, one action is selected randomly and executed. This continues until a fault has been found or until a stopping criterion is reached (G). In each state, all widgets are combined in a tree structure, the widget tree. Based on this widget tree, actions are derived, and one is selected. This way, the state of the GUI is continuously obtained and actions are selected based on the current implementation of the SUT [1, 19].

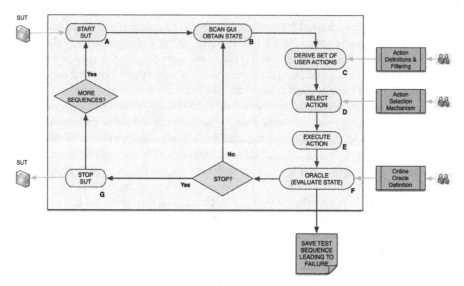

Fig. 1. The operational flow of TESTAR

The default configuration of TESTAR includes random selection of actions and implicit oracles for the detecting the violation of general-purpose system requirements, e.g., that the SUT should not crash, the SUT should not find itself in an unresponsive state (freeze), and the UI state should not contain any widget with suspicious titles, like *error*, *problem* or *exception*.

3.4 Subjects in the Case Study

In the case study, three subjects (test practitioners) were involved. These subjects were certified technical or functional testers working at case companies.

Within the companies, a technical tester is considered to have knowledge of programming (reading and writing code) and understands the operation of an application; moreover, he or she can view and interpret the logs of applications. A functional tester, on the other hand, tests the SUT through the GUI level and has limited knowledge on the technical implementation of an application.

The *technical tester* subject is identified as subject 1 and is graduated from a master's degree in computer science. This subject has 7 years of experience with software testing, of which 2 years in the rail sector. The functional tester subjects are identified as 2 and

3. Subject 2 has 12 years' experience with functional software testing and worked all these years in the rail sector. Subject 3 has four years of experience with functional software testing. Again, all four years the subject worked within the rail sector. The two subjects (2 and 3) with functional background have a bachelor degree in another field than computer science.

The SUT has been under development for 2 years. Subjects 2 and 3 have been involved from the start. All subjects have tested the SUT at least once.

3.5 Phases of the Case Study

The preparation consisted of 3 parts:

- *Deployment* (implementation) consisted of setting up the test environment such that the GUI widgets of the SUT were properly detected by TESTAR and actions on the GUI could be automated in a sandbox.
- *Training* consisted of reviewing the user manual and viewing an instructional video about TESTAR. Subsequently, three sessions of training were given. After the three sessions, the level of knowledge was measured using a questionnaire about TESTAR.
- *Hands-on learning* process makes the subjects work towards a configuration of TES-TAR that was applicable to start testing the SUT. Basically, this means that action filtering and oracle definitions have to be put in place. The final working version was used to test the SUT and the results were evaluated with the exit criteria. This review took place with the trainer.

During the execution and evaluation phase, TESTAR was run, data was collected and both TESTAR and the manual test approach were compared. For TESTAR, the execution phase took a minimum of 24 h, as this has been shown in previous studies to reach a certain test coverage [12, 13]. The following sections discuss the data collected from the runs and the evaluation.

3.6 Variables and Metrics

3.6.1 Effectiveness

Effectiveness shows the ability of the approach to detect faults in the SUT [16]. Some studies evaluate test approaches by injecting known faults into the SUT [12] and calculating the (injected) fault detection rate. In this study, it was not allowed to inject faults into the SUT because this would represent a risk in the test environment for other projects, because there is a complex IT landscape and the applications are connected with each other. Hence we have used surrogate measures like coverage [1, 18, 21, 22] to measure the percentage of the total code of an application has been tested with the test execution. In our study, effectiveness was measured in terms of:

- Number of detected faults during testing with both test approaches.
- Impact or severity of the relevant faults if the SUT was released in the production environment. This impact consists of cosmetic (low), disturbing (middle), serious

(high), and production-blocking (top) faults. The case organization is using these categories to determine the severity.

- Functional test coverage of both test approaches. This was measured by dividing the number of tested functionalities by the total number of functionalities.

Moreover, three subjects are interviewed with semi-structured interviews [16] to complement our measurements with qualitative data.

3.6.2   Learnability

We measured the learning process using the level-based strategy method [1], as well as the time required to learn TESTAR [17]. In this way, we can investigate the learnability step by step in each level. The level-based strategy method consists of reaction, learning, and performance:

- Reaction: interviews and observations were used to evaluate how the subject reacted to the learning process. After the training, the level of knowledge was examined with a questionnaire.
- Learning: the hands-on learning process was recorded in a working diary where all activities and time needed for them are logged. Through the log and observations, knowledge growth was measured.
- Performance: the TESTAR version, delivered in the hands-on learning process, was checked through exit criteria. The exit criteria were conditions based on the hands-on learning process, and were determined as follows:

  - The protocol (Java code) does not provide errors after execution the compiler;
  - TESTAR run for more than 24 h;
  - TESTAR performed more than 50,000 actions.

3.6.3   Efficiency

Efficiency was measured by monitoring the time required for the test activities during the preparation, implementation, and evaluation phases. During the execution, all observations were also recorded in a working diary [1, 8, 12, 13, 17–19, 21–24].

3.6.4   Subjective Satisfaction

Subjective satisfaction is measured using reaction cards and semi-structured interviews. Semi-structured interviews were conducted with all three subjects. Questions and topics were related to ease of use, understandability of the user manual, positive/negative reactions, loyalty and overall satisfaction.

The *reaction cards* are a collection of words from which the subjects can choose (e.g., too technical, time-saving, stressful, efficient, high quality, etc.) that have been used successfully to measure subjective satisfaction [25]. The subjects had the opportunity to choose five keywords that they associated with the test approaches.

4 Results

4.1 RQ1: Effectiveness of Both Test Approaches

4.1.1 Functional Coverage

Functional test coverage was determined using the logs of the SUT. When executing a determined functionality, the SUT registers its status and detail in a log file. Table 1 shows that the functional test coverage of TESTAR is between 33% and 80%. The functional test coverage varies because it depends on the duration of the test, type of algorithm and number of actions has an impact on the functionality. The third run achieved the highest functional coverage, 80%, and all exit criteria were met. In comparison with TESTAR, the manual test approach only had a functional coverage of 73% (see Table 2). This is the first study and context where functional coverage or TESTAR out performs the manual approach.

Table 1. Run results of TESTAR

Run	1	2	3
Duration (hours)	18	33	71
Number of sequences	276	12	192
Action selection (type of algorithm)	Random	Random	Random
Functional coverage	33%	51%	80%
Number of actions	21.377	47.487	98.081
Number of faults	0	1	2
Reproducibility	–	No	Yes

Table 2. Effectiveness of both test approaches

Description	Manual test approach	All runs of TESTAR
Number of faults detected	0	4
Impact of the fault(s)	–	High
Reproducibility fault(s)	–	3 out of 4
Functional coverage	73%	80%
Required time for preparation	43	44
Execution time (hours)	6	71 (run 3)
Required time for evaluation/analysis	2	5
Number of test cases/number of test sequences	100	192

In runs 1 and 2, TESTAR ran for 18 and 33 h, respectively. These runs were experimental and intended for the training phase. In run 3, TESTAR ran for 71 h. Although

TESTAR needed time to achieve high functional coverage, no human resources were needed.

4.1.2 Faults Found and Severity

As shown in Table 2, TESTAR detected three faults with random action selection, three of which were reproducible. In contrast, the manual test approach did not detect any faults. The type of the reproducible faults that were found by TESTAR were:

- one *null pointer exception* due to clicking multiple times on a button;
- one *functional fault* while exporting to Excel to release the day plan;
- one *concurrent modification exception* when clicking two times on a button in a row without waiting.

All the three faults were unique and assigned high severity since they forced the end user to restore the application for further use. The criteria for assigning the severity is based on the impact of the fault on the business processes and end user. In this context, the end user must do actions, therefore the faults are classified as high (serious). The severity-level is defined this way in the context of the case organization and the subjects classified the faults based on the criteria similar to their daily practice.

TESTAR used random action selection in the first three runs. Random selection has no limitations and clicks anywhere on the GUI level. Run 3 showed that random selection is capable of achieving high functional coverage [26].

4.1.3 Qualitative Data

Based on the interviews, we find that the subjects feel that the manual test approach provides more structure and focus, since the effectiveness of TESTAR depends on the configurations and settings. However, they appreciate the fact that TESTAR can test automatically, and offers a variety in the coverage of functionalities. This allows for a higher functional test coverage to be achieved.

Finally, it appears that the preparation of both test approaches takes a similar amount of time, although TESTAR can test the implementation without the use of resources; see Fig. 2 for the qualitative comparison between both test approaches.

Summarizing, the effectiveness of TESTAR is higher compared to that of the manual test approach: more faults were found, and the functional test coverage was higher.

4.2 RQ2: Learnability of TESTAR

The second research question looks for answers related to the learnability of TESTAR for test practitioners in the described industrial context. Our findings are shown in each level: reaction, learning and performance.

4.2.1 Reaction – Learning TESTAR

Initially, the test approach and purpose of TESTAR was not entirely clear to the subjects. According to them, this information was not described in the user manual. Their first

Manual test approach	TESTAR
continuous functional coverage. Provides focus because specific situations and boundaries can be tested. The ability to find faults depends on the test techniques. Based on the test cases, what has been accurately tested (and which paths) is traceable. It takes time and resources because it must be done manually.	coverage can be achieved. Provides variety in the tests, testing the functionalities that are not in the existing test suite. The ability to find faults depends on the configuration and settings of the tool. Based on the state graph, it is clear which widgets have been tested. It takes time to learn and configure the tool. After that it can be used

Fig. 2. Qualitative comparison obtained from the interviews

experience made them somewhat sceptical about TESTAR. However, during the training sessions, while the subjects practiced using TESTAR, their scepticism disappeared and their enthusiasm grew. The subjects gained more of an understanding of the test approach of TESTAR. This is valuable feedback for the TESTAR team to enhance the manual and make people enthusiastic. Concerning the training and the time needed. The level of understanding that the participants had of TESTAR in order to be able to start testing proved sufficient after training. Altogether, learning TESTAR took about 10 h.

4.2.2 Learning – Hands on Learning Process

Although the subjects encountered challenges during the learning process, the trainer's support solved all the problems, enabling the subjects to effectively learn. The subjects configured TESTAR separately and created oracles (suspicious titles and crash) and filters (filtering exit and browser buttons). Later, they merged the TESTAR modifications and came to one modified version.

Subjects 2 and 3 worked together because they struggled to edit the protocol having less programming experience. Finally, during the hands-on learning process, the subjects' knowledge level grew. Particularly after solving the problems, they gained significantly more knowledge about TESTAR.

4.2.3 Performance of TESTAR

The first version ran for 18 h and was validated with the defined exit criteria. In the second run of TESTAR, the protocol and oracles worked well. To meet the exit criterion regarding test actions (more than 50,000) we needed to run TESTAR autonomously for longer than 33 h. Consequently, with 33 h, the exit criterion regarding the hours (more than 24 h) was also met.

In the third run, TESTAR ran autonomously for 71 h, and the exit criteria were also reached.

4.3 RQ3: Efficiency of Both Test Approaches

The third research question investigated TESTAR's contribution to the efficiency when used in a real-life industrial context and compared to the current test approach.

Table 3 shows the duration of each of the phases in this study. For the manual test approach, this was data obtained from estimations of the subjects. For TESTAR, a working diary was kept which recorded the activities of the three subjects in each phase together with the time they spent on them.

Table 3. Time required for the phases

Manual test approach		TESTAR	
Phase	Hours	Phase	Hours
Preparation phase	43	Preparation phase	44
Detail intake	8	Implementation phase	2
Specify	35	Training phase - reaction	10
		Training phase - learning - hands-on	17
		Training phase - performance	13
Execution phase	6	Execution phase (run 3)	71
Evaluation phase	2	Evaluation phase (run 3)	5

The efficiency results show that the preparation time for the two test approaches is similar. During the preparation phase of TESTAR ten hours were spent on training to level up the knowledge of the subjects. This time is a one-time investment.

TESTAR autonomously spends 71 h testing while the manual test approach takes six hours to complete. However, as TESTAR needs no human resources to execute the tests, the test execution has no additional human costs.

The time spent during the evaluation phase of TESTAR was evidently higher than that of the manual test approach, since the latter did not find any faults. For each of the faults found with TESTAR, time was needed to reproduce them and find their type.

Summarizing, in terms of efficiency, the preparation time is similar for both approaches, but TESTAR can execute tests without the need for human resources. This means that no additional human costs are incurred, which contributes significantly to efficiency.

4.4 RQ4: Subjective Satisfaction

The last research question is about the satisfaction of the subjects. Our findings from the interviews are as follows.

4.4.1 The Interview Results

Based on the conducted interviews, we found the following.

Easy to Use. The subjects were satisfied with the logging facilities of TESTAR. In this context, the state graph was found to be highly powerful because it provided an overview of the executed test actions. On the other hand, the subjects lost a great deal of time analysing the logs. In this case, they would have appreciated a kind of dashboard to summarize the run results (number of faults, number of tests, duration and test coverage), which could save time in the analysis. The subjects reported that "regression testing with TESTAR could save time on maintenance of test cases compared to the manual test approach". This is because after a change, they experienced the maintenance and adjustment of test cases as labour-intensive with the manual test approach. Also, the subjects found the flexibility of TESTAR to be good, because it is easily transferable in various test environments. Subject 1 was satisfied with the features of the approach, such as the oracles, filters and protocol. This was because it allows new functionalities to be added. Subjects 2 and 3 were unsatisfied with the protocol, because they were not technical enough to add sophisticated oracles with Java programming. They expected more of a functional layer to provide the possibility to easily add functionalities or oracles. All in all, the subjects found TESTAR to be a refreshing and time-saving tool.

Understandability of User Manual. The manual was found to be insufficient to understand TESTAR. Although the user manual was improved after the other studies, it still is not clear enough for the industrialists in this case study. The academics were urged again to put more effort into a clear manual. For example, the use and detection of logging faults is only explained to a limited extent. Also, the oracles and the needed Java programming again in this study seems to be a barrier. Although some of it might be solved with a better user manual section on that, the fact is still that in industry most testers do not have programming skills.

Positive/Negative Reactions. The subjects' first impression of TESTAR was less positive, because the purpose of the approach was unclear to them and did not fit with their traditional ways of automated testing. Now that they were faced with a completely different test approach, they needed explanation and guidance. They were not familiar with the functionalities and possibilities of TESTAR. Their doubts further increased when they initially encountered the user manual. Because the way of working remained unclear. However, after the training, they developed a positive impression of the approach. This included the explanation during training and the run results that were booked. The subjects gained more confidence from the results that were achieved.

Loyalty. The subjects were asked if they would recommend the tool to the management and to colleagues. The first subject would definitely recommend the tool to management; the second subject wanted to wait to do so; and the third believed that TESTAR should have a chance to develop. Subject 1 recommended TESTAR probably because he had a technical background and because of that gave a higher satisfaction rating compared to the subjects with a functional background (subjects 2 and 3).

Overall Satisfaction. Both test approaches scored a 7 on satisfaction. The first subject gave TESTAR an 8, and the manual test approach a 6. This subject considered the manual test approach to be rigid, and TESTAR powerful. Whereas, the other two subjects found the manual test approach to be traceable and to provide structure, and therefore gave it an 8. In contrast, they gave TESTAR a 7. They both indicated that TESTAR could score a higher satisfaction rating if it was more user-friendly.

4.4.2 Response Cards

Finally, the response cards showed that TESTAR and the manual test approach were generally associated with keywords that have a positive charge. The manual test approach also contained one negative point: "time-consuming in use". In addition, the subjects found TESTAR too technical in use, because of the protocol which needs programming skills.

Overall, the test practitioners in the real-life setting were equally satisfied with both test approaches (see Fig. 3).

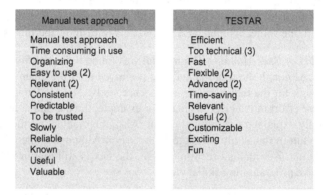

Manual test approach	TESTAR
Manual test approach	Efficient
Time consuming in use	Too technical (3)
Organizing	Fast
Easy to use (2)	Flexible (2)
Relevant (2)	Advanced (2)
Consistent	Time-saving
Predictable	Relevant
To be trusted	Useful (2)
Slowly	Customizable
Reliable	Exciting
Known	Fun
Useful	
Valuable	

Fig. 3. Results of the chosen reaction cards

5 Threats to Validity

Construct validity reflects to what extent our operational measures really represent what is investigated according to the research questions [28]. The learnability evaluation was based on a four-level strategy and we used logs for the learning level. Most of the collected data was based on subjects' responses (interviews, post questionnaires, working diaries). However, in order to reduce possible misinterpretations of formulated questions and answers gathered, data analysed and interpreted by the second author was also validated by the subjects. Regarding effectiveness and efficiency, we used well-known defined metrics used also in the previous studies.

Internal validity is the extent to which a causal relationship between the variables is justified [28]. To mitigate this threat:

- The interviewees were informed about both the interview itself and the interview topic. As a result, they had enough time to prepare and were less quickly surprised by a question. This reduced the likelihood of unnecessary mistakes.

- The interviews took place in an area where no others were present. If a colleague or manager had been in the room, then the subjects would have been likely to give socially desirable answers. Furthermore, the anonymity of the subjects was ensured.
- The (semi-structured) interview questions concerning effectiveness and satisfaction were formulated to be open to obtain input from the subjects. We actively requested details of the activities and events that the subjects had experienced. Moreover, the critical incidence method was applied [30 p. 230]. Finally, the interview questions and results were reported to allow for replication.

External validity concerns the generalization of results [28]. As indicated before, this research is context-driven and hence not undertaken with the goal of generalizability. However, the more studies of this type we do, the more chance of eventual generalizability will be established through secondary studies.

To ensure the **reliability** of the research, all the procedures, questions, logs, were reviewed by another researcher.

6 Discussion, Conclusion and Implications

6.1 Discussion and Conclusion

In the current literature, four case studies have been reported on evaluating TESTAR in industry. In this case study, we did an evaluation with a Java-based web application (BGS). Also, the rail sector has not been studied in the previous case studies.

One case study in the literature (SOFTEAM) showed that the difference in preparation time between test approaches was approximately equal and execution of manual test approach took 1 h [12]. While TESTAR took 77 h without the use of resources. The results of our study are similar. TESTAR was used to test for 71 h, and the manual test approach for 6. For future work, it is interesting to compare in more companies to see whether the preparation time for both test approaches are approximately the same, but TESTAR can be executed without the use of human resources.

During the training, the subjects without a technical background needed more time to learn the oracles. It appears to be too difficult for functional testers with limited programming experience to learn to extend the protocol and develop oracles. Also, the case study in the literature showed that the subjects had some difficulties with programming oracles [12]. An important question that arises here is whether we can expect test engineers to have programming skills. It sounds almost logical, but in practice it turns out that not all testers have programming skills.

The main question of this research was as follows: How does the test approach of TESTAR compare to that of the manual test approach?

Looking at the results, the test approach of TESTAR was found to be more effective and efficient than that of the manual test approach. This was because TESTAR detected more faults than the manual test approach, and also showed higher functional test coverage. Thereby, the test execution can be realized without the use of human resources.

Regarding satisfaction, both test approaches were found to be identical. TESTAR needs improvements in user-friendliness, as it is too technical in use, and some points could improve its usability. On the other hand, TESTAR was found to be learnable. It scored significantly higher on the variables of effectivity and efficiency compared to the manual test approach.

6.2   Theoretical and Practical Implications

A limitation of this type of research is that the results cannot be fully generalized, since a single case study was conducted. When the research is placed in a broader perspective, it appears that the results only apply to a Java-based web application. However, the study was very useful for technology transfer purposes: some remarks during the interviews indicate that TESTAR would not have been evaluated in so much depth if it would not have been backed up by our case study design. For follow-up research, it is advisable to repeat this research with multiple case studies and with different types of applications, so that the results can be generalized. Finally, having only a few real subjects available, this study took several weeks to complete and hence we overcame the problem of getting too much information too late.

In this study, TESTAR was compared to the manual test approach. In further research it is advised to involve a second GUI test automation tool. In doing so, the results of the case study could be explored in a broader perspective than only comparing it to the manual test approach.

The benefits of both test approaches can be extracted and combined during testing. TESTAR can be used to perform flexible and automated regression testing, while the manual test approach can be used to test a specific scenario. Based on this complementary use, cost and resources can be saved. Based on this case study the company will use TESTAR complementary with another test approach. In the future, the company is interested in follow-up research to determine if it can replace the current test approaches.

Acknowledgments. We would like to acknowledge the help of the case study companies They have been supporting our research, answering our questions, and validating our analyses. We would also like to thank the involved universities. This work was partially funded by the ITEA3 TESTOMAT project and the H2020 DECODER project.

References

1. Vos, T.E.J., et al.: TESTAR: tool support for test automation at the user interface level. Int. J. Inf. Syst. Model. Des. **6** (2015)
2. Kresse, A., Kruse, P.M.: Development and maintenance efforts testing graphical user interfaces: a comparison. In: Proceedings of the 7th International Workshop on Automating Test Case Design, Selection, and Evaluation (A-TEST 2016), pp. 52–58 (2016)
3. Grechanik, M., Xie, Q., Fu, C.: Experimental assessment of manual versus tool-based maintenance of GUI-directed test scripts. In: ICSM (2009)
4. Nguyen, B.N., Robbins, B., Banerjee, I., Memon, A.: GUITAR: an innovative tool for automated testing of GUI-driven software. Autom. Softw. Eng. **21**(1), 65–105 (2013). https://doi.org/10.1007/s10515-013-0128-9

5. Garousi, V., et al.: Comparing automated visual GUI testing tools: an industrial case study. In: ACM SIGSOFT International Workshop on Automated Software Testing (A-TEST 2017), pp. 21–28 (2017)
6. Aho, P., et al.: Evolution of automated regression testing of software systems through the graphical user interface. In: International Conference on Advances in Computation, Communications and Services (2016)
7. Leotta, M., et al.: Capture-replay vs. programmable web testing: an empirical assessment during test case evolution. In: Conference on Reverse Engineering, pp. 272–281 (2013)
8. Alégroth, E., Nass, M., Olsson, H.H.: JAutomate: a tool for system- and acceptance-test automation. In: Proceedings - IEEE 6th International Conference on Software Testing, Verification and Validation. ICST 2013, pp. 439–446 (2013)
9. Alégroth, E., Feldt, R., Ryrholm, L.: Visual GUI Testing in Practice: Challenges, Problems and Limitations. Empir. Softw. Eng. J. **20**(3), 694–744 (2015). https://doi.org/10.1007/s10 664-013-9293-5
10. Kitchenham, B., Pickard, L., Pfleeger, S.: Case studies for method and tool evaluation. IEEE Softw. **12**, 52–62 (1995)
11. Briand, L., et al.: The case for context-driven software engineering research: generalizability is overrated. IEEE Softw. **34**(5), 72–75 (2017)
12. Bauersfeld, S., et al.: Evaluating the TESTAR tool in an industrial case study. In: Proceedings of the 8th ACM/IEEE International Symposium on Empirical Software Engineering and Measurement - ESEM 2014, pp. 1–9. ACM Press, New York (2014)
13. Bauersfeld, S., de Rojas, A., Vos, T.E.J.: Evaluating rogue user testing in industry: an experience report. Universitat Politecnica de Valencia, Valencia 2014
14. Martinez, M., Esparcia, A.I., Rueda, U., Vos, T.E.J., Ortega, C.: Automated localisation testing in industry with test*. In: Wotawa, F., Nica, M., Kushik, N. (eds.) ICTSS 2016. LNCS, vol. 9976, pp. 241–248. Springer, Cham (2016). https://doi.org/10.1007/978-3-319-47443-4_17
15. Runeson, P., Host, M.: Guidelines for conducting and reporting case study research in software engineering. Empir. Softw. Eng. **14**(2), 131–164 (2009). https://doi.org/10.1007/s10664-008-9102-8
16. Vos, T.E.J., et al.: A methodological framework for evaluating software testing techniques and tools. In: 2012 12th International Conference on Quality Software, pp. 230–239 (2012)
17. Condori-Fernández, N., et al.: Combinatorial testing in an industrial environment - analyzing the applicability of a tool. In: Proceedings - 2014 9th International Conference on the Quality of Information and Communications Technology, QUATIC 2014, pp. 210–215 (2014)
18. Borjesson, E., Feldt, R.: Automated system testing using visual GUI testing tools: a comparative study in industry. In: ICST 2012 Proceedings of the 2012 IEEE Fifth International Conference on Software Testing, Verification and Validation, pp. 350–359 (2012)
19. Nguyen, C.D., et al.: Evaluating the FITTEST automated testing tools: an industrial case study. In: 2013 ACM/IEEE International Symposium on Empirical Software Engineering and Measurement, pp. 332–339 (2013)
20. Rueda, U., et al.: TESTAR -from academic prototype towards an industry-ready tool for automated testing at the User interface level (2014)
21. Imparato, G.: A combined technique of GUI ripping and input perturbation testing for Android apps. In: Proceedings - International Conference on Software Engineering, pp. 760–762 (2015)
22. Vos, T.E.J., et al.: Industrial scaled automated structural testing with the evolutionary testing tool. In: ICST 2010 – 3rd International Conference on Software Testing, Verification and Validation, pp. 175–184 (2010)
23. Bae, G., Rothermel, G., Bae, D.-H.: Comparing model-based and dynamic event-extraction based GUI testing techniques: An empirical study. J. Syst. Softw. **97**, 15–46 (2014)

24. Marchetto, A., Ricca, F., Tonella, P.: A case study-based comparison of web testing techniques applied to AJAX web applications. Int. J. Softw. Tools Technol. Transf. **10**, 477–492 (2008). https://doi.org/10.1007/s10009-008-0086-x
25. Benedek, J., Miner, T.: Measuring desirability new methods for evaluating desirability in a usability lab setting. Microsoft Corporation (2002)
26. Esparcia-Alcazar, A., et al.: Q-learning strategies for action selection in the TESTAR automated testing tool. In: Proceedings of the 6th International Conference on Metaheuristics and Nature Inspired Computing. META (2016)
27. Bohme, M., Paul, S.: Probabilistic analysis of the efficiency of automated software testing. IEEE Trans. Softw. Eng. **42**, 345–360 (2016)
28. Wieringa, R., Daneva, M.: Six strategies for generalizing software engineering theories. Sci. Comput. Program. **101**, 136–152 (2015). https://doi.org/10.1016/j.scico.2014.11.013. ISSN 0167-6423

Improving Performance and Scalability of Model-Driven Generated Web Applications

An Experience Report

Gioele Moretti, Marcela Ruiz$^{(\boxtimes)}$ (iD), and Jürgen Spielberger

Zurich University of Applied Sciences, Winterthur, Switzerland
{gioele.moretti,marcela.ruiz,juergen.spielberger}@zhaw.ch

Abstract. Context. Performance and scalability are of critical value for distributed and multiuser systems like web applications. Posity is a model-driven development tool that allows software engineers to specify a set of graphical diagrams for the automatic generation of web and/or desktop software applications. Posity provides the benefits of model-driven engineering (MDE) tools in terms of high-quality code generation, implementation speed, support for traceability and debuggability, etc. However, web applications generated with Posity do not scale properly to satisfy unpredictable performance demands. As a result, Posity industrial adoption is hindered. **Objective**. Design a treatment for improving performance and scalability of web applications generated with Posity. **Method**. We investigate current problems of web applications generated with Posity. Results from our investigation suggest candidate architectures, which we evaluate by applying the architecture trade-off analysis method (ATAM). The outcome of the ATAM evaluation guides the design and implementation of a thick-client architecture for the Posity runtime environment for web applications; which we validate by means of a laboratory demonstration. **Results**. i) we contribute with criteria for selecting a proper architecture for solving performance and scalability problems, and ii) we report on the experience of designing, developing and validating an architecture for Posity runtime environment. **Conclusions**. Results from the laboratory demonstration show tangible improvements in terms of performance and scalability of web applications generated by Posity. These advancements are promising and motivate further development of the thick-client architecture for Posity runtime environment for web applications. This experience report concludes with lessons learnt on promoting the adoption of model-driven development tools.

Keywords: Model-Driven Web Engineering · Model-driven development · Web development · Posity · Thick-client architecture · Performance · Scalability

1 Introduction

Model-Driven Web Engineering (MDWE) is a software development paradigm dealing with the automatic generation of executable web applications from graphical abstract diagrams representing information systems' business logic, data structures, business

© Springer Nature Switzerland AG 2020
F. Dalpiaz et al. (Eds.): RCIS 2020, LNBIP 385, pp. 285–301, 2020.
https://doi.org/10.1007/978-3-030-50316-1_17

rules, graphical user interface, etc. [1]. MDWE enables automatic generation of executable web applications by means of incremental diagram transformations until code is generated. As such, MDWE approaches ensure code quality, proper alignment with requirements specified in graphical diagrams, development speed, separation of information systems' business logic from underlying platform technologies, level of abstraction of software systems, etc. However, recent studies show that performance and scalability problems of developed web applications from MDWE approaches are among the main problems that hinder MDWE role in industry [2]. Moreover, no criteria or modernisation processes for improving performance and scalability of generated applications from MDWE approaches have been proposed yet.

Posity is a business, database-centric model-driven development tool for the automatic generation of software applications [3]. Posity allows software engineers to specify the abstract representation of information systems in a set of six diagrams types, which can be executed in the Posity runtime environment for web and/or desktop applications [4]. Though software engineers can specify complete information systems requirements (related to business and database aspects) and generate software application themselves, we observe that resulting software applications used in web browsers are not suitable for industrial application because of the following issues:

- **Scalability**. Software applications developed with Posity require an excessive amount of resources (CPU memory, database connection, etc.) when executed on a web runtime environment. Currently, web applications are limited to a few concurrent users.
- **Performance.** Web applications generated from Posity may take several seconds for providing feedback to the user input (**response time**). When application's state changes, user input is blocked. This slowness leads to insufficient user experience.
- **Individualisation**. Posity gives little scope for personalising the design of an application running in a web browser. The style of user interfaces is mostly predefined and can be adapted only with great effort. Despite the PDS provides options for extending GUI diagrams with CSS styles [5], this feature is rarely used because it requires the use of external tools for CSS that are not integrated in the PDS.

In this paper we present our experience in improving performance and scalability of web applications generated with Posity. Our main research goal is: *How to design a treatment for improving performance and scalability of web applications generated by Posity?* To answer this main research question, our research method follows the cycles prescribed by the Design Science Method [6]; encompassing the phases and tasks of problem investigation, treatment design, and treatment validation presented in Fig. 1. Results from the problem investigation suggest providing an architecture as a treatment. This paper details the experience on designing an architecture to mitigate performance and scalability challenges (see design cycle (DC1)). Results from DC1 motivates the design cycle DC2 for developing a prototype that can be used in practice. Currently we are conducting an iterative incremental development process where DC2 is followed several times until the prototype is ready to be transferred (treatment implementation phase according to the design science method) to industrial settings. Treatment implementation and implementation validation are phases considered for future work.

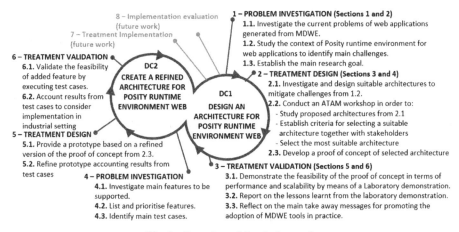

Fig. 1. Overview of the design cycle

In this paper we describe the following contributions pointing to their corresponding sections:

- We analyse the context of the MDWE tool Posity, which is currently used in industrial settings. We report our observations regarding challenges and opportunities for establishing Posity in the market (see Sect. 2).
- We discuss the modernisation process applied to Posity to satisfy performance and scalability requirements for web applications. The modernisation process involves investigation and design of suitable architectures and their corresponding evaluation by applying the architecture trade-off analysis method (ATAM) [7]. As a result, we present criteria for selecting a suitable architecture (see Sect. 3.1).
- We present a proof of concept architecture for Posity runtime environment for web applications (see Sect. 3.2), and illustrate the execution of the proposed architecture by means of a laboratory demonstration (see Sect. 3.2).
- We report on the experience from designing and developing an architecture for Posity runtime environment. Finally, we conclude the paper by discussing lessons learnt, future lines of work, and the main take away messages for promoting the adoption of model-driven development tools in practice (see Sect. 4).

2   The Context and Running Example

This section presents an overview of Posity and main challenges. Throughout the paper, we use a running example based on the case of building a summation calculator with Posity, which takes as input two numbers and returns the total sum. For the sake of brevity, the focus of the example is on the graphical user interface and business logic for the summation calculator. We conclude this section by discussing related work.

2.1 Posity in a Nutshell

Posity is a business and database-centric model-driven development tool supported by the company Posity AG[1]. Posity consists of the Posity Design Studio (PDS) and the Posity Runtime Environment (PRE). The PDS is an integrated development environment (IDE) that facilitates the specification of six graphical diagram types for software development [4]: data diagram (DD), query diagram (QD), graphical user interface (GUI) diagram (GD), module diagram (MD), process diagram (PD), and organisation diagram (OD). Once diagrams have been specified in the PDS, Posity provides an engine to automatically transform modelled diagrams into data tables, SQL [8] and an intermediate language named Functional Code (FCode), which is based on Bytecode [9] (see Fig. 2). As a result, software engineers can specify requirements and automatically generate software applications without the need of programming [4]. Further details related to the Posity architecture and development aspects can be found at [3].

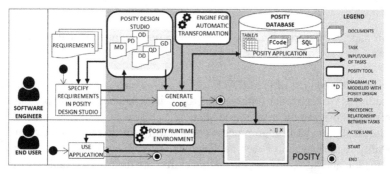

Fig. 2. Software engineers specify requirements by using the PDS. Resulting diagrams are then transformed into FCode, SQL, and data tables that are stored in the Posity database.

Posity Application

The engine for automatic transformation takes as input diagrams modelled in the PDS and compiles them into a Posity application composed by FCode, SQL, and data tables (see Fig. 2).

FCode is a set of instructions with compact numeric tokens, commands, partial tokens, constants and references that encode the results of a compiler or parser. Unlike human-readable source code, the compact instructions are designed for efficient execution but not for human analysis. For illustrative purposes, Table 1 presents a snapshot of FCode with explanatory comments.

The **SQL** generated by the engine are subroutines saved and executed into the database (stored procedures). They are used by the PRE for interacting with the database, for example for retrieving a specific FCode file. The **data tables** are simple database tables containing the data of the application.

---

[1] https://posity.ch/.

The Posity runtime environment executes web or desktop applications using the generated FCode, SQL and data tables.

Posity Runtime Environment

The Posity Runtime Environment (PRE) is responsible for executing Posity applications (FCode and SQL) modelled with the Posity Design Studio. Figure 3 illustrates an abstract architecture on how the different Posity application code fragments (which are derived from diagrams specified in the PDS) are processed by the PRE. A *process* component is started by the user, process and organization Posity application code fragments (*PD* and *OD*) provide appropriate configurations for users' access rights and profile. Once the *process* is started, the *module* component that contains the information related to the business logic and rules is initialised. The *Form* component returns the necessary GUI and triggers required business rules. The *dataset* component stores SQL statements and connections to the database for allowing access to data. The PRE is further enriched for the execution of Posity applications both as a desktop (PRE-Desktop) and/or web (PRE-Web) application. The focus of this paper is on the PRE-Web.

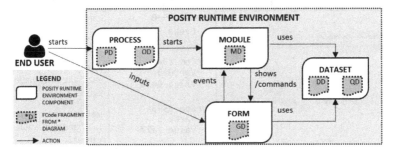

Fig. 3. Overview of an application running in the Posity Runtime Environment.

2.2 Running Example

For illustration purposes, we present how to build a simple application called summation calculator. The summation calculator takes two numeric values and returns their summation. Table 1 and Table 2 present the GUI and module diagrams specified using the PDS, together with their corresponding generated FCode ready for execution.

Executing the Summation Application and Main Problems Observed in the Current PRE-Web

Figure 4 presents a snippet of the execution of the summation calculator in the current PRE-Web. It works as expected: when the user clicks on the sum ("+") button, the values in fields "number 1" and "number 2" are summed. The resulting value appears in the "Result" field (see Fig. 4).

The current architecture of PRE-Web is based on a thin-client architecture, where the application server creates an instance of the PRE-Web each time a user opens the

Table 1. GUI diagram for the summation calculator and snapshot of its corresponding FCode

GUI Diagram	FCode	Comments
	AttSha 1a77 VaNa number1	Variable 'number1' with id '1a77'
	AttSha ea2d VaNa number2	Variable 'number2' with id 'ea2d'

	ButSha 902a
	  Event Sum
	  Labl +
		Button with label '+' When clicked, it calls the event 'Sum'.

	AttSha 95f2 VaNa result	Variable 'result' with id '95f2'

Table 2. Module diagram for the summation event and snapshot of its corresponding FCode

Module Diagram	FCode	Comments
	EventG 39e0 EveNa Sum	Start Event 'Sum'

	VarCom a040
	  VarOu 3
	  Value ea2d
		Read value from variable 'ea2d' and write value in register 3.

	VarCom 3598
	  VarOu 5
	  Value 1a77
		Read value from variable '1a77' and write value in register 5.

	StdCom c69f
	  SubTy NumberAdd
	  NumIn 5
	  NumIn 3
	  NumOu 0
		'NumberAdd' operation: Add values from register 5 and 3. Then write result in register 0.

	VarCom d7e0
	  VarIn 0
	  Value 95f2
		Read value in register 0. Then write it in variable '95f2'.

	EventE 39e0	
		End of event

summation calculator in the web browser. The PRE-Web instance on the server generates a static HTML page and sends it to the web browser for rendering the GUI every time the sum button is clicked. Figure 5 presents the current PRE-Web architecture exemplifying how one application is instantiated by two different users. The architecture of PRE-Desktop is also presented to illustrate how one application can be executed as desktop and web applications.

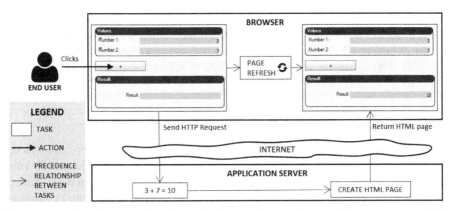

Fig. 4. A snippet of the execution of the calculator application in the web browser (current PRE-Web).

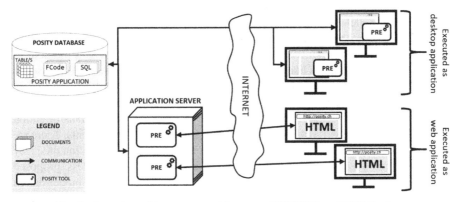

Fig. 5. Overview of the current architecture of PRE-Web and PRE-Desktop

When executing Posity applications in the PRE-Web we observed two main problems in terms of performance and scalability:

Performance problems

After the click on the "+" button, the user may wait up to several seconds before seeing the new page with the result. The reason for this is the long and resource-demanding roundtrip to the server. The performance problem is brought to the extreme from the fact that there is an excessive number of roundtrips to the server. Resizing the web browser window or just selecting a row in a data table causes a new roundtrip. At each roundtrip, the web browser replaces the current GUI with the one in the new HTML page. This performance is unacceptable for modern web applications. Besides, it deteriorates the user experience of Posity AG customers [10].

Scalability problems

The current version of the PRE-Web is not able to execute multiple applications simultaneously. Each instance of the PRE-Web can execute only one application (for a single user) at a time. Therefore, when a user executes an application in the web browser, the application server instantiates a new PRE-Web instance. Each instance can occupy several dozens or hundreds of MB of memory. Furthermore, clients send a considerable number of unnecessary requests. For each request, the server generates a new HTML document. This excessive and inefficient usage of server resources compromises the scalability of the PRE-Web solution.

2.3 Related Work

Industrial studies showed that by 2024 model-driven application development will be responsible for more than 65% of software application development activity [11]. This forecast possess big challenges for main market leaders of model-driven development tools [11]. For example, Appian is a model-driven tool that focuses on complex business process and applications requiring sophisticated automation and analytics capabilities [12]. Outsystems provides a rapid application development environment with a focus on enterprise application development [13]. Both leaders face low scores when user experience is evaluated regarding deployment functionality [11].

Mendix is a model-driven development tool that focuses on business-IT collaboration and application life cycle management [14]. Mendix's reference customers scored it below the average for satisfaction with its platform [11]. Scalability is a problem of niche players and visionaries like Kintone [15].

In summary, the challenges from the studies mentioned above evidence the need to improve end-user experience of model-driven generated software applications. Although the challenges are diverse, they motivate potential modernisation of IDEs, transformation engines, software architectures, model interpreters and runtime environments. There are various research reports proposing methods and techniques for modernisation of legacy software systems based on quality attribute scenarios [16–18]. Nevertheless, proposed solutions do not discuss their potential applicability in the context of model-driven engineering tools. Specifically, in this paper we report on our research experience on modernising Posity, which is a model-driven tool for which desktop generated applications have been successfully adopted in practice. Nevertheless, the lack of flexibility and poor performance when executing diagrams in different platforms like web browsers is hindering the opportunities of Posity to become a big player in the market. The Posity tool has been selected for this research because its development is supported by a continuous collaboration between Posity AG and the Zurich University of Applied Sciences; which is the main affiliation of the authors of this paper.

3 Posity Modernisation Process

The constant growth in the importance of web applications is pushing Posity AG toward the necessity of facing the PRE-Web challenges enlightened in Sect. 2.2. For this, together with Posity AG Stakeholders we have conducted a modernisation process aligned with our research method presented in Fig. 1. The modernisation process encompasses four tasks (see Fig. 6): i) propose treatment, ii) develop proof of concept, iii) conduct laboratory demonstration (Lab-demo), and iv) iterative task for prototype development.

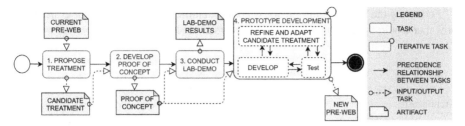

Fig. 6. Overview of the modernization process.

3.1 Task 1: Propose Treatment

The first task of the modernization process aims to identify a solution suitable to the necessities and priorities of Posity AG. This task has been executed in two steps (see Fig. 7). First, a set of possible treatments has been identified and described (see Table 3). Secondly, the set of possible treatments has been evaluated by applying the architecture trade-off analysis method (ATAM) [7]. Finally, the most suitable treatment has been chosen to be validated in a laboratory demonstration.

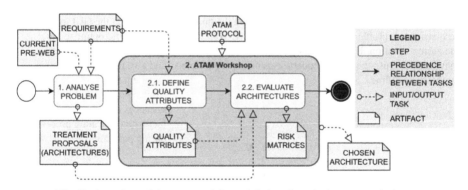

Fig. 7. Overview of the process followed during the solution proposal phase.

Analyse Problem
The goal of the problem analysis is to fully understand the problem and propose a set of possible treatments for solving it. The treatments proposed for the PRE-Web had to satisfy as best as possible the following requirements proposed by Posity Stakeholders:

- The existing code should be reused as much as possible.
- It must be possible to implement all features of the current version of the PRE.
- There is no plan to replace the current PRE-Desktop. Therefore, the PRE-Web must coexist with it.
- The new solution should be able to stay in use for at least ten years.
- Open standards should be consistently applied during the implementation.

Following the list of requirements, we have identified 3 possible candidate architectures that would improve the current situation (see Table 3).

Table 3. Candidate architectures

Architectures		
Architecture 1 - Thick-client	Architecture 2 - Current architecture with optimizations	Architecture 3 - GUI interpreter in client and containerization
Move from a thin-client to a thick-client architecture. The PRE is executed in a web browser A lightweight application server is used as an interface between client and database. (See Fig. 8)	Try to reduce the long response times using modern technologies like asynchronous communication between client and server	The interpretation of the application GUI is moved into the web browser. The GUI communicates with the business logic of its PRE instance through a web API. Each instance of the PRE runs in its own container. (See Fig. 9)
Advantages		
It solves the scalability and responsiveness problems of the current solution. Users may be able to use the applications offline	It aims to improve the quality of the current PRE-Web while reusing the existing PRE codebase as much as possible	Interpreting the GUI in the client should optimize the resources used on the server and give the user a smoother experience. Containerizing the PRE instances on the server, should facilitate the scaling process during peak hours
Drawbacks		
It requires a rewrite of the entire PRE-Web and would create an additional codebase to maintain	The scalability problem stays unchanged. Furthermore, there is no guarantee that performance will improve	It does not scale as good as Architecture 1 because the server still needs to handle the business logic and the application state of each user

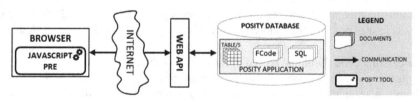

Fig. 8. Architecture 1. PRE-Web with a thick-client architecture.

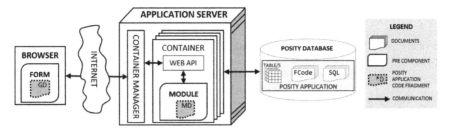

Fig. 9. Architecture 3. Architecture with GUI interpreter in client and containerization

ATAM Workshop
We have conducted a workshop inspired by the method for architecture evaluation ATAM [7]. The workshop was divided into 2 main activities: First, the team formed by Posity's Stakeholders (CEO, and 2 experts in Posity's architecture) and researchers (First author of this paper and a collaborator from the same research group) define a set of quality attributes and their priorities. Posity stakeholders played a key role in the definition of the main quality attributes by listing main problems, needs and desires. Secondly, the team evaluates the risk of each proposed solution.

Quality Attributes
As a first step, together with the stakeholders we delineated a list of quality attributes and their priorities (see Table 4). The quality attributes are necessary for defining the risk matrices. Furthermore, they become useful for validating the success of the developed architecture during the prototype development cycle (see DC2 in Fig. 1).

Risk Matrices
The team of stakeholders discussed the hypothetical satisfaction of the quality attributes in each proposed architecture. As a result, the risks of each quality attribute for each proposed architecture was evaluated.

Stakeholders' knowledge and experience helps the researchers to configure risk matrices (see Fig. 10).

As an example, we may consider the quality attribute 1 (cheap and scalable architecture). A thick-client architecture is probably the best architecture for having a cheap and scalable web application infrastructure. Therefore, it has been assigned with risk "unlikely" in the matrix of architecture 1. Nevertheless, the same quality attribute has a high risk in the other two architectures, since they do not solve the fact that the current solution is cumbersome to scale.

The Chosen Solution
After finalising the risk matrices, the thick-client architecture is clearly the solution with the lowest risk on the most important quality attributes. It has high risk only on attributes with lower priority. Therefore, we develop a proof of concept to evaluate its feasibility.

Table 4. Quality attributes

Extremely important	1. Cheap and scalable infrastructure: The infrastructure should be easy to arrange and maintain. Optimise resources to be able to serve as many clients with minimal infrastructure. Costs associated to use of resources (CPU time, bandwidth, and data transfer, etc.) should be reduced by 20% 2. Performance: The application should in 90% of the cases respond to the user input in less than 0.5 s
Very important	3. Maintainability: The deployment of the PRE should be simple and less error-prone than the current solution. The applications should be easy to debug. Changes in an application should take effect in less than 2 s. The deployment of an application should be simple and should take less than 1 h 4. Security and data integrity: Data and programs should not be changed by external elements. It is guaranteed that the data stays consistent 5. Stability: The PRE-Web should have a smaller or equal error rate than the current PRE-Desktop. Applications can run with an unstable internet connection 6. Usability: Applications should offer a modern appearance and they should be intuitive to operate. The GUIs could be individually designed
Important	7. Implementation time: A first version should be built in one year. All functionalities should be implemented in less than two years and a half 8. Stable technology: The used technologies should be stable for at least 10 years 9. Extensibility: Implementation of new functionalities is not more difficult than in the current solution. The range of functions should be at least as large as the one of the current PRE-Desktop

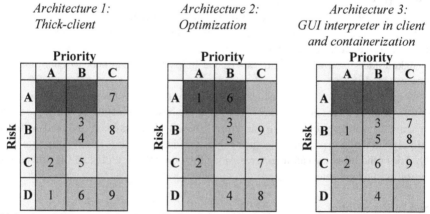

Risk: A = Almost certain, B = Likely, C = Possible, D = Unlikely.
Priority: A = Extremely important, B = Very important, C = Important.

Fig. 10. Risk matrices of the proposed architectures.

3.2   Task 2 and 3: Develop Proof of Concept and Conduct Laboratory Demonstration

The chosen solution requires an (almost) complete rewrite of the current PRE-web. Consequently, it is necessary to verify that it would be possible to execute a Posity application using a thick-client architecture in a web browser. We develop a proof of concept that has a minimal amount of features necessary for verifying that the thick-client architecture can indeed solve performance and scalability problems while satisfying the quality attributes (see Table 4). For this purpose, the proof of concept needs to replicate the behaviour of the calculator example (see Sect. 2.2).

The Objective of the Proof of Concept is to develop a PRE able to have the same behaviour of the PRE-Desktop while executing the calculator example into a web browser. Therefore, the proof of concept must support the following tasks:

- Task 1: Initializing the PRE (starting the module, parsing the FCode and rendering the form)
- Task 2: Executing the PRE (calculating the sum of two numeric inputs, updating the data in the form).

Achieving this objective would demonstrate the feasibility of the thick-client architecture and justify the further development of the new PRE-Web.

Proof of Concept Architecture
We illustrate the execution of the proof of concept of the mentioned architecture by means of the summation calculator example.

Task 1: Initializing the PRE
An instance of a process starts the execution of its module. A parser, which is a component of the PRE-Web, initializes the module by reading the FCode. Once the module is initialized, it is executed. In our example, the module has a command which triggers the rendering of the form. As a consequence, the form is rendered (see Fig. 13).

   The parser reads the values in the FCode commands and sets them in the corresponding PRE-Components. Thereby, after the initialization all the components know what to do when they are executed. For example, the command that executes the sum (NumberAddCmd), knows where it will find the two input values and where it will write the output value. The button knows that its label value is "+" and that when it is clicked, it will trigger the event "Sum" (See Fig. 11).

Task 2: Executing the PRE
When the user clicks on the button "+", it starts the execution of the "Sum" event in the module. Then the module reads the two input values and calculates their sum. Finally, the result is set into the form (see Fig. 12 and Fig. 14).

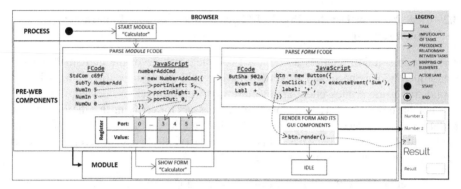

Fig. 11. Starting the calculator

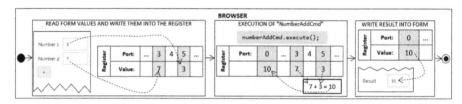

Fig. 12. Execution of the event "Sum" in the calculator module.

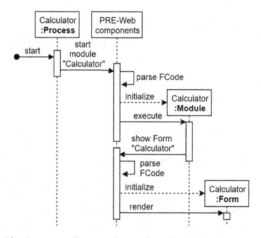

Fig. 13. Sequence diagram for starting the "Calculator" module.

Measuring the Performance of the Two PRE-Web Versions: A Laboratory Demonstration

We measured the response time for a simple calculation using the two versions of the PRE-Web. Both PRE were being executed locally, on the same machine using the same web browser. For measuring the response time we used the DevTools performance panel

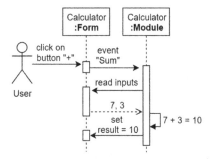

Fig. 14. Sequence diagram for executing the "Sum" event in the "Calculator" module.

of Chrome [19]. We measured the interval between the first frame that shows the button has been clicked and the first frame that shows the value "10" inside the result box (see Fig. 15).

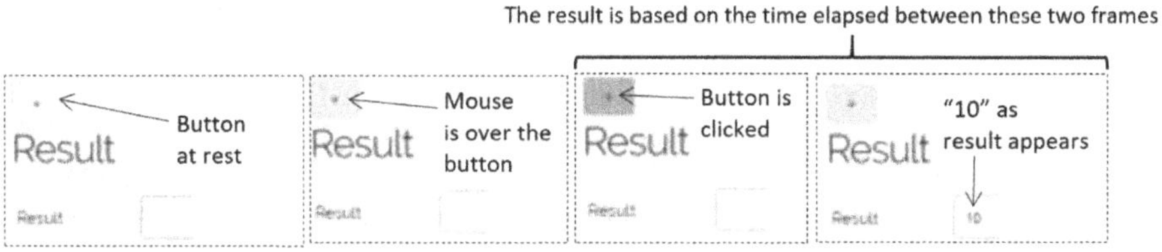

Fig. 15. The sequence of frames during the performance measurements of the new PRE-Web.

Results. The improvement in performance is clear. The response time using the thick-client architecture is more than 17 times shorter than the current PRE-Web (see Fig. 16). Since the application server is running locally, the trip of the client requests and server responses through the internet has been spared. Therefore, it can be assumed that the response time of the old PRE-Web would be even longer in a normal use case.

Fig. 16. Timeline of the response time of the two PRE-Web versions.

The scalability is likewise supposed to improve due to the reduction of server resources consumption that the nature of the thick-client architecture brings:

- Requests from the client to the server are considerably reduced.
- The application server does not need to start a new instance of the PRE for each connecting client.
- The execution of the business logic is now using the resources of the clients.

Finally, we conclude that the new PRE-Web can provide an improved user experience because the application reacts far faster and does not continuously refresh the page [10]. At this point, despite results are promising we recognise a threat to the generalisability of the results. Since the new PRE-Web depends on clients' hardware and operative system, subsequent tests should be conducted. Results motivate our current efforts on developing a prototype to further test performance and scalability values in production environments.

4 Lessons Learnt and Future Work

In this paper we present the results of an investigation we have conducted together with Posity AG, a software development company that supports the model-driven development tool Posity. Posity has been already transferred to industrial settings where desktop applications developed with Posity are used by various customers. Posity AG aims at being able to provide model-driven generated software applications to be executed in different platforms like web browsers. However, web applications generated with Posity do not satisfy actual demands in terms of performance and scalability. For this context problem, our main research question states: *How to design a treatment for improving performance and scalability of web applications generated by Posity?* We investigated the current context of Posity and the issues of generated web applications. As a result, we designed the proof of concept of a thick-client architecture. Additionally, we conducted a laboratory demonstration which revealed performance improvements with a response time 17 times shorter, and scalability growths. Some lessons learnt and future work are summarised below:

Development Challenges. The Posity runtime environment for web applications needs to interpret graphical models that have been already transformed into FCode (byte-code). Given that there is not a clear specification on how model interpretation needs to be conducted, it was necessary to re-engineer the behaviour of the existing interpreter for executing desktop applications. MDWE tools need to provide the specification of model interpreters and facilitate their interoperability with other technologies. This would greatly help during modernisation processes.

Security Concerns. A thick-client architecture brings security concerns from the fact that the entire application is being executed in web browsers with JavaScript. This may be dangerous because a malicious user could tamper with the programmed behaviour of the application. MDWE tools need to consider possible misuse of generated applications. For this, MDWE tools need to provide engineers with the facilities to model security attributes when applications are specified.

Future Work. Results obtained from the laboratory demonstration (see Sect. 3.2) justify further development of the PRE-Web with a thick-client architecture. However, the validation process must go forward to transfer the proposed architecture to practical settings. We plan to investigate which are the most important attributes that model-driven generated web applications should satisfy. Results will pave the way for successful model-driven engineering tools.

References

1. Rossi, G., Urbieta, M., Distante, D., Rivero, J.M., Firmenich, S.: 25 years of model-driven web engineering: what we achieved, what is missing. CLEI Electron. J. (2016). https://doi.org/10.19153/cleiej.19.3.1
2. Robles Luna, E., Sánchez Begines, J.M., Matías Rivero, J., Morales, L., Enríquez, J.G., Rossi, G.: Challenges for the adoption of model-driven web engineering approaches in industry. J. Web Eng. 17(3–4), 183–205 (2018). https://doi.org/10.5220/0006382704150421
3. "Posity AG - database applications for the cloud. https://posity.ch/index.html. Accessed 15 Jan 2020
4. Spielberger, J., Baertschi-Rusch, M., Mürner, M., Perellano, G., Wüst, R.: Rapid Development of ICT Business Services by Business Engineers Independent of Computer Scientists (2014)
5. HTML & CSS - W3C. https://www.w3.org/standards/webdesign/htmlcss.html. Accessed 30 Jan 2020
6. Wieringa, R.J.: Design Science Methodology: For Information Systems and Software Engineering. Springer, Berlin Heidelberg (2014). https://doi.org/10.1007/978-3-662-43839-8
7. Kazman, R., Klein, M., Clements, P.: ATAM : method for architecture evaluation. Cmusei No. (CMU/SEI-2000-TR-004, ADA382629) 4, 83 (2000)
8. ISO - ISO/IEC 9075-1:2016 - Information technology—Database languages—SQL—Part 1: Framework (SQL/Framework). https://www.iso.org/standard/63555.html. Accessed 30 Jan 2020
9. Bannwart, F., Müller, P.: A program logic for bytecode. Electron. Notes Theor. Comput. Sci. 141(1), 255–273 (2005). https://doi.org/10.1016/j.entcs.2005.02.026
10. Moody, D.L.: The method evaluation model: a theoretical model for validating information systems design methods (2003)
11. Vincent, P., Lijima, K., Driver, M., Wong, J., Yefim, N.: Gartner Reprint (2019)
12. Appian: Appian: Low-Code - Enterprise Application Development - BPM Software. https://www.appian.com/. Accessed 03 Feb 2020
13. OutSystems: The #1 Low-Code Platform for Digital Transformation|OutSystems. https://www.outsystems.com/. Accessed 03 Feb 2020
14. Mendix: Low-code Application Development Platform - Build Apps Fast & Efficiently|Mendix. https://www.mendix.com/. Accessed 03 Feb 2020
15. Kintone: No-Code/Low-Code Application Platform for Teams|Kintone. https://www.kintone.com/. Accessed 03 Feb 2020
16. Ali, N., Martínez-Martínez, A., Ayuso-Pérez, L., Espinoza, A.: Self-adaptive quality requirement elicitation process for legacy systems: a case study in healthcare. In: Proceedings of the ACM Symposium on Applied Computing, vol. Part F1280, pp. 1102–1107 (2017). https://doi.org/10.1145/3019612.3019751
17. Kephart, J.O., Chess, D.M.: The vision of autonomic computing. Comput. (Long. Beach. Calif.) 36(1) (2003). https://doi.org/10.1109/mc.2003.1160055
18. Oreizy, P., et al.: An architecture-based approach to self-adaptive software. IEEE Intell. Syst. 14(3), 54–62 (1999). https://doi.org/10.1109/5254.769885
19. Basques, K.: Performance Analysis Reference (2019)

TesCaV: An Approach for Learning Model-Based Testing and Coverage in Practice

Beatriz Marín[1](✉), Sofía Alarcón[1], Giovanni Giachetti[2], and Monique Snoeck[3]

[1] Universidad Diego Portales, Santiago, Chile
{beatriz.marin,sofia.alarcon}@mail.udp.cl
[2] Universidad Tecnológica de Chile INACAP, Santiago, Chile
ggiachetti@inacap.cl
[3] KU Leuven, Leuven, Belgium
monique.snoeck@kuleuven.be

Abstract. Academy and industry permanently remark the importance of software-testing techniques to improve software quality and to reduce development and maintenance costs. A testing method to be considered for this purpose is Model-Based Testing (MBT), which generates test cases from a model that represents the structure and the behavior of the system to be developed. The generated test suite is easier to maintain and adapt to changes in requirements or evolution of the developed system. However, teaching and learning MBT techniques are not easy tasks; students need to know the different testing techniques to assure that the requirements are fulfilled as well as to identify any failure in the software system modeled. In this work, we present *TesCaV*, an MBT teaching tool for university students, which is based on a model-driven technology for the automatic software generation from UML diagrams. *TesCaV* allows validating the test cases defined by students and graphically determines the level of testing coverage over the system modeled. Preliminary results show *TesCaV* as a promising approach for MBT teaching/learning processes.

Keywords: Teaching/learning testing · Model-Based Testing · Coverage · Lessons learned

1 Introduction

Model-Driven approaches use conceptual modeling during design and testing in order to automate the generation and verification of the software related to the products modeled in a partial or complete way [25, 33]. Thus, any defect introduced in the system's model can produce low quality software that does not meet the customers' requirements or presents unstable behavior. Learning conceptual modeling and testing are not easy tasks. Conceptual modeling implies abstracting from reality, identifying the business concepts, and then expressing them in a conceptual model. As identified in the CaMeLOT framework for learning objectives on Conceptual modelling [6], being able to validate a model is a prerequisite for learning to build the model correctly. Testing

© Springer Nature Switzerland AG 2020
F. Dalpiaz et al. (Eds.): RCIS 2020, LNBIP 385, pp. 302–317, 2020.
https://doi.org/10.1007/978-3-030-50316-1_18

skills are thus of primary importance, also in teaching Conceptual Modelling. Testing implies the assurance of the compliance of the requirements and the consideration of any scenario that may provoke the failure of the system modeled.

Teaching support for conceptual modeling ranges from the use of serious games (learning by playing) [21] to the application of specific model-driven tools [25, 30] to create and compile a conceptual model. An example of the latter are the JMermaid/MERLIN tool [19], which uses UML [24] and the Merode approach [32] for modeling class diagrams and state-transition diagrams that are compiled into java applications. The generated Java application allows to create, modify, and work with all the objects modeled. Thus, students can see how the modeled software works.

Concepts and techniques for software testing are commonly explained through lecturing and later, students must apply these techniques with some small or toy-example projects. Another common alternative is to perform testing on a predefined case guided by the teacher in the classroom. In both cases, students are applying testing concepts; however, they do not receive feedback to properly distinguish which part of the system is already tested from the part of the system that must be still tested. Such feedback is related to testing coverage, which must be considered for an effective testing process. In [1], authors analyze the common mistakes that students make when learning testing, resulting in the test coverage being the most frequent problem, since students commonly miss test cases, write incorrect test cases, or do not provide all the expected test cases. A high testing coverage indicates that most of the developed software has been tested, therefore, reducing the quality issues that the final software product may have. In case of code generation from models by means of proven transformations, coverage should refer to the model rather than to the code. The visualization of the coverage of testing on the basis of the model is however still is an open issue. It is however a relevant technique for proper learning and application of testing techniques.

In this paper, we present a tool that implements a specific approach for visualizing testing coverage on a model, which is called TesCaV (TESt CoverAge Visualization). This tool has been specifically implemented to improve the teaching and learning of Model-Based Testing (MBT) [36]. TesCaV is used to generate test cases from the conceptual model of a software system and to graphically visualize the coverage of the test cases defined by the students on the model used for software development. Thus, students identify the cases necessary to complete the software testing by considering the gap between their case studies from those automatically generated by the TesCaV platform. The approach has been validated in an explorative way with undergraduate students of software engineering courses, and shows promising results.

The rest of the paper is organized as follows. Section 2 presents related work. Section 3 introduces the TesCAV approach and tool, and Sect. 4 shows the empirical evaluation of the tool. Section 5 presents some lessons learned. Finally, Sect. 6 summarizes our main conclusions and future work.

2   Related Work

This section briefly presents MERODE code generator, the model-driven tool used as the starting point for implementing the TesCaV approach, as well as the foundations of Model-Based Testing and some relevant related works.

2.1 The MERODE Code Generator

The MERODE code generator is a Model-Driven Development (MDD) tool created to facilitate the conceptual modeling learning process. The tool uses conceptual models specified with the UML or MERODE modeling languages and can automatically generate a fully working application that can be used as a simulator by the students to create instances of the objects modeled, to edit instances, and to evaluate the behavior of the software system modeled.

The MERODE code-generator uses an XML representation for the conceptual constructs defined in the MERODE metamodel. This XML file is used as input by a code-generation tool to obtain the implementation (source code) of the application modeled. More details about the MERODE tools can be found in [19].

2.2 Model-Based Testing

Model-Based Testing (MBT) approaches automate the design and execution of test cases, which are generated by using model-driven techniques applied to the conceptual models of the reference software systems. For this reason, the MBT techniques can be perfectly aligned with MDD approaches [20] related to software development. Figure 1 shows the common steps related to MBT techniques:

(1) Model the software system in an abstract way by using a general-purpose modeling language such as UML or a Domain-Specific Modeling Language;
(2) Generate abstract test cases from the conceptual models defined by using a testing criterion related to the coverage of the model;
(3) Generate concrete test cases from the abstract test cases in the target programming language of the software system;
(4) Execute the concrete test cases and register the results obtained; and
(5) Analyze the results obtained to evaluate the testing coverage and effectiveness.

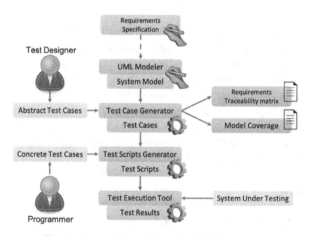

Fig. 1. General description of an MBT process.

Furthermore, an MBT process requires the definition of test criteria, which are used to identify the conceptual constructs and to define the generation rules to obtain test cases from the system modeled. For instance, we identified the following general criteria in object-oriented MBT approaches:

- Transition-based criteria, which generate test cases from the transitions and the different states of an object defined in a state-machine model.
- Class diagram criteria, which are used to test the associations, multiplicity, attributes, and instances of classes.
- Data-based criteria, which are used to select and define data sets for the test case executions.

2.3 Teaching Support for Software Testing

In practice, software testing continues to be the primary approach to quality assessment of software development, and more than 60% of the development cost is assigned to testing [40]. Major reasons of this high cost are not only the amount of testing but also how the testing is doing. A significant amount of testers have not been properly prepared for this task. This is one of the root causes of the current suboptimal state of practice in software testing and this is a motivation for exploring and improving the teaching of testing.

In many Computer Science programs, software testing is an elective rather than a mandatory course, resulting in many students being insufficiently trained in testing [39]. Moreover, due to the large number of topics that must be reviewed in software engineering courses and curricula, testing is not seen as a key topic [9]. In [18] it is suggested that the practice of testing should be an embedded part of the educational experience, and therefore each course in the curriculum should include one or more testing techniques. Nevertheless, even when programs include software testing topics, it is important to pay attention to how to teach these topics.

The *just in time teaching* (JiTT) is a strategy applied to improve the learning of non-traditional students, which was applied in a software testing course [22], where the out-of-class component was related to questions that students must answer before the class, and the in-class component was related to explain the misconceptions and problems in the answer. The authors conclude that JiTT is a technique that is particularly useful in theoretical courses.

In [35], case base learning (CBL) was used in order to teach testing in practice. In order to answer the case questions, students had to investigate the problem and apply the concepts previously learnt. Results indicate that students approve this teaching approach but the planning of CBL takes a great effort and the selection of the appropriate testing topics must be taught in the traditional way prior to the CBL sessions. ·

The use of serious games has also been explored to motivate students to learn testing. A card game is presented in [5], where the students play the role of a test analyst who must decide to apply acceptance testing, stress testing, functional testing, security testing or usability testing over the cases presented in other cards. In this case, students learn the different types of testing but they do not learn how to apply testing techniques to do that. In [37], the Testing game is presented, which focuses on functional testing, structural testing, and defect-based testing. The students must understand the techniques and eliminate the invalid test cases for a bubble sort program. The game does not address the concept of test coverage. TestEG [23] is a videogame, where students take the role of testing chief in a simulated project. However, the game does not address the different types of testing, the identification of test cases or the coverage of testing.

Several studies related to teaching software testing are oriented to start testing learning at early stages. This allows students to develop a testing culture, something that is difficult to achieve at later stages of their careers. This is the case of the work presented by Elbaum et al. [12], which teaches black and white box techniques in initial computer science courses by using the bug hunt web application. The works presented in [10, 14] are also oriented to black and white box testing by providing a repository with different tutorials (called virtual learning environments). These tutorials are oriented to testing concepts without alternatives for students to do testing practices through the WReSTT-CyLE virtual learning.

The works presented in [11] and [8] show the Web-Cat tool that considers aspects such as test coverage; however, the proper definition of test cases is not considered. In [7], these authors have introduced promotion mechanisms to strengthen the teaching of Test-Driven Development (TDD) techniques. The tool presented in [31] allows the students to define their own test cases that are later executed over applications already defined by the teacher. These applications present some failures that must be identified by the students' tests. In [27], a two-players serious game, named Code Defenders, is presented, whose purpose is to teach mutation-based testing techniques. The game considers an attacker that creates java-code mutations, called "mutants", which are "killed" when the defender detects the mutants by means of specific JUnit tests.

Other approaches propose some techniques for improving teaching testing, but without providing supporting tools. This is the case of the approach presented by Barbosa et al. [3], which considers the use of Class Responsibility Collaborator (CRC) cards. This approach is based on class diagrams; thus, it has a certain proximity to Model-Based Testing. The approach of Gotel et al. [16] considers pair review practice to validate unitary tests and acceptation tests among students. The work presented in [34] shows a card game for implementing an active learning method for teaching software testing. The approach presented in [17], called coding dojo, proposes group-oriented study techniques for learning agile practices, in particular, TDD for software testing.

In summary, most of the analyzed approaches consider traditional black and white box testing techniques and few provide automation elements or tools for test-case definitions. The approaches are more oriented to teaching testing concepts or improving knowledge about traditional testing techniques, than teaching novel testing approaches. The only approach that differs in this respect is Code Defender [27], which provides automation mechanisms for teaching mutation-based testing. Moreover, all the analyzed approaches and tools are related to code-oriented testing. Model-based testing thus remains a gap in the current state of the art, as well as techniques to teach testing for non-coders, in particular from a requirement engineering of business and functional analysts' perspective. This work addresses this gap by presenting a teaching approach for Model-Based Testing geared to conceptual modelers, and with special focus on the coverage of the test cases performed by the students. In a previous work [26], we presented the proof-of-concept of the tool without validation. In this paper, we present the improved version, including technical details and an exploratory empirical evaluation with students.

3   The TesCaV Approach

TesCaV is a Model-Based Testing tool that allows the automatic generation of concrete test cases starting from MERODE conceptual models. TesCaV is implemented as a module available in the generated application which adds graphical feedback to students about how much of the generated application has been tested. Using the same models that the students created in the modelling tool to describe the software application, TesCaV indicates graphically what part of the system has yet to be tested (for example, by indicating what transitions of a state machine have not been used for the objects created so far). TesCaV uses MBT to generate the test cases that the student must cover. TesCaV can be download from http://merode.econ.kuleuven.be/Research.html.

TesCaV implements ten different criteria related class to class diagram-based criteria, transition-based criteria and data-based criteria: TesCaV implements test criteria related to class attributes, association-end-multiplicity, and generalization criteria related to the class diagram; It also implements the all-states, all-transitions, all-transitions-pair, all-loop-free-paths, all-one-loop-paths, and all-configurations criteria related to the state transition diagram; Finally, TesCaV implements the one-value criterion related to data. The algorithms used to implement each criterion are similar to those presented in [20]. For instance, for the class attribute criterion, TesCaV creates one test case with valid values of each attribute of each class in the model in order to test the feasibility to create instances of all the classes modelled. Another example is the all-states criterion, for which TesCaV creates test cases that execute one event defined for each class in order to reach the first state, and from that state, TesCaV executes the next event needed to reach another state, considering that all the defined states must be reachable by some event. If not, then the model is defective, and the generated application as well.

TesCaV is implemented in Java and Swing, since the code generator and the generated applications use these programming languages as well. TesCaV reads the model of the application, takes into account the MERODE metamodel, and stores the information in a structure that facilitates the execution of the algorithms of each implemented MBT criterion (see Fig. 2).

The conceptual model of the software application needs to be specified according to the MERODE metamodel in order to properly execute TesCaV. In order to apply TesCaV to other modeling languages with different metamodels, it is important to note that these languages must support class diagrams and state-transition diagrams, since they provide the information to apply the MBT criteria mentioned before. To minimize the impact of applying TesCaV to other modeling languages, an integration metamodel can be used, similar to the approach presented in [15].

Regarding the execution of TesCaV, the code generator of the modeling tool must generate the application. TesCaV can be added as a package in the generated application. Since we use MERODE, the Code Generator must generate the application in Java first. Then, a button to execute TesCaV appears in the generated application (see Fig. 3).

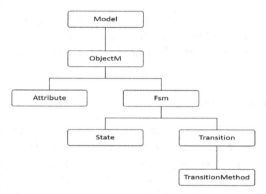

Fig. 2. Structure of the model elements that are used in the automatic generation of test cases.

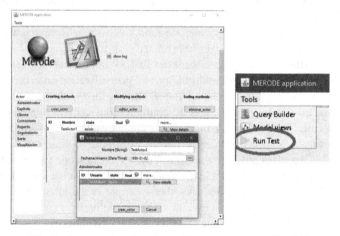

Fig. 3. Generated application and button to execute TesCaV.

When a student tests the generated application by using self-defined scenarios, the tool keeps a log of performed test actions. TesCaV will provide feedback to the students about the quality of the performed tests to improve the learning process. To verify the quality of the testing performed so far, the student will perform the following actions:

First, the student clicks the button *Run Test*, and the TesCaV tool generates automatically the test cases according to the implemented MBT criteria. TesCaV informs if the executed test cases have full coverage over the system implemented (Fig. 4A), or by contrast, if there are still test cases that must be defined to assure the coverage of all the system (Fig. 4B).

Second, the TesCaV tool identifies the interactions that the student has already performed. To do this, the TesCaV tool reviews the logs of the application usage and identifies the objects created by the students, and the events related to these objects, which correspond to transitions of the state-transition diagram. As a result, the TesCaV tool shows a summary of the coverage of each MBT criterion of each object modeled

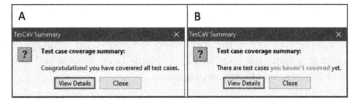

Fig. 4. General feedback of the coverage of the executed test cases.

in the MERODE modelling tool. For instance, Fig. 5 shows the coverage of the concept *Serie* in the application generated.

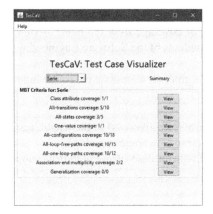

Fig. 5. Example of coverage of test cases executed for an object.

Third, the students can click the *view button* of each criterion, and TesCaV shows the objects that have not been created, the states that have not been visited, and the transitions that have not been executed in red. Figure 6 shows objects not created and the states not visited by the test cases executed by the students.

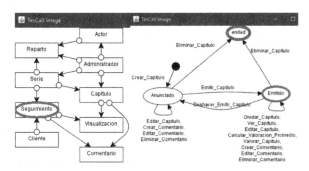

Fig. 6. Example of visualization of objects and states not covered by the student.

We advocate that with the visualization of the objects, states, and transitions not covered by the test cases executed by the students, the students can clearly observe what they have missed testing in the application to improve the coverage. Hence, the students are able to acquire the knowledge of Model-Based Testing and to understand the relevance of the coverage metric in practice.

4   Evaluation of TesCaV

We performed an exploratory empirical study to evaluate students' perception of the use of TesCaV by following the well-known guidelines provided by [38] and [28]. We used the Goal-Question-Metric template [4] to define the goal of the evaluation as follow: *Analyze* the TesCaV approach *for the purpose of* evaluation *with respect to* the perceived usefulness to put in practice the Model-Based Testing approach as well as to understand the concept of coverage *from the point of view* of the researcher *in the context of* undergraduate students of the Software Engineering course at Diego Portales University.

Taking into account this goal, we formulate the following research questions for the study:

RQ1: Do students find utility (effectiveness) in the use of TesCaV for learning Model-based testing and understand the coverage meaning?

RQ2: Are students satisfied with the ease-of-use of the tool support provided by TesCaV?

4.1   Study Planning

The context of the study is the software engineering course, which is a 4th year course of the Computer Engineering degree at Diego Portales University in Chile. This course is obligatory. In this course, the students learn how to model a software system with BPMN and UML by using process diagrams, use case diagrams, class diagrams, state-transition diagrams, components' diagrams and deployment diagrams. In this course students also learn how to test a software system by means of traditional lectures, i.e., by using PowerPoints to explain the concepts of different testing techniques (such as model-based testing, mutation testing and search based testing) and then they do testing exercises on paper. In the study, students must design and execute test cases for a software already modeled in in MERODE with class diagrams and state transition diagrams, and later, students must indicate their opinion about the testing process using TesCaV.

The independent variables correspond to the models and the generated application with their intrinsic complexity. The dependent variables correspond to the perceived usefulness of using TesCaV to learn model-based testing and to understand the meaning of the coverage. To obtain the perceived usefulness of TestCaV, we used the UMUX [13] questionnaire, which has 4 statements that are related to effectiveness, efficiency, satisfaction and overall usefulness perception. This questionnaire uses a 5-point Likert scale, which goes form strongly disagree to strongly agree. The statements of the UMUX questionnaire are the following:

Q1 Effectiveness: TesCaV capabilities meet my requirements, i.e., it allows to put in practice model-based testing and understand coverage.

Q2 Satisfaction: Using TesCaV is a frustrating experience.

Q3 Overall: TesCaV is easy to use.

Q4 Efficiency: I have to spend too much time correcting things with TesCaV.

The empirical study was set up as follows: Each student receives the application to test, the models that have been used to automatically generate the application, and a brief explanation about the study. Students must understand the application and then, they must design and execute test cases in the application, as many as they need to completely test the application. Next, students run the TesCaV to visualize the test cases correctly executed and the test cases that are needed but the student didn't design. After that, they can design and execute more test cases to improve the coverage and they can execute TesCaV again. In the end, students should answer the UMUX questionnaire to evaluate the perception of using TesCaV. Also, they can provide open comments at the end of the questionnaire if they want.

The case corresponds to a system that allows users to visualize and add comments to TV series, with the corresponding chapters and actors that participate in the serie. We selected this case since students are familiar with this domain.

4.2 Study Operation

The study was performed with 25 undergraduate students of the Engineering Faculty of Diego Portales University who were enrolled in the Software Engineering course during the second semester of 2018. At the end of the course (December), we invited students to participate in the study. This activity was not related to the approval of the course nor with any course evaluation. Nevertheless, we encouraged students to do their best when using the tool.

First, we briefly presented the goal of the study to the students, which was related to investigate the usefulness of TesCaV to put in practice model-based testing as well as to understand the concept of coverage. We explained the case modeled in the MERODE modelling tool. At this point, it is important to mention that even though students have had conceptual modeling classes, they never had used this tool. Hence, we created the model in JMermaid in order to mitigate the difficulty perceptions that are not related to the TesCaV tool and we explained the case.

Students had 30 min to understand the generated application and also to design and execute test cases that they believed could test the generated applications completely. The majority of students completed this task in less than 30 min. Next, they ran the TesCaV tool and visualized the coverage of their preformed testing. After that, they could design and execute more test cases to improve the coverage for 10 min if they wanted, and they could execute TesCaV again. This repetitive process allows students to realize the importance of coverage when design test cases. Finally, students answered the UMUX questionnaire to evaluate their perception of using TesCaV.

Students answered this questionnaire using a 5-point Likert scale (see Fig. 7). Results show that 92% of students agreed or strongly agreed with Q1, i.e., TesCaV allows to put in practice model-based testing and understand coverage. There is a strong tendency (82%)

that TesCaV is not a frustrating experience (Q2). Overall, 80% of students found that TesCaV is easy to use. Regarding efficiency (Q3), 68% of students strongly disagree or disagree that they have to spend too much time correcting things with TesCaV. In summary, students found the use of TesCaV and the visualization of coverage useful to put model-based testing in practice and to improve the testing process (RQ1). Students were also satisfied with the general usability of the tool (RQ2).

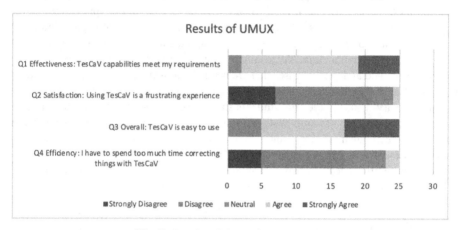

Fig. 7. Results of the exploratory study.

Regarding comments, not all the students provided comments. Some students (5) indicated that it was difficult to use the generated application, and a tutorial could be included to better understand how it works. Other comments (5) were related to improving the visualization of the coverage metric by using graphs or percentages. Currently, TesCaV shows the number of test cases executed/number of all the test cases. Finally, 8 comments stated that TesCaV is a good tool to understand how to test and also to understand how the coverage is measured, which strengthens the answers for RQ1 and RQ2. The data of this experiment is publicly available via the Zenodo platform at https://doi.org/10.5281/zenodo.3727619.

4.3   Threats to Validity

Despite the efforts to assure the validity of our findings, there are some threats to validity that may affect our study.

The students' lack of experience on using the MERODE tools may affect the *internal validity* since it impacts their interaction with the application. In order to decrease this threat, we provided the case already modelled to the students in order to allow them to focus just on the testing part and not on the modeling part. Another internal validity threat is related to the models selected to generate the test cases, since different models have different conceptual constructs and may not require all the testing criteria implemented by TesCaV. To manage this threat, we designed a case that included 89% of the testing criteria implemented in TesCaV. As a result, the students needed to design test cases using the large majority of the testing criteria, which improved their knowledge of model-based testing. The threat of information exchange between students was mitigated by the fact that all the students worked in a lab with separate work spaces and the professor was present during the entire study.

Regarding the *external validity*, the representativeness of the subject is a threat since the lack of representativeness of our sample of participants may affect the results. We selected students with all a same level of knowledge about testing since they are in the same course to mitigate this threat. To reduce the threat of evaluation apprehension, the students were informed that the participation was voluntary without any incidence in the approval of the course. While the students' level of testing knowledge may be considered representative for junior software developers, repeating the study with other students will help to ensure the generalizability of the results.

5 Lessons Learned

The development and validation of TesCaV allowed gaining some lessons learned about teaching model-based testing and coverage, which support our perception that the obtained results are promising.

Lesson 1: Teaching testing in practice. For the proper learning of testing, it is really important to not focus just on the theoretical part, but to let students experience how to do it in practice. In this paper we presented the TesCaV tool which allows to understand model-based testing by means of practice. The use of TestCaV reveals the importance of having tools and methods for the practical teaching of testing: we have observed that this is a more challenging and attractive strategy for students while at the same time they develop more advanced capabilities for adapting the testing concepts to real development scenarios. Moreover, we have preliminary evidence that the knowledge acquired by means of practical experience is more perdurable and easier to put in practice than the theoretically acquired knowledge.

Lesson 2: Visualization of coverage allows to interiorize and understand the different coverage metrics: it helps the students to realize what part of the model has not been tested, and thus may have quality issues left. Or at least, the students know the weak points of the testing performed since the coverage is not fully achieved, and, hence, are aware of the fact that potential failures may still be present in the system for the functionalities that have not been tested. The graphic information in red allows to easily understand the objects, states and transitions that have not been tested yet. This is aligned with the constructivist perspective, where to reach the learning goals textual (verbal) and visual information are the key to generate knowledge [29].

Lesson 3: The TestCaV approach provides a straightforward way to demonstrate to the students the implications of model defects in the final system, which improves their learning process. The student can visualize in an agile and clear way the importance of a well-defined model, and how to test the different system concepts defined at model-level. Testing demands analysis skills, which are reinforced with the visualization of the models and the traceability from these models to the generated application.

Lesson 4: Providing different scenarios strengthens the knowledge of the testing process. We embedded the TesCaV tool in the MERODE code generator, which allows to generate a working application from any conceptual model, in order to allow students to test different applications. This contrasts to existing solutions where the testing exercises are developed based on a single predefined application. We advocate that being able to exercise the skills on multiple applications is important to the practice of the testing process, since by applying model-based testing on different applications, we avoid memorizing the computed solutions that are available in the tools of the state of the art. Thus, students can strengthen their knowledge about model-based testing and the coverage metric.

Lesson 5: Even though implementing the graphical representation of the testing coverage in a concrete model-driven tool is a hard task, which demands more time than preparing a regular testing class centered on teaching testing concepts, the learning is improved. The learning curve is reduced since students can understand testing concepts faster and put them into practice. Moreover, the evaluation process is also improved since the professor can clearly observe those students that have properly applied testing concepts and graphically demonstrate why their defined testing cases are complete or not. Nevertheless, further empirical studies are needed to evaluate the correlation between the use of the tool with the learning performance.

Lesson 6: Considering the importance of including testing competences as mandatory in computer science curricula, the use of TesCaV leads to students being better prepared (better trained) to perform testing in software systems, using their conceptual model as a starting point. We observed that the use of TestCaV facilitates not only the inclusion of testing skills in different courses but also provides a guide to the professor and students to properly apply testing techniques. In practice, it also reduces the effort from the professor/student for the teaching/learning of the complex and abstract concepts that are involved in the correct testing definition and execution.

Besides these important lessons learned, we also identify some limitations of our approach.

A limitation of using TesCaV for learning model-based testing in practice is that TesCaV has been created specifically to run with MERODE models. Even though it uses class diagrams and state-transition diagrams that are widely supported by different modeling languages, each language has different elements in the definition of the conceptual constructs. In order to reduce this limitation, TesCaV can be integrated to other tools though the use of a Testing profile [2].

Another limitation of the TesCaV approach is that is related only to model-based testing and specifically focuses on test coverage. In order to reduce this limitation, we will explore other testing techniques that fit well with model-based testing in order to incorporate them to TesCaV.

Another limitation is related to the exploratory study: we only explored perceived utility and perceived ease of use. More research questions can be investigated in future experiments, for instance: Does the students' behavior (regarding attending to a class) change when they have tools to practice testing?, Do students characteristics (gender, age, previous courses) affect in the efficiency doing testing?, and Is the teacher an influential factor for the learning performance when the students use the TesCaV approach?, among others.

6 Conclusions

In this paper, we present TesCaV, a model-based testing tool that allows the visualization of the test case coverage. TesCaV has been developed to help in the teaching/learning process. To do that, TesCaV has been embedded in the MERODE code generator, which uses the model-driven engineering paradigm to automatically generate Java applications from MERODE conceptual models.

TesCaV puts into practice the model-based testing paradigm since it uses the MERODE conceptual models to automatically generate abstract and concrete test cases. TesCaV does not automate the test case execution since the focus of this tool is to help in the learning process. Even though all the test cases that allow for 100% coverage of the generated application are concretized automatically with TesCaV, the students can execute own test cases and then TesCaV compares the test cases used by the student with the automatically generated test cases in order to show the part of the system that has not been tested yet. This is the most important contribution of TesCaV: the visualization of the test case coverage. The coverage metric helps the students realizing that they need to test more to generate better confidence in the results of the testing performed or to test the correct elements.

We performed an exploratory study to evaluate the benefits of using TesCaV in the learning process, and results indicate that students perceive TesCaV as helpful for their learning process and that it is easy to use. Moreover, we provide six lessons learned that can be useful for other researchers that are interested in teaching model-based testing. Some of these lessons can be applicable to other fields, such as lesson 1and lesson 5, the remainder are specific for model-based testing and we advocate that are valuable knowledge for other researchers.

As future work, we plan to improve the code generator in order to include the TesCaV tool automatically when the java application is generated. Moreover, taking into account the results of this exploratory study, we plan to improve the visualization of the coverage, highlighting the student test cases that pass in green and maintaining the test cases that are not yet executed by the student in the red with a small description of the test cases that are missing. We also plan to graphically present the percentage of test case coverage as suggested in the comments of the exploratory study. Finally, we plan to perform an experiment in order to better understand the benefits of using TesCaV in the teaching/learning process of university students.

Acknowledgement. This work was funded by CONICYT project ENSE REDI170020, 2017–2019.

References

1. Aniche, M., Hermans, F., Deursen, A.V.: Pragmatic software testing education. In: Proceedings of Proceedings of the 50th ACM Technical Symposium on Computer Science Education, pp. 414–420. Association for Computing Machinery (2019)

2. Baker, P., Dai, Z.R., Grabowski, J., Haugen, Ø., Schieferdecker, I., Williams, C.: Model-Driven Testing: Using the UML Testing Profile. Springer, Heidelberg (2008). https://doi.org/10.1007/978-3-540-72563-3

3. Barbosa, E.F., Maldonado, J.C., LeBlanc, R., Guzdial, M.: Introducing testing practices into objects and design course. In: 2003 16th Conference on Software Engineering Education and Training, (CSEE&T 2003), pp. 279–286. IEEE (2003)

4. Basili, V., Caldeira, G., Rombach, H.D.: The Goal Question Metric Paradigm. Encycl. Softw. Eng. **2**, 528–532 (1994)

5. Beppe, T.A., de Araujo, I.L., Aragao, B.S., Santos, I.D., Ximenes, D., Andrade, R.M.C.: GreaTest: A Card Game to Motivate the Software Testing Learning. ACM (2018)

6. Bogdanova, D., Snoeck, M.: CaMeLOT: an educational framework for conceptual data modelling. Inf. Softw. Technol. **110**, 92–107 (2019)

7. Buffardi, K., Edwards, S.H.: A formative study of influences on student testing behaviors. In: 45th ACM Technical Symposium on Computer Science Education, pp. 597–602. ACM (2014)

8. Buffardi, K., Edwards, S.H.: Responses to adaptive feedback for software testing. In: 2014 Conference on Innovation & Technology in Computer Science Education, pp. 165–170. ACM (2014)

9. Clarke, P.J., Davis, D., King, T.M., Pava, J., Jones, E.L.: Integrating testing into software engineering courses supported by a collaborative learning environment. ACM Trans. Comput. Educ. **14**(3), 1–33 (2014). Article 18

10. Clarke, P.J., Pava, J., Davis, D., Hernandez, F., King, T.M.: Using WReSTT in SE courses: an empirical study. In: 43rd ACM Technical Symposium on Computer Science Education, pp. 307–312. ACM (2012)

11. Edwards, S.H., Pérez-Quiñones, M.A.: Experiences using test-driven development with an automated grader. J. Comput. Sci. Coll. **22**(3), 44–50 (2007)

12. Elbaum, S., Person, S., Dokulil, J., Jorde, M.: Bug hunt: making early software testing lessons engaging and affordable. In: 29th International Conference on Software Engineering, pp. 688–697. IEEE Computer Society (2007)

13. Finstad, K.: The usability metric for user experience. Interact. Comput. **22**(5), 323–327 (2010)

14. Fu, Y., Clarke, P.: Gamification-based cyber-enabled learning environment of software testing. In: ASEE Annual Conference and Expo (2016)

15. Giachetti, G., Marín, B., López, L., Franch, X., Pastor, O.: Verifying goal-oriented specifications used in model-driven development processes. Inf. Syst. **64**, 41–62 (2017)

16. Gotel, O., Scharff, C., Wildenberg, A.: Teaching software quality assurance by encouraging student contributions to an open source web-based system for the assessment of programming assignments. ACM SIGCSE Bull. **40**(3), 214–218 (2008)

17. Heinonen, K., Hirvikoski, K., Luukkainen, M., Vihavainen, A.: Learning agile software engineering practices using coding dojo. In: 14th Annual ACM SIGITE Conference on Information Technology Education, pp. 97–102. ACM (2013)

18. Jones, E.L.: An experiential approach to incorporating software testing into the computer science curriculum. In: 31st Annual Frontiers in Education Conference. Impact on Engineering and Science Education, pp. F3D-7-F3D-11. IEEE (2001)

19. KU-Leuven: JMermaid/MERLIN tool. http://merode.econ.kuleuven.be/Tools.html

20. Marín, B., Gallardo, C., Quiroga, D., Giachetti, G., Serral, E.: Testing of model-driven development applications. Softw. Qual. J. **25**(2), 407–435 (2017)

21. Marín, B., Larenas, F., Giachetti, G.: Learning conceptual modeling design through the Classutopia serious game. Int. J. Softw. Eng. Knowl. Eng. **28**(11n12), 1679–1699 (2018)

22. Martinez, A.: Use of JiTT in a graduate software testing course: an experience report. In: 2018 IEEE/ACM 40th International Conference on Software Engineering: Software Engineering Education and Training, pp. 108–115. IEEE (2018)

23. Oliveira, B., Afonso, P., Costa, H.: TestEG - a computational game for teaching of software testing. In: 2016 35th International Conference of the Chilean Computer Science Society. IEEE (2016)
24. OMG: Unified modeling language (UML) 2.5 specification. http://www.omg.org/spec/UML/2.5/
25. Pastor, O., Molina, J.C.: Model-Driven Architecture in Practice: A Software Production Environment Based on Conceptual Modeling. Springer, Heidelberg (2007). https://doi.org/10.1007/978-3-540-71868-0
26. Reyes-Garcia, F., Marín, B., Alarcón-Bañados, S.: Visualization of MBT testing coverage. In: 13th International Conference on Research Challenges in Information Science (RCIS), pp. 1–2. IEEE (2019). ISBN 978-1-7281-4844-1
27. Rojas, J.M., Fraser, G.: Teaching software testing with a mutation testing game. In: Proceedings of PPIG, p. 23 (2016)
28. Runeson, P., Host, M.: Guidelines for conducting and reporting case study research in software engineering. Empir. Softw. Eng. J. **14**(2), 131–164 (2009)
29. Schnotz, W.: An integrated model of multimedia learning. In: Mayer, R.E. (ed.) The Cambridge Handbook of Multimedia Learning, pp. 49–69. Cambridge University Press, New York (2005)
30. Selic, B.: The pragmatics of model-driven development. IEEE Softw. **20**(5), 19–25 (2003)
31. Smith, R., Tang, T., Warren, J., Rixner, S.: An automated system for interactively learning software testing. In: 2017 ACM Conference on Innovation and Technology in Computer Science Education, pp. 98–103. ACM (2017)
32. Snoeck, M.: Enterprise Information Systems Engineering. Springer, Cham (2014). https://doi.org/10.1007/978-3-319-10145-3
33. Sommerville, I.: Software Engineering 9th Edition, vol. 137035152 (2011). ISBN-10
34. Soska, A., Mottok, J., Wolff, C.: An experimental card game for software testing: development, design and evaluation of a physical card game to deepen the knowledge of students in academic software testing education. In: Proceedings of 2016 IEEE Global Engineering Education Conference (EDUCON), pp. 576–584. IEEE (2016)
35. Tiwari, S., Saini, V., Singh, P., Sureka, A.: A Case Study on the Application of Case-Based Learning in Software Testing. ACM (2018)
36. Utting, M., Legeard, B.: Practical Model-Based Testing: A Tools Approach. Elsevier, Amsterdam (2010)
37. Valle, P.H.D., Toda, A.M., Barbosa, E.F., Maldonado, J.C.: Educational games: a contribution to software testing education. In: 2017 IEEE Frontiers in Education Conference. IEEE (2017)
38. Wohlin, C., Runeson, P., Host, M., Ohlsson, M., Regnell, B.: Experimentation in Software Engineering. Springer, Heidelberg (2012). https://doi.org/10.1007/978-3-642-29044-2
39. Wong, E.: Improving the state of undergraduate software testing education. In: ASEE Annual Conference & Exposition, pp. 25.754.1-25.754.12 (2012). ISSN 2153-5965
40. Wong, W.E., Bertolino, A., Debroy, V., Mathur, A., Offutt, J., Vouk, M.: Teaching Software Testing: Experiences, Lessons Learned and the Path Forward. IEEE (2011)

Machine Learning and Text Processing

Automatic Classification Rules for Anomaly Detection in Time-Series

Ines Ben Kraiem[1(✉)], Faiza Ghozzi[3], Andre Peninou[1],
Geoffrey Roman-Jimenez[2], and Olivier Teste[1]

[1] University of Toulouse, UT2J, IRIT, Toulouse, France
{ines.ben-kraiem,andre.peninou,olivier.teste}@irit.fr
[2] University of Toulouse, CNRS, IRIT, Toulouse, France
geoffrey.roman-jimenez@irit.fr
[3] University of Sfax, ISIMS, MIRACL, Sfax, Tunisia
faiza.ghozzi@isims.usf.tn

Abstract. Anomaly detection in time-series is an important issue in many applications. It is particularly hard to accurately detect multiple anomalies in time-series. Pattern discovery and rule extraction are effective solutions for allowing multiple anomaly detection. In this paper, we define a Composition-based Decision Tree algorithm that automatically discovers and generates human-understandable classification rules for multiple anomaly detection in time-series. To evaluate our solution, our algorithm is compared to other anomaly detection algorithms on real datasets and benchmarks.

Keywords: Anomaly detection · Classification rules · Pattern-based method · Decision Tree · Time-series

1 Introduction

To detect unusual or interesting events, data supervision and monitoring are used in many fields, such as industries, computer systems, web traffic, financial and medical data, and many others [1].

In the industrial field, sensors networks are used to provide data from different sources for example temperature and pressure monitors, energy sensors, and others. Various users such as engineers, technicians, automation engineers, explore the time-series produced by sensor networks in order to analyze them, extract knowledge and detect anomalies that occur as a result of abnormal events or unusual behavior suchlike shutdown, failures, and sensor change or even shutdowns. Such a context produces time-series with multiple anomalies. In general, using their domain knowledge, experts analyze curves and detect *remarkable points*, which represent unusual signals in time-series. Such remarkable points lead them to analyze the surrounding points in order to determine the exact position of existing anomaly/ies if they exist.

© Springer Nature Switzerland AG 2020
F. Dalpiaz et al. (Eds.): RCIS 2020, LNBIP 385, pp. 321–337, 2020.
https://doi.org/10.1007/978-3-030-50316-1_19

We previously defined in [2] CoRP "Composition of Remarkable Points", a configurable approach for the simultaneous detection of multiple anomalies. CoRP evaluates a set of patterns in order to label the remarkable points using patterns and then it evaluates a set of label compositions to precisely detect the anomalies. Not only does this algorithm simultaneously detect various anomalies categories, but also it uses human-readable detection rules (label compositions) that help in doing so. Nevertheless, its main drawback is that the whole process requires professionals and their expertise to define patterns and composition rules.

Our goal in this paper is to be able to automatically obtain human-readable detection rules that can be further modified or adjusted by experts in the long run. Thus, we propose a rule-based approach that can automatically generate human-comprehensible rules to detect multiple anomalies. We propose a general point labeling approach, and we define a modified decision tree algorithm to learn label composition rules in order to detect anomalies in time-series.

This work makes the following contributions:

1. It proposes a modified decision tree algorithm to generate anomaly detection rules through combinations of labels.
2. The generated rules are human-readable and can easily be understood by experts. Moreover, these rules perform relevant time-series anomaly detection with good results.
3. The generated rules can simultaneously detect several types of anomalies for different application domains whereas classical methods of the literature fail to detect [2].

The rest of the paper is organized as follows. In Sect. 2, we discuss the related work on the machine learning method for anomaly detection. Section 3 details the proposed approach for anomaly detection. Section 4 presents experimental results and discussion and Sect. 5 provides our conclusion and an outlook for future research.

2   Related Work

Time-series anomaly detection has been characterized as a special case of time-series data mining, which also includes problems such as classification, clustering, machine learning and rule discovery. Important related work on using data mining and machine learning techniques had been covered under various surveys, review articles and books [3–8].

In this paper, we use supervised learning to build a model to classify anomalies and to learn rules. For this reason, we focus in this section on classification based on anomaly detection.

Classification is a classic data mining technique based on machine learning. It used to build a model from a set of labeled data instances and then, classify a test instance into one of the classes using the learned model (testing). There are a handful of techniques for classification such as decision trees, linear programming, Support Vector Machines (SVMs), Bayesian networks and neural networks [5].

Classification by decision tree was well researched and several algorithms have been designed [9,10]. Several classifiers based on the decision tree have been explored in [10] for anomaly detection such as Best-first, Decision Tree, Functional Tree, Logistic Model Tree, J48 and Random Forest decision tree. Based on their study, they showed that the Random Forest decision tree has outperformed other decision tree-based classifiers in terms of correct classification rate.

In [11], the authors proposed an anomaly detection technique by combining decision trees and parametric densities. During the tree construction process, the anomaly class densities are used directly in the split point algorithm. This method avoids generating artificial samples of the missing class in the training set. Instead, it uses a parametric distribution of the anomaly class when determining share points. The authors in [12] proposed an anomaly detection method using K-Means clustering and C4.5 decision tree to classify anomalous and normal activities in a computer network. k-Means is used first to partition learning instances into k clusters using Euclidean distance similarity. Then, C4.5 is applied to each cluster, containing normal instances or anomalies, to refine the decision.

Kim et al. used a C-LSTM neural networks algorithm to perform anomaly detection in web traffic data [13]. They combined a convolutional neural network (CNN), long short-term memory (LSTM), and deep neural network (DNN) to model the spatial and temporal information contained in traffic data. The transformed the temporal context using a CNN layer. Then, they used the output of this CNN layer as the input for several LSTM layers to reduce temporal variations. The output of the final LSTM layer is fed into several fully connected DNN layers in order to classify the output. As a result, they obtained high classification performance for anomalies but the disadvantage of neural networks is their "black box" nature.

By comparison, algorithms like decision trees are very interpretable. This is important because in some domains, interpretability is important to explain the root cause of anomalies. This further encourages us to adapt it in our approach.

3 Composition-Based Decision Tree

To supervise the sensor networks, the experts analyze the curves and detect the local points that have unusual behaviors. These points, called remarkable points, are unusual variations between some successive points in a time series, generally three points. Then, they analyze the neighborhood of each remarkable point to decide if it represents an anomaly. In this context, we created a method to label the remarkable points of a time series, depending on the analysis of three successive points, and we proposed a Composition-based Decision Tree (CDT) to generate automatic rules for anomaly detection.

3.1   Problem Statement

In [2], according to how experts analyze time-series, we define a two-step approach to detect anomalies (more details in Sect. 3.2):

- labeling of each point of a time-series based on a set of patterns. Each pattern considers three successive points and gives threshold comparisons to tag the middle point. When it fires on three successive points, a pattern tags the middle point with a label (word);
- a grammar is used to create compositions of labels on successive points in order to detect multiple anomalies. The grammar allows for the composition of successive points with repetition and alternatives [2]. For example, a valid rule is L1.(L2 AND NOT L3).L4*.L5 which means tag L1, next to L2 (but not L3), next to zero or more L4, next to L5.

Figure 1 illustrates an example of a labeled time series. It contains four examples of patterns (Normal, Ptpicpos, Ptpicneg, Changniv) used to detect the labeled points. Let denote the value of three successive points at index 2, 3 and 4 as v_2, v_3 and v_4 respectively. a is the difference between v_3 and v_2 whereas b is the difference between v_3 and v_4. If a and $b > 0$ then the point v_3 is labelled as "Ptpicpos" by the corresponding pattern.

The index points from 2 to 5, 8 to 11 and 13 to 16 present the compositions of labels defined through the grammar to detect the anomalies. For example, the composition Normal.Ptpicpos.Ptpicneg.Normal applies for points 13 to 16 and defines an anomaly at points 2 and 3 of the composition (14 and 15 in the example). Thus, the combination of both labeled points and compositions of labels allow to find anomalies. Labels (and thus patterns) alone do not allow us to decide for anomalies as shown in points 2 to 5 and 8 to 11.

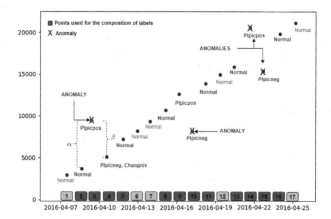

Fig. 1. Time-series labeling and anomaly detection using composition [2].

The creation of these label compositions requires good expertise in the application field and many efforts of investigation on time-series. Our goal is to make this task automatic by using decision trees to get automatic rules.

We firstly used classical decision tree algorithms to find rules, applied on times series values, or labels series. The results are not reported in this paper. They lead to good results for anomaly detection while the resulting rules were very hard to understand by an expert. Although decision trees are designed to produce understandable rules, this is not always the case, and they are not suited to our needs:

- The rules can become unintelligible if trees are large and consequently they are difficult to interpret and may not make sense to the user. Moreover, the resulting rules may contain a great part of negative tests that are very hard to understand by an expert.
- The decision tree considers features without any order when splitting the dataset. Conversely, experts in anomalies always think based on successive points. Hence, we adapt the decision tree to take into consideration the order between the features. Therefore, we seek to build the rules based on the compositions of ordered labels very similar to the proposed grammar when we transform the tree branches to rules.

3.2 The Proposed Method

To resolve the issues mentioned above, we propose the following method. First, we improve the manual labeling that was proposed in [2] by an automatic labeling to detect the remarkable points in the time-series. Second, we propose a Composition-based Decision Tree (CDT) to generate automatic rules for anomaly detection.

Time-Series. We first define time-series for the scope of this paper.

Definition 1. *Time-series* Ts is an ordered sequence of n real-valued variables collected sequentially in time at a regular interval. These observations represent the measures that are associated with a timestamp indicating the time of its collection [2]. $Ts = \{y_1, ..., y_n\}$ is an uni-variate time-series, $y_i \in \mathbb{R}$ such that values y_i are uniformly spaced in time. Let us notice that, for the scope of this paper, we suppose that the time-series are linearly normalized in the interval $[0, 1]$.

Definition 2. *A Labeled time-series* is a time-series of points where each point contains one label. $Tsb = \{l_1, ..., l_m\}$ is a labeled time-series of m labels, with $l_i \in \mathcal{L}$, $\mathcal{L}$ being the set of possible labels.

Automatic Labeling of Time-Series. This step consists of labeling the time-series through patterns.

In [2], we define a *pattern* by a triple (l, *a*, *b*) where l is a label that characterizes the pattern. *a* and *b* are two thresholds used to decide if a point is remarkable (or not) by this pattern[1]. A pattern is applied to three successive points y_{i-1}, y_i, y_{i+1} of a time-series. *a* is the difference between y_i and y_{i-1} whereas *b* is the difference between y_i and y_{i+1}. A positive *a* means an increasing value between y_{i-1} and y_i, a negative *a* means a decreasing value, whereas $a = 0$ means a constant value (unchanged value). Conversely, a negative *b* means an increasing value between y_i and y_{i+1}, a positive *b* means a decreasing value, whereas $b = 0$ means a constant value (unchanged value). As stated in [2], this definition works well when experts define both labels and thresholds.

In this paper, we generalize the definition of labels and patterns. A pattern considers 3 points, and we create labels for each possible variations of these 3 points, for example positive variation when values always increase on the three points. We then define 9 general patterns (in fact labels), illustrated in Table 1, namely PP (Positive Peak), PN (Negative Peak), SCP (Start Constant Positive), SCN (Start Constant Negative), ECP (End Constant Positive), ECN (End Constant Negative), CST (Constant), VP (Variation Positive) and VN (Variation Negative).

Each of these of this general pattern is supplemented with two intervals indicating the possible variations of values: α is an interval characterising the difference of y_i and y_{i-1} ($y_i - y_{i-1}$) and β is an interval characterising the difference of y_i and y_{i+1} ($y_i - y_{i+1}$). We then define 8 intervals according to the signs of ($y_i - y_{i-1}$), and ($y_i - y_{i+1}$):

- for ($y_i - y_{i-1}$) > 0 and ($y_i - y_{i+1}$) > 0, we create 4 intervals between 0 and 1 for α and β, noted Low (L), Medium Low (ML), Medium High (MH), High (H) where $L =]0, 0.25]$, $ML =]0.25, 0.5]$, $MH =]0.5, 0.75]$, $H =]0.75, 1]$.
- for ($y_i - y_{i-1}$) < 0 and ($y_i - y_{i+1}$) < 0, we create 4 intervals between −1 and 0 for α and β, noted −Low (−L), −Medium Low (−ML), −Medium High (−MH), −High (−H) where $-L = [-0.25, 0[$, $-ML = [-0.50, -0.25[$, $-MH = [-0.75, -0.50[$, $-H = [-1, -0.75[$.

Note that in the scope of this paper, we fixed with experts the interval number to 8, to keep the labeling discriminating enough while keeping the generated rules easily interpretable. However, the approach is flexible and it is possible to vary this interval number. This is a future work for this research to automatically learn the relevant interval number.

Definition 3. We define a pattern P = (l, α, β) where l (label) is a name identifying the pattern, and α and β are two possible intervals into $[-1, 1]$. For each successive points y_{i-1}, y_i, y_{i+1}, the point y_i is checked by a pattern only if $y_i - y_{i-1} \in \alpha \wedge y_i - y_{i+1} \in \beta$. In this case, y_i is labeled with l.

We designed the patterns as listed in Table 1. This list is also inspired by the Global Constraint Catalogue presented in [14] which describes Time-Series

---

[1] Let us notice that *a* and *b* were previously denoted α and β in [2].

Constraints through patterns. These 9 general patterns are combined with their respective possible intervals for α and β to generate 81 possibilities. Let us notice that for a given pattern, the resulting label is now the pattern name concatenated with the interval of α and β for the pattern. For example, the label $PP_{ML,H}$ stands for the pattern PP (positive peak) with $\alpha = ML$ and $\beta = H$.

Example Fig. 2 illustrates a sequence of remarkable points represented by different patterns namely $PP_{ML,H}$, $PN_{-H,-MH}$, $SCN_{MH,0}$.

- $PP_{ML,H}$ is a positive peak such as: $\alpha = ML$ and $\beta = H$;
- $PN_{-H,-MH}$ is a negative peak such as: $\alpha = -H$ and $\beta = -MH$;
- $SCP_{MH,0}$ is a constant positive start such as: $\alpha = MH$ and $\beta = 0$.

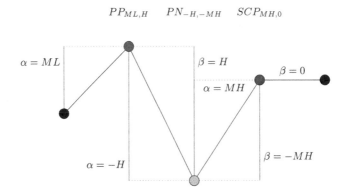

Fig. 2. An example of different patterns.

Construction of Composition-Based Decision Tree. This step consists in building a Composition-based Decision Tree (CDT) using sequences of labels (compositions) as attributes to generate automatic rules for anomaly detection.

Definition 4. We denote $\mathcal{L} = \{PP_{L,L}, PP_{L,ML}, ..., VN_{-H,H}\}$ the set of 81 labels corresponding to different patterns defined in Table 1.

Definition 5. *An observation* D is an ordered set (sequence) of labels that is associated with a given class c (e.g. *normal* or *anomaly*). $D = \{l_1, ..., l_k\}$, with $l_i \in \mathcal{L}$, is an observation associated with a class $c \in \{1, ..., M\}$. Note that, in this paper we consider that an observation D is associated with only one class c (no overlapping between classes across the sliding windows).

Definition 6. *A composition* C is an ordered set of labels representing a subsequence of an observation. We denote $C \subseteq_o D$ the presence of an ordered subset C within an ordered set D, such that C is a subsequence of D. The symbol $\subseteq_o$ signifies an inclusion of a subset C in a set D, while respecting the order of D. A composition should have a minimal length of 2.

Table 1. Types of patterns for labeling.

Pattern	Definition	Representation	Example
PP	$\alpha, \beta \in \{L, ML, MH, H\}$	 $PP_{\alpha,\beta}$	 $PP_{ML,MH}$
PN	$\alpha, \beta \in \{-L, -ML, -MH, -H\}$	 $PN_{\alpha,\beta}$	 $PN_{-MH,-H}$
SCN	$\alpha \in \{-L, -ML, -MH, -H\}$ $\beta = 0$	 $SCN_{\alpha,\beta}$	 $SCN_{-MH,0}$
SCP	$\alpha \in \{L, ML, MH, H\}$ $\beta = 0$	 $SCP_{\alpha,\beta}$	 $SCP_{MH,0}$
ECN	$\beta \in \{L, ML, MH, H\}$ $\alpha = 0$	 $ECN_{\alpha,\beta}$	 $ECN_{0,MH}$
ECP	$\beta \in \{-L, -ML, -MH, -H\}$ $\alpha = 0$	 $ECP_{\alpha,\beta}$	 $ECP_{0,-MH}$
CST	$\alpha = 0, \beta = 0$	 $CST_{\alpha,\beta}$	 $CST_{0,0}$
VP	$\alpha \in \{L, ML, MH, H\}$ $\beta \in \{-L, -ML, -MH, -H\}$	 $VP_{\alpha,\beta}$	 $VP_{ML,-MH}$
VN	$\alpha \in \{-L, -ML, -MH, -H\}$ $\beta \in \{L, ML, MH, H\}$	 $VN_{\alpha,\beta}$	 $VN_{-ML,MH}$

with $L =]0, 0.25]$, $ML =]0.25, 0.50]$, $MH =]0.50, 0.75]$, $H =]0.75, 1]$

Examples

- $C = \{l_2, l_3, l_4\} \subseteq_o D = \{l_1, l_2, l_3, l_4, l_5, l_6\}$.
- $C = \{l_3, l_2, l_4\} \not\subseteq_o D = \{l_1, l_2, l_3, l_5, l_5, l_6\}$.
- $C = \{l_1, l_2, l_3, l_4, l_5, l_6\} \subseteq_o D = \{l_1, l_2, l_3, l_4, l_5, l_6\}$.

Definition 7. *An impurity metric provides a measure of the quality of a set of observations* $\mathcal{D} = \{D_1, ..., D_n\}$ *regarding the distribution of classes that it is* composed of. The impurity metric is minimal if a set contains only observations of one class, and is maximal if the set contains equally observations of all classes. In this paper, we used the Gini impurity index as an impurity metric [15]. For a given set of observation $\mathcal{D}$, the Gini impurity index $G(\mathcal{D})$ is computed as:

$$G(\mathcal{D}) = \sum_{i=1}^{M} p_i(1 - p_i),$$ (1)

where p_i is the fraction of observations categorized as class i in $\mathcal{D}$.

Starting from the labeled time-series Tsb, we construct the set of N observations $\mathcal{D}(s, w) = \{D_1, ..., D_N\}$ using a sliding window algorithm, and where w and s are respectively the size and the stride of the sliding window. $\mathcal{D}(s, w)$ is also called $\mathcal{D}$. Each observation D_i is associated with a class of anomaly c and is composed of a set of labels $\{l_{i+s+1}, ..., l_{i+s+w}\}$, with $l_{i+s+j} \in Tsb$.

The aim of the CDT is to build a set of subsets $\mathcal{S} = \{S_1, S_2, ..., S_r\}$ where $S_i \subset \mathcal{D}$, with $S_i \cap S_{j \neq i} = \emptyset$ and $S_1 \cup S_2... \cup S_r = \mathcal{D}$, such that a given impurity metric for each set S_i is minimal. These subsets are called the "leaves" of the CDT. To do so, we iteratively split a given set of observations $\mathcal{D}^l$ (starting with $\mathcal{D}$) into two subsets $\mathcal{D}^m$ and $\mathcal{D}^n$ based on the presence of a composition C^l, such that $\mathcal{D}^m = \{D_i^m / C^l \subseteq_o D_i^m, D_i^m \in \mathcal{D}^l\}$ and $\mathcal{D}^n = \{D_i^n / C^l \not\subseteq_o D_i^n, D_i^n \in \mathcal{D}^l\}$. The composition C^l can take its value among all possible subsequences existing in any $D_i \in \mathcal{D}^l$. At each split, the composition C^l is selected to maximize the information gain $I_G(\mathcal{D}^l, C^l)$ computed as:

$$I_G(\mathcal{D}^l, C^l) = G(\mathcal{D}^l) - (\frac{N_m}{N_l}G(\mathcal{D}^m) + \frac{N_n}{N_l}G(\mathcal{D}^n)),$$ (2)

where N_l, N_m and N_n are respectively the size of $\mathcal{D}^l$, $\mathcal{D}^m$ and $\mathcal{D}^n$. If $G(\mathcal{D}^l) = 0$ or $max(I_G(\mathcal{D}^l, C^l)) = 0$, $\mathcal{D}^l$ is defined as a "leaf" of the CDT and is denoted S_l. Splitting iteratively the resulting subsets of a split, the construction of the CDT continues until each subset $\mathcal{D}^l$ is defined as a leaf S_l. Figure 3 shows a schematic representation of the construction process of the CDT.

Rule Generation. Once a decision tree has been constructed, we convert it into a set of rules for decisions. More precisely, the set for branches of the DT, leading to a given class, can be interpreted as the set of individual classification rules for this class.

Definition 8. *A* *rule* *R is a logical combination of compositions that can be used to classify an observation to a given class. A rule from a leaf* S_i *is denoted* R_{S_i} *and is constructed by combining the compositions from the root node to the leaf such that* $R_{S_i} = C \wedge C^0 \wedge ... \wedge C^i$.

Definition 9. *A* *global rule* *$\mathcal{R}$ is a logical combination of all rules leading to a given class. Given a set of rules* $\{R_{S_i}\}$*, each one leading to a class c, the global rule for the class c is denoted* $\mathcal{R}_c$ *and is constructed by combining all the rules of the set* $\{R_{S_i}\}$ *such that* $\mathcal{R}_c = R_{S_0} \vee R_{S_1} \vee ... \vee R_{S_n}$.

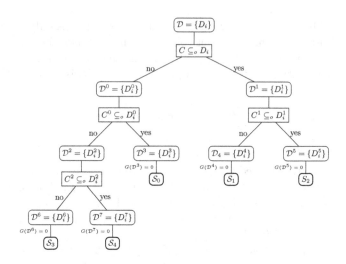

Fig. 3. Example of a composition-based decision tree (CDT). $\mathcal{D}$ represents the whole set of observations used for the construction of the CDT. The CDT is composed of 4 splits constructing a set of 5 leaves $\mathcal{S} = \{S_0, S_1, S_2, S_3, S_4\}$.

4   Experiments

Our goal in doing the experiments is twofold: (1) evaluate if the rules that Composition-based DT produces are human-readable and can be interpreted by experts, (ii) evaluate if, while producing relevant rules, we can also get relevant results in anomalies detection when compared with other learning methods that do not produce rules.

In this section, we discuss the experimental setup, our case study and the benchmark datasets used to evaluate the performances of Composition-based Decision Tree against other state-of-the-art machine learning techniques. We used the Waikato Environment for Knowledge Acquisition (WEKA) version 3.8 as a simulation tool. The experiments are performed on a machine running Windows 10 professional and optimized by an Intel (R) Core (TM) i5 processor and 16GB of RAM and the programming language is Python 3.7.

The Case Study: SGE DataSets. The SGE (Management and Exploitation Service of Rangueil Campus attached to the Rectorate of Toulouse) operates and manages the distribution of fluids (e.g., energy, water, compressed air) on different campuses. It relies on distribution devices equipped with sensors that regularly collect data (e.g., meter values, fluid temperatures, valve conditions) [2]. In this mass of data, meter data are used to calculate the consumption of buildings. The measurements of these meters are reassembled at a regular frequency and represent the *indexes* (readings of meters) which are used to measure the quantities of energy consumed, *consumptions* (by successive indexes differences). For this paper, we handle anomalies on calorie consumption datasets

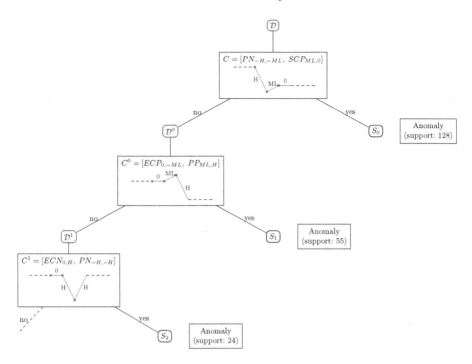

Fig. 4. Composition-based decision tree constructed from the SGE dataset.

that were calculated based on index data (readings of meters) by successive value differences.

We explored 25 time-series generated from different sensors annotated by the experts (in total 33536 observations). These time-series contain 586 anomalies of different types such as positives peaks, negatives peaks and sudden variations (negative or positive).

The Benchmark: Yahoo's S5 Webscope Dataset. In order to evaluate the performance of the proposed method in another application domain, we used Yahoo's S5 Webscope dataset in our experiments to compare with other machine learning algorithms. This dataset is an anomaly detection benchmark that is publicly available in [16]. It contains 371 files divided into four classes, named A1/A2/A3 and A4, each one containing respectively, 67/100/100/100 files. A1 Benchmark is based on real production traffic from actual web services while classes A2, A3, and A4 contain synthetic anomaly data. In this paper, we utilized the A1 class to validate the proposed anomaly detection method. This data is represented by time-series in one-hour units. Abnormal values were labeled manually and the data has a relatively large variation in traffic compared to other available datasets. There are a total of 94778 traffic values in 67 different files and 1669 of these values are abnormal.

4.1   Experiments

WEKA is an open-source software tool for implementing machine-learning algorithms (e.g., classification, clustering and association rules). We used J48, which is an implementation of the C4.5 algorithm in WEKA for constructing a decision tree. We used as competitors: (i) K-nearest neighbor (KNN) and we set the number of neighbors to 5, (i) random forest within the number of trees in the forest set to 100 (iii) multilayer perceptron (MLP) with the default configuration of WEKA and (iv) Support vector machine (SVM) the default configuration of WEKA.

For the training of the model, we randomly split the dataset into 33% testing and 67% training sets. For the SGE dataset, the training and testing set are composed respectively of 18 files (containing 23696 observations) and 7 files (containing 9840 observations). For the Yahoo dataset, the training and testing set are composed respectively of 45 files (containing 63927 observations) and 22 files (containing 30851 observations).

We normalize the values to get values between 0 and 1. For all algorithms, we applied the same sliding window on time-series to set up observations for learning. Classification performances of algorithms were evaluated using Precision, Recall, and F-Measure metrics. We report these evaluation metrics on the test datasets.

Results and Analysis for SGE DataSets. In our experiment, we fixed the length of the window $w = 5$ equivalent to 5 days. Figure 4 illustrates the first part of the CDT constructed on the SGE Dataset. The leaves are the rules found in different windows and their supports indicate the number of occurrences of observations firing the rules. In this example, we can observe that the 3 first leaves of the CDT lead to the class *anomaly*. From this tree, we can thus generate 3 rules leading to an *anomaly*:

- $R_{S_0} : C = [PN_{-H,-ML}, SCP_{ML,0}]$
- $R_{S_1} : \neg C \wedge C^0 = \neg[PN_{-H,-ML}, SCP_{ML,0}] \wedge [ECP_{0,-ML}, PP_{ML,H}]$
- $R_{S_2} : \neg C \wedge \neg C^0 \wedge C^1 = \neg[PN_{-H,-ML}, SCP_{ML,0}] \wedge \neg[ECP_{0,-ML}, PP_{ML,H}] \wedge [ECN_{0,H}, PN_{-H,-H}]$.

From these 3 listed rules, we can come up with a global rule $\mathcal{R}_{anomaly}$ that can be calculated as follows:

$$\mathcal{R}_{anomaly} = R_{S_0} \vee R_{S_1} \vee R_{S_2} \tag{3}$$

$$= C \vee (\neg C \wedge C^0) \vee (\neg C \wedge \neg C^0 \wedge C^1) \tag{4}$$

$$= C \vee C^0 \vee C^1, \tag{5}$$

and thus

$$\mathcal{R}_{anomaly} = [PN_{-H,-ML}, SCP_{ML,0}] \tag{6}$$

$$\vee [ECP_{0,-ML}, PP_{ML,H}] \tag{7}$$

$$\vee [ECN_{0,H}, PN_{-H,-H}], \tag{8}$$

which leads to a simple and readable rule that can be interpreted by a domain-expert to detect and identify the different types of anomalies occurring within the SGE dataset. Table 2 presents a representation of some rules generated by our CDT, associated with an expert interpretation of these rules. Let us notice that the produced rules are very close to those proposed by experts in the manual mode of our approach detailed in [2] and are considered as equivalent by these experts meanwhile patterns to label points are somewhat different.

Table 2. Rules generated for anomaly detection in the SGE datasets.

Rules	Support	Representation	Expert Interpretation
$[PN_{-H,-ML}, SCP_{-ML,0}]$	128		The negative peak represents an anomaly since the energy consumption in a building cannot be negative.
$[ECP_{0,-ML}, PP_{ML,H}]$	55		The anomaly is the positive peak which occurred following a stop of the meter (constant value).
$[ECN_{0,H}, PN_{-H,-H}]$	24		A negative peak which followed by a constant plateau represents a level shift caused by a change of sensor.
$[PN_{-H,-H}, PP_{H,H}]$	8		There are 2 anomalies here, a positive peak followed by a negative peak. This is due to a fault in the reading of the sensors.

Table 3 reports the classification performance of the different machine learning techniques (namely Decision Tree, Random Forest, KNN and MLP) and our CDT. Best results were found with the CDT with a precision of 1 a recall of 0.81 and an F-measure of 0.89. Overall, The CDT and the Random Forest yields a better recall (0.81) than MLP, KNN and the Decision Tree. However, a precision of 0.54 for the Random Forest suggests that the algorithm was not able to capture discriminant rules. In fact, Random Forest's performance decreases when learning from an unbalanced training data set. It tends to focus on the accuracy of predictions from the majority class, which generates poor precision for the minority class [17]. Although MLP detected anomaly with a precision of 1.00, a recall of 0.41 indicates a important false negative rate, suggesting that the algorithm was unable to construct rules for different types of anomaly (such as the ones presented in Table 2).

Table 3. Evaluation of anomaly detection methods in the SGE datasets.

Evaluation	Precision	Recall	F-measure
CDT	**1.00**	**0.81**	**0.89**
Decision Tree	0.94	0.68	0.79
Random Forest	0.54	0.81	0.65
KNN	0.90	0.79	0.84
MLP	1.00	0.41	0.58

Results and Analysis for Yahoo's S5 Webscope Dataset. Figure 5 presents an example of anomalies observed in web traffic datasets. As we can see, there are different types of anomalies: (i) global anomaly in which the anomaly appears outside the traffic and presents a peak, (ii) local anomaly when the anomaly exists inside the traffic, (iii) collective anomaly that presents long-term irregularities. The collective anomaly can last almost 2 days (more than 40 observations). To be able to handle this type of "long" anomaly, we need to represent it as a point anomaly to guarantee a normal neighborhood around it. Therefore, we downsampled time-series data to a lower frequency such as from hour to days and summarize the higher frequency observations. For the experiments, each new data point is the mean of the raw data within those 48 h. Then, we apply a sliding window of length 15.

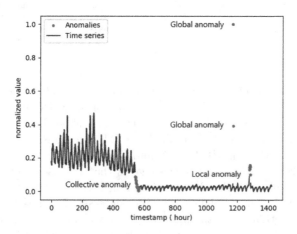

Fig. 5. Example of yahoo DataSets (Web traffic anomaly).

Table 4 gives a summary of the comparative analysis of algorithms. It shows that our algorithm performance achieves higher precision compared to other competing approaches such as classical decision tree, random forest and MLP. In addition, it has a higher recall compared with the decision tree, KNN, and

MLP. Even though the recall and F-measure scores are lower compared to the random forest, our method outperforms it in the precision metric. Moreover, our method has the advantage that we can interpret the learning process and we can generate interpretable and simple rules for anomaly detection.

Table 4. Evaluation of anomaly detection methods in the Yahoo S5 Webscope Dataset.

Evaluation	Precision	Recall	F-measure
CDT	**0.74**	0.72	0.73
Decision Tree	0.73	0.65	0.69
Random Forest	0.72	**0.80**	**0.76**
KNN	0.76	0.67	0.71
MLP	0.73	0.63	0.68

4.2 Discussion

In our comparative study, we show that our algorithm outperforms other state-of-the-art machine learning techniques in the SGE dataset. However, this is not the case for the Yahoo benchmark dataset, Random forest providing a better Recall and F-measure. Although it provides better classification performances, Random Forest does not provide a direct way to extract the rule explaining the classification process, leading to the black-box problem. Our advantage over all other algorithms, which is also our overall goal, is that we generate interpretable and simple rules with good anomaly detection performances. With such output, experts can analyze and explain the detection rules to make a decision or even adjust the rules (e.g., combine rules, generalize rules). Hence, these "hand-tighted" rules are more likely to cover a larger domain than the training dataset, reducing the overfitting problem and avoiding a higher false positive rate in test datasets.

Limitations of CDT. Although the proposed CDT provides the possibility to generate interpretable rules for anomaly detection, some limitations should be noted. First, CDT is sensitive to the labeling process. Indeed, with the Yahoo benchmark dataset, the CDT performs lower than a more generic such as Random Forest, which uses real-valued variables from the time series. This leads us to conclude that the variety of labels is too constrained to construct discriminating rules.

Second, the quality of the detection rules generated by the CDT remains sensitive on the choice of parameters such as i) the size of downsampling, which assign a minimal time interval for anomaly detection and ii) the size of the sliding window, which fixes the maximal size of rules to explain anomalies. The choice of such parameters depends on the type and domain of the considered time-series and it is difficult to ensure an optimal unique choice of them for every domain. For example, in our experiments, the Yahoo benchmark dataset, which is composed of time-series corresponding to various types of web traffic services, led to lower classification performances than with the SGE dataset, which is only composed of energy consumption time series.

5   Conclusion

In this paper, we propose a Composition-based decision tree (CDT) for anomaly detection in univariate time-series. Our method is based on two steps: firstly, it tags (labels) remarkable points using different patterns and, secondly, it constructs a decision tree based on compositions of these labels. Thus, we used CDT to automatically generate classification rules to detect various anomalies. It is efficient for generating rules which are simple and interpretable by the experts. Our case study is based on a real context: consumption sensor datasets and web traffic datasets. We demonstrated the usefulness of our method when compared to other machine learning methods.

Future work will concern, the improvement of the generated rules and the detection using this model. For example, we will investigate how to combine rules by generalization or how to simplify rules by logic simplifications. Another part of the work will be dedicated to learning patterns and their parameters, which is to learn the meta parameters of the approach: optimal size of siding-window, relevant values intervals for patterns, necessary down-sampling of data. Our results have also to be compared with dedicated anomaly detection methods. Finally, we will study how to detect the exact location (point or points) of the anomaly in the composition of a rule.

Acknowledgment. This PhD. was supported by the Management and Exploitation Service (SGE) of the Rangueil campus attached to the Rectorate of Toulouse and the research is made in the context of the neOCampus project (Paul Sabatier University, Toulouse). The authors thank the SGE for providing access to actual sensor data.

References

1. Puttagunta, V., Kalpakis, K: Adaptive methods for activity monitoring of streaming data. In: ICMLA, vol. 2, pp. 197–203, June 2002
2. Ben Kraiem, I., Ghozzi, F., Péninou, A., Teste, O: Pattern-based method for anomaly detection in sensor networks. In: International Conference on Enterprise Information Systems, vol. 1, pp. 104–113, May 2019
3. Witten, I.H., Frank, E., Hall, M.A., Pal, C.J.: Data Mining: Practical Machine Learning Tools and Techniques, 4th edn. Morgan Kaufmann, Burlington (2016)
4. Agrawal, S., Agrawal, J.: Survey on anomaly detection using data mining techniques. Procedia Comput. Sci. **60**, 708–713 (2015)
5. Omar, S., Ngadi, A., Jebur, H.H: Machine learning techniques for anomaly detection: an overview. Int. J. Comput. Appl. **79**(2) (2013)
6. Parmar, J.D., Patel, J.T: Anomaly detection in data mining: a review. Int. J. Adv. Res. Comput. Sci. Softw. Eng. **7**(4) (2017)

7. Däubener, S., Schmitt, S., Wang, H., Krause, P., Bäck, T.: Anomaly detection in univariate time series: an empirical comparison of machine learning algorithms. In: ICDM (2019)
8. Braei, M., Wagner, S.: Anomaly Detection in Univariate Time-series: A Survey on the State-of-the-Art. arXiv preprint arXiv:2004.00433 (2020)
9. Gupta, B., Rawat, A., Jain, A., Arora, A., Dhami, N.: Analysis of various decision tree algorithms for classification in data mining. Int. J. Comput. Appl. **163**(8), 15–19 (2017)
10. Sinwar, D., Kumar, M: Anomaly detection using decision tree based classifiers. Int. J. Mod. Trends Eng. Res. (IJMTER) **3** (2016)
11. Reif, M., Goldstein, M., Stahl, A., Breuel, T.M: Anomaly detection by combining decision trees and parametric densities. In: 2008 19th International Conference on Pattern Recognition, pp. 1–4. IEEE, December 2008
12. Muniyandi, A.P., Rajeswari, R., Rajaram, R.: Network anomaly detection by cascading k-means clustering and C4. 5 decision tree algorithm. Procedia Eng. **30**, 174–182 (2012)
13. Kim, T.Y., Cho, S.B.: Web traffic anomaly detection using C-LSTM neural networks. Expert Syst. Appl. **106**, 66–76 (2018)
14. Arafailova, E., Beldiceanu, N., et al.: Global constraint catalog, volume ii, time-series constraints. arXiv preprint arXiv:1609.08925 (2016)
15. Singh, S., Gupta, P.: Comparative study ID3, cart and C4. 5 decision tree algorithm: a survey. Int. J. Adv. Inf. Sci. Technol. (IJAIST) **27**(27), 97–103 (2014)
16. Laptev, N., Amizadeh, S: A labeled anomaly detection dataset S5 Yahoo Research, v1. https://webscope.sandbox.yahoo.com/catalog.php?datatype=s&did=70
17. Chen, C., Liaw, A., Breiman, L.: Using random forest to learn imbalanced data. Univ. Calif. Berkeley **110**(1–12), 24 (2004)

Text Embeddings for Retrieval from a Large Knowledge Base

Tolgahan Cakaloglu[1,3]([✉]), Christian Szegedy[2], and Xiaowei Xu[3]

[1] Walmart Labs, Bentonville, USA
tolgahan.cakaloglu@walmart.com
[2] Google, Mountain View, USA
szegedy@google.com
[3] University of Arkansas, Fayetteville, USA
{txcakaloglu,xwxu}@ualr.edu

Abstract. Text embedding representing natural language documents in a semantic vector space can be used for document retrieval using nearest neighbor lookup. In order to study the feasibility of neural models specialized for retrieval in a semantically meaningful way, we suggest the use of the Stanford Question Answering Dataset (SQuAD) in an open-domain question answering context, where the first task is to find paragraphs useful for answering a given question. First, we compare the quality of various text-embedding methods on the performance of retrieval and give an extensive empirical comparison on the performance of various non-augmented base embedding with, and without IDF weighting. Our main results are that by training deep residual neural models, specifically for retrieval purposes, can yield significant gains when it is used to augment existing embeddings. We also establish that deeper models are superior to this task. The best base baseline embeddings augmented by our learned neural approach improves the top-1 paragraph recall of the system by 14%.

Keywords: Deep learning · Ad-hoc retrieval · Learning representations · Ranking · Text matching

1 Introduction

The goal of open domain question answering is to answer questions posed in natural language, using an unstructured collection of natural language documents such as Wikipedia. Given the recent successes of increasingly sophisticated neural attention based question answering models, such as [35], it is natural to break the task of answering a question into two subtasks as suggested in [7]:

- Retrieval: Retrieval of the paragraph most likely to contain all the information to answer the question correctly.
- Extraction: Utilizing one of the above question-answering models to extract the answer to the question from the retrieved paragraphs.

© Springer Nature Switzerland AG 2020
F. Dalpiaz et al. (Eds.): RCIS 2020, LNBIP 385, pp. 338–351, 2020.
https://doi.org/10.1007/978-3-030-50316-1_20

In our case, we use the collection of all SQuAD [24] paragraphs as our knowledge base and try to answer the questions without knowing to which paragraphs they correspond. We do not benchmark the quality of the extraction phase but study the quality of text retrieval methods and the feasibility of learning specialized neural models text retrieval purposes. Due to the complexity of natural languages, a good text embedding that represents the natural language documents in a semantic vector space is critical for the performance of the retrieval model. We constrain our attention to approaches that use a nearest neighbor look-up over a database of embeddings, using some embedding method (Fig. 1).

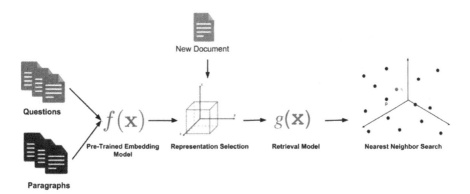

Fig. 1. The workflow of the proposed approach for retrieval.

We describe the implementation details utilizing the pre-trained embeddings to create, semantically, more meaningful text embedding improved by utilizing an extra knowledge base; hence, improving the quality of a target NLP retrieval task. Our solution is based on refining existing text embeddings trained on huge text corpora in an unsupervised manner. Given those embeddings, we learn residual neural models to improve their retrieval performance. For this purpose, we utilize the triplet learning methodology with hard negative mining [26].

The first question studied here is whether having advanced and refined embedding may provide higher recall for retrieval in the external knowledge base. Therefore, we benchmark most popular available embedding models and compare their performance on the retrieval task. First, we start with a review of recent advances in text embeddings in Sect. 2. In Sect. 3 we describe our proposed approach. The core idea is to augment precomputed text embedding models with an extra deep residual model for retrieval purposes. We present an empirical study of the proposed method in comparison with our baselines, which utilize the most popular word embedding models. We report the experiments and results in Sect. 4, 4.1 and 4.2 respectively. Finally, we conclude the paper with some future work in Sect. 5.

2   Related Work

There are various types of applications of word embedding in the literature that was well covered by [22]. The influential Word2Vec [19] is one of the first popular approaches of word embedding based on neural networks that was built on top of guiding work by [1] on the neural language model for distributed word representations. This type of implementation is able to conserve semantic relationships between words and their context; in other terms, surrounding neighboring words. Two different approaches are proposed in Word2Vec to compute word representations. One of the approaches is called Skip-gram that predicts surrounding neighboring words, given a target word; the other approach is called Continuous Bag-of-Words that predicts a target word using a bag-of-words context. The following study, Global Vectors (GloVe) [21], reduces some limitations of Word2Vec by focusing on the global context instead of surrounding nearby words for learning the representations. The global context is calculated by utilizing the word co-occurrences in a corpus. During this calculation, a count-based approach is functioned, unlike the prediction-based method in Word2Vec. On the other hand, fastText [2], is also announced recently. It has the same principles as others that focus on extracting word embedding from a large corpus. fastText is very similar to Word2Vec, except handling each word as a formation of character n-grams. That formation accelerates fastText to learn representation more efficiently.

Nonetheless, an important problem still exists on extracting high-quality and more meaningful representations—how to seize the semantic, syntactic and the different meanings in different contexts. This is also the point where our journey is getting started. Embedding from Language Models (ELMO) [23] newly-proposed in order to tackle that question. ELMO extracts representations from a bi-directional Long Short Term Memory (LSTM) [13] that is trained with a language model (LM) objective on a very large text dataset. ELMO representations are a function of the internal layers of the bi-directional Language Model (biLM) that outputs good and diverse representations about the words/token (a CNN over characters). ELMO is also incorporating character n-grams like in fastText but there are some constitutional differences between ELMO and its predecessors. The reason why we focused on ELMO is that it can generate more refined and detailed representations of the words due to utilizing internal representations of the LSTM network. As we mentioned before, ELMO is built on top of an LM, and each word/token representation is a function of the entire input, which makes it different than the other methods and also eliminates the others' restrictions, where each word/token is a mean of multiple contexts.

There are some other embedding methods which are not used as a baseline in the field; therefore, we did not discuss them in detail. Skip-Thought Vectors [16] uses encoder-decoder RNNs that predicts the nearby sentence of a given sentence. The other one is InferSent [9], that utilizes a supervised training for the sentence embeddings, unlike Skip-Thought. They used BiLSTM encoders to generate embeddings. p-mean [25] is built to tackle the unfairness of the Skip-Thought that is taking the mean of the word/token embeddings with different dimensions. There are other methods, such as [17]'s Doc2Vec/Paragraph2Vec, [12]'s fastSent, and [20]'s Sent2Vec.

Furthermore, we also include the newly-announced Universal Sentence Encoder [4] in our comparisons. Universal Sentence Encoder is built on top of two different models. Initially, the transformer-based attentive encoder model [30] was implemented to get high accuracy and the other model takes the benefit of the deep averaging network (DAN) [14]. As a result, averages of words/token embeddings and bi-grams can be provided as input to a DAN, where the sentence embeddings are getting computed. According to the authors, their sentence-level embeddings exceeds the performance of transfer learning, using word/token embeddings alone.

Last, but not least, distance metric learning is designed to amend the representation of the data in a way that retains the related points close to each other while separating unrelated points on the vector space as stated by different experiments such as [3,18,34]. Instead of utilizing a standard distance metric learning, a non-linear embedding of the data—using deep networks—has demonstrated important improvements by learning representations, using triplet loss [8,10], contrastive loss by [5,33], angular loss [32], and n-pair loss [27] for some influential studies by [26,28,29,31].

After providing a brief review of the latest trends in the field, we describe the details of our approach and experimental results in the following sections.

3 Proposed Approach

3.1 Embedding Model

After examining the latest advanced work in word embedding, and since ELMO outperforms the other approaches for all important NLP tasks, we included the pre-trained ELMO contextual word representations into our benchmark to discover the embedding model for the retrieval task that produces the best result. The pre-trained ELMO model used the raw 1 Billion Word Benchmark dataset [6], and the vocabulary of 79347 tokens.

By having all the requirements set, it was time to compute ELMO representations for the SQuAD dev set, using the pre-trained ELMO model. Before explaining the implementation strategies, we would like to mention the details of ELMO representation calculations. As expressed in the equation below, a L-layer biLM computes a set of $2L + 1$ representations for each token t_i.

$$\mathsf{L}_i = \{\boldsymbol{x}_i^{LM}, \overrightarrow{\boldsymbol{h}}_{i,j}^{LM}, \overleftarrow{\boldsymbol{h}}_{i,j}^{LM} | j = 1, ..., L\} = \{\overleftrightarrow{\boldsymbol{h}}_{i,j}^{LM} | j = 0, ..., L\}$$

where $\boldsymbol{x}_i^{LM}$, a context-indepedent token representation, is computed via a CNN over characters. These representations are then transmitted to L layers of forward and backward LSTMs (or BiDirectional LSTMs-$biLSTMs$). Each LSTM layer provides a context-dependent vector representation $\overleftrightarrow{\boldsymbol{h}}_{i,j}^{LM}$ where $j = 0, ..., L$. While the top layer LSTM results $\overrightarrow{\boldsymbol{h}}_{i,j}^{LM}$, presents the prediction of the next token t_{i+1}, likewise, $\overleftarrow{h}_{i,j}^{LM}$ represents the prediction of the previous token t_{i-1} by using a Softmax layer. The general approach would be a weighting of all biLM layers to get ELMO representations of the corpus. For our task, we generated the representations for the corpus, not only considering the results from the weighting of all biLM layers ($ELMO$), but also other individual layers, such as token layer, biLSTM layer 1 and biLSTM layer 2.

As a result, we build the tensors based on tokens instead of documents; but documents can also be sliced from these tensors. To this end, we created a mapping dictionary for keeping the document's index and length (number of tokens). In this way, a token is represented as the tensor of a shape $[1, 3, 1, 1024]$. To improve the traceability, the tensors were reshaped by swapping axis to become the tensor of a shape $[1, 3, 1024]$. We, then, stacked all these computed tokens, resulting with the tensor of a shape $[416909, 3, 1024]$ where 416909 is the number of tokens in the corpus (in other words, 416909 represents the 12637 documents in the corpus). Therefore, any document could be extracted from this tensor, using the previously-created mapping dictionary. For example, let us assume that doc_1 has an index of 126 and a length of 236, so doc_1 can be extracted by slicing the tensor, using the format $[126 : 126 + 236, :, :]$. In terms of math expression, we built a tensor $T_{i,j,d}$ where i is representing the total documents in the corpus, j is representing the layers, and d is a dimension space of a vector. T is based on tokens instead of documents, but documents can also be sliced from that tensor.

To achieve a good embedding, the main question was about identifying the most critical components that contain the most valuable information for the document. Since the new tensor of a shape $[12637, 3, 1024]$ has 3 components, in order to extract the most valuable slice(s), we defined a new weight tensor $W_{1,j,1}$ where the j had the a same dimension as in the tensor T. For our experiment, we set the j to 3 as the same dimension value in which the pre-trained ELMo word representations were used. The elements of the vector j of the tensor W was symbolized as a, b, and c, where $a + b + c = 1$. In order to find the right combination within the elements of the weight tensor W for the best embedding matrix M, we calculated the following function:

$$M' = ||mean(\mathsf{T} * \mathsf{W}; \theta = 1)||$$

where $M' = \{M_1', M_2', \ldots, M_n'\}$, $\mathsf{W}' = \{\mathsf{W}_1', \mathsf{W}_2', \ldots, \mathsf{W}_n'\}$, n is the number of documents in the set and θ represents the axis argument of the function. Last, but not least, all candidate embedding was normalized by L2-Norm. With this setup, we were able to create the candidate embedding matrices represented by M' for further experiments to get the ultimate best embedding E. Each embedding in the embedding matrix is symbolized by $f(x) \in \mathbb{R}^d$. Therefore, it was able to embed a document x into a d-dimensional Euclidean space.

In order to capture the best combination of W' (in other words, finding the best a, b, and c values), we calculated the pair-wise distances between questions and paragraphs embedding, represented Q' and P' respectively, that were sliced from M'. The performance of finding the correct question-paragraph embedding pair is measured by *recall@k*. The reason why we used the *recall@k* is that we wanted to compute the hitting performance of the true paragraph (answers) to the particular question, whether it is in the top-k closest paragraphs or not. We used the ranks of top $1, 2, 3, 5, 10$, and, 50. In order to calculate the recall values, we had to deal with $20M$ question-paragraph embedding pairs ($10K$ questions x $2K$ answers) in the dev dataset. We primarily looked at the Receiver Operating Characteristic (ROC) curve and used Area Under Curve (AUC) as the target metric for tuning the embedding. Therefore, we sorted the retrieved samples by their distance (the paragraphs to the question) and then we computed recall and precision at each threshold. After having the precision numbers from the computations, we observed that our precision numbers became very low values because of having only $10k$ correct pairs and a high amount of negative paragraphs. We decided to switch to other methods; namely, Precision-Recall curve and Average Precision.

Additionally, we took one further step. We wanted to inject the inverse document frequency (IDF) weights of each token into the embedding M to observe whether it creates any positive impact on the representation or not since the IDF is calculated using the following function: $IDF(t) = log_e(\frac{\#of\,documents}{\#of\,docs.w/term})$, Where we calculated the IDF weights from each tokenized documents. Then we multiplied newly-computed token IDF weights with the original token embedding extracted from the pre-trained model to have the final injected token embedding.

Similar to both the ELMO and extension of ELMO with IDF weights steps, we followed the same pipeline for the GloVe since it is one of the important baselines for this type of research. We specially utilized the *"glove-840B-300d"* pre-trained word vectors, where it was trained on using the common crawl within 840B tokens, 2.2M vocab, cased, 300d vectors. We created the GloVe representation for our corpus and also extended it with IDF weights.

3.2   Retrieval Model

The retrieval model aims to improve the *recall@1* score by selecting the correct pair among all possible options. While pursuing this goal, it is developing embedding accuracy by minimizing the distance from the questions to the true paragraphs after embedding both questions and paragraphs to the semantic space.

The model architectures we designed to implement our idea are presented in Fig. 2 and Fig. 3. Question embedding Q^b (*b is representing the batch of question embedding*) were provided as inputs to the models. The output layer was wrapped with [11]'s residual layer by scaling the previous layer's output with a constant scalar factor sf. Finally, the ultimate output from the residual layer was also normalized by L2. The normalized question embedding and the corresponding paragraph embedding are processed by the model that is optimized, using a loss function $\mathcal{L}$. For this reason, we proposed and also utilized several loss functions. The main reason for this was to move the true $q \in Q^b, p \in P^b$ pairs closer to each other, while keeping the wrong pairs further from each other. Using a constant margin value m would be also helpful to create an enhanced effect on this goal.

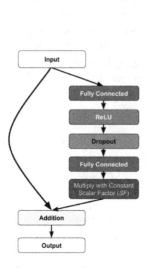

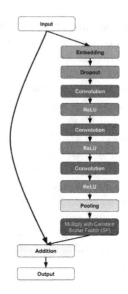

Fig. 2. The layer architectures in the *Fully Connected Residual Retrieval Network* (**FCRR**).

Fig. 3. The layer architectures in the *Convolutional Residual Retrieval Network* (**ConvRR**).

The first function we defined was a **quadratic regression conditional loss**. With this $\mathcal{L}_{\text{quadratic regression conditionally}}$, we aimed to use a conditional margin as below.

$$m'(m, d) = \begin{cases} m, & \text{if } d > m. \\ 0, & \text{otherwise.} \end{cases} \tag{1}$$

$$\mathcal{L}_{\text{quadratic regression conditional}} = [||\boldsymbol{q} - \boldsymbol{p}||^2 - m]^+ + m'(m, ||\boldsymbol{q} - \boldsymbol{p}||^2)$$

The latter loss function we utilized was the **triplet loss**. With this setup, we not only consider the positive pairs but also negative pairs in the batch. Our aim was that a particular question $\boldsymbol{q}_{\text{anchor}}$ would be a question close in proximity to a paragraph $\boldsymbol{p}_{\text{positive}}$ as the answer to the same question than to any paragraph $\boldsymbol{p}_{\text{negative}}$ as they are answers to other questions. The key point of the $\mathcal{L}_{\text{triplet}}$ was building the correct triplet structure, which should not meet the restraint of the following equation easily $||\boldsymbol{q}_{\text{anchor}} - \boldsymbol{p}_{\text{positive}}||^2 + m < ||\boldsymbol{q}_{\text{anchor}} - \boldsymbol{p}_{\text{negative}}||^2$. Therefore, for each anchor, we took the positive $\boldsymbol{p}_{\text{positive}}$ in such a way arg $\max_{\boldsymbol{p}_{\text{positive}}} ||\boldsymbol{q}_{\text{anchor}} - \boldsymbol{p}_{\text{positive}}||^2$ and likewise, the hardest negative $\boldsymbol{p}_{\text{negative}}$ in such a way that arg $\min_{\boldsymbol{p}_{\text{negative}}} ||\boldsymbol{q}_{\text{anchor}} - \boldsymbol{p}_{\text{negative}}||^2$ to form a triplet. This triplet selection strategy is called *hard triplets mining*.

$$\mathcal{L}_{\text{triplet}} = [||\boldsymbol{q}_{\text{anchor}} - \boldsymbol{p}_{\text{positive}}||^2 - ||\boldsymbol{q}_{\text{anchor}} - \boldsymbol{p}_{\text{negative}}||^2 + m]^+$$

During all our experiments, we have utilized [15]'s ADAM optimizer with a learning rate of 10^-3. For the sake of equal comparison, we have fixed the seed of randomization. We have also observed that a weight decay 10^-3 and/or a dropout 10^-1 is the optimum value for all types of model architectures to tackle over-fitting. In addition to that, the batch size b of question-paragraph embedding pairs has been set to 512 during the training. We trained the networks with a range of between 50 to 200 iterations.

Specifically, we designed our FCRR model as a stack of multi-layers. During the observation of the experiments, the simple but the efficient configuration was emerged as 2-layers. Likewise, we used 1024 filters, 5 as a length of the 1D convolution window, and 2 as a length of the convolution in our ConvRR model. Last, but not least, the scaling factor is set to 1 for both models.

4   Experiment

We did an empirical study of the proposed question-answering method in comparison with major state-of-the-art methods in terms of both text embedding and question answering. In the subsequent, we are going to describe details for the dataset, the model comparison, and the results.

4.1   SQuAD Dataset

For the empirical study of the performance of text embedding and question answering, we use the Stanford Question Answering Dataset (SQuAD) [24]. The SQuAD is a benchmark dataset, consisting of questions posed by crowd-workers on a set of Wikipedia articles, where the answer to every question is a segment of text from the corresponding reading passage. The number of documents in the dataset is stated in the following Table 1.

Table 1. Number of documents in the SQuAD dataset.

Set name	# of Ques.	# of Par.	# of Tot. Cont
Dev	10570	2067	12637
Train	87599	18896	106495

4.2   Embedding Comparison

We wanted to observe trade-off between Precision and Recall and AP value to compare performances of each candidate embedding M'. $recall@k$ was calculated for each embedding matrix M' by using grid search over the a, b, c components presented in Table 2.

Table 2. The grid search results for both *recall@1* and average *recalls* among top 1, 2, 5, 10, 20, 50 recalls to find the best layer for the task.

Layer name	**W'** Configuration	*recall@1*	*avg recalls*
Token Layer	$a = 1, b = 0, c = 0$	$41.50\% \pm 0.03\%$	$66.40\% \pm 0.02\%$
biLSTM Layer 1	$a = 0, b = 1, c = 0$	$26.20\% \pm 0.01\%$	$54.30\% \pm 0.05\%$
biLSTM Layer 2	$a = 0, b = 0, c = 1$	$19.60\% \pm 0.07\%$	$48.00\% \pm 0.04\%$
ELMO	$a = 0.33, b = 0.33, c = 0.33$	$21.20\% \pm 0.01\%$	$48.30\% \pm 0.02\%$

Table 3. *recall@ks* of GloVe.

recall@k	# of docs	%
1	3246	30.7%
2	4318	40.8%
5	5713	54.0%
10	6747	63.8%
20	7602	71.9%
50	8524	80.6%

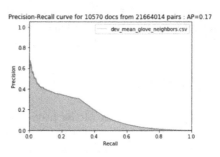

Fig. 4. P-R Curve for GloVe.

Table 4. *recall@ks* of Extension of GloVe with IDF weights.

recall@k	# of docs	%
1	3688	34.8%
2	4819	45.5%
5	6293	59.5%
10	7251	68.5%
20	8076	76.4%
50	8919	84.3%

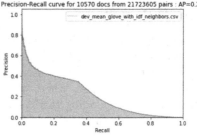

Fig. 5. P-R Curve for extension of GloVe with IDF weights.

The best component combination emerged as $a = 1$, $b = 0$, $c = 0$ that provides the best setting to represent the corpus. In other words, token layer is the most useful layer. Finally, question and paragraph embedding are represented $Q = \{q_1, q_2, \ldots, q_x\}$ and $P = \{p_1, p_2, \ldots, p_{(n-x)}\}$, where x represents the number of questions within the corpus. In other terms $[0 : 10570, 1024]$ belongs to questions while $[10570 :, 1024]$ belongs to paragraphs for the dev dataset.

We can now start to compare the results of the *recall@k* of the pair-wise embedding that are derived from different models for the **dev corpus** in order to measure the embedding quality. The *recall@k* tables and the Precision-Recall curve from each of the embedding structure are presented in the section below (Figs. 4, 5, 6 and 7) (Tables 3, 4, 5 and 6).

The average-precision scores of each embedding structure is listed in Table 7.

Table 5. *recall@k*s of ELMO.

recall@k	# of docs	%
1	4391	41.5%
2	5508	52.1%
5	6793	64.2%
10	7684	72.6%
20	8474	80.1%
50	9271	87.7%

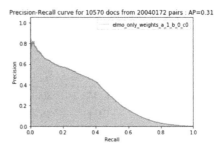

Fig. 6. P-R Curve for ELMO.

Table 6. *recall@k*s of Extension of ELMO with IDF weights.

recall@k	# of docs	%
1	4755	44.9%
2	5933	56.3%
5	7208	68.1%
10	8040	76.0%
20	8806	83.3%
50	9492	89.8%

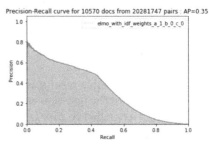

Fig. 7. P-R Curve for extension of ELMO with IDF weights.

Table 7. Average precision list.

Model name	Average Precision (AP)
GloVe	0.17
Extension GloVe W/ IDF w.	0.22
ELMO	0.31
Extension ELMO W/ IDF w.	0.35

By following the same pipeline, we applied the defined best model to the **train set**. As an initial step, we randomly selected 5K question embedding and corresponding paragraph embedding from the corpus as our validation set. The remaining part of the set is defined to be used as a training data. The results from the best model (*Extension of ELMO w/ IDF weights*) and baseline model (*Only ELMO*) are presented in Table 8.

As presented in Table 8, we were able to improve the representation performance of the embeddings increased by 4% on a *recall@1* and 4.7% on an *average recall* for our task by injecting the IDF weights into the ELMO token embedding.

Table 8. *recall@k*s of Extension of ELMO w/ IDF weights and Only ELMO from the train set..

recall@k	ELMO		Ext. of ELMO w/ IDF	
	# of docs	%	# of docs	%
1	1445	30.38%	1723	34.46%
2	1918	38.36%	2128	42.56%
5	2424	48.48%	2688	53.76%
10	2820	56.40%	3045	60.90%
20	3143	62.86%	3388	67.76%
50	3545	70.90%	3792	75.84%

4.3   Model for Retrieval

After having the best possible results as a new baseline, we aimed to improve the representation quality of the question embedding. In order to train our models for the retrieval task, we decided to **merge the SQuAD dev and train datasets** to create the larger corpus. By executing that step, we have a total of 98169 questions and 20963 paragraphs. We randomly selected 5K question embedding and corresponding paragraph embedding from the corpus as our validation set for the recall task and similarly 10K as our validation set for the loss calculation task. The remaining part of the set is defined as the training data.

The intuition was that the correct pairs should be closer in proximity to one another so that closest paragraph embedding to the question embedding would be correct in an ideal scenario. With this goal; *1)* the question embedding is fine-tuned by our retrieval models so that the closest paragraph embedding would be the true pair for the corresponding question embedding, *2)* similarly, the paragraph embedding is also fine-tuned by our retrieval model so that the closest question embedding would be the true pair for the corresponding paragraph embedding, and finally *3)* on top of previous steps, we further fine-tuned question embedding, using the combination of improved question and paragraph embedding stated in step 1 & 2.

As shown in Table 9 and Table 10, we were able to improve the question and paragraph embedding in such a way that the retrieval performance for the question side increased by $9.36\% \pm 0.11\%$ on a *recall@1* result and $11.60\% \pm 0.12\%$ on an *average recall* compared to our new baseline that is an extension of ELMO w/ IDF. In addition to that, if we compare our best results with the original ELMO baseline results, we observe that the representation performance increased by $13.56\% \pm 0.15\%$ on a *recall@1* and $16.10\% \pm 0.08\%$ on an *average recall*. Similarly, the retrieval performance for the paragraph side increased by $8.85\% \pm 0.03\%$ on a *recall@1* result and $16.00\% \pm 0.07\%$ on an *average recall* compared to our new baseline that is an extension of ELMO w/ IDF. In addition to that, if we compare our best results with the original ELMO baseline results,

Table 9. The highest *recall@1* and average *recalls* among top 1, 2, 5, 10, 20, 50 results from the best models including the baseline model for question embedding.

Model	Question embedding			
	recall@1	improv. (%)	avg *recalls*	improv. (%)
Only ELMO	28.40% ± 0.06%	–	49.70% ± 0.02%	–
ELMO w/ IDF	32.60% ± 0.04%	4.20% ± 0.1%	54.20% ± 0.06%	4.50% ± 0.08%
FCRR	40.50% ± 0.02%	12.10% ± 0.08%	64.30% ± 0.03%	14.60% ± 0.05%
FCRR + ConvRR	41.60% ± 0.06%	13.20% ± 0.12%	65.50% ± 0.04%	15.80% ± 0.06%
FCRR + ConvRR + w/ fine-tuned Paragraph embed.	41.96% ± 0.07%	13.56% ± 0.15%	65.80% ± 0.06%	16.10% ± 0.08%

Table 10. The highest *recall@1* and average *recalls* among top 1, 2, 5, 10, 20, 50 results from the best models including the baseline model for paragraph embedding.

Model	Paragraph embedding			
	recall@1	improv. (%)	avg *recalls*	improv. (%)
Only ELMO	6.70% ± 0.07%	–	22.50% ± 0.09%	–
ELMO w/ IDF	8.80% ± 0.02%	2.10% ± 0.09%	26.70% ± 0.04%	4.20% ± 0.13%
FCRR	13.60% ± 0.05%	6.90% ± 0.12%	41.40% ± 0.08%	18.90% ± 0.17%
FCRR + ConvRR	14.00% ± 0.02%	7.30% ± 0.09%	42.10% ± 0.04%	19.60% ± 0.13%
FCRR + ConvRR + w/ fine-tuned Question embed.	14.65% ± 0.01%	7.95% ± 0.08%	42.70% ± 0.03%	20.20% ± 0.12%

we observe that the representation performance increased by $7.95\% \pm 0.08\%$ on an *recall@1* and $20.20\% \pm 0.12\%$ on an *average recall*

On the other hand, $\mathscr{L}_{\text{quadratic regression conditional}}$ didn't show any performance improvement compared to $\mathscr{L}_{\text{triplet}}$. Last, but not least, during our experiments, we also wanted to compare the quality of our embedding with the embedding derived from USE. Although our best model with the $\mathscr{L}_{\text{triplet}}$ was able to improve the representation performance of the USE document embedding for the retrieval task, it was still far from achieving our state-of-the-art fine-tuned result.

5   Conclusion

We developed a new question answering framework for retrieval answers from a knowledge base. The critical part of the framework is text embedding. The state-of-the-art embedding uses the output of the embedding model as the representation. We developed a representation selection method for determining the optimal combination of representations from a multi-layered language model. In addition, we designed deep learning based retrieval models, which further improved the performance of question answering by optimizing the distance from the source to the target. The empirical study, using the SQuAD benchmark dataset, shows a significant performance gain in terms of the recall. In the future, we plan to apply the proposed framework for other information retrieval and ranking tasks. We also want to improve the performance of the current retrieval models, by applying and developing new loss functions.

Acknowledgments. This study used the Google Cloud Computing Platform (GCP) which is supported by Google AI research grant.

References

1. Bengio, Y., Ducharme, R., Vincent, P., Janvin, C.: A neural probabilistic language model. J. Mach. Learn. Res. **3**, 1137–1155 (2003)
2. Bojanowski, P., Grave, E., Joulin, A., Mikolov, T.: Enriching word vectors with subword information. Trans. Assoc. Comput. Linguist. **5**, 135–146 (2017)
3. Cao, Q., Ying, Y., Li, P.: Similarity metric learning for face recognition. In: 2013 IEEE International Conference on Computer Vision, pp. 2408–2415 (2013)
4. Cer, D., et al.: Universal sentence encoder (2018)
5. Chechik, G., Sharma, V., Shalit, U., Bengio, S.: Large scale online learning of image similarity through ranking. J. Mach. Learn. Res. **11**, 1109–1135 (2010)
6. Chelba, C., et al.: One billion word benchmark for measuring progress in statistical language modeling. Technical report (2013)
7. Chen, D., Fisch, A., Weston, J., Bordes, A.: Reading wikipedia to answer open-domain questions. arXiv preprint arXiv:1704.00051 (2017)
8. Chopra, S., Hadsell, R., LeCun, Y.: Learning a similarity metric discriminatively, with application to face verification, vol. 1, pp. 539–546 (2005)
9. Conneau, A., Kiela, D., Schwenk, H., Barrault, L., Bordes, A.: Supervised learning of universal sentence representations from natural language inference data. In: Proceedings of the 2017 Conference on Empirical Methods in Natural Language Processing, pp. 670–680 (2017)
10. Hadsell, R., Chopra, S., LeCun, Y.: Dimensionality reduction by learning an invariant mapping. In: CVPR 2006, pp. 1735–1742 (2006)
11. He, K., Zhang, X., Ren, S., Sun, J.: Deep residual learning for image recognition. In: 2016 IEEE Conference on Computer Vision and Pattern Recognition (CVPR), pp. 770–778 (2016)
12. Hill, F., Cho, K., Korhonen, A.: Learning distributed representations of sentences from unlabelled data. In: Proceedings of the 2016 Conference of the North American Chapter of the Association for Computational Linguistics: Human Language Technologies, pp. 1367–1377 (2016)
13. Hochreiter, S., Schmidhuber, J.: Long short-term memory. Neural Comput. **9**(8), 1735–1780 (1997)
14. Iyyer, M., Manjunatha, V., Boyd-Graber, J.L., III, H.D.: Deep unordered composition rivals syntactic methods for text classification. In: ACL, no. 1, pp. 1681–1691 (2015)
15. Kingma, D.P., Ba, J.: Adam: a method for stochastic optimization. arXiv preprint arXiv:1412.6980 (2014)
16. Kiros, R., et al.: Skip-thought vectors. In: Advances in Neural Information Processing Systems, vol. 28, pp. 3294–3302 (2015)

17. Le, Q.V., Mikolov, T.: Distributed representations of sentences and documents. In: ICML, vol. 32, pp. 1188–1196 (2014)
18. Lowe, D.G.: Similarity metric learning for a variable-kernel classifier. Neural Comput. **7**(1), 72–85 (1995)
19. Mikolov, T., Sutskever, I., Chen, K., Corrado, G.S., Dean, J.: Distributed representations of words and phrases and their compositionality. In: Advances in Neural Information Processing Systems, vol. 26, pp. 3111–3119 (2013)
20. Pagliardini, M., Gupta, P., Jaggi, M.: Unsupervised learning of sentence embeddings using compositional n-gram features. In: Proceedings of the 2018 Conference of the North American Chapter of the Association for Computational Linguistics: Human Language Technologies, vol. 1 (Long Papers), pp. 528–540 (2018)
21. Pennington, J., Socher, R., Manning, C.D.: Glove: global vectors for word representation. In: Empirical Methods in Natural Language Processing (EMNLP), pp. 1532–1543 (2014)
22. Perone, C.S., Silveira, R., Paula, T.S.: Evaluation of sentence embeddings in downstream and linguistic probing tasks. arXiv preprint arXiv:1806.06259 (2018)
23. Peters, M., Neumann, M., Iyyer, M., Gardner, M., Clark, C., Lee, K., Zettlemoyer, L.: Deep contextualized word representations. In: Proceedings of the 2018 Conference of the North American Chapter of the Association for Computational Linguistics: Human Language Technologies, vol. 1 (Long Papers), pp. 2227–2237 (2018)
24. Rajpurkar, P., Zhang, J., Lopyrev, K., Liang, P.: Squad: 100,000+ questions for machine comprehension of text. arXiv preprint arXiv:1606.05250 (2016)
25. Rücklé, A., Eger, S., Peyrard, M., Gurevych, I.: Concatenated p-mean word embeddings as universal cross-lingual sentence representations. arXiv preprint arXiv:1803.01400 (2018)
26. Schroff, F., Kalenichenko, D., Philbin, J.: Facenet: a unified embedding for face recognition and clustering, pp. 815–823 (2015)
27. Sohn, K.: Improved deep metric learning with multi-class n-pair loss objective. In: NIPS 2016, pp. 1857–1865 (2016)
28. Sun, Y., Chen, Y., Wang, X., Tang, X.: Deep learning face representation by joint identification-verification, pp. 1988–1996 (2014)
29. Taigman, Y., Yang, M., Ranzato, M., Wolf, L.: Deepface: closing the gap to human-level performance in face verification. In: CVPR 2014, pp. 1701–1708 (2014)
30. Vaswani, A., et al.: Attention is all you need. In: Advances in Neural Information Processing Systems, vol. 30, pp. 5998–6008 (2017)
31. Wang, J., et al.: Learning fine-grained image similarity with deep ranking, pp. 1386–1393 (2014)
32. Wang, J., Zhou, F., Wen, S., Liu, X., Lin, Y.: Deep metric learning with angular loss (2017)
33. Weinberger, K.Q., Saul, L.K.: Distance metric learning for large margin nearest neighbor classification, vol. 10, pp. 207–244 (2009)
34. Xing, E.P., Ng, A.Y., Jordan, M.I., Russell, S.: Distance metric learning, with application to clustering with side-information. In: NIPS 2002, pp. 521–528 (2002)
35. Yu, A.W., et al.: Qanet: combining local convolution with global self-attention for reading comprehension. arXiv preprint arXiv:1804.09541 (2018)

Predicting Unemployment with Machine Learning Based on Registry Data

Markus Viljanen$^{(\boxtimes)}$ and Tapio Pahikkala

Turun Yliopisto, Turku, Finland
majuvi@utu.fi

Abstract. Many statistical models have been developed to understand the causes of unemployment, but predicting unemployment has received less attention. In this study, we develop a model to predict the labour market state of a person based on machine learning trained with a large administrative unemployment registry. The model specifies individuals as Markov chains with person specific transition rates. We evaluate the model on three tasks, where the goal is to predict who has the highest risk of escaping unemployment, becoming unemployed, and being unemployed at any given time. We obtain good performance (AUC: 0.80) for the machine learning model of lifetime unemployment, and very good performance (AUC: 0.90+) to the near future when we know the recent labour market state of a person. We find that person information affects the predictions in an intuitive way, but there still are significant differences that can be learned by utilizing labour market histories.

Keywords: Unemployment · Machine learning · Prediction

1 Introduction

Understanding and predicting unemployment is very important for societies and individuals alike. Identifying at risk individuals and the total amount of unemployment is a central topic of interest, regardless of the context. To understand how unemployment is experienced at the individual level, we need to consider the full labor market history of each person. These histories consists of recurrent spells of unemployment and other labor market states, which together determine the total time person spends in unemployment. When we have a well-founded model for the labor market histories, we can predict these the transitions in and out of unemployment, including the resulting lifetime unemployment.

In this study, we develop a model for the sequence of labour market states of a person. We focus on prediction and evaluate models on three related prediction tasks: what is the probability that a person exits unemployment, becomes unemployed, and is unemployed at any given time? To do this, we model the unemployment status as a Markov chain with person specific transition rates. The prediction of a person's unemployment status is then given by the state probabilities of the Markov chain. The steady state probabilities imply that,

© Springer Nature Switzerland AG 2020
F. Dalpiaz et al. (Eds.): RCIS 2020, LNBIP 385, pp. 352–368, 2020.
https://doi.org/10.1007/978-3-030-50316-1_21

in the long run, an individual can be predicted to spend a certain amount of their lifetime on unemployment. We investigate both a statistical model and a machine learning model for the transition rates in different settings, where predictions can be required for a future time or a completely new person. As a result, we obtain predictive models for unemployment dynamics at the individual level, using simple models trained with few years of historical data.

2 Related Work

Macroeconometric research has studied unemployment trends using historical time series and aggregate labor market statistics. See for example a review [1], which summarized the current state of research on unemployment dynamics in macroeconomic models. It is possible to explain the unemployment rate in terms of the unemployment entry and exit flows, which often correlate with changes in the economy [2]. However, it has been pointed out that individuals have significant heterogeneity, which this analysis ignores [3]. In our Finnish study region of Varsinais-Suomi, the ELY-center (Centre for Economic Development, Transport and the Environment) is required by law to publish the total number of job seekers and basic statistics related to them each month. Recently, KELA (The Social Insurance Institution of Finland) published a working paper which used macroeconometric data to produce estimates on the total amount of lifetime unemployment in the population [4]. However, macroeconometric statistics cannot be used for prediction at the individual level.

Microeconometric studies have been used to develop models at the individual level. In these studies, regression is often used to assess the effect of a variable of interest, such as a policy change in unemployment benefits. The most common application of person-level data is the study of unemployment duration. For example, an older review [5] summarized many studies on how health, age, gender, unemployment benefits, etc. affect unemployment. A recent study [6] reviewed the accumulated evidence of the individual experience of unemployment, predictors of exiting unemployment, and the effect of interventions. In Finland, studies have reported how individual characteristics influence the risk of exiting unemployment [7–9] and the risk of becoming unemployed [10,11]. Studies have also investigated the flows of individuals between different labor market states, where Finnish studies have been performed on both aggregate [12] and person-level data [13].

Modeling unemployment with Markov Chain models, which is an idea underlying our model, has been considered in a statistical context [14–16]. These studies have focused on the dynamics of unemployment and the effect of different variables, not on the predictive ability of the model. In the predictive task, several studies have investigated the predictive power of Google searches in forecasting the unemployment rate, see for example the references in [17]. In the Finnish context, work at ETLA (The Research Institute of the Finnish Economy) has also predicted the unemployment rate using Google searches [18]. In addition to standard time-series models, machine learning can be applied to macroeconomic time-series prediction [19]. At the individual level, multiple studies have predicted the Long-Term Unemployment (LTU) status of a person, see for example the references in [20]. This is a simpler task of binary prediction whether an individual would fall under the classification 'long-term unemployed'. The unemployment exit rate was recently studied in [21]. Studies have traditionally used logistic regression, but machine learning algorithms such as gradient boosting or random forest have been found to perform slightly better.

3   Data Set

Our data set is based on individual-level administrative data collected in the Varsinais-Suomi ELY-centre, based in turn on the URA-registry collected in the local employment and business services office (TE services). Unlike many other unemployment studies, we do not have a separate questionnaire or other data sets merged into this data set. The registry contains all job seekers registered at the unemployment agencies, which they are required to do in order to receive unemployment benefits. For this reason, practically all unemployed persons can be considered to belong to the registry. For example, the official unemployment statistics produced by the Ministry of Labour (TEM) are based on the number of people in these registries. The administrative registry is not biased by sample selection or subjective reporting. However, if we wish to apply the model to predict unemployment for the Varsinais-Suomi population, the training set should strictly be a random sample of the population. In the appendix, we investigate how the unemployment registry differs from this population.

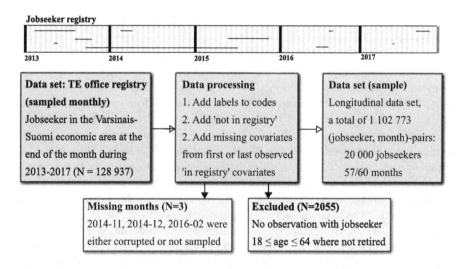

Fig. 1. Process of transforming the unemployment registry to the study data set.

The registry was sampled at the weekday following the end of each month, from the beginning of 2013 to the end of 2017, as illustrated in Fig. 1. This resulted in one sample per month over 5 years, in principle 60 monthly samples. The data acquired for this research turned out to have some missed samples due missed manual collection or data corruption, with 57 total monthly samples. The models we use are designed to handle censoring, so this does not bias the results. Each entry identifies the individual by their social security number, records their labor market state and collects some background information. The social security number was replaced by an ordinal userid before analysis due to data protection laws. The original data set had 128 937 potential persons, of which the study used a random sample of 20 000.

The labor market state of a job seeker is recorded as employed on placement, employed, unemployed, laid off, shortened workweek, outside the labour force, and unemployment retirement. If a person is employed or outside the labor market they may be missing from the registry, because they do not have to report to the unemployment office. We have therefore denoted the state of missing from the data with a new code 'not in registry' and filled these observations with covariates primarily forward and secondarily backward from the last observed covariates. We also created a new category of 'censored' observations. These included samples which were either not collected or where the person's age would have been smaller than 18 or over 64.

The individual registry entry has information such as gender, age, work experience, level of education, field of education, field of profession, mother tongue, and citizenship. This information varies over time and these are the possible time-varying covariates to include in the model. However, some of the information has a high degree of identifiability, so we had to use the following higher level covariates: gender, work experience, age in 5 year buckets, level of education, field of education. The background information is recorded in the registry as codes displayed in Table 1, so we attached human readable labels from Statistics of Finland descriptions. If a code was missing or the corresponding label did not exist, we replaced the covariate value by the 'unknown' category.

Table 1. The following covariates were included in the model.

Registry entry	Covariate (categories)	Example values
henkilotunnus	userid (20000)	1,2,3
supukoodi	gender (2)	M, F
ika	age (10)	[18,20), [20,25), ..., [60,65)
tyokokemuskoodi	work experience (3)	None, Some, Sufficient
koulutuskoodi	level of education (16)	Early Education, Basic 1–6, ..., PhD
	field of education (12)	Preparatory, Education, ..., Services
vvvvkk	time (59)	2013-01, 2013-02, ..., 2017-12
voimolevatyollkoodi	labour market status (7)	Employed, Unemployed, ..., Censored

It is well-known that unemployment is influenced by many economic factors: economic growth, labour market conditions, regulation, unemployment benefits, etc. The unemployment rate also fluctuates significantly with the economic cycle. It would be possible to include macroeconomic indicators. However, if one wants to predict future unemployment instead of historical unemployment, one needs to know these variables in the future. This is of course not possible, and predicting them accurately is very difficult. Our data consists of a complete economic cycle in the local unemployment rate (Appendix Fig. 6), which implies that the future predictions are time-averaged. This suits us well since we are interested in the long run individual unemployment and do not wish to model the economic cycle. In addition, our evaluation metric depends only on the relative unemployment; it should not affect the performance estimates in any case.

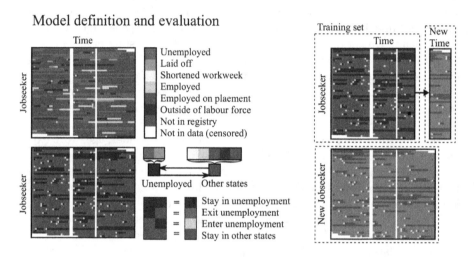

Fig. 2. Model definition and evaluation from the sequence of labor market states.

4   Model

4.1   Mathematical Framework

The model is motivated by the visualization of labor market histories in Fig. 2. For the purpose of this study, we define the labour market status as either unemployed or not unemployed. We treat persons that were either unemployed or laid off as 'unemployed' and other labor market states as 'not unemployed'. Each labour market history therefore is a binary vector of 'unemployed' states $x_i(t) \in \{0,1\}$ of the individual $i = 1, \ldots, N$ at months $t = 1, \ldots, T$. We describe the labour market history of each person is a stochastic process $\{X_i(t), t \geq 0\}$ where the random variable $X_i(t) \in \{0,1\}$ is the unemployment status of the individual i at time t. The random vector $P_i(t) = (P(X_i(t) = 0), P(X_i(t) = 1))$ is the state probability vector, giving the probability of being either in or out of unemployment at a given time. At the prediction time, we know the current state of a person and wish to predict the future state of the person. For this reason, we define the transition probability matrix:

$$\mathbb{P}_i(s,t) = \begin{pmatrix} P(X_i(t) = 0 | X_i(s) = 0) & P(X_i(t) = 1 | X_i(s) = 0) \\ P(X_i(t) = 0 | X_i(s) = 1) & P(X_i(t) = 1 | X_i(s) = 1) \end{pmatrix} \tag{1}$$

The labor market history of a person does not appear to consist of randomly dispersed unemployment events, but rather consecutive months of unemployment which can be characterized as unemployment spells. In addition, some persons seem to have considerably longer unemployment spells than others. This observation is the basis of our model. Every calendar month, a person either remains in the current state or transitions into unemployment (entry) or out of unemployment (exit). We consider that only one transition occurs within each calendar month and that the transition probabilities are person specific. In other words, we hypothesize that the data set is a Markov Chain with person specific transition rates.

If the labor market states at $X_i(t)$ and $X_i(t + dt)$ are different, this means that either of two transition events occurred in $(t, t+dt]$: exit from unemployment or entry into unemployment. Transition rates are defined through the instantaneous probability of a transition. Define the person specific rate of unemployment exit $\lambda_i(t)$ and the rate of unemployment entry $\mu_i(t)$:

$$\begin{aligned} \lambda_i(t) &= \lim_{dt \to 0} P(X_i(t + dt) = 0 | X_i(t) = 1)/dt \\ \mu_i(t) &= \lim_{dt \to 0} P(X_i(t + dt) = 1 | X_i(t) = 0)/dt \end{aligned} \tag{2}$$

The Markov Chain is then defined by a rate matrix $d\mathbb{A}_i(t) = \begin{pmatrix} -\mu_i(t) & \mu_i(t) \\ \lambda_i(t) & -\lambda_i(t) \end{pmatrix} dt$. It can be shown that the transition probability matrix $\mathbb{P}_i(s,t)$ can be computed as the following matrix-valued product integral [22]:

$$\mathbb{P}_i(s,t) = \prod_{u \in (s,t]} (\mathbb{I} + d\mathbb{A}_i(u)) \tag{3}$$

We train the model using time-varying transition rates. However, we predict to the future using last known covariates so that the predicted future rates are constant. Under the assumption of constant rates, we can derive the following interesting results for person's lifetime unemployment using well-known properties of the Markov Chain. The lifetime unemployment is defined as the proportion of the working age life that a person spends in unemployment. Denote the rate of unemployment exit by λ_i and the rate of unemployment entry by μ_i. At prediction time, we wish to predict the future state $\mathbb{P}_i(t + \delta t, t)$ given δt months forward from the last known state $X_i(t)$. In this case, we can explicitly derive a closed form expression for the transition probability matrix to obtain [26]:

$$\mathbb{P}_i(t, t + \delta t) = \begin{pmatrix} \frac{\lambda_i}{\lambda_i + \mu_i} + \frac{\mu_i}{\lambda_i + \mu_i} e^{-(\lambda_i + \mu_i)\delta t} & \frac{\mu_i}{\lambda_i + \mu_i} - \frac{\mu_i}{\lambda_i + \mu_i} e^{-(\lambda_i + \mu_i)\delta t} \\ \frac{\lambda_i}{\lambda_i + \mu_i} - \frac{\lambda_i}{\lambda_i + \mu_i} e^{-(\lambda_i + \mu_i)\delta t} & \frac{\mu_i}{\lambda_i + \mu_i} + \frac{\lambda}{\lambda_i + \mu_i} e^{-(\lambda_i + \mu_i)\delta t} \end{pmatrix} \tag{4}$$

Regardless whether the person is unemployed at the last observation, the transition probability matrix implies that the probability of being unemployed converges over time to:

$$\lim_{\delta t \longrightarrow \infty} P_i(t + \delta t) = \left(\frac{\lambda_i}{\lambda_i + \mu_i}, \frac{\mu_i}{\lambda_i + \mu_i} \right) \tag{5}$$

In the long run, the person with rates λ_i and μ_i can be expected to be unemployed $\frac{\mu_i}{\lambda_i + \mu_i}$ of the time. We call this the individual's unemployment prevalence implied by the transition rates. This observation also means that we lose predictive information the longer we predict to the future.

4.2   Training Models

We train the models using the probabilities implied by the mathematical framework. The framework is defined in continuous time, but our data is recorded using one month granularity and we assume that there can be only one transition within a given month. If different months are coded as integers $t = 0, 1, \ldots$ and $\lambda_i(t)$ or $\mu_i(t)$ define the transition rates within that month, we have the probability of a transition [23]:

$$\begin{aligned} P(X_i(t) = 1 | X_i(t - 1) = 0) = 1 - \exp(-\lambda_i(t)) \\ P(X_i(t) = 0 | X_i(t - 1) = 1) = 1 - \exp(-\mu_i(t)) \end{aligned} \tag{6}$$

To fit the model, we think of each labour market history as a sequence of transitions between unemployment and employment as demonstrated in Fig. 2. Denote by $c_i(t) \in \{0, 1\}$ the observability status of a transition, with $c_i(t) = 1$ indicating that months t and $t - 1$ were observable for person i and $c_i(t) = 0$ when either was censored. The likelihood of the sequence can be split into two parts. First, the part when the previous observation month t is unemployed where $\mathbb{N}_{i,1} = \{t \in \mathbb{N} : x_i(t - 1) = 1, c_i(t) = 1\}$:

$$L_{\lambda_i}(x_i(t)) = \prod_{t \in \mathbb{N}_{i,1}} (1 - \exp(-\lambda_i(t)))^{\mathbb{I}(x_i(t)=0)} \exp(-\lambda_i(t))^{\mathbb{I}(x_i(t)=1)} \tag{7}$$

Second, the part when the previous observation month t is not unemployed where $\mathbb{N}_{i,0} = \{t \in \mathbb{N} : x_i(t - 1) = 0, c_i(t) = 1\}$:

$$L_{\mu_i}(x_i(t)) = \prod_{t \in \mathbb{N}_{i,0}} (1 - \exp(-\mu_i(t)))^{\mathbb{I}(x_i(t)=1)} \exp(-\mu_i(t))^{\mathbb{I}(x_i(t)=0)} \tag{8}$$

The likelihood of a person's labour market history is then:

$$L_{\lambda_i, \mu_i}(x_i(t)) = L_{\lambda_i}(x_i(t)) L_{\mu_i}(x_i(t)) \tag{9}$$

We still have to model the person specific transition rates $\lambda_i(t)$ and $\mu_i(t)$. We assume that the transitions are determined by observed characteristics (covariates), unobserved characteristics and randomness in finding or exiting a job. The observed characteristics influence the transition rates through a time-varying covariate vector $z_i(t)$ and a parameter vector α or β, depending on the transition. The unobserved characteristics are modelled by person-specific intercept

u_i or v_i, depending on the transition. For example, there could differences in the demand for the occupations, motivations in finding a job, personal issues, etc. We assume that the transition rates follow a proportional rates assumption. This is equivalent to the proportional hazards model in a survival analysis of a single spell with a subject-specific frailty term [24]. The model then defines the person specific transition rates:

$$\lambda_i(t) = \exp(\alpha^T z_i(t) + u_i)$$
$$\mu_i(t) = \exp(\beta^T z_i(t) + v_i)$$

(10)

Interestingly, the prevalence $P(X_i(t) = 1) = \frac{\mu_i}{\lambda_i + \mu_i}$ and time-invariant covariates z_i imply a logistic regression model of lifetime unemployment prevalence:

$$\frac{P(X_i(t) = 1)}{1 - P(X_i(t) = 1)} = \frac{\mu_i}{\lambda_i} = \exp((\beta - \alpha)^T z_i + (v_i - u_i))$$

(11)

In a statistical model, the covariates are known as fixed effects and the person specific intercepts are random effects. The model is therefore a two-state mixed effects model. To model the random effects, we assume that they follow a multivariate normal distribution $(u_i, v_i) \sim \text{Normal}(\gamma, \Sigma)$ with a 2×1 mean vector γ and a 2×2 covariance matrix Σ as unknown parameters. This allows a correlation between the unemployment entry and exit rates, since it is possible that persons who have a difficult time of finding employment might also find it difficult to remain employed. Given a data set $D = \{x_i(t)\}_{i=1,\dots,N}$, we define the unconditional data likelihood by integrating out the unknown random effects using the normal distribution density function $f_{\gamma, \Sigma}(u_i, v_i)$ [25]:

$$L_{\alpha, \beta, \gamma, \Sigma}(D) = \prod_{i=1,\dots,N} \int_{u_i, v_i} L_{\lambda_i, \mu_i}(x_i(t)) f_{\gamma, \Sigma}(u_i, v_i) du_i dv_i$$

(12)

The model is then fit by minimizing the negative log likelihood:

$$\text{argmin}_{\alpha, \beta, \gamma, \Sigma}[-\log(L_{\alpha, \beta, \gamma, \Sigma}(D))]$$

(13)

In a machine learning model, we assume that the person specific intercepts u_i or v_i are the elements of a model parameter vector u or v, just like α or β, and make the problem well-conditioned by regularization. This means that we fit the maximum likelihood with a penalty term which is multiplied by a constant C. We set the optimal constant with 10-fold cross-validation by splitting the training set into train and validation sets. However, as long as the solution is defined for $C > 0$, the evaluation was not sensitive to the choice of regularization and we report results for the default value of $C = 1$. We define the conditional data likelihood by assuming that the person specific rates are model parameters:

$$L_{\alpha, \beta, u, v}(D) = \prod_{i=1,\dots,N} L_{\lambda_i, \mu_i}(x_i(t))$$

(14)

The model is then fit by minimizing the penalized negative log likelihood:

$$\text{argmin}_{\alpha, \beta, u, v}[-\log(L_{\alpha, \beta, u, v}(D)) + C(\|\alpha\|^2 + \|\beta\|^2 + \|u\|^2 + \|v\|^2)]$$

(15)

The statistical model and the machine learning model result in surprisingly similar estimators. The person specific intercepts u_i and v_i, which make application of straightforward regression ill-conditioned, are 'shrunk' toward the population averages. The machine learning model is considerably faster to train and yields almost equivalent predictions, though it is not based on a statistical analysis of the problem in question.

5   Results

5.1   Prediction Tasks

There are three natural prediction tasks that our model answers:

1. Exit: Who has the highest risk of exiting unemployment?
2. Entry: Who has the highest risk of entering unemployment?
3. Prevalence: Who has the highest risk of being unemployed?

The model can used to predict the person specific exit and entry rates $\lambda_i(t)$ and $\mu_i(t)$. The first and the second answer are then given by the exit and entry probabilities in formula 6. The third answer corresponds to the lifetime unemployment of a person, which is the prevalence probability in formula 5. However, we can do even better if the last known state is u and the prediction is δt months to the future. We then use the transition probabilities in formula 4. Note that all these probabilities are implied by the same model.

We evaluate the model with a straightforward train and test set split. We investigate two different types of test sets, as plotted in the Fig. 2:

1. Predict to the future: we train the model using 10000 persons in years 2013–2016 and take the year 2017 as the test set. We predict for the persons present in the training set, but require predictions for a future time.
2. Predict to new persons: we train the model using the 10000 persons in 2013–2016, and take another set of 10000 persons that the model has not seen and predict for them over the observation period 2013–2017.

The Receiver Operating Characteristic (ROC) curve illustrates the diagnostic ability of a binary classifier for different threshold values. We use the Area Under the ROC Curve (AUC) to evaluate the model performance. This is the probability that the model ranks a randomly chosen positive example higher than a randomly chosen negative example. For example, assume that the task is to predict who has the highest risk of escaping unemployment. We compute separately for every month in how many of the pairs where one person escaped unemployment and one did not, the exit rate prediction for the one who escaped was higher.

5.2 Predictive Accuracy

In Table 2 we present the time-stratified AUC of three different models, measured separately in the training set and the two tests sets. The Linear Model (LM) includes only the covariates but not the subject specific intercepts, the Linear Mixed Effects (LME) model is the statistical model, and Linear Machine Learning (LML) model is the machine learning version. We evaluate them on the three different prediction tasks: predict the risk of unemployment exit (Exit), unemployment entry (Entry) and the unemployment prevalence (Prevalence). The training set (Train) consists of years 2013–2016 with a sample of 10000 persons. The first test set (Test) consists of the year 2017 on the same persons, and the cold start test set (Cold) contains the years 2013–2017 for a different data set of 10000 persons.

Table 2. Time-Stratified AUCs of the models, evaluated in three different prediction tasks in one train and two test sets.

Model	Linear			Mixed effects			Machine learning		
	Train	Test	Cold	Train	Test	Cold	Train	Test	Cold
Exit	0.65	0.63	0.64	0.79	0.67	0.64	0.81	0.67	0.64
Entry	0.56	0.59	0.56	0.70	0.68	0.56	0.74	0.69	0.56
Prevalence	0.64	0.64	0.64	0.81	0.78	0.64	0.83	0.80	0.64

We make the following observations. First, the cold start prediction performance $(0.64, 0.56, 0.64)$ is the same for all of the three models. This is not suprising, since the LME and LML models are not able to learn the person specific intercepts for persons they have not seen. The rate prediction is based on the covariates only; the prediction formulas of these linear models are identical without the person specific intercepts and the learned parameters are very close to each other. The overall prediction performance is modest when we are forced to rely on the covarites only, but it is significantly better than random.

Second, the future test set predictions are improved significantly by using the LME and LML models $(0.63 \rightarrow 0.67, 0.59 \rightarrow 0.69, 0.64 \rightarrow 0.80)$ that include the person specific intercept. Part of this improvement could captured by including more detailed covariates in the model, but some part of it probably represents the person's characteristics that are difficult to measure. It is therefore useful to utilize the labour market histories with models that exploit this information. While predicting the exact timing of the transitions is still difficult $(0.67, 0.69)$, the overall unemployment prevalence can be predicted quite well (0.80) from the machine learning model.

Third, the training set provides overoptimistic performance measures in the LME and LML models that have a larger flexibility to fit the training set. This is probably due to the fact that the actual transitions to be predicted belong to training set. The differences on transition rates in the training set imply that we actually know to some extent who had a transition and who did not, and this is reflected in the prediction accuracy.

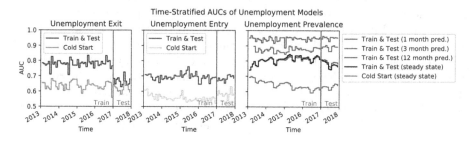

Fig. 3. Time-Stratified AUCs plotted separately for each month and prediction task.

Next we analyze the predictive performance over time, and whether the Markov Chain assumption enables even better predictions of who is unemployed at a given time. In Fig. 3, we report the LME model performance separately for every month. The predictive performance seems stable over time for unemployment exit and entry, taking into account that predicting unseen unemployment exists in the test set is considerably harder. The difficulty of predicting unemployment prevalence seems to correlate with the unemployment rate. When unemployment is high in general, the task is easier for the model that includes the person specific effects and more difficult for the model that doesn't.

In the unemployment prevalence plot, we included predictions that utilize the mathematical properties of the Markov Chain. We assume that we know the state 1, 3, or 12 months ago and use the transition probability matrix to calculate predictions for the future state. If one knows the past unemployment status, the task of predicting unemployment clearly becomes easier: it is very easy 1 month forward with AUCs in the range of 0.95, quite easy 3 months forward with AUCs up to 0.90, and rapidly more difficult with 12 months forward with AUCs of 0.80 being almost the same as the prevalence prediction performance.

5.3   Model Interpretation

The linear models can be used to interpret the results. Every prediction is based on two sources of information: person's covariates (gender, work experience, age, level of education, field of education) and the person's labour market history. Some part of the person specific unemployment entry and exit rates are explained by the covariates and the rest can be inferred from the labour market history.

First we interpret the effect of covariates. We used the contrast sum coding when fitting the LME model, so that within a categorical covariate the parameters are constrained to sum to zero. Each parameter then estimates the risk of the covariate value, relative to the average of all values. We have plotted $\exp(\alpha)$, $\exp(\beta)$ and the implied prevalence $\exp(\alpha - \beta)$ on a logarithmic scale in Fig. 4.

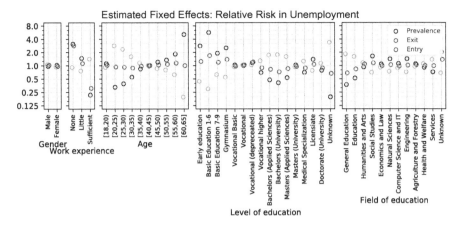

Fig. 4. Model parameters $\exp(\alpha)$, $\exp(\beta)$, $\exp(\beta - \alpha)$ corresponding to covariates $z_i(t)$.

For example, having age in the bucket $[55,60)$ is predicted to result in two times the unemployment prevalence relative to the baseline.

It seems that gender is not a significant predictor. Having no work experience results in significantly higher unemployment entry and sufficient experience in significantly lower entry. The effect on unemployment exit is smaller, with experienced workers exiting faster. The result on unemployment prevalence is drastic: having no work experience predicts almost four times, whereas sufficient work experience predicts under a fourth, of the baseline. Younger adults have significantly better chances, and the persons close to retirement have significantly worse chances, of exiting unemployment. There is a slightly higher entry risk for both young and old people. As a result, the unemployment prevalence raises almost linearly with age and the effect for old or young people is again almost four times greater or smaller. Education is a reasonable predictor, where people with little education have higher prevalence because of both lower unemployment exit and higher entry, and people with higher education have significantly lower prevalence due to both higher exit and lower entry. The field of education is another reasonable predictor, with the person's degree implying a somewhat higher or lower exit rate from unemployment. These findings account for some of the differences in predicted transition rates.

Another component is the subject specific random effect, which we can predict from the model. We plot the pairs $\exp(u_i)$, $\exp(v_i)$ in Fig. 5. The estimated normally distributed random effects show some skewness and a significant negative correlation: a person with a higher unemployment exit rate tends to have a lower unemployment entry rate. The normal distribution mean vector is $\gamma = (-2.85, -1.79)$, and the estimated covariance matrix Σ implies a standard deviation 0.41 of the entry rate and 0.86 of the exit rate, with a correlation of -0.71. There is significant variation left between individuals even after accounting for their covariates.

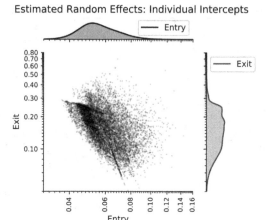

Fig. 5. Predicted random effects $\exp(u_i)$ and $\exp(v_i)$.

6   Conclusion

In this study, we developed a model to predict the labour market state of a person. Our main focus was on prediction and we evaluated the model on three different prediction tasks: predict the risk of escaping unemployment, the risk of becoming unemployed, and the risk of being unemployed at any given time.

We used a Markov chain model with person specific transition rates. The transition rates were predicted by fitting three linear models to an unemployment registry: the simple linear model, the linear mixed effects model, and the linear machine learning model. We evaluated the models using time-stratified AUC on two test sets; one in the future and the second with unseen persons in the cold start setting. The person specific Markov chain assumption improves predictions significantly. The cold start problem is the hardest because one cannot use person history, and the models have a modest performance. On the other hand, predicting to the future for known persons is easier. It is still difficult to predict the exact timing of unemployment entry and exit, but we obtained good performance for the machine learning model of lifetime unemployment. Very good performance could be obtained to the near future given the last known state. The statistical model and the machine learning model result in similar predictions. The covariates have intuitive effects that are consistent with previous findings in the literature, but there is still considerable heterogeneity in the unemployment histories that can be used to improve predictions.

Our study has its own challenges and possibilities for future research. While registry data has many advantages, it is not necessarily reflective of the entire population in a given area. We investigated these biases in the appendix. Additional research could improve the predictive performance we have obtained with more detailed person information and non-linear models. Machine learning has many models for high-dimensional data and non-linear relationships, but it would be useful to work with more detailed person level information to fully exploit their potential.

Appendix

Unemployment registry data has a number of potential biases if we want to generalize the results to the entire population. In that case, the training set should contain all 18 to 64 year olds currently residing in Varsinais-Suomi with their recurrent unemployment and employment spells. However, the unemployment registry is sampled monthly and contains only people who have been jobseekers at least once during the sampling.

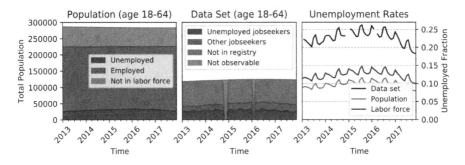

Fig. 6. Registry data set compared to the full population in Varsinais-Suomi.

The Data Set Includes Only People Who Have Been Unemployed

Persons who have not been job seekers during 2013 to 2017 in the unemployment agencies are missing from the original data set because they do not have a registry entry. This is the case for people who have not been unemployed. We compared the data set to the official yearly statistics in Fig. 6, where we find that about 50% of the labour force in Varsinais-Suomi is missing. The unemployment exit rate is not biased, because every unemployed person is included. However, the baseline unemployment entry rate and prevalence are too high, because many people who are never unemployed are missing as negative examples. In other words, by definition we are analyzing unemployment among all people who experience unemployment at least once during the follow-up period.

It is still possible to estimate the true person specific rates from model predictions. Assume that the true unemployment entry rate is μ_i and the exit rate is λ_i for person i. Denote the length of a 'not unemployed' spell as T and the length of follow-up as t. The probability of missing from the data corresponds to probability of starting outside unemployment and remaining at that state the entire time: $P(\{X_i(t) = 0\}_{t=0,1,...}) = P(X_i(0) = 0)P(T > t)$. The data contains all of the 'unemployed' observations $P(X_i(t) = 1) = \frac{\mu_i}{\lambda_i + \mu_i}$ but the proportion of 'not unemployed' observations included is only $P(X_i(t) = 0) - P(\{X_i(t) = 1\}_{t=0,1,\dots}) = P(X_i(0) = 0)P(T \leq t) = \frac{\lambda_i}{\lambda_i + \mu_i}(1 - e^{\mu_i t})$. Denote the observed odds of unemployment $\frac{\mu_i^*}{\lambda_i}$, which should be equal to the odds $P(X_i(t) = 1)/P(X_i(t) = 0)P(T \leq t) = \frac{\mu_i}{\lambda_i(1 - e^{-\mu_i t})}$. This means we can solve:

$$\frac{\mu_i}{1 - e^{-\mu_i t}} = \mu_i^* \tag{16}$$

We then obtain the true rate μ_i that produces the observed unemployment entry rate μ_i^*. With increasing follow-up $t \longrightarrow \infty$ we gather all samples.

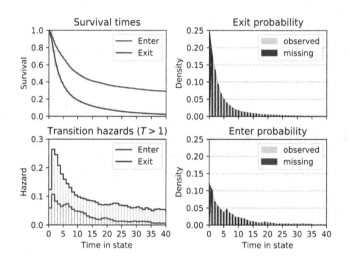

Fig. 7. Survival functions, hazards and probability densities of the unemployment (exit) and non-unemployment (enter) spell lengths, estimated from the first spell.

The Data Set Excludes Some Short Spells

Spells shorter than one calendar month are undersampled because the registry status is recorded monthly. Such persons may enter and exit unemployment in between monthly measurements without being recorded. We estimate how many percent of spells are missing by calculating the Kaplan-Meier estimate $S(t) = P(T > t)$ of the first spell length T in Fig. 7. The second month hazard can be used to estimate the true first month hazard, as shown in the bottom left figure. For example, assuming that first month hazards should be 0.25/month (exit) and 0.12/month (entry), the percentage of spells that end in the first month should be $1 - e^{-0.25} \approx 22\%$ (exit) and $1 - e^{-0.12} \approx 11\%$ (entry) instead of the $1 - e^{-0.12} \approx 11\%$ (exit) and $1 - e^{(} - 0.06) \approx 6\%$ (entry) that were observed. These spells are a small subset of the data set, and short spells do not meaningfully contribute to the total amount of unemployment

The Data Set Includes Some People Who have a Moved Out

Finally, we have no knowledge of who remain or move out of the Varsinais-Suomi area. The data set may include persons who have moved out and are not at risk of being recorded in the unemployment registry. This bias can be estimated with a simple Monte Carlo simulation. From the government movement statistics in the years 2013-2017 (StatFin) we can calculate the migration rates within Finland. Each year on average 2.1% of the Varsinais-Suomi population moved into other economic areas, and 0.21% of the population in other areas moved into Varsinais-Suomi. We assume that the migration of people follows a Markov chain with the corresponding monthly transition probabilities. We then overlay the movement patterns generated from this Markov Chain into the data set as seen in the left of Fig. 8, and calculate the percentage of people that are outside Varsinais-Suomi each month in the right of Fig. 8. This implies that about 6% of the samples at each time were probably outside Varsinais-Suomi.

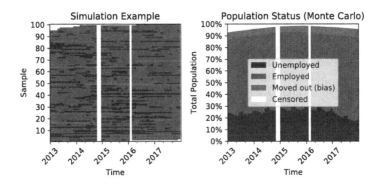

Fig. 8. The real world moving out bias is estimated with a monte carlo simulation.

References

1. Ernst, E., Rani, U.: Understanding unemployment flows. Oxford Rev. Econ. Pol. **27**(2), 268–294 (2011)
2. Shimer, R.: Reassessing the ins and outs of unemployment. Rev. Econ. Dyn. **15**(2), 127–148 (2012)
3. Ahn, H.J., Hamilton, J.D.: Heterogeneity and unemployment dynamics. J. Bus. Econ. Stat. 1–26 (2019)
4. Honkanen, P.: Odotelaskelmat työllisyyden, työttömyyden ja eläkeajan arvioinnissa. KELA Working Papers, No. 137 (2018)
5. Pedersen, P.J., Westergård-Nielsen, N.C.: Unemployment. A review of the evidence from panel data. In: Economics of Unemployment. Edward Elgar Publishing (2000)
6. Wanberg, C.R.: The individual experience of unemployment. Ann. Rev. Psychol. **63**, 369–396 (2012)

7. Kettunen, J.: Education and unemployment duration. Econ. Educ. Rev. **16**(2), 163–170 (1997)
8. Ollikainen, V.: The determinants of unemployment duration by gender in Finland. VATT Discussion Papers, No. 316 (2003)
9. Kyyrä, T.: Partial unemployment insurance benefits and the transition rate to regular work. Eur. Econ. Rev. **54**(7), 911–930 (2010)
10. Rokkanen, M., Uusitalo, R.: Changes in job stability: evidence from lifetime job histories. IZA Discussion Papers, No. 4721 (2010)
11. Asplund, R.: Unemployment among finnish manufacturing workers. Who gets unemployed and from where? ETLA Discussion Papers, No. 711 (2000)
12. Eriksson, T., Pehkonen, J.: Unemployment flows in Finland, 1969–95: a time series analysis. Labour **12**(3), 571–593 (1998)
13. Peltola, M.: Työmarkkinasiirtymät Suomessa. Työllisyyden päättymisen jälkeinen työmarkkinasiirtymien dynamiikka vuosina 1995–1999. VATT Discussion Papers, No. 360 (2005)
14. Heckman, J.J., Borjas, G.J.: Does unemployment cause future unemployment? Definitions, questions and answers from a continuous time model of heterogeneity and state dependence. Economica **47**(187), 247–283 (1980)
15. Flinn, C.J., Heckman, J.J.: New methods for analyzing individual event histories. Sociol. Methodol. **13**, 99–140 (1982)
16. Mühleisen, M., Zimmermann, K.F.: A panel analysis of job changes and unemployment. Eur. Econ. Rev. **38**(3–4), 793–801 (1994)
17. D'Amuri, F., Marcucci, J.: The predictive power of Google searches in forecasting US unemployment. Int. J. Forecast. **33**(4), 801–816 (2017)
18. Tuhkuri, J.: ETLAnow: a model for forecasting with big data-forecasting unemployment with Google searches in Europe. No. 54. ETLA Report (2016)
19. Katris, C.: Prediction of unemployment rates with time series and machine learning techniques. Comput. Econ. **55**, 673–706 (2019). https://doi.org/10.1007/s10614-019-09908-9
20. de Troya, Í.M.R., et al.: Predicting, explaining and understanding risk of long-term unemployment. In: 32nd Conference on Neural Information Processing Systems (2018)
21. Kütük, Y., Güloğlu, B.: Prediction of transition probabilities from unemployment to employment for Turkey via machine learning and econometrics: a comparative study. J. Res. Econ. **3**(1), 58–75 (2019)
22. Beyersmann, J., Allignol, A., Schumacher, M.: Competing Risks and Multistate Models with R. Springer, Heidelberg (2011). https://doi.org/10.1007/978-1-4614-2035-4
23. Tutz, G., Schmid, M.: Modeling Discrete Time-to-Event Data. Springer, Cham (2016). https://doi.org/10.1007/978-3-319-28158-2
24. Duchateau, L., Janssen, P.: The Frailty Model. Springer, Heidelberg (2007). https://doi.org/10.1007/978-0-387-72835-3
25. Cook, R.J., Lawless, J.: The Statistical Analysis of Recurrent Events. Springer, Heidelberg (2007). https://doi.org/10.1007/978-0-387-69810-6
26. Rausand, M., Høyland, A.: System Reliability Theory: Models, Statistical Methods, and Applications, vol. 396. Wiley, Hoboken (2003)

Anomaly Detection on Data Streams
– A LSTM's Diary

Christoph Augenstein[1]([⊠]) and Bogdan Franczyk[2]

[1] Information Systems Institute, Leipzig University, Grimmaische Strasse 12, Leipzig, Germany
augenstein@wifa.uni-leipzig.de
[2] Wroclaw University of Economics, ul. Komandorska 118/120, Wroclaw, Poland
franczyk@wifa.uni-leipzig.de

Abstract. In the past years, the importance of processing data streams increased with the emergence of new technologies and application domains. The Internet of Things provides many examples, in which processing and analyzing data streams are critical success factors. An important use case is to identify anomalies, i.e. something that is different or unexpected. We often have to cope with anomaly detection use cases in sequences within data streams, for instance in network intrusion, in predictive analytics or in forecasting.

Sequence analysis can be performed using recurrent neural nets and in particular, we use long short-term memory (LSTM) neural nets. An LSTM is not only capable of storing a sequence of data but also of deciding to forget certain parts of it. Unfortunately, the internal representation of learned data does not clearly illustrate what was learned. Moreover, like many neural net-based approaches, these nets tend to need a high volume of data in order to produce valuable insights.

In this paper, we want to present an experimental setting, comprising an architecture, a structured way of producing sample data and end-to-end pipelines to store and evaluate the hidden state of a LSTM per training batch. Main purpose is to extract the hidden state as well as to analyze changes during training and thus to identify patterns in the hidden state as well as anomalies.

Keywords: Machine learning · Neural nets · Sequence analysis · Anomaly detection

1 Introduction

Threats, anomalies and outliers are growing challenges for almost all companies. Since they occur in every corner of operations, like in their sensor and computer networks, or in business processes, companies have to be aware of intrusions and other abnormal or malicious activities on many different levels. According to the Oxford dictionary, anomalies are deviations from what is regarded as normal, or more specifically, describe events or measurements that are extraordinary, whether they are exceptional or not [14]. In data mining, the term describes data objects that are not compliant with the general behavior or model of the data [7].

© Springer Nature Switzerland AG 2020
F. Dalpiaz et al. (Eds.): RCIS 2020, LNBIP 385, pp. 369–377, 2020.
https://doi.org/10.1007/978-3-030-50316-1_22

In [1] we developed a multipurpose architecture for identifying anomalies in data streams based on Docker and Kubernetes. The goal was to identify and build common components that are reusable for a given task in preprocessing, model building and training or for model deployment and inferencing. Aside from preprocessing, feature engineering and model building are the most challenging tasks. For instance, detecting threats in computer networks, i.e. network intrusion detection, leads us to gather data from network interfaces (i.e. a data stream) and process them to a set of sequences of explainable features (e.g. source/target ports, addresses, flags, etc.).

Recurrent neural nets and especially long short-term memories (LSTM) are capable of analyzing such sequences. In fact, many newer approaches for intrusion detection or similar tasks tend to use LSTM-based architectures (cf. Sect. 2). Dependent on the effectiveness of the modeled sequences, these nets have a good accuracy and perform well. However, the explanatory power of a trained net is only as good as we can derive information from the made predictions, i.e. we can understand why a net made a certain prediction. For instance, we can easily measure the effectiveness of a LSTM using accuracy, f-score or something similar but the decision of the net is somehow blurred in terms of the internal state of the net (especially the hidden units). To be able to identify anomalies in data streams precisely, we want to understand the prediction and classifications of the nets we use in our use cases better. Therefore, the research questions are: *(1) Does the hidden state reflect patterns from input data, i.e. what (exactly) is in the hidden state and (2) are we able to extract learned representations from the hidden state and use it to get a better understanding for anomalies?*

In this setting, we want to enhance our existing anomaly detection in that we want to reuse architecture and components to analyze the hidden state of neural nets and of LSTMs in particular. Our goal is to derive insights into the training process and especially in the changes of the hidden state. Reasons for this are twofold. On the one hand, we can analyze the features and patterns a LSTM builds during training and consequently improve our anomaly detection. On the other hand, and based on the first, we might be able to reduce amount of training data by carefully selecting data that mostly influences the training process (similar to active learning [4]). In this paper, we want to present the overall process of our experiment, a brief description of the components, and the method to train and analyze a LSTM. Hence, the next Sect. 2 contains a short introduction to LSTMs and related work. In Sect. 3, we then present the experimental setting, components and the process of gathering and analyzing data. In Sect. 4, we will conclude the paper with actual findings and the next steps.

2 Related Work

This section contains background information on neural nets and LSTMs respectively. In addition, we will handle autoencoder approaches, a special form of neural nets that are capable of building their own feature representation through dimensionality reduction. Finally, we will cope with approaches, which want to solve the problem of analyzing the hidden state of neural nets. Due to the lack of space, we will only provide prominent examples and will not present every aspect in detail.

In accordance with the exploding advances in the machine learning and artificial intelligence area, a recent trend for anomaly detection is to use deep learning methods to model normal behavior and search for anomalies in data. Neural nets outperform other machine learning approaches in several fashions. For instance, a simple feed-forward net, is capable of identifying non-linear relationships in a dataset [19]. Deeper nets with many hidden layers are even more powerful [11]. Another interesting feature, relevant for anomaly detection, is the so called "course of dimensionality" [6], at which deep learning can tackle high dimensional data much better than other algorithms.

Neural nets described above are usually so called feed-forward nets, i.e. data flows from input to output without loops or backward flows. This implies that these nets have no capability to store information about the history or context in general. However, to analyze sequences it is important that nets have this capability. Hence, recurrent nets were developed. Based on the de-facto standard backpropagation for updating the internal state, recurrent nets had another problem: vanishing or exploding gradients [2], i.e. weights change dramatically between training steps potentially leading to unstable net states. The solution to this kind of problem were so called gated nets like a LSTM [9], which at least succeed in the vanishing gradient problem.

Solving the problem of anomaly detection in data streams, we need a neural net that is capable of filtering data and extracting relevant features. Autoencoders [8] succeed in a comparable task: reducing dimensionality of data and thereby learning a simplified encoding of the data. Specifically in the field of anomaly detection, there are plenty of examples using autoencoders like [12] and [5] (network intrusion detection), [26] (deep auto encoders for feature engineering), [18] (anomalies in videos) or [16] (fraud detection). Finally, [13] present an autoencoder approach that works without prior knowledge about considered processes and anomalies to classify business events. The task of filtering explainable features can significantly be improved using kernel filters from convolutional neural nets. Depending on the dimension of input data, one or two-dimensional convolutions are acceptable. An approach that uses such a CNN-RNN combination is [3]. The CNN part therefore amplifies features in the data stream and thus supports the RNN in choosing the relevant information.

The task now remains how to extract or to explicate the trained feature representation in order to learn from the net or at least to understand the inherent connections in the data found by the trained net. As humans are not good in handling complex relationships in mere numbers, many approaches use visualization techniques. This is especially true and widely used for convolutional neural nets to understand object identification or segmentation tasks performed on pictures by these nets (e.g. [24, 25]). Similar but more general is the approach of [22]. They try to visualize changes in the different layers in terms of weight changes. If the net is small enough, this could be a promising way to extract such information. However, all the presented approaches so far handle feed-forward nets only. Fortunately, for recurrent nets and especially for LSTM there also approaches visualizing the hidden states. For instance, [21] present a complex toolset that highlights hidden states in comparison to selected words. Moreover, they present a stakeholder driven analysis, in that they developed different views dependent on the stakeholder's perspective. Another word based approach is [20]. In contrast to the former, they focus on a comparison of probabilistic distributions between the hidden state and the output, trying to visualize the predictive power. Finally, [15] use a LSTM in the field of action recognition. In their approach, they actively manipulate input data with activation maximization method and proceed with a sensitivity analysis of the resulting changes in the hidden state and with a comparison of the resulting skeleton model. Based on this background and with ideas from related work, we want to present first steps towards mapping input and hidden state as well as extracting learned feature representations from the hidden state.

3   Experiment

The basic setting for our experiment is derived from our architecture presented in [1]. We intensively use the interactive tooling based on Jupyter notebooks, the model server and of course the preprocessing components. The experiment we conduct is split up into two parts: At first, we use our architectural solution and build a pipeline for gathering necessary data and secondly we use architectural components in order to build a pipeline to process data and derive insights.

3.1   Data Gathering

To be able to analyze the hidden state of a LSTM and the learned feature representation, we chose to construct a simple autoencoder model based on two LSTM layers, a repeat vector and a time distributed dense output to predict elements of a given sequence. We use this simplified architecture to especially focus on a plain vanilla LSTM cell. The aforementioned CNN-RNN combinations will be introduced in later versions of the experiment. With this setup, we can feed specific data into the encoder part of the net, let it learn a feature representation and with the help of the decoder part, we can assure that it correctly learned provided data. Figure 1 shows the initial configuration.

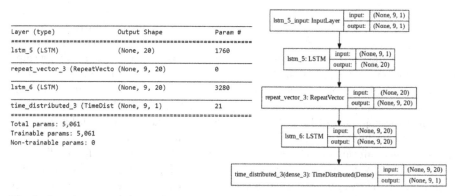

Fig. 1. Sample autoencoder configuration (Keras implementation), optimizer: adam, loss: mse

We use widespread and proven optimizer and loss functions to start with in our experiment. In a latter version of the experiment, we might change these. We feed a fixed-length Fibonacci sequence of length nine into the autoencoder and provide both LSTMs with 20 hidden units (encoder and decoder always have same amount). In the first version of this experiment, we try to restrict the number of neurons in contrast to Sect. 2 for the following reasons. If the autoencoder succeeds in its job and is capable of learning the sequence, we belief that with fewer neurons it is easier for us to detect relevant patterns in the hidden state and the search is even better manageable. In addition, a smaller number of neurons tend to generalize better and the risk of overfitting can be reduced [23]. In the end, the number of neurons used has to be adapted to the task of generating a representation of a Fibonacci sequence (cf. Sect. 4).

During training (300 epochs in the example above), a pipeline processes the autoencoder configuration and especially the contained weights and stores them away and put them into an InfluxDB for further processing. With the Keras implementation, it is easy to get the trained weights per layer from the neural net. The calculation of the respective gates at a given point in time t is:

$$\text{Forget gate: } f_t = \sigma(W_f x_t + U_f h_{t-1} + b_f) \tag{1}$$

$$\text{Input gate : } i_t = \sigma(W_i x_t + U_i h_{t-1} + b_i) \tag{2}$$

$$\text{Output gate : } o_t = \sigma(W_o x_t + U_o h_{t-1} + b_o) \tag{3}$$

$$\text{Cell state : } c_t = f_t \bigcirc c_{t-1} + i_t \bigcirc \sigma(W_c x_t + U_c h_{t-1} + b_c) \tag{4}$$

$$\text{Output : } h_t = o_t \bigcirc \sigma_h(c_t) \tag{5}$$

Each training is carried out ten times to gather relevant data. In addition, and to get more data, we either change the amount of hidden units or the specific Fibonacci sequence (i.e. we do not always use the first nine numbers) or both after a full training job and test if autoencoder predicts well. For the latter analysis, we store the different matrices (data) along with the following metadata: the input sequence, number of hidden units, number of epochs and the output sequence from the prediction.

3.2 Data Analysis

We build a second pipeline to do the analysis of the gathered data. At first, we take each training series from the database and test the prediction result. A prediction is correct if the deviation between sequence number and corresponding prediction is within a given range. Another possibility would be to sum up two consecutive numbers and see if the result is the next sequence number. A third possibility is to test, whether a number divided by its predecessor in the sequence produces a value nearby the golden ratio. All three approaches are still focal point of interest. With deviation and summation, we have to cope with the fact that we need to adjust boundaries with increasing sequence numbers. Calculation of the golden ratio also has its drawback as the calculation on the original sequence only converges with higher sequence numbers. In that case, we might also test, whether golden ratio of the original and of the prediction are within a given range.

For an initial analysis, we only use results that passed this first test. Further analysis is done with the help of principal component analysis (PCA, cf. [8, 21]). In contrast to [5] we do not analyze the input data with the help of PCA, but we want to identify the most prominent hidden units for a given sequence and try to find patterns in the training process. Especially, we are interested in finding state activation patterns and their change during the training process. From the related work (cf. [21, 22, 25]) we start the experiment using heatmaps as a visualization. We build them using the results of the PCA with a coloring inferred from the discriminative power. We belief that this might lead us to identify possible patterns in the state activation. The overall process is shown in Fig. 2.

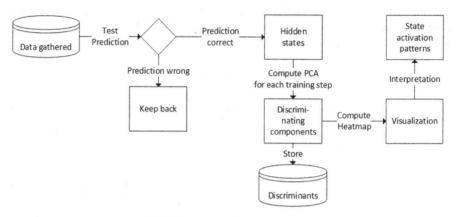

Fig. 2. Data analysis process

As we built our architecture based on Docker and Kubernetes, we can benefit from parallelization in that we, for instance compute the PCA per training step in paral-lel through multiple instances of a PCA Docker container. Thus, we can speed up experimental process and quickly gain insights.

4   Findings and Next Steps

At current stage, we are in the phase of building pipelines and commencing first interactive tests with the autoencoder. From this state, we can draw preliminary findings:

- A fixed-length Fibonacci sequence (e.g. 1, 1, ... , 34) needs significantly more hidden units per LSTM than a fixed-length range sequence (e.g. 1, 2, ... , 10) to correctly reproduce or predict the sequence.
- A Fibonacci sequence of higher numbers (e.g. 10th–19th) requires significantly more hidden units than a sequence of lower numbers (e.g. 0th–9th), i.e. the size of numbers correlates with memory capacity.
- A Fibonacci sequence with higher numbers should be trained longer (more epochs) to produce acceptable prediction results.
- The more hidden units, the less training time can be used, but this can also be due to overfitting (cf. [23]), i.e. needs further investigation.

This already provides valuable information to our first research question of the content of the hidden states in a LSTM. Complexity or rather size of input (number of digits) matters and also the kind of input pattern. If the autoencoder, similar to feed-forward nets, produced a function approximation (cf. [10]) the higher resource requirements could be derived from the irrational components in the approximate solution (cf. Binet's formula). However, at this point this too speculative and needs further investigation. Our focus is on building an autoencoder with a minimal set of neurons that succeeds in the job but allows us to analyze the hidden states efficiently. The fewer neurons the better we might be able to identify changes in activation patterns per neuron and thus get insights into the way a LSTM stores and changes information during learning. If we managed to identify most prominent features this way, we would also be able to provide data sets that are more effective in terms of specifically selected features and thus reduce the total amount of data needed.

Latter versions of the experiment will significantly change the autoencoder's architecture. Especially, we want to overcome the limitation of fixed-length input of autoencoders using concepts like attention [17] and beyond that want to get a better understanding of the relationship between inputs and the internal feature representation. The attention concept seems to be a promising and already tested way to achieve this. Another variant might be the combination of CNN and RNN to amplify features. We managed to test this combination already in another use case and could improve a classification task significantly. Point of origin for our research yet had to be a simple and a primordial implementation to analyze the hidden units without side effects from other techniques.

Next steps involve finding optimal parameters for the number of hidden units and training epochs especially for sequences with higher Fibonacci numbers to avoid overfitting of the net. In parallel, we build the pipelines to store and analyze hidden states of the encoding LSTM. Therefore, we need to build Docker containers with source code of the autoencoder for automation. Further, we build a container for the PCA analysis based on the scikit-learn package. To store and load we already have the InfluxDB and only need to configure this for the specific job.

Acknowledgements. The work presented in this paper is partly funded by the European Social Fund (ESF) and the Free State of Saxony (Sächsische Aufbaubank - SAB).

References

1. Augenstein, C., Spangenberg, N., Franczyk, B.: An architectural blueprint for a multi-purpose anomaly detection on data streams. In: Filipe, J. (ed.) Proceedings of the 21st International Conference on Enterprise Information Systems: ICEIS 2019, vol. 2 [S. l.], pp. 470–476. SciTePress (2019)
2. Bengio, Y., Simard, P., Frasconi, P.: Learning long-term dependencies with gradient descent is difficult. IEEE Trans. Neural Netw. **5**(2), 157–166 (1994). https://doi.org/10.1109/72.279181
3. Canizo, M., Triguero, I., Conde, A., et al.: Multi-head CNN–RNN for multi-time series anomaly detection: An industrial case study. Neurocomputing **363**, 246–260 (2019). https://doi.org/10.1016/j.neucom.2019.07.034
4. Cohn, D., Atlas, L., Ladner, R.: Improving generalization with active learning. Mach. Learn. **15**(2), 201–221 (1994). https://doi.org/10.1007/BF00993277

5. Gao, Z.S., Su, Y., Ding, Y., Liu, Y.D., Wang, X.A., Shen, J.W.: Key technologies of anomaly detection using PCA-LSTM. In: Barolli, L., Xhafa, F., Hussain, O.K. (eds.) IMIS 2019. AISC, vol. 994, pp. 246–254. Springer, Cham (2020). https://doi.org/10.1007/978-3-030-22263-5_24
6. Goodfellow, I., Bengio, Y., Courville, A.: Deep Learning. MIT Press, Cambridge (2016)
7. Han, J., Pei, J., Kamber, M.: Data Mining: Concepts and Techniques. Elsevier, Amsterdam (2011)
8. Hinton, G.E., Salakhutdinov, R.R.: Reducing the dimensionality of data with neural networks. Science 313(5786), 504–507 (2006). https://doi.org/10.1126/science.1127647
9. Hochreiter, S., Schmidhuber, J.: Long short-term memory. Neural Comput. 9(8), 1735–1780 (1997). https://doi.org/10.1162/neco.1997.9.8.1735
10. Jones, R.D., Lee, Y.C., Barnes, C.W., et al.: Function approximation and time series prediction with neural networks. In: Proceedings of 1990 IJCNN International Joint Conference on Neural Networks, vol. 1, pp. 649–665. IEEE (1990)
11. LeCun, Y., Bengio, Y., Hinton, G.: Deep learning. Nature 521(7553), 436–444 (2015). https://doi.org/10.1038/nature14539
12. Mirza, A.H., Cosan, S.: Computer network intrusion detection using sequential LSTM Neural Networks autoencoders. In: Proceedings of the 2018, 26th IEEE Signal Processing and Communications Applications Conference, May 2018, pp 1–4. IEEE, Piscataway (2018). 26. IEEE Sinyal İşleme ve İletişim Uygulamaları Kurultayı. 2-5 Mayıs, Altın Yunus Resort ve Thermal Hotel, Çesme - Izmir
13. Nolle, T., Luettgen, S., Seeliger, A., et al.: Analyzing business process anomalies using autoencoders. Mach. Learn. 107(11), 1875–1893 (2018)
14. Oxford Dictionaries: Anomaly (2019). https://en.oxforddictionaries.com/definition/anomaly Accessed 23 Jan 2019
15. Patil, D., Draper, B.A., Beveridge, J.R.: Looking under the hood: visualizing what LSTMs learn. In: Karray, F., Campilho, A., Yu, A. (eds.) ICIAR 2019. LNCS, vol. 11663, pp. 67–80. Springer, Cham (2019). https://doi.org/10.1007/978-3-030-27272-2_6
16. Paula, E., Ladeira, M., Carvalho, R., et al.: Deep learning anomaly detection as support fraud investigation in Brazilian exports and anti-money laundering. In: Proceedings of the 15th IEEE International Conference on Machine Learning and Applications, pp. 954–960, Anaheim, California, 18–20 December 2016. IEEE (2016)
17. Pereira, J., Silveira, M.: Unsupervised anomaly detection in energy time series data using variational recurrent autoencoders with attention. In: Wani, M.A. (ed.) Proceedings of the 17th IEEE International Conference on Machine Learning and Applications: ICMLA 2018, pp. 1275–1282, Orlando, Florida, USA, 17–20 December 2018. IEEE Computer Society, Conference Publishing Services, Los Alamitos (2018)
18. Revathi, A.R., Kumar, D.: An efficient system for anomaly detection using deep learning classifier. SIViP 11(2), 291–299 (2017). https://doi.org/10.1007/s11760-016-0935-0
19. Sadegh, N.: A perceptron network for functional identification and control of nonlinear systems. IEEE Trans. Neural Netw. 4(6), 982–988 (1993). https://doi.org/10.1109/72.286893
20. Sawatzky, L., Bergner, S., Popowich, F.: Visualizing RNN states with predictive semantic encodings. In: Proceedings of the 2019 IEEE Visualization Conference (VIS), pp. 156–160. IEEE (2019)
21. Strobelt, H., Gehrmann, S., Pfister, H., et al.: LSTMVis: a tool for visual analysis of hidden state dynamics in recurrent neural networks. IEEE Trans. Vis. Comput. Graph. 24(1), 667–676 (2018). https://doi.org/10.1109/TVCG.2017.2744158
22. Tzeng, F.-Y., Ma, K.-L.: Opening the black box - data driven visualization of neural networks. In: Silva, C.T., Gröller, E., Rushmeier, H.E. (eds.) Proceedings of the VIS 05: IEEE Visualization 2005, pp. 383–390, Minneapolis, Minnesota, 23–28 October 2005. Institute of Electrical and Electronics Engineers, Piscataway (2005)

23. Wilamowski, B.: Neural network architectures and learning algorithms. EEE Ind. Electron. Mag. **3**(4), 56–63 (2009). https://doi.org/10.1109/MIE.2009.934790
24. Zeiler, M.D., Fergus, R.: Visualizing and understanding convolutional networks. In: Fleet, D., Pajdla, T., Schiele, B., Tuytelaars, T. (eds.) ECCV 2014. LNCS, vol. 8689, pp. 818–833. Springer, Cham (2014). https://doi.org/10.1007/978-3-319-10590-1_53
25. Zhou, C., Paffenroth, R.C.: Anomaly detection with robust deep autoencoders. In: Matwin, S., Yu, S., Farooq, F. (eds.) Proceedings of the KDD2017, pp. 665–674, Halifax, NS, Canada, 13–17 August 2017. ACM, New York (2017)

Process Mining, Discovery, and Simulation

Discovering Business Process Simulation Models in the Presence of Multitasking

Bedilia Estrada-Torres[1,2](✉) [iD], Manuel Camargo[1] [iD], Marlon Dumas[1] [iD], and Maksym Yerokhin[1]

[1] University of Tartu, Tartu, Estonia
{estrada,manuel.camargo,marlon.dumas,maksym.yerokhin}@ut.ee
[2] Universidad de Sevilla, Sevilla, Spain
iestrada@us.es

Abstract. Business process simulation is a versatile technique for analyzing business processes from a quantitative perspective. A well-known limitation of process simulation is that the accuracy of the simulation results is limited by the faithfulness of the process model and simulation parameters given as input to the simulator. To tackle this limitation, several authors have proposed to discover simulation models from process execution logs so that the resulting simulation models more closely match reality. Existing techniques in this field assume that each resource in the process performs one task at a time. In reality, however, resources may engage in multitasking behavior. Traditional simulation approaches do not handle multitasking. Instead, they rely on a resource allocation approach wherein a task instance is only assigned to a resource when the resource is free. This inability to handle multitasking leads to an overestimation of execution times. This paper proposes an approach to discover multitasking in business process execution logs and to generate a simulation model that takes into account the discovered multitasking behavior. The key idea is to adjust the processing times of tasks in such a way that executing the multitasked tasks sequentially with the adjusted times is equivalent to executing them concurrently with the original processing times. The proposed approach is evaluated using a real-life dataset and synthetic datasets with different levels of multitasking. The results show that, in the presence of multitasking, the approach improves the accuracy of simulation models discovered from execution logs.

Keywords: Multitasking · Process simulation · Process mining

1 Introduction

Business process simulation (BPS) is a widely used technique for analyzing quantitative properties of business processes. The basic idea of BPS is to execute a large number of instances of a process, based on a process model and a number of simulation parameters, in order to collect performance measures such as waiting times of tasks, processing times, execution cost, and cycle time [1,10]. BPS

© Springer Nature Switzerland AG 2020
F. Dalpiaz et al. (Eds.): RCIS 2020, LNBIP 385, pp. 381–397, 2020.
https://doi.org/10.1007/978-3-030-50316-1_23

tools (simulators) allow analysts to identify performance bottlenecks [18] and to estimate how a given change to a process may affect its performance [16].

The accuracy of a process simulation, and hence the usefulness of the conclusions drawn from it, is to a large extent dependent on how faithfully the process model and simulation parameters capture the observed reality. Traditionally, process models are manually designed by analysts for the purpose of communication and documentation. As such, these models do not capture all the intricacies of how the process is actually performed. In particular, manually designed process models tend to focus on frequent pathways, leaving aside exceptions. Yet, in many cases, exceptions occur in a non-negligible percentage of instances of a process. Moreover, simulation parameters for BPS are traditionally estimated based on expert intuition, sampling, and manual curve fitting, which do not always lead to an accurate reflection of reality [18].

To tackle these limitations, several authors have advocated the idea of automatically discovering simulation models from business process execution logs (also known as *event logs*) [8,13]. Simulation models discovered in this way are generally more faithful since they capture not only common pathways, but also exceptional behavior. Moreover, automated approaches to simulation model discovery typically explore a larger space of options when tuning the simulation parameters compared to what an analyst is able to explore manually.

The automated discovery of BPS models from event logs opens up the possibility of capturing resource behavior at a finer granularity than manual BPS modeling approaches. In particular, Martin et al. [14] demonstrated the possibility of discovering fine-grained resource availability timetables from event logs and the benefits of using these timetables to enhance the accuracy of BPS models.

Inspired by this possibility, this paper studies the problem of discovering another type of resource behavior, namely multitasking, from an event log. Multitasking refers to the situation where a resource executes multiple task instances simultaneously, meaning that the resource divides its attention across multiple active task instances [15]. The inability to capture multitasking behavior has been identified as a limitation of existing BPS approaches, for example in [2].

Concretely, the paper proposes an approach to discover multitasking behavior from an event log and to generate a BPS model that takes into account the discovered multitasking behavior. The key idea is to adjust the processing times of task instances in such a way that executing the multitasked task instances sequentially with the adjusted times is equivalent to executing them concurrently with the original processing times. Once the event log is adjusted is this way, we discover a BPS model using existing BPS model discovery techniques, namely those embedded in the SIMOD tool [9]. The proposed approach is evaluated using a real-life dataset and synthetic datasets with different levels of multitasking.

The rest of this article is structured as follows. Section 2 motivates our research. Section 3 introduces basic concepts and related work. Section 4 describes the proposed approach. Finally, Sect. 5 reports on the evaluation of the approach while Sect. 6 draws conclusions and outlines directions for future work.

2   Motivation

During business process execution, certain events are recorded which capture, for example, the moment when a task instance started and ended, the resource that executed the task instance, etc. Such events are stored in *event logs*, which can be used to analyze the performance of the process or to discover process models that faitfully reflect the actual execution of the process.

Sometimes, the events associated to a given resource in an event log may show that the resource started a task instance before completing a previous one. Hence, during some period of time, the resource performs multiple task instances simultaneously, a situation known as *multitasking*. Multitasking arises, for example, when a resource postpones the completion of a task due to missing information. While this information becomes available, the resource may start another task instance to avoid idle times.

Figure 1 represents a subset of four tasks carried out by resource $R1$, where each continuous line represents the duration of each task. These four tasks result in seven execution intervals. In intervals $A(0–10)$, $C(75–95)$ and $G(140–150)$ only one task is executed, T1, T1 and T3, respectively. Other segments reflect multi-task execution: in $B(10–75)$, $D(95–110)$ and $F(130–140)$ two tasks are executed (T1, T2), (T1, T3) and (T3, T4), respectively; and in interval $E(110–130)$ multi-tasking is performed between three tasks (T1, T3, T4). These tasks may belong to one or more traces. A *trace* contains the ordered sequence of events observed for a given process instance [10]. An event log is composed of one or more traces.

Given the data of this event log segment, a traditional simulator would calculate a total execution time of 280 min, because it would take each duration individually, one task after the other. However, in Fig. 1, it is possible to see that all tasks are executed between the 0 and the 150 min. This means that during certain intervals, the resource $R1$ divided its time and attention into more than one task. Therefore, it would not be correct to consider as total task execution time the time between the start and end record of the task, but the time should be distributed among all the tasks that overlap in a given period.

Since there is usually no detailed record of the specific time that each resource spends on the execution of each task in multitasking scenarios, we consider it necessary to propose a mechanism to adjust processing times to reflect the time spent by each resource more accurately.

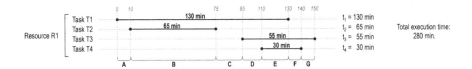

Fig. 1. Example of multitasking for the resource $R1$

3   Background and Related Work

In a simulation scenario, a *work item* is created during a process simulation, when a task is ready to be executed, which can be seen as an instance of a task that will be executed [19]. A simulator tries to assign each *work item* to a resource. Once that it is been assigned, the simulator determines the *work item* duration and that *work item* is placed in suspend mode during the assigned duration time. When the duration time ends, the *work item* is considered completed and the resource is again available to be used by another *work item* [10].

Many efforts have been made to try to simulate process models as close to reality as possible. However, simplifications of these processes are still needed due to the technical limitations of certain simulators [3]. One of the areas of interest that still has deficiencies is related to the behavior of resources involved in a process execution. Several workflow resource patterns are presented in [19], describing how resources are represented and used in a workflow. However, behaviors such as described in [1] and [2] have not yet been fully incorporated into simulation techniques. On the basis of patterns described in [19], Afifi et al. presented in [5] and [4], the extension of BPSim, the Business Process Simulation Standard [20]. BPSim provides a metamodel and an electronic file format to define process models including simulation-specific parameters. However, a tool to support for this proposal is suggested as future work.

Ling et al. [11] propose a prototype simulation tool that considers differences between resources based on their experience and on personnel movements such as recruitment, transfer and resignation. However, this proposal does not consider the possibility of performing more than one task in a given time instant. Although Ouyang et al. [15] point out that real business processes are resource-intensive, where multitasking situations are typical, their study focuses on proposing a conceptual model, in which its possible to model and schedule the use of shared material resources, such as surgical material that is shared by several doctors during a surgical operation; but unlike our proposal, the authors do not analyze real execution data, nor do they simulate proposals for the use of shared resources, since their implementation is proposed as future work.

In the approach proposed by Rusinaite et al. in [18], resources (human or not) are classified as *shareable resource*, to indicate a resource can be used by several activities simultaneously; and *non-shareable resource*, when a resource is allocated to only one activity at a time. For the modeling and simulation a resource is defined by means of attributes of *capacity* (reusable or consumable) and *shareability* (shareable and non-shareable). A simulation engine was used to validate the proposal, where authors found that when two or more resources are available, average time decreased considerably as shared resources are used. From the shared use of five resources, the difference in time was less noticeable. Authors do not specify how shared times are defined and calculated. One inconvenience of this proposal is the need to know beforehand the characteristics of the resource being used. On the contrary, in our proposal, we use event logs to identify if a (human) resource has been running simultaneous tasks and to determine the fragments of time in which the tasks were executed simultaneously.

4   Approach

As explained in Sect. 2, a resource can start a *work item* before finishing one or more *work item* he/she started before, but simulators are not capable of taking this behavior into account. To cope with this lack, we propose to pre-process event logs to adjust the processing times, which is to proportionally divide the interval of execution time where different tasks intersect by the number of tasks involved. In this way, multitasking can be approached without modifying the structure and operations of the simulators. Figure 2 shows how the duration of multitasked intervals (Fig. 1) are distributed proportionally among the number of tasks in each interval. For example, in interval B, the total time (65 min) is divided proportionally between tasks T1 and T2 (32.5 min for each); or in segment C, three tasks are executed, so the 20 min of its duration are divided between tasks T1, T3 and T4. In this way, the new task execution times are more similar to the real dedication of the resource.

Fig. 2. Example of time adjustments derived from multitasking

The objective of pre-processing event log is, on the one hand, to identify the resources that perform multitasking, determine in which time periods the multitasking execution is performed and to make an adjustment of the *work item* duration times according to the multitasking periods. And, on the other hand, to determine how the multitasking execution intervals influence the general performance of the business process. We assume that resources are involved in only one business process at a time.

The following definitions describe step-by-step how the event log is pre-processed. To do this, we begin by formally defining the concepts of *event, trace, event log* and *work item*.

Definition 1 (Events, Attribute). *Let $\mathcal{E}$ be the set of all possible events that occur during a process execution. Let's assume an event e can be described by means of a set of attributes att, where $att = \{id, type, r, st, et\}$, id is the identifier of the event; type represents the event type, the activity name; r represents the resource that performs the event; st indicates the event start timestamp; et indicates the event end timestamp. In such a way that, for example, $att_r(e) = e_r = r_1$, where r_1 is a particular resource performing e.*

Definition 2 (Trace). *Let $\mathcal{T}$ be the set of all possible traces defined as a sequence of events, such that, $\sigma \in \mathcal{T}, \sigma = <e_1, e_2, ..., e_n>$*

Definition 3 (Event Log). *An event log can be defined as a set of traces,* $\mathcal{L} \subseteq \mathcal{T}$, *where* $\mathcal{L} = <\sigma_1, \sigma_2, ..., \sigma_n>$

Definition 4 (Work Item). *Let* wi *be a work item representing an event in a process simulation, in such a way that* $wi \approx e$. *Therefore, a trace can be represented as a sequence of work items, such that* $\sigma \in \mathcal{T}, \sigma = <wi_1, wi_2, ..., wi_n>$.

As with events, a work item has the set of attributes att. For example, $att_r(wi) = wi_r = r_1$, *where* r_1 *is the resource that has the wi assigned to it.*

Multitasking can be generated by *work items* generated in a single trace or by *work items* belonging to different traces. In this proposal, the broadest case is considered, so all traces in which each resource participates is considered. In order to identify the task (and *work items*) in which a resource perform multitasking, the log $\mathcal{L}$ is divided into as many *Segment per Resource* as there are resources in log. Each segment consists of all the *work items* of each resource in $\mathcal{L}$, which will be ordered according to the start timestamp of each *work item* (wi_{st}). Figure 1 represents one *Segment per Resource* (sr_1) with four *work items* for resource $R1$.

Definition 5 (Segment per Resource). *Given an event log* $\mathcal{L}$, $\mathcal{R}$ *represents the set of all possible resources that execute at least one work item in any trace in a log* $\mathcal{L}$. *Such that,* $\forall r \in \mathcal{R}, \exists wi \subseteq \mathcal{T} \subseteq \mathcal{L} \mid wi_r = r$.

Then, let $\mathcal{S}$ *be the set of all possible ordered subsets of work items conforming the traces of a log, in such a way that* $\mathcal{L} = \{sr_1, sr_2, ..., sr_n\}$, *where* $\forall sr_i \in \mathcal{S}, sr_i = <wi_{ij}, ..., wi_m> \mid (wi_{j_r} = wi_{j+1_r} = \cdots = wi_{m_r}) \wedge (wi_{j_{st}} \leq wi_{j+1_{st}} \leq \cdots < wi_{m_{st}})$, *where* $1 \leq j \leq n$.

Having divided $\mathcal{L}$ into different (sr_i), the *Sweep Line algorithm* [6] is applied to each sr_i to identify intersection points between *work items* determined by their start and end timestamps. For each pair of intersection points between the different *work items*, *auxiliary work items* ($wiaux$) are created.

To identify the set of $wiaux$, first, for each *segment per resource* sr_i an ordered list of time ($ordtimes$) is created, where $ordtimes = \{ point_1, point_2, ..., point_n \}$. Each element of the list, called *points*, is a tuple $point_i = (tstamp_i, wiid_i, symbol_i)$, where $tstam_i$ could be a start timestamp or an end timestamp of any of the work items in sr_i; $wi_{i_{id}}$ is the identifier of the work item with start or end timestamp equals to $tstamp_i$; $symbol_i$ could be '+' if $tstamp_i$ corresponds to a start timestamp, or '-' if it is an end timestamp; and wi_i is the complete *work item* used to obtain the other values of the tuple.

Definition 6 (Ordered List of Times). $\forall sr_i \subseteq \mathcal{L}, \exists times_i, ordtimes_i \mid \{(wi_{j_{st}}, wi_{j_{id}}, '+'), (wi_{j_{et}}, wi_{j_{id}}, '-'), ..., (wi_{n_{st}}, wi_{n_{id}}, '+'), (wi_{n_{et}}, wi_{n_{id}}, '-')\} \wedge$
$ordtimes_i = \{(tstamp_k, wiid_k, symbol_k), (tstamp_{k+1}, wiid_{k+1}, symbol_{k+1}), ..., (tstamp_l, wiid_l, symbol_l)\} \wedge tstamp_k \leq tstamp_{k+1} \leq \cdots \leq tstamp_l \wedge |times_i| = |ordtimes_i|$, *where* $(tstamp_x = wi_{x_{st}} \vee tstamp_x = wi_{x_{et}}); wiid_x = wi_{x_{id}}; symbol_x \subset \{'+', '-'\}$.

Once the $ordtimes_i$ has been created, concrete intervals of time $intervals_i$ are specified, identifying also the work items wi_n that are being executed for each interval, $intervals_i = \{(start\_int_1, end\_int_1, list\_wiids_1), ...,$

Algorithm 1: Creating $wiaux$ elements in a $lwiaux$

Input: Ordered list of times $ordtimes_i$
Output: List of auxiliar work items $lwiaux$
1 temp_ids = []; intervals = []; lwiaux = []; id = 1
2 **for** i *in range(0,len(ordtimes)-1)* **do**
3   **if** *(exists(ordtimes[i+1]))* **then**
4   **if** *ordtimes[i]['symbol'] == '+')* **then**
5   temp_ids.append(ordtimes[i]['wiid'])

6   **else**
7   temp_ids.remove(ordtimes[i]['wiid'])

8   intervals.append(ordtimes[i]['tstamp'], ordtimes[i+1]['tstamp'], temp_ids)

9 **for** *interval in intervals* **do**
10   **for** *wiid in interval['list_wiid']* **do**
11   lwiaux.append(id, interval['start_int'], interval['end_int'], interval[list_wiid]['wiid'])
12   id += 1

$(start\_int_k, end\_int_k,\ list_w iids_k)\}$, where $start\_int$ and end_int represent the start and end timestamp of the intersected work items collected in $list\_wiids$. For each element in $list\_wiids$ an auxiliar work item $wiaux$ is created, in such a way that $wiaux = (start\_int, end\_int, id, duration)$, where $wi = \{wiaux_1, \ldots, wiaux_n\}$ and $wi_{et} - wi_{st} = \sum_{n=1}^{n} wiaux_{n_d}$. The $duration$ of each $wiaux$ is determined by the number of $wiaux$ generated from a given $interval, duration = (end\_int - start\_int)/ len(list_w iids)$. For example, from $interval = (10, 75, 'wi_1, wi_2')$ two $wiaux$ are generated $wiaux_1 = (10, 75, 'wi_1', 32.5)$, $wiaux_2 = (10, 75, 'wi_2', 32.5)$. The list $lwiaux$ contains all $wiaux$ generated.

Based on the above definitions, Algorithm 1 describes how the adjustment of task execution times is performed taking into account the number of tasks that are simultaneously executed by a resource, by means of the creation of the $lwiaux$ list. Applying the Definition 6 and the Algorithm 1 to the scenario depicted in Figs. 1 and 2, the set of values presented in Table 1 are obtained.

Table 1. Intermediate values obtained from Definition 6 and Algorithm 1

ordtimes =	{(0, A, '+'), (10, B, '+'), (75, B, '-'), (95, C, '+'), (110, D, '+'), (130, A, '-'), (140, D, '-'), (150, C, '-')}
intervals =	{(0, 10, 'A'), (10, 75, 'A,B'), (75, 95, 'A'), (95, 110, 'A,C'), (110, 130, 'A,C,D'), (130, 140, 'C,D'), (140, 150, 'C')}
lwiaux =	{(0, 10, 'A', 10), (10, 75, 'A', 32.5), (10, 75, 'B', 32.5), (75, 95, 'A', 20), (95, 110, 'A', 7.5), (95, 110, 'C', 7.5), (110, 130, 'A', 6.67), (110, 130, 'C', 6.67), (110, 130, 'D', 6.67), (130, 140, 'C', 5), (130, 140, 'D', 5), (140, 150, 'C', 10)}

Given an event log $\mathcal{L}, len(\mathcal{L})$ indicates the number of work items in $\mathcal{L}$. And according to the above definitions it is possible to state that $lwiaux = \mathcal{L}'$, where $\mathcal{L}'$ is defined as:

Definition 7 (Auxiliar Event Log ($\mathcal{L}'$)). *Given a* $\mathcal{L}$, $\forall \mathcal{L} = <wi_1, wi_2, ...,$ $wi_n>, \exists \mathcal{L}' \mid \mathcal{L} \equiv \mathcal{L}' \wedge \mathcal{L}' = <wiaux_1, wiaux_2, ..., wiaux_m>,$ *where* $wi_i = $ $<wiaux_j, ..., wiaux_k>, 1 \leq i \leq n, 1 \leq j \leq k, m \geq len(\mathcal{L}).$

From $\mathcal{L}'$ it is possible to generate a "coalescing log" $\mathcal{L}''$ that contains a set of coalesing work items *wicoal*. Each *wicoal* is the result of the sum of the pre-processed times (*wiaux*) of each original *wi* in $\mathcal{L}$.

Definition 8 (Coalescing Log ($\mathcal{L}''$)). $\forall \mathcal{L} = <wi_1, ..., wi_n>, \mathcal{L}' = <wiaux_1,$ $..., wiaux_m> \exists \mathcal{L}'' = <wicoal_1, ..., wicoal_n> \mid wicoal_{i_{id}} = wi_{i_{id}} \wedge$ $wicoal_{i_{type}} = wi_{i_{type}} \wedge wicoal_{i_r} = wi_{i_r} \wedge wicoal_{i_{st}} = wi_{i_{st}} \wedge wicoal_{i_{et}} = $ $(wicoal_{i_{st}} + sum_{t=1}^{m} wiaux_{t_d}) \wedge len(\mathcal{L}) = len(\mathcal{L}'') \wedge [sum_{t=1}^{n}(wi_{t_{et}} - wi_{t_{st}}) = $ $sum_{t=1}^{n}(wicoal_{t_{et}} - wicoal_{t_{st}})].$

From the above definitions we can deduce that: $\forall \mathcal{L} \exists \mathcal{L}', \mathcal{L}'' \mid \mathcal{L} \equiv \mathcal{L}' \equiv \mathcal{L}'' \wedge$ $len(\mathcal{L}) \leq len(\mathcal{L}') \wedge len(\mathcal{L}') \geq len(\mathcal{L}'') \wedge len(\mathcal{L}) = len(\mathcal{L}'').$

In addition, if $len(\mathcal{L}) == len(\mathcal{L}')$ there is no multitasking, because the execution times do not intersect for any work item of any resource in the event log $\mathcal{L}$ and $\forall wi_i \in \mathcal{L} \mid wi_i = \{wiaux_i\}.$

The level of multitasking in a given log, is determined by the amount of overlap between the execution times of pairs of events in a log, for a given resource, in proportion to the number of total pairs of events that can be formed between the work items of each sr_i. In order to determine the level of multitasking in a given log $\mathcal{L}$, we propose a measure called ***Multitasking Log Index*** (*MTLI*). To calculate the *MTLI* of a log $\mathcal{L}$, we based on the idea that a log is divided by grouping all the work items of a given resource (r), generating $sr_i \in \mathcal{S}$ (See Definition 5). The multitasking of a log is derived from the overlap between the execution times of two work items executed by the same resource. Therefore, for each sr_i, let WI_{sr} be the set of all possible work items in sr_i and $SRWI_r$ be the set of all possible pairs of work items in sr_i.

$$SRWI_r = \{(wi_1, wi_2) \in WI_{sr} \times WI_{sr} \mid wi_1 \neq wi_2 \wedge wi_1.r = wi_2.r\}$$

For each pair of events $(wi_1, wi_2)_i \in SRWI_r$, $1 < i <\mid SRWI_r \mid$, an overlap function is calculated as the maximum between the zero and the difference of the minimum of the end timestamps of the work items and the maximum of their start timestamps; divided by the maximum value of the duration of the two work items.

$$overlap(wi_1, wi_2)_i = \frac{max((min(wi_1.et, wi_2.et) - max(wi_1.st, wi_2.st)), 0)}{max((wi_1.et - wi_1.st), (wi_2.et - wi_2.st))}$$

With the previous information it is possible to calculate the *Multitasking Resource Index (MTRI$_r$)*, as the index of multitasking for each sr_i in the log. For each sr_i, all overlap values are summed; and that sum is multiplied by the value of 1 divided number of pair of events in $SRWI_r$.

$$MTRI_r = \frac{1}{|SRWI_r|} \sum_{(wi_1, wi_2)_i \in SRWI_r}^{|SRWI_r|} overlap(wi_1, wi_2)_i$$

Finally, $MTLI$ is calculated as the average of all $MTRI_r$ in the log.

$$MTLI = \frac{\sum_{j=1}^{|S|} MTRI_j}{|S|}, S = \{sr_1, \ldots, sr_n\}$$

The **Multitasking Work Items Index (MTWII)** is another measure related to multitasking that is calculated in a very similar way that $MTLI$, but in this case, only overlapped pairs of events are considered. The set of all possible overlapped pairs of events for a resource is defined as follows.

$$RWI_{o_r} = \{(wi_1, wi_2) \in WI_{sr} \times WI_{sr} \mid wi_1 \neq wi_2 \wedge wi_1.r = wi_2.r$$
$$\wedge (min(wi_1.et, wi_2.et) - max(wi_1.st, wi_2.st)) > 0\}$$

The function $overlap(wi_1, wi_2)$ is calculated the same way. Now, the value of $MTRI_r$ is calculated only for those pairs of events overlapped ($MTRI_{o_r}$).

$$MTRI_{o_r} = \frac{1}{|RWI_{o_r}|} \sum_{(wi_1, wi_2)_i \in RWI_{o_r}}^{|RWI_{o_r}|} overlap(wi_1, wi_2)_i$$

Finally, $MTWII$ is calculated as the average of all $MTRI_{o_r}$, where S_o represents the set of all resources that have at least on pair of work items with multitasking. $S_o = \{sr_{o_1}, \ldots, sr_{o_j}\}$, where $1 < i < j$; $sr_{o_i} = \{wi_1, \ldots, wi_k\}$ | $\exists(wi_n, wi_m) \in MTRI_{o_r}$, where $1 < n, m < j$; $win \neq wi_m$.

$$MTWII = \frac{\sum_{r=1}^{|S_o|} MTRI_{o_r}}{|S_o|}$$

5   Evaluation

The pre-processing of an event log for the identification of multitasking *work items*, the overlapping time periods, the adjustment of the execution times for these *work items* and the calculation of multitasking indexes is done by means of a *Sweeper* Python script. It receives as input a base event log ($\mathcal{L}$) in eXtensible Event Stream (XES) format and generates as output an event log with the adjusted times according to the multitasking previously identified ($\mathcal{L}''$). The $\mathcal{L}$ must contain *work items* with at least the task name, the resources that executed the *work item*, and the start and end timestamps for each *work item*. An identifier for each *work item* is assigned during pre-processing. In addition, the events in the log must reflect multitasking in order to perform the analysis. Based on these restrictions, the evaluation was twofold and was performed using a real event log and a set of synthetic logs. Event logs[1] and scripts[2] are available online. The experiments were carried out on a computer using Windows 10 Enterprise (64-bit), a processor Inter Core i5-6200U, CPU 2.3 GHz and 16.0 GB RAM.

In both real and synthetic cases, after generating the event logs with the adjusted times derived from multitasking, the SIMOD tool [9] was used to discover business process simulation models. This tool uses the hyper-parameter optimization technique "to search in the space of possible configurations in order to maximize the similarity between the behavior of the simulation model and the behavior observed in the log". Process models are discovered using the Split Miner algorithm [7], which considers different levels of sensibility and depends on two parameters: the parallelism threshold, epsilon (ϵ) that determines the quantity of concurrent relations between events to be captured; and the percentile for frequency threshold, eta (η), that acts as a filter over the incoming and outgoing edges of each node and retains only the most frequent percentiles. Both parameters are defined in a range between 0 and 1. The resulting simulation models can be executed using Scylla [17] and BIMP [12]. As in [8], we use BIMP because it allows a wider set of distribution probabilities to be used, thus widening the space for configuration options. During SIMOD executions, an objective evaluation of the results is made by means of similarity measures which will be described in more detail in the following subsections.

5.1   Evaluation Based on a Real-Life Event Log

The objective of this section is to identify the actual accuracy gains of the proposal, using a real-life event log. The hypothesis in this scenario is that adjusting execution times derived from multitasking provides more accurate execution results, reduces the total execution time of tasks and processes; avoid over-utilization of resources due to sequential simulation of task execution; and maintains the correct alignment of the model generated according to the original model derived from the log. The real event log represents an academic credentials recognition (*ACR log*) process in an University during the first semester of 2016. This log has 954 traces, 18 tasks, 6870 events and involves 561 resources.

Experimental Setup. The validation process is divided into the following steps:

1. *Create the adjusted log.* Execute the *sweeper.py* script using the *ACR log* to generate a new event log with the adjusted times (*ACR adjusted log*).

---

2. *Calculate measures.*
   - The execution of the *Sweeper* script also provides a set of values and indexes to identify the level of multitasking in the *ACR log*.
   - The hyper-parameter optimization of SIMOD was used with both logs to obtain similarity measures in each case. 50 BPS models were generated using different setup combinations of processing parameters. Parameters ϵ and η varied from 0.0 to 1.0. Each BPS model was executed 5 times, for that, 250 simulations were evaluated for each of the both event logs.
   - Finally, Apromore[3] can be used for the comparison of processing times and BIMP[4] to analyze resource utilization values.
3. *Analyze the results.* Compare values between two logs.

Analysis of Results. Executing SIMOD using the *ACR log*, very similar results were obtained to those presented in [8], using half number of simulations. In that proposal, the similarity measure Timed String Distance (TSD) is calculated. TSD is a modification of the distance measure called Demerau-Levinstein (DL) that assesses the similarity between two process traces. TSD allows to include a penalty related to the time difference in processing and waiting times providing a single measure of accuracy. In [8], TSD is equal to *0.9167*. In our experiment, TSD is equal to *0.906* with $\epsilon = 0.615$ and $\eta = 0.559$. Executing *ACR adjusted log*, similarity measure is equal to *0.929* with $\epsilon = 0.484$ and $\eta = 0.591$.

The difference between similarity values of both logs is *2.54%*. Although this value may seem low, it should not be seen by itself; it should be analyzed in relation to the amount of multitasking identified in the log. Table 2 shows the characteristics related to the content of the event log. Out of the 18 tasks in the event log, 17 are overlapped in at least one instance (work item) within the log. From the 6870 events (*work items*), 1267 are overlap with at least one other event. Out of the 561 resources involved in the log, 76 executed at least one event with multitasking. Finally, after grouping all events according to the resource that executed them, 1116776 pairs of events were identified. Of all of them, 1036 are overlapped in some period of their execution time. This last feature is very significant as it indicates that the log used for this analysis actually has a low amount of multitasked events. This is a possible reason why the percentage of similarity improvement was quite low (2.54%). In addition, from the BPS model results generated by SIMOD, it is possible to extract the *Average Cycle Time* of each simulation. When comparing the results of both logs, an improvement of approximate 14% of the *ACR adjusted log* with respect to *ACR log* was obtained.

As mentioned in Sect. 4, *Multitasking Log Index (MTLI)* is another measure that helps identify the percentage of multitasking in the entire event log. For the *ACR log*, $MTLI = 1.05\%$. If *MTLI* is low, one would expect the rate of improvement in the analysis to be low as well, but as the level of multitasking in the log increases, the measure should improve proportionally. This indicates

---

[3] http://apromore.cs.ut.ee/.
[4] http://bimp.cs.ut.ee/.

Table 2. Differences between original log features and features reflecting multitasking

	Task	Events	Resources	Event-pairs
Original log characteristics	18	6870	561	1116776
Multitasking log characteristics	17	1267	76	1039
% of characteristics with multitasking	94.4%	18.4%	13.5%	0.09%

that when analyzing all possible pairs of events, only the 1.05% of the time of those events were overlapped, which represents low level of multitasking. For the same log, the *Multitasking Work Item Index* is $MTWII = 58.54\%$, that indicates that, for those events where multitasking has been identified, the pairs of events are overlapping by 58.54% of their total duration.

Using Apromore, *ACR log* and *ACR adjusted log* were analyzed and compared in terms of time. Figure 3 shows the average duration of process tasks. Blue bars represent the average time duration of *ACR log* tasks and red bars the average time duration of *ACR adjusted log* tasks. Both *RD* and *HGR* reflect a difference of 0.6 hours (h), followed by *HGR* with 0.43 h; *EC* and *CC* with 0.35h; *CS*, *VBPC* and *RC* with 0.15 h; *VS* 0.07; *VSPH* 0.04; *VF* with 0.02 h; *RSH* does not show improvement; and the last 6 task do not reflect improvement either, but can be considered activities of instant duration. Finally, using BIMP, three resource pools were identified and slight differences in the percentage of resource utilization were noticed.

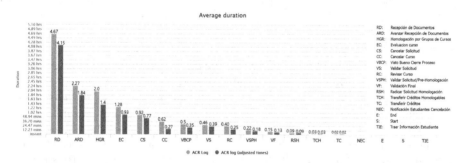

Fig. 3. Comparison of average duration between *ACR log* and *ACR adjusted log*

In general, the above results show that with the pre-processing of log it is possible to effectively reduce processing times of tasks and to maintain and/or improve similarity between traces involved in each log. Besides, we figured that the level of improvement in the results depends on the multitasking level in the log: the number of event pairs overlapped and the percentage of overlap between each event pair. As we have only been able to identify and use one real-life log with multitasking characteristics to show dependence between the amount of multitasking and the result improvements, in the following subsection, a synthetic log was modified to generate a log set with different multitasking levels.

5.2 Evaluation Based on a Synthetic Log

The objective of this section is to identify how the level of multitasking affects the discovery and simulation of BPS models. Our hypothesis is based on the assumption that the results of BPS models vary and are enhanced depending on the amount of overlap identified in each log. This scenario is composed of a set of event logs derived from a synthetic log called *PurchasingExample.xes*. This is one of the public event logs available through the SIMOD distribution [9] that was generated from a purchase-to-pay process model not available to the authors. This event log, which does not contain multitasking characteristics (*PE_OP_log*), has 608 traces, 21 tasks, 9119 events and involves 27 resources.

Experimental Setup. The validation process if divided into the following steps:

1. *Selection and preparation of the base log.* The *PE_OP_log* base log does not contain multitasking characteristics. Therefore, when calculating their multitasking indexes they have a value of zero. New logs were generated using different percentage of shifting (overlap between events or *work items*) for each log. To generate the new event logs, we implemented a Python script (*percentage.py*) that, given a percentage of shifting (between 0.0 and 1.0) generates a new event log in XES format including events overlapped in that percentage of their processing times. The script algorithm works as follows.
   - The base event log is divided by grouping the events that are executed by a particular resource (see Description 5, *segment per resource*).
   - The events of each *segment per resource* are ordered according to their start timestamps.
   - For each *segment per resource*, the first event is taken as the pivot and the next adjacent event is searched among the remaining events. Two events (e_1, e_2) are adjacent events if the end timestamp of e_1 has the same value as the start timestamp of e_2. In Fig. 4.a, the first pair of events shown are adjacent events.
   - When a pair of adjacent events are identified, the timestamps are shifted depending on the percentage assigned. In Fig. 4.b, 20% of shifting is applied, while in Fig. 4.c, the shifting is 40%.
   - The two events of a pair of adjacent events are excluded from the following search. The next event in the *segment per resource* is taken as pivot and the search is repeated. If no adjacent event is found, it is not modified and the search is repeated with a new pivot.
   - The search of adjacent events is repeated for all *segment per resources*.
   - The resulting log will have a multitasking percentage *MTWII* similar to the percentage of shifting indicated in the script, although we will comment this value may vary. However, the total percentage of multitasking in the log (*MTLI*), depends on the number of adjacent events identified.

2. *Generate the set of adjusted logs.* The *Sweeper* script is run on each of the logs generated in the previous step.
3. *Calculate measures.*
   - Using the *Sweeper* script the multitasking indexes in the log were calculated (*MTWII* and *MTLI*).
   - The hyper-parameter optimization of SIMOD was used with each log to obtain similarity measures in each case. To do that, 100 BPS models were generated using different setup combinations of processing parameters. Parameters *epsilon* and *eta* varied from 0.0 to 1.0. Each simulation model was executed 5 times, for that, 500 simulations were evaluated for each log in the set.
   - BIMP can be used to analyze the resource utilization percentages.
4. *Comparison and analysis of results.*

Fig. 4. Overlapping of events according to a percentage of shifting.

Analysis of the Results. The set of synthetic event logs was made up of 6 logs. The *PE_OP_log* and 5 more logs built using the *Percentage* script with the *PE_OP_log* as a base log and using a percentage of shifting of 5%, 10%, 15%, 20% and 25%. With regard to resources, in *PE_OP_log* participate 27 resources and 11 of them reflect multitasking. From the 9119 events in *PE_OP_log*, 2625561 pairs of events were identified. From these, 789 are adjacent events to be used for time shifting of the logs, excluding in this set all instantaneous events.

Table 3 shows the percentage of shifting applied to the adjacent events in each generated log; the multitasking indexes (*MTWII* and *MTLI*) for each log in the set; the number of pairs of events in which overlapping was identified (multitasking); and the value of two similarity measures obtained using SIMOD. *DL-Mean Absolute Error* (*DL-MAE*) assesses the similarity between two traces evaluating an attribute, in this case the *cycle time* of traces, and the *Mean Absolute Error* (*MAE*) of the cycle time traces expressed in seconds.

The percentage reflected in the column *MTWII* should be the same as *Shifting*, because the number of adjacent events on which the shifts were made was the same for all the logs. However, certain *MTWII* values are slightly higher since the shifting of some events may generate overlapping between events that initially were not adjacent. This is also reflected in the column *Overlapping Pairs*, where the number of pairs of events overlapped is greater than 789 and increases as the shifting increases. Above a certain amount of shifting, the value of *MTWII* is less than the percentage of shifting. This is because a shift can cause one event to be embedded within another (Fig. 4.c), and if the shifting increases, the event is still embedded and does not provide more multitasking to the log. As could be deduced by identifying the number of events in the log, the *MTLI* is quite low. However, like *MTWII*, it increases when the percentages of shifting increase. Similarly, since the amount of multitasking in the log is low, the difference between *DL_MAE* values varies and improves slightly for those cases where the percentage of shifting is quite similar to *MTWII* (0, 5, 10, 15) and worsen slightly for those cases where the shifting and index vary more. Finally, when calculating the MAE we see that although there is a significant difference between a log with and without multitasking, as the multitasking is increased, and the adjustment in the logs, the MAE is gradually reduced, which means that the discovered BPS models are more accuracy. BPS models were simulated using BIMP. 5 resource pools were discovered, two of them with high percentage of resource utilization (RU). The RU in BPS models derived from multitasking is reduced, especially for those resource pools where the RU is higher.

Table 3. Comparison between the synthetic logs created using a percentage of shifting.

Shifting (%)	MTWII (%)	MTLI	Overlapping pairs	DL_MAE	MAE (segs)
0	0	0	0	0.8883	1073208
5	5.596	1.468e−05	876	0.8889	1145181
10	10.381	2.754e−05	950	0.8893	1098788
15	14.694	3.953e−05	1006	0.8895	1091332
20	18.860	5.087e−05	1041	0.8841	1049593
25	22.266	6.147e−05	1073	0.8866	1117721

6   Conclusion

This paper outlined an approach to discover BPS models that take into account multitasking behavior. Specifically the paper showed how to pre-process an event log in order to discover multitasking behavior and how to adjust the processing times of tasks in such a way that the resulting log does not contain multitasking behavior, yet the resource utilization in the resulting log is equivalent to that in the original log. In this way, the BPS model discovered from the pre-processed log takes into account the multitasking behavior but can be simulated using a traditional process simulator (e.g. BIMP).

The evaluation showed that, in the presence of multitasking, the approach improves the accuracy of BPS models. We also identified that the greater the percentage of overlap in multitasking events in a log, the more the approach improves the accuracy of the generated BPS models. The experimental evaluation was restricted to one real-life and the amount of multitasking in this logs was low, so it was difficult to generalize the results. The evaluation on synthetic logs partially addressed this limitation by introducing varying levels of multi-tasking. Still, the obtained levels of multitasking remained relatively low due to the approach employed to add multitasking behavior in the synthetic log.

The discovery of simulation models is key to the setup of as-is scenarios that allow the reliable evaluation of what-if scenarios focused on process optimization. Processes are dynamic and the results of their execution may vary over time, largely due to the behavior of the human resources involved, and this characteristic is independent of the defined process model. Even in those cases in which the process is not clearly defined and only execution records are available, simulation models obtained allow the analysis of processing times or resource utilization rates, which can be influenced by human behavior such as multitasking, batching or delaying of low-priority tasks.

A possible direction for future work is to extend the evaluation to other real-life logs with higher levels of multitasking. The challenge here is that event logs where both the start and end times of tasks are available are generally not available in the public domain. An alternative approach is to design new methods for generating realistic synthetic logs with high levels of multitasking.

The present work was limited to multitasking across multiple instances of one business process. Another avenue for future work is to discover and handle multitasking across multiple business processes. The latter would require the ability to simulate multiple business processes simultaneously.

Acknowledgments. This research is funded by the European Research Council (ERC Advanced Grant - Project PIX 834141) and the European Commission (FEDER) and the Spanish R&D&I programmes (grants P12–TIC-1867 (COPAS), RTI2018-101204-B-C22 (OPHELIA)).

References

1. van der Aalst, W.M.P.: Business process simulation revisited. In: Barjis, J. (ed.) EOMAS 2010. LNBIP, vol. 63, pp. 1–14. Springer, Heidelberg (2010). https://doi.org/10.1007/978-3-642-15723-3_1
2. van der Aalst, W.M.P.: Business process simulation survival guide. In: vom Brocke, J., Rosemann, M. (eds.) Handbook on Business Process Management 1. IHIS, pp. 337–370. Springer, Heidelberg (2015). https://doi.org/10.1007/978-3-642-45100-3_15
3. van der Aalst, W.M.P., Nakatumba, J., Rozinat, A., Russell, N.: Business process simulation: how to get it right? BPM Center Report BPM-08-07. BPMcenter. org **285**, 286–291 (2008)
4. Afifi, N., Awad, A., Abdelsalam, H.M.: Extending BPSim based on workflow resource patterns. In: Abramowicz, W., Paschke, A. (eds.) BIS 2018. LNBIP, vol. 320, pp. 206–222. Springer, Cham (2018). https://doi.org/10.1007/978-3-319-93931-5_15
5. Afifi, N., Awad, A., Abdelsalam, H.M.: RBPSim: a resource-aware extension of BPSim using workflow resource patterns. In: Proceedings of CEUR-WS, pp. 32–39 (2018)

6. Arge, L., Procopiuc, O., Ramaswamy, S., Suel, T., Vitter, J.S.: Scalable sweeping-based spatial join. In: Proceedings of VLDB, pp. 570–581 (1998)

7. Augusto, A., Conforti, R., Dumas, M., Rosa, M.L.: Split Miner: Discovering Accurate and Simple Business Process Models from Event Logs. In: Proceedings of ICDM, pp. 1–10 (2017)

8. Camargo, M., Dumas, M., González-Rojas, O.: Automated discovery of business process simulation models from event logs. Decis. Support Syst. 113284 (2020)

9. Camargo, M., Dumas, M., Rojas, O.G.: Simod: A Tool for Automated Discovery of Business Process Simulation Models. In: Proceedings of Demonstration Track - BPM 2019, pp. 139–143 (2019)

10. Dumas, M., Rosa, M.L., Mendling, J., Reijers, H.A.: Fundamentals of Business Process Management. Springer, Heidelberg (2018). https://doi.org/10.1007/978-3-662-56509-4

11. Ling, J., Feng, Q., Zhang, L.: A business process simulation method supporting resource evolution. In: Proceedings of ICSSP 2014, pp. 169–177 (2014)

12. Madis, A.: Lightning Fast Business Process Simulator. Master's thesis, University of Tartu (2011)

13. Martin, N., Depaire, B., Caris, A.: The use of process mining in business process simulation model construction - structuring the field. Bus. Inf. Syst. Eng. 58(1), 73–87 (2016)

14. Martin, N., Depaire, B., Caris, A., Schepers, D.: Retrieving the resource availability calendars of a process from an event log. Inf. Syst. 88, 101463 (2020)

15. Ouyang, C., Wynn, M.T., Fidge, C., ter Hofstede, A.H., Kuhr, J.C.: Modelling complex resource requirements in business process management systems. In: Proceedings of ACIS 2010. ACIS, December 2010

16. Peters, S., Dijkman, R.M., Grefen, P.: Quantitative effects of advanced resource constructs in business process simulation. In: Proceedings of EDOC, pp. 115–122 (2018)

17. Pufahl, L., Wong, T.Y., Weske, M.: Design of an extensible BPMN process simulator. In: Teniente, E., Weidlich, M. (eds.) BPM 2017. LNBIP, vol. 308, pp. 782–795. Springer, Cham (2018). https://doi.org/10.1007/978-3-319-74030-0_62

18. Rusinaite, T., Vasilecas, O., Savickas, T., Vysockis, T., Normantas, K.: An approach for allocation of shared resources in the rule-based business process simulation. In: Proceedings of CompSysTech 2016, pp. 25–32 (2016)

19. Russell, N., van der Aalst, W.M.P., ter Hofstede, A.H.M., Edmond, D.: Workflow Resource Patterns: Identification, Representation and Tool Support. In: Pastor, O., Falcão e Cunha, J. (eds.) CAiSE 2005. LNCS, vol. 3520, pp. 216–232. Springer, Heidelberg (2005). https://doi.org/10.1007/11431855_16

20. (WfMC), W.M.C.: Business Process Simulation Specification (2016). http://www.bpsim.org/specifications/2.0/WFMC-BPSWG-2016-01.pdf

TLKC-Privacy Model for Process Mining

Majid Rafiei$^{(\boxtimes)}$ ⓘ, Miriam Wagner ⓘ, and Wil M. P. van der Aalst ⓘ

Chair of Process and Data Science, RWTH Aachen University, Aachen, Germany
majid.rafiei@pads.rwth-aachen.de

Abstract. Process mining aims to provide insights into the actual processes based on event data. These data are widely available and often contain private information about individuals. Consider for example health-care information systems recording highly sensitive data related to diagnosis and treatment activities. Process mining should reveal insights in the form of annotated models, yet, at the same time, should not reveal sensitive information about individuals. In this paper, we discuss the challenges regarding directly applying existing well-known privacy-preserving techniques to event data. We introduce the *TLKC*-privacy model for process mining that provides privacy guarantees in terms of group-based anonymization. It extends and customizes the LKC-privacy model presented to deal with high-dimensional, sparse, and sequential trajectory data. Experiments on real-life event data demonstrate that our privacy model maintains a high utility for process discovery and performance analyses while preserving the privacy of the cases.

Keywords: Responsible process mining · Privacy preservation · Process discovery · Performance analyses

1 Introduction

Event logs are used by process mining algorithms to discover and analyze the real processes. An event log is a collection of events and such information is widely available in current information systems [1]. Each event is described by its attributes and typical attributes required for process mining algorithms are *case id*, *activity*, *timestamp*, and *resource*. The minimal requirements for process mining are that any event can be related to both a case and activity and that the events that belong to a case are ordered, which is often done by means of timestamps [1]. Therefore, *timestamps* play a crucial role in process mining algorithms and need to be stored and processed. However, the event data containing accurate timestamps (in milliseconds) are highly sensitive.

Moreover, some of the event attributes may refer to individuals, e.g., in the health-care context, the *case id* may refer to the patient whose data is recorded, and the *resource* may refer to the employees performing activities for the patients, e.g., nurses or surgeons. When the individuals' data are explicitly or implicitly included, privacy issues arise. According to regulations such as the

© Springer Nature Switzerland AG 2020
F. Dalpiaz et al. (Eds.): RCIS 2020, LNBIP 385, pp. 398–416, 2020.
https://doi.org/10.1007/978-3-030-50316-1_24

European General Data Protection Regulation (GDPR) [21], organizations are obliged to consider the privacy of individuals.

Regarding the four main attributes of events, two different perspectives for privacy in process mining can be considered; *resource perspective* and *case perspective*. The *resource perspective* refers to the privacy of the individuals performing the activities, and the *case perspective* considers the privacy of the individuals whose data is recorded and analyzed. Depending on the context, the relative importance of these perspectives may vary. However, often the *case perspective* is more important than the *resource perspective*. For example, in the health-care context, the activity performers could be publicly available. However, what happens for a specific patient and her/his personal information should be kept private. In this paper, we focus on the *case perspective*.

There are many activities and techniques in process mining such as *process discovery, conformance checking, social network analyses, prediction*, etc. However, the three basic types of process mining are; *process discovery, conformance checking*, and *enhancement* [1]. The proposed privacy model focuses on process discovery and a subfield of enhancement called performance analyses. Since the event data used by process mining algorithms are high-dimensional sparse data, privacy preservation with high data utility is significantly challenging.

The aim of this paper is to provide a privacy-preserving model for process mining protecting the privacy of *cases*, yet, at the same time, maintains the utility of the process discovery and performance analyses. The utility is preserved in terms of similarity of the results provided by the privacy-preserving approach to the results obtained from the original data. We introduce *TLKC*-privacy model, which exploits some restrictions regarding the availability of the background knowledge in the real world to deal with process mining-specific challenges. Our model is an extension for the *LKC*-privacy model [8,16], which was presented to deal with privacy challenges of the trajectory data. The *LKC*-privacy model generalizes several traditional privacy models, such as k-anonymity, confidence bounding, (α,k)-anonymity, and l-diversity, which are inherited by our model. We evaluate our approach with respect to the typical trade-off between privacy guarantees and the loss of accuracy. The approach is evaluated on a real-life event data belonging to a hospital (Sepsis) containing infrequent behavior. Our experiments show that our approach maintains a high utility, assuming realistic background knowledge while using tunable privacy parameters.

The rest of the paper is organized as follows. In Sect. 2, we explain the motivation and challenges. In Sect. 3, formal models are presented for event log and attack scenarios. We explain the *TLKC*-privacy model in Sect. 4. In Sect. 5, the implementation and evaluation are described. Section 6 outlines related work, and Sect. 7 concludes the paper.

2   Motivation

To motivate the necessity to deal with privacy issues in process mining, we illustrate the problem with an example in health-care context. Suppose that Table 1 shows a part of an event log recorded by an information system in a hospital. Assuming that an adversary knows that patient's data are in the event log (as a *case*), with little information about the activities having been done for the patient, the adversary is easily able to connect the patient to the corresponding *Case Id* and find the complete sequence of activities having been performed for the patient. For example, if the adversary knows that two blood tests have been performed for the patient, the only matching case is case 2. We call this attack *case linkage* attack. Note that the complete sequence of activities having been done for a patient is considered as the sensitive person-specific information which can be disclosed by the *case linkage* attack. Moreover, if we consider some attributes in the event log as sensitive, e.g., diagnosis and test results, the adversary can go further and link the sensitive information as well. For example, the disease that belongs to case 2 is infection. This attack is called *attribute linkage*. Note that the *attribute linkage* attack does not necessarily need to be done after the *case linkage*, i.e., if more than one case corresponds to the adversaries knowledge while all the cases have the same value as the sensitive attribute, the *attribute linkage* could happen without a successful *case linkage*.

Many privacy models, such as k-anonymity and its extensions [12], have been introduced to deal with the aforementioned attacks in the context of relational databases. In these privacy models, the data attributes are classified into four main categories including; *explicit identifier, quasi-identifier, sensitive attributes*, and *non-sensitive attributes*. The *explicit identifier* is a set of attributes containing information that explicitly identifies the data owner, the *quasi-identifier* is a set of attributes that could potentially identify the data owner, the *sensitive attributes* consist of sensitive person-specific information such as disease, and the *non-sensitive attributes* contain all the attributes that do not fall into the previous three categories [3]. In the group-based privacy models, the idea is to disorient potential linkages by generalizing the records into equivalence classes having the same values on the *quasi-identifier*. These privacy models are effective for anonymizing relational data. However, they are not easily applicable to event data due to some specific properties of event data.

In process mining, the *explicit identifiers* do not need to be stored and processed. By identifier, we often refer to a dummy identifier, e.g., incremental IDs, created to distinguish cases. As already mentioned, the minimal required information for process mining is the sequence of activities having been performed for each case, known as a *trace*. Therefore, an event log can be defined as a multiset of traces, i.e., a multiset of sequences of activities. Considering this minimal required information, the first challenge is that a trace can be considered as a *quasi-identifier* and, at the same time, as a *sensitive attribute*. In other words, a complete sequence of activities belonging to a case, is sensitive person-specific information, at the same time, part of a trace, i.e., only some of the activities, can be utilized as a *quasi-identifier* to identify the trace owner.

The *quasi-identifier* role of traces in process mining causes significant challenges for group-based anonymization techniques because of two specific properties of event data; *high variability* and *Pareto distribution*. In an event log the

Table 1. Sample event log (each row represents an event).

Case Id	Activity	Timestamp	Resource	Age	Disease
1	Registration (RE)	01.01.2019-08:30:00	Employee1	22	Flu
1	Visit (V)	01.01.2019-08:45:00	Doctor1	22	Flu
2	Registration (RE)	01.01.2019-08:46:00	Employee1	30	Infection
3	Registration (RE)	01.01.2019-08:50:00	Employee1	32	Infection
4	Registration (RE)	01.01.2019-08:55:00	Employee4	29	Poisoning
1	Release (RL)	01.01.2019-08:58:00	Employee2	22	Flu
5	Registration (RE)	01.01.2019-09:00:00	Employee1	35	Cancer
6	Registration (RE)	01.01.2019-09:05:00	Employee4	35	Hypotension
4	Visit (V)	01.01.2019-09:10:00	Doctor2	29	Poisoning
5	Visit (V)	01.01.2019-09:20:00	Doctor4	35	Cancer
4	Infusion (IN)	01.01.2019-09:30:00	Nurse2	29	Poisoning
2	Hospitalization (HO)	01.01.2019-09:46:00	Employee3	30	Infection
3	Hospitalization (HO)	01.01.2019-10:00:00	Employee3	32	Infection
5	Hospitalization (HO)	01.01.2019-09:55:00	Employee6	35	Cancer
2	Blood Test (BT)	01.01.2019-10:00:00	Nurse1	30	Infection
5	Blood Test (BT)	01.01.2019-10:10:00	Nurse2	35	Cancer
3	Blood Test (BT)	01.01.2019-10:15:00	Nurse1	32	Infection
6	Visit (V)	01.01.2019-10:20:00	Doctor3	35	Hypotension
4	Release (RL)	01.01.2019-10:30:00	Employee2	29	Poisoning
6	Release (RL)	01.01.2019-14:20:00	Employee2	35	Hypotension
2	Blood Test (BT)	01.02.2019-08:00:00	Nurse2	30	Infection
2	Visit (V)	01.02.2019-10:00:00	Doctor2	30	Infection
3	Visit (V)	01.02.2019-10:15:00	Doctor3	32	Infection
2	Release (RL)	01.02.2019-14:00:00	Employee2	30	Infection
3	Release (RL)	01.02.2019-14:15:00	Employee5	32	Infection
5	Release (RL)	01.02.2019-16:00:00	Employee5	35	Cancer

variability of traces is high because: (1) There could be tens of different activities happening in any order, (2) One activity or a bunch of activities could happen repetitively, and (3) Some traces could contain a few activities compared to all possible activities. In an event log, trace variants are often distributed similarly to the Pareto distribution, i.e., few trace variants are frequent and many trace variants are unique. Enforcing k-anonymity on little-overlapping traces in a high-dimensional space is a significant challenge, and the majority part of the data have to be suppressed in order to achieve the desired anonymization.

3 Preliminaries (Formal Models)

In this section, we provide formal models for event logs and possible attacks. These formal models will be used in the remainder for describing the approach.

3.1   Event Log Model

For a given set A, A^* is the set of all finite sequences over A, and $\mathcal{B}(A)$ is the set of all multisets over the set A. A finite sequence over A of length n is a mapping $\sigma \in \{1, ..., n\} \rightarrow A$, represented as $\sigma = \langle a_1, a_2, ..., a_n \rangle$ where $\sigma_i = a_i = \sigma(i)$ for any $1 \leq i \leq n$. $|\sigma|$ denotes the length of the sequence. For $\sigma_1, \sigma_2 \in A^*$, $\sigma_1 \sqsubseteq \sigma_2$ if σ_1 is a subsequence of σ_2, e.g., $\langle a, b, c, x \rangle \sqsubseteq \langle z, x, a, b, b, c, a, b, c, x \rangle$. For $\sigma \in A^*$, $\{a \in \sigma\}$ is the set of elements in σ, and $[a \in \sigma]$ is the multiset of elements in σ, e.g., $[a \in \langle x, y, z, x, y \rangle] = [x^2, y^2, z]$. For $x = (a_1, a_2, ..., a_n) \in A_1 \times A_2 \times ... \times A_n$, $\pi_k(x) = a_k$, i.e., the k-th element of the tuple. For $\sigma \in (A_1 \times A_2 \times ... \times A_n)^*$, $\pi_k(\sigma) = \langle \pi_k(x) \mid x \in \sigma \rangle$, i.e., the sequence projected on the k-th element. For example, $\pi_1(\langle (a_1, t_1), (a_2, t_2), ..., (a_n, t_n) \rangle) = \langle a_1, a_2, ..., a_n \rangle$. These notations can be combined, e.g., $[a \in \pi_k(\sigma)]$ is the multiset of elements for the sequence projected on the k-th element.

Definition 1 (Event, Event Log). *An event is a tuple $e = (a, r, c, t, d_1, ..., d_m)$, where $a \in \mathcal{A}$ is the activity associated with the event, $r \in \mathcal{R}$ is the resource, who is performing the activity, $c \in \mathcal{C}$ is the case id, $t \in \mathcal{T}$ is the event timestamp, and $d_1, ..., d_m$ is a list of additional attributes values, where for any $1 \leq i \leq m, d_i \in \mathcal{D}_i$ (domain of attributes). We call $\xi = \mathcal{A} \times \mathcal{R} \times \mathcal{C} \times \mathcal{T} \times \mathcal{D}_1 \times ... \times \mathcal{D}_m$ the event universe. An **event log** is $EL \subseteq \xi$ where each event can appear only once, i.e., events are uniquely identifiable by their attributes.*

Definition 2 (Simple Process Instance, Simple Trace, Simple Event). *We define $\mathcal{P} = \mathcal{C} \times (\mathcal{A} \times \mathcal{T})^* \times \mathcal{S}$ as the universe of all simple process instances, where $\mathcal{S}$ is the domain of the sensitive attribute. Each simple process instance $p = (c, \sigma, s) \in \mathcal{P}$ represents a **simple trace** $\sigma = \langle (a_1, t_1), (a_2, t_1), ..., (a_n, t_n) \rangle$, which is a sequence of **simple events**, containing activities and timestamps, belonging to the case c with s as the sensitive attribute value.*

Definition 3 (Simple Event Log). *Let $\mathcal{P} = \mathcal{C} \times (\mathcal{A} \times \mathcal{T})^* \times \mathcal{S}$ be the universe of simple process instances. A simple event log is $EL \subseteq \mathcal{P}$ such that if $(c_1, \sigma_1, s_1) \in EL$, $(c_2, \sigma_2, s_2) \in EL$, and $c_1 = c_2$, then $\sigma_1 = \sigma_2$ and $s_1 = s_2$.*

Table 2 shows a simple event log derived from Table 1, where timestamps are represented as "day-hour:minute". In this event log, "Disease" is the attribute which is considered as the sensitive attribute. In the remainder, by event log, trace, and event, we refer to Definition 2 and Definition 3.

3.2   Attack Model

Considering the typical scenario of data collection and data publishing [7], we assume the *trusted model*, where the *data holder* (here, a hospital) is trustworthy. However, the *data recipient* (here, a process miner) is not trustworthy, i.e., a process miner may attempt to identify sensitive information from record owners. In

Table 2. A simple event log derived from Table 1 (each row represents a simple process instance).

Case Id	Simple Trace	Disease
1	$\langle$(RE,01-08:30),(V,01-08:45),(RL,01-08:58)$\rangle$	Flu
2	$\langle$(RE,01-08:46),(HO,01-09:46),(BT,01-10:00),(BT,02-08:00),(V,02-10:00),(RL,02-14:00)$\rangle$	HIV
3	$\langle$(RE,01-08:50),(HO,01-10:00),(BT,01-10:15),(V,02-10:15),(RL,02-14:15)$\rangle$	Infection
4	$\langle$(RE,01-08:55),(V,01-09:10),(IN,01-09:30),(RL,01-10:30)$\rangle$	Poisoning
5	$\langle$(RE,01-09:00),(V,01-09:20),(HO,01-09:55),(BT,01-10:10),(RL,02-16:00)$\rangle$	Cancer
6	$\langle$(RE,01-09:05),(V,01-10:20),(RL,01-14:20)$\rangle$	Hypotension

this subsection, we explain the real attack scenarios based on the *quasi-identifier* role of traces. Note that the examples used in the following definitions are based on Table 2.

Definition 4 (Background Knowledge 1 - bk_{set}^{EL}). *In the first scenario, we assume that the adversary knows a subset of activities having been done for the case, and this information can lead to the case (attribute) linkage attack. Let EL be an event log, we formalize this background knowledge by a function $bk_{set}^{EL} : 2^{\mathcal{A}} \to 2^{EL}$. For $A \subseteq \mathcal{A}$, $bk_{set}^{EL}(A) = \{(c, \sigma, s) \in EL \mid A \subseteq \{a \in \pi_1(\sigma)\}\}$.*

For example, if the adversary knows that $\{V, IN\}$ is the subset of activities having been done for a case, the only matching case is case 4. Therefore, the whole sequence of activities and the sensitive attribute are disclosed.

Definition 5 (Background Knowledge 2 - bk_{mult}^{EL}). *In this scenario, we assume that the adversary knows not only a subset of activities having been done for the case, but also the frequency of each activity. Let EL be an event log, we formalize this background knowledge by a function $bk_{mult}^{EL} : \mathcal{B}(\mathcal{A}) \to 2^{EL}$. For $B \in \mathcal{B}(\mathcal{A})$, $bk_{mult}^{EL}(B) = \{(c, \sigma, s) \in EL \mid B \subseteq [a \in \pi_1(\sigma)]\}$.*

For example, if the adversary knows that $[HO^1, BT^2]$ is the multiset of activities having been performed for a case, the only matching case is case 2. Consequently, the whole sequence of activities and the diseases are disclosed.

Definition 6 (Background Knowledge 3 - bk_{seq}^{EL}). *In this scenario, we assume that the adversary knows a subsequence of activities having been done for the case, and this information can lead to the case (attribute) linkage attack. Let EL be an event log, we formalize this background knowledge by a function $bk_{seq}^{EL} : \mathcal{A}^* \to 2^{EL}$. For $\sigma \in \mathcal{A}^*$, $bk_{seq}^{EL}(\sigma) = \{(c, \sigma', s) \in EL \mid \sigma \sqsubseteq \pi_1(\sigma')\}$.*

For example, if the adversary knows that $\langle RE, V, HO \rangle$ is the subsequence of activities having been performed for a case, the only matching case is case

5. Note that case 3 and case 5 have the same set of activities and by assuming bk_{set}^{EL}, the adversary is not able to single out a case, and since the matching cases have different values as the sensitive attribute, the adversary cannot certainly deduce the actual value of the sensitive attribute.

As can be seen, case 1 and case 6 are not distinguishable according to the defined types of background knowledge, i.e., the *case linkage* attack is not possible. However, by considering the timestamps, another attack scenario can be considered. In order to avoid revealing the exact timestamps of events, we assume that the timestamps are relative rather than absolute.

Definition 7 (Relative Timestamps). *Let* $\sigma = \langle (a_1, t_1), (a_2, t_2), ..., (a_n, t_n) \rangle$ *be a trace and* t_0 *be an initial timestamp,* $rel(\sigma) = \langle (a_1, t_1'), (a_2, t_2'), ..., (a_n, t_n') \rangle$ *is the trace with relative timestamps such that* $t_1' = t_0$ *and for each* $1 < i \leq n$, $t_i' = t_i - t_1 + t_0$.

Definition 8 (Background Knowledge 4 - bk_{rel}^{EL}). *In this scenario, we assume that the adversary knows not only a subsequence of activities, but also the time difference between the activities. Let* EL *be an event log, we formalize this background knowledge by a function* $bk_{rel}^{EL} : (\mathcal{A} \times \mathcal{T})^* \rightarrow 2^{EL}$. *For* $\sigma \in (\mathcal{A} \times \mathcal{T})^*$, $bk_{rel}^{EL}(\sigma) = \{(c, \sigma', s) \in EL \mid rel(\sigma) \sqsubseteq rel(\sigma')\}$.

For example, case 1 and case 6 have the same sequence of activities. However, if the adversary knows that for a victim case, it took almost four hours to get released after visiting by a doctor, the corresponding possible cases narrow down to only one case, which is case 6. The defined types of background knowledge can be categorized from more general and easily achievable to more specific and difficult to achieve, i.e., bk_{set}^{EL} is the most general and easier to gain by an adversary, and bk_{rel}^{EL} is the most specific one. Corresponds to the four defined types of background knowledge and considering a trace in an event log, we define four types of quasi-identifiers w.r.t. the trace and four matching sets for the trace.

Definition 9 (Trace-based Quasi-identifiers - QID_{set}^σ, QID_{mult}^σ, QID_{seq}^σ, QID_{rel}^σ). *Let* EL *be an event log and* σ *be a trace such that* $(c, \sigma, s) \in EL$. *Given the four defined types of background knowledge,* $QID_{set}^\sigma = \{a \in \pi_1(\sigma)\}$, $QID_{mult}^\sigma = [a \in \pi_1(\sigma)]$, $QID_{seq}^\sigma = \pi_1(\sigma)$, *and* $QID_{rel}^\sigma = rel(\sigma)$.

Definition 10 (Matching Sets - EL_{set}^σ, EL_{mult}^σ, EL_{seq}^σ, EL_{rel}^σ). *Let* EL *be an event log and* σ *be a trace such that* $(c, \sigma, s) \in EL$. *Given the four defined types of background knowledge,* $EL_{set}^\sigma = \{bk_{set}^{EL}(A) \mid A \subseteq QID_{set}^\sigma\}$, $EL_{mult}^\sigma = \{bk_{mult}^{EL}(B) \mid B \subseteq QID_{mult}^\sigma\}$, $EL_{seq}^\sigma = \{bk_{seq}^{EL}(\sigma') \mid \sigma' \sqsubseteq QID_{seq}^\sigma\}$, *and* $EL_{rel}^\sigma = \{bk_{rel}^{EL}(\sigma') \mid rel(\sigma') \sqsubseteq QID_{rel}^\sigma\}$.

4   TLKC-Privacy Model

Regular k-anonymity and its extended privacy models assume that an adversary could use all of the quasi-identifier attributes as background knowledge to launch the attacks. However, in reality, it is almost impossible for an adversary to acquire all the information of a target victim, and it requires non-trivial effort to gather each piece of background knowledge. The *LKC*-privacy model exploits this limitation and assume that the adversary's background knowledge is bounded by at most L values of the quasi-identifier.

Based on the bounded background knowledge, proposed by the *LKC*-privacy model [16], we introduce *TLKC*-privacy model for process mining. In the *LKC*-privacy model, L refers to the power of background knowledge, i.e., the length of a sequence, K refers to the k in the k-anonymity definition, and C refers to the bound of confidence regarding the sensitive attribute values in an equivalence class. In the *TLKC*-privacy model $T \in \{seconds, minutes, hours, days\}$ is added which refers to the accuracy of timestamps. For example, when $T = hours$, the accuracy of timestamps is limited at *hours* level. We denote $EL(T)$ as the event log with the accuracy of timestamps at the level T. The general idea of *TLKC*-privacy is to ensure that the background knowledge with maximum length L in $EL(T)$ is shared by at least K cases, and the confidence of inferring any sensitive value in S given the quasi-identifier is not greater than C.

Definition 11 (*TLKC*-Privacy). *Let EL be an event log, L be the maximum length of background knowledge, $T \in \{seconds, minutes, hours, days\}$ be the accuracy of timestamps, and type $\in \{set, mult, seq, rel\}$. $EL(T)$ satisfies TLKC-privacy if and only if for any trace $\sigma \sqsubseteq \sigma'$, $(c, \sigma', s) \in EL$, and $0 < |\sigma| \leq L$:*

- $|EL(T)^\sigma_{type}| \geq K$, *where* $K \in \mathbb{N}_{>0}$, *and*
- $Pr(s|QID^\sigma_{type}) = \frac{|[s' \in \pi_3(p)|p \in EL(T)^\sigma_{type} \wedge s' = s]|}{|EL(T)^\sigma_{type}|} \leq C$ *for any* $s \in S$, *where* $0 < C \leq 1$ *is a real number as the confidence threshold.*

TLKC-privacy inherits several properties from *LKC*-privacy that makes it suitable for anonymizing high-dimensional sparse event data. First, it provides a major relaxation from traditional k-anonymity based on a reasonable assumption that the adversary has restricted knowledge. Second, it generalizes several privacy models including; k-anonymity, confidence bounding, (α, k)-anonymity, and l-diversity. Third, it provides the flexibility to adjust the trade-off between data privacy and data utility, and between an adversary's power and data utility.

4.1 Utility Measure

The measure of data utility depends on the task which is supposed to be performed. However, in process mining, and specifically for process discovery, we want to preserve the maximal frequent traces which are defined as follows.

Definition 12 (Maximal Frequent Trace - MFT). *Let EL be an event log. For a given minimum support threshold Θ, a non-empty trace $\sigma \sqsubseteq \sigma'$ such that $(c, \sigma', s) \in EL$ is maximal frequent in the EL if σ is frequent, i.e., the frequency of σ is greater than or equal to Θ, and no supertrace of σ is frequent in the EL.*

The goal of data utility is to preserve as many MFT as possible. We denote the set of MFT in an event log EL by MFT_{EL}, which is much smaller than the set of frequent traces in the event log EL. Note that any subtrace of an MFT is also a frequent trace, and once all the MFT have been discovered, the support counts of any frequent subtrace can be computed by scanning the data once.

4.2   The Algorithm

The first step is to find all traces that violate the given $TLKC$-privacy requirement. We define a violating trace as follows.

Definition 13 (Violating Trace). *Let EL be an event log, $\sigma \sqsubseteq \sigma'$ such that $(c, \sigma', s) \in EL$, L be the maximum length of the background knowledge, $T \in \{seconds, minutes, hours, days\}$ be the accuracy of timestamps, type $\in \{set, mult, seq, rel\}$, and $0 < |\sigma| \leq L$. σ is violating with respect to $TLKC$-privacy requirements if $|EL(T)_{type}^\sigma| < K$ or $Pr(s|QID_{type}^\sigma) > C$ for any $s \in S$.*

An event log satisfies $TLKC$-privacy, if all violating traces w.r.t. the given privacy requirement are removed. A naïve approach is to determine all possible violating traces and remove them. However, this approach is inefficient because of the numerous number of violating traces, even for a weak privacy requirement.

Table 3. A simple event log with relative timestamps for monotonic property.

Case Id	Trace	Disease
1	$\sigma_1 = \langle(\text{RE},01\text{-}00\text{:}00\text{:}00),(\text{V},01\text{-}01\text{:}02\text{:}00)\rangle$	Flu
2	$\sigma_2 = \langle(\text{RE},01\text{-}00\text{:}00\text{:}00),(\text{V},01\text{-}01\text{:}02\text{:}00),(\text{RL},01\text{-}01\text{:}10\text{:}00)\rangle$	Flu
3	$\sigma_3 = \langle(\text{RE},01\text{-}00\text{:}00\text{:}00),(\text{V},01\text{-}01\text{:}02\text{:}00),(\text{RL},01\text{-}01\text{:}10\text{:}00)\rangle$	HIV

In [16], the authors demonstrate that LKC-privacy is not monotonic w.r.t. L, which holds for $TLKC$-privacy as well. The anonymity threshold K is monotonic w.r.t. L, i.e., if $L' \leq L$ and $C = 100\%$, an event log EL satisfying $TLKC$-privacy must satisfy $TL'KC$-privacy. However, confidence threshold C is not monotonic w.r.t. L, i.e., if σ is non-violating trace, its subtrace may or may not be a non-violating trace. For example, in Table 3, for $L = 3$ and $C = 75\%$, trace σ_2 satisfies $Pr(Flu|\sigma_2) \leq 75\%$. However, its subtrace σ_1 with $L' = 2$ does not satisfy $Pr(Flu|\sigma_1) \leq 75\%$. Therefore, in order to satisfy the second condition in Definition 11, it is insufficient to ensure that every trace σ in EL satisfies $Pr(s|QID_{type}^\sigma) \leq C$ for $|\sigma| = L$, and the condition should hold for $0 < |\sigma| \leq L$. To this end, the *minimal violating traces* are defined.

Definition 14 (Minimal Violating Trace - MVT). *Let EL be an event log, a violating trace $\sigma \sqsubseteq \sigma'$ such that $(c, \sigma', s) \in EL$ is a minimal violating trace in the EL if every proper subtrace of σ is not a violating trace in the EL.*

Algorithm 1. TLKC-Privacy Algorithm

Input: Original event log EL
Input: T, L, K, C, and Θ
Input: Sensitive values S
Output: Anonymized event log EL' which satisfies $TLKC$-privacy
1 generate MFT_{EL} and MVT_{EL};
2 generate MFT_{tree} and MVT_{tree} as the prefix trees for MFT_{EL} and MVT_{EL};
3 **while** *there is node (event) in* MVT_{tree} **do**
4 | select an event (node) e_w that has the highest score to suppress;
5 | delete all the MVT and MFT containing the event e_w from MVT_{tree} and MFT_{tree};
6 | update $Socre(e)$ for all the remaining events (nodes) in MVT_{tree};
7 | add e_w to the suppression set Sup_{EL};
8 **end**
9 **foreach** $e \in Sup_{EL}$ **do**
10 | suppress all instances of e from EL;
11 **end**
12 return suppressed EL as EL';

Every violating trace in an event log is either an MVT or it contains an MVT. Therefore, if an event log EL contains no MVT, then EL contains no violating trace. We denote the set of MVT in an event log EL by MVT_{EL}, which is much smaller than the set of violating traces in the event log EL. A greedy function $Score : \xi \rightarrow \mathbb{R}_{>0}$ is defined to choose an event e to suppress such that it maximizes the number of removed minimal violating traces (privacy gain), but minimizes the number of removed maximal frequent traces (utility loss). For $e \in \xi$, $Score(e) = {}^{PG(e)}/_{UL(e)+1}$. $PG(e)$ is the number of MVT containing the event e, and $UL(e)$ is the number of MFT containing the event e. In order to avoid diving by zero (when e does not belong to any MFT), 1 is added to the denominator. The event e with the highest score is called the *winner* event, denoted by e_w. Algorithm 1 summarizes all the steps of $TLKC$-privacy.

Table 4. A simple event log where timestamps are represented by integer values.

Case id	Trace	Disease
1	$\langle (RE, 1), (HO, 4), (V, 5), (BT, 7), (V, 8) \rangle$	Cancer
2	$\langle (BT, 7), (V, 8), (RL, 9) \rangle$	Infection
3	$\langle (HO, 4), (V, 5), (BT, 7), (RL, 9) \rangle$	Poisoning
4	$\langle (RE, 1), (V, 6), (V, 8), (RL, 9) \rangle$	Infection
5	$\langle (HO, 4), (V, 8), (RL, 9) \rangle$	Poisoning
6	$\langle (V, 6), (BT, 7), (RL, 9) \rangle$	Flu
7	$\langle (RE, 1), (BT, 7), (V, 8), (RL, 9) \rangle$	Flu
8	$\langle (RE, 1), (V, 6), (BT, 7), (V, 8) \rangle$	Cancer

Suppose that Table 4 shows a simple event log EL where timestamps are represented by integer values as hours. The first line in Algorithm 1 generates the set of maximal frequent traces (MFT_{EL}) and the set of minimal violating traces (MVT_{EL}) from the event log EL with $T = hours$, $L = 2$, $K = 2$, $C = 50\%$, $\Theta = 25\%$, $Disease$ as the sensitive attribute S, and bk_{rel}^{EL} as the background knowledge. $MFT_{EL} = \{\langle (RE, 1), (V, 6), (V, 8)\rangle, \langle (RE, 1), (BT, 7), (V, 8)\rangle, \langle (RE, 1), (V, 8), (RL, 9)\rangle, \langle (HO, 4), V, 5), (BT, 7)\rangle, \langle (BT, 7), (V, 8), (RL, 9)\rangle, \langle (V, 6), (BT, 7)\rangle, \langle (V, 6), (RL, 9)\rangle, \langle (HO, 4), (V, 8)\rangle, \langle (HO, 4), (RL, 9)\rangle\}$, and $MVT_{EL} = \{\langle (RE, 1), (HO, 4)\rangle, \langle (RE, 1), (V, 5)\rangle, \langle (RE, 1), (BT, 7)\rangle, \langle (V, 5), (V, 8)\rangle, \langle (V, 5), (RL, 9)\rangle\}$.

Figure 1 shows the MFT_{tree} and MVT_{tree} generated by line 2 in Algorithm 1, where each root-to-leaf path represents one trace, and each node represents an event in a trace with the frequency of occurrence. Table 5 shows the initial $Score(e)$ of every event (node) in the MVT_{tree}. Line 4 determines the winner event e_w which is $(V, 5)$. Line 5 deletes all the MVT and MFT containing the winner event e_w, i.e., subtree 2 and the path $\langle (RE, 1), (V, 5)\rangle$ of subtree 1 in the MVT_{tree} as well as the path $\langle (HO, 4), (V, 5), (BT, 7)\rangle$ of subtree 4 in the MFT_{tree} are removed and frequencies get updated. Line 6 updates the scores based on the new frequencies of events. Table 6 shows the remaining events in MVT_{tree} with the updated scores. Line 7 adds the winner event to a suppression set Sup_{EL}. Lines 4–7 is repeated until there is no node in MVT_{tree}. According to Table 6 the next winner event is $(RE, 1)$, and after deleting all the MVT and MFT containing this event, MVT_{tree} is empty. Therefore, at the end of the *while* loop, the suppression set $Sup_{EL} = \{(V, 5), (RE, 1)\}$. The **foreach** loop suppresses all the instances of the events (*global suppression*) in the Sup_{EL} from the EL, and the last line returns the suppressed EL as the anonymized event log EL' which is shown by Table 7. Table 8 shows the result by applying the traditional k-anonymity with $k = 2$ on the event log Table 4. One can see that even for a weak privacy requirement, much information needs to be suppressed compared to the results provided by $TLKC$-privacy.

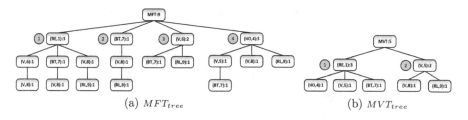

(a) MFT_{tree} (b) MVT_{tree}

Fig. 1. The MFT_{tree} and MVT_{tree} generated for the event log Table 4 with $T = hours$, $L = 2$, $K = 2$, $C = 50\%$, $\Theta = 25\%$, $S = Disease$, and bk_{rel}^{EL}.

5   Evaluation

We evaluate our proposed privacy protection model by applying it on a real-life event log and exploring the effect on the accuracy of the process discovery and

Table 5. The initial scores for the events in Fig. 1b.

	(RE, 1)	(HO, 4)	(V, 5)	(BT, 7)	(V, 8)	(RL, 9)
$PG(e)$	3	1	3	1	1	1
$UL(e)$+1	4	4	2	5	6	5
$Score(e)$	0.75	0.25	1.50	0.20	0.16	0.20

Table 6. The first updated scores.

	(RE, 1)	(HO, 4)	(BT, 7)
$PG(e)$	2	1	1
$UL(e)$+1	4	3	4
$Score(e)$	0.5	0.33	0.25

Table 7. The anonymized event log for Table 4 with $T = hours$, $L = 2$, $K = 2$, $C = 50\%$, $\Theta = 25\%$, $S = Disease$, and bk_{rel}^{EL}.

Case Id	Trace	Disease
1	$\langle (HO, 4), (BT, 7), (V, 8) \rangle$	Cancer
2	$\langle (BT, 7), (V, 8), (RL, 9) \rangle$	Infection
3	$\langle (HO, 4), (BT, 7), (RL, 9) \rangle$	Poisoning
4	$\langle (V, 6), (V, 8), (RL, 9) \rangle$	Infection
5	$\langle (HO, 4), (V, 8), (RL, 9) \rangle$	Poisoning
6	$\langle (V, 6), (BT, 7), (RL, 9) \rangle$	Flu
7	$\langle (BT, 7), (V, 8), (RL, 9) \rangle$	Flu
8	$\langle (V, 6), (BT, 7), (V, 8) \rangle$	Cancer

Table 8. The traditional 2-anonymity event log for Table 4.

Case Id	Trace	Disease
1	$\langle (BT, 7), (V, 8) \rangle$	Cancer
2	$\langle (BT, 7), (V, 8), (RL, 9) \rangle$	Infection
3	$\langle (BT, 7), (RL, 9) \rangle$	Poisoning
4	$\langle (V, 8), (RL, 9) \rangle$	Infection
5	$\langle (V, 8), (RL, 9) \rangle$	Poisoning
6	$\langle (BT, 7), (RL, 9) \rangle$	Flu
7	$\langle (BT, 7), (V, 8), (RL, 9) \rangle$	Flu
8	$\langle (BT, 7), (V, 8) \rangle$	Cancer

performance analysis compared to the ground truth. As the ground truth we use the original process model discovered from the original event log. We employed *Sepsis Case* [13] to conduct our experiments due to some challenging features that it has for process discovery. This event data is a hospital event log containing 16 unique activities, 1050 traces, and 846 variants, which are unique traces, i.e., 80% of traces are unique. The maximum number of traces per variant is 35, the maximum trace length is 185, on average the traces contain 14.5 events, i.e., the average length of traces is 14.5. Note that we provide privacy guarantees w.r.t. the power of background knowledge (L), i.e., all the subtraces having the maximal length L should fulfill the *TLKC*-privacy requirements (Definition 11). Since 80% of traces are unique, this event log is significantly challenging for privacy-preserving process discovery algorithms [6,14].

Overall 1536 experiments have been done for four different types of background knowledge, 384 per each background knowledge, using $T \in \{hours, minu\text{-}tes\}$, $L \in \{2, 4, 8, 16\}$, $K \in \{10, 20, 40, 80\}$, $C \in \{0.2, 0.3, 0.4, 0.5\}$, and $\Theta \in \{0.7, 0.8, 0.9\}$. We consider "disease" and "age" as the sensitive case attributes in the *Sepcis* event log. The confidence value C should not be greater than 0.5, i.e., there are at least two different sensitive values for a victim case. We convert the numerical attributes to categorical using *Boxplots* such that all the values greater than the upper quartile are categorized as *high*, the values less than the lower quartile are categorized as *low*, and the values in between are categorized as *middle*. Regarding the number of unique activities in this event log, it is not realistic to consider the power of background knowledge greater than

16. This is the maximal *set* background knowledge, i.e., an adversary knows all the activities that can be done. Moreover, the length of 75% of the traces in this event log is maximal 16. We consider two settings as representatives to interpret the results in detail; *weak setting* and *strong setting*. For the *weak setting*, we use $T = hours$, $L = 2$, $K = 10$, $C = 0.5$, and $\Theta \in \{0.7, 0.8, 0.9\}$. For the *strong setting*, we use $T = minutes$, $L = 8$, $K = 80$, $C = 0.2$, and $\Theta \in \{0.7, 0.8, 0.9\}$. The implementation as a Python program is available on Github.[1]

5.1   Process Discovery

To evaluate the effect of applying our method on the accuracy of discovered models, we consider three main questions. **Q1:** How accurately do the discovered process models capture the behavior of the original event log? **Q2:** How similar are the discovered process models to the original process model in terms of some quality measures? **Q3:** How is the content of the original event log preserved by the privacy model? To answer Q1, we first discover a process model M' from an anonymized event log EL'. Then, for M', we calculate *fitness*, *precision*, and *f1-score* [1], as some model quality measures, w.r.t. the original event log EL. *Fitness* quantifies the extent to which the discovered model can reproduce the traces recorded in the event log. *Precision* quantifies the fraction of the traces allowed by the model which is not seen in the event log, and *f1-score* combines the fitness and precision $f1\text{-}score = 2 \times precision \times fitness/precision + fitness$. To answer Q2, we discover two process models; the original process model M from the original event log EL and a process model M' from an anonymized event log EL'. Then, we calculate *fitness*, *precision*, and *f1-score* of M and M' w.r.t. EL. At the end, we compare the results to analyze the similarity of the quality measures. We use the *inductive miner infrequent* [10] with the default parameters as the process discovery algorithm. To answer Q3, we compare the number of *variants*, which are the unique traces in the event log, after applying our method with the actual number of variants. Note that applying privacy-preserving algorithms may result in high *precision* and probably high *f1-score*. However, high values for some quality measures do not necessarily mean that the privacy-preserving algorithm preserves the data utility, since the aim is to provide as similar results as possible not to improve the quality of discovered models.

As we discuss in Sect. 6, $PRETSA$ is the only similar algorithm which applies k-anonymity and t-closeness on event data for privacy-aware process discovery. However, $PRETSA$ focuses on the *resource perspective* of privacy while we focus on the *case perspective* of privacy. To compare our method with similar methods, we have developed a variant of $PRETSA$ algorithm $PRETSA_{case}$ where only the k-anonymity part is considered, and the focus is on the privacy of *cases* rather than *resources*. The background knowledge assumed by $PRETSA$ is a prefix of the sequence of executed activities. We have also developed two naïve baseline algorithms. *baseline1* is a naïve k-anonymity algorithm, where we remove all

---

[1] https://github.com/Widderiru/TLKC-privacy/tree/master/home_version.

the traces that occur less than k times in the event log. *baseline2* considers k-anonymity and maps each violating trace to the most similar non-violating subtrace by removing events. For the baseline algorithms and $PRETSA_{case}$ only K is considered from the *settings*.

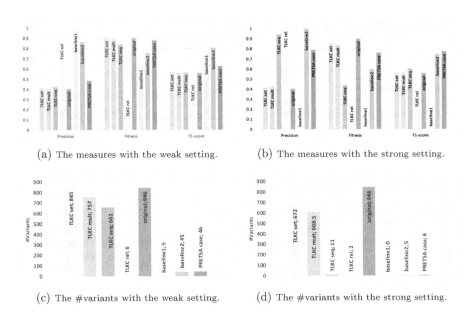

(a) The measures with the weak setting.

(b) The measures with the strong setting.

(c) The #variants with the weak setting.

(d) The #variants with the strong setting.

Fig. 2. The number of variants and quality measures comparison between the four variants of *TLKC*-privacy, the original results, $PRETSA_{case}$, and the baseline algorithms.

Figure 2a shows how the mentioned quality measures are affected by applying our method with the weak setting (average of three experiments regarding Θ), while we consider four variants of our privacy model based on the introduced types of background knowledge including; $TLKC_{set}$, $TLKC_{mult}$, $TLKC_{seq}$, and $TLKC_{rel}$. We compare the measures with the results from the original process model, two baseline algorithms, and $PRETSA_{case}$. If we only consider Q1, the baseline algorithms should be marked as the best ones, since they result in better *f1-score* values. However, as can be seen in Fig. 2c, the baseline algorithms remove many variants from the original event log. Consequently, the corresponding anonymized event logs contain significantly less behavior compared to the original event log, and the resulting models have high *precision*, which in turn results in high *f1-score*. Figure 2a and Fig. 2c show that the results from our privacy model are considerably similar to the original results, except for $TLKC_{rel}$. $TLKC_{rel}$ removes many variants compared to the other variants which is not surprising regarding the assumed background knowledge which is considerably strong, but, difficult to achieve in reality.

Figure 2b and Fig. 2d show the same experiments based on the mentioned quality measures with the strong setting (average of three experiments regarding Θ). Figure 2d shows that even for the strong setting, our privacy model preserves a considerably high amount of content of the original event log considering more general types of background knowledge (bk_{set}^{EL} and bk_{mult}^{EL}). However, $TLKC_{seq}$ preserves fewer variants with the strong setting which results in high precision. Note that the baseline algorithms and $PRETSA_{case}$ do not protect event data against the *attribute linkage* attack and provide weaker privacy guarantees.

5.2   Performance

The effect on performance analyses is evaluated by analyzing the bottlenecks w.r.t. the mean duration of cases between activities. Since the privacy-preserving algorithm may have removal activities, we cannot compare the bottlenecks in the original process model with the bottlenecks in a process model discovered from an anonymized event log. Therefore, we first project the original event log on the activities existing in the anonymized event log. Then, we discover a performance-annotated directly follows graph DFG from the projected event log and compare it with the performance-annotated directly follows graph DFG' from the anonymized event log. A DFG is a graph where the nodes represent activities and the arcs represent causalities. Activities "a" and "b" are connected by an arrow when "a" is frequently followed by "b" [11].

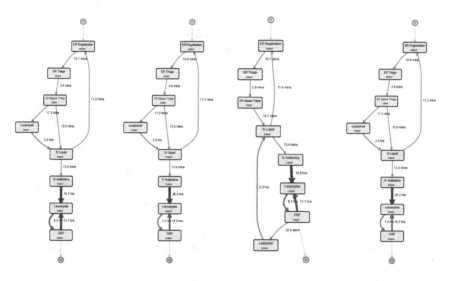

(a) $DFG'\text{-}TLKC_{set}$ (b) $DFG\text{-}TLKC_{set}$ (c) $DFG'\text{-}TLKC_{mult}$ (d) $DFG\text{-}TLKC_{mult}$

Fig. 3. The performance-annotated DFGs from the projected event log (DFG) and an anonymized event log (DFG') for $TLKC_{set}$ and $TLKC_{mult}$ with the strong setting where $\Theta = 0.7$.

Here, we show the results for the strong setting with $\Theta = 0.7$ in Fig. 3 and Fig. 4.[2] As can be seen, the bottlenecks in DFG and DFG' are the same for all the variants except for $TLKC_{rel}$, where the assumed background knowledge is significantly strong and only a few variants remain after applying the method. Note that the mean duration of the cases are different in DFG and DFG' because of the use of relative timestamps in the anonymized event logs. This experiment shows the similarity of the results in terms of real process models.

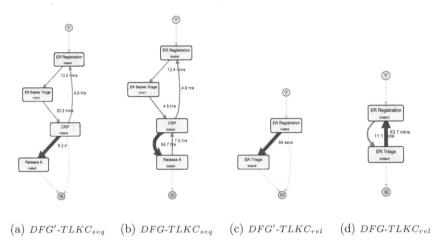

(a) DFG'-$TLKC_{seq}$ (b) DFG-$TLKC_{seq}$ (c) DFG'-$TLKC_{rel}$ (d) DFG-$TLKC_{rel}$

Fig. 4. The performance-annotated DFGs from the projected event log (DFG) and an anonymized event log (DFG') for $TLKC_{seq}$ and $TLKC_{rel}$ with the strong setting where $\Theta = 0.7$.

6   Related Work

During the last decades, privacy issues have received increasing attention. The privacy challenges in process mining are more similar to the privacy-preserving sequential pattern mining [4,9] and anonymizing trajectory data [16,17]. The privacy model, presented in this paper, extends the LKC-privacy model [16], both in the parameters and the type of background knowledge, to be fitted in the context of process mining. In process mining research, confidentiality and privacy received less attention. In [2], *Responsible Process Mining* (RPM) is introduced as the sub-discipline focusing on possible negative side-effects of applying process mining. RPM addresses concerns related to Fairness, Accuracy, Confidentiality, and Transparency (FACT). In [15], the authors propose a privacy-preserving system design for process mining, where a user-centered view is considered to track personal data. In [19,20], a framework is introduced, which provides a

---

[2] These results have been provided by Disco (https://fluxicon.com/disco/) with the sliders set to the maximal number of activities and the minimal paths.

generic scheme for confidentiality in process mining. In [18], the aim is to provide a privacy-preserving method for discovering roles from event data.

Most related to our work are [6] and [14], where the authors propose privacy-preserving techniques for process discovery. Therefore, we pinpoint the differences with $TLKC$-privacy model. In [6], the authors apply k-anonymity and t-closeness [12] on event data to preserve the privacy of *resources* while we focus on the *case perspective*. Also, the assumed background knowledge is a prefix of sequence of activities which is restrictively specific. In [14], the authors employ the notion of differential privacy [5]. This research focuses on *case perspective* of privacy in process mining which is similar to our research from this point of view. However, the type of privacy guarantee is noise-based. As shown in [14], applying the noise-based privacy guarantees on event data is challenging when the process models are unstructured and the majority of traces are unique. Moreover, noise-based techniques do not preserve the *truthfulness* of values at the case level [8], i.e., for some cases there is no corresponding individual in real life. Also, the performance aspect is not considered by this research.

7   Conclusions

In this paper, we introduced two perspectives for privacy in process mining (*case perspective* and *resource perspective*), and we discussed privacy challenges in process mining. We demonstrated that existing well-known privacy-preserving techniques cannot be directly applied to event data. We introduced the $TLKC$-privacy model for process mining which is an extension for the LKC-privacy model. Our proposed model preserves the privacy of the cases whose data is processed in process mining, particularly for process discovery and performance analyses. It counteracts both the *case linkage* and the *attribute linkage* attacks.

We implemented four variants of $TLKC$-privacy w.r.t. the four different types of background knowledge. All the variants have been evaluated based on a real-life event log which is highly challenging for process discovery techniques in terms of unique traces ratio. 384 experiments were performed per each type of background knowledge, and the results were given for a weak and a strong setting. Our experiments demonstrate that $TLKC$-privacy model preserves the data utility in terms of similarity of the results to the actual results. Specifically, for the more general types of background knowledge. Moreover, we showed that how the cost of privacy increases w.r.t. the strength of background knowledge.

For the *multiset* variant of $TLKC$ ($TLKC_{mult}$) many potential minimal violating traces with the length longer than one can be generated by the presented algorithm, which results in long computation times. In the future, smarter pruning algorithms could be explored to generate a smaller potential set of minimal violating traces. Moreover, some algorithms could be designed to automatically generate reasonable values for the parameters used by our algorithm.

Acknowledgment. Funded under the Excellence Strategy of the Federal Government and the Länder. We also thank the Alexander von Humboldt (AvH) Stiftung for supporting our research.

References

1. van der Aalst, W.M.P.: Process Mining - Data Science in Action, Second edn. Springer, Heidelberg (2016). https://doi.org/10.1007/978-3-662-49851-4
2. Aalst, W.M.P.: Responsible data science: using event data in a "people friendly" manner. In: Hammoudi, S., Maciaszek, L.A., Missikoff, M.M., Camp, O., Cordeiro, J. (eds.) ICEIS 2016. LNBIP, vol. 291, pp. 3–28. Springer, Cham (2017). https://doi.org/10.1007/978-3-319-62386-3_1
3. Aggarwal, C.C., Philip, S.Y.: Privacy-Preserving Data Mining: Models and Algorithms. Springer, Heidelberg (2008). https://doi.org/10.1007/978-0-387-70992-5
4. Bonomi, L., Xiong, L.: A two-phase algorithm for mining sequential patterns with differential privacy. In: Proceedings of the 22nd ACM International Conference on Information & Knowledge Management. ACM (2013)
5. Dwork, C.: Differential privacy: a survey of results. In: Agrawal, M., Du, D., Duan, Z., Li, A. (eds.) TAMC 2008. LNCS, vol. 4978, pp. 1–19. Springer, Heidelberg (2008). https://doi.org/10.1007/978-3-540-79228-4_1
6. Fahrenkrog-Petersen, S.A., van der Aa, H., Weidlich, M.: PRETSA: event log sanitization for privacy-aware process discovery. In: International Conference on Process Mining, ICPM 2019, Aachen, Germany, 24–26 June 2019, pp. 1–8 (2019)
7. Fung, B.C., Wang, K., Chen, R., Yu, P.S.: Privacy-preserving data publishing: a survey of recent developments. ACM Comput. Surv. (Csur) **42**(4), 1–53 (2010)
8. Fung, B.C., Wang, K., Fu, A.W.C., Philip, S.Y.: Introduction to Privacy-Preserving Data Publishing: Concepts and Techniques. Chapman and Hall/CRC, London (2010)
9. Kapoor, V., Poncelet, P., Trousset, F., Teisseire, M.: Privacy preserving sequential pattern mining in distributed databases. In: Proceedings of the 15th ACM International Conference on Information and Knowledge Management. ACM (2006)
10. Leemans, S.J.J., Fahland, D., van der Aalst, W.M.P.: Discovering block-structured process models from event logs containing infrequent behaviour. In: Business Process Management Workshops - BPM International Workshops, pp. 66–78 (2013)
11. Leemans, S.J.J., Fahland, D., van der Aalst, W.M.P.: Scalable process discovery and conformance checking. Softw. Syst. Model. **17**(2), 599–631 (2016). https://doi.org/10.1007/s10270-016-0545-x
12. Li, N., Li, T., Venkatasubramanian, S.: t-closeness: privacy beyond k-anonymity and l-diversity. In: Proceedings of the 23rd International Conference on Data Engineering, ICDE 2007, The Marmara Hotel, Istanbul, Turkey, 15–20 April 2007
13. Mannhardt, F.: Sepsis cases-event log. Eindhoven University of Technology (2016)
14. Mannhardt, F., Koschmider, A., Baracaldo, N., Weidlich, M., Michael, J.: Privacy-preserving process mining - differential privacy for event logs. Bus. Inf. Syst. Eng. **61**(5), 595–614 (2019)
15. Michael, J., Koschmider, A., Mannhardt, F., Baracaldo, N., Rumpe, B.: User-centered and privacy-driven process mining system design for IoT. In: Cappiello, C., Ruiz, M. (eds.) CAiSE 2019. LNCS, vol. 350, pp. 194–206. Springer, Heidelberg (2019). https://doi.org/10.1007/978-3-030-21297-1_17
16. Mohammed, N., Fung, B.C., Hung, P.C., Lee, C.k.: Anonymizing healthcare data: a case study on the blood transfusion service. In: Proceedings of the 15th ACM SIGKDD International Conference on Knowledge Discovery and Data Mining, KDD 2009, pp. 1285–1294. ACM, New York (2009)
17. Nergiz, M.E., Atzori, M., Saygin, Y.: Towards trajectory anonymization: a generalization-based approach. In: Proceedings of the SIGSPATIAL ACM GIS 2008 International Workshop on Security and Privacy in GIS and LBS (2008)

18. Rafiei, M., van der Aalst, W.M.P.: Mining roles from event logs while preserving privacy. In: Di Francescomarino, C., Dijkman, R., Zdun, U. (eds.) BPM 2019. LNBIP, vol. 362, pp. 676–689. Springer, Cham (2019). https://doi.org/10.1007/978-3-030-37453-2_54

19. Rafiei, M., von Waldthausen, L., van der Aalst, W.M.P.: Ensuring confidentiality in process mining. In: Proceedings of the 8th International Symposium on Data-Driven Process Discovery and Analysis (SIMPDA 2018), Seville, Spain (2018)

20. Rafiei, M., von Waldthausen, L., van der Aalst, W.M.P.: Supporting confidentiality in process mining using abstraction and encryption. In: Ceravolo, P., van Keulen, M., Gómez-López, M.T. (eds.) SIMPDA 2018-2019. LNBIP, vol. 379, pp. 101–123. Springer, Cham (2020). https://doi.org/10.1007/978-3-030-46633-6_6

21. Voss, W.G.: European union data privacy law reform: general data protection regulation, privacy shield, and the right to delisting. Bus. Lawyer **72**(1), 221–234 (2016)

Incremental Discovery of Hierarchical Process Models

Daniel Schuster[1(✉)], Sebastiaan J. van Zelst[1,2], and Wil M. P. van der Aalst[1,2]

[1] Fraunhofer Institute for Applied Information Technology FIT,
Sankt Augustin, Germany
{daniel.schuster,sebastiaan.van.zelst}@fit.fraunhofer.de
[2] RWTH Aachen University, Aachen, Germany
{s.j.v.zelst,wvdaalst}@pads.rwth-aachen.de

Abstract. Many of today's information systems record the execution of
(business) processes in great detail. Process mining utilizes such data and
aims to extract valuable insights. Process discovery, a key research area
in process mining, deals with the construction of process models based
on recorded process behavior. Existing process discovery algorithms aim
to provide a "push-button-technology", i.e., the algorithms discover a
process model in a completely automated fashion. However, real data
often contain noisy and/or infrequent complex behavioral patterns. As a
result, the incorporation of all behavior leads to very imprecise or overly
complex process models. At the same time, data pre-processing techniques have shown to be able to improve the precision of process models,
i.e., without explicitly using domain knowledge. Yet, to obtain superior
process discovery results, human input is still required. Therefore, we
propose a discovery algorithm that allows a user to incrementally extend
a process model by new behavior. The proposed algorithm is designed to
localize and repair nonconforming process model parts by exploiting the
hierarchical structure of the given process model. The evaluation shows
that the process models obtained with our algorithm, which allows for
incremental extension of a process model, have, in many cases, superior characteristics in comparison to process models obtained by using
existing process discovery and model repair techniques.

Keywords: Process mining · Incremental process discovery · Process
trees · Process model repair

1 Introduction

Process discovery is one of the three main fields in *process mining*, along with
conformance checking and *process enhancement* [4]. In process discovery, the
data generated during process executions and stored in information systems are
utilized to generate a process model that describes the observed behavior. We
refer to such data as *event data*. The obtained process models are used for a
variety of purposes, e.g., to provide insights about the actual process performed
and to analyze and improve performance and compliance problems.

© Springer Nature Switzerland AG 2020
F. Dalpiaz et al. (Eds.): RCIS 2020, LNBIP 385, pp. 417–433, 2020.
https://doi.org/10.1007/978-3-030-50316-1_25

Most process discovery techniques are fully automated, i.e., no interaction with the algorithm is possible during discovery. These techniques require event data as input and return a process model that describes the given observed behavior. Moreover, it is not directly possible, i.e., using process discovery techniques, to extend an existing process model with additional behavior, except by re-applying the algorithm to the entire extended event data. *Process model repair* techniques have been developed to add additional behavior to an existing model. However, they are not designed to be applied iteratively to a given event log to mimic an (incremental) process discovery algorithm.

In this paper, we propose an approach to *incrementally* discover process models. The algorithm allows the user to incrementally discover a process model by adding the behavior, trace by trace, to an existing process model. Thereby, the process model under construction gets incrementally extended. Hence, our approach combines the usually separate phases of event data filtering and discovery. In addition, the algorithm offers the possibility at any point in time to "autocomplete", i.e., observed behavior not yet processed is automatically added to the process model under construction. Our approach takes behavior that is not yet described by the process model and detects which parts of the process model must be altered. We focus on hierarchical, also called block-structured, process models and exploit their structure to determine the process model parts that must be changed. The evaluation of our proposed approach shows that the obtained process models have a comparable and in many cases superior quality compared to non-incremental process discovery algorithms, which have to be executed on the whole extended event data each time behavior is added. Furthermore, the conducted experiments show that our proposed approach outperforms an existing process model repair technique [12] in many cases.

The remainder of the paper is structured as follows. We present related work in Sect. 2. In Sect. 3, we present concepts, notations and definitions used throughout the paper. In Sect. 4, we present our novel approach to incrementally discover process models. Afterwards, we discuss the results of the conducted experiments in Sect. 5. Finally, we summarize the paper in Sect. 6.

2   Related Work

Various process discovery algorithms exist. An overview is beyond the scope of this paper, hence, we refer to [11]. We mainly focus on process model repair techniques, incremental and interactive process discovery.

The term *process model repair* was introduced in [12] and an extended algorithm to repair a process model was presented in [13]. In the paper, an event log L and a process model P is assumed, i.e., a Petri net, which does not accept all traces in L. The goal is to find a process model P' that accepts L. In comparison to our proposed approach, an essential goal for the authors is that the repaired model P' is structurally similar to the original model P since their focus is on model repair and not on process discovery. Since our proposed approach is an incremental algorithm for process discovery, similarity of the resulting model to the original model is not a requirement.

In [15], an *incremental process discovery* architecture was introduced that is based on merging new discovered process models into existing ones. In detail, an existing process model P is assumed and, for unseen behavior, a new process model is discovered and then merged into the existing model P. Furthermore, the approach is explicitly designed to work in an automated fashion. Two other approaches [14,19] calculate ordering relations of activities based on the given process model and on a yet unprocessed event log. The two obtained relations are then merged together and are used to retrieve a model. In [7] the authors describe a repair approach that incrementally highlights deviations in a process model with respect to a given event log. The user has to manually repair this deviations under the guidance of the algorithm.

Next to incremental process discovery algorithms, there is the field of *interactive process mining* [9]. In [10] an interactive process discovery algorithm is presented that assumes constant feedback from a user. Moreover, the user controls the algorithm by specifying how the process model should be altered. The algorithm supports the user by indicating favourable actions, e.g, where to place an activity in the process model (and also provides an "auto-complete option"). Furthermore, the algorithm ensures that the process model under construction retains certain properties, i.e., soundness.

3   Background

In this section, we introduce notations and definitions used in this paper.

Given an arbitrary set X, we denote the set of all sequences over X as X^*, e.g., $\langle a, b, b \rangle \in \{a, b, c\}^*$. We denote the empty sequence by $\langle \rangle$. For a given sequence σ, we denote its length as $|\sigma|$ and for $i \in \{1, \ldots, |\sigma|\}$, $\sigma(i)$ represents the i-th element of σ. Given two sequences σ and σ', we denote the concatenation of these two sequences by $\sigma \cdot \sigma'$. For instance, $\langle a \rangle \cdot \langle b, c \rangle = \langle a, b, c \rangle$. We extend the $\cdot$ operator to sets of sequences, i.e., let $S_1, S_2 \subseteq X^*$ then $S_1 \cdot S_2 = \{\sigma_1 \cdot \sigma_2 \,|\, \sigma_1 \in S_1 \wedge \sigma_2 \in S_2\}$. For given traces σ, σ', the set of all interleaved sequences is denoted by $\sigma \diamond \sigma'$. For example, $\langle a, b \rangle \diamond \langle c \rangle = \{\langle a, b, c \rangle, \langle a, c, b \rangle, \langle c, a, b \rangle\}$. We extend the $\diamond$ operator to sets of sequences. Let S_1, S_2 be two sets of sequences. $S_1 \diamond S_2$ denotes the set of interleaved sequences, i.e., $S_1 \diamond S_2 = \{\sigma_1 \diamond \sigma_2 \,|\, \sigma_1 \in S_1 \wedge \sigma_2 \in S_2\}$.

For a set X, a multi-set over X allows multiple appearances of the same element. Formally, a multi-set is a function $f : X \rightarrow \mathbb{N}_0$ that assigns a multiplicity to each element in X. For instance, given $X = \{a, b, c\}$, a multi-set over X is $[a^3, c]$, which contains three times an element a, no b and one c. We denote all possible multi-sets over X as $\mathcal{B}(X)$. Furthermore, given two multi-sets X and Y, $X \uplus Y$ denotes the union of two multi-sets, e.g., $[x^2, a] \uplus [x, y^2] = [x^3, a, y^2]$.

Next, we introduce projection functions. Given a set X, a sequence $\sigma \in X^*$ and $X' \subseteq X$. We recursively define $\sigma_{\downarrow_{X'}} \in X'^*$ with: $\langle \rangle_{\downarrow_{X'}} = \langle \rangle$, $(\langle x \rangle \cdot \sigma)_{\downarrow_{X'}} = \langle x \rangle \cdot \sigma_{\downarrow_{X'}}$ if $x \in X'$ and $(\langle x \rangle \cdot \sigma)_{\downarrow_{X'}} = \sigma_{\downarrow_{X'}}$ otherwise.

Let $t = (x_1, \ldots, x_n) \in X_1 \times \ldots \times X_n$ be an n-tuple over n sets. We define projection functions that extract a specific element of t, i.e., $\pi_1(t) = x_1, \ldots, \pi_n(t) = x_n$. For example, $\pi_2((a, b, c)) = b$.

Table 1. Example of an event log

Event-id	Case-id	Activity name	Timestamp	$\cdots$
$\cdots$	$\cdots$	$\cdots$	$\cdots$	$\cdots$
200	13	create order (c)	2020-01-02 15:29:24	$\cdots$
201	27	receive payment (r)	2020-01-02 15:44:34	$\cdots$
202	43	dispatch order (d)	2020-01-02 16:29:24	$\cdots$
203	13	pack order (p)	2020-01-02 19:12:13	$\cdots$
204	13	cancel order (a)	2020-01-03 11:32:21	$\cdots$
$\cdots$	$\cdots$	$\cdots$	$\cdots$	$\cdots$

Analogously, given a sequence of length m with n-tuples $\sigma = \langle(x_1^1,\ldots,x_n^1),\ldots,(x_1^m,\ldots,x_n^m)\rangle$, we define $\pi_1^*(\sigma) = \langle x_1^1,\ldots,x_1^m\rangle,\ldots,\pi_n^*(\sigma) = \langle x_n^1,\ldots,x_n^m\rangle$. For instance, $\pi_2^*(\langle(a,b),(a,c),(b,a)\rangle) = \langle b,c,a\rangle$.

3.1   Event Data and Event Logs

The execution of (business) processes generates event data in the corresponding information systems. Such data describe the activities performed, which process instance they belong to and they contain various metadata about the activities performed. Activities performed in the context of a specific process instance are referred to as a *trace*, i.e., a sequence of activities.

Consider Table 1 in which we present an example of an event log. For instance, if we consider all events related to the case-id 13, we observe the trace ⟨create order (c), pack order (p), cancel order (a)⟩. For simplicity, we abbreviate activities with letters. A *variant* describes a unique sequence of activities which can occur several times in an event log. Since, in the context of this paper, we are only interested in the traces that occurred, we define an event log as a multiset of traces. Note that, event data as depicted in Table 1 can be translated easily into a multiset of traces.

Definition 1 (Event Log). *Let $\mathcal{A}$ denote the universe of activities. An* event log *is a multiset of sequences over $\mathcal{A}$, i.e., $L \in \mathcal{B}(\mathcal{A}^*)$.*

3.2   Process Models

A process model describes the (intended) behavior of a process. Many process modeling formalisms exist, ranging from informal textual descriptions to mathematical models with exact execution semantics. In the field of process mining, *workflow nets* [1] are often used to represent process models since concurrent behavior can be modelled in a compact manner. In this paper we focus on *process trees* that represent hierarchical structured, sound workflow nets, i.e., block-structured workflow nets [16]. We formally define process trees in Definition 2.

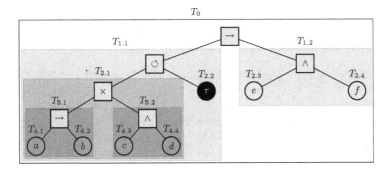

Fig. 1. Example of a process tree T_0

Definition 2 (Process Tree). *Let $\mathcal{A}$ be the universe of activities and let $\tau \notin \mathcal{A}$. Let $\oplus = \{\rightarrow, \times, \wedge, \circlearrowleft\}$ be the set of process tree operators.*

- *given an arbitrary $a \in \mathcal{A} \cup \{\tau\}$, a is a process tree*
- *given $n \geq 1$ process trees $T_1, T_2, \ldots, T_n$ and an operator $\bullet \in \{\rightarrow, \times, \wedge\}$, $T = \bullet(T_1, T_2, \ldots, T_n)$ is a process tree*
- *given two process trees T_1, T_2, $T = \circlearrowleft (T_1, T_2)$ is a process tree*

We denote the set of all process trees over $\mathcal{A}$ as $\mathcal{T}_\mathcal{A}$. Furthermore, we denote for a process tree T the set of its leaf nodes by L_T. Note that, by definition, leaf nodes always contain activities or the silent activity τ, and inner nodes and the root node always contain process tree operators. Consider Fig. 1 which shows an example of a process tree T_0. Note that the tree can also be presented textually: $\rightarrow (\circlearrowleft (\times(\rightarrow (a,b), \wedge(c,d)), \tau), \wedge(e,f))$.

For given process trees T and T', we call T' a *subtree* of T if T' is contained in T. For instance, $T_{3.2}$ is a subtree of $T_{1.1}$ (Fig. 1). Given two subtrees T_x, T_y of a tree T, we define the *lowest common ancestor (LCA)* as the tree T_{LCA} such that the distance between T's root node and T_{LCA}'s root node is maximal and T_x, T_y are contained in T_{LCA}. For example, given the two subtrees $T_{4.2}$ and $T_{2.2}$ of T_0 (Fig. 1), $T_{1.1}$ is the LCA of $T_{4.2}$ and $T_{2.2}$.

In the following, we first informally describe the semantics of a process tree and afterwards, present formal definitions. The sequence operator $\rightarrow$ indicates that the subtrees have to be sequentially executed. For example, the root of process tree T_0 is a sequence operator. Hence, the left subtree $T_{1.1}$ has to be executed before the right one $T_{1.2}$. The loop operator $\circlearrowleft$, which has by definition two subtrees, contains a loop body which is the first subtree and a redo part, the second subtree. The loop body has to be executed at least once. Afterwards, the redo part can be optionally executed. In case the redo part is executed, the loop body must be executed afterwards again. The choice operator $\times$, i.e., exclusive or, indicates that exactly one subtree must be executed. The parallel operator $\wedge$ indicates a parallel (interleaved) execution of the subtrees. For instance, for the tree $T_{1.2}$ the activities e and f can be executed in any order.

a	b	$\gg$	$\gg$	c	f	$\gg$
a	b	τ	d	c	f	e
$(T_{4.1})$	$(T_{4.2})$	$(T_{2.2})$	$(T_{4.4})$	$(T_{4.3})$	$(T_{2.4})$	$(T_{2.3})$

a	$\gg$	b	c	f	$\gg$
$\gg$	a	b	$\gg$	f	e
	$(T_{4.1})$	$(T_{4.2})$		$(T_{2.4})$	$(T_{2.3})$

Fig. 2. Two possible alignments for process tree T_0 (Fig. 1) and $\langle a, b, c, f \rangle$

We denote the language of a process tree $T \in \mathcal{T}_A$, i.e., the set of accepted traces over $\mathcal{A}$, as $\mathcal{L}(T)$. For instance, $\langle a,b,f,e \rangle, \langle d,c,a,b,e,f \rangle \in \mathcal{L}(T_0)$ and $\langle d,c,a,e,f \rangle, \langle a,c,e,f \rangle \notin \mathcal{L}(T_0)$. Next, we define the semantics of process trees based on [4].

Definition 3 (Semantics of Process Trees). *For a process tree $T \in \mathcal{T}_A$, we recursively define its language $\mathcal{L}(T)$.*

- *if $T = a \in \mathcal{A}$, $\mathcal{L}(T) = \{\langle a \rangle\}$*
- *if $T = \tau$, $\mathcal{L}(T) = \{\langle\rangle\}$*
- *if $T = \rightarrow(T_1, \ldots, T_n)$, $\mathcal{L}(T) = \mathcal{L}(T_1) \cdot \ldots \cdot \mathcal{L}(T_n)$*
- *if $T = \wedge(T_1, \ldots, T_n)$, $\mathcal{L}(T) = \mathcal{L}(T_1) \diamond \ldots \diamond \mathcal{L}(T_n)$*
- *if $T = \times(T_1, \ldots, T_n)$, $\mathcal{L}(T) = \mathcal{L}(T_1) \cup \ldots \cup \mathcal{L}(T_n)$*
- *if $T = \circlearrowleft(T_1, T_2)$, $\mathcal{L}(T) = \{\sigma_1 \cdot \sigma_1' \cdot \sigma_2 \cdot \sigma_2' \ldots \cdot \sigma_m \mid m \geq 1 \wedge \forall 1 \leq i \leq m(\sigma_i \in \mathcal{L}(T_1)) \wedge \forall 1 \leq i \leq m(\sigma_i' \in \mathcal{L}(T_2))\}$*

3.3   Alignments

Alignments have been developed to map observed behavior onto modeled behavior [5]. They are used to determine if a given trace conforms to a given process model. In the case of deviations, alignments indicate the detected deviations in the process model and in the trace.

In Fig. 2, two possible alignments for the process tree T_0 (Fig. 1) and the trace $\langle a, b, c, f \rangle$ are given. The first row, the trace part, always corresponds to the given trace (ignoring the skip symbol $\gg$). The second row, the model part, always corresponds to a trace that is accepted by the given process model (ignoring $\gg$).

An alignment move corresponds to a single column in Fig. 2. We distinguish four different alignment moves. Synchronous moves, highlighted in light gray, indicate that the observed behavior in the trace can be replayed in the process model. For example, the first two moves of the left alignment in Fig. 2 represent synchronous moves, i.e., the observed activities a and b could be replayed in the process model. Log moves, highlighted in black, indicate additional observed behavior that cannot be replayed in the process model and therefore represent a deviation. Model moves, highlighted in dark gray, indicate that behavior is missing in the given trace according to the process model. Model moves can be further differentiated into visible and invisible model moves. Given the first alignment from Fig. 2, the first model move represents an invisible model move because the executed activity is the silent activity τ. Note that invisible model moves do not represent deviations. The second model move represents a visible

a	b	≫	c	d	≫	a	b	e	f
a	b	τ	c	d	τ	a	b	e	f
$(T_{4.1})$	$(T_{4.2})$	$(T_{2.2})$	$(T_{4.3})$	$(T_{4.4})$	$(T_{2.2})$	$(T_{4.1})$	$(T_{4.2})$	$(T_{2.3})$	$(T_{2.4})$
T_0	T_0	T_0	T_0	T_0	T_0	T_0	T_0	T_0	T_0
$T_{1.1}$	$T_{1.1}$	$T_{1.1}$	$T_{1.1}$	$T_{1.1}$	$T_{1.1}$	$T_{1.1}$	$T_{1.1}$		
$T_{2.1}$	$T_{2.1}$		$T_{2.1}$	$T_{2.1}$		$T_{2.1}$	$T_{2.1}$		
$T_{3.1}$	$T_{3.1}$					$T_{3.1}$	$T_{3.1}$		
			$T_{3.2}$	$T_{3.2}$					
								$T_{1.2}$	$T_{1.2}$

T_0	$[\langle a,b,c,d,a,b,e,f\rangle]$
$T_{1.1}$	$[\langle a,b,c,d,a,b\rangle]$
$T_{2.1}$	$[\langle a,b\rangle^2, \langle c,d\rangle]$
$T_{3.1}$	$[\langle a,b\rangle^2]$
$T_{3.2}$	$[\langle c,d\rangle]$
$T_{1.2}$	$[\langle e,f\rangle]$

(a) Alignment and listing of subtrees containing the executed process tree leave nodes

(b) Sub event logs

Fig. 3. Calculation of the sub event log for T_0 (Fig. 1) and $L = [\langle a,b,c,d,a,b,e,f\rangle]$

model move since the executed activity $d \neq \tau$. Visible model moves represent deviations because a modeled activity was not observed.

Definition 4 (Alignment). *Let $\mathcal{A}$ denote the universe of activities, let $\sigma \in \mathcal{A}^*$ be a trace and let $T \in \mathcal{T}_\mathcal{A}$ be a process tree with the set of leaf nodes L_T. A sequence $\gamma \in ((\mathcal{A}\cup\{\gg\}) \times (L_T\cup\{\gg\}))^*$ is an alignment iff:*

1. $\sigma = \pi_1^*(\gamma)_{\downarrow_\mathcal{A}}$
2. $\pi_2^*(\gamma)_{\downarrow_{L_T}} \in \mathcal{L}(T)$
3. $(\gg, \gg) \notin \gamma$
4. $(a_1, a_2) \notin \gamma$ for $a_1 \in \mathcal{A}, a_2 \in L_T$ s.t. $a_1 \neq a_2$

For given T and σ, the set of all possible alignments is denoted by $\Gamma(\sigma, T)$. Since many alignments exist for a given trace and a process model, there is the concept of optimal alignments. In general, an optimal alignment minimizes the number of mismatches between the process model and the trace. To determine optimal alignments, costs are assigned to alignment moves. A cost minimal alignment for a given trace and a process model is considered to be an optimal alignment. In this paper, we assume the *standard cost function* that assigns cost 0 to synchronous and invisible model moves. Furthermore, it assigns cost 1 to visible model and log moves. Note that there can be several optimal alignments for a given model and trace. The calculation of optimal alignments was shown to be reducible to the shortest path problem [5]. Note that there can be several optimal alignments.

We denote the set of optimal alignments for σ and T by $\bar{\Gamma}(\sigma, T)$. Observe that, under the standard cost function, an alignment $\gamma \in \bar{\Gamma}(\sigma, T)$ indicates a deviation between the trace σ and the process tree T if the costs are higher than 0.

3.4 Sub Event Logs for Process Trees

In this section, we define the concept of a sub event log. Assume a process tree T and a perfectly fitting event log L, i.e., $\{\sigma \in L\} \subseteq \mathcal{L}(T)$. We define for each

---

Algorithm 1. Calculation of sub event logs for process trees

Input: $L{\in}\mathcal{B}(\mathcal{A}^*), T{\in}\mathcal{T}_\mathcal{A}$ (Assumption: $\{\sigma{\in}L\}{\subseteq}\mathcal{L}(T)))$
Output: sub event log for each subtree of T, i.e., $s : \mathcal{T}_\mathcal{A} \to \mathcal{B}(\mathcal{A}^*)$
begin

  1   **forall the** *subtrees* T' *of* T **do**
  2       $s(T') \leftarrow []$ // initialize sub event logs

  3   **forall the** $\sigma{\in}L$ **do**
  4   let $\gamma{\in}\bar{\Gamma}(\sigma, T)$ // calculate optimal alignment for σ and T
  5   **forall the** *subtrees* T' *of* T **do**
  6          $t(T') \leftarrow \langle\rangle$ // initialize trace for each subtree
  7   **for** $i{\in}\{1,\ldots,|\gamma|\}$ **do**
  8          $m \leftarrow \gamma(i)$ // extract i-th alignment move
  9          $T_l \leftarrow \pi_2(m)$ // extract executed process leaf node
 10   **forall the** *subtrees* T' *of* T **do**
 11   **if** T_l *is subtree of* $T' \vee T_l{=}T'$ **then**
 12              $t(T') \leftarrow t(T'){\cdot}\langle\pi_2(m)\rangle$ // add executed activity to T''s trace
 13   **else if** $t(T'){\neq}\langle\rangle$ **then**
 14              $s(T') \leftarrow s(T'){\uplus}[t(T')]$ // add trace to T''s sub event log
 15              $t(T') \leftarrow \langle\rangle$ // reset trace

 16   **return** s

---

subtree in T a sub event log that reflects which parts of the given traces from L are handled by the subtree.

Assume the event log $L = [\langle a, b, c, d, a, b, e, f\rangle]$ and the process tree T_0 (Fig. 1). The event log L is perfectly fitting because the only trace $\sigma = \langle a, b, c, d, a, b, e, f\rangle$ in L is accepted by T_0, i.e., $\sigma \in \mathcal{L}(T_0)$. To calculate sub event logs, we first calculate alignments for each trace in the given event log. The alignment of σ and T_0 is depicted in the upper part of Fig. 3a. Since σ is accepted by T_0, we only observe invisible model moves and synchronous moves. Below the depicted alignment, all subtrees are listed that contain the executed leaf nodes. For example, the first executed leaf node a ($T_{4.1}$) is a subtree of $T_0, T_{1.1}, T_{2.1}$ and $T_{3.1}$.

Obviously, all executed leaf nodes are subtrees of T_0. Hence, we add the complete trace to T_0's sub event log (Fig. 3b). Note that the sub event log of the whole process tree, i.e., T_0, is always equal to the given event log. The subtree $T_{1.1}$ contains all executed leaf nodes from the 1st leaf a ($T_{4.1}$) to the last execution of b ($T_{4.2}$). This sequence of executed leaf nodes corresponds to the trace $\langle a, b, c, d, a, b\rangle$ that is added to $T_{1.1}$'s sub event log. The subtree $T_{2.1}$ contains the first two executed leaf nodes, i.e., a ($T_{4.1}$) and b ($T_{4.2}$). The 3rd executed leaf node τ ($T_{2.2}$) is not contained in $T_{2.1}$. Therefore, we add the trace that corresponds to the first two executed leaf nodes, i.e., $\langle a, b\rangle$, to $T_{2.1}$'s sub event log. The 4th and 5th executed leaf nodes are again a subtree of $T_{2.1}$, but not the 6th leaf node. Hence, we add the trace $\langle c, d\rangle$, which corresponds to the 4th and 5th executed leaf node, to $T_{2.1}$'s sub event log. The 7th and 8th executed leaf nodes are again subtrees of $T_{2.1}$, and therefore, we add the trace $\langle a, b \rangle$ to $T_{2.1}$'s sub event log. By processing the alignment for each subtree in the presented way, we obtain sub event logs for each subtree in T_0 as shown in Fig. 3b.

In Algorithm 1 we present a formal description of the sub event log calculation. We successively calculate an alignment for each trace in L (line 4). First, we initialize an empty trace for each subtree T' of T that will be eventually added to T''s sub log (line 6). Next, we iterate over the alignment, i.e., the executed process tree leaf nodes since the alignment contains only synchronous and invisible model moves. For every subtree that contains the current executed leaf node, we add the corresponding activity to its trace (line 14). If the current executed leaf node is not contained in a subtree T', we add the corresponding trace, if it is not empty, to T''s sub log (line 14) and reset the trace (line 15).

4 Incremental Discovery of Process Trees

In this section, we present our approach to incrementally discover process trees. In general, we assume an initially given process tree T, which is incrementally modified trace by trace. If a new trace σ_i is not accepted by the current process tree T, we calculate an optimal alignment and localize the nonconforming parts in T. We then modify the identified process tree part(s) to make the obtained process tree T' accept σ_i. Afterwards, we continue with T' and process the next trace σ_{i+1} analogously. In case a trace is already accepted by the current process tree, we move on to the next trace without modifying the current process tree.

The remainder of this section is structured as follows. First, we introduce an approach to repair a single deviation. We then present a more advanced approach that additionally handles blocks of deviations and uses the previously mentioned approach as a fallback option.

4.1 Repairing Single Deviations

In this section, we present an approach to repair a single alignment move which corresponds to a deviation in a process tree. We assume that a process tree T, a trace σ and an alignment $\gamma \in \bar{\Gamma}(T, \sigma)$ are given. Moreover, we assume that potential deviations in the given alignment γ are repaired from left to right. Next, we present process tree modifications to repair various deviations.

Assume that the given alignment contains a visible model move, i.e., $\gamma = \frac{\cdots \gg \cdots}{\cdots \boxed{a} \cdots}$. Since a model move indicates that a modeled activity was not observed, we make the corresponding leaf node a optional. Therefore, we replace the leaf node a by the choice construct $\times(a, \tau)$ (Fig. 4a). This ensures that the activity is optional in the process model and no longer causes a model move.

If the alignment contains a log move, we have to differentiate two cases, i.e., the standard case and the root case. For the standard case the alignment is of the form $\gamma = \frac{\cdots \boxed{a}\, b \cdots}{\cdots \boxed{a}\, \gg \cdots}$ or $\gamma = \frac{\cdots \gg \boxed{b} \cdots}{\cdots \tau\, \gg \cdots}$, i.e., directly before the deviation,

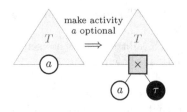

(a) Repairing a visible model move

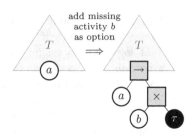

(b) Repairing a log move with preceding synchronous move

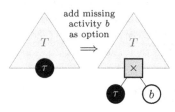

(c) Repairing a log move with preceding invisible model move

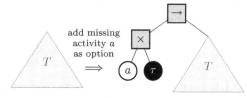

(d) Repairing a log move (root case)

Fig. 4. Repairing a single deviation - process tree repair modifications

there is either a synchronous or an invisible model move. In this case, we extend the process tree such that we ensure that after the activity a or τ it is possible to optionally execute the missing activity in the process model. Therefore, we replace the leaf node a by $\rightarrow (a, \times(b, \tau))$ (Fig. 4b). Accordingly, we change the process tree for a preceding invisible model movement, i.e., we replace τ by $\times(\tau, b)$ (Fig. 4c). In the other case, the root case, the log move is at the beginning of the alignment, i.e., $\gamma = \begin{array}{c} a \\ \gg \end{array} \begin{array}{c} \cdots \\ \cdots \end{array}$. In this case, we add the possibility to optionally execute the missing activity a before the current tree. Let T be the given process tree, we alter T to $\rightarrow (\times(a, \tau), T)$ (Fig. 4d), i.e., we extend the given process tree at the root node. Since we assume that deviations in an alignment are repaired from left to right, one of the two cases always applies to log moves.

The presented approach allows us to fix multiple deviations in an alignment by separately repairing all deviations from left to right. Furthermore, the approach is deterministic because in each iteration we repair a deviation of the given alignment. Moreover, we always add behavior to the process tree and never remove behavior, i.e., we always extend the language of accepted traces. In the next section, we present a further approach that additionally handles blocks of deviations and uses the presented approach as a fallback option.

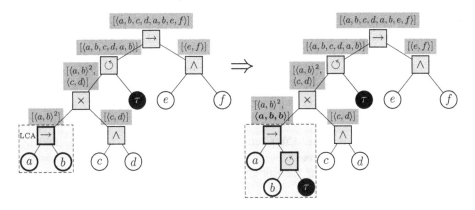

Fig. 5. Conceptual idea of the proposed LCA approach

4.2 Repairing Blocks of Deviations

In this section, we present our more advanced approach that additionally handles blocks of deviations. First, we present the conceptual idea and an example. Afterwards, we introduce the algorithm.

Conceptual Idea. The proposed LCA approach assumes an initial process tree T, a perfectly fitting event log L, i.e., $\{\sigma \in L\} \subseteq \mathcal{L}(T)$, and a trace σ. The event log L represents the traces processed so far, i.e., traces that must be accepted by the process tree T. Furthermore, the LCA approach assumes a process tree discovery algorithm $disc : \mathcal{B}(\mathcal{A}^*) \to \mathcal{T}_\mathcal{A}$ that, given any event log, returns a perfectly fitting process tree.[1] The proposed LCA approach returns a process tree T' such that the given trace σ and the log L are accepted.

Assume the process tree T_0 (Fig. 1), the event log $L = [\langle a, b, c, d, a, b, e, f \rangle]$ and the trace $\sigma = \langle a, b, e, f \rangle$, which is not accepted by T_0. When we apply the LCA approach, we first calculate an optimal alignment.

a	b	b	e	f
a		b	e	f
$(T_{4.1})$	$\gg$	$(T_{4.2})$	$(T_{2.3})$	$(T_{2.4})$

We always repair the first occurring (block of successively occurring) deviation(s). In the given example, we observe a log move on b and before and after the deviation a synchronous move. Next, we calculate the LCA of a ($T_{4.1}$) and b ($T_{4.2}$) that encompass the deviation. The LCA is $T_{3.1}$ and its sub event log is $[\langle a, b \rangle^2]$ as depicted in the left process tree in Fig. 5. The calculated LCA corresponds to a subtree that causes the deviation and must therefore be changed. Hence, we add the trace $\langle a, b, b \rangle$ to $T_{3.1}$'s sub event log and apply the given $disc$ algorithm on the extended sub event log. For instance, we could get $\to (a, \circlearrowleft (b, \tau))$ depending

---

[1] For example, the Inductive Miner algorithm [16] fulfills the listed requirements.

on the concrete instantiation of $disc$. Finally, we replace $T_{3.1}$ by the discovered process tree, i.e., $T_0' = \to (\circlearrowright (\times(\to(a, \circlearrowright(b, \tau)), \wedge(c, d)), \tau), \wedge(e, f))$.

Next, we again compute an alignment of the updated process tree T_0' and γ. In case of further deviations, we repair them in the above-described manner. Otherwise, we return the modified process tree and the extended event log $L' = L \uplus [\langle a, b, b, e, f \rangle]$. Hereinafter, we formally describe the algorithm in detail.

Algorithmic Description. First, an optimal alignment is calculated for the given trace σ and the process tree T, i.e., $\gamma \in \bar{\Gamma}(T, \sigma)$. In case there exist no deviations, we return T. In case of deviations, we repair the first (block of) deviation(s). Assume the alignment is of the form as depicted below.

$$\gamma = \frac{\cdots |x_i'| \cdots |x_i| \cdots deviation(s) \cdots |x_j| \cdots |x_j'| \cdots}{\cdots |T_i'| \cdots |T_i| \cdots deviation(s) \cdots |T_j| \cdots |T_j'| \cdots}$$

We have a (block of) deviation(s), i.e., visible model moves and/or log moves, and directly before and after the (block of) deviation(s) there is no deviation, i.e., either a synchronous move or an invisible model move in each position. Let T_i be the process tree leaf node executed before the deviation(s) and T_j be the one after the deviation(s). We then calculate the LCA of T_i and T_j, hereinafter referred to as T_{LCA}. Note that T_i and T_j are subtrees of T_{LCA}.

Next, we check which of the executed process tree leaf nodes preceding T_i are also a subtree of T_{LCA}. Assume T_i' is a subtree of T_{LCA} and all process tree leafs from T_i' until T_i are a subtree of T_{LCA} too. Besides, either the process tree leaf node executed before T_i' is not a subtree of T_{LCA}, or T_i' is the first executed leaf node in the alignment. Since we repair the first occurring (block of) deviation(s), we know that before T_i only synchronous or invisible model moves occur.

Analogously, we check which executed process tree leaf nodes after T_j are a subtree of T_{LCA}. Note that there is a difference because log moves and visible model moves potentially occur after T_j because we always repair the first (block of) deviation(s). However, except that we ignore log moves, we proceed as described above. Let T_j' be the last leaf node s.t. all executed leaf nodes from T_j to T_j' are a subtree of T_{LCA}. In addition, either the next executed leaf node after T_j' is not a subtree of T_{LCA} or there exist no more executed tree leaves after T_j'.

Given T_i' and T_j', we add the trace $\langle x_i', \ldots, x_j' \rangle \downarrow_{\mathcal{A}}$ (ignoring $\gg$) to T_{LCA}'s sub event log $L_{T_{LCA}}$, i.e., $L'_{T_{LCA}} = L_{T_{LCA}} \uplus [\langle x_i', \ldots, x_j' \rangle \downarrow_{\mathcal{A}}]$. Next, we apply the given $disc$ algorithm on $L'_{T_{LCA}}$ and replace T_{LCA} by the newly discovered process tree $disc(L'_{T_{LCA}})$. Since the process tree $disc(L'_{T_{LCA}})$ accepts the trace $\langle x_i', \ldots, x_j' \rangle \downarrow_{\mathcal{A}}$, we repaired the first (block of) deviation(s). Afterwards, we again calculate an optimal alignment on the updated process tree and σ. If there are still deviations, we again repair the first (block of) deviation(s).

In the case that before or after the (block of) deviation(s) no process tree leaf node was executed and hence, we cannot compute a LCA, we apply the repair approach from the previous section, which repairs a single deviation, on the first log or visible model move. Afterwards, we apply the above described algorithm

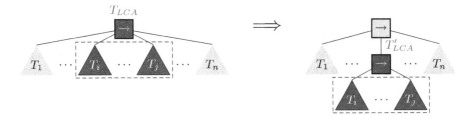

Fig. 6. Pulling down a sequence LCA in the process tree hierarchy

again on the updated process tree. Thereby, we ensure that the proposed LCA approach is deterministic since in every iteration a (block of) deviation(s) is repaired either by rediscovering the determined LCA or by applying the single deviation repair approach. Next, we refine the calculation of a LCA to minimize the affected subtrees getting altered.

Lowering an LCA in the Tree Hierarchy. For a process tree with a low height, it is likely that the proposed LCA approach determines the root as LCA and therefore, re-discovers the entire process tree. This behavior is not desirable since in this case the quality of the returned process tree solely depends on the given *disc* algorithm and most often, deviations can be repaired at a lower subtree.

To keep the affected subtrees that get rediscovered small, we introduce expansion rules to lower the detected LCA in the tree hierarchy. For this purpose, we use language preserving reduction rules in the reverse direction [17].

Assume that the determined LCA, denoted by T_{LCA}, contains the sequence operator and has n child nodes. Furthermore, assume that the deviation was localized between two children of T_{LCA}, i.e., between T_i and T_j. Hence, the process tree is of the form $T_{LCA} = \rightarrow (T_1, \ldots, T_i, \ldots, T_j, \ldots T_n)$. Then we know that all child nodes of T_{LCA} which are not between T_i and T_j are not responsible for the deviation. Hence, we can cut $T_i, \ldots, T_j$ and replace the nodes by a new sequence operator with the cut subtrees as children, i.e., $\rightarrow (T_1, \ldots, \rightarrow (T_i, \ldots, T_j), \ldots T_n)$ (Fig. 6). If we re-compute the LCA, we will get $T'_{LCA} = \rightarrow (T_i, \ldots, T_j)$.

In case the LCA contains the parallel or choice operator, we lower the detected LCA in a similar manner. Assume the deviation was localized between two children of T_{LCA}, i.e., between T_i and T_j, and that T_{LCA} has n child nodes. Hence, the process tree is of the form $T_{LCA} = \bullet(T_1, \ldots, T_i, \ldots, T_j, \ldots T_n)$ for $\bullet \in \{\times, \wedge\}$. In this case, we extract the two child nodes T_i and T_j and pull them one level down in the process tree: $T_{LCA} = \bullet(T_1, \ldots, \bullet(T_i, T_j), \ldots T_n)$.

5   Evaluation

We evaluated the proposed LCA approach on the basis of a publicly available, real event log. In the following section, we present the experimental setup. Subsequently, we present and discuss the results of the conducted experiments.

5.1   Experimental Setup

In the experiments, we compare the LCA approach against the Inductive Miner (IM) [16], which discovers a process tree that accepts the given event log, and the model repair approach presented in [13]. Note that the repair algorithm does not guarantee to return a hierarchical process model. We implemented the LCA approach extending *PM4Py* [8], a process mining library for Python. Since both the LCA approach and the IM algorithm guarantee the above mentioned properties for the returned process tree, we use the IM algorithm as a comparison algorithm. Furthermore, we use the IM algorithm inside our LCA approach as an instantiation of the *disc*-algorithm, which is used for rediscovering subtrees.

As input, we use a publicly available event log that contains data about a road fine management process [18]. We use the complete event log, e.g., we do not filter outliers. We sorted the event log based on variant frequencies in descending order, i.e., the most occurring variant first. We chose this sorting since in real applications it is common to consider first the most frequent behavior and filter out infrequent behavior. Note that the order of traces influences the resulting process model in our approach and in the model repair approach.

To compare the obtained process models, we use the f-measure regarding the whole event log. The f-measure takes the harmonic mean of the precision and the fitness of a process model with respect to a given event log. Fitness reflects how good a process model can replay a given event log. In contrast, precision reflects how much additional behavior next to the given event log is accepted by the process model. The aim is that both the fitness and the precision and thus, the f-measure are close to 1. We use alignment-based approaches for fitness [2] and precision calculation [6].

The procedure of the conducted experiments is described below. First, we discover a process tree on the first variant with the IM algorithm since the LCA approach and the model repair algorithm require an initial process model. Note that the LCA approach can be used with any initial model. Afterwards, we add variant by variant to the initially given process model with the LCA approach. Analogously, we repair the initially given process model trace by trace with the model repair algorithm. In addition, we iteratively apply the IM algorithm on the 1st variant, the 1st + 2nd variant, etc.

5.2   Results

In Fig. 7 we present the obtained results. We observe that the f-measures (Fig. 7a) of the process models obtained by the LCA approach are higher compared to models obtained by the IM and the model repair algorithm for the majority of processed variants. Note that the IM algorithm returns process trees with a higher f-measure in the end. However, for real process discovery applications it is unusual to incorporate the entire behavior in an event log. Reasons for not trying to incorporate all observed behavior are data quality issues, outliers and incomplete behavior. Furthermore, observe that after processing the first 15% of all variants, we already cover >99% of all recorded traces (Fig. 7b) and obtain

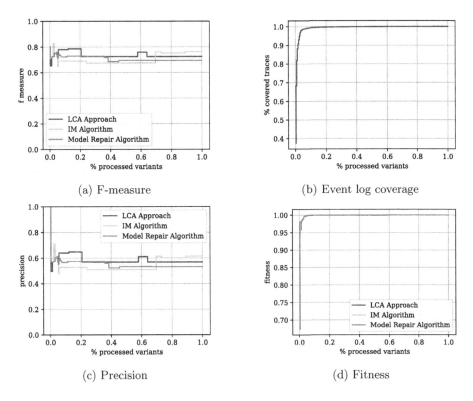

(a) F-measure

(b) Event log coverage

(c) Precision

(d) Fitness

Fig. 7. Results on f-measure, precision, fitness and event log coverage

a process model with the LCA approach that outperforms the other techniques (Fig. 7a). The jump in the f-measure for the IM algorithm at 70% processed variants results from the fact that the IM gets more behavior as input, i.e., a larger event log, and therefore, detects a more suited pattern which leads to a more precise process tree in this case.

In Fig. 7c the precision values are depicted. These influence the f-measure most because we guarantee perfect fitness w.r.t. the added trace variants. Also here we can see that for most of the processed variants the LCA approach delivers more precise models. However, if we add more than 70% of all variants, the IM algorithm suddenly delivers more precise models. For fitness (Fig. 7d) the differences between LCA and IM are minor.

The higher f-measure of the LCA approach in many cases compared to the IM algorithm can be explained by the differences in the *representational bias* [3]. The LCA approach may return models that have duplicate labels, i.e., the same activity can occur in multiple leaf nodes. In comparison, the models returned by the IM algorithm do not allow for duplicate labels. Note that also the model repair algorithm allows duplicate labels.

6   Conclusion

In this paper, we presented a novel algorithm to incrementally discover a process tree. The approach utilizes the hierarchical structure of a process tree to localize the deviating subtree and rediscovers it. The conducted experiments show that the obtained process models have in many cases better quality in comparison to models produced by a process discovery and model repair algorithm with same guarantees about the resulting model, i.e., replay fitness. Actually, it is surprising that our incremental discovery approach works so well. We do not use domain knowledge and see many ways to improve the technique. The potential to outperform existing approaches even further is therefore high.

While most process discovery algorithms are fully automated, i.e., they assume an event log and return a process model, the LCA approach is able to incrementally add behavior to an existing model. Therefore, it can be used to evolve a process model trace by trace. This makes it easy for the user to see the impact on the process model when a trace is added. Thus, by the incremental selection of traces by a user, the usually separated phases of event data filtering and process discovery are connected. Hence, our approach enables the user to interactively discover a process model by selecting iteratively which behavior should be covered by the process model.

As future work, we plan to investigate both the impact of the initially given model and the ordering of traces incrementally given to the LCA approach on the resulting process model. Furthermore, we plan to explore different strategies for determining the deviating subtree next to the LCA calculation. We also plan to further develop this algorithm into an advanced interactive process discovery algorithm that provides further user interaction possibilities next to the incremental selection of traces/observed behavior.

References

1. van der Aalst, W.M.P.: The application of petri nets to workflow management. J. Circ. Syst. Comput. **8**(1), 21–66 (1998). https://doi.org/10.1142/S0218126698000043
2. van der Aalst, W.M.P., Adriansyah, A., van Dongen, B.F.: Replaying history on process models for conformance checking and performance analysis. Wiley Interdiscip. Rev. Data Min. Knowl. Discov. **2**(2), 182–192 (2012). https://doi.org/10.1002/widm.1045
3. van der Aalst, W.M.P.: On the representational bias in process mining. In: Reddy, S., Tata, S. (eds.) Proceedings of the 20th IEEE International Workshops on Enabling Technologies: Infrastructures for Collaborative Enterprises, WETICE 2011, Paris, France, 27–29 June 2011, pp. 2–7. IEEE Computer Society (2011). https://doi.org/10.1109/WETICE.2011.64
4. van der Aalst, W.M.P.: Process Mining: Data Science in Action, 2nd edn. Springer, Heidelberg (2016). https://doi.org/10.1007/978-3-662-49851-4
5. Adriansyah, A.: Aligning Observed and Modeled Behavior. Ph.D. thesis, Eindhoven University of Technology, Department of Mathematics and Computer Science, July 2014. https://doi.org/10.6100/IR770080

6. Adriansyah, A., Munoz-Gama, J., Carmona, J., van Dongen, B.F., van der Aalst, W.M.P.: Measuring precision of modeled behavior. Inf. Syst. E-Bus. Manag. **13**(1), 37–67 (2015). https://doi.org/10.1007/s10257-014-0234-7

7. Armas Cervantes, A., van Beest, N.R.T.P., La Rosa, M., Dumas, M., García-Bañuelos, L.: Interactive and incremental business process model repair. In: Panetto, H., Debruyne, C., Gaaloul, W., Papazoglou, M., Paschke, A., Ardagna, C.A., Meersman, R. (eds.) OTM 2017. LNCS, vol. 10573, pp. 53–74. Springer, Cham (2017). https://doi.org/10.1007/978-3-319-69462-7_5

8. Berti, A., Zelstvan Zelst, S.J., Aalstvan der Aalst, W.M.P.: Process mining for python (PM4Py): bridging the gap between process-and data science. In: Proceedings of the ICPM Demo Track 2019, Co-Located with 1st International Conference on Process Mining (ICPM 2019), Aachen, Germany, 24–26 June 2019, pp. 13–16 (2019). http://ceur-ws.org/Vol-2374/

9. Dixit, P.: Interactive process mining. Ph.D. thesis, Department of Mathematics and Computer Science, June 2019

10. Dixit, P.M., Verbeek, H.M.W., Buijs, J.C.A.M., van der Aalst, W.M.P.: Interactive data-driven process model construction. In: Trujillo, J.C., Davis, K.C., Du, X., Li, Z., Ling, T.W., Li, G., Lee, M.L. (eds.) ER 2018. LNCS, vol. 11157, pp. 251–265. Springer, Cham (2018). https://doi.org/10.1007/978-3-030-00847-5_19

11. van Dongen, B.F., Alves de Medeiros, A.K., Wen, L.: Process mining: overview and outlook of petri net discovery algorithms. In: Jensen, K., van der Aalst, W.M.P. (eds.) Transactions on Petri Nets and Other Models of Concurrency II. LNCS, vol. 5460, pp. 225–242. Springer, Heidelberg (2009). https://doi.org/10.1007/978-3-642-00899-3_13

12. Fahland, D., van der Aalst, W.M.P.: Repairing process models to reflect reality. In: Barros, A., Gal, A., Kindler, E. (eds.) BPM 2012. LNCS, vol. 7481, pp. 229–245. Springer, Heidelberg (2012). https://doi.org/10.1007/978-3-642-32885-5_19

13. Fahland, D., van der Aalst, W.M.P.: Model repair: aligning process models to reality. Inf. Syst. **47**, 220–243 (2015). https://doi.org/10.1016/j.is.2013.12.007

14. Kalsing, A., do Nascimento, G.S., Iochpe, C., Thom, L.H.: An incremental process mining approach to extract knowledge from legacy systems. In: Proceedings of the 14th IEEE International Enterprise Distributed Object Computing Conference, EDOC 2010, Vitória, Brazil, 25–29 October 2010, pp. 79–88. IEEE Computer Society (2010). https://doi.org/10.1109/EDOC.2010.13

15. Kindler, E., Rubin, V., Schäfer, W.: Incremental workflow mining based on document versioning information. In: Li, M., Boëhm, B., Osterweil, L.J. (eds.) SPW 2005. LNCS, vol. 3840, pp. 287–301. Springer, Heidelberg (2006). https://doi.org/10.1007/11608035_25

16. Leemans, S.J.J., Fahland, D., van der Aalst, W.M.P.: Discovering block-structured process models from event logs - a constructive approach. In: Colom, J.-M., Desel, J. (eds.) PETRI NETS 2013. LNCS, vol. 7927, pp. 311–329. Springer, Heidelberg (2013). https://doi.org/10.1007/978-3-642-38697-8_17

17. Leemans, S.J.J., Fahland, D., van der Aalst, W.M.P.: Scalable process discovery and conformance checking. Softw. Syst. Model. **17**(2), 599–631 (2018). https://doi.org/10.1007/s10270-016-0545-x

18. Leonide Leoni, M., Mannhardt, F.: Road traffic fine management process - event log. 4TU.Centre for Research Data (2015), https://doi.org/10.4121/uuid:270fd440-1057-4fb9-89a9-b699b47990f5. Accessed 12 Oct 2019

19. Sun, W., Li, T., Peng, W., Sun, T.: Incremental workflow mining with optional patterns and its application to production printing process. Int. J. Intell. Control Syst. **12**, 45–55 (2007)

Security and Privacy

Ontology Evolution in the Context of Model-Based Secure Software Engineering

Jens Bürger[1,2]([☒]) [ID], Timo Kehrer[3] [ID], and Jan Jürjens[2,4] [ID]

[1] Knipp Medien und Kommunikation GmbH, Dortmund, Germany
jbuerger@knipp.de
[2] University of Koblenz-Landau, Koblenz, Germany
[3] Humboldt-Universität zu Berlin, Berlin, Germany
[4] Fraunhofer Institute ISST, Dortmund, Germany

Abstract. Ontologies as a means to formally specify the knowledge of a domain of interest have made their way into information and communication technology. Most often, such knowledge is subject to continuous change, which demands for consistent evolution of ontologies and dependent artifacts. In this paper, we study ontology evolution in the context of a model-based approach to engineering of secure software, where ontologies are used to formalize the security context knowledge which is needed to come up with software systems which can be considered secure. In this application scenario, techniques for detecting ontology changes and determining their semantic impact are faced with a couple of challenging requirements which are not met by existing solutions. To overcome these shortcomings, we adapt a state-based approach to model differencing to OWL ontologies. Our solution is capable of detecting semantic editing patterns which may be customly defined using graph transformation rules, but it does not depend on information about editing processes such as persistently managed change logs. We showcase how to leverage semantic editing patterns for the sake of system model co-evolution in response to changing security context knowledge, and demonstrate the feasibility of the approach using a realistic medical information system.

Keywords: Software engineering · Model-based security · Security context knowledge · Ontology evolution · Semantic editing patterns

1 Introduction

Ontologies as a means for formal and explicit specification of knowledge of a domain of interest have made their way into contemporary information and communication technology, e.g., to foster information semantics and semantic interoperability in various kinds of information systems [9]. Often, the knowledge of a domain is subject to continuous change. This demands for continuous evolution of the respective ontologies and, depending on the application scenario, the consistent co-evolution of dependent artifacts. Managing such ontology evolution is faced with a multitude of technical and organizational challenges [7,19].

© Springer Nature Switzerland AG 2020
F. Dalpiaz et al. (Eds.): RCIS 2020, LNBIP 385, pp. 437–454, 2020.
https://doi.org/10.1007/978-3-030-50316-1_26

In this paper, we focus on the task of detecting ontology changes and determining their semantic impact, which must be supported by a technical solution that accommodates application-specific requirements [27]. We study ontology evolution in the context of a model-based approach to secure software engineering called S^{2}EC^{2}O (Secure Software in Evolving Contexts via CO-evolution) [4]. Developing secure software systems requires expert knowledge which is independent of the actual system. Such knowledge, referred to as *Security Context Knowledge (SCK)* in the sequel, comprises, e.g., information on which encryption algorithms can be considered secure and which are known to be compromized. In S^{2}EC^{2}O, ontologies are used as a means to formally capture and exploit SCK. However, SCK changes over time due to, e.g., newly discovered attacks or regulatory changes. In case the system is insecure regarding the evolved knowledge, it needs to be co-evolved such that the essential security requirements are preserved. In this application scenario, tool support for managing ontological change is faced with a set of requirements which may be summarized as follows (cf. literature pointers for a more detailed discussion of each of the requirements):

(1) Atomic, low-level changes such as adding or deleting single ontology elements are too fine-grained to determine their semantic impact. Instead, changes must be handled on the level of more coarse-grained, *semantic editing patterns*, also referred to as composite, complex or high-level changes [21,25].

(2) Since changes to the knowledge base may occur ad-hoc and largely undocumented, occurrences of semantic editing patterns must be *detected after the fact* by comparing the old and new version of an ontology. In particular, they cannot be recorded through a controlled change management process and tool chain [29].

(3) The set of semantic editing patterns supported by the change detection facility must be *customizable and extensible*. This enables the configuration of domain- and system-specific countermeasures addressing different kinds of security threats [5].

(4) To (semi-)automatically execute configured countermeasures, occurrences of detected semantic editing patterns must be *amenable to model-driven engineering tools* [3].

While a number of approaches to support ontology evolution have been presented that cope with the lifting of atomic ontological changes to semantic editing patterns [6,12,13,21,24–27] (requirement (1)), none of them meets all of the above mentioned requirements. Most of them [6,12,13,21,26,27] rely on a well-defined ontology evolution process and assume all ontological changes to be captured through a dedicated tool and/or persistently managed in form of a change log. Ad-hoc changes and exchanging ontologies across tool boundaries, which demand for a state-based comparison after the fact (requirement (2)), are not supported. Some approaches [24,25] get rid of the restriction of persistently managed change logs, however, only support a fixed set of semantic editing patterns which cannot be adapted (requirement (3)). None of the proposed approaches reports occurrences of semantic editing patterns in a form which is amenable to model-driven engineering tools (requirement (4)).

To overcome these shortcomings, our technical solution to detect ontological changes draws from recent advances in the field of model comparison and versioning. In particular, we adopt a state-based approach to model differencing which assumes the old and new version of an ontology to be available, but no information about editing processes such as the existence of a change log [18]. We work on a structural, graph-based representation of ontological models using a fixed meta-model as type graph. Thereupon, graph transformation rules are used as an intuitive means for specifying semantic editing patterns. In summary, the paper makes the following contributions:

- An approach to detect occurrences of semantic editing patterns, specified as graph transformation rules, between two versions of an ontology formulated using the Web Ontology Language (OWL) [23].
- A prototypical implementation of the approach based on the Eclipse Modeling Framework (EMF) technology stack [30], along with an open catalog of semantic editing patterns on OWL ontologies implemented in the Henshin transformation language [31].
- A case study of how to leverage semantic editing patterns for the sake of system model co-evolution in model-based secure software engineering, including an application to the medical information system iTrust [10].

We introduce our application scenario and resulting problem motivation in more detail in Sect. 2. Sections 3 and 4 are dedicated to our contributions. Related work is considered in Sect. 5 before we conclude the paper in Sect. 6.

2 Background and Problem Motivation

2.1 The S^2EC^2O Approach to Secure Software Engineering

Model-based secure software engineering fosters the usage of modeling languages such as UMLsec to gradually refine and transform high-level requirements into executable software, incorporating security requirements into software development from the very beginning [14]. A particular feature of the S^2EC^2O approach (Secure Software in Evolving Contexts via CO-evolution) is that it accommodates the fact that a system's security may be affected by external security knowledge. Consider an information system which processes private data and which shall meet the Essential Security Requirement (ESR) that all database communications must be encrypted using a secure encryption algorithm. Obviously, what can be considered a secure encryption algorithm is not system-specific but part of a more general body of knowledge to which we refer as SCK. ESRs are called *essential* since they cover abstract, technology-independent security needs, while the SCK provides the knowledge required to properly implement ESRs for a specific system. In our example, the SCK provides information on which encryption algorithms can be considered secure.

In S^2EC^2O, ESRs are refined to concrete security requirements using the SCK. These security requirements can then be linked to appropriate security

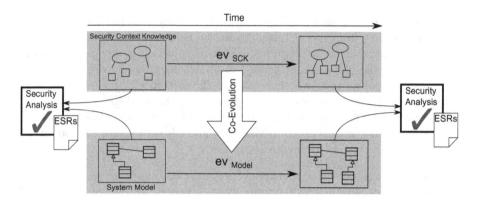

Fig. 1. Objective of the S^2EC^2O approach to model-based secure software engineering.

mechanisms and finally to model-based system implementations through a series of design decisions and using well-established approaches for secure, model-based software engineering. This includes the selection of concrete implementation technologies. We refer to the design artifacts describing a concrete software system in terms of architecture and/or behavior as *system model*.

Figure 1 illustrates the relation between the SCK (top) and the system model (bottom). When a system is initially developed, it is ideally compliant with all of its ESRs regarding the security knowledge, i.e., it passes a security analysis (middle left) [14]. However, SCK changes over time due to, e.g., newly discovered attacks or regulatory changes. When the SCK evolves (ev_{SCK}), an appropriate co-evolution (ev_{Model}) needs to be determined such that the co-evolved system model passes the security analysis again. The overall goal of S^2EC^2O is to detect security-relevant changes to the SCK, determine the impact on the system's security, and to facilitate co-evolutions to recover the compliance with the ESRs.

2.2   Ontological Modeling of Security Context Knowledge

A basic prerequisite of S^2EC^2O is the formal and explicit representation of SCK. To that end, S^2EC^2O adopts an ontological approach leveraging the Web Ontology Language (OWL) as standardized by the W3C [23].

While its semantics is based on description logics (DLs) [1], the OWL notation is largely motivated by terminology known from object-oriented programming: Objects (or entities) are called *individuals*, and each object is an *instance of* a dedicated *class*. On the type level, OWL supports the definition of inheritance hierarchies through *subclass* relationships. On the instance level, so-called *object properties* may be attached to an individual by relating it to other individuals. Type and instance level correspond to what is usually referred to as TBox ("terminological part") and ABox ("assertional part") in DLs, respectively.

An ontological model of SCK is structured into three layers, each of them having a specific security focus. Lower layers may import and use the concepts

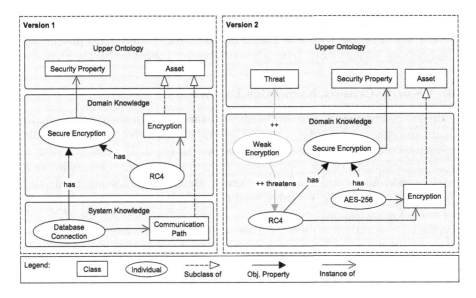

Fig. 2. Example of an ontological model of security context knowledge subject to evolution: an encryption algorithm is discovered to be vulnerable.

defined by upper layers (in DL terminology, elements of the upper ontology are part of the TBox, domain and system ontologies can contain elements of both TBox and ABox):

Upper The upper ontology is independent of a particular software domain or application. It represents the most general software security concepts, such as *security property* or *attack* [5,8].

Domain Domain ontologies capture domain knowledge as well as concrete security issues and measures. They have to be created for each domain anew and can be shared by different systems in the same domain.

System System ontologies express the security-relevant knowledge about a concrete system. They can be produced or enriched from existing artifacts, such as a UML-based system model.

Figure 2 shows an excerpt of an ontological model of SCK which is relevant for our example. In the initial version 1 on the left, it includes elements from different layers, namely a security property (`Secure Encryption`), system components and concepts (`Database Connection`, `Communication Path`), and an encryption algorithm (`RC4`) which is considered to provide secure encryption.

SCK is usually gathered from natural language documents of various kinds, e.g., the IT baseline protection guidelines proposed by the German Federal Office for Information Security[1], or attack and vulnerability reports as provided in the Common Vulnerabilities and Exposures (CVE) database[2]. Moreover, community

---

[1] https://www.bsi.bund.de/EN/Topics/ITGrundschutz/itgrundschutz_node.html.
[2] https://cve.mitre.org.

knowledge regarding known vulnerabilities and mitigations is available, e.g., in terms of the Common Weakness Enumeration (CWE) database[3]. Finally, individual persons such as white hats or developers can contribute to the SCK.

2.3 Security Context Knowledge Evolution

As already mentioned, SCK may change over time. This holds in particular for domain and system knowledge, while we assume the upper ontology to be stable. An example of such SCK evolution is illustrated in Fig. 2. The initial version of the ontological model evolves into version 2 shown on the right. Essentially, Weak Encryption of RC4 is added as a new Threat. Detecting such semantic changes is faced with the following organizational and technical challenges.

From an organizational point of view, ontologies representing the SCK may be updated by a variety of different tools and processes in a largely uncontrolled and ad-hoc manner. In some cases, parts of the ontological model of SCK are automatically extracted from external knowledge sources [11], which means that there is no dedicated editing process at all but parts of the SCK are simply replaced by a new version. As a consequence, occurrences of semantic editing patterns as the one in our example must be detected after the fact, i.e., by comparing the old and new version of an ontology [29]. They cannot be recorded through a dedicated tool or software library such as the OWL API of Protégé[4].

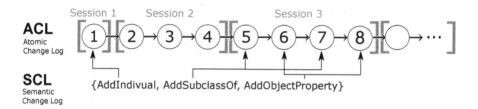

Fig. 3. Low-level change log (top) vs. semantic editing patterns (bottom) comprising a set of intermixed low-level changes.

Technically, even if all changes would be applied through a common tool or API, the generated change logs capture ontological changes on a level of granularity which is way too fine-grained to determine the semantic impact of the recorded changes [24,25]. Moreover, different semantic editing patterns can be performed in an interleaved manner [29]. As an example, consider the changes between the two ontology versions 1 and 2 in Fig. 2. Assume that, according to the illustration in Fig. 3, a security expert performs this task in two editing sessions (Session 1 and Session 3) which are interrupted by an externally triggered change (Session 2)[5]. In Session 1, (s)he adds the individual WeakEncryption,

---

[3] https://cwe.mitre.org.
[4] https://protege.stanford.edu.
[5] The effect of Session 2 is not illustrated in Fig. 2.

and (s)he completes the editing task in Session 3 by declaring `WeakEncryption` as an instance of class `Threat` and by adding an object property targeting `RC4`. Logging through the OWL API would result in a stream of low-level changes as illustrated in the upper part of Fig. 3. Note that in OWL, relationships are represented as first class citizens connected to their source and target elements. Thus, the addition of each of the relationships introduced in Session 3 boils down to first adding the element representing a relationship which is then connected to its source and target. Consequently, all low-level changes need to be grouped to form occurrences of pre-defined semantic editing patterns such as "addEncryptionThreat", as the lower half of Fig. 3 exemplifies.

3 Approach

3.1 Structural Representation of Ontologies

As illustrated in the previous section, semantic editing patterns rely on a structural, graph-based representation of ontologies. To that end, we adopt the concept of meta-modeling that has been established in model-based software engineering. Following this approach, an ontology is considered as a typed attributed graph, the meta-model defines the allowed types of the nodes and edges. Conceptually irrelevant details, notably the layout of an external diagram notation such as the one used in Fig. 2, are ignored. In our prototypical implementation, we work with a MOF[6]-based meta-model for OWL[7]. MOF-based meta-models are based on basic principles of object-oriented modeling. In particular, node types are specified by classes which can be related by generalization relationships. Edge types are specified by associations equipped with multiplicity constraints.

Figure 4 shows an excerpt of our MOF-based OWL meta-model. Entities, i.e., `NamedIndividuals`, `Classes` and `ObjectProperties`, do not have attributes that make them distinguishable directly, but their "identity" is given by relating them to a `URI` node via an edge of type `entityURI`. Instance-of relationships are represented by `ClassAssertions` relating an individual to its class via edges of type `individual` and `classExpression`. `ObjectProperties` relate two individuals via edges of type `sourceIndividual` and `targetIndividual`.

3.2 Rule-Based Specification of Semantic Editing Patterns

Using a graph-based representation of ontologies, we consider the effect of applying a semantic editing pattern as an in-place graph transformation and use the transformation language Henshin [31] for specifying editing patterns of interest. Henshin is based on graph transformation concepts, which enables us to specify editing patterns as declarative graph transformation rules. A Henshin rule $r : L \rightarrow R$ consists of two graphs L and R referred to as left-hand side and

---

[6] https://www.omg.org/mof.
[7] https://www.w3.org/2007/OWL/wiki/MOF-Based_Metamodel.

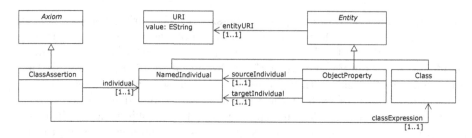

Fig. 4. MOF-based meta-model serving as type graph for the structural, graph-based representation of OWL ontologies.

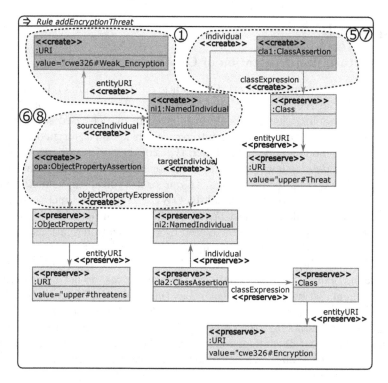

Fig. 5. Rule-based specification of a semantic editing pattern updating the SCK: Addition of a *Threat* to an existing *Encryption* of the Security Context Knowledge.

right-hand side, respectively. The notation $L \to R$ symbolizes a partial mapping which, by adopting notations from set theory loosely, induces the graph patterns to be found and preserved ($L \cap R$), to be deleted ($L \setminus R$), and to be created ($R \setminus L$) by a rule. In the visual Henshin transformation language, the left- and right-hand side of a rule are integrated in a "unified graph", the graph patterns $L \cap R$, $L \setminus R$ and $R \setminus L$ are marked by stereotypes «preserve», «delete» and «create», respectively.

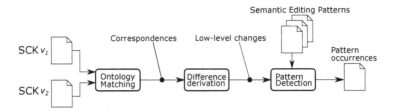

Fig. 6. Processing pipeline of the model differencing tool SiLift [16] adapted to detect occurrences of semantic editing patterns in evolving OWL ontologies.

To give an example, Fig. 5 shows the Henshin rule *addEncryptionThreat*, which formally specifies the semantic editing pattern turning version 1 of the ontology shown in Fig. 2 into its revised version 2. The parts which specify the changes illustrated in Fig. 3 are indicated by dashed ellipses. Change actions indicated by ① specify the creation of an individual named *WeakEncryption* (represented by nodes of type `Class` and `URI` with value `cwe326#Weak_Encryption`). Change actions indicated by ⑤ and ⑦ specify the creation of an instance-of relationship (node of type `ClassAssertion`) which declares the new individual to be an instance of *Threat* (represented by nodes of type `Class` and `URI` with value `upper#Threat`). The class *Threat* itself already exists, it is imported from the upper ontology. Change actions indicated by ⑥ and ⑧ specify the attachment of the object property *threatens* (nodes of type `ObjectProperty` and `URI` with value `upper#threatens`) to the new individual. The object property targets an individual (node of type `NamedIndividual`) which is an instance of *Encryption* (represented by nodes of type `ClassAssertion`, `Class` and `URI` with value `cwe326#Encryption`. Analogously to the class *Threat*, the object property *threatens* as well as the individual which is an instance of *Encryption* already exist (imported from the upper ontology).

Note that the manual specification of semantic editing patterns may be supported by semi-automated techniques, e.g., by learning from examples [15] or past evolutions [20]. Their exploration is out of the scope of this paper.

3.3   Recognition of Pattern Occurrences

Our approach to recognizing occurrences of semantic editing patterns between two versions of the structural representation of an OWL ontology adopts the model differencing approach and tool known as SiLift [16]. The differencing pipeline implemented in SiLift basically consists of the three successive steps depicted in Fig. 6. While a detailed description of the generic aspects of each of these steps is out of the scope of this paper and maybe found in [18], we give a brief illustration for the sake of self-containedness, concentrating on how we adapt the pipeline to OWL ontologies.

In the the first step, a model matcher identifies the corresponding elements which are considered "the same" in both versions v_1 and v_2. The matcher is an exchangeable component within the SiLift framework. Currently, we use a rather simple one which matches entities based on their URIs, relying on the assumption that equally named entities refer to the same conceptual elements. Relationships are matched if they connect the same source and target elements. In principle, this rather simple matching strategy implemented in our research prototype can be replaced by more sophisticated matchers, such as an adaptable model matcher [17] or more semantically oriented ontology matcher [22].

Subsequently, a low-level difference is derived from the matching. Elements of v_1 which do not have a corresponding element in v_2 are considered to be deleted. Analogously, elements exclusively comprised by v_2 are considered to be created. The low-level difference derivator is a generic component which can be adopted from the SiLift framework without the need for any adaptation.

Finally, a pattern detection algorithm recognizes occurrences of semantic editing patterns in a given low-level difference. The pattern detection engine is configured by formal specifications of semantic editing patterns using the Henshin transformation language, as presented in the previous section. Essentially, SiLift exploits the fact that the application of a semantic editing pattern leads to well-defined change pattern in the given low-level difference. All low-level changes involved in such a change pattern are grouped to a so-called semantic change set, a set of low-level changes as indicated by the semantic editing log in the lower part of Fig. 3.

Pattern occurrences may be accessed through the SiLift API. Basically, all rule graph elements comprised by the respective Henshin rule can be traced to their occurrence in the low-level difference between the two versions v_1 and v_2. Hence, semantic editing pattern occurrences being observable in the evolution of the SCK can be automatically processed in subsequent steps of S^2EC^2O, as we will illustrate in the case study presented in the following section.

4   Case Study

In what follows, we will introduce a concrete security evolution scenario and show how semantic editing patterns detect the addition of threats and how this can be leveraged to co-evolve dependent artifacts of a subject system.

4.1   Security Vulnerability by Context Evolution

The evolution of security-relevant context knowledge indicated by the example shown in Fig. 2 represents a security vulnerability that has actually taken place, broke assumptions and led to the necessity that software systems needed to be adapted. The cipher suite RC4 has been popular over a long period of time and was used in Transport Layer Security (TLS) to provide security for HTTP sessions. However, after the publication of an attack that could be carried out in merely 75 h [32], the use of RC4 has been prohibited in a Request for Comments

(RFC) by the Internet Engineering Task Force [28]. At that time, the estimation of TLS traffic relying on RC4 was approximately 30%. Moreover, numerous business applications communicating through HTTP-based REST-APIs were affected by this vulnerability. All of the affected web servers and distributed systems needed to be adapted.

4.2 Maintaining Security by Leveraging Semantic Editing Patterns

To mitigate security vulnerabilities as introduced in the previous section, S^2EC^2O follows a rule-based approach to security maintenance using so-called Security Maintenance Rules (SMRs) [2]. The goal of a SMR is to recover the security of a system when a threat is discovered w.r.t. an ESR. Therefore, a SMR proposes possible adaptations of the system model mitigating the threat. In general, SMRs follow the *Event-Condition-Action* principle: An external event triggers a SMR which, if its condition evaluates to true, causes a set of adaptations to be carried out as the action part of the SMR. In particular, SMRs may be triggered by changes in the SCK, and they may leverage occurrences of semantic editing patterns to determine possible adaptations.

SMRs are specified by implementing three hook methods, each of them is dedicated to a specific part of the Event-Condition-Action principle. While the event part may be implemented in a generic way by polling for changes in the SCK, we concentrate on the condition and action part which need to be tailored for a particular threat:

- checkConditions(deltaList DeltaList) is used to realize the *Condition* part. By using the parameter deltaList, the SMR may access occurrences of semantic editing patterns on the evolving SCK and, if a threat is discovered, generate proposals on how to mitigate the treat.
- As soon as the user or an algorithm has selected a proposal, the method apply(proposal Proposal) is called, realizing the *Action* part. The proposal which is to be used by the SMR to co-evolve the system model is supplied as a parameter.

```
1  checkConditions(DeltaList deltaList) {
2    currentAlgorithms = queryModelForUsedAlgorithms();
3    alternativeAlgorithms = querySckForAlternativeAlgorithms();
4    for (pattern : d.getSemanticEditingPatterns()){
5      if (pattern.getName().equals("addEncryptionThreat")){
6        threatened = pattern.getParameter("alg");
7        threatenedAlgorithms.add(threatened);
8        if (currentAlgorithms.contains(threatened)){
9          for (alternative : alternativeAlgorithms){
10           Proposal.addAlternative("Replace" + threatened + " by " +
               alternative);
11         }
12       }
13     }
14   }
15 }
16
17 apply(Proposal p) {
18   for (cp : queryModelForCommunicationPaths) {
```

```
19    if (threatenedAlgorithms.contains(cp.getAlgorithm)){
20      alterModel(p.getChoice());
21    }
22  }
23 }
```

Listing 1.1. Condition and action part of the SMR mitigating the detection of a weak encryption algorithm in the evolving SCK.

To give an example, Listing 1.1 shows the SMR which is dedicated to the knowledge evolution declaring RC4 as a weak encryption algorithm. Its condition and action part are illustrated using pesudo-code.

In the condition part, first, all currently used encryption algorithms are queried from the system model (line 2). After that, all alternative algorithms are gathered (line 3). Therefore, the SCK is queried for encryption algorithms that are currently not threatened. Next, we walk through the changes in the SCK (for-each loop in line 4), checking for the occurrence of the semantic editing pattern "addEncryptionThreat" (line 5). The threatened encryption algorithms are obtained from the occurrence of the semantic editing pattern through the SiLift API (line 6) and added to a globally accessible collection (line 7). Next, the SMR checks whether the threatened algorithm is currently also used in the system model (line 8). If so, for every possible combination of exchanging this specific algorithm with a non-threatened one, a proposal mitigating the threat is generated and added to the collection of proposals (line 10).

After a developer has made a choice on which proposal shall be selected to adapt the system, the action part of the SMR is being executed (lines 17–21). It iterates over all communication paths of the system model, and every threatened encryption algorithm is replaced according to the chosen proposal.

4.3   Prototypical Tool Support

The S^2EC^2O tool is realized as an extension of the Eclipse platform. Figure 7 gives an overview of the part of the architecture which we use in this paper.

The tool architecture consists of two sub-systems and uses a set of external components (arrows between components represent dependencies):

Process is the main component of the *core* sub-system. It realizes an engine for the S^2EC^2O process, supporting both automated and interactive parts. Moreover, the core sub-system provides access to the SCK and ESRs.

We implemented three components to support the *evolution and co-evolution* of OWL ontologies (representing the SCK) and system models (realized as UML(sec) models). **OWL Evolution** is responsible for the transformation from API-based representations of OWL ontologies to instantiations of the EMF-based OWL meta-model, i.e., the structural representation we work with (see Sect. 3). **OWL Rulebase** adapts the SiLift model differencing framework in order to recognize occurrences of semantic editing patterns in evolving OWL ontologies. The component **UML Evolution** realizes model co-evolution for UMLsec models by interpreting Security Maintenance Rules, as illustrated in the previous sub-section.

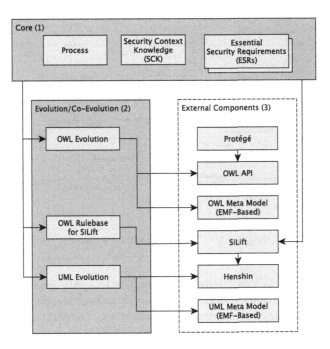

Fig. 7. Overview of the used prototype components.

As for *external* tools, we chose Protégé to manage OWL knowledge bases, and we use EMF-based implementations of the OWL and UML meta-model, respectively. Finally, the model transformation framework Henshin is not only used by SiLift, but also used by the S^2EC^2O tool (e.g., for a declarative specification of Security Maintenance Rules).

4.4 Application to a Larger Subject System

To apply S^2EC^2O to a larger subject system, we chose the medical information system iTrust [10], which supports the electronic communication of all participants (patients, doctors, lab technicians, etc.) of the medical processing in a smart hospital. To date, iTrust comprises 39 use cases being implemented in about 120k lines of code distributed over more than 900 Java classes. Thus, the system is of a size that bares the risk of overlooking details when managing security without proper tool support.

Figure 8 shows a deployment diagram of iTrust. Its concrete security requirements are specified using the UMLsec approach and its « secure links » annotation. Concrete encryption algorithms are annotated. The deployment reflects the typical setting of a distributed information system: There is an application server, executing the iTrust application as well as the database. Apart from that, there are two kinds of devices (medical staff and patients) to act as clients, both running a browser. The database runs on the same node as the iTrust appli-

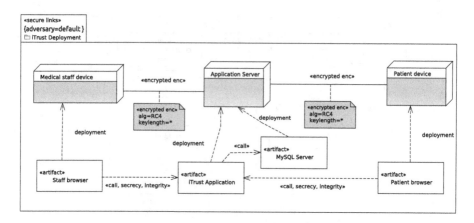

Fig. 8. Deployment diagram for iTrust with security annotation « secure links ».

cation, and it thus does not require communication path encryption. On the contrary, the communication between the server and the clients shall ensure the integrity and the secrecy of the data transmitted over the communication paths.

At a point in time before the vulnerability of RC4 is discovered, according to the SCK, RC4 is selected as the encryption algorithm to secure the communication paths between the application server and the client devices' browsers. As illustrated in the previous sections, the vulnerability of RC4 is identified by detecting an occurrence of the semantic editing pattern "addEncryptionThreat" in the evolving SCK, being a trigger for the SMR shown in Listing 1.1. In subsequent steps, S^2EC^2O first checks if a risky encryption algorithm is in use and, if so, guides the user to selecting appropriate, state-of-the-art alternatives (again, by using the SCK). This way, the iTrust system model could be successfully adapted in a (semi-)automated fashion.

In sum, we analyzed three kinds of context changes that have the potential to put security on stake: changes to privacy laws, trust in external libraries, and encryption algorithm exploits. For full details of the study, we refer to [4]. We investigated concrete contextual changes that lead to the following security vulnerabilities, all of them can be categorized in CWE catalog entries (the vulnerability of RC4 is categorized by CWE-327):

- CWE-284: Improper Access Control,
- CWE-311*: Missing Encryption of Sensitive Data,
- CWE-732*: Incorrect Permission Assignment for Critical Resource,
- CWE-327*: Use of a Broken or Risky Cryptographic Algorithm,
- CWE-20: Improper Input Validation, and
- CWE-502: Deserialization of Untrusted Data.

The entries with an asterisk are among the 2011 CWE/SANS 25 most dangerous software errors[8]. In every case, we were able to show that changes leading to these

---

[8] http://cwe.mitre.org/top25/.

vulnerabilities can be detected by analyzing evolution in ontologies, and S^2EC^2O guided the user to manage the risk by recommending alternatives.

We used Protégé to analyze the complexity of the ontologies representing the SCK in our study. The highest complexity measure was identified as $\mathcal{ALU}$ (attributive language with concept union). However, the complexity regarding the description logic is not relevant for SiLift, which works on a syntactical level rather than inferring logical relations. Regarding the runtime performance of our tooling, detecting semantic editing patterns took at most 17 s for the considered evolution scenarios. The time for a complete run of S^2EC^2O, including the generation of co-evolution proposals, took no longer than 30 seconds. Given that we are experimenting with a research prototype which is not optimized for performance, we believe that the obtained results demonstrate the applicability of our approach in a real-world setting.

5   Related Work

Ontology evolution as the process to adapt and change ontologies and dependent artifacts in a consistent manner has been studied in the literature for many years, surveys can be found in [7,19,33,34]. Various techniques have been proposed to support dedicated tasks of this process. The most closely related approaches to ours deal with the management of changes. The first approach which distinguishes changes on an atomic, composite and complex level has been presented by Maedche et al. [21], where ontological changes are recorded through a dedicated tool known as OntoLogging. A configurable approach to detect ontological changes has been presented by Plessers et al. [26,27]. They introduce a change definition language which allows tool users to define sets of change patterns. The detection is realized by interpreting change definitions as temporal queries on a persitently managed ontology version log. Thus, in contrast to ours, their approach is still bound to the restriction of logging ontology change information through a dedicated tool environment. The same limitation applies to approaches which have been later proposed by Djedidi et al. [6] and Javed et al. [12,13]. The approach proposed by Papavassiliou et al. [24,25] gets rid of this limitation, however, only supports a fixed set of semantic editing patterns which cannot be extended by customly defined change patterns. In sum, none of the proposed approaches fully meets our specific requirements described in the introduction.

6   Conclusion

We presented an approach and prototypical implementation to detect occurrences of semantic editing patterns in evolving OWL ontologies. Compared to existing approaches that aim at semantic lifting of low-level ontological changes, the most distinguishing features of our approach are that it does not rely on tool-specific information such as persistently managed edit logs, and that the set of supported semantic editing patterns can be easily customized and extended.

We motivated the need for these features in the context of a model-based security engineering approach which incorporates so-called security context knowledge into system design and evolution, and a case study on a medical information system demonstrates the applicability and usefulness of the developed techniques. However, application scenarios leading to similar requirements can be found in other areas as well. In software engineering, for example, knowledge management is increasingly considered as a key aspect having a strong impact on the maintainability of various quality attributes of software systems. Besides traditional development artifacts, manifold information such as rationale for development decisions may need to be gathered. Whenever such knowledge is documented and exploited through the use of ontologies which may undergo uncontrolled and ad-hoc change over time, we believe that our approach provides a suitable basis for successfully managing the respective ontology evolution.

References

1. Baader, F., Horrocks, I., Sattler, U.: Description logics. In: Staab, S., Studer R. (eds.) Handbook on Ontologies, pp. 3–28. Springer, Heidelberg (2004). https://doi.org/10.1007/978-3-540-24750-0_1
2. Bürger, J., Jürjens, J., Ruhroth, T., Gärtner, S., Schneider, K.: Model-based security engineering: managed co-evolution of security knowledge and software models. In: Aldini, A., Lopez, J., Martinelli, F. (eds.) FOSAD 2012-2013. LNCS, vol. 8604, pp. 34–53. Springer, Cham (2014). https://doi.org/10.1007/978-3-319-10082-1_2
3. Bürger, J., Jürjens, J., Wenzel, S.: Restoring security of evolving software models using graph transformation. Int. J. Softw. Tools Technol. Transf. **17**(3), 267–289 (2014). https://doi.org/10.1007/s10009-014-0364-8
4. Bürger, J.: Recovering security in model-based software engineering by context-driven co-evolution. Ph.D. thesis, University of Koblenz-Landau (2019)
5. Bürger, J., Strüber, D., Gärtner, S., Ruhroth, T., Jürjens, J., Schneider, K.: A framework for semi-automated co-evolution of security knowledge and system models. J. Syst. Softw. **139**, 142–160 (2018)
6. Djedidi, R., Aufaure, M.A.: Ontology change management. In: I-SEMANTICS, pp. 611–621 (2009)
7. Djedidi, R., Aufaure, M.A.: Ontology evolution: state of the art and future directions. In: Ontology Theory, Management and Design: Advanced Tools and Models. IGI Global (2010)
8. Gärtner, S., Ruhroth, T., Bürger, J., Schneider, K., Jürjens, J.: Maintaining requirements for long-living software systems by incorporating security knowledge. In: 22nd IEEE International Requirements Engineering Conference. IEEE (2014)
9. Gruber, T.R.: A translation approach to portable ontology specifications. Knowl. Acquis. **5**(2), 199–220 (1993)
10. Heckman, S., Stolee, K., Parnin, C.: 10+ years of teaching software engineering with iTrust: the good, the bad, and the ugly. In: International Conference on Software Engineering Education and Training, pp. 1–4. IEEE (2018)
11. Hesse, T.M., Gärtner, S., Roehm, T., Paech, B., Schneider, K., Bruegge, B.: Semi-automatic security requirements engineering and evolution using decision documentation, heuristics, and user monitoring. In: International Workshop on Evolving Security and Privacy Requirements Engineering, pp. 1–6. IEEE (2014)

12. Javed, M., Abgaz, Y.M., Pahl, C.: A pattern-based framework of change operators for ontology evolution. In: Meersman, R., Herrero, P., Dillon, T. (eds.) OTM 2009. LNCS, vol. 5872, pp. 544–553. Springer, Heidelberg (2009). https://doi.org/10. 1007/978-3-642-05290-3_68

13. Javed, M., Abgaz, Y.M., Pahl, C.: Ontology change management and identification of change patterns. J. Data Semant. **2**(2–3), 119–143 (2013)

14. Jürjens, J.: Secure Systems Development with UML. Springer, Heidelberg (2005)

15. Kehrer, T., Alshanqiti, A., Heckel, R.: Automatic inference of rule-based specifications of complex in-place model transformations. In: Guerra, E., van den Brand, M. (eds.) ICMT 2017. LNCS, vol. 10374, pp. 92–107. Springer, Cham (2017). https:// doi.org/10.1007/978-3-319-61473-1_7

16. Kehrer, T., Kelter, U., Ohrndorf, M., Sollbach, T.: Understanding model evolution through semantically lifting model differences with SiLift. In: International Conference on Software Maintenance (2012)

17. Kehrer, T., Kelter, U., Pietsch, P., Schmidt, M.: Adaptability of model comparison tools. In: International Conference on Automated Software Engineering, pp. 306–309. IEEE (2012)

18. Kehrer, T., Kelter, U., Taentzer, G.: A rule-based approach to the semantic lifting of model differences in the context of model versioning. In: International Conference on Automated Software Engineering (2011)

19. Khattak, A.M., Batool, R., Pervez, Z., Khan, A.M., Lee, S.: Ontology evolution and challenges. J. Inf. Sci. Eng. **29**(5), 851–871 (2013)

20. Kögel, S., et al.: Learning from evolution for evolution. Managed Software Evolution, pp. 255–308. Springer, Cham (2019). https://doi.org/10.1007/978-3-030-13499-0_10

21. Maedche, A., Motik, B., Stojanovic, L., Studer, R., Volz, R.: Managing multiple ontologies and ontology evolution in ontologging. In: Musen, M.A., Neumann, B., Studer, R. (eds.) IIP 2002. ITIFIP, vol. 93, pp. 51–63. Springer, Boston, MA (2002). https://doi.org/10.1007/978-0-387-35602-0_6

22. Otero-Cerdeira, L., Rodríguez-Martínez, F.J., Gómez-Rodríguez, A.: Ontology matching: a literature review. Expert Syst. Appl. **42**(2), 949–971 (2015)

23. OWL Working Group, W.: OWL 2 Web Ontology Language: Document Overview. W3C Recommendation (2009)

24. Papavassiliou, V., Flouris, G., Fundulaki, I., Kotzinos, D., Christophides, V.: On Detecting high-level changes in RDF/S KBs. In: Bernstein, A., et al. (eds.) ISWC 2009. LNCS, vol. 5823, pp. 473–488. Springer, Heidelberg (2009). https://doi.org/ 10.1007/978-3-642-04930-9_30

25. Papavassiliou, V., Flouris, G., Fundulaki, I., Kotzinos, D., Christophides, V.: High-level change detection. ACM Trans. Database Syst. (TODS) **38**(1), 1 (2013)

26. Plessers, P., De Troyer, O.: Ontology change detection using a version log. In: Gil, Y., Motta, E., Benjamins, V.R., Musen, M.A. (eds.) ISWC 2005. LNCS, vol. 3729, pp. 578–592. Springer, Heidelberg (2005). https://doi.org/10.1007/11574620_42

27. Plessers, P., De Troyer, O., Casteleyn, S.: Understanding ontology evolution: a change detection approach. Web Semant.: Sci. Serv. Agents World Wide Web **5**(1), 39–49 (2007)

28. Popov, A.: RFC 7465: Prohibiting RC4 cipher suite, February 2015. https://tools. ietf.org/html/rfc7465. Accessed 24 Apr 2020

29. Ruhroth, T., Gärtner, S., Bürger, J., Jürjens, J., Schneider, K.: Versioning and evolution requirements for model-based system development. In: International Workshop on Comparison and Versioning of Software Models (2014)

30. Steinberg, D., Budinsky, F., Merks, E., Paternostro, M.: EMF: Eclipse Modeling Framework. Pearson Education, London (2008)
31. Strüber, D., et al.: Henshin: a usability-focused framework for EMF model transformation development. In: de Lara, J., Plump, D. (eds.) ICGT 2017. LNCS, vol. 10373, pp. 196–208. Springer, Cham (2017). https://doi.org/10.1007/978-3-319-61470-0_12
32. Vanhoef, M., Piessens, F.: All your biases belong to us: Breaking RC4 in WPA-TKIP and TLS. In: USENIX Security Symposium, pp. 97–112 (2015)
33. Wardhana, H., Ashari, A., Sari, A.K.: Review of ontology evolution process. J. Comput. Appl. **45**, 26–33 (2018)
34. Zablith, F., et al.: Ontology evolution: a process-centric survey. knowl. Eng. Rev. **30**(1), 45–75 (2015)

Blockchain-Based Personal Health Records for Patients' Empowerment

Omar El Rifai[1,3](✉), Maelle Biotteau[2,3], Xavier de Boissezon[2,3],
Imen Megdiche[1], Franck Ravat[1], and Olivier Teste[1]

[1] Institut de Recherche en Informatique de Toulouse, CNRS (UMR 5505),
Université de Toulouse, Toulouse, France
{omar.el-rifai,imen.megdiche,franck.ravat,olivier.teste}@irit.fr
[2] ToNIC, Toulouse NeuroImaging Center, Université de Toulouse, Inserm, UPS,
Toulouse, France
maelle.biotteau@inserm.fr
[3] Centre hospitalier universitaire de Toulouse, Toulouse, France
deboissezon.xavier@chu-toulouse.fr

Abstract. With the current trend of patient-centric health-care, blockchain-based Personal Health Records (PHRs) frameworks have been emerging. The adoption of these frameworks is still in its infancy stage and is dependent on a broad range of factors. In this paper we look at some of the typical concerns raised from a centralized medical records solution such as the one deployed in France. Based on the state of the art literature in terms of Electronic Health Records (EHRs) and PHRs, we discuss the main implementation bottlenecks that can be encountered when deploying a blockchain solution and how to avoid them. In particular, we explore these bottlenecks in the context of the French PHR system and suggest some recommendations for a paradigm shift towards patients' empowerment.

Keywords: Blockchain · Empowerment · Health-care · PHR · DMP-France

1 Introduction

In recent years, there has been a clear interest to modernize and digitalize health-care services. Many health-care projects have been geared toward information systems advances. Specifically, we have seen developments in the area Electronic Health Records (EHRs) and Personal Health Records (PHRs). The Harvard School of Public Health website, defines the difference between EHRs and PHRs as follows: "Whereas an electronic health record (EHR) is a computer record that originates with and is controlled by doctors, a personal health record (PHR) can be generated by physicians, patients, hospitals, pharmacies, and other sources but is controlled by the patient". Patients are then responsible of managing their own PHR, which is in step with the concept of patients' empowerment

© Springer Nature Switzerland AG 2020
F. Dalpiaz et al. (Eds.): RCIS 2020, LNBIP 385, pp. 455–471, 2020.
https://doi.org/10.1007/978-3-030-50316-1_27

[2]. Empowerment is defined by the World Health Organization (WHO) as "a proactive partnership and patient self-care strategy to improve health outcomes and quality of life among the chronically ill" [3]. Patients are no longer only the passive recipient of treatments, but also share an active role with health practitioners. In terms of data management, this can be translated to patients' ownership of their medical records and autonomy in terms of data access control policies. These ownership and control points are crucial in the health-care sector where patients' data are particularly sensitive.

In this paper we look at challenges faced by a centralized PHR solution. The situation is illustrated by analyzing the French use case and the specific issues of the French context. We elaborate on the key problems and establish relationships with state of the art solutions that use the blockchain to secure patients' data and empower them. Indeed, the blockchain was designed as a "system based on cryptographic proof instead of trust, allowing any two willing parties to transact directly with each other without the need for a trusted third party" [23]. This concept of decentralized trust was used in the context of medical records as we see in the later sections.

The paper is organised as follows: Sect. 2 explains the context of personal health records in France along with relevant aspects of the current architecture. In Sect. 3, we detail some fundamental concepts of the blockchain. Then, in Sect. 4, we present the related blockchain-based solutions for EHR/PHR as they provide answers to some of the current shortcomings. Finally, in Sect. 5, we propose enhancements to the current architecture and conclude with some general recommendations.

2   PHR Solution in France

Among the efforts that have been made towards digital health-care data in France, we note the following.

1. In 2004, the French ministry devised a plan to create a generalized digital personal health record, ("Dossier Médical Partagé" or DMP)[1]. The primary aim of this initiative was to have a unique centralized source of information for every patients.
2. Due to the project lack of momentum in its early stages, the French minister of Health decided in 2013 to overhaul the project with a second generation DMP. With this overhaul, the focus shifted from a generalized PHR to a more modest objective of primarily focusing on the elderly and patients with chronic diseases.
3. A national health-care road-map planned for 2022 ("Ma santé 2022") is deployed for the advancement of medical data digitalization. Among other aims, this road map seeks to accelerate the deployment of numerical services such as the DMP. [7].

---

[1] The official websites describes the project as a "carnet de santé numérique" which is owned by patients in its paper form.

The French DMP contains all records relevant to patients' care. This includes physician's diagnosis results, medical (biological, imaging) test results, allergies and any other relevant background medical data[2]. Furthermore, the DMP can be used by patients to enter personal medical data they deem relevant. According to the article R1111-26 of the French Civil Code[3], the DMP is "designed to encourage a preventive, qualitative, constant and coordinated healthcare service"[4]. The DMP has elements of both EHRs and PHRs [20]. It is an EHR to the extent that health care providers can use the DMP once authorized, and some content can be made temporarily invisible to the patient for medical reasons. It is a PHR as the initial creation is dependent on patient's initiative, and they can feed-in additional content.

An illustration of the current centralized PHR is presented in Fig. 1. Most of the data records are stored in government accredited servers and are accessed using unique identifiers. For patients, these identifiers are the French national insurance numbers ("numéro de carte vitale") whereas health-care professionals (HCP) use a health-care specific national registration number "carte CPS". In the next section, we detail some key elements relevant to patients' empowerment in this architecture.

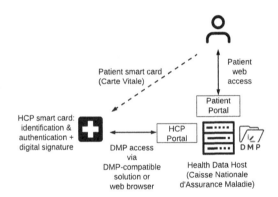

Fig. 1. An illustration of the current architecture

2.1   Patients' Empowerment in the Current Technical Architecture

We look at three points in the DMP architecture that are relevant to patients' empowerment. Namely, we look at the ownership status, access right management rules and usage transparency.

---

[2] https://www.ameli.fr/haute-garonne/medecin/sante-prevention/dossier-medical-partage/dmp-tout-ce-que-professionnels-de-sante-doivent-savoir.

[3] https://www.legifrance.gouv.fr/affichCodeArticle.do?idArticle=LEGIARTI0000328 43719.

[4] The translation is by the authors.

Patients are the legal owners of their DMP [25]. But in reality, there is an ambiguous ownership status whereby despite the legal status, patients lack the tools for exercising their agency over their data. The ambiguous status of the ownership is illustrated by two examples.

1. Without a derogation, DMP holders can not refuse data entry to their DMP if the HCP deems the data important for the patient's care. The definition of a valid derogation is not detailed in the text and is open to interpretation.
2. Second, upon requesting the deletion of the DMP, the regular process is executed only 10 years after the demand is made. Patients need to make a specific request for prompt deletion [25].

Similarly, access rights are managed by patients. They can choose to grant or revoke access to every piece of information to HCP. However, consent for access is given orally and is thus difficult to prove. Also, by default, the access right is defined at the "health-care unit level". This means that patients granting access to one particular physician are implicitly granting access to the entire health-care team [25].

The DMP also offers a mechanism for usage transparency and traceability. Indeed, time stamped access logs and transactions are recorded in the DMP [25]. This provides users with a historical log that helps them ensure their privacy is respected. According to the current regulations, in addition to the patient, the patient's treating physician and the data entry author can access these logs. These logs, as the points mentioned above, are a step towards increasing patients' power over their data and hence their empowerment. However, there still remains some challenges for a paradigm where patients are actors in the system and not only users. We detail in the next section some of these challenges.

2.2 Current Challenges

Some studies have raised concerns regarding data ownership and control in the context of centralized solutions [24]. These concerns are not unjustified. For instance, the French health ministry kick-started in December 2019, a project entitled "health data hub" which serves as a platform for data science projects to exploit the national collection of medical data. The platform guarantees the security of the data by having the code of the different projects run within the platform itself without exporting patients' data [5]. Nevertheless, this initiative has been taken without explicit consent from patients and still raises ownership questions.

The early adoption of the DMP has been hindered primarily by agency and security concerns [24]. In terms of agency, the governance of the DMP and hence the inherent governance of the critical medical data is entrusted to the French government insurance organization ("Caisse Nationale d'Assurance Maladie" or CNAM). Technically, the data are hosted on a national server for the most part and in specialized health organizations for others [24]. However, decisions regarding the access and control mechanisms remain one sided and constitute administrative and technical barrier to patients' empowerment. For example, if legislation's regarding the access rights of data were to change, patients would potentially not be included in the decision making process.

Similarly, because of the centralized governance of data, no real guarantees of records security and immutability can be provided. A successful attack on the hosting servers would potentially compromise the entire national database. Access logs are a step towards transparency but suffer the same centralization weakness. Some example privacy infringements with regards to medical records in France have been advanced in [24]. For instance, on the 16th of June 2011, The French National Commission on Informatics and Liberty raised formal complaints about the SMG society for a lack of sufficient security measures with regards to patients' data [24].

Recently, the blockchain has emerged as a technology that addresses the above issues by relying on a decentralized consensus mechanism. This decentralized mechanism can serve towards more transparency and users' participation which is a step towards patients' empowerment. Even if this technology had been initially designed with crypto currencies in mind, it has evolved towards different use cases among which we find EHRs/PHRs. In other countries, some initiatives have already been taken to use the blockchain at state level to counterbalance the perceived disadvantages of a centralized solution. The Estonian government is largely believed to have been the first to consider blockchain technology as a security layer for protecting patients' data [22]. Similarly, a national health-care project in the United Arab Emirate's was recently launched to have a blockchain system for recording and sharing health-care data [15].

3   Technical Concepts of Blockchain

A myriad of blockchain implementations, both public and private are now developed. The blockchain sparked interest both inside and outside of cryptography. The trend was accentuated by financial speculations on crypto-currencies which somewhat tarnished the reputation of the technology and shifted the focus away from the real advantages. Nonetheless, the increased interest also pushed for the development of valuable technology that rest on the technical properties of the blockchain. We explain in this section some of the important aspects that need to be understood for the development of blockchain-based applications [8,27].

The blockchain can be thought of as a secure decentralized ledger. The ledger is duplicated across a public network of peers that are globally responsible for maintaining the integrity of the records. At the heart of the blockchain, lies a consensus protocol first formalized in [23], which ensures that the ledger is immutable, transparent, and privacy preserving. These algorithmic properties are essential for performing transactions at large scale without relying on trusted third parties (such as banks or state institutions) for guarantees.

3.1   Cryptographic Primitives

Two concepts from cryptography, hash functions and digital signatures, are used as building blocks for the blockchain.

Cryptographic Hash Functions (CHF). A mathematical algorithm that maps an arbitrary size input to a fixed size output. In the context of the blockchain, hash functions are used to uniquely identify data (fingerprint) and ensure integrity. A successful CHF should be *deterministic, distributed, efficient, pre-image-resistant* and *collision-resistant* [11].

Digital Signatures. Digital signatures are codes attached to electronic documents which authenticate a persons' identity. Using public key cryptography, a simple digital signature protocol can be made whereby the sender encrypts a message (or the hash of the message) using his private key and the receiver attempts to decrypt the message using the sender's public key. If the decryption succeeds, the receiver can authenticate the sender's identity.

3.2   Consensus Protocol

The consensus protocol serves to find an agreement (consensus) between the nodes so that they all have the same version of the ledger. In the bitcoin's blockchain implementation, the protocol used is called Proof of Work (PoW). The computational effort needed to verify nodes comes in the form of a mathematical puzzle nodes need to solve. The puzzle consists of finding a number (nonce), that if hashed with the blockchain ledger, produces a binary hash smaller than the current target of the network. As a reward for validating transactions (mining), nodes receive bitcoins. Figure 2 illustrates this mechanism with three user (nodes). In addition to the PoW, new blocks need to reference hashes of past transactions.

The bitcoins' PoW consensus protocol works well for public blockchains with many participants as the robustness of the mechanism relies on having voting capacity proportional to computational power. In the context of medical records, the number of participants may be limited, especially in a first phase. And thus a PoW protocol can be risky as any attacker with 51% computational power could cause a denial of service. For private (or permissioned) blockchain (with read and/or write access restrictions to some participants) the PoW consensus protocol may not be the most suitable. Other implementations such as Proof of Stake (PoS) or Byzantine Fault Tolerance (BFT) exist and the choice should be based on the intended usage of the blockchain. A list of consensus protocols are described in [17] in the context of health-care applications.

3.3   Smart Contracts (SC)

SC expand the initial idea of financial transactions to a more complete set of instructions that are distributedly run on the blockchain. With SC, the properties

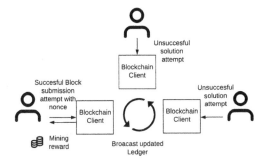

Fig. 2. An illustration of the Proof of Work (PoW) consensus protocol

that were true of bitcoin's transactions, now extend to complex protocols. In the health-care sector, smart contracts have been used, among other things, for health insurance, health records and tele-medicine. For instance, a patient can now subscribe to an insurance plan through a smart contract and avoid going through lengthy and often varying procedures for filing an insurance claim. The patient only needs to comply to the conditions he first agreed upon on signing to have guarantees that a prompt and automatic reimbursement will take place.

Although simple in appearance, the blockchain has had a radical impact on the way we perceive data transfers. Whereas before, it was difficult for digital assets to inspire trust, the blockchain made digital assets unique and non reproducible. From these properties, technologies that where previously impossible have been put to practice.

4   Related Work

Electronic health-care initiatives have been extensively used for translating the empowerment concept into concrete measures [2]. Hordern et al. [14] classify these initiatives into five main categories (Peer-to-peer online support Groups/ Health Related Virtual Communities, Self Management/Self Monitoring, Decision Aids, Personal Health Records and Internet Use). PHRs has been shown to be linked to empowerment [2,14] and particularly among frequent users of the health-care system. Some of the advantages reported by these patients are an easier access to data from different sources and a larger sense of control over the care process.

The blockchain furthers these advantages by allowing the development of a patient-centric solution. Especially, the blockchain improves upon server-based or cloud based solutions in terms of data integrity, digital access rules, and data audit. In the next sections, we present some of the relevant studies on blockchain in the health-care sector in general, then focus on PHR/EHR solutions.

4.1 The Blockchain in the Health Sector

Because of the properties it possesses, the blockchain has been recently investigated in relations with medical applications [1,8]. Especially, there has been an increased interest in using the blockchain for storing health or medical records. Although the hype seems justified, a lack of proper understanding of the mechanisms to put it in place have thus far prevented the technology from being broadly adopted [16].

The authors of [22], introduced some of the efforts that have been made towards using the blockchain in the health-care sector. They emphasize "the disruptive character which underlies blockchain technology, [which] will strongly affect the balance of powers between existing market players in the health-care". Similarly, Gordon et al. [13] discusses the shift towards more "patient mediated" and "patient driven" health data exchange in EHRs. The authors argue that a blockchain-based solution can help bridge the gap between the increasing need of data liquidity and interoperability and the privacy and security issues associated with patient-centric solutions.

Esposito et al. [10] also look at blockchain-based solutions for storing PHRs but they focus on the challenges that need to be faced for it to be a viable option. For instance, they ask what certification of validity can be obtained for data collected by patients. Further, they also ask whom should be legally responsible for misdiagnosis based on inaccurate information in the PHRs. These an other relevant questions need to be addressed for a solution to be applied in practice.

In a review paper of the use of blockchain in the biomedical domain, Drosatos et al. [8] classify the reasons that have been advanced in the literature for the use of the blockchain. For studies dealing with Medical records or Personal records, the main reasons presented are:

1. **Data Integrity:** data should be tamper-proof.
2. **Access Control:** ownership should be restricted and provable
3. **Data Audit:** audit operations should be made easy and verifiable.

In the next section, we look at how these issues were solved in the EHR/PHR literature and highlight some relevant studies with frameworks that could be implemented in the DMP context. In particular, we look at studies that focus on blockchain-based solutions.

4.2 EHR/PHR Solutions

A fundamental paper by Zyskind et al. [30] addresses the above three points and offers a solution that exploits the advantages of the blockchain for data sharing. The authors suggest an architecture whereby personal data remain outside the blockchain while data pointers (in the form of hashes), and access rights policies are stored on the blockchain. With the addition of these mechanism on the blockchain, users can establish data ownership, define personalised access rules and verify access transactions. Indeed, even though with the proposed architecture data records remain physically stored on external servers, users can claim and prove ownership easily by fingerprinting and digitally signing records. The authors also outline a data encryption scheme that can be used in such a platform. They suggest that data stored outside the blockchain be encrypted using a symmetric key and that data owners shares this symmetric key with every user authorized to view the data using an asymmetric key exchange protocol. Based on the above mentioned ideas, a host of papers were published that develop more or less similar lines.

Ekblaw et al. [9] implemented a solution for blockchain-based EHRs using the Ethereum blockchain. The solution proposed contains three modules that handle identity registration, access management, and transactions history logs to offer patients a summary view of their data. Other studies improved upon this scheme by introducing complementary cryptographic protocols in the architecture. Liu et al. [19] for example, suggest adding a cryptography scheme called Cascaded Encryption Scheme (CES) to an architecture similar to that of Ekblaw et al. [9]. Their idea is that medical documents can contain several pieces of personal information which a user might not want to disclose entirely to every access recipient. The scheme encrypts and signs the documents in several parts so that access is given in a modular way. Dagher et al. [6] improve on the architecture primarily by adding a proxy re-encryption scheme whereby encryption keys are stored on the blockchain. This protocol is explained in [4] as follows: "A proxy re-encryption scheme allows an untrusted party to convert ciphertext between keys without access to either the original message or to the secret component of the old key or the new key." The idea is to create an additional "proxy key" $P(A, B)$ which, when coupled with the encrypted message, converts the message intended to be decrypted by user's A public key, to a message decryptable by user's B public key This is handy in the context of blockchains where such schemes can be hosted in smart contracts simplifying the exchange of data.

Other solutions focused more on the practical and legal aspects of blockchains. For instance, Zhang et al. [29] approach the problem from the legal point of view. They propose a solution to cater for the technical requirements from the Office of the National Coordinator for Health Information Technology (ONC). Their proposal details every requirement for a health data system by the ONC and suggests a blockchain-based architecture that satisfies it. Similarly, in [6], the authors design their solution for meeting the Health Insurance Portability and Accountability Act (HIPAA) requirements.

Regardless of the focus point, the fundamental idea behind blockchain-based health records remains constant. Medical records are stored off chain and hash pointers to the data sources are stored on a decentralized ledger. In Table 1 we summarize the main components of each of the relevant papers. In terms of implementation, most solutions use Ethereum for its inherent Smart Contracts (SC) functionality that we will explain in Sect. 3. In terms of external storage, recommendation are mostly dependent on the problem context and can either consist of specific service provider databases or cloud storage solutions. The use-cases found all revolve around registering access policies on the blockchain along with some sort of digitally signed data pointers to the records themselves. These mechanisms constitute the crux of the proposals and are complemented with other functionalities such as logs of transactions, identity management mechanisms, or advanced encryption policies.

4.3   Discussion: Technical Difficulties in the Health-Care Domain

From the above properties, it is tempting to think of the blockchain as a panacea for electronic health records management. But before going further, some of these properties can be challenges in themselves as we have seen in the related literature. First transparency in the health-care context is double edged. Indeed, as every node can potentially verify every transaction in the blockchain, all nodes have access to the entire data contained in the blockchain. This is obviously problematic in the context of health-care records as patients may not want to share their medical history with the entire network. Second, transactions in the blockchain often consist of very simple data transfers. Large volumes of data are not handled well by design as the data is duplicated on every node in the network. However, health-care data are often prohibitively voluminous with records ranging from large unstructured documents to imaging results. Third, in the context of the European General Data Protection Regulation (GDPR), users have the right to request the deletion of their data at any moment. This principle goes against the immutability property is of the blockchain ledger and would of course not be possible if medical records were to be stored directly on the blockchain. All of these issues have been dealt with using data pointers as we have seen in the related literature. However, there remains institutional and market challenges that have been rarely addressed in the literature. We look at all these points in the next section. Also, we explain some of the technical details underlying the blockchain technology. These concepts will then allow us to suggest improvements on the current French framework.

5   Lessons Learned and Recommendations: A Blockchain Framework

To counteract some of the limitations of a centralized PHR solutions and head towards a patients' empowerment paradigm, we offer suggestions on technical, institutional and market factors that can hinder the deployment of a blockchain-based solution [16]. Specifically, we follow on the guidelines of Janssen et al. [16] that recommend "an integrated understanding of the various factors ranging from governance to technology to create blockchain applications that work, fulfil the benefits of users and service providers and are acceptable by the society". By facing these challenges, the solution could be more inline with a balanced distribution of power.

5.1   Institutional Factors

Because of the paradigm shift the blockchain operates on electronic data, legislative, cultural and governance considerations have to be taken into account. As

Table 1. Properties of related blockchain-based EHR/PHR framework in the literature

Article	Blockchain use	External storage	Blockchain technology	Cryptographic protocols
[30]	Data access policies	Distributed Hash Table NoSQL	Bitcoin	Symmetric and asymmetric key encryption
[9]	Identity management Access policies Reference pointers Summary logs	Providers DB storage	Ethereum	Digital signatures Encryption (no details)
[28]	DB actions log for auditing	Existing DB infrastructure Authenticator Server	Proprietary	Digital signature Asymmetric encryption
[12]	Reference pointers Hash of EMRs Summary logs	Providers DB (unspecified)	Proprietary	Digital signature Symmetric and asymmetric key encryption
[6]	Identity management Hashes of reference pointers History summary Access policies Proxy re-encryption	Providers' DB storage	Ethereum	Symmetric and asymmetric key encryption Proxy re-encryption signature
[19]	Access policies Reference pointers Access logs	Cloud storage	Smart Contract based - unspecified	Symmetric and asymmetric key encryption Content Extraction Signature
[29]	Identity Verification Access policies Reference pointer	Providers' DB storage	Ethereum	Digital Signature Symmetric and asymmetric key encryption

far as legislation, the European General Data Protection Regulation (GDPR) imposes strict rules for data protection and users' privacy insurance [26]. Among those rules we can mention "the right to be forgotten" which requires data controllers to remove users' data either on their request or if the data is no longer relevant for the initial intended usage. The right to provide data exports of users' data, the ability for users to easily give and revoke access, and necessary encryption and pseudonymisation mechanisms [26].

But as we have seen in related literature, the blockchain layer need not contain any medical record in itself but only pointers and hashes of data. As such these requirements are implicitly satisfied. In addition, security features such as encryption mechanisms and pseudonymity are inherent in the blockchain mechanisms. Data hosts such as the CNAM are already government accredited and strictly observe the GDPR requirements.

5.2   Market Factors

Janssen et al. [16] define market factors as "the operating of an organisation in its environment' and suggest to be mindful of related changes that could occur when implementing blockchain technologies. In particular, the authors address changes in market structure, contracts and agreements and business processes. In terms of market structure, the maintenance of a blockchain-based EHR system requires bandwidths and processing power to validate the blocks and secure the network. As one possible solution, the authors of [9] suggest that health data providers handle the validation process singlehandedly arguing that they are already the "trusted keepers of medical data". This approach nonetheless concentrates agency in the hand of healthcare data providers. Alternatively, patient's or patient's union could participate by providing the required processing power with the incentive of increased agency over their data. For, contracts and agreements, there would be inevitable changes as exchanges between patients and HCP would have to be redefined and encoded in SC. However, as the terms of those SC would be accessible and transparent to everyone, they are likely to be more readily and widely adopted. Finally, in terms of business processes, both patients and HCP could improve their experience as HCP could be alleviated from some service provision tasks now processed directly from the SCs and patients would gain agency and decision power. Additionally, if patients feel more empowered, it is likely that they will be more willing to register for the DMP, which has been a one major blocking point for the development of the project until now [21].

5.3   Technical Factors

Adding a blockchain layer to the DMP architecture is not disruptive with respect to the existing data hosting solution. Indeed, we do not suggest moving patients' data to the blockchain but instead using the blockchain for developing an additional layer that adds security and transparency guarantees as recommended in the blockchain-based PHR literature [1,8,30].

Most blockchain implementations come with many resources to facilitate the development of SC. For instance, on the Ethereum blockchain, development is made easy with a Turing-complete programming language called "Solidity". Once the SC are developed, framework for interfacing with them are also widely available and are usually packaged into a user-friendly interface in the form of a website.

To illustrate an example architecture, we detail below SC that could be implemented on an Ethereum blockchain implementation to guarantee decentralized identity management, data integrity guarantees, access control, and data audit capacities.

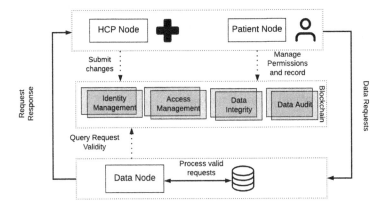

Fig. 3. An illustration of the proposed architecture with the added blockchain layer. Transactions are shown in dashed lines.

- **Identity Management:**
  Registration of patients to the DMP currently passes through the CNAM servers. They authenticate patients and maintain a list of registered patients. Managing the identity of patients on the blockchain instead would serve a double purpose. First it would democratize the governance of the registration process and render the rules for registration clear and transparent. Second, it would serve as a platform for authenticating patients and HCP and allowing them to prove their identity so that they can participate in the consensus protocol and in other SC functionalities. In an nutshell the blockchain can serve as a secure decentralized certificate of authority. For instance, a blockchain system was developed by the United Nations (UN) to help refugees without identity papers and qualifications to hold a certificate of identity [18].
- **Access Management:**
  For access management, the blockchain could store user-defined access control policies in the form of SC. Access control policies stored on the blockchain would serve as immutable references for the access rights of the different actors to the different aspects of users' data. For instance, whenever a HCP

would request access to some patient's data, the patient could add the HCP in the list of authorized users for the duration of intervention. Patients would then be the sole accountable for modifying these access rights. Encryption mechanisms such as those described below could also be coupled to the access control policies so that encryption and decryption tools secure the exchange of data.

- **Data Integrity:**
  The blockchain can host data hashes to ensure data integrity. Data hashes allow user to fingerprint their medical records guaranteeing that the original copy is never tampered with. Modifications to the data on the server would produce a completely different hash result and be a mark of data alteration. In addition, the proxy re-encryption scheme [6] and the Content Extraction Signature (CES) scheme [19] are two powerful mechanisms that can be used to facilitate secure data sharing. The CES scheme allows user to share specific parts instead of whole records to designated recipients. The proxy re-encryption scheme facilitates data sharing by allowing a SC to re-encrypt a already encrypted message with a new recipient's public key without disclosing any content of the original message.

- **Data Audit:**
  As transactions are natively immutable on the blockchain, data audit becomes much simpler and secure. A "Summary Logs" SC could serve as a breadcrumb mechanism as suggested in [9] for patients to verify the usage history of their PHR. The advantage of having the summary logs inside the blockchain instead of on the DMP, is that patients are guaranteed that the logs are not tampered with.

The overall architecture of the system is illustrated in Fig. 3. The blockchain layer consists of the SC detailed above and which, once deployed, serve as an interface between the users and the data providers. The user layer consists of the patients and the HCP which interact with the deployed SC. As mentioned above, this interaction can be done through a web interface or mobile app connecting to the smart contracts using one of the many freely available interface frameworks (e.g web3.js for the Ethereum blockchain). Finally, the data layer serves only as a data provider which checks for access permissions and logs access history through the blockchain. A "database keeper" such as the one described in [9] can be deployed on the Data Host layer to listen to incoming data requests, query the smart contracts for access rights, and respond appropriately to the users.

6   Conclusion

In this paper we analyzed the main challenges encountered with a centralized framework for health records. The context of the DMP project in France was used to illustrate these challenges. Based on this analysis, we suggested adding a blockchain layer following from the state of the art literature of blockchain-based EHRs/PHRs solutions. The blockchain-based layer adds security and transparency guarantees to traditional EHR/PHR platforms as well as introduces the decentralization paradigm. This paradigm is a step towards patients' empowerment in the sense that with it, patients become actors of their security and their data.

For a blockchain solution to remain user-centric and keep the properties and guarantees that makes it attractive, it is essential that it'd be used in accordance with the original principles of its founders. Consequently, even in private blockchains, the consensus protocol should not be designed to be exclusively in the hand of a single-interest party. Having a biased consensus protocol would defeat the purpose of the technology and serve the classical paradigm of a centralized authority.

Similarly, the code developed for the different SC should be optional for patients to use. The smart contracts described only serve as example tools that work in favor of patient guarantees for transparency and access management. Ideally, computer savvy users would develop their own SC and host them on an open platform where patients can choose from. This is already in line with the way SC are deployed today whereby any user can anonymously choose to participate after reviewing the specifications.

We organized the recommendations in terms of technical, institutional and market factors to address the complete picture of challenges faced when implementing this new framework and provide an overall vision on the challenges that can serve to enact these changes.

Funding Source. This work was supported by a grant from the Roche Fundation 2018.

References

1. Agbo, C., Mahmoud, Q., Eklund, J.: Blockchain technology in healthcare: a systematic review. Healthcare **7**(2), 56 (2019)
2. Alpay, L., Van Der Boog, P., Dumaij, A.: An empowerment-based approach to developing innovative e-healthtools for self-management. Health Inform. J. **17**(4), 247–255 (2011)
3. Aymé, S., Kole, A., Groft, S.: Empowerment of patients: lessons from the rare diseases community. The Lancet **371**(9629), 2048–2051 (2008)
4. Blaze, M., Bleumer, G., Strauss, M.: Divertible protocols and atomic proxy cryptography. In: Nyberg, K. (ed.) EUROCRYPT 1998. LNCS, vol. 1403, pp. 127–144. Springer, Heidelberg (1998). https://doi.org/10.1007/BFb0054122
5. Cuggia, M., Combes, S.: The French health data hub and the German medical informatics initiatives: two national projects to promote data sharing in healthcare. Yearb. Med. Inform. **28**(01), 195–202 (2019)
6. Dagher, G.G., Mohler, J., Milojkovic, M., Marella, P.B.: Ancile: privacy-preserving framework for access control and interoperability of electronic health records using blockchain technology. Sustain. Cities Soc. **39**, 283–297 (2018)
7. Ministère des Solidarités et de la Santé. Ma santé 2022: un engagement collectif. https://solidarites-sante.gouv.fr/systeme-de-sante-et-medico-social/masante2022/. Accessed 10 Jan 2020

8. Drosatos, G., Kaldoudi, E.: Blockchain applications in the biomedical domain: a scoping review. Comput. Struct. Biotechnol. J. **17**, 229–240 (2019)
9. Ekblaw, A., Azaria, A., Halamka, J.D., Lippman, A.: A case study for blockchain in healthcare: "MedRec" prototype for electronic health records and medical research data. In: Proceedings of IEEE Open & Big Data Conference, vol. 13, p. 13 (2016)
10. Esposito, C., De Santis, A., Tortora, G., Chang, H., Choo, K.K.R.: Blockchain: a panacea for healthcare cloud-based data security and privacy? IEEE Cloud Comput. **5**(1), 31–37 (2018)
11. Faber, B., Michelet, G.C., Weidmann, N., Mukkamala, R.R., Vatrapu, R.: BPDIMS: a blockchain-based personal data and identity management system. In: Proceedings of the 52nd Hawaii International Conference on System Sciences (2019)
12. Fan, K., Wang, S., Ren, Y., Li, H., Yang, Y.: MedBlock: efficient and secure medical data sharing via blockchain. J. Med. Syst. **42**(8), 1–11 (2018). https://doi.org/10.1007/s10916-018-0993-7
13. Gordon, W.J., Catalini, C.: Blockchain technology for healthcare: facilitating the transition to patient-driven interoperability. Comput. Struct. Biotechnol. J. **16**, 224–230 (2018)
14. Hordern, A., Georgiou, A., Whetton, S., Prgomet, M.: Consumer e-health: an overview of research evidence and implications for future policy. Health Inf. Manag. J. **40**(2), 6–14 (2011)
15. Hughes, E.: Unlocking blockchain: embracing new technologies to drive efficiency and empower the citizen. J. Br. Blockchain Assoc. **1**(2), 1–15 (2018)
16. Janssen, M., Weerakkody, V., Ismagilova, E., Sivarajah, U., Irani, Z.: A framework for analysing blockchain technology adoption: integrating institutional, market and technical factors. Int. J. Inf. Manag. **50**, 302–309 (2020)
17. Kuo, T.T., Zavaleta Rojas, H., Ohno-Machado, L.: Comparison of blockchain platforms: a systematic review and healthcare examples. J. Am. Med. Inform. Assoc. **26**(5), 462–478 (2019)
18. Leeming, G., Cunningham, J., Ainsworth, J.: A ledger of me: personalizing healthcare using blockchain technology. Front. Med. **6**, 1–10 (2019)
19. Liu, J., Li, X., Ye, L., Zhang, H., Du, X., Guizani, M.: BPDS: a blockchain based privacy-preserving data sharing for electronic medical records. In: Proceedings of 2018 IEEE Global Communications Conference, GLOBECOM 2018 (2018)
20. Macary, F.: The French PHR/EHR: creation, usage and lessons learnt with a national e-health record. HIMSS Europe (2013)
21. Manaouil, C.: Le dossier médical personnel (DMP): "autopsie" d'un projet ambitieux? Médecine Droit **2009**(94), 24–41 (2009)
22. Mettler, M.: Blockchain technology in healthcare: the revolution starts here. In: 2016 IEEE 18th International Conference on e-Health Networking, Applications and Services, Healthcom 2016, pp. 1–3 (2016)
23. Nakamoto, S.: Bitcoin: a peer-to-peer electronic cash system (2008). http://bitcoin.org/bitcoin.pdf
24. Schweitzer, L.: Le DMP ou comment constituer un gigantesque fichier des données de santé. Terminal. Technologie de l'information Cult. société **111**, 91–111 (2012)
25. l'Assurance Maladie Sécurité Sociale. FAQ. https://www.dmp.fr/patient/faq. Accessed 2020
26. Tankard, C.: What the GDPR means for businesses. Netw. Secur. **2016**(6), 5–8 (2016)

27. Sarah Underwood: Blockchain beyond bitcoin (2016)
28. Xia, Q., Sifah, E.B., Asamoah, K.O., Gao, J., Du, X., Guizani, M.: MeDShare: trust-less medical data sharing among cloud service providers via blockchain. IEEE Access **5**, 14757–14767 (2017)
29. Zhang, P., White, J., Schmidt, D.C., Lenz, G., Rosenbloom, S.T.: FHIRChain: applying blockchain to securely and scalably share clinical data. Comput. Struct. Biotechnol. J. **16**, 267–278 (2018)
30. Zyskind, G., Nathan, O., Pentland, A.S.: Decentralizing privacy: using blockchain to protect personal data. In: Proceedings of the 2015 IEEE Security and Privacy Workshops, SPW 2015, pp. 180–184 (2015)

COPri - A Core Ontology for Privacy Requirements Engineering

Mohamad Gharib[1]([⊠]), John Mylopoulos[2], and Paolo Giorgini[2]

[1] University of Florence - DiMaI, Viale Morgagni 65, Florence, Italy
mohamad.gharib@unifi.it
[2] University of Trento - DISI, 38123 Povo, Trento, Italy
{john.mylopoulos,paolo.giorgini}@unitn.it

Abstract. In their daily practice, most enterprises collect, store, and manage personal information for customers in order to deliver their services. In such a setting, privacy has emerged as a key concern as companies often neglect or even misuse personal data. In response to this, governments around the world have enacted laws and regulations for privacy protection. These laws dictate privacy requirements for any system that acquires and manages personal data. Unfortunately, these requirements are often incomplete and/or inaccurate as many RE practitioners might be unsure of what exactly are privacy requirements and how are they different from other requirements, such as security. To tackle this problem, we developed a comprehensive ontology for privacy requirements. To make it comprehensive, we base our ontology on a systematic review of the literature on privacy requirements. The contributions of this work include the derivation of an ontology from a previously conducted systematic literature review, an implementation using an ontology definition tool (Protégé), a demonstration of its coverage through an extensive example on Ambient Assisted Living, and a validation through a competence questionnaire answered by lexical semantics experts as well as privacy and security researchers.

Keywords: Privacy ontology · Privacy requirements · PbD · Conceptual modeling

1 Introduction

It is common practice for most companies today to collect, store, and manage personal information to deliver their services. Therefore, privacy has emerged as a key concern since such companies need to protect the privacy of personal information in order to comply with various privacy laws and regulations (e.g., GDPR in the EU [1]) that many governments have enacted for privacy protection. Accordingly, dealing with privacy concerns is a must these days [2]. However, most of such concerns can be tackled if the privacy requirements of the system-to-be were considered and addressed properly during requirements engineering [3,4]. Unfortunately, most requirements engineers are unfamiliar with

© Springer Nature Switzerland AG 2020
F. Dalpiaz et al. (Eds.): RCIS 2020, LNBIP 385, pp. 472–489, 2020.
https://doi.org/10.1007/978-3-030-50316-1_28

privacy requirements and how they differ from other requirements, such as security or vanilla quality requirements [5]. Even when requirements engineers have familiarity with privacy concerns, they focus mainly on confidentiality, and overlooking important privacy aspects such as unlinkability, unobservability [3].

Although privacy concepts have been studied for more than a century, they are still elusive and vague concepts to grasp [3,6]. In recent years, there have been numerous attempts to define privacy based on various related concepts such as confidentiality, anonymity, risk, transparency, etc. [6–9]. However, there is no consensus on the definitions of many of these concepts nor which of them should be used to analyze privacy [6]. In addition, many of these concepts are overlapping, thereby contributing to the confusion while dealing with privacy. Ontologies have proven to be a key factor for reducing the conceptual vagueness and terminological confusion by providing a shared understanding of related concepts [10]. In this context, the main objective of this work is to propose, implement, evaluate and validate a well-defined ontology that captures key privacy-related concepts.

Privacy is a social concept in that it depends on how others treat an individual's personal information and it strongly depends on the social context where that information is captured and used [5]. Accordingly, the privacy ontology should conceptualize privacy in their social and organizational context. In previous research [5], we worked toward addressing this problem by proposing a preliminary ontology for privacy requirements that has been mined through a systematic literature review.

In this paper, we propose COPri (a Core Ontology for Privacy requirements engineering) that has been mined from the results of what is proposed in [5] with new and more refined concepts concerning both personal information and privacy. Moreover, we implement the ontology, apply it to an Ambient-Assisted Living (AAL) illustrative example, and then validate it by querying the ontology instance (the AAL example) depending on a set of competency questions. Finally, we evaluate the ontology against common pitfalls in ontologies with the help of some tools, lexical semantics experts, and privacy and security researchers.

The rest of the paper is organized as follows; Sect. 2 presents an illustrative example, and we describe the process we followed for developing COPri in Sect. 3. Section 4 presents the conceptual model of COPri, and we implement and validate COPri in Sect. 5 and 6 respectively. We evaluate the ontology in Sect. 7. Related work is presented in Sect. 8, and we conclude and discuss future work in Sect. 9.

2   Illustrating Example: The Ambient-Assisted Living (AAL) System

Our motivating example concerns an old person called Jack that suffers from diabetes disease. Jack lives in a home that is equipped with an AAL system, which relies on various interconnected body sensors (e.g., Continuous Glucose Monitoring (CGM), location, and motion sensors). These sensors collect various information about Jack's vital signs, location, and activities. This information is transmitted to Jack's Personal Digital Assistant (PDA) that assesses his health situation and provides required notifications accordingly. Jack's PDA may also forward such information to a nearby caring center, where a nurse called Sarah can monitor such information, and she can also monitor some of Jack's activities (e.g., watching TV, sleeping, etc.) by collecting location and motion related-information. Sarah can detect unusual situations and react accordingly, she also has access to all Jack's health records and she may contact the required medical professional that might be needed depending on Jack's situation. Jack, like many other users, wants to preserve his privacy by controlling what is collected and shared concerning his personal information, who is using such information, and for which reasons.

3   The Process for Developing the COPri Ontology

The process for developing COPri (depicted in Fig. 1) has been constructed based on [11,12], and it is composed of five main phases, two of them (in gray) were addressed in [5] while the remaining three are addressed in this paper:

- *Step 1. Scope & objective identification,* COPri aims at assisting software engineers while designing privacy-aware systems by providing a generic and expressive set of key privacy concepts and relationships, which enable for capturing privacy requirements in their social and organizational context.
- *Step 2. Knowledge acquisition* aims at identifying and collecting knowledge needed for the construction of the ontology. In [5], we have conducted a systematic literature review for identifying the concepts and relationships used in the literature for capturing privacy requirements as well as the semantic mappings between them[1]. The systematic literature review has identified 38 privacy-related concepts and relationships.
- *Step 3. Conceptualization* aims at deriving an ontology that consists of key concepts and relationships for privacy [12]. In [5], we have proposed a preliminary ontology consisting of 38 concepts and relationships. In this paper, we extend and refine our earlier proposal to a comprehensive ontology consisting of 52 concepts and relationships.
- *Step 4. Implementation* aims at codifying the ontology in a formal language. This requires an environment that guarantees the absence of lexical and syntactic errors from the ontology, and an automated reasoner to detect inconsistencies and redundant knowledge.
- *Step 5. Evaluation and Validation* aims at ensuring that the resulting ontology meets the needs of its usage [12]. Following [13], we validated COPri by applying it to the Ambient-Assisted Living (AAL) illustrating example and querying the ontology instances depending on Competency Questions (CQs). Then, evaluating whether the ontology captures enough detailed knowledge about the targeted domain to fulfill the needs of its intended use.

---

[1] A detailed version of the systematic literature review can be found at [14].

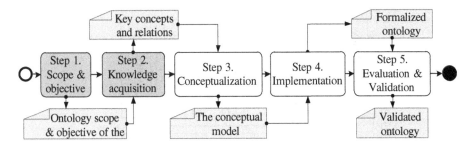

Fig. 1. The process for developing the COPri ontology

4 The COPri Ontology

The ontology is presented as a UML class diagram in Fig. 2. For reasons of readability, multiplicity and other constraints have been left out. The concepts of the ontology are organized into four main dimensions:

(1) Organizational dimension includes concepts for capturing the social and organizational aspects of the system, which are organized into several categories:

 Agentive entities captures the active entities of the system, and it includes the following concepts: *Actor* represents an autonomous entity that has intentionality and strategic goals, and it covers two entities: a *Role* represents an abstract characterization of an actor in terms of a set of behaviors and functionalities. A role can be a specialization (*is_a*) of one another; an *Agent* represents an autonomous entity that has a specific manifestation, and it can *play* a role or more, where an agent inherits the properties of the roles it plays.

 Intentional entities includes the following concepts: *a goal* is a state of affairs that an actor **aims** to achieve. When a goal is too coarse to be achieved, it can be refined through *and/or-decompositions* of a root goal into finer subgoals, where the first implies that the achievement of the root-goal requires the achievement of all of its sub-goals, and the latter implies that the achievement of the root-goal requires the achievement of any of its sub-goals.

 Informational entities includes the following concepts: *Information* represents a statement provided or learned about something or someone. Information can be atomic or composed of several parts, and we rely on *partOf* relationship to capture the relationship between an information entity and its sub-parts. We differentiate between two types of information: *Public information,* any information that cannot be *related* (directly or indirectly) to an identified or identifiable legal entity, and *Personal information,* any information that can be *related* to an identified or identifiable legal entity (e.g., medical records).

 Sensitivity level & situation, personal information has a *sensitivity level* [4,15]. Based on [16], we adopt four different sensitivity levels ordered as *(R)estricted, (C)onfidential, (S)ensitive,* and *Secre(T),* where *Secre(T)* is the most sensitive. Moreover, the sensitivity of personal information can be linked to when and where such information has been collected and for what purposes,

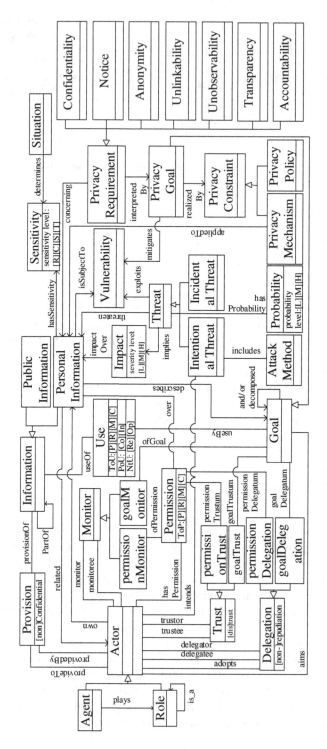

Fig. 2. The conceptual model of COPri

i.e., the context/state of affairs related to such information. Thus, we also adopt the concept of *situation* as a mean to determine the sensitivity level.

Information use is a relationship between a goal and information, and it has three attributes: *(1) Type of Use (ToU)*, our ontology provide four types of use, we consider sufficient for covering main information processing tasks: *Produce, Read, Modify*, and *Collect*, indicates that information is created, consumed, altered and acquired respectively. *(2) Need to Use (NtU)* captures the necessary of use that has two types: *Require* and *Optional*, wherein the first the use of information is required for the goal achievement, and in the later is not [17]. *(3) Purpose of Use (PoU)*, we differentiate between two types: *Compatible* and *Incompatible*, where the first indicates that the purpose for which information is used is compliant with the rules that guarantee the best interest of its owner; and in the later, it is not compliant.

Describes is a relationship where information characterizes a goal (activity) while it is being pursued by some actor[2].

Ownership & Permissions includes the following concepts: *Own* indicates that an actor is the legitimate owner of information. *Permission* is a consent that identifies a particular use of a particular information in a system. Information owner (data subject[3]) has full control over the use of information it owns, and it depends on *permissions* for such control. In COPri, a permission has a type that can take as values (P)roduce, (R)ead, (M)odify and (C)ollect, which cover the four relationships between goals and information that our ontology proposes.

Entity interactions: the ontology adopts three types of interactions: *(1) Information provision* captures the transmission of information among actors, and it has a type that can be either *confidential* or *nonConfidential*, where the former guarantee the confidentiality of the transmitted information, while the last does not. *(2) Delegation* indicates that actors can delegate obligations and entitlements to others, where the source of delegation called the delegator, the destination is called delegatee, and the subject of delegation is called delegatum. The concept of *delegation* is further specialized into two concepts: *Goal delegation*, where the delegatum is a goal; and *Permission delegation*, where the delegatum is a permission. *(3) Adoption* is considered a key component of social commitment, and it indicates that an actor accepts to take responsibility for the delegated objectives and/ or entitlements from another actor.

Entities social trust: the need for trust arises when actors depend on one another for goals or permissions since such dependencies might entail risk [18]. *Trust* has a type that can be either: *(1) Trust* means the trustor expects that the trustee will behave as expected considering the trustum (e.g., a trustee will not misuse the trustum), and *(2) Distrust* means the trustor expects that the trustee may not behave as expected considering the trustum. Moreover, the concept of

---

[2] The Ontology has been extended with *Collect* and *Describes* to capture situations when information *describing* some activities performed by a data subject (personal information) is being *collected* by others.

[3] We treat "information owner" and "data subject" as synonyms.

Trust is further specialized into two concepts *GoalTrust,* where the trustum is a goal; and *PermissionTrust,* where the trustum is a permission.

Monitoring: is the process of observing and analyzing the performance of an actor in order to detect any undesirable performance. We adopt the concept of *monitoring* to compensate for the lack of trust or distrust in the trustee concerning the trustum. The concept of *monitor* is further specialized into two concepts *GoalMonitor,* where the subject of the monitoring is a goal; and *PermissionMonitor,* where the subject of the monitoring is a permission.

(2) Risk dimension includes risk related concepts that might endanger privacy needs at the social and organizational levels:

A vulnerability is a weakness in the current state-of-affairs that may be *exploited* by a *threat.*

A threat is a potential incident that *threatens* personal information by *exploiting* a *vulnerability* concerning such information [19]. *Threat* has a *probability* that measures the likelihood of its occurrence, and it is characterized by three different values *high, medium* or *low.* In COPri, we differentiate between two types of threat: *(1) Incidental threat* that is a casual, natural or accidental threat that is not caused by a *threat actor* nor does it require an *attack method.* *(2) Intentional threat* is a threat that require a *threat actor* and *includes* a presumed *attack method* [14].

Threat actor is an actor that intends to achieve an *intentional threat* [19].

Attack method is a standard means by which a *threat actor* carries out an *intentional threat* [10,19].

Impact is the expected consequence of a *threat* over the personal information. An *impact* has a *severity* that captures the level of the impact [10], and takes values *high, medium* or *low.*

(3) Treatment dimension includes concepts to mitigate risks:

A privacy goal defines an intention to counter threats and prevent harm to personal information by satisfying privacy properties.

A privacy constraint is a design restriction that is used to realize/satisfy a privacy goal, constraints can be either a privacy policy or privacy mechanism.

A privacy policy defines permitted and forbidden actions to be carried out by actors toward information.

A privacy mechanism is a concrete technique that operationalizes a privacy goal. Some mechanisms can be directly *applied to personal information* (e.g., anonymity, unlinkability).

(4) Privacy dimension includes concepts to capture the actors' privacy requirements/needs concerning their personal information:

Privacy requirements capture information owners' privacy needs. *Privacy requirements* can be *interpretedBy* privacy goals, and it is further specialized into seven more refined concepts[4]:

Confidentiality means personal information should remain inaccessible to incidental or intentional threats [4,6,15]. We rely on three principles to analyze confidentiality: *(1) Non-disclosure,* personal information can only be disclosed if the owner's consent is provided [4,6,15]. Therefore, *non-disclosure* can be analyzed depending on the existence of read permission as well as the confidentiality of information provision. *(2) Need to Know (NtK),* can be analyzed depending on *Need to Use (NtU)* that captures the necessity of use, i.e., personal information can only be used if it is strictly necessary for completing a certain task [4]. *(3) Purpose of Use (PoU),* personal information can only be used for specific legitimate purposes and not in ways that are incompatible with those purposes [6,15], i.e., if the *PoU* is *compatible* with the rules that guarantee the best interest of its owner.

Anonymity means personal information can be used without disclosing the identity of its owner [6,7,15]. Personal information can be *anonymized* (e.g., removing identifiers) depending on some *privacy mechanism.*

Unlinkability means that it should not be possible to link personal information back to its owner [3,7,20]. A *privacy mechanism* can be used to remove any linkage between personal information and its owner.

Unobservability means the identity of information owner should not be observed by others, while performing an activity [3,7]. *Unobservability* can be analyzed relying on the *describes* relationship, which enables for detecting situations where personal information that describes an activity (goal) being pursued by a data subject is being collected by some other actor [21].

Notice means information owner should be notified when its information is being collected [6,15]. *Notice* can be analyzed depending on collect relationship and its corresponding permission. In the case where personal information is being collected and there is no permission to collect it, a notice violation will be raised. Providing a permission to collect implies that the actor has been already notified.and agreed upon the collection of his information.

Transparency means information owner should be able to know who is using its information and for what purposes [15], we rely on two principles to analyze transparency: *(1) Authentication* a mechanism aims at verifying whether actors are who they claim they are, and it can be analyzed by verifying whether i) the actor is playing a role that enables the identification of its main responsibilities; and ii) the actor is not playing any threat actor role. *(2) Authorization* a mechanism aims at verifying whether actors can use information in accordance with their credentials [15].

Accountability means information owner should be able to hold information users accountable for their actions concerning its information [15]. We rely

---

[4] The right to erasure (right to be forgotten) is essential in several privacy laws, yet we did not consider it since the use of information is limited to a specific, explicit, legitimate purpose (a goal), i.e., information will not be kept after achieving the goal.

on the *non-repudiation* principle to analyze accountability, which can be analyzed relying on the adoption relationship, i.e., if a delegatee did not adopt the delegatum, a *non-repudiation* violation can be raised.

This ontology extends the one proposed in [5] by new concepts concerning personal information and privacy requirements. Accordingly, we have extended and refined the organizational, risk, treatment and privacy dimensions to cover the new extensions, and to allow for performing a more comprehensive analysis.

5   The Implementation of COPri[5]

We have implemented the COPri ontology[6] using the on Protégé tool[7] that supports the creation, modification, visualization and consistency-checking for an ontology. Protégé also offers a plug-in for using SPARQL to query an ontology. In particular, we have implemented COPri relying on classes and object properties (relationships) in Protégé, had to amend and/or create new classes and relationships during this process. Moreover, for each class that has attributes with quantitative values, we have created a class (called a Value Partition pattern) to present such attributes, and several individuals (instances) to cover all quantitative values of their corresponding attributes.

In our implementation, all *primitive siblings* classes (e.g., Personal and Public Information) have been made *disjoint*, which helps the reasoner to detect inconsistencies. Moreover, we have used Probe Classes, which are classes that are subclasses of two or more disjoint classes to test and ensure that the ontology does not include inconsistencies. Additionally, we have used a covering axiom to solve the open-world assumption in OWL-based ontologies, where a covering axiom is a class that results from the union of the classes being covered. Properties are used to link individuals from domain to range classes. Thus, we have defined the domain and range for each of the object properties, which can be used by the reasoner to make inferences and detect inconsistencies. Moreover, we defined only one inverse property to minimize the number of object properties. Finally, we have used cardinality restrictions to specify the number of relationships between classes depending on at *least*, at *most* or *exactly* keywords.

6   The Validation of COPri[8]

We validated the COPri ontology by applying it to the AAL illustrating example, and then query the ontology instance relying on Competency Questions (CQs) and check whether these queries can return comprehensive answers. In particular,

---

[5] Available in greater detail in [22].
[6] The COPri ontology is available in OWL formal at https://goo.gl/AaqUxx.
[7] http://protege.stanford.edu/.
[8] Available in greater detail in [22], formalization of the CQs (SPARQL queries), and the validation we performed.

CQs represent a set of queries that the ontology must be capable of answering to be considered competent for conceptualizing the domain it was intended for [11,13]. The CQs are meant to assist and guide requirements engineers while dealing with privacy requirements by capturing main wrong/bad design decisions (we call *violations*) related to the four dimensions of our ontology. 26 CQs[9] have been defined (shown in Table 1), which we consider sufficient for capturing all violations to the privacy requirements considered in our ontology.

In particular, **CQ1–3** are dedicated for organizational aspects, e.g., identifying violations related to permissions delegation without trust or monitoring (*CQ1*), the existing of trust and monitoring concerning the same trustum that is considered as a bad design decision (*CQ2*), and *CQ3* can be used for returning different sets of personal information based on their sensitivity levels (e.g., Secret, Sensitive, etc.).

CQ4–13 are dedicated for risk aspects, e.g., identify violations related to existing vulnerabilities and information subject to them (*CQ4*), threats that can exploit such vulnerabilities (*CQ5*), unmitigated vulnerabilities (*CQ6*), existing threats (*CQ7*), and *CQ8* can be used to identify threats based on the severity levels of their impact (e.g., Low, Medium, or High). *CQ9–11* can be used to identify existing intentional threats, threat actors and attack methods respectively. While *CQ12* can be used to identify existing incidental threats, and *CQ13* is used to identify different sets of threats based on their probability levels (Low, Medium, or High).

CQ14–15 are dedicated for treatment aspects, e.g., identify violations related to unrealized privacy goals (*CQ14*) and *CQ15* can be used to identify privacy mechanisms and personal information that such mechanisms are applied to.

CQ16–26 are dedicated for privacy requirements violations. In particular, *CQ16–19* are used for analyzing *Confidentiality*, where *CQ16–17* are used for analyzing non-disclosure by detecting and reporting when personal information is read without the owner's permission (*CQ16*), or it has been transferred relying on non-confidential transmission means (*CQ17*). *CQ18* is used for analyzing Need to Know (NtK) principle by verifying whether personal information is strictly required by goals using them, i.e., if the Need to Use (NtU) of the goal is optional, *CQ18* will report such violation. *CQ19* is used for analyzing the Purpose of Use (PoU) principle by verifying whether personal information is used for specific, explicit, legitimate purposes that have been permitted to be used for, i.e., if the PoU is incompatible, *CQ19* will report such violation. *CQ20* is used for analyzing *Anonymity* by verifying whether the identity of information owner can be sufficiently identified, i.e., if personal information has not been anonymized relying on a privacy mechanism, *CQ20* will report such violation. *CQ21* is used for analyzing *Unlinkability* by verifying whether it is possible to link personal information back to its owner, i.e., if an unlinkability mechanism has not been applied to personal information, *CQ21* will report such violation.

CQ22 is used for analyzing *Unobservability* by verifying whether the identity of information owner can be observed by others while performing some activity.

---

[9] Note that the main focus of the CQs is privacy requirements, not goal analysis.

Table 1. Competency questions for validating the COPri ontology

Organizational dimension

CQ1. Who are the delegators that delegate produce, read, modify, or collect permission, which is not accompanied by trust nor monitoring?

CQ2. Who are the delegators that delegate produce, read, modify, or collect permission accompanied by both trust and monitoring?

CQ3. Which is the personal information of sensitivity Restricted [Confidential, Sensitive or Secret]?

Risk dimension

CQ4. Which are the existing vulnerabilities and which personal information are subject to them?

CQ5. Which are the existing vulnerabilities and which are the threats that can exploit them?

CQ6. Which are the existing vulnerabilities that are not mitigated by privacy goals?

CQ7. Which are the existing threats and which is the personal information that are threatened by them?

CQ8. Which are the existing threats that have an impact with severity level Low [Medium, High] over personal information?

CQ9. Which are the existing intentional threats and which is the personal information that are threatened by them?

CQ10. Who are the threat actors and which are the intentional threats that they intend to perform?

CQ11. Which are the existing attack methods and to which intentional threats they can be used for?

CQ12. Which are the existing incidental threats and which is the personal information that are threatened by them?

CQ13. Which are the existing threats of probability Low [Medium | High]?

Treatment dimension

CQ14. Which are the privacy goals that are realized by privacy constraints?

CQ15. Which are the existing privacy mechanisms and which is the personal information that such mechanisms are applied to?

Privacy dimension

CQ16. Which is the personal information that is read without read permission?

CQ17. Which is the personal information that is transferred relying on non-confidential provision?

CQ18. Which is the personal information that is used by a goal, where their usage (NtU) is not strictly required (i.e., optional)?

CQ19. Which is the personal information that is used by goals, where their purpose of use (PoU) is incompatible with the best interest of its owner?

CQ20. Which is the personal information that is not anonymized?

CQ21. Which is the personal information that can be linked back to their owners?

CQ22. Which is the personal information that describes a goal, and it is also being collected by some actor?

CQ23. Who are the actors that are collecting personal information without collect permissions?

CQ24. Who are the actors that do not play any role or they play a threat actor role?

CQ25. Who are the actors that are using (producing, reading, modifying, or collecting) personal information without the required permission?

CQ26. Who are the delegatees that have not adopted their delegatum?

Consider for example that Jack does not want his activities to be monitored while he is in the bathroom. Then, "Jack's location" should not be collected when he is in the bathroom since such information can be used to infer activities that Jack does not want it to be observed. If such information is collected, *CQ22* will report such violation. *CQ23* is used for analyzing *Notice* by verifying whether personal information is being collected without notifying its owner. In case, personal information is being collected and there is no permission to collect, *CQ23* will detect and report such violation.

CQ24–C25 are used for analyzing *Transparency*, where *CQ24* analyzes the authentication principle by verifying whether an actor can be authenticated based on the role(s) she/he is playing[10]. Accordingly, *CQ24* will report whether an actor can be authenticated. While *CQ25* analyzes the authorization principle by verifying that actors are not using personal information without the required permissions. Finally, *CQ26* is used for analyzing *Accountability* relying on the non-repudiation principle by verifying that actors cannot repudiate that they accepted delegations, which can be done depending on the adoption concept, if there exists a delegatee without an adopt relationship to the delegatum, *CQ26* will detect and report such violation.

The formulation of the CQs was an iterative process i.e., several CQs have been refined before having the final set of CQs. Note that the concepts of the ontology have been refined and extended as well while formulating the CQs because some limitations in the ontology have been revealed.

7   Evaluation

We evaluate the COPri ontology against the common pitfalls for ontologies identified in [23], where the authors classify 20 of these pitfalls by criteria under 1 - *Consistency pitfalls* verify whether the ontology includes or allows for any inconsistencies; 2 - *Completeness pitfalls* verify whether the domain of interest is appropriately covered; and 3 - *Conciseness pitfalls* verify whether the ontology includes irrelevant elements or redundant representations of some elements with respect to the domain to be covered. The pitfalls classification by criteria is shown in Table 2, where we can also identify the four different methods we followed to evaluate the COPri ontology:

1 - Protégé & HermiT Reasoner[11]: Both Protégé & HermiT have been used. In particular, HermiT is able to detect cycles in the hierarchy (*P6.*). *P4.* has been verified depending on OntoGraf plug-in that enables for visualizing the ontology. Concerning *P10.*, we have already made all *primitive siblings* classes *disjoint*. We have manually checked whether the domain and range of all object properties have been defined (*P11.*). Moreover, we verified *P14.* depending on Probe Classes. COPri ontology cannot suffer from *P15.* since we did not use complement operators to describe/define any of the classes, i.e., all defined classes have been defined depending on both necessary and sufficient conditions. The concepts of the ontology are general enough to avoid both *P17.* and *P18.*. No miscellaneous class have been identified (*P21.*), since the names of all classes and their sub-classes have been carefully chosen.

---

[10] If an actor is not playing any role, it will be impossible to authenticate it.
[11] http://www.hermit-reasoner.com/.

2 - Evaluation with OntOlogy Pitfall Scanner (OOPS!): OOPS! is a web-based ontology evaluation tool[12] for detecting common pitfalls in ontologies. The COPri ontology was uploaded to the OOPS! pitfall scanner, which returned an evaluation report[13]. In particular, two suggestions have been returned, proposing to characterize both is_a and partOf relationships as symmetric or transitive. We took these suggestions into account, characterizing both of these relationships as transitive. 53 minor pitfalls (*P13.*) have been identified. However, as mentioned earlier we defined only one inverse property to minimize the number of properties/relationships in the ontology. Finally, only one critical pitfall has been identified stating that we are using is_a relationship instead of using OWL primitives for representing the subclass relationship (rdfs:subClassOf). However, is_a relationship is used in most Goal-based modeling languages, where we have adopted many of the concepts and relationships of the COPri ontology. Therefore, we chose not to replace it with the subClassOf relationship.

Table 2. Pitfalls classification by criteria and how they were evaluated

		Protégé	OOPS!	Experts	Researchers
Consistency	**P1.** Creating polysemous elements	-	-	✓	-
	P5. Defining wrong inverse relationships	-	✓	-	-
	P6. Including cycles in the hierarchy	✓	✓	-	-
	P7. Merging different concepts in the same class	-	✓	✓	-
	P14. Misusing "allValuesFrom"	✓	-	-	-
	P15. Misusing "not some" and "some not"	✓	-	-	-
	P18. Specifying too much the domain or the range	✓	-	-	-
	P19. Swapping intersection and union	-	✓	-	-
	P24. Using recursive definition	-	✓	✓	-
Completeness	**P4.** Creating unconnected ontology elements	✓	✓	-	-
	P9. Missing basic information	-	-	-	✓
	P10. Missing disjointness	✓	✓	-	-
	P11. Missing domain or range in properties	✓	✓	-	-
	P12. Missing equivalent properties	-	✓	-	-
	P13. Missing inverse relationships	-	✓	-	-
	P16. Misusing primitive and defined classes	✓	-	-	-
Conciseness	**P2.** Creating synonyms as classes	-	✓	✓	-
	P3. Creating the relationship "is" instead of using "subclassOf", "instanceOf" or "sameIndividual"	-	✓	-	-
	P17. Specializing too much a hierarchy	✓	-	✓	-
	P21. Using a miscellaneous class	✓	✓	✓	-

---

[12] http://oops.linkeddata.es/index.jsp.

[13] Evaluation with OOPS! has been performed after evaluating the ontology with Protégé & HermiT, i.e., several pitfalls have been already detected and corrected.

3 - Lexical semantics experts: Two lexical semantics experts with main focus on Natural Language Processing (NLP) have been provided with the COPri ontology, and they were asked to check whether the ontology suffers from *P1, P2, P7, P17, P21*, and *P24* pitfalls[14]. Several issues have been raised by the experts concerning *P2, P21* and *P24*. Each of these issues has been properly addressed. The experts' feedback and how it was addressed can be found in [22].

4 - A survey with researchers: The main purpose of this survey was evaluating the adequacy and completeness of the COPri ontology in terms of its concepts and relationships for dealing with privacy requirements in their social and organizational context (*P9.*). The survey was closed, i.e., it was accessible through a special link that is provided to the invited participants only to avoid unintended participants. In total 25 potential participants were contacted to complete the survey, and they were asked to forward the email to anyone who fits in the participating criteria (e.g., has good experience in privacy and/or security). We have received 16 responses (64% response rate). The survey template[15] is composed of four main sections: *S1. General information about the survey, S2. Participant demographics, S3. Evaluation questions*, and *S4. Final remarks*.

S2. Result of Demographic Questions: 15 (93.8%) of the participants are researchers and 1 (6.2%) is a student. Concerning experience with privacy and/or security: 2 (12.5%) of the participants have both academic and industrial experience, and 14 (87.5%) have pure academic experience. Moreover, 3 (18.8%) have less than one year, 7 (43.8%) have between one and four years, and 6 (37.5%) have more than four years of experience.

S3. Result of Evaluation Questions: This section is composed of 10 subsections, each of them is dedicated to collect feedback concerning the adequacy and completeness of a specific dimension/category of concepts and relationships. In each of these subsections, we provide the definitions of the concepts and relationships of the targeted dimension/category as well as a diagram representing them. Followed by a mandatory question, asking the participant to grade the completeness of the presented concepts and relationships with respect to system aspects they aim to capture on a scale from 1 (incomplete) to 5 (incomplete). The result of the evaluation for each of these sections is summarized in Table 3. The result tends to demonstrate that most of the targeted dimension/category of concepts and relationships are properly covering the aspects they aim to represent.

Additionally, we have added an optional question in each of the 10 sections to evaluate the adequacy of the concepts and relationships by collecting suggestions to improve the category/dimension under evaluation. Some feedback suggested to refine, include or exclude some of the concepts/relationships, we took some of these suggestions into account while developing the final ontology.

S4. Result of Remarks Question: Most of the feedback was valuable, has raised important issues and ranged from complementing to criticizing. For example, among the encouraging feedback, we received *"COPri covers a wide range of*

---

[14] The experts evaluation template can be found at https://goo.gl/ZEhLnN.
[15] The survey template can be found at https://goo.gl/bro8nG.

privacy-related concepts, with actor and goal-oriented perspectives, which looks promising. We look forward to seeing it used to capture real-world privacy problem context". Another feedback and suggestion was *"I think it is very precise and very good work. Maybe some other concepts could be expressed somewhere".* One of the comments we received was *"How satisfaction of privacy requirements can be verified using it?".* We also received criticisms such as the following one *"I have no idea how good it is unless it is applied to many real cases. I'm concerned that it is not grounded in reality. It's also very complicated, which makes it hard to apply in the industry".* However, such criticism opens the way for future research directions.

Table 3. The result of the evaluation

	Strongly disagree	Disagree	N. agree/n. disagree	Agree	Strongly agree
Q1. Agentive cat.	0 (0%)	1 (6.3%)	3 (18.8%)	6 (37.5%)	6 (37.5%)
Q2. Intentional cat.	0 (0%)	1 (6.3%)	4 (25.0%)	7 (43.8%)	4 (25.0%)
Q3. Informational cat.	0 (0%)	2 (12.5%)	4 (25.0%)	4 (25.0%)	6 (37.5%)
Q4. Goals & info cat.	0 (0%)	2 (12.5%)	2 (12.5%)	6 (37.5%)	6 (37.5%)
Q5. Ownership cat.	0 (0%)	1 (6.3%)	1 (6.3%)	5 (31.3%)	9 (56.3%)
Q6. Interactions cat.	0 (0%)	1 (6.3%)	1 (6.3%)	6 (37.5%)	8 (50.0%)
Q7. Social Trust cat.	0 (0%)	0 (0.0%)	4 (25.0%)	7 (43.8%)	5 (31.3%)
Q8. Risk dim.	0 (0%)	3 (18.8%)	0 (0.0%)	8 (50.0%)	5 (31.3%)
Q9. Treatment dim.	0 (0%)	0 (0.0%)	3 (18.8%)	7 (43.8%)	6 (37.5%)
Q10. Privacy dim.	0 (0%)	2 (12.5%)	2 (12.5%)	5 (31.3%)	7 (43.8%)

Threats to the validity of our study, we have identified the following threats: *1. Authors' background,* the authors have good experience in goal modeling (especially in *i** languages). This may have influenced the selection and definitions of the concepts of the ontology. However, *i** languages have been developed to capture requirements in their social and organizational context, which is also a main objective of our ontology. *2. Survey result validity,* the number of participants can raise concerns about the validity of the result. However, most of them are experts with good experience in privacy. *3. Extensive evaluation,* the ontology has been evaluated against the common pitfalls in ontologies with the help of some tools, lexical semantics experts, and privacy researchers, yet it has not been applied in industry. However, applying our ontology to real case studies from different domains is on our list for future work.

8   Related Work

Several ontologies have been proposed for dealing with privacy and security. For example, Palmirani et al. [24] proposed PrOnto, a first draft privacy ontology for supporting researchers and regulators while analyzing privacy policies through SPARQL queries. Oltramari et al. [25] developed PrivOnto, a semantic framework for analyzing privacy policies, which rely on an ontology developed to represent privacy-related issues to users and/or legal experts. On the other hand, Kalloniatis et al. [3] introduce PriS, a security requirements engineering method that considers users' privacy requirements as business goals and provides a methodological approach for analyzing their effect on the organizational processes. Dritsas et al. [15] developed an ontology for developing a set of security patterns that can be used to deal with security requirements for e-health applications. In addition, Labda et al. [4] propose a privacy-aware Business Processes framework for modeling, reasoning and enforcing privacy constraints. In summary, most existing works do not appropriately cover all four concept categories (e.g., organizational, risk, treatment, and privacy) we consider in this work, which was clear based on the results of the systematic literature review we conduct.

9   Conclusions and Future Work

We proposed the COPri ontology for privacy requirements, and since it is based on a systematic literature review; it is more comprehensive in coverage than all ontologies included in our systematic review. Moreover, the ontology has been implemented and applied to an AAL illustrative example. In addition, we have validated it depending on CQs. Finally, we have evaluated the ontology against common pitfalls for ontologies with the help of some software tools, lexical semantics experts, and privacy and security researchers. The main purpose of developing COPri is assisting requirements engineers while eliciting privacy requirements for systems that handle personal data by providing a comprehensive set of necessary and sufficient concepts that allow for analyzing privacy requirements in their social and organizational context.

In this paper, we provide a preliminary validity check for the comprehensiveness of our proposal, which needs to be complemented in the future with empirical validation through controlled studies. The next step in this work is to develop a tool and a systematic methodology for privacy requirements that are founded on the COPri ontology. We also aim at better analyzing how the sensitivity level can be determined based on the situation, and how it can be used to facilitate the identification of privacy requirements. We will refine the analysis of the *PoU* property as *compatible/compatible* are too abstract to characterize such important property, and we will investigate how *PoU* can be determined based on the characteristics of the goal. Additionally, we are planning to develop a goal-oriented framework based on our ontology to be used for eliciting and analyzing privacy requirements.

References

1. General Data Protection Regulation: Regulation (EU) 2016/679 of the European Parliament and of the Council of 27 April 2016, and repealing Directive 95/46. Official J. Eur. Union (OJ) **59**, 1–88 (2016)

2. Gharib, M., et al.: Privacy requirements: findings and lessons learned in developing a privacy platform. In: Proceedings - 24th International Requirements Engineering Conference, RE, pp. 256–265. IEEE (2016)
3. Kalloniatis, C., Kavakli, E., Gritzalis, S.: Addressing privacy requirements in system design: the PriS method. Requir. Eng. **13**(3), 241–255 (2008). https://doi.org/10.1007/s00766-008-0067-3
4. Labda, W., Mehandjiev, N., Sampaio, P.: Modeling of privacy-aware business processes in BPMN to protect personal data. In: Proceedings of the 29th Annual ACM Symposium on Applied Computing, pp. 1399–1405. ACM (2014)
5. Gharib, M., Giorgini, P., Mylopoulos, J.: Towards an ontology for privacy requirements via a systematic literature review. In: Mayr, H.C., Guizzardi, G., Ma, H., Pastor, O. (eds.) ER 2017. LNCS, vol. 10650, pp. 193–208. Springer, Cham (2017). https://doi.org/10.1007/978-3-319-69904-2_16
6. Solove, D.J.: A taxonomy of privacy. Univ. PA Law Rev. **154**(3), 477 (2006)
7. Pfitzmann, A., Hansen, M.: A terminology for talking about privacy by data minimization: anonymity, unlinkability, undetectability, unobservability, pseudonymity, and identity management, pp. 1–98. Dresden University (2010)
8. Krasnova, H., Spiekermann, S., Koroleva, K., Hildebrand, T.: Online social networks: why we disclose. J. Inf. Technol. **25**(2), 109–125 (2010)
9. Awad, K.: The personalization privacy paradox: an empirical evaluation of information transparency and the willingness to be profiled online for personalization. MIS Q. **30**(1), 13 (2006)
10. Souag, A., Salinesi, C., Mazo, R., Comyn-Wattiau, I.: A security ontology for security requirements elicitation. In: Piessens, F., Caballero, J., Bielova, N. (eds.) ESSoS 2015. LNCS, vol. 8978, pp. 157–177. Springer, Cham (2015). https://doi.org/10.1007/978-3-319-15618-7_13
11. Uschold, M.: Building ontologies: towards a unified methodology. In: Proceedings Expert Systems 1996, The 16th Annual Conference of the British Computer Society Specialist Group on Expert Systems, pp. 1–18 (1996)
12. Fernández-López, M., Gómez-Pérez, A., Juristo, N.: Methontology: from ontological art towards ontological engineering. In: AAAI-97 Spring Symposium Series SS-97-06, pp. 33–40 (1997)
13. Dong, H., Hussain, F.K., Chang, E.: Application of Protégé and SPARQL in the field of project knowledge management. In: Second International Conference on Systems and Networks Communications, ICSNC 2007 (2007)
14. Gharib, M., Giorgini, P., Mylopoulos, J.: Ontologies for privacy requirements engineering: a systematic literature review. preprint arXiv:1611.10097 (2016)
15. Dritsas, S., et al.: A knowledge-based approach to security requirements for e-health applications. J. E-Commer. Tools Appl. **2**, 1–24 (2006)
16. Turn, R.: Classification of personal information for privacy protection purposes, p. 301 (1976)
17. Gharib, M., Giorgini, P.: Modeling and reasoning about information quality requirements. In: Fricker, S.A., Schneider, K. (eds.) REFSQ 2015. LNCS, vol. 9013, pp. 49–64. Springer, Cham (2015). https://doi.org/10.1007/978-3-319-16101-3_4
18. Gharib, M., Giorgini, P.: Analyzing trust requirements in socio-technical systems: a belief-based approach. In: Ralyté, J., España, S., Pastor, Ó. (eds.) PoEM 2015. LNBIP, vol. 235, pp. 254–270. Springer, Cham (2015). https://doi.org/10.1007/978-3-319-25897-3_17
19. Mayer, N.: Model-based management of information system security risk. Ph.D. thesis, University of Namur (2009)

20. Mouratidis, H., Giorgini, P.: Secure Tropos: a security-oriented extension of the Tropos methodology. J. Softw. Eng. Knowl. Eng. **17**(2), 285–309 (2007)
21. Gharib, M., Lollini, P., Bondavalli, A.: A conceptual model for analyzing information quality in System-of-Systems. In: 12th System of Systems Engineering Conference, SoSE 2017, pp. 1–6. IEEE (2017)
22. Gharib, M., Mylopoulos, J.: A Core Ontology for Privacy Requirements Engineering. preprint arXiv:1811.12621 (2018)
23. Poveda, M., Suárez-Figueroa, M.C., Gómez-Pérez, A.: A double classification of common pitfalls in ontologies. In: OntoQual 2010 - Workshop on Ontology Quality. CEUR Workshop Proceedings, Lisbon, Portugal, pp. 1–12 (2010). ISBN: ISSN 1613-0073
24. Palmirani, M., Martoni, M., Rossi, A., Bartolini, C., Robaldo, L.: PrOnto: privacy ontology for legal reasoning. In: Kő, A., Francesconi, E. (eds.) EGOVIS 2018. LNCS, vol. 11032, pp. 139–152. Springer, Cham (2018). https://doi.org/10.1007/978-3-319-98349-3_11
25. Oltramari, A., et al.: PrivOnto: a semantic framework for the analysis of privacy policies. Semant. Web **9**(2), 185–203 (2018)

Privacy Preserving Real-Time Video Stream Change Detection Based on the Orthogonal Tensor Decomposition Models

Bogusław Cyganek[✉]

AGH University of Science and Technology, Al. Mickiewicza 30, 30-059 Kraków, Poland
cyganek@agh.edu.pl

Abstract. In this paper the video change detection method that allows for data privacy protection is proposed. Signal change detection is based on the tensor models constructed in the orthogonal tensor subspaces. Tensor methods allow for processing of any kind of multi-dimensional signals since computation of special features is not required. The proposed signal encoding method makes that person identification in the processed signal is very difficult or impossible for the unauthorized personnel. It is demonstrated that despite the input being distorted for encryption, the proposed tensor based method can still correctly identify video shots in real-time. Compared with the non-distorted signals, the obtained accuracy is only slightly lower, at the same time providing data privacy.

Keywords: Data privacy · Image encryption · Video analysis · Tensor models · HOSVD · Real-time algorithms

1 Introduction

Signal change detection in video signals finds application mostly in the surveillance systems, in the video summarization platforms, as well as in the search engines, to name a few. For this purpose many methods were proposed, which either specialize in certain type of video sequences, such as sport and news, or try to operate on general video signals. We only outline the problem here – a broader treatment of the subject of video summarization can be accessed in many works, such as [2, 10, 14, 21, 22, 24]. However, there are at least two significant problems related to this task. First is a great variety of video content, as well as problems with clear definition of a video signal change. The second problem is the requirement on data privacy protection. In this paper we address both problems by proposing an extension to the recently developed tensor based video change detection method that also allows for data privacy protection.

Details of the aforementioned video change detection method are provided in the paper by Cyganek [10]. Here we only outline its basic properties and present details of its extensions that allows for data privacy protection. The method treats input signals as multi-dimensional tensors and does not assume any feature detection. It starts with composition of the input tensors, from which the model is computed based on construction of the orthogonal tensor subspace (OTS). In the next steps, the incoming tensors

© Springer Nature Switzerland AG 2020
F. Dalpiaz et al. (Eds.): RCIS 2020, LNBIP 385, pp. 490–499, 2020.
https://doi.org/10.1007/978-3-030-50316-1_29

(frames) are compared with the current model; It is then is either updated or entirely rebuilt, based on the statistical inference procedure. The method was shown to reach the topmost performance both, in accuracy, as well as in the execution time, allowing for the real-time operation. However, to ensure data privacy protection – which gained on importance in the video surveillance, as discussed in many papers [3–5, 7, 12, 13, 19, 23] – the aforementioned method has been endowed with the data encryption module. Its primary role is a reliable data protection with the de-identification option. However, special attention has also been devoted to the availability of behavior recognition and also to the recoverability. The latter option allows person identification but only to the authorized persons e.g. for the law enforcement, etc. In this paper we outline connection of the two modules, as well as we show its operation, properties, as well as the future directions.

2   Method Description

In this section the basic architecture of the proposed method is presented. More concretely, we start with the overall view of the main processing blocks. After that descriptions of the tensor shot detection and data encryption methods follow.

Figure 1(a) presents a general view on the method proposed in this paper. There are two main blocks: (I) the visual data preprocessing module, which does data encryption in order to preserve the required level of data privacy and (II) the video stream shot detector, which reveals remarkable scene changes in the encrypted signal, still allowing for further video analysis and summarization.

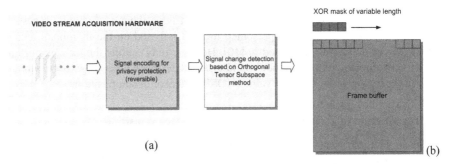

Fig. 1. Overall architecture of the video shot detection method assuring data privacy (a). The XOR based color image encoding scheme which allows data protection, behavior analysis and recoverability to the authorized users (b).

Figure 2 depicts an overall view of the proposed tensor based method for video stream analysis from Fig. 1(a). The input video stream is split into a number of contiguous partitions, from which the tensor model is built. If the consecutive tensor-frames fit to this model, then the model is only updated; Otherwise, it is rebuilt. The method is able to operate on signals encrypted for data privacy protection, as will be discussed.

As already mentioned, the method relies on a tensor analysis which will be outlined in the next section.

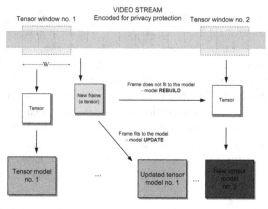

Fig. 2. Scheme of the tensor based method for video stream analysis.

Operation of the tensor based video shot detection method is as follows. The input multi-dimensional video signal is modelled as a tensor – that is, as a stream of multi-dimensional cubes of data. From these, an initial window of the width W is composed, which constitutes an input to the tensor model. The input tensor is then decomposed to form the OTS, which can be viewed as a multi-dimensional equivalent to the well known orthogonal vector subspaces. OTS has a number of useful features. First of all, it allows for a multi-dimensional signal representation in a succinct form.

A model based on the OTS can be also used to measure a fitness of the incoming tensor-frames from the input video stream. In a consequence, each new frame which conforms to the model is used for its update. On the other hand, frames that significantly differ from the model, which indicate a signal shot, trigger the model rebuilt process.

As alluded to previously, the presented method is based on the thumbnail tensor method, whose details are presented in [10]. Here we only outline the most important steps of OTS construction and model build and update procedures (Fig. 2), which are based on the higher-order singular value (HOSVD) tensor decomposition.

2.1 Introduction to Tensor Representation and Decomposition

Tensors are mathematical objects which fulfill precise transformation rules on a change of the coordinate systems [1, 15]. However, in the multi-dimensional data analysis tensors represent cubes of data in which each dimension corresponds to a different measurement. Since video streams are four dimensional, without much loss of generality let's start with the definition of a 4D *tensor* [1, 8–10, 15, 20].

$$\mathcal{T} \in \Re^{N_1 \times N_2 \times N_3 \times N_4}, \tag{1}$$

where N_j stands for a j-th dimension of $\mathcal{T}$ ($1 \le j \le 4$). However, with no loss of information each tensor can be represented in a matrix representation, known as *a tensor flattening*. Namely, for a tensor $\mathcal{T}$, its flattening alongside its k-th dimension is defined as follows:

$$\mathbf{T}_{(k)} \in \Re^{N_k \times (N_1 \dots N_{k-1} N_{k+1} \dots N_4)}. \tag{2}$$

It is obtained from the tensor $\mathcal{T}$ by selecting its k-th dimension for the row dimension of $\mathbf{T}_{(k)}$, while a product of all other indices makes its column dimension.

The next concept is the k-th *modal product* of a tensor $\mathcal{T} \in \Re^{N_1 \times \dots \times N_4}$ and a matrix $\mathbf{M} \in \Re^{Q \times N_k}$: The result of this product is a tensor $\mathcal{S} \in \Re^{N_1 \times \dots N_{k-1} \times Q \times N_{k+1} \times \dots N_4}$ whose elements are defined as follows [8]:

$$\mathcal{S}_{n_1 \dots n_{k-1} q n_{k+1} \dots n_4} = (\mathcal{T} \times_k \mathbf{M})_{n_1 \dots n_{k-1} q n_{k+1} \dots n_4} = \sum_{n_k=1}^{N_k} t_{n_1 \dots n_{k-1} n_k n_{k+1} \dots n_4} m_{q n_k}. \quad (3)$$

Consequently, the HOSVD decomposition of $\mathcal{T}$ can be defined as follows [20, 10]

$$\mathcal{T} = \mathcal{Z} \times_1 \mathbf{S}_1 \times_2 \mathbf{S}_2 \times_3 \mathbf{S}_3 \times_4 \mathbf{S}_4, \quad (4)$$

where $\mathbf{S}_k$ are $N_k \times N_k$ unitary matrices, $\times_k$ is a k-th order tensor matrix product. On the other hand, the tensor $\mathcal{Z} \in \Re^{N_1 \times N_2 \times \dots N_m \times \dots N_n \times \dots N_P}$ represents the core tensor, fulfilling the sub-tensor orthogonality and decreasing energy value properties [10]. Computation of the HOSVD requires a series of SVD decompositions on flattenings (2) of $\mathcal{T}$.

What is important, due to the commutative properties of the k-mode multiplication, for each mode matrix $\mathbf{S}_i$ in (4) the following sum can be constructed

$$\mathcal{T} = \sum_{h=1}^{N_4=W} \mathcal{D}_h \times_4 \mathbf{s}_4^h. \quad (5)$$

Further, it can be shown that the tensors [8, 10]

$$\mathcal{D}_h = \mathcal{Z}(:, :, :, h) \times_1 \mathbf{S}_1 \times_2 \mathbf{S}_2 \times_3 \mathbf{S}_3 \quad (6)$$

are orthogonal, while the vectors $\mathbf{s}_P^h$ are columns of the unitary matrix $\mathbf{S}_P$ [10]. Because of the orthogonal property, they form *the orthogonal base*, spanning a subspace (OTS). This space is used to construct the tensor based model of the consecutive frames in the video stream, as depicted in Fig. 3.

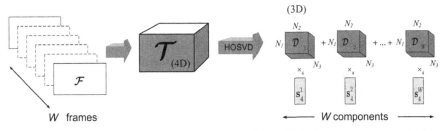

Fig. 3. Tensor model construction framework. The W frames in the input stream are stacked into the 4D model tensor $\mathcal{T}$. After its HOSVD decomposition the W bases $\mathcal{D}_w$ are obtained. A distance of a test tensor to the model tensor $\mathcal{T}$ is measured as its projection onto the subset of bases $\{\mathcal{D}_w\}$.

2.2 Frame to the Tensor Model Fitness Measure

A series of the W input frames is modelled as a subspace spanned by the tensors $\mathcal{D}_h$ defined in (6). The subset of $\mathcal{D}_h$ is then used to compare the incoming frames (tensors). That is, a distance of a test frame $\mathcal{F}$ to the tensor model, is computed as follows [10]:

$$R = \sum_{u=1}^{U \leq W} \langle \mathcal{D}_u, \mathcal{F} \rangle^2, \tag{7}$$

where $U \leq W$ is a method parameter. The values of R computed for the model frames, as well as computed for all other frames in the video, are used for the statistical analysis of abrupt signal changes in that video. Namely, the differences ΔR are used for this purpose. More concretely, the following error function is proposed

$$\Delta R_i \equiv R_i - R_{i-1}. \tag{8}$$

For detection of the video shots with slowly changing content, the following statistical measure is used

$$\left\| \Delta R_{\mathcal{F}} - \bar{R}_\Delta \right\| < a\sigma_\Delta + b. \tag{9}$$

where $a \in [3.0\text{--}4.0]$, and b is an additive component in the range $(0.5\text{--}2.5)$. The parameters $\bar{R}_\Delta$ and σ_Δ stand for the mean and standard deviation obtained from the *differences* of the fit measure in (8) for the model. These are computed as follows

$$\bar{R}_\Delta = \frac{1}{W} \sum_{w=1}^{W} R_{\Delta w}, \quad \sigma_\Delta^2 = \frac{1}{W-1} \sum_{w=1}^{W} \left(R_{\Delta w} - \bar{R}_\Delta \right)^2. \tag{10}$$

Each new tensor is checked to fit to the above model in accordance with (10). If it does not fit, the model is rebuilt. Further details on operation of the video shot detection method are provided in [10].

2.3 Video Encryption Method

In this work for the privacy encryption the pixel-by-pixel exclusive-or (XOR) encoding is proposed, as shown in Fig. 1(b). Although XOR is not a strong data encryption method, in our system it fulfills all of the requirements, that is: (1) the method allows a sufficient privacy (person identity protection), (2) it is fast, (3) it can be implemented close to the camera's sensor, (4) it allows for behavior analysis or scene shot observation, as well as (5) it is recoverable. For the latter, a value of the mask needs to be known. Moreover, longer masks can be used which provide the higher encryption levels. However, in our system a practical trade-off of 1–3 bytes is sufficient. We experimented with various permutations of the bytes from the set $\{0xAA, 0x55, 0xCD\}$. In the future, more advanced encryption methods are planned to be investigated as well.

3   Experimental Results

The proposed method was implemented in C++. The experiments were run out on the computer with 64 GB RAM, the Intel® Xeon E-2186 processor, and Windows® 10. For tensor decomposition the *DeRecLib* framework was used [11].

Figure 4 shows results of image encoding with the proposed XOR masking of pixels in each of the color channels with only 1 byte in the mask. The method is extremely simple and fast, at the same time allowing for the high level of privacy protection, as visible. On the other hand, behavior patterns in the stream can be still discernible.

Fig. 4. Color data encoding for privacy protection. Each color channel is independently processed with a 1 byte XOR mask. This encoding is fast, can be implemented in hardware and makes person's and object's details identification very difficult or impossible (right). Images from the Open Video Database [16] (left) – 'The Voyage of the Lee', segments 05 and 15.

Due to the color mangling, personal details of face and person posture are not possible for identification. Similarly, some texts and other details identifying objects are also concealed, as shown in the last row in Fig. 4. Nevertheless, the proposed simple XOR'ing method is relatively easy to be broken (decoded). Therefore, further research will be devoted to the development and investigation of other data encryption methods, which allow for efficient video shot detection, at the same time ensuring a sufficient level of data protection. Exemplary plots of the detected scene shots computed by the presented tensor based method, operating on the encrypted video sequence no 60 and 61 from the 'The Voyage of the Lee', segments 05 and 15, of the Open Video Database [16], are shown in Fig. 5, respectively. Detailed results for each video from the database are presented in Table 1. For measurements the ground truth data from the work by de Avila *et al.* [6] has been employed. The measures $CUS_A = n_{AU}/n_U$ and $CUS_E = {\sim}n_{AU}/n_U$ are used, where n_A denotes a number of *matching* keyframes from the automatic summary (*AS*) and the user annotated summary, ${\sim}n_{AU}$ is the complement of this set, whereas n_U is a total number of keyframes from the user summary only (*US*). Also the P (precision), R (recall) and F measures are used [9, 10, 17, 18, 21, 24]. An average F measure of the proposed method is 0.75, which is only by 0.03 less than the average F measure obtained on the not encrypted (pure) video signals presented in the paper [10]. This shows that both research tasks were fulfilled. That is, the sufficient level of data encryption, which disallows person identification, joined with an efficient tensor based real-time method of signal change detection were attained.

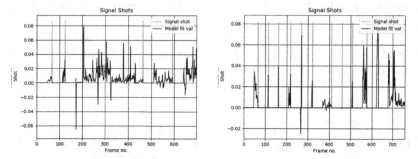

Fig. 5. Plots of the detected scene shots computed in the privacy encrypted video sequences no. 60 and no. 61 from the Open Video Database. These frames are shown in Fig. 4.

Table 1. Results of the proposed tensor based change detection method obtained on the privacy encoded video streams from the Open-Video Database.

Video No.	CUS_A	CUS_E	P	R	F
21	0.64	0.36	0.64	0.64	0.64
22	0.75	0.25	0.75	0.75	0.75
23	0.88	0.13	0.88	0.88	0.88
24	0.55	0.18	0.75	0.55	0.63
25	0.50	0.08	0.86	0.50	0.63
26	0.63	0.38	0.63	0.63	0.63
27	0.75	0.19	0.80	0.75	0.77
28	0.74	0.09	0.89	0.74	0.81
29	0.63	0.13	0.83	0.63	0.71
30	0.60	0.10	0.86	0.60	0.71
31	0.85	0.08	0.92	0.85	0.88
32	0.67	0.56	0.55	0.67	0.60
33	0.67	0.17	0.80	0.67	0.73
34	1.00	0.00	1.00	1.00	1.00
35	0.42	0.25	0.63	0.42	0.50
36	0.60	1.20	0.33	0.60	0.43
37	1.00	0.40	0.71	1.00	0.83
38	0.85	0.46	0.65	0.85	0.73

(*continued*)

Table 1. (*continued*)

Video No.	CUS$_A$	CUS$_E$	P	R	F
39	0.83	0.25	0.77	0.83	0.80
40	1.00	0.50	0.67	1.00	0.80
41	0.92	0.33	0.73	0.92	0.81
42	0.89	0.33	0.73	0.89	0.80
43	0.89	0.22	0.80	0.89	0.84
44	0.90	0.30	0.75	0.90	0.82
45	0.89	0.33	0.73	0.89	0.80
46	0.50	0.50	0.50	0.50	0.50
47	0.80	0.00	1.00	0.80	0.89
48	0.88	0.75	0.54	0.88	0.67
49	0.87	0.20	0.81	0.87	0.84
50	0.89	0.78	0.53	0.89	0.67
51	0.71	0.29	0.71	0.71	0.71
52	1.00	0.38	0.73	1.00	0.84
53	0.83	0.33	0.71	0.83	0.77
54	0.86	0.00	1.00	0.86	0.92
55	0.80	0.20	0.80	0.80	0.80
56	0.78	0.11	0.88	0.78	0.82
57	0.86	0.29	0.75	0.86	0.80
58	0.69	0.00	1.00	0.69	0.82
59	0.80	0.00	1.00	0.80	0.89
60	0.50	0.00	1.00	0.50	0.67
61	1.00	0.43	0.70	1.00	0.82
62	1.00	0.00	1.00	1.00	1.00
63	0.86	0.29	0.75	0.86	0.80
64	0.69	0.25	0.73	0.69	0.71
65	0.88	0.50	0.64	0.88	0.74
66	0.75	0.38	0.67	0.75	0.71
67	0.63	0.63	0.50	0.63	0.56
68	0.75	0.25	0.75	0.75	0.75
69	0.80	0.50	0.62	0.80	0.70
70	0.60	0.20	0.75	0.60	0.67
					F_av = **0.75**

The above results place the propose method at the top of the state-of-the-art methods in the field of video shot detection. A detailed comparison of the thumbnail tensor approach with other methods can be found in the paper [10]. However, contrary to other methods, the proposed one allows for seamless operation in the domain of data encoded for privacy protection. This is the main novelty presented in this paper. Moreover, the method allows up to 160 frames/s, placing it in the group of fastest real-time methods.

4   Conclusions

The paper presents a video stream change detection method based on the orthogonal tensor decomposition models. The method fulfills the of data privacy constraint and allows for real-time operation on encoded signals. One of the characteristic features of the proposed tensor method is operation on multi-dimensional signals without any specific feature extraction. Thanks to this universality, the method is able to work also with encrypted data in order to attain data privacy protection. For the latter, the XOR masking is proposed, which achieves a number of goals. Although it is not a strong encryption method, it allows for reliable and reversible operations by the authorized personnel. On the other hand, XOR can be efficiently implemented, very close to the image sensor, allowing for high data privacy protection and fast in-hardware operation. To some extend this paper opens the subject of video signal change analysis in an encrypted domain, which surely will gain on attention. Further research will be devoted to an analysis of other encryption methods, which fulfill the stated goals of video analysis and data privacy protection at the same time. Also, an important research direction is operation in a domain of signals preprocessed with properly trained deep networks, which allow for more in-depth treatment of semantic data properties.

Acknowledgement. This work was supported by the Polish National Science Center NCN under the grant no. 2016/21/B/ST6/01461.

References

1. Aja-Fernández, S., de Luis Garcia, R., Tao, D., Li, X.: Tensors in Image Processing and Computer Vision. Springer, Heidelberg (2009). https://doi.org/10.1007/978-1-84882-299-3
2. Asghar, M.N., Hussain, F., Manton, R.: Video indexing: a survey. Int. J. Comput. Inf. Technol. **03**(01), 148–169 (2014)
3. Baaziz, N., Lolo, N., Padilla, O., Petngang, F.: Security and privacy protection for automated video surveillance. In: 2007 IEEE International Symposium on Signal Processing and Information Technology, Giza, pp. 17–22 (2007)
4. Boult, T.E.: PICO: privacy through invertible cryptographic obscuration. In: Computer Vision for Interactive and Intelligent Environment (CVIIE 2005), USA, pp. 27–38 (2005)
5. Çiftçi, S., Akyüz, A.O., Ebrahimi, T.: A reliable and reversible image privacy protection based on false colors. IEEE Trans. Multimedia **20**(1), 68–81 (2018)
6. de Avila, S.E.F., Lopes, A.P.B., Luz da Jr., A., Araújo, A.A.: VSUMM: a mechanism designed to produce static video summaries and a novel evaluation method. Pattern Recogn. Lett. **32**, 56–68 (2011)

7. Chu, K.-Y., Kuo Y.-H., Hsu, W.H.: Real-time privacy-preserving moving object detection in the cloud. In: Proceedings of the 21st ACM International Conference on Multimedia, Association for Computing Machinery, NY, USA, pp. 597–600 (2013)
8. Cyganek, B.: Object Detection and Recognition in Digital Images: Theory and Practice. Wiley, Hoboken (2013)
9. Cyganek, B.: Hybrid ensemble of classifiers for logo and trademark symbols recognition. Soft. Comput. **19**(12), 3413–3430 (2015)
10. Cyganek, B.: Thumbnail tensor - a method for multidimensional data streams clustering with an efficient tensor subspace model in the scale-space. Sensors **19**, 4088 (2019)
11. DeRecLib. http://www.wiley.com/go/cyganekobject. Accessed 21 Mar 2020
12. Domingo-Ferrer, J., Farràs, O., Ribes-González, J., Sánchez, D.: Privacy-preserving cloud computing on sensitive data: a survey of methods, products and challenges. Comput. Commun. **140–141**, 38–60 (2019)
13. Du, L., Zhang, W., Fu, H., Ren, W., Zhang, X.. An efficient privacy protection scheme for data security in video surveillance. J. Vis. Commun. Image Repr. **59** (2019)
14. Del Fabro, M., Böszörmenyi, L.: State-of-the-art and future challenges in video scene detection: a survey. Multimedia Syst. **19**(5), 427–454 (2013)
15. Grabek, J., Cyganek, B.: Speckle noise filtering in side-scan sonar images based on the Tucker tensor decomposition. Sensors **19**, 2903 (2019)
16. https://open-video.org/
17. https://sites.google.com/site/vsummsite/home
18. https://sites.google.com/site/vscansite/home
19. Korshunov, P., Ebrahimi, T.: Using warping for privacy protection in video surveillance. In: 18th International Conference on Digital Signal Processing (DSP), Fira, pp. 1–6 (2013)
20. de Lathauwer, L., de Moor, B., Vandewalle, J.: A multilinear singular value decomposition. SIAM J. Matrix Anal. Appl. **21**(4), 1253–1278 (2000)
21. Mahmoud, K.M., Ismail, M.A., Ghanem, N.M.: VSCAN: an enhanced video summarization using density-based spatial clustering. In: Petrosino, A. (ed.) ICIAP 2013. LNCS, vol. 8156, pp. 733–742. Springer, Heidelberg (2013). https://doi.org/10.1007/978-3-642-41181-6_74
22. Ou, S.-H., Lee, C.-H., Somayazulu, V.S., Chen, Y-K., Chien S-Y.: On-line multi-view video summarization for wireless video sensor network. IEEE J. Sel. Topics Sig. Process. **9**(1), 165–179 (2015)
23. Padilla-Lopez, J.R., Chaaraoui, A.A., Florez-Revuelta, F.: Visual privacy protection methods: a survey. Expert Syst. Appl. **42**, 4177–4195 (2016)
24. Qayyum, H., Majid, M., Haq, E., Anwar, S.: Generation of personalized video summaries by detecting viewer's emotion using electroencephalography. J. Vis. Com. Image **65**, 102672 (2019)

Posters and Demos

How the Anti-TrustRank Algorithm Can Help to Protect the Reputation of Financial Institutions

Irina Astrova[✉]

Department of Software Science, School of IT, Tallinn University of Technology,
Akadeemia tee 21, 12618 Tallinn, Estonia
irina@cs.ioc.ee

Abstract. When financial institutions are found to have their customers conduct money laundering through them, they are subjected to large fines. Moreover, the reputation of those institutions suffers greatly through public exposure. Consequently, financial institutions invest significant resources in building systems to automatically detect money laundering in order to minimize the negative impact of money launderers on their reputation. This paper investigates a graph algorithm called Anti-TrustRank and demonstrates how it can be used to identify money launderers. Our approach to using Anti-TrustRank is not replacing money laundering detection systems, rather is generating additional inputs to feed into such systems in order to improve their overall detection accuracy.

Keywords: Financial institutions · Money laundering · Terrorist financing · Money laundering detection systems · PageRank · TrustRank · Anti-TrustRank

1 Introduction

A graph-as-a-service is one that uses a knowledge graph to enable interrelated data to be retrieved, using the concepts of nodes, edges and properties to represent and store those data. A well-known example is Google's knowledge graph, which is used by its search engine. Another example is a financial knowledge graph, which is a network of data and relationships between them that matter to financial institutions.

Today financial institutions regularly store and retrieve transaction and payment data. As a result, they can utilize those data to improve their ability to identify money launderers. While human experts can identify suspicious transactions, a manual review of transactions is impractical due to the amount of data. Therefore, in a typical scenario, money laundering detection systems will automatically identify a suspicious transaction, raise a flag, and route the transaction to human experts, who will confirm that the transaction is money laundering [5].

Many existing money laundering detection systems are based on a set of business rules that detect suspicious transactions or anomalous payment events. For example, a business rule might look for payments for a given customer where the amount is significantly above the average payment for that customer. Although these rules are

© Springer Nature Switzerland AG 2020
F. Dalpiaz et al. (Eds.): RCIS 2020, LNBIP 385, pp. 503–508, 2020.
https://doi.org/10.1007/978-3-030-50316-1_30

effective for some cases, money launderers can often circumvent such rules. Moreover, the rules often cannot automatically discover new patterns of money laundering, are not scalable and are difficult to maintain and update over time [4].

Therefore, more recently financial institutions have been applying machine learning techniques to identify money launderers. For example, a financial institution might utilize a supervised learning model that uses various features of the current transaction as well as historical transaction stream to detect a suspicious transaction. However, many existing money laundering detection systems have been directed toward supervised machine learning techniques such as regression modelling, decision trees or random forests as well as unsupervised machine learning techniques such as clustering, whereas graph algorithms are relatively new and not as widely used [5].

In this paper, we will explore a graph algorithm called Anti-TrustRank and demonstrate how financial institutions can apply it for the purpose of money laundering detection.

2 Anti-TrustRank

Anti-TrustRank is a variant of TrustRank, which in its turn is a variant of PageRank.

PageRank [1] is a graph algorithm used by Google in its search engine to determine the order in which pages will be shown in the search results. Pages that appear near the top of search results are more worthy to visit, whereas pages that are shown at the bottom are likely to be spam pages. The algorithm views the web as a graph, where pages are nodes and links between pages are edges. The algorithm computes scores for each page. These scores indicate the "goodness" of pages: the higher score a page has, the more likely a web surfer will visit that page. The surfer starts from a random page on the web and follows a sequence of steps. In each step, the surfer may take one of two possible actions: (1) choose one of the links on the page and follow it; or (2) "jump" to a randomly selected page. Therefore, the score of a page is the probability that the surfer will end up at that page.

The basic idea of PageRank is that a page is good if it is linked by many other good pages. Initially, each page is assigned the same non-zero score. After computation, good pages will get high scores, whereas spam pages will get low scores.

The formula for computation of a page score is:

$$\mathbf{p} = \alpha \cdot \mathbf{T} \times \mathbf{p} + (1 - \alpha) \cdot \mathbf{d}$$

where $\mathbf{p}$ is a page score vector, $\mathbf{T}$ is a transition matrix – it is built from the graph, α is a damping factor (usually 0.85) – it is needed to limit an effect of loops in the graph, $\mathbf{d}$ is a uniformly distributed random vector. Instead of following links to other pages, a web surfer can just jump to a random page chosen according to $\mathbf{d}$.

Since PageRank computes page scores based upon the link structure of the web, one popular technique for increasing the scores of spam pages is through complex linking structures called spam farms. TrustRank [2] seeks to combat spam farms. It is a topic-sensitive PageRank, where the "topic" is a set of pages believed to be trustworthy. A web surfer can start only from a page in the topic and can jump only to a page included in that topic.

The basic idea of TrustRank is that good pages seldom link to spam pages. If we trust good pages, we can also trust pages pointed by good pages. This way trustability can be propagated through the link structure of the web. Before computation, a "topic" of highly trustworthy pages is created as a seed set, which a very small set of all pages on the web. Each of the pages in the seed set is assigned the same non-zero initial score, whereas other pages are initialized with a zero score. After computation, good pages will get high scores, whereas spam pages will get low scores.

The formula for computation of a page score is:

$$\mathbf{t} = \alpha \cdot \mathbf{T} \times \mathbf{t} + (1 - \alpha) \cdot \mathbf{d}^\tau$$

where $\mathbf{t}$ is a page score vector, $\mathbf{T}$ is a transition matrix, α is a damping factor (usually 0.85), $\mathbf{S}$ is a seed set.

$$d_p^\tau = \begin{cases} 1/\|S\|, & \text{if } p \text{ is in trust seed set } S \\ 0, & \text{otherwise} \end{cases}.$$

Anti-TrustRank [3] is the inverse of TrustRank. The formula for computation of a page score is the same as that for TrustRank. The only difference is that the seed set consists of pages that are already known to be spam. After computation, spam pages will get high scores, whereas good pages will get low scores.

3   Using Anti-TrustRank in Money Laundering Detection

Traditionally, Anti-TrustRank is used to find out spam pages. However, applications of the algorithm are not limited to the web. In this paper, we demonstrate that the algorithm can also be used to detect money laundering based on the link structure of the ownership. In practice, even one or two money launderers in the ownership structure are a good indicator of money laundering.

In our approach to using Anti-TrustRank, customers are viewed as pages, and there is a link between customers if these customers are related in terms of shares. Given the postulate "Customers related to money launderers are more likely to be themselves money launderers", we look for money launderers (spam pages) that appear near to a seed set of customers who make suspicious transactions or anomalous payments. In this context, money laundering detection is supervised, as some customers are already labeled as money launderers. After running the algorithm, the customers who are not yet labeled as money launderers but have high scores are the ones we want to find. The higher scores of customers, the more vulnerable those customers to money laundering.

Our approach goes through the following steps:

1. Compute an ownership structure. This is a directed graph of shareholder relations between customers, where customers are nodes and shareholder relations are indicated by edges, which display the direction of ownership.
2. Create a transition matrix from the graph.
3. Select customers who are already known to be money launderers and label them as a seed set.

4. Run the algorithm against the transition matrix and the seed set.
5. Find customers with high scores.

Figure 1 shows an example of customer scores for a sample ownership structure. Customers from the seed set are shown in black, whereas customers identified by Anti-TrustRank as vulnerable to money laundering are shown in grey. As can be seen, the probability of money laundering diminishes with increase in distance between customers and the seed set.

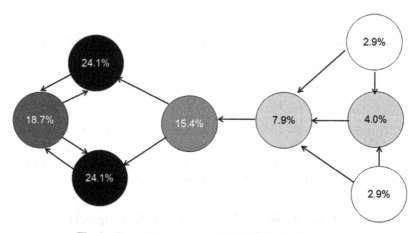

Fig. 1. Ownership structure with Anti-TrustRank scores.

4 Related Work

Money laundering detection started in 1970 when financial institutes began reporting suspicious transactions to their governments. Statistical methods such as Bayesian models and temporal sequence matching were used in late 1990s to detect money laundering [6]. Since 2004 machine-learning techniques such as C4.5 decision tree algorithms, support vector machines and radial-based function neural network models have been applied [7–9].

Recently, graph-based approaches have gained popularity. For example, Awasthi et al. [10] combined a graph-mining algorithm with clustering techniques to find money-laundering communities. Chen et al. [11] applied fuzzy logic on various attributes of transactions such as their timestamp and the amount transferred to detect suspicious transactions.

Efficient methods to reduce the size of the original data set is crucial to money laundering detection because large amounts of transaction and payment data are produced daily from e-businesses, e-commerce and other online financial activities [4]. Therefore, we proposed to take a different approach: instead of analyzing transactions and money launderers communities, we analyzed the shareholder relations by using Anti-TrustRank.

5 Conclusion

Financial institutions may greatly benefit from using graph algorithms to identify customers who may expose the institutions to money laundering. In this paper, we investigated one of such algorithms: Anti-TrustRank. This algorithm calls for selecting a very small set of customers to be evaluated by human experts as money launderers. Once this set has been identified, the algorithm seeks out customers linked (either directly or indirectly) to those money launderers. As a result, the reputation of financial institutions will be better protected.

Our approach in using Anti-TrustRank has been evaluated against synthetic data. In the future work, we plan to conduct experiments on real data gathered by financial institutions. However, to protect the privacy of their customers and to maintain the confidentiality of the customers activities, financial institutions safeguard transaction and payment data with utmost diligence [12].

Furthermore, not only Anti-TrustRank can be used to combat money laundering, but also to fight the financing of terrorism – even one or two terrorists in the ownership structure are a good indicator of terrorist financing. Thus, in the future, Anti-TrustRank can be used to prevent financial institutions from being misused for these purposes as well.

Acknowledgement. Irina Astrova's work was supported by the Estonian Ministry of Education and Research institutional research grant IUT33-13.

References

1. Page, L., Brin, S., Motwani, R., Winograd, T.: The PageRank citation ranking: bringing order to the web. In: Proceedings of the 7th International World Wide Web Conference (1998)
2. Gyöngyi, Z., Garcia-Molina, H., Pedersen, J.: Combating web spam with TrustRank. In: Proceedings of the 30th International Conference on Very Large Databases (VLDB) (2004)
3. Krishnan, V., Raj, R.: Web spam detection with Anti-Trust rank. In: Proceedings of 2nd International Workshop on Adversarial Information Retrieval on the Web (AIRWeb) (2006)
4. Soltani, R., Nguyen, U., Yang, Y., Faghani, M., Yagoub, A., An, A.: A new algorithm for money laundering detection based on structural similarity. In: Proceedings of IEEE 7th Annual Ubiquitous Computing, Electronics and Mobile Communication Conference (UEMCON) (2016)
5. Mendelevitch, O.: Using PageRank to detect anomalies and fraud in healthcare (2015). https://hortonworks.com/blog/using-pagerank-detect-anomalies-fraud-healthcare/
6. Phua, C., Lee, V., Smith, K., Gayler, R.: A comprehensive survey of data mining-based accounting-fraud detection research. Technical report, Clayton School of Information Technology, Monash University, pp. 1–27 (2005)
7. Wang, S., Yang, J.: A money laundering risk evaluation method based on decision tree. In: Proceedings of International Conference on Machine Learning and Cybernetics, vol. 1. IEEE (2007)
8. Tang, J., Yin, J.: Developing an intelligent data discriminating system of anti-money laundering based on SVM. In: Proceedings of International Conference on Machine Learning and Cybernetics, vol. 6. IEEE (2005)

9. Lv, L., Ji, N., Zhang, J.: A RBF neural network model for anti-money laundering. In: International Conference on Wavelet Analysis and Pattern Recognition, vol. 1. IEEE (2008)
10. Awasthi, A.: Clustering algorithms for anti-money laundering using graph theory and social network analysis (2012)
11. Chen, Y., Mathe, J.: Fuzzy computing applications for anti-money laundering and distributed storage system load monitoring. Knowl. Inf. Syst. **57**(2), 245–285 (2018)
12. Barse, E., Kvarnstrom, H., Jonsson, E.: Synthesizing test data for fraud detection systems. In: Proceedings of 19th Computer Security Applications Conference. IEEE (2003)

Punctuation Restoration System for Slovene Language

Marko Bajec[1](✉), Marko Janković[1,2], Slavko Žitnik[1], and Iztok Lebar Bajec[1]

[1] Faculty of Computer and Information Science, University of Ljubljana, Ljubljana, Slovenia
Marko.bajec@fri.uni-lj.si
[2] Vitasis d.o.o., Rakek, Slovenia

Abstract. Punctuation restoration is the process of adding punctuation symbols to raw text. It is typically used as a post-processing task of Automatic Speech Recognition (ASR) systems. In this paper we present an approach for punctuation restoration for texts in Slovene language. The system is trained using bi-directional Recurrent Neural Networks fed by word embeddings only. The evaluation results show our approach is capable of restoring punctuations with a high *recall* and *precision*. The F1 score is specifically high for *commas* and *periods*, which are considered most important punctuation symbols for the understanding of the ASR based transcripts.

Keywords: Punctuation restoration · Automatic speech recognition · Text processing

1 Introduction

The goal of punctuation restoration is to identify positions in raw text where punctuation symbols are missing or could be added to improve the readability and semantic value of text. It is typically used in combination with ASR systems that produce sequences of words without any punctuation symbols. The text is then improved by the insertion of punctuation symbols to positions where they fit according to specific rules.

The ability to accurately restor punctuations is found to be very important, not just for an understanding of the recognized text, but also for further processing such as providing quality translations. In this paper we describe an approach for punctuation restoration that uses bi-directional neural networks for punctuation predictions.

The rest of the paper is structured as follows: Sect. 2 provides related works, Sect. 3 the method used, Sect. 4 the dataset that we used and Sect. 5 the evaluation results. Short conclusion is given in Sect. 6.

2 Related Works

The challenge of punctuation restoration is not new. A lot of efforts have been made to restore punctuation symbols automatically. In terms of how the punctuation restoration

© Springer Nature Switzerland AG 2020
F. Dalpiaz et al. (Eds.): RCIS 2020, LNBIP 385, pp. 509–514, 2020.
https://doi.org/10.1007/978-3-030-50316-1_31

problem is modeled, the existing approaches can be categorized into three categories [1]. The first category comprises approaches that model punctuations as hidden inter-word states and use *n-gram* language models or *hidden Markov chains* to restore punctuations [2]. Approaches in the second category deal with the punctuation restoration as with a *sequence labeling task* where labels are punctuations, and words are objects to which labels are assigned. It has been shown in the literature that feature-rich models such as *Condition Random Fields* (CRFs) are specifically suited for the task at hand. Approaches that are based on CRFs achieve F1 scores around 55% for English datasets [3]. In the third category there are approaches that use *neural networks* (NN), specifically *deep neural networks* (DNN) to predict punctuations in text.

As for many other Natural Language Processing (NLP) tasks, it has been shown also for the punctuation restoration problem that NNs outperform other known approaches. Several NN architectures have been proposed in the literature for this purpose. Improvements in punctuation restoration accuracy have been demonstrated with different NN-based architectures, such as *convolutional* NN [4], *long short-term memory* NN [5], *bi-directional recurrent* NN with *attention mechanism* [6], *recurrent* NN *encoder-decoder* architecture with *attention layer* [7], etc.

In this paper we focus on the punctuation restoration for Slovene language. The approach that we describe is based on NN, with a bi-directional recurrent architecture and attention mechanism. On the input we only use lexical features, including *word embeddings*. We are not aware of any prior work that would address the problem of punctuation restoration for Slovene texts. The only known attempt that we are aware of was focused on *comma replacement* and *correction* [8] employing various machine learning techniques. As we show in this paper, our approach is superior as it achieves considerably higher accuracy for the comma prediction problem. Moreover, the prediction accuracy of punctuation restoration is in general better for Slovene texts than it is usually reported for English (cf. [3–7]). Although this comparison does not necessarily make sense, as linguistic features differ from language to language, it may represent an interesting observation, worthy of further research. Most importantly, the prediction accuracy is in particular high for commas and periods that are considered the most important punctuation symbols for improving human readability of ASR generated texts and its further machine processing.

3 Method

The model that we use in our approach is built along the NN architecture suggested by O. Tilk and T. Alumäe in [6]. In simple words, the model works as follows: at each step t the model calculates the probabilities of missing punctuation symbols p_t between the current input word x_t and previous input word x_{t-1}. The sequence of words $X = (x_1, x_2, \ldots x_T)$, in which each word is represented as a *one-hot encoded* vector x_i, is first processed by two recurrent layers. One processing the sequence in forward and the other in backward direction. Optionally, if we want pre-trained word embeddings to replace one-hot encoded word vectors, the two recurrent layers are preceded by a *shared embedding layer* with weights W_e.

The hidden state at step t of the forward recurrent layer is calculated with GRU where *tanh* is used for the activation function: $\boldsymbol{hidden\_f}_t = GRU\left(\boldsymbol{hidden\_f}_{t-1}, x_t * W_e\right)$.

The hidden state of the backward recurrent layer $hidden\_b_t$ is computed in the same way, except that for a reverse input sequence order. Then both hidden states $hidden\_f_t$ and $hidden\_b_t$ are concatenated: $hidden_t = concat(hidden\_f_t, hidden\_b_t)$.

Like suggested in [6], the bi-directional recurrent layer is proceeded by a unidirectional GRU layer with an attention mechanism. While the GRU layer sequentially processes the states of the previous layers and keeps track of the position in the sequence, the attention mechanism focuses on potential relationships among words before and after the current position, signaling important information for the punctuation decisions. The output state s at step t is then calculated as $s_t = GRU(hidden_t, s_{t-1})$. The state s is finally *late fused* [12] into f_t and fed to the output layer.

The punctuation probabilities y_t at position t are calculated using *Softmax* function as follows: $y_t = Softmax(f_t * W_y + b_y)$, where b_y is a bias vector.

4 Dataset and Data Preparation

To train NN, large datasets are usually required. In our case we used the corpus Gigafida 2.0, which represents a reference corpus of written Slovene [9]. The corpus is comprised of articles from newspapers, magazines, a selection of web texts, and excerpts from different types of publications, i.e. fiction, schoolbooks, and non-fiction. Altogether it includes 60 million sentences out of which 40 million were used for training.

Prior to the training process, we labeled sentences in the corpus with information on *predictive classes*, i.e. which tokens represent punctuation symbols that we would like to learn how to predict. We did that by replacing punctuations with special labels, defined for each punctuation symbol separately. By these transformations we assured that punctuation symbols would be treated as separate tokens rather than as being additional characters of words. In addition, we decapitalized all sentences, since this information is not available in ASR generated texts and we did not want the NN to become dependent on it.

In the data preparation phase, we also trained word embeddings. We did the training from scratch (using GloVe [14]) since all the embeddings that are available for Slovene language capture semantic similarity of words only.

5 Experiments and Results

5.1 Punctuation Restoration Accuracy

For the experimentation, 10% of the Gigafida 2.0 dataset was reserved for validation and testing and the rest for training. We experimented with several word representations, including one-hot encoding, pre-trained GloVe embeddings for Slovene language, and GloVe embeddings, specifically trained for the purpose of punctuation restoration.

For the NN hyperparameters, such as *learning rate* and the *number of hidden layers*, we followed suggestions reported in related works. We used 256 hidden layers and a learning rate of 0.02.

The results are shown in the table below. The numbers noWe column correspond to experiments, in which we did not use word embeddings. The vocabulary was created from 200.000 most frequently used words in the corpus. Columns PreWe and SpecWe with pre-trained and newly trained GloVe embeddings, respectively.

As it can be noticed, best performance can be achieved with embeddings that are specifically trained for the punctuation restoration task. This was expected, as words in the pre-trained embeddings appear in their *lemmatized* form, while for the punctuation restoration we assume it is better to distinguish between different forms of the same word. Slovene is one of the languages where word forms may depend on cases – a feature that is known for Balto-Slavic languages plus few others, like German. In German, cases are mostly marked on articles and adjectives, while in Balto-Slavic languages they are marked on nouns. With lemmatization we lose this information, which might not be irrelevant for predicting punctuation positions in a text (Table 1).

Table 1. Punctuation restoration results

Punctuation	Precision			Recall			F1 measure		
	noWe	PreWe	SpecWe	noWe	PreWe	SpecWe	noWe	PreWe	SpecWe
Comma	0.776	0.864	**0.905**	0.692	0.798	**0.872**	0.731	0.830	**0.888**
Period	0.661	0.798	**0.862**	0.545	0.834	**0.869**	0.598	0.816	**0.865**
Ques. m.	0.352	0.655	**0.722**	0.027	0.487	**0.527**	0.050	0.559	**0.609**
Exc. m.	–	–	**0.520**	–	–	**0.030**	–	–	**0.070**
Overall	*0.731*	*0.823*	*0.881*	*0.620*	*0.799*	*0.859*	*0.671*	*0.811*	*0.870*

5.2 Comparison with the Best-Known Results for Slovene

In Table 2 we compare our results with the best-known results for punctuation restoration in Slovene texts. We are not aware of any other work to compare with except for the one in [8], where the authors deal with the problem of *comma placement* and *correction* while other punctuations are not considered. Hence, the comparison was performed only for punctuation symbol *comma*. In [8] the authors evaluate various machine learning approaches by using *grammar-based features* that they generate specifically for the problem at hand. The classification methods they test are *random forests, support vector machines, naive Bayesian classifier, RBF network, alternating decision trees, AdaBoost.M1*, and *decision table*. The best performing methods are random forests, alternating decision trees, and decision table. The results in Table 2 show that our model significantly improves accuracy for the *comma placement* problem on the same dataset, i.e. Šolar[1].

5.3 Comparison with Punctuation Restoration Accuracy for Other Languages

Table 3 provides results of punctuation restoration for three different languages, Estonian, English and Slovene. The results for English and Estonian are taken from [6].

---

[1] http://eng.slovenscina.eu/korpusi/solar.

Table 2. Comparison between supervised ML approaches and bi-directional RNN with attention mechanism for comma restoration problem on the dataset Šolar

Punctuation	Precision	Recall	F1
NaiveBayes	0.269	0.861	0.410
RandomForest	0.913	0.542	0.680
ADTree	0.916	0.426	0.581
DecisionTable	**0.920**	0.577	0.709
Bi-directional RNN	0.890	**0.837**	**0.863**

Table 3. Comparison between languages

Language	Precision		Recall		F1	
	Comma	Period	Comma	Period	Comma	Period
English	0.655	0.733	0.471	0.725	0.548	0.729
Estonian	0.816	0.738	0.754	0.773	0.784	0.755
Slovene	**0.905**	**0.862**	**0.872**	**0.869**	**0.888**	**0.865**

Even though the results do not reveal much about the methods used, as they were in all the three cases similar, i.e. a bi-directional RNN with attention mechanism, it is interesting to notice that for Slovene language we can achieve a much higher punctuation restoration accuracy than for the other two languages. The relatively high difference can be attributed to different reasons, but we believe it indicates that the Slovene grammar is relatively rich comparing to English and Estonian language in terms of information the NN can exploit when learning how to predict punctuation places in Slovenian text.

6   Conclusion

Punctuation restoration is an important process that is typically used in combination with ASR systems to place missing punctuations in the output text of the recognizer. The punctuations that set sentence boundaries are particularly important, as they improve the readability of the output text and facilitate further machine processing, such as for example machine translation.

In this paper we focused on the problem of punctuation restoration for Slovene language that has not been addressed yet in this manner. Taking into account the findings of related works that deal with the same challenge on other languages, we employed DNN to predict missing punctuations. The NN architecture uses recurrent GRU gates in bi-directional mode, plus an attention mechanism to give the network additional context information for punctuation decisions. The evaluation results show the suggested model is able to achieve a much higher prediction accuracy than previously evaluated machine learning techniques. More surprisingly, the results demonstrate using nearly the same

NN architectures significantly higher prediction accuracy can be achieved for Slovene than for English or Estonian language.

References

1. Yi, J., Tao, J.: Self-attention based model for punctuation prediction using word and speech embeddings. In: Proceedings of ICASSP 2019 – 2019 IEEE International Conference on Acoustics, Speech and Signal Processing (ICASSP), pp. 7270–7274 (2019)
2. Stolcke, A., et al.: Automatic detection of sentence boundaries and disfluencies based on recognized words. In: IC-SLP 1998, Sydney (1998)
3. Ueffing, N., Bisani, M., Vozila, P.: Improved models for automatic punctuation prediction for spoken and written text. In: INTERSPEECH, pp. 3097–3101 (2013)
4. Che, X.et al.: Punctuation prediction for unsegmented transcript based on word vector. In: Proceedings of the LREC, pp. 654–658 (2016)
5. Tilk, O., Alumae, T.: LSTM for punctuation restoration in speech transcripts. In: INTER-SPEECH, pp. 683–687 (2015)
6. Tilk, O., Alumae, T.: Bidirectional recurrent neural network with attention mechanism for punctuation restoration. In: INTERSPEECH, pp. 3047–3051 (2016)
7. Klejch, O., Bell, P., Renals, S.: Sequence-to-sequence models for punctuated transcription combining lexical and acoustic features. In: ICASSP, pp. 5700–5704 (2017)
8. Krajnc, A., Robnik-Sikonja, M.: Postavljanje vejic v Slovenščini s pomočjo strojnega učenja in izboljšanega korpusa Šolar. In: Darja Fišer slovenščina na spletu in v novih medijih, pp. 38–43 (2015)
9. Logar, N.: Reference corpora revisited: expansion of the Gigafida corpus. In: Gorjanc, V., et al. (eds.) Dictionary of modern Slovene: problems and solutions (Book series Prevodoslovje in uporabno jezikoslovje), 1st edn. Ljubljana University Press, Ljubljana, pp. 96–119 (2017)
10. Luong, T., Hieu, P., Manning, C.D.: Effective approaches to attention-based neural machine translation. In: Proceedings of the 2015 Conference on Empirical Methods in Natural Language Processing, pp. 1412–1421, Lisbon. Association for Computational Linguistics (2015)
11. Yuan, G., Glowacka, D.: Deep gate recurrent neural network. In: Proceedings of ACML, pp. 350–365 (2016)
12. Snoek, C.G., Worring, M., Smeulders, A.W.: Early versus late fusion in semantic video analysis. In: Proceedings of the 13th Annual ACM International Conference on Multimedia, pp. 399–402. ACM (2005)
13. Khattak, F.K., Jeblee, S., Pou-Prom, C., Abdalla, M., Meaney, C., Rudzicz, F.: A survey of word embeddings for clinical text. J. Biomed. Inform.: X 4, 100057 (2019). ISSN 2590-177X
14. Pennington, J., Socher, R., Manning, C.D.: GloVe: global vectors for word representation. In: Proceedings of the 2014 Conference on Empirical Methods in Natural Language Processing (EMNLP), pp. 1532–1543, Doha. Association for Computational Linguistics (2014)

Practice and Challenges of (De-)Anonymisation for Data Sharing

Alexandros Bampoulidis[1]([✉]), Alessandro Bruni[2], Ioannis Markopoulos[3], and Mihai Lupu[1]

[1] Research Studio Data Science, RSA FG, Vienna, Austria
{alexandros.bampoulidis,mihai.lupu}@researchstudio.at
[2] Center for IT & IP Law, KU Leuven, Leuven, Belgium
alessandro.bruni@kuleuven.be
[3] Forthnet S.A., Athens, Greece
jmarkopo@forthnet.gr

Abstract. Personal data is a necessity in many fields for research and innovation purposes, and when such data is shared, the data controller carries the responsibility of protecting the privacy of the individuals contained in their dataset. The removal of direct identifiers, such as full name and address, is not enough to secure the privacy of individuals as shown by de-anonymisation methods in the scientific literature. Data controllers need to become aware of the risks of de-anonymisation and apply the appropriate anonymisation measures before sharing their datasets, in order to comply with privacy regulations. To address this need, we defined a procedure that makes data controllers aware of the de-anonymisation risks and helps them in deciding the anonymisation measures that need to be taken in order to comply with the General Data Protection Regulation (GDPR). We showcase this procedure with a customer relationship management (CRM) dataset provided by a telecommunications provider. Finally, we recount the challenges we identified during the definition of this procedure and by putting existing knowledge and tools into practice.

Keywords: Anonymisation · De-anonymisation · Data sharing · GDPR

1 Introduction

Personal data contains information about individuals and is used for the advancement of many research fields and for fostering innovation in the industry. Trace data being used for the optimisation of public transportation and query logs for improving information search are some of the benefits of collecting and processing personal data. However, such data contains private, sensitive information about individuals whose privacy must be protected. The data controllers carry the responsibility of protecting the privacy of the individuals in their datasets, and

© Springer Nature Switzerland AG 2020
F. Dalpiaz et al. (Eds.): RCIS 2020, LNBIP 385, pp. 515–521, 2020.
https://doi.org/10.1007/978-3-030-50316-1_32

they need to be cautious when collecting, processing, and sharing such datasets, while being able to extract value from them, and complying with regulations.

Simply removing direct identifiers, such as full name and address, is not enough to protect the privacy of the individuals, because of the quasi-identifiers (QIs). QIs are attributes that do not directly identify individuals, but, when combined, could serve as a unique identifier. Research on de-anonymisation has proven that only a few QIs can uniquely identify the majority of individuals in a dataset. For instance, the combination of ZIP code, date of birth, and gender uniquely identifies 87% of the U.S. population [10], and four data points of location and time uniquely identify 95% of the individuals in a trace dataset [2].

In order to counter the risks of de-anonymisation, privacy models that rely on modifying the original values of a dataset have been introduced. The most prevalent of which are k-anonymity [11], l-diversity [8], and differential privacy [3]. Such models define a privacy principle that a dataset needs to conform to, and offer various degrees of privacy represented by parameters. We refer to Ji et. al's survey [6] for a broad and diverse overview on the topics of anonymisation and de-anonymisation.

Conforming to such anonymity models, however, results in the decrease in the utility of the dataset and, therefore, the value one can extract from it; the higher the privacy is, the more distorted the original values are. Before sharing their datasets, data controllers need to reach a decision on how much privacy is enough, while still having a valuable dataset. While there exists literature on quantifying this trade-off [7], this topic remains highly subjective due to the dynamic context of, and the value one intends to extract from data sharing.

The de-anonymisation of an individual is considered a privacy breach and it is subject to legal action against the data controller. Many regulations worldwide have been put in place addressing this issue and, in this paper, we take into consideration the General Data Protection Regulation (GDPR), and the opinions published by the Article 29 Working Party (WP29). Recital 26 of the GDPR and Opinion (Op.) 05/2014 of WP29 call for the data controller becoming aware of the risks of de-anonymisation in their datasets, the effort, in terms of cost, time, and know-how, required for it, its likelihood, and the severity of its consequences. Op. 05/2014 states that this knowledge should be used in deciding the extent to which anonymisation measures are applied and that the *"the optimal solution should be decided on a case-by-case basis"*.

In the context of the Horizon 2020 (H2020) Safe-DEED research project, we need to investigate the de-anonymisation and anonymisation of the use-case data of the project in a data sharing setting, in order to raise privacy "red flags". To do so, we defined a procedure that takes into account the GDPR, raises the awareness of data controllers on the de-anonymisation risks in their datasets and helps them in deciding the appropriate anonymisation measures. While there exist anonymisation guidelines published by the WP29 and other authorities [5], we did not follow any specific one, but we incorporated elements from most of them in our defined procedure.

Table 1. *Assets* table example.

Assets												
Customer ID	Asset ID	Activation Date	Deactivation Date	Asset Status ID	Initiation Channel	Initiation Dealer ID	Portability	Loop Type	Asset Status Reason	Asset Status Reason Descr.	Provider Dest.	Provider Source
U9ECH9	1YTZDN9	25/01/2013	02/04/2019	0	Store	NS Chania	Yes	Active	Termination	Unpaid Bills	HOL	OTE
B6CCF1	ZZANCX4	17/12/2013	-	1	Store	NS Irakleio	Yes	Active	-	-	-	OTE

Table 2. *Invoices* and *Support Requests (SRs)* tables examples

Invoices				Support Requests (SRs)	
Month	AssetID	Revenue Type	Revenue	Contact Type	Contacts
10/2014	1YTZDN9	Monthly Fee	20.08	Technical Problems Internet	3
10/2014	1YTZDN9	Usage International	4.36	Technical Problems TV	1

In Sect. 2 we describe the use-case dataset of Safe-DEED, and in Sect. 3 we present the aforementioned procedure and describe how we applied it on the provided dataset. In Sect. 4 we recount the challenges we identified during the definition and execution of this procedure. We conclude the paper in Sect. 5.

2   Use-Case Dataset

Forthnet (FNET) is a Greek telecom provider that offers telephony, internet and TV services. Through their participation in Safe-DEED, FNET applied all the necessary GDPR processes and provided an anonymised customer relationship management (CRM) dataset, that did not contain any direct identifiers of individuals, for a limited time (May 6–10, 2019) on their premises, allowing us to apply the procedure described in Sect. 3. The provided dataset consisted of 3 data tables (Tables 1 and 2): *assets*, *invoices*, and *support requests (SRs)*.

The table *assets* contains information about FNET's customers contracts, whether active or not. The table contains, among other attributes, the activation and deactivation date of a contract and an identifier of the initiator which, also, contains information on the customer's city of residence. *Assets* contains 11 QIs - all attributes except *Customer ID* and *Asset ID*. The table *invoices* contains the monthly invoices FNET sends out to its customers for offering their services, i.e. the revenue FNET generates per month per contract. The provided subset consisted of all the invoices sent out between October 2018 and March 2019, resulting in a total of 48 QIs (6 months x 8 revenue types). The table *SRs* contains the support requests customers have made to FNET regarding their contracts. The provided subset consisted of all the SRs made between October 2018 and April 2019, resulting in a total of 91 QIs (7 months x 13 SRs types).

FNET provided ∼1.25 million lines of the table assets, out of which ∼570k had at least one invoice and ∼480k had at least one SR. The merging of the 3 tables resulted in a sparse 150-dimensional dataset.

3   The (De-)Anonymisation Procedure

In this section, we present the procedure we defined in order to investigate the (de-)anonymisation of datasets and we describe how we applied it on the provided CRM dataset. The procedure consists of 3 steps: data landscape analysis, threat analysis, and anonymisation measures.

3.1   Data Landscape Analysis

In this step, the data controllers become aware of the de-anonymisation risks in their dataset, the effort, in terms of time, costs, and know-how required for a de-anonymisation, and they get to know how an attacker would de-anonymise individuals in their dataset. This step consists of manual work and includes:

1) **Gathering external information:** The data controller needs to spend time looking for sources of information that could be matched to the information contained in their dataset. The search for personal information indicates the effort an attacker would have to make to acquire enough information for a de-anonymisation. The costs of de-anonymising individuals are indicated in the case where private information, that could de-anonymise individuals, may be purchased from companies or data brokers. The most prominent sources of publicly available information, where individuals share many potential QIs, are social media platforms, such as Facebook, and forums, such as Quora.

2) **Processing the data:** After gathering as much information as possible, data controllers need to know how this information could be matched to their datasets. More specifically, they need to become aware of the know-how required in order to process their dataset in a way that would de-anonymise individuals with the acquired information. The processing could be as simple as importing a file into a database, or it could require complex methods in order to extract further information from the dataset (e.g. sentiment analysis for product reviews).

For FNET's dataset, we searched for personal information on FNET's Facebook and Twitter feeds, Youtube channel and a tech forum where FNET's customers ask for support and FNET provides it. In this step, FNET became aware of the information their customers publicly reveal, and the effort required to process their dataset and match the gathered information to their dataset.

3.2   Threat Analysis

In this step, data controllers become aware of the likelihood of de-anonymisation by an attacker that already possesses enough information for a de-anonymisation. This step is carried out with the help of tools that analyse the de-anonymisation risks of a dataset from a statistical point of view. The state-of-the-art anonymisation tool ARX [9] contains such risk analysis modules, and to meet one of the requirements of Safe-DEED, i.e. the potential future integration of (de-)anonymisation tools in a data market platform, we developed a risk analysis tool[1], which we also applied on FNET's dataset. Such tools reveal the extent to which a dataset is de-anonymisable and the QIs that are critical in de-anonymisation.

3.3 Anonymisation Measures

After becoming aware of the de-anonymisation risks and judging the severity of a de-anonymisation in their dataset, data controllers need to take the appropriate anonymisation measures. Data controllers should follow anonymisation guidelines published by authorities (e.g. [5]) to decide the appropriate anonymisation measures for their dataset in order to protect the privacy of the individuals.

Additionally, the data controllers are helped by the output of the previous two steps in deciding the extent to which the anonymisation measures should be applied; the degree of privacy their dataset conforms to, while still being useful. For instance, if, through *data landscape analysis*, the data controller finds that information about certain QIs can be easily acquired, then they might consider not releasing them or distorting them more than the rest of the QIs.

After studying anonymisation guidelines and literature, we had to decide which anonymisation measures should be taken for FNET's dataset. Since we investigate data sharing in a setting where a dataset is handed over to a recipient, giving them complete control of the dataset, and since the dataset does not contain any sensitive attributes, conforming to k-anonymity is a good enough measure to mitigate the de-anonymisation risks. In order to achieve as less loss of information as possible, we decided to use local recoding as a transformation method, through generalisation and suppression.

For k-anonymising FNET's dataset, we used ARX [9] which, among others, offers local recoding k-anonymity. However, its latest version (3.7.1), at the time of the given access to FNET's dataset, could not handle the complete dataset due to its high dimensionality (150 dimensions). Therefore, we decided to k-anonymise the *assets* table for k∈[2,10], and generate aggregate information of the tables *invoices* and *SRs*: sum of revenue per type of revenue per contract, and sum of requests per type of request per contract, respectively.

4 Challenges

During the definition of the procedure in Sect. 3 and by putting existing knowledge and tools into practice, we identified the following challenges.

Lack of Awareness on (De-)anonymisation: In general, laypeople are not aware of the risks of de-anonymisation, and anonymity is viewed as simply removing the direct identifiers. The same situation, unfortunately, exists in the industry as well, as reported by popular news media[2].

---

[1] https://github.com/alex-bampoulidis/safe-deed-risk-analysis.
[2] https://www.nytimes.com/2019/07/23/health/data-privacy-protection.html.

Lack of Detailed Guidelines: Privacy in data sharing is a complex issue and it should be studied in more detail and have a broader coverage in the regulations and guidelines. Even though WP29 and other authorities provide such guidelines, more details should be provided on anonymising datasets case-by-case and, especially, on the balance between privacy and utility.

Lack of Open-Source Tools for Complex Data: As mentioned in Sect. 3.3, we could not k-anonymise the complete FNET dataset due to its high-dimensionality. The scientific literature on anonymisation [6] consists of many methods that could anonymise high-dimensional datasets whose source code, however, is not open-source or not available. For example, Ghinita et. al's [4] method could be adapted to FNET's dataset and be used to anonymise it with an acceptable information loss, but its source code is not available.

5   Conclusion

In this paper, we presented the procedure we defined taking into consideration the GDPR, and which a data controller should follow before selling, releasing, or exchanging their datasets, and showcased this procedure on a CRM dataset. While defining and applying this procedure, we identified certain challenges which may be faced by: 1) authorities and news media promoting awareness on the dangers of de-anonymisation and appropriate anonymisation measures, 2) authorities providing more detailed guidelines on anonymising datasets, and 3) researchers and developers reproducing existing anonymisation methods and developing them as open-source tools.

We are going to revisit this procedure in the context of the H2020 TRUSTS project, apply it on its use-case datasets, and use PrioPrivacy [1], the anonymisation tool we developed, inspired by applying this procedure on FNET's data, and which is capable of outperforming ARX.

Acknowledgments. The authors are partially supported by the H2020 projects Safe-DEED (GA 825225) and TRUSTS (GA 871481), funded by the EC.

References

1. Bampoulidis, A., Markopoulos, I., Lupu, M.: Prioprivacy: a local recoding k-anonymity tool for prioritised quasi-identifiers. In: WI (Companion) (2019)
2. De Montjoye, Y.A., Hidalgo, C.A., Verleysen, M., Blondel, V.D.: Unique in the crowd: the privacy bounds of human mobility. Sci. Rep. **3**, 1376 (2013)
3. Dwork, C.: Differential privacy: a survey of results. In: Agrawal, M., Du, D., Duan, Z., Li, A. (eds.) TAMC 2008. LNCS, vol. 4978, pp. 1–19. Springer, Heidelberg (2008). https://doi.org/10.1007/978-3-540-79228-4_1
4. Ghinita, G., Tao, Y., Kalnis, P.: On the anonymization of sparse high-dimensional data. In: IEEE ICDE (2008)
5. Graham, C.: Anonymisation: Managing Data Protection Risk Code of Practice. Information Commissioner's Office (2012)

6. Ji, S., Mittal, P., Beyah, R.: Graph data anonymization, de-anonymization attacks, and de-anonymizability quantification: a survey. IEEE ComST **19**(2), 1305–1326 (2016)
7. Li, T., Li, N.: On the tradeoff between privacy and utility in data publishing. In: ACM SIGKDD (2009)
8. Machanavajjhala, A., Kifer, D., Gehrke, J., Venkitasubramaniam, M.: L-diversity: privacy beyond k-anondymity. ACM TKDD **1**, 3-es (2007)
9. Prasser, F., Kohlmayer, F.: Putting statistical disclosure control into practice: the ARX data anonymization tool. In: Gkoulalas-Divanis, A., Loukides, G. (eds.) Medical Data Privacy Handbook, pp. 111–148. Springer, Cham (2015). https://doi.org/10.1007/978-3-319-23633-9_6
10. Sweeney, L.: Simple Demographics Often Identify People Uniquely (2000)
11. Sweeney, L.: k-anonymity: a model for protecting privacy. Int. J. Uncertainty Fuzziness Knowl. Based Syst. **10**(05), 571–588 (2002)

A Study of Text Summarization Techniques for Generating Meeting Minutes

Tu My Doan, Francois Jacquenet[✉], Christine Largeron, and Marc Bernard

Univ Lyon, UJM-Saint-Etienne, CNRS, Institut d'Optique Graduate School,
Laboratoire Hubert Curien UMR 5516, 42023 Saint-Etienne, France
{Francois.Jacquenet,Christine.Largeron,
Marc.Bernard}@univ-st-etienne.fr

Abstract. A lot of research has been conducted all over the world in the domain of automatic text summarization and more specifically using machine learning techniques. Many state of the art prototypes partially solve this problem so we decided to use some of them to build a tool for automatic generation of meeting minutes. In fact, this was not an easy work and this paper presents various experiments that we did using Deep Learning, GANs and Transformers to achieve this goal as well as dead ends we have encountered during this study. We think providing such a feedback may be useful to other researchers who would like to undertake the same type of work to allow them to know where to go and where not to go.

Keywords: Text summarization · Text generation · GAN · Deep learning · Meeting summarization

1 Introduction

According to a Microsoft survey[1], employees globally spend an average of 5.6 hours a week in meetings and, one of the most sensitive and unpleasant things to do in a meeting is probably to write its minutes. However, in any organization, writing meeting minutes is essential for the life of project teams in order to keep track of what was said throughout the projects, the decisions made, the tasks performed, etc. Generating meeting minutes is within the scope of text summarization [8,11,15], a subfield of natural language processing. Two main approaches can be distinguished: *extractive summarization* and *abstractive summarization*. In the first approach, the main idea is to extract the top-k sentences of an input text, that is, the most important ones, and merge them to produce the summary as an output. In the second approach, the ultimate goal is

---

This work has been carried out as part of the REUS project funded under the FUI 22 by BPI France, the Auvergne Rhône-Alpes Region and the Grenoble metropolitan area, with the support of the competitiveness clusters Minalogic, Cap Digital and TES.
[1] https://tinyurl.com/yx2bz6pv.

F. Dalpiaz et al. (Eds.): RCIS 2020, LNBIP 385, pp. 522–528, 2020.
https://doi.org/10.1007/978-3-030-50316-1_33

to understand the meaning of the most important ideas developped in the input text and then produce, as an output, the summary of those ideas using words or sentences that may not be in the input text.

Obviously, abstractive summarization is far more difficult than extractive summarization. Nevertheless, the latter approach doesn't fit the task of summarizing meetings. Indeed, meetings are made up of dialogues, especially follow-up project meetings that we want to address. Therefore, the structure of a meeting is very different from the structure of normal texts and this can be a difficult problem. The issue with a dialogue is that an extractive method just copies parts of the input text without understanding the important underlying relationships between them and thus the underlying meaning of the whole conversation. This is why we focus on abstractive summarization techniques and the reader interested in a detailed survey on that domain can refer to [6]. Thus, the aim of this paper is twofold. Firstly, it presents experiments we did to design a tool for generating automatically the minutes of meetings. Secondly, it describes the dead ends encountered to solve this issue.

2 Supervised Deep Learning Approaches

2.1 Using the Bottom-Up Abstractive Summarization System

In the context of our study of text summarization techniques for meeting minutes generation, we decided to use the Bottom-up Abstractive Summarization prototype presented by Gehrmann et al. in [3]. It combines extractive and abstractive summarization techniques. In a first part, the system is trained to learn an extractive summarizer that is used to extract the most significant parts of the text. In a second part, the system uses the selected parts of the text to build an abstractive summary. It integrates the most advanced techniques of the moment (seq2seq, attention, pointer-generator, language models, etc.) and can be considered as an improved version of the system presented by See et al. in [16].

There are many parameters to tune for the training step[2] to efficiently run the prototype. We followed the authors' recommendations and used a 128-dimensional word-embedding, and 512-dimensional one layer LSTM. On the encoder side, as the prototype uses a bidirectional LSTM, the 512 dimensions were split into 256 dimensions per direction. The maximum norm of the gradient was set to 2, and a renormalization was done if the gradient norm exceeded this value and there was no dropout.

To apply this supervised approach, we need as an input some pairs of texts with their associated summaries. Various datasets have been used in that context such as the DUC dataset [14], the Gigaword dataset [13] or the CNN/Daily Mail dataset [7,12] to cite the most famous ones but for meeting summarization, there exists only one dataset called the AMI dataset [1]. It is made up of 142 written transcriptions of meetings with their associated abstractive summaries

---

[2] More details can be found here: http://opennmt.net/OpenNMT-py/Summarization.html.

written by humans. Those meetings are real meetings that were held as role-playing games, each of them having an approximate average duration of one hour. We mainly carried out three experiments, the results of which are presented in Table 1 in terms of the ROUGE measure [9]. First we trained the system on 80% of the AMI dataset and tested it on the remaining 20% (first column). Second we trained the system on CNN/DM and tested it AMI (second column). Finally we trained the system on a part of CNN/DM and tested it on this dataset (third column) to confirm the results presented in [3].

Table 1. Performance of the system trained and tested on the AMI and CNN/DM datasets

Metric	AMI AMI	CNN/DM AMI	CNN/DM CNN/DM
ROUGE-1 Recall	0.21788	0.03991	0.43652
ROUGE-1 Precision	0.69117	0.23391	0.41798
ROUGE-1 F-measure	0.32103	0.06540	0.41323
ROUGE-2 Recall	0.07578	0.00676	0.19465
ROUGE-2 Precision	0.25072	0.04199	0.18575
ROUGE-2 F-measure	0.11241	0.01145	0.18376
ROUGE-L Recall	0.20664	0.03490	0.40367
ROUGE-L Precision	0.65332	0.20982	0.38710
ROUGE-L F-measure	0.30406	0.05748	0.38239

In the first column we can observe that the precision is quite good at 69.11% but the recall is only equal to 21.78% according to ROUGE-1, this is due to a training step on a really small dataset that does not provide enough vocabulary and an important variety of sentences. This is why we tried to solve this issue by training the system on CNN/DM and the second column of values shows that the results were very poor in terms of recall. In fact, the vocabulary and the style of sentences in CNN/DM have nothing to do with those of the AMI dataset, that explains the fact that the system is not able to generate interesting sentences. The third column confirms that the system has quite good performances (with a F-measure equals to 0.41 compared to 0.065 or 0.32 obtained previously) when trained on CNN/DM and tested on CNN/DM the most popular dataset for text summarization research that is quite large.

2.2   Enlarging the Dataset

Based on those unsatisfying results, we then thought it was necessary to find a way to increase the size of the AMI dataset. Thus, we first investigated the GAN approach [4] and more specifically the LeakGAN [5] system which is the state of the art in the domain of GANs for generating texts. Unfortunately, LeakGAN performed badly on the AMI dataset. Thus, we decided to explore another approach consisting of paraphrasing texts. Unfortunately, to build a model for paraphrasing, we need a dataset composed of pairs *(source/target)* where *source* is an original sentence and *target* is a paraphrase, but AMI was not designed for that purpose. To tackle the above problem, we decided to use the ParaNMT-50M dataset [17] to train a model that can paraphrase any sentence into another semantically similar sentence. By using this model on the AMI dataset we have been able to generate new meetings similar to the ones of the AMI dataset.

Table 2 shows a comparison of the ROUGE score of the abstractive bottom-up summarization model built on the AMI dataset and on the AMI + paraphrased AMI dataset.

Table 2. ROUGE scores of the Bottom-up model learned on AMI (col. 2) or AMI+ParaAMI (col. 3) datasets and BertSUM (col. 4)

Metric	AMI	AMI+ParaAMI	BertSUM
ROUGE-1 Recall	0.21788	**0.30832**	0.32509
ROUGE-1 Precision	0.69117	0.49864	0.48588
ROUGE-1 F-measure	0.32103	**0.37215**	0.37622
ROUGE-2 Recall	0.07578	**0.08704**	0.09100
ROUGE-2 Precision	0.25072	0.13995	0.13852
ROUGE-2 F-measure	0.11241	0.10463	0.10684
ROUGE-L Recall	0.20664	**0.28506**	0.29171
ROUGE-L Precision	0.65332	0.46423	0.44001
ROUGE-L F-measure	0.30406	**0.34554**	0.33987

It can be easily seen that there are some significant improvements in terms of recall but obviously the precision decreases. Nevertheless, if we consider the F-measure, we can observe a very significant improvement of this one for ROUGE-1 and ROUGE-L.

2.3 Using Transformers

As text summarization has been recently addressed with models based on transformers such as BERT [2] or an extended version, BertSUM [10] able to generate abstractive text summaries, we decided to use this last one in the context of meeting minutes generation.

As for the use of Bottom-up, we used the AMI+ParaAMI dataset split into training, validation and test sets as previously. Table 2 Column 2 shows the results we obtained on this dataset with BertSUM and we can see that the results obtained with BertSUM are quite similar to those obtained with Bottom-up which is a little bit disappointing given the promises about transformers in the literature.

In fact, as all meetings of the AMI+ParaAMI dataset are very long, we thought that it was difficult for BertSUM (as well as for Bottom-up) to capture the entire content of each meeting. To overcome this problem and try to improve the results provided by BertSUM, we decided to preprocess each meeting of the AMI+paraAMI dataset to select the more relevant sentences given its associated summary. So first, we split each meeting in the training set of AMI+paraAMI into sentences, tokenized them and learned their representation vector using the BERT model. For each meeting summary, we also learned a representation vector using BERT. Then, for each meeting of the training set, we compared the representation vector of each sentence with the representation vector of its associated summary using the cosine similarity measure. Finally, we kept any sentence that had a cosine similarity value greater than a given threshold. After this preprocessing, we ran the BertSUM system on these new training sets. Table 3 presents the results obtained with AMI and ParaAMI preprocessed with the most significant values of the threshold, that is 0.7, 0.75 and 0.8. The column labelled BertSUM recalls the results of BertSUM applied on the AMI+ParaAMI dataset without any preprocessing while the three columns on its right show the results of BertSUM applied on the AMI+ParaAMI dataset after the preprocessing step where the threshold has been fixed respectively to 0.7, 0.75 and 0.8.

Table 3. ROUGE scores for the BertSUM and improved BertSUM models, trained and tested on AMI+ParaAMI

Metric/Model	BertSUM	BertSUM (0.7)	BertSUM (0.75)	BertSUM (0.8)
ROUGE-1 Average_R	0.32509	0.30876	**0.35090**	0.32499
ROUGE-1 Average_P	0.48588	**0.51284**	0.50482	0.50407
ROUGE-1 Average_F	0.37622	0.37579	**0.40448**	0.38385
ROUGE-2 Average_R	0.09100	0.09331	**0.10237**	0.09682
ROUGE-2 Average_P	0.13852	**0.15712**	0.14665	0.14280
ROUGE-2 Average_F	0.10684	0.11425	**0.11737**	0.11081
ROUGE-L Average_R	0.29171	0.27736	**0.31751**	0.29574
ROUGE-L Average_P	0.44001	**0.46260**	0.45962	0.45628
ROUGE-L Average_F	0.33987	0.33801	**0.36729**	0.34840

As we can see, the best values in terms of the recall and F1 ROUGE measures are obtained with a threshold equals to 0.75. In that context, the BertSUM system obtains a value of F1 measure improved by 10% compared to the results obtained without any preprocessing of the AMI+ParaAMI dataset (0.40448 versus 0.37622 for ROUGE-1 for example). Moreover, when we read the content of the summaries that are generated, we can observe that the information provided is more accurate and the sentences are more grammatically correct.

3   Conclusion

A tool that can generate meeting minutes would be invaluable to companies today because of the importance of meetings in their daily lives and the human cost that this task can have if done carefully. This is why we tried to build such a tool using state of the art technologies. We hope we have convinced the reader that the task is not easy but we have provided guidance on what kind of approach can work and what kind of limitations such state of the art tools may have. We think it is clear that this research field still needs a great amount of work before we can provide an operational tool.

References

1. Carletta, J., et al.: The AMI meeting corpus: a pre-announcement. In: Renals, S., Bengio, S. (eds.) MLMI 2005. LNCS, vol. 3869, pp. 28–39. Springer, Heidelberg (2006). https://doi.org/10.1007/11677482_3
2. Devlin, J., Chang, M., Lee, K., Toutanova, K.: BERT: pre-training of deep bidirectional transformers for language understanding. In: Proceedings of the Conference of the North American Chapter of the Association for Computational Linguistics: Human Language Technologies, pp. 4171–4186 (2019)
3. Gehrmann, S., Deng, Y., Rush, A.M.: Bottom-up abstractive summarization. In: Proceedings of the Conference on Empirical Methods in Natural, pp. 4098–4109 (2018)
4. Goodfellow, I.J., et al.: Generative adversarial nets. In: Proceedings of the Conference on Neural Information Processing Systems, pp. 2672–2680 (2014)
5. Guo, J., Lu, S., Cai, H., Zhang, W., Yu, Y., Wang, J.: Long text generation via adversarial training with leaked information. In: Proceedings of the Thirty-Second AAAI Conference on Artificial Intelligence, pp. 5141–5148. AAAI Press (2018)
6. Gupta, S., Gupta, S.K.: Abstractive summarization: an overview of the state of the art. Expert Syst. Appl. **121**, 49–65 (2019)
7. Hermann, K.M., et al.: Teaching machines to read and comprehend. In: Proceedings of the Conference on Neural Information Processing Systems, pp. 1693–1701 (2015)
8. Jones, K.S.: Automatic summarising: the state of the art. Inf. Process. Manag. **43**(6), 1449–1481 (2007)
9. Lin, C., Hovy, E.H.: Automatic evaluation of summaries using N-gram co-occurrence statistics. In: Proceedings of the Conference of the North American Chapter of the Association for Computational Linguistics: Human Language Technologies, pp. 150–157. ACL (2003)
10. Liu, Y., Lapata, M.: Text summarization with pretrained encoders. In: Proceedings of the Conference on Empirical Methods in Natural, pp. 3728–3738 (2019)
11. Lloret, E., Palomar, M.: Text summarisation in progress: a literature review. Artif. Intell. Rev. **37**(1), 1–41 (2012)
12. Nallapati, R., Zhou, B., dos Santos, C.N., Gülçehre, Ç., Xiang, B.: Abstractive text summarization using sequence-to-sequence RNNs and beyond. In: Proceedings of the Conference on Computational Natural Language Learning, pp. 280–290 (2016)
13. Napoles, C., Gormley, M.R., Durme, B.V.: Annotated Gigaword. In: Workshop Automatic Knowledge Base Construction and Web-scale Knowledge Extraction, pp. 95–100 (2012)

14. Over, P., Dang, H., Harman, D.: DUC in context. Inf. Process. Manag. **43**(6), 1506–1520 (2007)
15. Saggion, H., Poibeau, T.: Automatic text summarization: past, present and future. In: Poibeau, T., Saggion, H., Piskorski, J., Yangarber, R. (eds.) Multi-source, Multilingual Information Extraction and Summarization, pp. 3–21. Springer, Heidelberg (2013). https://doi.org/10.1007/978-3-642-28569-1_1
16. See, A., Liu, P., Manning, C.: Get to the point: summarization with pointer-generator networks. In: Proceedings of the 55th Annual Meeting of the Association for Computational Linguistics, pp. 1073–1083 (2017)
17. Wieting, J., Gimpel, K.: ParaNMT-50M: pushing the limits of paraphrastic sentence embeddings with millions of machine translations. In: Proceedings of the 56th Annual Meeting of the Association for Computational Linguistics, pp. 451–462 (2018)

CCOnto: Towards an Ontology-Based Model for Character Computing

Alia El Bolock[1,2(✉)], Cornelia Herbert[2], and Slim Abdennadher[1]

[1] German University in Cairo, Cairo, Egypt
{alia.elbolock,slim.abdennadher}@guc.edu.eg
[2] Ulm University, Ulm, Germany
cornelia.herbert@uni-ulm.de

Abstract. Our lives are rewritten by technology and data, making it crucial for machines to understand humans and their behavior and react accordingly. Technology systems could adapt to different factors such as affect (Affective Computing), personality (Personality Computing), or character (Character Computing). Character consists of personality, affect, socio-cultural embedding, cognitive abilities, health, and all other attributes distinguishing one individual from another. Ontology-based conceptual models representing individuals i.e. their character and resulting behavior in situations is needed for providing a unified framework for building truly interactive and adaptive systems. We propose CCOnto, an ontology for Character Computing that models human character. The ontology is to be used for adaptive interactive systems to understand and predict an individual's behavior in a given situation, more specifically their performance in different tasks. The developed ontology models the different character attributes, their building blocks, and interactions with each other and with a person's performance in different tasks.

Keywords: Character Computing · Ontology · Personality · Affect

1 Introduction

Nowadays, where technology and data are an integral part of our lives, it is necessary for machines to understand humans to predict and adapt to their behavior more now than ever. Accordingly, frameworks for developing adaptive systems are in high demand. Many approaches for adapting to affect and personality already exist. While Affective Computing [16] and Personality Computing [19] focus on affect and personality, respectively, Character Computing [8,10,12,13] advocates that affect and personality alone are not enough to capture the essence of a person and their behavior. Modeling affect and personality on their own is a complex task. However, adding other factors to it (e.g. culture, health) as well as distinguishing between different situations, makes it exponentially more complex. Developing conceptual models, i.e. ontologies, is one often used approach for representing and modeling such a complex interaction. Several approaches

© Springer Nature Switzerland AG 2020
F. Dalpiaz et al. (Eds.): RCIS 2020, LNBIP 385, pp. 529–535, 2020.
https://doi.org/10.1007/978-3-030-50316-1_34

have been proposed for using ontologies in similar endeavors related to human personality, emotions, and behavior. For example, EmOCA, an emotion ontology can be used to reason about philia and phobia based on emotion expression in a context-aware manner [5]. EmotionsOnto is another emotions ontology for developing affective applications and detecting emotions [3]. In [2], an ontology of psychological user profiles (mainly personality traits and facets) is presented. LifeOn is an "ubiquitous lifelong learner model ontology" (with a highlight on learner personality) for adaptive learning systems [15]. An ontology for insider threat risk detection and mitigation through individual (personality, affect, ideology and other similar attributes) and organizational sociotechnical factors is presented in [14]. For different extensive overviews of ontologies related to human behavior and affective states refer to [1,6]. An ontology of human character is necessary to enable machines to understand people and people to understand themselves and each other. It also provides a unified foundation for building adaptive systems that interact with users, moving persons further to the center of computing. The character is the individual person with all his/her defining or describing features, such as stable personality traits, variable affective, cognitive and motivational states, history, morals, beliefs, skills, appearance, and socio-cultural embeddings. However, the character cannot be understood alone but rather has to be investigated through its effect on behavior in a given situation (denoted the Character-Behavior-Situation (CBS) triad [9]). The developed ontology, CCOnto, serves as a formal foundation for understanding and sharing knowledge about human character and its interactions. It is also a unified, reusable knowledge base which can be leveraged in building various adaptive or interactive systems within the framework of Character Computing (see [11]). The ontology model is based on the behavior of a specific individual in a given situation. Currently, the situation is constrained to performing specific tasks and the behavior is measured as the score or the performance within these tasks.

2   CCOnto Model

The model of CCOnto distinguishes between three main concepts: situation, behavior, and character. As discussed above, for the purpose of this paper, we only consider the performance (behavior) of an individual within a specific task (situation), measured by a score. The person is the central concept of the ontology relating all the others together. One can think of it in terms of a person with character x performing task y (situation) and has score z (behavior). The x in turn consists of many components $x_1, x_2, ..., x_n$ representing the personality, affect, emotion, culture, etc. Based on the different character attributes, persons can be further categorized into different subsets, as will be discussed below. The character attributes can be divided into two sets of groups: stable traits and variable states. Most of the states have trait counterparts e.g. affect (trait) and emotions (state) or general and current health. We represent these attributes through the same concepts (classes) and only distinguish between them through different properties (representing the stable and variable counterparts). We focus on the more commonly represented components to be able to compare the results to other work and evaluate CCOnto. As such, the top-level concepts for these character attributes are added into the ontology without going into their representation details. The most relevant character traits and states that are extensively represented in the CCOnto ontology are personality traits, affect, and emotions. Initial steps to support cognitive capabilities, socio-economic standard, and culture are also taken. CCOnto distinguishes between person "types" based on certain character components which eases querying the ontology and applying rules to it which is needed for any application. Distinguishing persons based on personality traits (e.g., extrovert, introvert or energetic, laidback) is taken from the Personality Insights project by IBM. We also distinguish between individuals based on culture and age. The ontology is developed in a modular manner, enabling the addition of any further models representing the existing character attributes or adding new ones. The ontology design is based on common ontology development practices and makes use of already existing ontologies: the ontology of psychological terms [4] and the EmOCA ontology [5].

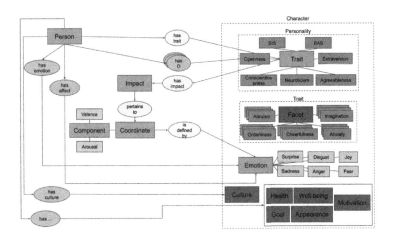

Fig. 1. An overview of character. The entities integrated from EmOCA are depicted in a different color. The dotted boxes represent components making up the header concept. Not all entities of character are represented due to space constraints.

3   CCOnto Implementation

The main purpose of this work is to provide a generic model ontology of character for developing applications that can model and adapt to a person's character when performing a specific task. The classes, and the properties between them, are derived based on our Character Computing model developed by the team of computer scientists and psychologists based on the research literature. The ontology is implemented using Protégé 5.2.0 and OWL 2. One main advantage

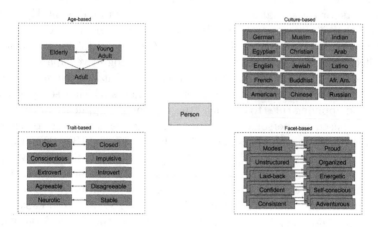

Fig. 2. An overview of the different human categories based on their character attributes. The categorization is based on personality traits, facets, culture, and age.

Table 1. A fragment of the classes representing traits, facets, emotions and tasks. Due to space constraints some subclasses/individuals were not included.

Class	Subclasses - Individuals
Trait	Openness - highOpenness, lowOpenness
	Conscientiousness - highConscientiousness, lowConscientiousness
	Extraversion - highExtraversion, lowExtraversion
	Agreeableness - highAgreeableness, lowAgreeableness
	Neuroticisms - highNeuroticisms, lowNeuroticisms
Facet	Imagination - highImagination, lowImagination
	Emotionality - highEmotionality, lowEmotionality
	Adventurousness - highAdventurousness, lowAdventurousness
	ArtisticInterests - highArtisticInterests, lowArtisticInterests
	Intellect - highIntellect, lowIntellect
	Liberalism - highLiberalism, lowLiberalism
Emotion	Anger, Disgust, Fear, Happiness, Sadness, Surprise (same naming for classes and individuals, for different modeling purposes)
Task	GfTask - Form Boards, Paper folding, Spatial Relations, Letter Sets, ..
	GcTask - WJ Picture Vocab, WAIS Vocab, Antonym Vocab, ..
	MemoryTask - Logical Memory, Paired Associations, Free Recall
	SpeedTask - Digit Symbol, Pattern Comparison, Letter Comparison

of using ontologies is ontology reuse. Of special relevance was the EmOCA ontology [5] from which the classes Person, Trait, Impact and Emotion were taken as a basis for modeling the interaction between the abstract version of persons with traits and emotions. Figure 1 shows EmOCA's main classes and how they were extended and embedded into the CCOnto ontology. The classes were integrated into the character hierarchy by specifying the emotion as part of the character and the trait as a super concept of the different personality traits available in the included models. All concepts that are already available in the APA Psychology Terms [4] ontology were reused to ensure inter-operability. Table 1 details the constructs that make up character, personality and emotion/affect, respectively. The categorization of the different implemented task types is integrated from [18]. To represent the score of every individual in a specific task i.e. the tertiary relationship between person, task and score, the class `TaskScore` is added. The different types of persons are shown in Fig. 2. We define which classes are disjoint with each other e.g., `Introvert` and `Extrovert`, which is necessary when querying or reasoning on the ontology. The relationships and interactions between the character attributes are represented through properties. All main relations related to character are shown in Fig. 1. `has impact`, `pertains to`, `is defined by` and `has trait` have been integrated from the EmOCA ontology. The behavior of the first three properties is the same as in the original ontology, which serves to represent emotions as they result from stimuli and are impacted by the personality traits of the Five Factor Model (FFM) [7]. To differentiate between stable trait-like emotions i.e. affect and variable state-like emotions we have the `hasAffect` and `hasEmotion` which both map a person to an emotion (either discrete or continuous). The `has trait` property has seven sub-classes representing the currently implemented traits (five from the FFM and two from the BIS/BAS [17]). The individual trait properties also indicate personality facets by mapping a person to the individuals of type facet (e.g. `x hasExtraversion ''highCheerfullness''`). Other important properties are the `belongsTo` and `ofTask` which map a TaskScore to a person and a task respectively and the Task's data property `hasScore` which maps it to a score (`xsd:int`). Additionally, a person has `hasCulture` and `hasAge` properties mapping to (one or many) `Culture` individual(s) and an age (`xsd:int`).

4   Conclusions and Future Work

We presented an ontology of character from the perspective of Character Computing. The main focus of the ontology was modeling personality and affect, alongside other character components and their relation to a person's performance in a specific task. The ontology is to be used for developing character-aware adaptive applications. The developed ontology can then be integrated into and extended for the purposes of any application that puts the individual at the center by considering different characteristics and their impact on the person's behavior. More models representing the included and remaining character attributes can still be added to CCOnto. Character-specific visualization and editing capabilities need to be added to facilitate the use by domain experts. The ontology should be applied to multiple adaptive and predictive applications and use-cases (validated by both Computer Scientists and Psychologists). This would enable us to evaluate the model and extend it accordingly.

References

1. Abaalkhail, R., Guthier, B., Alharthi, R., El Saddik, A.: Survey on ontologies for affective states and their influences. Semant. Web **9**(4), 441–458 (2018)
2. García-Vélez, R., et al.: Creating an ontological networks to support the inference of personality traits and facets. In: 2018 IEEE XXV International Conference on Electronics, Electrical Engineering and Computing (INTERCON), pp. 1–4. IEEE (2018)
3. López Gil, J.M., et al.: EmotionsOnto: an ontology for developing affective applications. J. Univ. Comput. Sci. **13**(20), 1813–1828 (2014)
4. Walker, A., Garcia, A., Galloway, I.: Psychology ontology. BioPortal (2014). https://bioportal.bioontology.org/ontologies/APAONTO
5. Berthelon, F., Sander, P.: Emotion ontology for context awareness. In: 4th International Conference on Cognitive Infocommunications (CogInfoCom), pp. 59–64. IEEE (2013)
6. Norris, E., Finnerty, A.N., Hastings, J., Stokes, G., Michie, S.: A scoping review of ontologies related to human behaviour change. Nat. Hum. Behav. **3**(2), 164–172 (2019)
7. Costa Jr, P.T., McCrae, R.R.: The Revised NEO Personality Inventory (NEO-PI-R). Sage Publications, Inc. (2008)
8. El Bolock, A.: Defining character computing from the perspective of computer science and psychology. In: Proceedings of the 17th International Conference on Mobile and Ubiquitous Multimedia, pp. 567–572. ACM (2018)
9. El Bolock, A.: What is character computing? In: El Bolock, A., Abdelrahman, Y., Abdennadher, S. (eds.) Character Computing. HIS, pp. 1–16. Springer, Cham (2020). https://doi.org/10.1007/978-3-030-15954-2_1
10. Bolock, A., Abdelrahman, Y., Abdennadher, S.: Character computing. In: Human–Computer Interaction Series. Springer International Publishing (2020)
11. El Bolock, A., Abdennadher, S., Herbert, C.: Applications of character computing from psychology to computer science. In: El Bolock, A., Abdelrahman, Y., Abdennadher, S. (eds.) Character Computing. HIS, pp. 53–71. Springer, Cham (2020). https://doi.org/10.1007/978-3-030-15954-2_4
12. El Bolock, A., Salah, J., Abdelrahman, Y., Herbert, C., Abdennadher, S.: Character computing: computer science meets psychology. In: 17th International Conference on Mobile and Ubiquitous Multimedia, pp. 557–562. ACM (2018)
13. El Bolock, A., Salah, J., Abdennadher, S., Abdelrahman, Y.: Character computing: challenges and opportunities. In: Proceedings of the 16th International Conference on Mobile and Ubiquitous Multimedia, pp. 555–559. ACM (2017)
14. Greitzer, F.L.: Developing an ontology for individual and organizational sociotechnical indicators of insider threat risk. In: STIDS, pp. 19–27 (2016)
15. Nurjanah, D.: LifeOn, a ubiquitous lifelong learner model ontology supporting adaptive learning. In: 2018 IEEE Global Engineering Education Conference (EDUCON), pp. 866–871. IEEE (2018)

16. Picard, R.W.: Affective computing: challenges. Int. J. Hum.-Comput. Stud. **59**(1–2), 55–64 (2003)
17. Pickering, A., Corr, P.J.: Gray's reinforcement sensitivity theory of personality. In: The SAGE Handbook of Personality Theory and Assessment, vol. 1, pp. 239–257 (2008)
18. Soubelet, A., Salthouse, T.A.: Personality-cognition relations across adulthood. Dev. Psychol. **47**(2), 303 (2011)
19. Vinciarelli, A., Mohammadi, G.: A survey of personality computing. IEEE Trans. Affect. Comput. **5**(3), 273–291 (2014)

A Tool for the Verification of Decision Model and Notation (DMN) Models

Faruk Hasić[1]([☒]), Carl Corea[2], Jonas Blatt[2], Patrick Delfmann[2], and Estefanía Serral[1]

[1] Research Centre for Information Systems Engineering (LIRIS),
KU Leuven, Brussels, Belgium
{faruk.hasic,estefania.serralasensio}@kuleuven.be

[2] Institute for IS Research, University of Koblenz-Landau, Koblenz, Germany
{ccorea,jonasblatt,delfmann}@uni-koblenz.de

Abstract. The Decision Model and Notation (DMN) is a decision modelling standard consisting of two levels: the decision requirement diagram (DRD) level which depicts the dependencies between elements involved in the decision model, and the decision logic level, which specifies the underlying decision logic, usually in the form of decision tables. As the decision tables and DRD are modelled in conjunction, the need to verify the consistency of both levels arises. While there have been some works geared towards the verification of decision tables, the DRD-level has been strongly neglected. In this work, we therefore present a tool for the model verification of DMN models at both the logic and the DRD level, along with the performance assessment of the tool.

Keywords: DMN · Decision model and notation · Tool support · Consistency checking · Automated feedback · Model evolution · Camunda

1 Introduction

The Decision Model and Notation (DMN) [14] has at its the core the business rule decision logic usually modelled by means of decision tables (*decision logic level*). The standard can also provide decision requirement diagrams (*DRD level*), which allow specifying the requirements and relations of decisions involved in the decision model [8,10,11].

While DMN standardizes how to represent decision logic and decision requirements, no means are provided to guide experts in consistently modelling the two levels. In result, modelling errors can easily occur. This can be seen in Fig. 1, which show an inconsistent DMN decision model. First, there are errors within the decision logic, specifically, the income conditions for rules 1 and 2 are overlapping (when the input is exactly 20). Second, the DRD level and the decision table are inconsistent because the *Assets* requirement is missing on the DRD level.

© Springer Nature Switzerland AG 2020
F. Dalpiaz et al. (Eds.): RCIS 2020, LNBIP 385, pp. 536–542, 2020.
https://doi.org/10.1007/978-3-030-50316-1_35

Fig. 1. DMN model: DRD (left) and decision table (right) with modelling errors.

Such modelling errors are a problem currently faced in practice, as proven by interviews with key practitioners who unanimously report problems in verifying the correctness of DMN models [15]. Also, empirical results on detected modelling errors within the decision logic of a large insurance company are presented in [1]. This calls for automated means to support companies in the verification of decision models.

Table 1 shows an overview of existing DMN verification approaches. As can be seen from the DRD level verification capabilities in Table 1, recent research is sparse. In a previous work [7], we presented means to detect a selection of decision logic level verification capabilities as proposed in the business rule management capability framework [15]. In the work at hand, we present novel verification capabilities for the DRD level, as well as some novel decision logic level capabilities derived from [9]. To the best of our knowledge, our tool is the first to provide such an extensive set of verification mechanisms. As can be seen from Table 1, this work extends the verification capabilities of [7] with the following verification capabilities: *unused predefined value verification, missing predefined value verification, missing in-/output value verification, missing in-/output column verification, idle data input data verification, missing input verification, multiple input verification* and *inconsistent type verification*. We will discuss these capabilities in detail in Sect. 2. We refer to the work in [7] for the decision logic level verification capabilities that were part of that work and are also incorporated in the tool presented here.

2   Tool Description and Usage Example

The developed tool relies on the camunda-dmn[1] library and is available for demonstration[2]. The tool allows to upload and analyze DMN models directly in the browser. The tool presented in this work extends the one presented in [7] with the following novel decision logic and DRD level verification capabilities derived from [9]:

---

[1] https://github.com/camunda/camunda-engine-dmn.
[2] https://bit.ly/2OEPEpH.

Table 1. Overview of verification capabilities covered by existing approaches (where X = full support, o = partial support. * = co-authors of this work).

Literature		Decision logic level											DRD level					
		Identical rules	Equivalent rules	Subsumed rules	Indeterminism	Overlapping conditions	Partial reduction	Missing rules	Unused predefined value	Missing predefined value	Missing input value	Missing output value	Missing input column	Missing output column	Idle data input	Missing (data) input	Multiple (data) input	Inconsistent types
Calvanese et al. (2016)	[4]	X	o	X		X		X										
Laurson et al. (2016)	[12]	X		X	o	X	o	X										
Batoulis et al. (2017)	[2]	X		X		X		X										
Calvanese et al. (2017)	[6]	X	o	X	o	X		X										
Ochoa et al. (2017)	[13]										X	X						
Batoulis et al. (2018)	[3]	X		X		X		o										
Calvanese et al. (2018)	[5]	X	o	X	o	X	o	X										
Corea et al. (2019)*	[7]	X	X	X	X	X	X	X										
This work		**X**	**X**	**X**	**X**	**X**	**X**	**X**	**X**	**X**	**X**	**X**	**X**	**X**	**X**	**X**	**X**	**X**

Decision Logic Verification Capabilities (Verification of Decision Logic Within a Decision Table):

- **Missing predefined value verification.** Detecting if there is a value in a rule which is not part of the predefined values.
- **Unused predefined value verification.** Detecting whether there are predefined values for a column, but no rule for that value.
- **Missing input value.** Detecting whether there is an output value of another table (where that table is an input to the table under consideration), but the table does not have a corresponding input value (missing rule).
- **Missing output value.** Detecting whether there is an input value in a table, but the subdecision does not have a corresponding output value (and thus, the current rule would be unreachable).

DRD Level Verification Capabilities (Verification of Interconnection Between Logic Modules, I.e., Between Different Decision Tables in the DRD, as Well as Between Input Data and Decision Tables):

- **Missing input column verification.** Given a decision and a subdecision, detecting whether the subdecision has an output column, but the decision table of the higher-level decision does not have a corresponding input column.
- **Missing output column verification.** Given a decision and a subdecision, detecting whether the higher-level decision has an input column, but the subdecision table does not have a corresponding output column.

- **Idle data input verification.** There is a data input node that is not used.
- **Missing (data) input verification.** There is (data or subdecision) input that is used in a decision, but it is missing in the DRD.
- **Multiple (data) input verification.** For any input column, detecting whether there are too many inputs.
- **Inconsistent type verification.** Given a decision and a subdecision, detecting whether the corresponding columns have the same data type.

Figure 2 provides a usage example of the tool. The user can upload and verify a DMN model (1). Note that modellers can easily switch from the DRD-level to the table level by clicking on an individual table. The tool identifies all errors based on the shown verification capabilities and displays error messages (2). The tool can highlight the errors and allows the user to quickly browse the issues. Next to this issue, the tool suggests actions to remedy the modeling issues and allows the modeller to select one, which is then automatically performed by the tool (3). Additionally, the modeller can then re-verify the resulting model (see checkbox next to (1)). This way, the modeller can incrementally apply actions to restore a consistent model. The tool can be used to verify arbitrary DMN models, but can also be connected to workflow engines such as Camunda. Here, the user can deploy the updated and verified decision model directly from the tool (4).

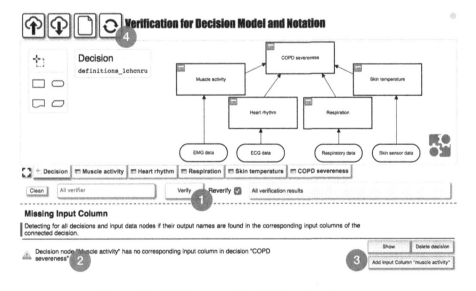

Fig. 2. The DRD view of the DMN verification tool.

3 Maturity and Outlook

For a preliminary evaluation, we performed run-time experiments and analysed a total of 900 synthetic decision models. As parameters for generating these models, our custom generator[3] accepts the number of rows and columns in a single decision table, as well as the number of overall nodes on a DRD level. As the novel DRD level capabilities are the focus of this work, we continue discussing the results for a varying number of DRD level nodes in the model. Please see [7] for further experiments on the decision logic verification capabilities with a varying number of columns and rows.

For the experiments, we selected {*18, 36, ..., 180*} as the number of nodes on the DRD level, and {*10,20, ..., 100*} as the number of rules per table from (i.e., 10 × 10 possible combinations). Note that most models in literature employ less than 20 nodes and at most a few tens of rules per node. For each of the 100 possible combinations of rows and nodes, we generated 9 decision models as follows: on the DRD-level, the decision tables and input nodes were connected at random, which allowed to create synthetic decision models with actual errors such as missing or redundant input data. The respective rules of these tables were generated by using random integer conditions (see [7] for details). The number of columns for each decision table ranged from 2 to 5 at random. Consequently, for each of the 10 × 10 combinations, we applied the verification tool for the 9 respective models and computed the average run-time for each parameter configuration, as shown in Fig. 3. The experiments were run on Ubuntu Xenial with E312 processor and 16GB RAM.

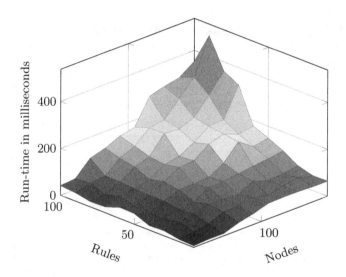

Fig. 3. Run-time statistics for the analyzed synthetic decision models with up to 180 nodes on the DRD-level and 100 rules per table.

As it can be seen in Fig. 3, the run-time for analysing a model with 180 DRD nodes and 100 rules per table averages to roughly 0.4 seconds. Thus, for the analysed data set, our tool allowed for a feasible analysis.

---

[3] An interface to use our generator can be found at https://bit.ly/31q1U2r.

4   Conclusion

The tool presented in this report allows to analyze DMN models both on a logic level and on a DRD level, which is a current issue faced in practice. As shown in Table 1, our work contributes to closing existing research gaps by implementing all depicted verification capabilities in a unified tool. Our tool supports the current DMN standard, allowing companies to perform model verification on their DMN models. Through a direct integration with workflow management systems, our tool can be used for consistent model evolution and thus facilitates sustainable business rule management. In future work, we aim to apply our tool to industrial data sets and to conduct usability studies with practitioners.

Acknowledgements. This work was supported by the DFG (grant DE 1983/9-1) and Internal Funds KU Leuven.

References

1. Batoulis, K., Nesterenko, A., Repitsch, G., Weske, M.: Decision management in the insurance industry: standards and tools. In: BPM (Industry Track), pp. 52–63 (2017)
2. Batoulis, K., Weske, M.: A tool for checking soundness of decision-aware business processes. In: BPM (Demos), pp. 1–5 (2017)
3. Batoulis, K., Weske, M.: Disambiguation of DMN decision tables. In: Abramowicz, W., Paschke, A. (eds.) BIS 2018. LNBIP, vol. 320, pp. 236–249. Springer, Cham (2018). https://doi.org/10.1007/978-3-319-93931-5_17
4. Calvanese, D., Dumas, M., Laurson, Ü., Maggi, F.M., Montali, M., Teinemaa, I.: Semantics and analysis of DMN decision tables. In: La Rosa, M., Loos, P., Pastor, O. (eds.) BPM 2016. LNCS, vol. 9850, pp. 217–233. Springer, Cham (2016). https://doi.org/10.1007/978-3-319-45348-4_13
5. Calvanese, D., Dumas, M., Laurson, Ü., Maggi, F.M., Montali, M., Teinemaa, I.: Semantics, analysis and simplification of DMN decision tables. Inf. Syst. **78**, 112–125 (2018)
6. Calvanese, D., Dumas, M., Maggi, F.M., Montali, M.: Semantic DMN: formalizing decision models with domain knowledge. In: Costantini, S., Franconi, E., Van Woensel, W., Kontchakov, R., Sadri, F., Roman, D. (eds.) RuleML+RR 2017. LNCS, vol. 10364, pp. 70–86. Springer, Cham (2017). https://doi.org/10.1007/978-3-319-61252-2_6
7. Corea, C., Blatt, J., Delfmann, P.: A tool for decision logic verification in DMN decision tables. In: BPM (Demo Track), pp. 1–5 (2019)
8. Deryck, M., Hasić, F., Vanthienen, J., Vennekens, J.: A case-based inquiry into the Decision Model and Notation (DMN) and the Knowledge Base (KB) paradigm. In: Benzmüller, C., Ricca, F., Parent, X., Roman, D. (eds.) RuleML+RR 2018. LNCS, vol. 11092, pp. 248–263. Springer, Cham (2018). https://doi.org/10.1007/978-3-319-99906-7_17
9. Hasić, F., Corea, C., Blatt, J., Delfmann, P., Serral, E.: Decision model change patterns for dynamic system evolution. Knowl. Inf. Syst. (2020). https://doi.org/10.1007/s10115-020-01469-w

10. Hasić, F., De Smedt, J., Vanthienen, J.: Developing a modelling and mining framework for integrated processes and decisions. In: Debruyne, C., et al. (eds.) OTM 2017. LNCS, vol. 10697, pp. 259–269. Springer, Cham (2018). https://doi.org/10.1007/978-3-319-73805-5_28
11. Hasić, F., Smedt, J.D., Vanthienen, J.: Augmenting processes with decision intelligence: principles for integrated modelling. Decis. Support Syst. **107**, 1–12 (2018)
12. Laurson, Ü., Maggi, F.M.: A tool for the analysis of DMN decision tables. In: BPM (Demo Track), pp. 56–60 (2016)
13. Ochoa, L., González-Rojas, O.: Analysis and re-configuration of decision logic in adaptive and data-intensive processes (short paper). In: Panetto, H., et al. (eds.) OTM 2017. LNCS, vol. 10573, pp. 306–313. Springer, Cham (2017). https://doi.org/10.1007/978-3-319-69462-7_20
14. OMG: Decision Model and Notation (DMN) 1.2 (2019)
15. Smit, K., Zoet, M., Berkhout, M.: Verification capabilities for business rules management in the Dutch governmental context. In: International Conference on Research and Innovation in Information Systems, pp. 1–6. IEEE (2017)

Text as Semantic Fields: Integration of an Enriched Language Conception in the Text Analysis Tool Evoq®

Isabelle Linden[1]([⊠])[iD], Anne Wallemacq[1,2], Bruno Dumas[1][iD], Guy Deville[2,3], Antoine Clarinval[1][iD], and Maxime Cauz[1][iD]

[1] NAmur Digital Institute (NADI), University of Namur, Namur, Belgium
{isabelle.linden,anne.wallemacq,bruno.dumas,
antoine.clarinval,maxime.cauz}@unamur.be
[2] NAmur Institute of Language, Text and Transmediality (NaLTT),
University of Namur, Namur, Belgium
guy.deville@unamur.be
[3] Institut de Recherches en Didactiques et Education de l'UNamur (IRDENa),
University of Namur, Namur, Belgium

Abstract. Analysis of interviews transcripts plays a key role in many human sciences research protocols. Numerous IT tools are already used to support this task. Most of them leave the interpretation task to the analyst, or involve an implicit conception of language which is rarely questioned.

Developed in the context of the EFFaTA-MeM (Evocative Framework For Text Analysis - Mediality Models) trans-disciplinary research project, the Evoq software takes a radically innovative approach. It voluntarily integrates concepts from post-structuralism theory which are thus offered as a reading sieve at the analyst's disposal.

This demo paper briefly introduces the main concepts of post-structuralism, then it presents how these concept are modelised in a formal system. Finally, it shows how this approach is integrated in the Evoq software and how the human scientist can benefit from its functionalities.

Keywords: Data analytic · Text analysis · Human sciences · Structural analysis · Evoq®

1 Yet Another Software to Support Text Analysis

Several pieces of software exist that support text analysis. In an in-depth study of their functionalities, Lejeune [1,2] organizes them into 5 families (lexicometry, concordance, automata, dictionaries/registers, reflexives) around 2 axes (compute/show and explore/analyse). In his conclusions, he underlines that even though these functionalities are really helpful, none of them replace the researcher's ability to bring out a stimulating interpretation of the text. Indeed, this ability requires a powerful theoretical and methodological framework.

© Springer Nature Switzerland AG 2020
F. Dalpiaz et al. (Eds.): RCIS 2020, LNBIP 385, pp. 543–548, 2020.
https://doi.org/10.1007/978-3-030-50316-1_36

If we look at text visualisation from the point of view of mediality [8], existing extraction and visualisation tools display an implicit conception of language which is rarely questioned. This question needs to be investigated, however, not only from an epistemological point of view but also from a heuristic point of view: How can a visualisation foster the analyst's creativity in developing a new understanding of a text? In typical visualisations (as these refered by [3]: enriched texts, line plots, ...), as a matter of fact, this conception is characterized by linearity, univocality, a firm distinction between author and reader – as producer/consumer –, low interaction, a frontal relation to the language and 2D visualisation. This conception leads to a reduction of natural language to a formal language understandable by a computer. In order to allow a novel understanding of the semantic universe built by a text, we propose to rely on a richer conception of language.

The EFFaTA-MeM Research Project explores a different approach. It intends to explore an enriched conception of language and wants to focus on the text with an approach to language that is more architectural, plurivocal, interactive, immersive and multi dimensional than what has been done until now. The research reported here relies on a conception of language developed in the structuralist theory and its reformulation in post-structuralism [4–7].

In this demo paper, we present the first step of the formalisation and specifically address the following research questions. On the one hand, a fundamental research question: how to express post-structuralism in a formal model. On the other hand, a more pragmatic question: how to integrate this formal model into a usable and pleasant tool?

The paper is structured as follows. Section 2 briefly introduces the main concepts of post-structuralism. Then, Sect. 3, addressing the first research question, introduces the formal concept of *Semantic Field* used to formalise post-structuralism. Next, proposing an answer to the second research question, Sect. 4 summarises the main elements of the implementation and introduces the Evoq tool. Finally, Sect. 5 draws some conclusion.

2   Post-structuralism

One of the essential goal of the EFFaTA-MeM project is to conceive ways of interacting and visualising texts that foster new insights in their analysis. This means that we investigate (i) the mediality of texts and of graphical and pictorial representations, (ii) the intermedial transposition from the textual semiotic system to a pictorial semiotic [9–13], and (iii) the meaning enrichment opportunities offered by this transposition.

The theoretical background used to develop the mediality presented in this paper is based on a deep reformulation of the post-structuralist principles. From a mediality point of view, post-structuralism is interesting because it fundamentally questions and re-frames the linearity of the text. Post-structuralism opens a very interesting conception of language that can be described as follows.

- The text is seen as a field of forces rather than a continuum extending from a beginning to an end. Structuralism will consider a text as synchronic. It means that the beginning and the end of the text are considered in the same way and with the same status.
- Rather than phrases or words, basic units of the text are couples of words[1] in opposition, such as White/Black. The couple is enriched by the whole cloud of cross evocations that are part of the discourse or implicitly supposed by it (White + pure + good/Black + dirty + bad).
- The meaning of words is therefore larger than the simple denotation. White is far more than a simple colour. Opposed to black it conveys the semantic universe of purity, angel, paradise, untouched.
- The meaning is no longer intrinsic but relational: it is based on its dynamic place in the system of the text. If White is now opposed to Red, its meaning changes: since Red is life, warmth, White becomes cold, death: a very different semantic field compared to the White/Black example.
- This system of opposition and association is called a semantic field. These are not always explicit but are more often assumed than explicitly mentioned. This refers to a famous structuralist distinction between the level of language and the level of discourse. In turn, it implies that a speaker never has a complete mastery of what he is saying since his discourse is embedded in these semantic fields that are collectively produced and taken for granted. The semantic field has thus to be considered as surrounding the speaker.
- As Derrida [6] puts it, these semantic fields are not a quiet equilibrium but always in power tension according to the idea that there are dominant relationships between competing semantic fields.
- The aim of structural analysis is to reveal the semantic fields underlying the explicit and conscious discourse together with the power relationship which takes place in the defining dominant world-vision underlying a text.

3 The Knowledge Model in Evoq

In the post-structuralist approach as presented in the previous section, a text becomes much more than a linear sequence of words. It involves a domain knowledge, implicit representations and tensions which are captured by relations. Before going to the development of a tool integrating this view, we developed a formal model to capture this approach and formalise it. In this model, the global object of the analysis is not only a text but a complete *Semantic Field*. This section presents the formal model which is composed of *Text*, *FieldWord*, *FieldRelation* and *Knowledge*.

Formally, the minimal definition of a semantic field can be given by a tuple (t, wl, rl, k) in $SemanticField = Text \times FieldWord^* \times FieldRelation^* \times Knowledge$ where

---

[1] For the sake of simplicity of the report we use "word" in this paper to denote "word or expression in their canonical form".

- $t \in Text$, is the text object of the analysis,
- $wl \in FieldWord^* = (Word \times Colours)^*$ is the list of purposeful words associated with colours,
- $rl \in FieldRelation^* = (Word \times Word \times Boolean)^*$ is a list of pairs of Words with a boolean denoting if the relation reflects an evocation or an opposition (also called association and dissociation),
- $k \in Knowledge$, is an embedded knowledge which basically consists in dictionaries, lemmatisers, synonyms dictionaries, antonyms dictionary and domain knowledge.

3.1 Enriched Views of a Semantic Field

Based on this minimal representation, enriched concepts are built that integrate various element of the Semantic Field tuple. So, for a given SemanticField (t, wl, rl, k), one defines the following objects.

- *Enriched Text*: the text in which the words that appear in wl (or whose lemma appears) are tagged and associated with the same colour as in wl.
- *Field Dictionary*: the list of purposeful words associated with their colour and a boolean denoting the presence/absence of the word in the text;
- *Field Relation Dictionary*: the relation field, rl, where each word is augmented with a boolean denoting is presence/absence in the text.

Direct access to these enriched objects provides to the human scientist an enriched perception of the text, and guides him into the interpretation process.

3.2 Semantic Field Construction

The model presented above formalises a post-structuralist enhanced model of a text, as the result of an analysis, and the enriched views on the information. The most challenging question remains to address: how to build such a model from a fresh text? Expressed in our formalism: how to transform an original $(t, \emptyset, \emptyset, k)$ into an analysis (t, wl, rl, k) and its associated enriched objects? This short paper does not offer the space to provide a full formalisation of this process. Let us mention here some of the main principles.

First of all, let us remind that we do not aim to offer a tool that will fully automate the analysis but a tool that will, on the one hand, stimulate the analyst and, on the other hand, facilitate some tasks of encoding or research. That is to say that only a part of the knowledge k requested to lead the analysis can be fully formalised and implemented, an important part of it remains in the analyst's brain.

With this in mind, the analysis process can be formalised as a sequence of transformation that will, step-by-step, transform a semantic field (t, wl, rl, k), and

- *extract words* from the text and/or the knowledge using the text and/or the (integrated or human) knowledge, and

- *add these words*, with their associated colour, to *wl*,
- *identify* relations among the words, from the text and/or the knowledge, and
- *add these relations*, with their associate boolean, to *rl*.

The support offered by Evoq mainly consists in (i) offering visualisations of the enriched concepts (ii) proposing interactions that give a user-friendly realisation of the operations described above (and their cancellation), and (iii) making propositions for words extraction and relations identification.

4   Implementation: Evoq

Figure 1 presents the analysis of *Zen in the art of archery* by *Herrigel* [14] realised with Evoq. The various (resizeable and re-positionable) panels present synchronised views of the Semantic Field resulting from the analysis. The top left panel presents the Enriched Text, where the words of the Field Dictionary are delineated in bold and colours. The bottom left panel presents the Field Relation Dictionary as a matrix. The right panel offers a presentation of the Field Relation Dictionary as a force-directed graph.

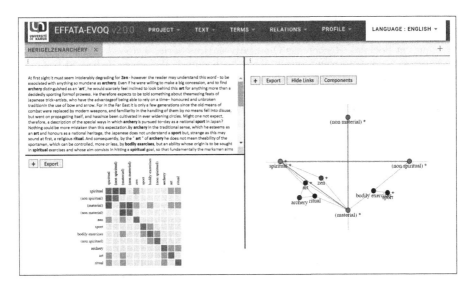

Fig. 1. Analysis of Zen in the art of Archery by Herrigel in Evoq®.

Each of these panels offers interactivity that supports field construction functionalities, mainly adding/modifying words in the Field dictionary and relations in the Field relations dictionary. The node-link diagram has a prominent role. Indeed, together with a very synthetic view on the Relation Field Dictionary, it offers interactions that suggest new relationships (by clicking on the + near the nodes). Moreover, the (relative) positions of the node express/suggest implicit knowledge that stimulate the analyst's thinking. (More on interaction in [15].)

5   Conclusion and Future Work

The Evoq software is an innovative tool to support human scientists in their text analysis. It embeds an approach based on a post-structural methodology in its visualisations and interaction. In this paper, we have introduced a formal model that translates this methodology and underlines its implementation in Evoq.

The software is currently available at https://projects.info.unamur.be/evoq, free account for research can be obtained by contacting the first author.

The usability of the interface and the user interaction process has been studied on V.1.0 of Evoq presented in [15], V2.0 results from the integration of the conclusion of this work. At the time of writing this paper, a campaign of user confrontation to the V.2.0 is being planned. Its aims are multiple: to assess the usability, to identify met/unmet user expectations, to enhance the contribution of the tool with respect to other tools Many questions are still open: what should be the initial position of the graph? Should other interactions be integrated? As many other questions which would bring us outside the size limit of this paper.

References

1. Lejeune, C.: Montrer, calculer, explorer, analyser. Ce que l'informatique fait (faire) à l'analyse qualitative, in: Logiciels pour l'analyse Qualitative: Innovations Techniques et Sociales. Recherches Qualitatives, Hors Série, **9**, 15–32 (2010)
2. Lejeune, C.: http://www.squash.ulg.ac.be/lejeune/. Web page dedicated to Qualitative Data Analysis Softwares
3. Kucher, K., Kerren, A.: Text visualization techniques: taxonomy, visual survey, and community insights. In: Proceedings of IEEE Pacific Visualization Symposium (PacificVis), pp. 117–121. IEEE, Hangzhou (2015)
4. Barthes, R.: Introduction à l'analyse structurale des récits. Communications **8**(1), 1–27 (1966)
5. Cooper, R.: Modernism, post modernism and organizational analysis 3. The contribution of Jacques Derrida. Organ. Stud. **10**(4), 479–502 (1989)
6. Derrida, J.: L'écriture et la différence. Éditions du Seuil, Paris (1967)
7. Piret, A., Nizet, J., Bourgeois, E.: L'analyse structurale: une méthode d'analyse de contenu pour les sciences humaines. De Boeck Supérieur, Brussels (1996)
8. Jäger, L., Linz, E., Schneider, I. (eds.): Media, Culture, and Mediality. New Insights into the Current State of Research. Bielefeld: transcript (2011)
9. Rajewski, I.: Intermedialität, Tübingen. A. Francke, Basel (2002)
10. Rajewski, I.: Intermediality, intertextuality, and remediation. A literary perspective on intermediality. Intermédialités **6**, 43–64 (2005)
11. Wolf, W.: The Musicalization of Fiction. A Study in the Theory and History of Inter mediality. Rodopi, Amsterdam (1999)
12. Ellestrom, L. (ed.): Media Borders, Multimodality and Intermediality. Palgrave Macmillan, Basingstoke (2010)
13. Ellestrom, L.: Media Transformation. The Transfer of Media Characteristics Among Media. Palgrave Macmillan, Basingstoke (2014)
14. Herrigel, E., Hull, R.: Zen in the Art of Archery. Pantheon Book, New York (1953)
15. Clarinval, A., Linden, I. Wallemacq, A., Dumas, B.: Evoq: a visualization tool to support structural analysis of text documents. In: Proceedings of the 2018 ACM Symposium on Document Engineering, pp. 1–10. ACM Press (2018)

MERLIN: An Intelligent Tool for Creating Domain Models

Monique Snoeck$^{(\boxtimes)}$ (iD)

Research Center on Information Systems Engineering, KU Leuven, Leuven, Belgium
monique.snoeck@kuleuven.be

Abstract. The complexity of modelling languages and the lack of intelligent tool support add unnecessary difficulties to the process of modelling, a process that is in itself already demanding, given the challenges associated to capturing user requirements and abstracting these in the correct way. In the past, the MERODE method has been developed to address the problem of UML's complexity and lack of formalization. In this paper, we demonstrate how the formalization of a multi-view modelling approach entails the possibility to create smart and user-friendly modelling support.

Keywords: Conceptual modelling · Modelling tool · UML · Model-driven engineering · Consistency checking

1 Modelling Difficulties

Model-driven engineering (MDE) aims to create software from models. One of the key assumptions behind MDE is that models can be made sufficiently complete and correct to generate code from them. While the "general purpose" character of UML makes it widely applicable, it is also its weakness. The UML contains a large number of constructs, making it difficult to use. And when those models are intended to generate code from them, the problem is exacerbated as generating code from a UML model is only possible if the models are sufficiently detailed, which requires a thorough knowledge of the UML. UML is not the only language facing a too large complexity. Several authors have already pointed out that many modelling languages (including the UML) are too "noisy" with various concepts, which inevitably results in creating erroneous models [1, 2]. Also modelling tools are complex, and pose additional challenges to modelers [3], even though good tool support had been proved to lower the likelihood of model quality problems [4].

The MERODE modelling method [5] targets conceptual modelling and addresses these challenges by offering a UML-based modelling approach that allows creating models that conceptual in nature (as opposed to technical designs), yet are sufficiently precise and complete to generate code from them with no more than three clicks. In addition, intelligent tool support has been developed to support the modeller in the best possible way while modelling. The goal of this demo is to demonstrate the features of the MERLIN modelling environment, including multi-view support and intelligent model

© Springer Nature Switzerland AG 2020
F. Dalpiaz et al. (Eds.): RCIS 2020, LNBIP 385, pp. 549–555, 2020.
https://doi.org/10.1007/978-3-030-50316-1_37

consistency checking. The modelling environment is freely available since January 2020 at http://www.merlin-academic.com.

2 Simplification of the Modelling Language

To ease the use of UML for conceptual modelling, the MERODE method uses a minimal set of concepts from UML required to capture domain models. Three views are supported: structural modelling by means of a UML class diagram, behavioural modelling by means of state charts, and interaction modelling, using a matrix-technique. The three views are directly supported by MERLIN.

In MERODE, the Class diagram only uses the concepts of class, binary association and inheritance associations. More complex concepts such as Association Class, composition and aggregation are deliberately not used so as to ease the modellers' task. Moreover, MERODE requires each binary association to be of a one-to-many or of one-to-one type, expressing existence dependency of one object type on the other. Transformation rules from a "classical" UML diagram to such an existence-dependency only class diagram are provided by the method. The following example illustrates the inherent difficulties associated to UML, and how such transformation process results in more precise models, while using a limited number of concepts.

Figure 1 identifies three object types[1] (customer, order and salesperson) and two associations: an order is placed by a customer, and is managed by a salesperson. Because both associations are graphically identical, they fail to capture the inherently different semantics of the underlying domain rules: Whereas the customer of an order remains the same for the whole duration of the order, the salesperson managing the order may change over time. In other words, the association end is placed by labelled with a "1" next to customer is not modifiable or frozen, whereas the association end is managed by labelled with a "1" (next to salesperson) is modifiable. Figure 1 is not incorrect but is incomplete as it does not allow to discern between frozen and modifiable association ends labelled with multiplicity "1". Depending on the transformation rules, both association ends would either be implemented as modifiable or as frozen, as there is no way to make a distinction based on the UML diagram. In order to obtain a model that captures this difference and can be correctly and automatically transformed to code, we need to express these different semantics by means of different modelling constructs.

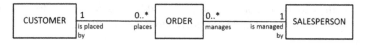

Fig. 1. Example class diagram

In this case, the MERODE rules dictate to reify the association between order and salesperson as show in Fig. 2, thus identifying the concept of 'Sales Person Duty' as

---

[1] In the remainder of this book we will follow the convention that object types are written in SMALLCAPS and that association names will be underlined.

a separate business concept. Reification is also advocated for many-to-many associations, shared aggregation and for composition associations not expressing existence dependency from the part on the whole.

State charts allow modelling a domain object's behaviour. The UML bases its state chart notation on Harel State charts, offering a rich pallet of concepts, including parallelism and decomposition. MERODE however uses only the basic notions: start, intermediate and end states, and requires each class to have just one state chart defining its behaviour.

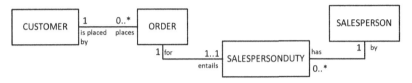

Fig. 2. Class diagram with reified association

Likewise, interaction modelling is simplified. In the UML, object interaction aspects are modelled by means of sequence charts and collaboration diagrams, thus forcing a conceptual modeller into premature commitments. In contrast, MERODE follows an event-driven approach that raises events to the same level of importance as objects, and recognizes them as a fundamental part of the structure of experience. In particular, "business events" are captured as the phenomena of interest at the interface between the real world and the information system [6]. An event-object interaction table, inspired from the "CRUD" matrix[2], allows defining the interaction between business events and business objects and using the events as triggers for state transitions in the state charts.

3 Intelligent Tool Support

Modelling typically requires describing the same socio-technical system from different perspectives (data, behaviour, authorisations, etc.). Some aspects may however be modelled in more than one scheme, e.g. a business object type appearing in a class diagram and as data object in a BPMN diagram. While many modelling tools focus on one particular diagram, the modelling environment of MERODE allows viewing two models side-by-side, see Fig. 3.

Obviously, some kind of consistency checking between different views is required to ensure the quality of the model [7, 8]. This consistency checking can vary from a simple syntactic correspondence to a full semantic match between diagrams. In the past, continuing efforts have been made to provide UML with the needed formal underpinning [9–14]. Nevertheless, these efforts have not entailed an agreed-upon set of consolidated rules, as a result of which authors define their own set of rules [8]. However, to achieve true consistency, the integration of different views is needed. Recently, the integration between the data and business process perspective is also gaining ground as exemplified by artefact centric approaches [15–17].

---

[2] Captures how processes create, read, update or delete data.

In MERODE, the concept of existence dependency is based on the notion of "life" of an object, and this induces a natural sequencing of creating and ending of objects [14]. A MERODE class diagram is therefore-in spite of its appearance- not a pure data model, but also defines a default behavioural model. This facilitates consistency checking with other diagrams intended to capture the behavioural aspects of the domain. In contrast with existing tools like Enterprise Architect, Visual Paradigm, etc. that treat the class diagram in a totally independent way from the behavioural models, MERODE defines consistency between the static model and the behavioural model [5]. In particular, MERODE sustains three modes of consistency checking [18]:

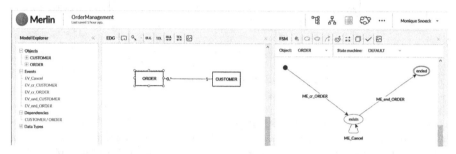

Fig. 3. Viewing the class diagram and state charts side by side.

- *Consistency by construction*, is the most powerful, and means that the tool "auto completes" model elements based on consistency rules. Figure 3, right, shows the default state chart that is automatically generated for each class, including the generation of default creating and ending events.
- *Consistency by analysis* means that an algorithm is used to detect all potential inconsistencies in the model. The modeller can thus construct the model without caring about temporary incompleteness or contradicting elements. Upon request, a verification algorithm can be run against the models to spot errors and/or incompleteness in the various views. Such verification could be done manually as well, but obviously automated support substantially eases model verification, and is likely to ensure more thorough verification as well. Assume for example, that in an Order Management model, the modeller created a state chart like in Fig. 4. Running a model checker will then result in a report mentioning the problems of non-determinism and backward inaccessible state shown in Fig. 5.

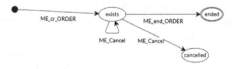

Fig. 4. Erroneous state chart

- *Consistency by monitoring*, allows checking new specification against correctness rules when entered in the tool. This allows to maintain the correctness of a model, but it should be used with parsimony as a too stringent verification procedure will turn the input of new model elements into a frustrating activity.

The major advantage of this consistency checking is that this saves a lot of input effort while improving the completeness of the model in one go. Moreover, the auto complete functionality avoids the input of inconsistent specifications by completing the entered specifications with their consistent consequences. The result is a much more user-friendly environment. Figure 6 shows how model settings in MERLIN allow the user switching on auto complete functionality, the first of which leads to the automatic creation of creating and ending business events and methods when adding a business object type to the class diagram.

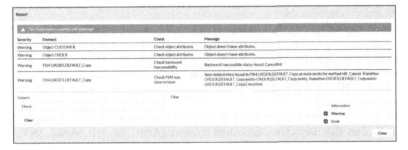

Fig. 5. Sample model checking report

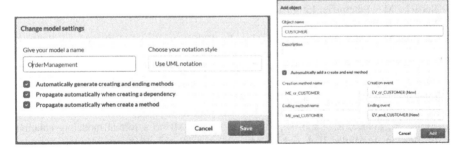

Fig. 6. Autocomplete functionality in MERLIN

4   Conclusion

The MERLIN modelling environment demonstrates how the formal underpinning of a modelling method, and the formal definition of consistency rules allows offering intelligent and user-friendly modelling support for creating domain models. Besides the benefit for the modeler in terms of modelling effort, the quality of the resulting models entails easy code generation. In the case of MERLIN, the files can be exported to an xml-format allowing the generation of full functional code with a single click. This contributes to model quality too as the generated application is enriched with didactic features helping the modeller to assess the quality of the model [19].

For the purpose of conceptual modelling, MERLIN offers more easy modelling compared to existing tools such as Visual Paradigm and Enterprise Architect: less input is required to achieve a model fit for code-generation, and more consistence checks are offered. On the downside, MERLIN offers a very limited set of modelling constructs, as result of which design choices (such as e.g. navigability of associations, sequence charts) are set by default or part of transformation process. In the future, we plan an XMI-export so that high-level MERLIN-models could be imported in commercial tools to detail the models further.

References

1. Erickson, J., Siau, K.: Can UML be simplified? Practitioner use of UML in separate domains. In: Proceedings of the 12th Workshop on Exploring Modeling Methods for Systems Analysis and Design (EMMSAD 2007), pp. 87–96, Trondheim, Norway (2007). Held in conjunction with the 19th Conference on Advanced Information Systems (CAiSE 2007)
2. Wilmont, I., Hengeveld, S., Barendsen, E., Hoppenbrouwers, S.: Cognitive mechanisms of conceptual modelling. In: Ng, W., Storey, V.C., Trujillo, J.C. (eds.) ER 2013. LNCS, vol. 8217, pp. 74–87. Springer, Heidelberg (2013). https://doi.org/10.1007/978-3-642-41924-9_7
3. Siau, K., Loo, P.-P.: Identifying difficulties in learning UML. Inf. Syst. Manag. **23**(3), 43–51 (2006)
4. Recker, J., et al.: How good is BPMN really? Insights from Theory and Practice. In: 14th European Conference on Information Systems, Goeteborg, Sweden. Association for Information Systems (2006)
5. Snoeck, M.: Enterprise Information Systems Engineering: The MERODE Approach. Springer, Berlin (2014)
6. Jackson, M.: The world and the machine. In: 17th International Conference on Software Engineering, p. 283, Seattle, Washington, USA (1995)
7. Paige, R., Ostroff, J.: The single model principle. J. Object Technol. **1**(5), 63–81 (2002)
8. Torrea, D., Labiche, Y., Genero, M., Elaasar, M.: A systematic identification of consistency rules for UML diagrams. J. Syst. Softw. **144**, 121–142 (2018)
9. pUML: The precise UML group. http://www.cs.york.ac.uk/puml/
10. Evans, A., France, R., Lano, K., Rumpe, B.: The UML as a formal modeling notation. In: Bézivin, J., Muller, P.-A. (eds.) UML 1998. LNCS, vol. 1618, pp. 336–348. Springer, Heidelberg (1999). https://doi.org/10.1007/978-3-540-48480-6_26
11. B., J.-M., L., Johan., M., Ana., France, R.B.: Defining precise semantics for UML. In: Goos, G., Hartmanis, J., van Leeuwen, J., Malenfant, J., Moisan, S., Moreira, A. (eds.) ECOOP 2000. LNCS, vol. 1964, pp. 113–122. Springer, Heidelberg (2000). https://doi.org/10.1007/3-540-44555-2_10
12. Cheung, K.S., Chow, K.O., Cheung, T.Y.: Consistency analysis on lifecycle model and interaction model. In: Proceedings of the International Conference on Object Oriented Information Systems, pp. 427–441, Paris (1998). https://doi.org/10.1007/978-1-4471-0895-5_26
13. Huzar, Z., Kuzniarz, L., Reggio, G., Sourrouille, J.L.: Consistency problems in UML-based software development. In: Jardim, N.N., Selic, B., Rodrigues da Silva, A., Toval Alvarez, A. (eds.) UML Modeling Languages and Applications: UML 2004. Lecture Notes in Computer

Science, vol. 3297, pp. 1–12. Springer, Berlin (2005). https://doi.org/10.1007/978-3-540-317
97-5_1

14. Snoeck, M., Dedene, G.: Existence dependency: the key to semantic integrity between
    structural and behavioral aspects of object types. IEEE Trans. Softw. Eng. **24**(4), 233–251
    (1998)

15. Dumas, M.: On the convergence of data and process engineering. In: Eder, J., Bielikova, M.,
    Tjoa, A.Min. (eds.) ADBIS 2011. LNCS, vol. 6909, pp. 19–26. Springer, Heidelberg (2011).
    https://doi.org/10.1007/978-3-642-23737-9_2

16. Calvanese, D., Montali, M., Patrizi, F., Rivkin A.: Modelling and In-Database Management
    of Relational, Data-Aware Processes ArXiv:1810.08062 [Cs], October (2018). http://arxiv.
    org/abs/1810.08062

17. Künzle, V., Reichert, M.: PHILharmonicFlows: towards a framework for object-aware process
    management. J. Softw. Maintenance Evol.: Res. Pract. **23**(4), 205–244 (2011)

18. Snoeck, M., Michiels, C., Dedene, G.: Consistency by construction: the case of MERODE.
    In: Jeusfeld, M.A., Pastor, Ó. (eds.) ER 2003. LNCS, vol. 2814, pp. 105–117. Springer,
    Heidelberg (2003). https://doi.org/10.1007/978-3-540-39597-3_11

19. Sedrakyan, G., Snoeck, M., Poelmans, S.: Assessing the effectiveness of feedback enabled
    simulation in teaching conceptual modeling. Comput. Educ. **78**, 367–382 (2014)

Business Intelligence and Analytics: On-demand ETL over Document Stores

Manel Souibgui[1,2(✉)], Faten Atigui[2], Sadok Ben Yahia[1,3],
and Samira Si-Said Cherfi[2]

[1] Faculty of Sciences of Tunis, LIPAH, University of Tunis El Manar, Tunis, Tunisia
`manel.souibgui@fst.utm.tn`
[2] Conservatoire National des Arts et Métiers, CEDRIC-CNAM, Paris, France
`{faten.atigui,samira.cherfi}@cnam.fr`
[3] Department of Software Science, Tallinn University of Technology, Tallinn, Estonia
`sadok.ben@taltech.ee`

Abstract. For many decades, Business Intelligence and Analytics (BI&A) has been associated with relational databases. In the era of big data and NoSQL stores, it is important to provide approaches and systems capable of analyzing this type of data for decision-making. In this paper, we present a new BI&A approach that both: *(i)* extracts, transforms and loads the required data for OLAP analysis (on-demand ETL) from document stores, and *(ii)* provides the models and the systems required for suitable OLAP analysis. We focus here, on the on-demand ETL stage where, unlike existing works, we consider the dispersion of data over two or more collections.

Keywords: Business Intelligence and Analytics · Document stores · ETL · OLAP

1 Introduction

With the advent of big data and NoSQL stores that have been primarily developed, more than a decade ago, NoSQL offered a new cost-effective method, schema-free and built on distributed systems, which makes it easy to scale and shard. While the use of NoSQL stores is widely accepted today, Business Intelligence & Analytics (BI&A) has long been associated with relational stores. In fact, from the earliest days of data warehousing, the qualities of the relational model have been highly valued in the quest for data consistency and quality. The question that quickly arose about NoSQL was how does this relate to BI&A? Can it be of use in data warehousing?[1]

Today, exploiting NoSQL data for analytical purposes lacks maturity, traceability, and metadata management. For this, we introduce a new approach that aims to extract, transform, and load NoSQL data sources on-demand. This approach is hybrid that has and takes into account both data sources schemaless

---

[1] https://www.dataversity.net/nosql-and-business-intelligence/.

© Springer Nature Switzerland AG 2020
F. Dalpiaz et al. (Eds.): RCIS 2020, LNBIP 385, pp. 556–561, 2020.
https://doi.org/10.1007/978-3-030-50316-1_38

nature and analytical needs in order to explore several NoSQL stores in an efficient way. Specifically, the distinguishing features of our approach are: *(i)* to the best of our knowledge, there does not exist a global BI&A approach dedicated to NoSQL data sources that covers all the decision-making chain starting from the ETL process and that reaches OLAP analysis; *(ii)* here, we focus on document stores (DSs), and unlike existing works, our approach is not limited to one collection, as we consider the dispersion of data across several collections; and *(iii)* we shed light on the on-demand ETL phase. We also enlighten the challenges triggered by the join operator of two schemaless sources.

The paper outline is as follows: In Sect. 2, we discuss the related literature. In Sect. 3, we give an overview of our approach, where its first stage is detailed in Sect. 4. Finally, we draw the conclusion in Sect. 5.

2   Related Work

As our main objective is to provide an on-demand ETL process over DSs, and to facilitate their OLAP analysis, we present, in this section, existing works that were carried out around this issue. We identify two main streams: *(i)* approaches that have dealt with the problem of ETL and schema extraction of DSs and *(ii)* approaches that have proposed contributions for OLAP analysis on DSs.

2.1   ETL over Document Stores

Few researchers have addressed the problem of ETL in the context of NoSQL stores, particularly the document-oriented ones [1]. For example, in [8], authors proposed a tool called *BigDimETL*. Data are extracted from a DS to be converted to a column-oriented store in order to apply partitioning techniques. Furthermore, the majority of prior research tended to focus on the transformation of a multidimensional conceptual model into a document-oriented one, rather than applying ETL phases over DSs [4,11].

On the other hand, several works have focused on how to extract a schema, i.e., a list of document fields with their types, from DSs. Since it is an essential step in an ETL process dealing with DSs, we have studied these different contributions. In [2], Baazizi et al. were interested in schema inference of massive JSON datasets. The distinguishing feature of their approach is that it is parametric and allows the user to specify the degree of preciseness and conciseness of the inferred schema. Besides, Gallunicci et al. [6] have extended the level of schema extraction of a collection of JSON documents with schema profiling techniques to capture the hidden rules explaining schema variants. Previous studies have almost exclusively focused on the early stage of the BI&A chain. In the following, we provide an overview of works dealing with OLAP analysis on DSs.

2.2   OLAP Analysis over Document Stores

Very few works have tried to find solutions for OLAP analysis on DSs. Chouder et al. [5] have proposed an approach to enable OLAP on a DS in the context of self-service BI. This approach extracts the global schema of one collection of nested JSON documents and generates a draft multidimensional schema. Then, the decision-maker can define his query, which is validated by mining approximate functional dependencies (FDs). Similarly, the approach proposed in [7] enables OLAP directly on a collection. But, unlike [5] where the research for FDs is done on-demand, this approach looks for all the approximate FDs.

Our study of the literature showed that several works have proposed solutions for the ETL and the schema extraction of DSs. Although they are almost similar, the distinction lies in how each work approaches the problem of schema discovery. On the other hand, existing works that have dealt with OLAP analysis on DSs, have considered only one single collection. However, in the context of BI&A, data are often scattered over several collections. Besides, On-demand approaches are worth of interest and are not yet used for the ETL in the context of DSs [3,10]. To the best of our knowledge, no prior works have proposed a global BI&A approach, based on the on-demand methodology, that starts from schema extraction of multiple DSs, performs ETL operations, and reaches OLAP analysis. In the following, we introduce our new approach that palliates this shortage.

3   Overview of Our Approach

We propose a new approach that have the advantage to both extract, transform, and load DSs and provide the dedicated solutions for OLAP analysis. As shown in Fig. 1, our approach operates in two main stages: (i) on-demand ETL where ETL operations are only performed on the pertinent data that meets the decision-maker requirements; and (ii) OLAP analysis of this data.

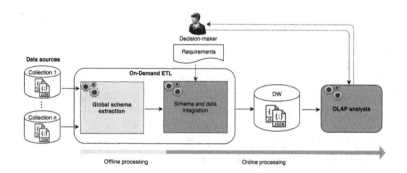

Fig. 1. Approach general architecture as a glance

In this paper, a first objective is to consider a document-oriented data model taking into account schema variety. We consider scattered data over several collections. Moreover, we take into account the three types of data storage model in JSON documents: (i) *normalized:* the JSON related objects are represented separately from the original document and are referenced using identifiers; (ii) *denormalized:* the JSON related objects are nested in the original document; and *(iii) semi-normalized:* there are both nested and separate objects. Fetching relevant data, often needs to access more than one collection of JSON documents. This multiple access is increasing the complexity since it requires finding the "pivot" connecting fields. To do so, our approach is built upon two main stages:

- **Stage 1: On-demand ETL** aims to extract, transform and load only, the relevant data for each specific analysis. It operates in two phases:
  - **Phase 1: Global schema extraction:** extracts the global schema of each collection, in order to deal with the schemaless and variety nature of DSs. This phase is automated and processed when the user is offline.
  - **Phase 2: Global schema and data integration** where Facts' measures and Dimensions' attributes (called multidimensional attributes) are extracted from one or more sources attributes. Starting from several collections, this phase aims to: *(i)* perform a mapping between multidimensional attributes and collections schemas; *(ii)* perform ETL operations; and *(iii)* create the DW which is a collection of JSON documents. It is worth mentioning that this phase is processed when the user is online, since it requires interaction with him, as depicted in Fig. 1.
- **Stage 2: OLAP analysis**: the aim of this stage is to ensure an OLAP analysis adapted to DSs. The decision-maker expresses OLAP queries that is then translated into a DS native query language. Due to space limitation the description of this stage is left to forthcoming paper and we introduce only the first stage in the following section.

4   On-demand ETL

In this section, we present the core stage of our approach, which is divided into two phases: *(i)* global schema extraction of DSs; and *(ii)* global schema and data integration.

4.1   Stage 1.1: Global Schema Extraction

DSs have a dynamic schema, mainly obvious through the presence or absence of certain fields with a variety of types. Inferring the overall schema of each collection is of paramount importance for the data integration. This latter is an upfront processing to extract the global schema of each collection (Definition 2). Obviously, the number of global schemas is less than or equal to the initial number of collections because several collections can share the same schema.

Definition 1. *Document flat schema: a list of fields with their associated types. Let $S_D = \{(p,t)_i / 1 < i < k\}$ be the schema associated to a JSON document D. It consists of k pairs (p,t), such that: (i) p is the field path from the document root. It is the unique identifier of each field; and (ii) t is the field type.*

Definition 2. *Collection global schema: the global schema of a collection C is $SG(C) = \bigcup_{j=1}^{l} S_{D_j}$, where S_{D_j} is the flat schema associated with a JSON document D_j that belongs to the collection C and l denoting the number of distinct documents schemas that exist in a collection C.*

4.2   Stage 1.2: Global Schema and Data Integration

This stage aims to extract relevant data that meets the analysis requirements. To do so, we have two main steps: *(i)* mapping; and *(ii)* performing ETL operations to load data into the DW.

Mapping. The goal of this phase is to ensure a mapping between collections global schemas and the multidimensional attributes so as to unveil the collections of interest that will be included as input in the rest of the phases.

Definition 3. *Decision-maker requirements: decision-maker requirements are expressed as a multidimensional schema. A multidimensional schema, denoted with MS, is a triple $MS = (D, M, f)$ where:*

- $D = \{d_i, 1 < i < l\}$: *a finite set of dimensions d_i. Each dimension is associated to a finite set of hierarchy levels $h_j(d_i)$.*
- $M = \{(m, o, a)_i, 1 <= i < n\}$: *the set of measures to be analysed, where:*
  m: label of the measure to be analysed.
  o:

$$o = \begin{cases} Computation\ formula, \\ \emptyset, & otherwise \end{cases}$$

  a: aggregation operator associated with each measure m_i (AVG, MAX, etc.).
- *f: a function that associates each measure to a finite set of grouping fields, such that $f : M \rightarrow G$ where G is a set of grouping fields.*

Definition 4. *Mapping: given the multidimensional schema and the set of collections global schemas, a mapping is defined by the function: $\varphi : \{G, M\} \rightarrow S^G$*
$$a \mapsto \varphi(a)$$
where: (i) $\{G, M\}$ is the set of multidimensional attributes, i.e., dimensions and measures; and (ii) S^G is the set of collections global schemas.

This phase is semi-automatic since it requires an interaction with the decision-maker. In fact, a multidimensional attribute can be found in more than one collection. In this case, the decision-maker validates manually the mapping proposed by the system.

Performing ETL Operations. ETL is a crucial part of the BI&A chain where most of the data curation is carried out [9]. The latter is made up of a set of operations. Since, our approach starts from several collections, a join operation is required. The latter is a complex operation to ensure, while no prior definition of foreign keys. While joining tables in relational data sources is assured by dint of a precise join key, in DSs, collections are unlikely to have an exact join key due to the absence of integrity constraints. So, identifying key fields that are necessary for joining two collections is a real challenge on which we are working. On the other hand, DW creation relies on ETL operations processing. In fact, the DW is a collection of JSON documents. Its collection schema is constructed by fetching each multidimensional attribute from the corresponding source collection.

5   Conclusion

In this paper, we have proposed a new BI&A approach, covering the hole chain, that extracts-transforms-and-loads only the data required for OLAP analysis from DSs with dispersed data across several collections. As part of our future work, we plan to improve our approach on both its theoretical ground and its technical implementation. We also intend to perform larger experimentations over real-life datasets to better study the efficiency and the boundaries of our approach. On the long run, we plan to consider the OLAP analysis stage and to extend our approach to support additional NoSQL data models.

References

1. Asanka, P.D.: ETL framework design for NoSQL databases in dataware housing. IJRCAR **3**, 67–75 (2015)
2. Baazizi, M.-A., Colazzo, D., Ghelli, G., Sartiani, C.: Parametric schema inference for massive JSON datasets. VLDB J. **28**(4), 497–521 (2019). https://doi.org/10.1007/s00778-018-0532-7
3. Baldacci, L., Golfarelli, M., Graziani, S., Rizzi, S.: QETL: an approach to on-demand ETL from non-owned data sources. Data Knowl. Eng. **112**, 17–37 (2017)
4. Chevalier, M., Malki, M.E., Kopliku, A., Teste, O., Tournier, R.: Document-oriented models for data warehouses - NoSQL document-oriented for data warehouses. In: ICEIS 2016 - Proceedings of the 18th International Conference on Enterprise Information Systems, Rome, Italy, 25–28 April, vol. 1, pp. 142–149 (2016)
5. Chouder, M.L., Rizzi, S., Chalal, R.: Exodus: exploratory OLAP over document stores. Inf. Syst. **79**, 44–57 (2019)
6. Gallinucci, E., Golfarelli, M., Rizzi, S.: Schema profiling of document-oriented databases. Inf. Syst. **75**, 13–25 (2018)
7. Gallinucci, E., Golfarelli, M., Rizzi, S.: Approximate OLAP of document-oriented databases: a variety-aware approach. Inf. Syst. **85**, 114–130 (2019)
8. Mallek, H., Ghozzi, F., Teste, O., Gargouri, F.: BigDimETL with NoSQL database. In: Knowledge-Based and Intelligent Information & Engineering Systems: Proceedings of the 22nd International Conference KES, Belgrade, Serbia, pp. 798–807 (2018)
9. Souibgui, M., Atigui, F., Zammali, S., Cherfi, S.S., Ben Yahia, S.: Data quality in ETL process: a preliminary study. In: Knowledge-Based and Intelligent Information & Engineering Systems: Proceedings of the 23rd International Conference KES-2019, Budapest, Hungary, pp. 676–687 (2019)
10. Yang, Y., Meneghetti, N., Fehling, R., Liu, Z.H., Kennedy, O.: Lenses: an on-demand approach to ETL. PVLDB **8**(12), 1578–1589 (2015)
11. Yangui, R., Nabli, A., Gargouri, F.: ETL based framework for NoSQL warehousing. In: Themistocleous, M., Morabito, V. (eds.) EMCIS 2017. LNBIP, vol. 299, pp. 40–53. Springer, Cham (2017). https://doi.org/10.1007/978-3-319-65930-5_4

Towards an Academic Abstract Sentence Classification System

Connor Stead[1]([✉]), Stephen Smith[1], Peter Busch[1], and Savanid Vatanasakdakul[2]

[1] Macquarie University, Sydney, NSW, Australia
connor.stead@hdr.mq.edu.au,
{stephen.smith,peter.busch}@mq.edu.au
[2] Carnegie Mellon University, Doha, Qatar
savanid@cmu.edu

Abstract. This research in progress paper introduces a novel academic abstract sentence classification system intended to improve researcher literature discovery efficiency. The system provides three key functions: 1) displays abstracts with visual identification of each sentence's indicated literature characteristic class, 2) conversion of unstructured abstracts into structured variants and 3) categorised class sentence extraction available for export to CSV alongside literature metadata. This functionality is made possible by a web application connected to a Python instance via PHP, integration with an open access literature index via an API and a deployed academic abstract sentence classification model. The contribution of the proposed system is its ability to enhance researcher literature discovery. This paper provides context and motivation behind the development of the system, outlines its functionality and provides an outlook for future research.

Keywords: Abstracts · Literature discovery · Abstract sentence classification

1 Introduction

As a result of the large volume of academic literature available on the Internet [9], identifying literature relevant to a research undertaking can be a tedious task. This is due to the information overload associated with unprecedented widespread accessibility to literature. Even though academic literature indices and databases provide access to a significant number of digitally accessible literature, junior researchers are often at a loss as to where to begin searching for content and experienced academics often find themselves in echo chambers seeking an alternative method to identify novel research.

This paper introduces a system which can assist researchers hone in on literature within their research scope. This is achieved through the novel deployment of academic abstract sentence classification modelling into a software system designed specifically for researchers. Such modelling is an artefact of the computer science research field of natural language programming, concerned with the classification of academic abstract sentences into structured abstract format classes. Examples of these classes include 'Purpose', 'Methodology', 'Findings' and 'Contributions'. The deployment of this modelling

© Springer Nature Switzerland AG 2020
F. Dalpiaz et al. (Eds.): RCIS 2020, LNBIP 385, pp. 562–568, 2020.
https://doi.org/10.1007/978-3-030-50316-1_39

capability enables the software to provide three primary functions: 1) display abstracts with visual identification of each sentence's indicated literature characteristic class, 2) conversion of unstructured abstracts into structured variants and 3) categorised class sentence extraction available for export to CSV alongside literature metadata. These functions are intended to enable researchers to utilize the advancements in academic abstract sentence classification modelling to enhance literature discovery capability and improve literature review efficiency. The system proposed is the first known example of the deployment of academic abstract sentence classification capability into a software system specifically for academic researchers and with demonstrated integration with an academic literature index.

This paper is structured as follows. Firstly, some context on structured abstracts and academic abstract sentence classification will be outlined as well as the motivations for the development of the system. The paper will then introduce the system, before outlining our ongoing research on its development and the study of its utilisation.

2 Background

This section will introduce structured abstracts and academic abstract sentence classification modelling, key concepts underpinning the utility of the proposed system.

The approach to authoring abstracts is not universal across academic disciplines. Some journals and conferences enforce a structured approach, requiring a set of literature characteristics to be explicitly identified. The set of characteristics utilised in a structured abstract is known as a format [13]. Common examples of structured abstract formats from the biomedical discipline include IMRAD ('Introduction', 'Methods', 'Results' and 'Discussion') and the 8-heading format, which varies from IMRAD with the inclusion of 'Setting', 'Patients', 'Interventions' and 'Outcome Measurements'.

The utility of structured abstracts has been well documented in the literature. Of particular note is the understanding that the adoption of structured abstracts increases relevant literature discovery capability [1, 7, 10, 11]. For example, Budgen et al. [2] conducted quantitative research on the utility of structured abstracts through a survey of 64 researchers and students. They determined that non-structured free text abstracts "are likely to omit substantial amounts of relevant information" (p. 457) and that structured variants "are significantly more complete and clearer than unstructured abstracts" (p. 457). These findings are supported by further research conducted by Budgen et al. [3].

The adoption of structured abstracts also benefits researchers in the computer science research field of natural language processing, as they provide a unique source of categorised sentence level observations suitable for training machine/deep learning models. These models are capable of classifying non-structured abstract sentences into structured heading format classes, such as 'Purpose', 'Method', 'Findings' and 'Contributions'. Table 1 outlines state-of-the-art academic abstract sentence classification models identifying the origin paper , algorithm/modelling approach adopted and some performance characteristics. The models shown demonstrate the high-performance capability of these artefacts, most of which reach ~90% precision when classifying biomedical structured abstract sentences sourced from the PubMed 20k/200k [5] datasets.

Table 1. Summary of state-of-the-art academic abstract sentence classification models

Paper	Algorithm	Performance
Dernoncourt et al. [6]	Neural Network	PubMed 200k [5]: F1-score: 89.9%
Cohan et al. [4]	Bidirectional Encoder Representations from Transformers (BERT)	PubMed 20k [5]: 92.9% accuracy
Gonçalves et al. [8]	Neural Network	PubMed 20k [5]: 90.9% precision, 90.8% recall/F1-score
Jiang et al. [12]	Text convolutional neural network (CNN) + bidirectional recurrent neural network (bi-RNN)	PubMed 200k [5]: 94.4% accuracy (p. 8)

3 Motivation

Our research has not identified a system that deploys academic abstract sentence classification modelling capability, particularly for academic researchers. We also have not identified a system that demonstrates the integration of abstract sentence classification with academic literature indices or databases for on demand abstract sentence classification. Having greater access to relevant literature will ultimately save researchers' valuable time and resources. Therefore, we propose a system that can enhance the ability of researchers to find relevant literature more accurately and efficiently. We are also motivated to contribute to the information systems and computer science bodies of knowledge through the demonstration of how academic abstract sentence classification capability can be operationalised, and how it's introduction and adoption in the literature discovery activity impacts the ability of researchers to acquire relevant material in their efforts to produce novel research.

4 Proposed System

The proposed system is dependent on two key components: 1) the framework enabling the classification of abstract sentences and 2) the deployed classification model(s). The framework comprises of a web application, connected via PHP to a Python instance running Flask (http://flask.palletsprojects.com/en/1.1.x/), a web framework enabling REST request dispatching. The Python instance processes queries from users via the web application, forwarding these on to the open source academic literature index DOAJ

(Directory of Open Access Journals) to retrieve literature metadata. The connection to DOAJ serves as an example of connectivity - other literature indexes/databases may be connected in the future. Flat files (CSVs) of exported metadata from academic literature index searches can also be loaded and queried. Figure 1 provides a high level overview of the framework.

Once retrieved, abstracts are scored by the model, which in preprocessing splits each abstract's sentences before classifying them according to the programmed structured abstract headings. The model also provides confidence scores for each classification. The web application is then served enriched metadata via the Python instance, allowing three functions to be performed. Firstly, the application can visually highlight sentences according to the classification indicated by the model, as demonstrated in Fig. 2. Secondly, the application can convert unstructured abstracts into structured variants, as shown in Fig. 3. Alternatively, a CSV can be exported which contains returned literature metadata, and for each row an extract of structured heading sentences appended together. An example is shown in Fig. 4, filtered on 'design/methodology/approach'.

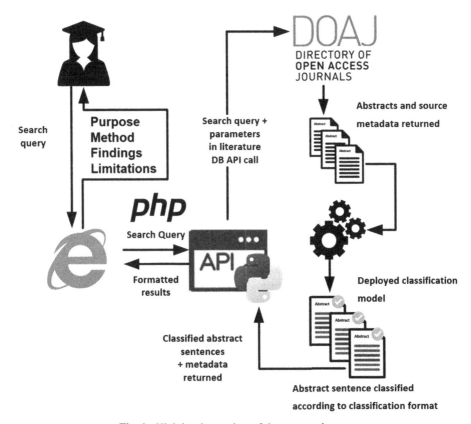

Fig. 1. High level overview of the proposed system

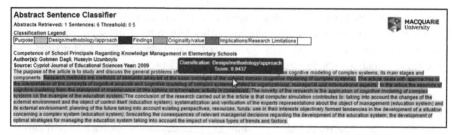

Fig. 2. Highlighting of sentences according to the classified structured abstract class.

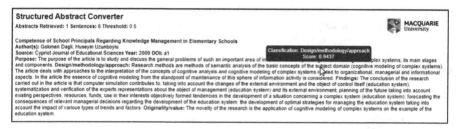

Fig. 3. Structuring of an unstructured abstract. Heading classes are identified in bold.

	title	author	source	year	doi	category	extract
1	Competence of Schoc	Gokmen C	Cypriot Jo	2009	a1	design_methodology_approach	Research methods are methods of semantic analysis of the basic concepts of the subject domain (cognitive modeling of complex systems). The article deals with approaches to the interpretation of the concepts of cognitive analysis and cognitive modeling of complex systems related to organizational, managerial and informational aspects. In the article the essence of cognitive modeling from the standpoint of maintenance of this sphere of information activity is considered.

Fig. 4. Structured class content and metadata extracted to CSV. Filtered on 'findings' extracts.

To demonstrate the utility of the system we trained a sentence classification model using the XLNet [15] modelling method, which has achieved state-of-the-art status for several classification challenges [15]. A XLNet model was trained using the Emerald 20k dataset [14], containing 201,452 classified sentences from 20,000 multidisciplinary abstracts. Sentences in the dataset are classified into the following structured abstract heading classes: purpose, design/methodology/approach, originality/value, practical implications, social implications and research limitations/implications. The model achieved 73.3% precision when tested on a holdout subset. Whilst performance of the model is not state-of-the-art, it served the purpose of demonstrating the system's ability to classify academic abstract sentences on demand. Future system development will look towards the deployment of state-of-the-art models, such as those identified in Table 1. This highlights the adaptability of the system, in that it permits the deployment of pre-trained models that enable classification via a Python instance. It is also possible to deploy several classification models and for alternate models to be used for scoring depending on characteristics of the abstract or query, such as the origin discipline.

5   Ongoing Research

We are conducting research exploring the utility of the system, specifically what role it plays as a facilitating tool in the literature discovery activity conducted by multidisciplinary researchers. Our examination will adopt a theoretical framework which permits the analysis of researchers adopting the system into their research efforts. We anticipate this research will yield both quantitative and qualitative insights into the value of the academic abstract sentence classification, thereby directing any future research and development into the deployment of such capability. We will also be working to enhance the system through state-of-the-art model deployment, user experience improvement as well as alternative academic literature index and database integration.

Acknowledgments. The authors wish to acknowledge the Australian Government Research Training Program Scholarship which enabled this research to take place.

References

1. Bayley, L., Eldredge, J.: The structured abstract: an essential tool for researchers. Hypothesis **17**(1), 11–13 (2003). PMID: 15858627
2. Budgen, D., Kitchenham, B.A., Charters, S.M., Turner, M., Brereton, P., Linkman, S.G.: Presenting software engineering results using structured abstracts: a randomised experiment. Empirical Softw. Eng. **13**(4), 435–468 (2008). https://doi.org/10.1007/s10664-008-9075-7
3. Budgen, D., Burn, A.J., Kitchenham, B.: Reporting computing projects through structured abstracts: a quasi-experiment. Empirical Softw. Eng. **16**(2), 244–277 (2011). https://doi.org/10.1007/s10664-010-9139-3
4. Cohan, A., Beltagy, I., King, D., Dalvi, B., Weld, D.S.: Pretrained language models for sequential sentence classification (2019). arXiv preprint arXiv:1909.04054
5. Dernoncourt, F., Lee, J.Y.: PubMed 200k RCT: a dataset for sequential sentence classification in medical abstracts (2017). arXiv preprint arXiv:1710.06071
6. Dernoncourt, F., Lee, J.Y., Szolovits, P.: Neural networks for joint sentence classification in medical paper abstracts (2016). arXiv preprint arXiv:1612.05251
7. Eldredge, J.: Evidence-based librarianship: the EBL process. Libr. Hi Tech **24**(3), 341–354 (2006). https://doi.org/10.1108/07378830610692118
8. Gonçalves, S., Cortez, P., Moro, S.: A deep learning classifier for sentence classification in biomedical and computer science abstracts. Neural Comput. Appl. **32**, 6793–6807 (2019). https://doi.org/10.1007/s00521-019-04334-2
9. Gusenbauer, M.: Google Scholar to overshadow them all? Comparing the sizes of 12 academic search engines and bibliographic databases. Scientometrics **118**(1), 177–214 (2019). https://doi.org/10.1007/s11192-018-2958-5
10. Hartley, J.: Is it appropriate to use structured abstracts in social science journals? Learn. Publish. **10**(4), 313–317 (1997). https://doi.org/10.1087/09531519750146789
11. Hartley, J., Sydes, M., Blurton, A.: Obtaining information accurately and quickly: are structured abstracts more efficient? J. Inform. Sci. **22**(5), 349–356 (1996). https://doi.org/10.1177/016555159602200503
12. Jiang, X., Zhang, B., Ye, Y., Liu, Z.: A hierarchical model with recurrent convolutional neural networks for sequential sentence classification. In: Tang, J., Kan, M.-Y., Zhao, D., Li, S., Zan, H. (eds.) NLPCC 2019. LNCS (LNAI), vol. 11839, pp. 78–89. Springer, Cham (2019). https://doi.org/10.1007/978-3-030-32236-6_7

13. Nakayama, T., Hirai, N., Yamazaki, S., Naito, M.: Adoption of structured abstracts by general medical journals and format for a structured abstract. J. Med. Libr. Assoc. **93**(2), 237 (2005). PMID: 15858627
14. Stead, C., Smith, S., Busch, P., Vatanasakdakul, S.: Emerald 110k: a multidisciplinary dataset for abstract sentence classification. Paper presented at the Proceedings of the 17th Annual Workshop of the Australasian Language Technology Association, pp. 120–125 (2019)
15. Yang, Z., Dai, Z., Yang, Y., Carbonell, J., Salakhutdinov, R., Le, Q.V.: XLNet: generalized autoregressive pretraining for language understanding. In: 33rd Conference on Neural Information Processing Systems, pp. 5754–5764 (2019)

Diálogop - A Language and a Graphical Tool for Formally Defining GDPR Purposes

Evangelia Vanezi[✉], Georgia M. Kapitsaki, Dimitrios Kouzapas,
Anna Philippou, and George A. Papadopoulos

Department of Computer Science, University of Cyprus, Nicosia, Cyprus
{evanez01,gkapi,dimitrios.kouzapas,annap,george}@cs.ucy.ac.cy

Abstract. The notion of *processing purpose*, as set out in the EU General Data Protection Regulation (GDPR), comprises a crucial part of a software system's privacy policy. Processing purposes are meant to characterize the usage of personal data within a system. In this work, we propose a formal type language for defining purposes as the communication exchanges between a system's entities, based on *session types* enhanced with privacy notions. In order to provide software engineers with the means to easily define processing purposes, we encode the formal language syntax to a UML-based domain model and we present Diálogop, a tool that supports the graphical model definition and subsequently translates it into formal language definitions.

1   Introduction

The European Union applied the General Data Protection Regulation (GDPR) [2] in order to face the challenge of protecting personal data. The GDPR imposes the notion of *purpose* in privacy policies, defining that *"personal data shall be collected for specified, explicit and legitimate purposes and not further processed in a manner that is incompatible with those purposes"*.

In software engineering, validation of privacy policies against software systems is either done by testing techniques, or by human auditing. Alternatively, a formal verification method can guarantee the compliance of a system to its privacy policy, by relying, for instance, on type checking techniques. Proposals for validating privacy requirements in software systems include [9], where automata are used as a formalism for designing and enforcing privacy policies on social networks. Other works aim to extract and model requirements out of regulatory text [12], or to model laws by using primitives, such as roles and norms, and the relationships between them [5]. In [8], the authors present RSLingo4Privacy Studio, a tool for supporting the specification and analysis of privacy policies in software systems, using the RSL-IL4Privacy domain specific language proposed in [1], for the specification of privacy-aware requirements. In turn, [7] employs UML diagrams to define the design of a software's architectural structure, facilitating software engineers in implementing the desired functionality and achieving

© Springer Nature Switzerland AG 2020
F. Dalpiaz et al. (Eds.): RCIS 2020, LNBIP 385, pp. 569–575, 2020.
https://doi.org/10.1007/978-3-030-50316-1_40

privacy by design and by default. Finally, we mention [11], where a two-tiered UML representation of the GDPR is presented, aiming towards a cost-effective method that will help the business sector systems achieve GDPR compliance.

Our work shares similar aims to the above-mentioned works and complements them by adopting a formal approach towards rigorously verifying that software systems comply to their privacy requirements. We propose thus, a language for formal specification of processing purposes in software systems based on session types [3,4,10] and the Privacy Calculus [6]. Furthermore, we propose a graphical modelling language for privacy policies and a methodology for transforming graphically defined privacy policies into formal type language definitions. We present DiálogoP, a tool for defining purposes as diagrams through a domain model and a toolbox, without requiring knowledge of the formal language. We utilise Domain Specific Languages (DSL) covering privacy purpose for any software system. Each diagram is translated into a formal specification using the introduced transformation process.

Use Case: A Healthcare System. As a use case, we consider an automated medical system for hospitals, for which the responsible authority, i.e. the Ministry of Health, defines the functionality and the privacy policy, and each hospital is responsible to implement its own system. A part of the system handles appointments as follows: the system knows the full name, the date of birth and the hospital id number of each patient that has an appointment. At the entrance, a patient scans her hospital identity card, which stores the above data. The system compares the data from the card and the booked appointment and, if they match, it allows the patient to proceed with the visit. The data cannot be used in any other way. The system retrieves from the database the patient's record, i.e. all visits and diagnoses, and forwards that information to the doctor without reading the data. The doctor reads the data, examines the patient and adds information for symptoms and latest diagnosis to the record.

2   A Formal Language for Defining Purposes

We build on *multiparty session types* [4], to formally define processing purposes, enriching them with the notion of personal data stores inspired by the Privacy Calculus [6]. Session types are based on message exchanges between the entities of the system. In our language, in each purpose definition a number of distinct sessions can be set up, able to run in parallel and be interleaved, the entities participating in each session and their interactions. Entities belonging to the same session can exchange messages including personal data either by directly sending them to each other, or based on conditions' evaluation. Such interactions should occur in a specific defined sequence within each session. In order to integrate the notion of *personal data* we exploit the structure of *personal data stores*, first defined in the Privacy Calculus [6], including a unique id and a set of data. Each store has an owner entity. Other entities of a system may obtain references to stores, and use them to access the respective personal data.

Figure 1 presents the syntax. Metavariable, g, denotes ground types such as integer and boolean. Exchange types, U, include ground types, g, annotations, α, and private data types, $\mathsf{pd}[\mathsf{U}]^\alpha$. Annotations, α, are identifiers used to annotate private data. Private data type, $\mathsf{pd}[\mathsf{U}]^\alpha$, is used to type a reference on private data storage that contains private data of type U. We also assume labels for true, $\mathtt{tt}$, and false, $\mathtt{ff}$, and a set of participants $\mathsf{p}, \mathsf{q}, \ldots \in \mathcal{P}$. A global type, G, defines a multiparty session type able to describe privacy purpose. Global type end is the termination type. Type $\mathsf{p} \rightarrow \mathsf{q} : U.G$ describe that participant p sends to participant q an exchange value U and then proceeds with global type G. Global types include $\alpha \rightarrow \mathsf{p} : U.G$ and $\mathsf{p} \rightarrow \alpha : U.G$ describing the reading from or the writing to a store annotated by α personal data of type U, respectively. Finally, conditional branching type, $\mathsf{p} \rightarrow \mathsf{q} : (U \; op \; U')\{\mathtt{tt} : G_1, \mathtt{ff} : G_2\}$, describes the choice that takes place on participant p based on the type of the expression $U \; op \; U'$ and, moreover, participant q is informed and proceeds accordingly.

Ground Types	g	$::=$	$\mathsf{int} \mid \mathsf{bool} \mid \ldots$	
Exchange Types	U	$::=$	$g \mid \mathsf{pd}[\mathsf{U}]^\alpha \mid \alpha$	
Global Types	G	$::=$	end	Termination
		$\mid$	$\mathsf{p} \rightarrow \mathsf{q} : U.G$	Value Exchange
		$\mid$	$\alpha \rightarrow \mathsf{p} : U.G$	Personal Data Read
		$\mid$	$\mathsf{p} \rightarrow \alpha : U.G$	Personal Data Storage
		$\mid$	$\mathsf{p} \rightarrow \mathsf{q} : (U \; op \; U')\{\mathtt{tt} : G_1, \mathtt{ff} : G_2\}$	
				Conditional Branching
Operators	op	$::=$	$= \mid \geq \mid \leq$	

Fig. 1. Multiparty session types for privacy purpose

3 DiálogoP - A Graphical Tool for Defining Purposes

Aiming to simplify the procedure of specifying purposes we elevate the definition to diagrams that are subsequently automatically translated to session types through DiálogoP. The tool was developed using Eclipse Sirius, through Obeo Designer[1] and EMF (Eclipse Modeling Framework) modelling.

Meta-Model. The first step was to create an EMF meta-model, shown in Fig. 2[2], the source code of which is then generated and imported into new modelling projects, allowing to define purposes as diagrams and dictating the structure that such diagrams should have. *PDataStoreReference*, *PersonalData*, and *Operator*, were defined as types. *Purpose* is the main kind of entity, composed of a set of *Sessions*, composed in turn out of one or more *Ends* and sets of *Communicating Entities*, *Messages*, and *Conditions*. Communicating entities may be

---

[1] https://www.obeodesigner.com/.
[2] Full-size figures can be found at http://www.cs.ucy.ac.cy/seit/dialogop/.

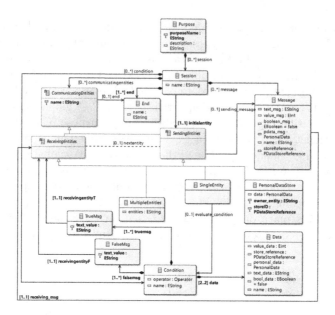

Fig. 2. DiálogoP metamodel

either *Receiving Entities* or *Sending Entities*. Each session needs to have precisely one initial entity, that will be a Sending Entity. Sending Entities may be *Single Entities* or *Personal Data Stores*. Receiving Entities may be *Single Entities*, *Personal Data Stores* or blocks of *Multiple Entities*. Conditions are composed of two sets of *Data* that will be compared based on an operator, as well as exactly one message for evaluating the condition as *True* and exactly one message for *False*. Sending Entities can be connected to at most one Condition or at most one Message, Messages can be connected to exactly one Receiving Entity, Receiving Entities can be connected directly to a Sending Entity, and all entities can be connected to an End.

Graphical Designer. New modelling projects can be created by the user in order to design models, either via the tree view or via the palette. The tree form allows the addition of children and siblings for each model entity. The tree structure root is a *Purpose* entity that can only have *Session* entities as children. In each *Session*, new children can be added including *Single Entities*, *Multiple Entities*, *Personal Data Stores*, *Messages*, *Conditions* and *Ends*, as shown in Fig. 3. All other entities cannot have any children added, except a *Condition* that can have *Data*, *True Message* and *False Message* entities as children. Each added entity has a set of properties that can be set up by the user, including its attributes values and relations with other entities. Different class instances are represented by different icons[3]. Figure 4 shows the palette that includes the

---

[3] Iconset source: https://www.iconfinder.com/iconsets/message-and-communication-sets, under Creative Commons License Attribution 3.0 Unported (CC BY 3.0).

Nodes section with all entities, and the *Edges* section, with all relations. The attributes are set. To add a node, one should first click on the respective icon from the palette, and then click on an already existing entity which is higher in the hierarchy and already placed on the canvas. Figure 5 displays the purpose diagram for the healthcare use case.

Translation into Formal Session Types. The purpose model is extracted in an XML (Extensible Markup Language) format and is fed into the custom made parser, implemented in Java, to be translated into session types definition. Two main classes, *PurposeEdge* and *PurposeEntity*, are used. The parser recognises all nodes and edges (with *xmi:type* equals to *"diagram:DEdge"*) by their *ownedDiagramElements* tag, and subsequently all inner tags *semanticElements*, from the XML document. All recognised objects with their data, are stored in lists. The lists are then parsed, recognising sessions, and the sequence of actions beginning with the initial entity and following all edges towards the end of the session by calling function *findPath*. Each situation is then handled in a different manner, e.g. in the case of conditional statements the function is called recursively for the two possible paths. Figure 6 shows the translation of the running use case to session types, as given automatically by the tool.

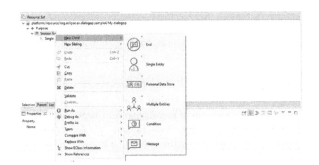

Fig. 3. New entities in a session

Fig. 4. Palette

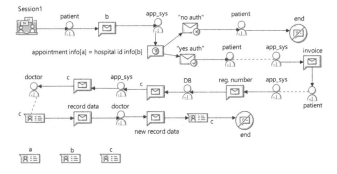

Fig. 5. The graphical purpose

Fig. 6. The translation output

4　Conclusions

We have presented our work towards an automated process for compliance of software systems to privacy policies, focusing on the GDPR notion of purpose. We have defined a formal language for purpose using session types, and we have created a graphical modelling environment that allows the definition of purposes for systems using the introduced meta-model, and the automatic transformation to the formal language. As future work, we intend to use the output to perform compliance analysis, and to extend our approach to other areas of GDPR.

References

1. Caramujo, J., da Silva, A.R., Monfared, S., Ribeiro, A., Calado, P., Breaux, T.: RSL-IL4Privacy: a domain-specific language for the rigorous specification of privacy policies. Requir. Eng. **24**(1), 1–26 (2019). https://doi.org/10.1007/s00766-018-0305-2
2. European Parliament and Council of the European Union: General data protection regulation (2015). Official Journal of the European Union
3. Honda, K., Vasconcelos, V.T., Kubo, M.: Language primitives and type discipline for structured communication-based programming. In: Hankin, C. (ed.) ESOP 1998. LNCS, vol. 1381, pp. 122–138. Springer, Heidelberg (1998). https://doi.org/10.1007/BFb0053567
4. Honda, K., Yoshida, N., Carbone, M.: Multiparty asynchronous session types. In: ACM SIGPLAN-SIGACT Symposium on Principles of Programming Languages, pp. 273–284 (2008)
5. Ingolfo, S., Siena, A., Mylopoulos, J.: Nómos 3: reasoning about regulatory compliance of requirements. In: IEEE Requirements Engineering Conference, pp. 313–314. IEEE (2014)
6. Kouzapas, D., Philippou, A.: Privacy by typing in the π-calculus. Logical Methods Comput. Sci. **13**(4), 1–42 (2017)
7. Mougiakou, E., Virvou, M.: Based on GDPR privacy in UML: case of e-learning program. In: International Conference on Information, Intelligence, Systems & Applications, pp. 1–8. IEEE (2017)
8. Ribeiro, A., da Silva, A.R.: RSLingo4Privacy studio-a tool to improve the specification and analysis of privacy policies. In: ICEIS, vol. 2, pp. 52–63 (2017)
9. Pardo, R., Colombo, C., Pace, G.J., Schneider, G.: An automata-based approach to evolving privacy policies for social networks. In: Falcone, Y., Sánchez, C. (eds.) RV 2016. LNCS, vol. 10012, pp. 285–301. Springer, Cham (2016). https://doi.org/10.1007/978-3-319-46982-9_18

10. Takeuchi, K., Honda, K., Kubo, M.: An interaction-based language and its typing system. In: Halatsis, C., Maritsas, D., Philokyprou, G., Theodoridis, S. (eds.) PARLE 1994. LNCS, vol. 817, pp. 398–413. Springer, Heidelberg (1994). https://doi.org/10.1007/3-540-58184-7_118

11. Torre, D., Soltana, G., Sabetzadeh, M., Briand, L.C., Auffinger, Y., Goes, P.: Using models to enable compliance checking against the GDPR: an experience report. In: 2019 ACM/IEEE International Conference on Model Driven Engineering Languages and Systems, pp. 1–11. IEEE (2019)

12. Zeni, N., Kiyavitskaya, N., Mich, L., Cordy, J.R., Mylopoulos, J.: GaiusT: supporting the extraction of rights and obligations for regulatory compliance. Requir. Eng. **20**(1), 1–22 (2015). https://doi.org/10.1007/s00766-013-0181-8

Identifying the Challenges and Requirements of Enterprise Architecture Frameworks for IoT Systems

Filip Vanhoorelbeke[1], Monique Snoeck[2], and Estefanía Serral[1](✉)

[1] KU Leuven, Warmoesberg 26, 1000 Brussels, Belgium
[2] KU Leuven, Naamsestraat 69, 3000 Leuven, Belgium

Abstract. Enterprise Architecture Frameworks (EAFs) have been around since the last decades of the 20th century. They are a proven practice to analyze, describe, organize, implement and manage changes in the global architecture of an enterprise's data, processes, applications and technology. Recently, new promising technologies such as big data, machine learning, and the always-and-everywhere connected Internet of Things (IoT), have made their way into all sorts of business-generating activities. The vast number of possible connectable devices, with almost infinite useful applications throughout an enterprise such as operations, human resource management, communications, and customer service, demonstrates the holistic nature of IoT. Because of that, making use of IoT cannot be treated in isolation, but should be integrated in all aspects of Enterprise Architecture. Therefore, this paper identifies the main architectural challenges and derived requirements of IoT systems for an EAF. A literature study and a questionnaire aimed at industry EA experts have been used as main data sources.

Keywords: Enterprise Architecture · Enterprise Architecture Frameworks · The Internet of Things · IoT

1 Introduction

Enterprise Architecture Frameworks (EAFs) have been around since the last decades of the 20th century, a time where memory and storage were very costly for an enterprise. However, technology has drastically evolved over the years, bringing along new types of business processes and data applications, and making unclear whether current EAFs are prepared to facilitate the management of such evolving technologies, data, and processes. One of the promising new technologies that finds itself in the adoption phase is the Internet of Things (IoT). More and more does IoT find its way in the daily lives of our society, opening a whole world of business opportunities.

IoT is still often seen as not more than a money-bleeding gimmick which has yet to prove itself as being a potential value-adding asset. It remains to be seen if the opportunities of IoT can outweigh the challenges it faces, or it becomes a liability instead of delivering business value. This is where an EAF could help by providing methodologies for constructing a to-be architecture including IoT, reference material to aid the process

© Springer Nature Switzerland AG 2020
F. Dalpiaz et al. (Eds.): RCIS 2020, LNBIP 385, pp. 576–581, 2020.
https://doi.org/10.1007/978-3-030-50316-1_41

of building such architecture, and means to inform and collect input from different kinds of stakeholders on different abstraction levels. The question is: can current EAFs support the new challenges that IoT brings? This paper will therefore focus on identifying the challenges that IoT brings for EAFs and to derive what requirements should be addressed to deal with those requirements.

The rest of this paper is organized as follows. Section 2 presents the methodology used in this paper to answer the research questions along with related works about EAFs, IoT, and EAFs specifically designed with IoT in mind. In Sect. 3, the results of the questionnaire and the interviews are elaborated on. Section 4 presents the identified IoT challenges and consequently the requirements for an EAF. Finally, this paper finishes with a discussion and possible future research in Sect. 5.

2 Research Method and Related Work

The methodology used in this paper is twofold. First, a literature study was performed to understand the current state of the art concerning IoT and EAFs, including those explicitly aimed at IoT. For the literature, around 30 papers on the topics of IoT, EAFs, EAFs for IoT, Enterprise modeling, IoT architecture, and Enterprise Architecture Management have been thoroughly researched using Google Scholar. Also, multiple surveys such as [1] have been used as source of input.

In the literature study, the challenges that IoT brings are identified. Based on these challenges, requirements that an EAF needs to satisfy to support IoT are determined. To identify the challenges, research was done on existing papers that focus on IoT challenges, e.g. [2–6]; papers that focus on EAFs' challenges, e.g. [7–9]; and papers that overlap in both topics, e.g. [10–13]. From these papers, a list of challenges was derived.

To allow for a more holistic approach towards the identification of requirements and challenges, a questionnaire aimed at Enterprise Architects was performed. Questions were asked to determine: 1) the professional profile of the expert, 2) strengths and weaknesses of the EAFs in use, 3) EAFs support for IoT. We also asked the experts if they would be willing to be interviewed. These interviews allowed for additional context on some of the responses that were given in the questionnaire. Both the literature study and the responses of the experts were used to refine the identified IoT challenges and requirements.

3 Experts' Responses

A total of 35 EAF experts answered the questionnaire of which 4 were interviewed. Their demographic information is provided in Table 1. Figure 1 shows the EAFs that were most used by these experts at their workplace. On the question whether IoT is being used or is planned on being used within the company of the experts, around 62% responded with 'definitely yes', 19% with 'probably yes', and 12% with 'might or might not'. Only 8% of the questioned experts indicate that the company they work at is not planning on using IoT to deliver business value. Over half of the respondents (58%) do not believe that new EAFs that would be specifically designed for IoT scenarios would be different from the existing EAFs, while 42% believes the opposite. While the opinion

Table 1. Demographic info

Demographic	Count	%
Number of respondents	35	
Average age	47.17	
Years of experience in EA field		
10+	24	69%
5–10	4	11%
2–5	4	11%
0–2	3	9%
Years of working experience		
10+	33	94%
5–10	1	3%
2–5	1	3%

(rounded to nearest integer, not all percentages add up to 100%)

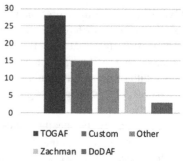

Fig. 1. EAFs in use at the respondents' company

of the experts is leaning towards the former, it is clear that there is no firm consensus on this topic yet. According to the experts who think current EAFs are not entirely suited for IoT, EAFs lack, among others: deployment models, device management, and reference architectures. The experts who think current EAFs are suited often cite that IoT is a technology as any other and that the EAFs they use have a high enough abstraction level to fit in new technologies.

4   IoT Challenges and Requirements for an EAF

This section presents the most important challenges that stem from the literature or were raised by the experts that were questioned. To define a set of requirements that an EAF needs to be able to address, the challenges that IoT brings need to be analyzed. In the following we summarize the challenges and the extracted requirements:

Multiple Stakeholder Perspectives: In an IoT system multiple stakeholders geographical distant and with a different level of interest and expertise often collaborate [3, 14]. Decision making can be a lengthy and a challenging process with multiple levels each required to approve a particular decision. Therefore, aligning the business objectives with IoT can be challenging from a governance perspective. To deal with this challenge, the EAF needs to provide a means of governance.
Primary requirements: life cycle management, governance, stakeholder management
Derived requirements: change management, reference architecture

Data Management: Devices of all kind, with diverse capabilities for IoT, can generate enormous amounts of data. This heterogeneous data needs to be processed and stored, often in a distributed way [15]. The management and storage of this data is a big challenge because current architectures are not prepared yet for this amount of information [2].

To address this challenge, an EAF needs to support adequate data management, data analytics, and device management.

Primary requirements: data management, complexity management

Derived requirements: change management, integration & interoperability, security, scalability & maintainability

Privacy and Security: Since many stakeholders are involved, a robust security strategy is required to ensure data privacy. The data that finds itself within the IoT system needs to be stored safely and with respect for privacy of the stakeholders. Especially in a European context, where the General Data Protection Regulation (GDPR, Regulation 2016/679) is in place since May 25, 2018, the way how data is handled is essential since failing to meet the requirements could have a severe financial impact on an enterprise.

Because of the severe impact a breach could have on data integrity and privacy, security is one of the most critical challenges that an EA faces [16].

Primary requirements: security, privacy

Derived requirements: change management, complexity management, risk management

Integration: Service-oriented architectures, which is the case with IoT, need integrations on multiple levels with a potentially enormous amount of different heterogeneous systems. A challenge is that different objects need to be able to work together in a standardized way. Today there is a lack of standardization and semantic interoperability on multiple levels. Because of the complexity of the involved systems, an EAF suited for IoT would benefit from reference architectures. Being able to model IoT-specific capabilities would be a valuable capability that an EAF could offer. To be able to react quickly, proper change management along with an agile supporting lifecycle management are required. Finally, it is also important to talk about the challenge of integrating IoT in an already existing architecture.

Primary requirements: integration & interoperability, complexity management, lifecycle management, reference architecture

Derived requirements: change management, governance, risk management, stakeholder management

Financial Cost: Implementing a new technology such as IoT brings along important investments. Estimating potential long-term effects of the implementation of an IoT system can be complicated. The uncertain nature of IT, the immaturity of IoT, and the rapid pace of technological advances are challenges that need proper risk assessment and control [2–17]. An EAF should be able to provide means to estimate the needed financial investment to develop the to-be EA.

Primary requirements: risk management

Derived requirements: change management, lifecycle management, stakeholder management

Reliability, Performance, and Scalability: Fallback systems are no unnecessary luxury. Not only high-availability is a must, but also the performance of communication between the different components is a crucial factor [16]. In addition, an EAF for IoT systems needs to address the fact that IoT systems can have a large scale of operations that require abstractions at different technology layers [16–18].

Primary requirements: quality management, scalability & maintainability
Derived requirements: change management, integration & interoperability, lifecycle management, risk management

EA Design Process Some EAFs have extensive reference architectures to aid the design of an architecture. It can be challenging to find adequate reference material that fits the wanted scenario. The reference models of these reference architectures can serve as templates and best-practices on how to build the system on an enterprise-scale [19]. Another challenge during the process of conceiving an architecture is that of the continuously changing business requirements.
Primary requirements: change management, lifecycle management, reference architecture
Derived requirements: complexity management

5   Conclusions, Discussion, and Future Research

The challenges and derived requirements of IoT that have been analyzed in this paper indicate that the needs of an IoT system are of a specific nature. Integration and interoperability are of the most important aspects that an EAF for IoT systems would need to address. Also, when addressing integration challenges, being able to model IoT-specific capabilities such as cloud integrations, wireless communication, and autonomous functionalities, would be a valuable EAF feature. For this, the requirement of architecture modeling is very important. Other important requirements that have been identified related to the integration challenge are security management, lifecycle management, change management and complexity management.

Remarkably, none of the experts stated explicitly the usability of a framework as an important requirement for an EAF. Usability should be a factor in the decision-making process on whether an existing EAF currently in use should be extended for IoT scenarios within a company or another more suited EAF should be chosen. However, the requirements of change management, lifecycle management, and risk management could be expanded to include this topic. Being able to quickly and effectively introduce and implement a new EAF, which could have a steep learning curve, into an enterprise is a factor that should not be underestimated. Depending on what EAF one is familiar with, and how deep one's knowledge is about an EAF, it is likely that one comes to a different conclusion on which EAF to finally use.

Future research would require deepening and refining the specifications of the identified requirements, and executing a complete comparison of established EAFs such as TOGAF, the Zachman Framework, DoDAF, and the UAF versus newer EAFs specifically aimed at IoT such as ESARC. These EAFs could be compared on basis of the identified requirements stated in this paper to determine the level of suitability of each EAF for IoT systems and to identify particular gaps that should be addressed to improve this suitability. Specifically, because the lack of best practices and reference architectures is a recurring theme amongst the inquired experts and current EAFs, future research in this area would be highly beneficial for EAFs in regard to IoT.

Acknowledgments. This research has been funded by Interne Fondsen KU Leuven / Internal Funds KU Leuven.

References

1. Gluhak, A., et al.: A survey on facilities for experimental internet of things research. IEEE Commun. Mag. **49**(11), 58–67 (2014)
2. Lee, I., Lee, K.: The Internet of Things (IoT): applications, investments, and challenges for enterprises. Bus. Horiz. **58**(4), 431–440 (2015)
3. van Kranenburg, R., Bassi, A.: IoT Challenges. Commun. Mob. Comput. **1**(1), 9 (2012)
4. Reyna, A., Martín, C., Chen, J., Soler, E., Díaz, M.: On blockchain and its integration with IoT. Challenges and opportunities. Futur. Gener. Comput. Syst. **88**(2018), 173–190 (2018)
5. Al-Fuqaha, A., Guizani, M., Mohammadi, M., Aledhari, M., Ayyash, M.: Internet of Things: a survey on enabling technologies, protocols, and applications. IEEE Commun. Surv. Tutorials **17**(4), 2347–2376 (2015)
6. Dyess, N.: Six IoT challenges, solutions. Control Eng., October, p. 21 (2018)
7. Romero, D., Vernadat, F.: Enterprise information systems state of the art: past, present and future trends. Comput. Ind. **79**, 3–13 (2016)
8. Buckl, S., Schweda, C.M.: On the state-of-the-art in enterprise architecture management literature. Technical report, p. 144 (2011)
9. Giachetti, R.: Design of Enterprise Systems. CRC Press, Florida (2010)
10. Pourzolfaghar, Z., Bastidas, V., Helfert, M.: Standardisation of enterprise architecture development for smart cities. J. Knowl. Econ., 1–22 (2019). https://doi.org/10.1007/s13132-019-00601-8
11. Dar, K., Taherkordi, A., Baraki, H., Eliassen, F., Geihs, K.: A resource oriented integration architecture for the internet of things: a business process perspective. Pervasive Mob. Comput. **20**, 145–159 (2015)
12. Baxter, R., Hastings, N., Law, A., Glass, E.J.: A rapid and robust sequence-based genotyping method for BoLA-DRB3 alleles in large numbers of heterozygous cattle. In: Uckelmann, D., Harrison, M., Michahelles, F. (eds.) Architecting the Internet of Things. Springer (2011)
13. Zimmermann, A., Schmidt, R., Sandkuhl, K., Wißotzki, M., Jugel, D., Möhring, M.: Digital enterprise architecture-transformation for the internet of things. EDOCW **2015**(October), 130–138 (2015)
14. Patel, P., Cassou, D.: Enabling high-level application development for the Internet of Things. J. Syst. Softw. **103**, 62–84 (2015)
15. Razzaque, M.A., Milojevic-Jevric, M., Palade, A., Cla, S.: Middleware for internet of things: a survey. IEEE Internet Things J. **3**(1), 70–95 (2016)
16. Udoh, I.S., Kotonya, G.: Developing IoT applications: challenges and frameworks. IET Cyber-Phys. Syst. Theory Appl. **3**(2), 65–72 (2017)
17. Fichman, R.G., Keil, M., Tiwana, A.: Beyond valuation: options thinking in it project management. Calif. Manage. Rev. **47**(2), 74–96 (2005)
18. Abdmeziem, M.R., Tandjaoui, D., Romdhani, I.: Architecting the internet of things: state of the art. In: Koubaa, A., Shakshuki, E. (eds.) Robots and Sensor Clouds. SSDC, vol. 36, pp. 55–75. Springer, Cham (2016). https://doi.org/10.1007/978-3-319-22168-7_3
19. Guinard, D., Trifa, V., Mattern, F., Wilde, E.: From the internet of things to the web of things: resource-oriented architecture and best practices. In: Uckelmann D., Harrison M., Michahelles F. (eds) Architecting the Internet of Things. Springer, Berlin (2011). https://doi.org/10.1007/978-3-642-19157-2_5

Doctoral Consortium

A Holistic Approach Towards Human Factors in Information Security and Risk

Omolola Fagbule[(✉)]

Bournemouth University, Poole, UK
ofagbule@bournemouth.ac.uk

Abstract. Businesses take various precautions and measures to protect their assets, and at the centre of their computer systems are users. Many data breaches originate from accidental human error, which has lasting damaging financial or reputation loss. Although companies intend to change behaviour, one of the biggest problems with this approach is the lack of Psychology informed theories to understand why and how users are targeted. To understand why users defy compliance procedures and policy, despite warnings and training, we need to understand every internal and external factor that contributes to such behaviour. The literature proposes that users are the main cause for system dysfunction, and this is accentuated by media headlines that portray users as the source of the problem. One of the biggest problems is that, research continues to evaluate surface level problems, rather than explore or acknowledge more systemic factors that can have damaging results. In this paper, we discuss factors, that could impact the way that information is processed and how this is translated into action or no action. Also we, identify how an environment can encourage or discourage desired behaviour.

Keywords: Human factors · Psychology · Cyber security

1 Introduction

There is a sporadic growth pertaining to Internet usage, with more than 3.9 billion worldwide users. The Office National Statistics release, 2019 suggest that [1], virtually all adults aged 16 to 44 years in the UK were recent internet users (99%). As the world embrace hyper-connected components, malicious groups exploit existing pathways and have created paths for numerous attacks to gain unauthorised access to the most sensitive information. Some businesses have taken precautionary steps to protect their assets; some enrol employees in cyber training courses, while others recruit specialists to manage their network. Despite the investment to educate users and in turn change behaviour, the business risk posture remain an easy target for cyber criminals. A criminologist, Ronald Akers, claimed that, people do not comply to security measures because they do not perceive the risks or they fail to fully understand the correct behaviour [2], and therefore act in ways best understood to them despite cyber security training.

© Springer Nature Switzerland AG 2020
F. Dalpiaz et al. (Eds.): RCIS 2020, LNBIP 385, pp. 585–594, 2020.
https://doi.org/10.1007/978-3-030-50316-1_42

The lack of noticeable change in behaviour creates uncertainty about the effectiveness of cyber security training. Although there are thousands of cyber security training aimed to increase user knowledge, and in turn minimise user risk to the business through user error. There is little work to interrogate the shortcomings of cyber security training from a Psychology perspective; a domain that centers attitudes and behaviours.

One of the ways to change behaviour is through fear appeals, these are defined as an aim to scare people by describing terrible things that will happen to them if they do not do what the message recommends [3]. In other words, it presents a risk, the vulnerability to the risk and a protective action. A common example from Health Psychology is the use of diseased lungs on cigarette packets. Research has proven this deterrent technique has falliable results, as these behaviours have not changed with lung cancer on the rise [4].

A fear appeal has similar inclinations as the Protection Motivation theory in Psychology, it is concerned with how individuals process threats and select responses to cope with the danger brought about by those threats [5]. Although fear appeals have good intentions there have been limited success, some have argued it creates fear, uncertainty and doubt, a concept in the computing realm that has proven to invoke maladaptive behaviour [6].

One of the main purposes for this paper is to evaluate existing literature, define the loopholes that do not encourage behaviour change, which will aid the sketch for furture. This paper aims to address this gap, we suggest individual differences need to be evaluated and encompass these in design to and how human factors in design can reduce unintentional user error. This study looks specifically at behaviour change in organisations, we consider the effectiveness of existing awareness and training courses for organisations and assess factors that inhibit memory retention from a psychology perspective. We examine literature corresponding to behaviour change and propose research questions to address loopholes in the literature in Sect. 2, then we evaluate risks to a business and how user error contribute to this in Sect. 3, followed by the effectiveness of cyber security training in Sect. 4, then we present the next phase of research methodology in Sect. 4.2, then we observe approaches to change behaviour in Sect. 5, followed by challenges from the presented cases in Sect. 6, and lastly future directions for future work in Sect. 6.1.

To tackle this problem, we propose to use Psychological models to show relationships between knowledge, attitudes and behaviour [7].

2   Research Questions

In this section, we foremost capture various schemes to develop mindfulness of the cyber security phenomena through training campaigns. Then we assess literature and loopholes with existing training campaigns and identify how these factors demote behaviour change. We propose research questions that could fill the missing link between users and a desired change towards cyber security.

2.1 Gender Related User Behaviour

The general consensus in the Information Security community is that human beings are the weakest link in a cybersecurity environment [8]. Some researchers have recognised the need to evaluate users to develop an effective cybersecurity training, and therefore propose to interrogate disparity in attitudes and behaviour towards cyber security from both men and women [9]. One research study examined compliance between men and women and identified that males appear to have lower security policy compliance intentions compared to females. This is an initial baseline to understand the differences between men and women, this research aim to take this a step further by investigating the drivers that compose this mindset [10]. A qualitative research approach will tailor questions to disparities and categorise them as part of the methodology. If the results suggest there is a difference, future training material can tailor this to fit the criterion.

– Research Question: Gender related user behaviourDoes gender impact user understanding for cyber security risks and training material?

2.2 External Influence on Behaviour

Cyber security awareness campaign and training material take a blanket approach, which is a one size fits all approach [11]. It is important that policy makers and commissioners take steps to address the social, environmental, economic and legislative factors that affect people's ability to change their behaviour [7]. The narrative suggests that the user context, i.e. their work environment is not considered in the design of cyber material [12]. Therefore, the next question we need to consider is, can the dynamics of a user environment affect how they respond to security warnings?

– Research Question: Can user environment contribute to how users interpret information?

2.3 Pyschology Theories

Until now, most training towards sustainable behaviour has focused on fulfilling functions, rather than aim to change the user profile into a more sustainable direction [13]. Research into behaviour change proposes that to change attitudes a persuasive appeal must be tailored to match the underlying attitude functions. [14]. The main reason to understand attitudes first is because attitude change is a precursor to behaviour change [15]. Since Psychology plays a pivotal role in the way the human mind works and how it influences behaviour [16], we would like to investigate how the study and implementation of Psychology theories and concepts such as, characteristics, behaviours and traits can enhance desired behaviour.

– Research Question: Can Psychology theories enhance behaviour change through awareness training?

3   Related Work

3.1   Human Error in Information Security

There is an increased state of inter-dependency which is pertinent to information sharing, from one user to another [17]. Yet, substantial research imply that a large proportion of security breach originate from inside the organisation mainly due to the users' ignorance or careless behaviours; some of which include sharing personal passwords and opening deceptive innocuous emails [18]. The general premise stakeholders and design architects hold about users, is they lack computer system knowledge. Many users lack the baseline knowledge of how operating systems, applications, email and web work or even how to distinguish the difference between them [19].

The Anti-Phishing Working Group, conducted a cognitive walkthrough on approximately 200 sample attacks within a "Phishing Archive" backdated from September 2003 [20]. The study depicted that users do not have the skills to distinguish forged from legitimate headers, nor do they have accurate knowledge of security indicators. For example, many users do not know that a closed padlock icon in the browser indicates that the page they are viewing was delivered securely by SSL.

Cyber criminals have identified loopholes in user systems, manipulated this for their own financial gain and exacerbate circumstances, by denying user entry and at times bring a system to a complete halt [14]. According to the National Institute of Standards and Technology [21] the people factor is paramount to providing an effective and appropriate level of security. However if people are the key, but are also a weak link, more attention must be paid to this, hence an increase for cyber security training.

4   Cyber Security Education Awareness and Training

History depicts that cybercriminals have moved away from the random type of attacks to more sophisticated methods, many of which consist of spying, hijacking and manipulating another person's computer [22]. As a result of this, 15% of these businesses and 17% of these charities have engaged in additional training and communications [23], with the expectation to equip employees to identify risks to the business. The objectives of these training campaigns tend to backfire, as they lack appropriate training cues, rewards and motivation to create and nourish a healthy security culture [14].

As organisations become ingrained in technology to achieve business objectives, some businesses have recognised the need to enhance the security awareness culture in organisations and to transform this culture into actual security conscious behaviours [24].

4.1   Reduce Human Error Through Education

Seven in ten businesses have taken, or are currently taking action to protect their organisation from further breaches [23]. Cyber security awareness campaigns are often disseminated through non-electronic methods (posters, newsletters and instructor-led training) and electronic communication methods (email notifications and eLearning) [25]. One of the biggest challenges this approach has to change behaviour is that it takes a blanket approach, it does not adopt Psychology theories that can help understand individuals, for example social choice theory or individual values [26]. One of the ways to ensure, this study does not repeat the error of the former is to use Psychology theories as a barometer to measure effectiveness in approach.

4.2 Approach

This paper adopts an inductive approach; a systematic procedure for analyzing the qualitative data in which the analysis refers to approaches that primarily use detailed readings of raw data to derive concepts, themes, or a model through interpretations made from the raw data [27].

The study adopts a mixed methodology approach, with quantitative and qualitative research strategy. The initial part of the research, will begin with quantitative research, this presents a survey that features a range of attitude and knowledge questions. The baseline results will enquire interview questions to further probe thoughts and feelings on the subject matter. The next stage of the research will be a qualitative study where we will adopt thematic analysis to compile common themes across participants. The little work in this research area means, this study will mirage trends and patterns from individuals, to propose a framework to train individuals and maintain retention and desired behaviour [28].

The qualitative phase of the study will adopt interviews as a data collection tool. Interviews are flexible, they are a useful method for data collection and effective for collecting participant experiences, beliefs and behaviours towards a particular subject area [29]. We considered alternative and additional data collection tools, such as overt observations, however research demonstrates that this method can create a hawthorne effect. This is where the researchers' presence can influence the participants behaviour due to assumption or apprehension, this has a way of manipulating data and in turn creates a set of unreliable data [30]. Similarly, we considered focus groups as a research strategy. It is defined as a planned series of discussions designed to gather perceptions on a particular subject area, in a non bias or non-threatening environment [31]. Generally, group members influence each other by responding to ideas and comments of others [32]. However, one of the biggest limitations with this approach is there is a tendency for certain types of socially acceptable opinions to arise [33], which means some individuals may withhold their true thoughts and feelings, in fear of being socially rejected. The collected data becomes questionable to whether it is inclusive of the minority, for example introverts who find it difficult to speak in public.

After a thorough evaluation of, it became pronounced that interviews are the most effective and appropiate for this research.

The inclusion criteria for the research are small and medium sized enterprises (SMEs) [34], operating within Dorset, UK with potentials to expand to the South West and have not already certified in Cyber Essentials.

5   Discussion

From the literature insight, one of the common themes identified is the lapse in user attentiveness to identify risks and how their actions can further populate opportunities for attackers misuse. The literature put a contentious onus on user flaws, and claim that users are completely incapable of understanding or using the technology. In this section, we explore areas where user interest is considered to change behaviour.

5.1   User Centred Design Approach

The development of User Centred Design (UCD) considers human interaction and usability as important drivers for a successful system design [35] and is often used alongside security by design to meet user requirements. The user requirements are often gathered at the initial phase of the design cycle, but there is limited scope to understand users from Psychology perspective. For example, the rational choice theory assume human actions are based on rational decisions; they are informed by the probable consequences of that actions, as supposed to what compliance or rules suggest [2]. We propose in the future work, to evaluate how users derive at their choice of reasoning from qualitative research and hone cyber security training to encompass these differences.

5.2   Psychology Approach to Change Behaviour

Although a business can adopt precautionary measures and invest in their Information Security infrastructure, it will not change situations, unless the users at the epitome of the system are fully understood. From a Psychological perspective, behaviour begins with an attitude. An attitude is a summary evaluation of an object of thought. An object can be anything a person favours or dislikes [10]. The importance of an attitude to behaviour in cyber security, is if users have a negative trigger towards cyber security they are likely to be unresponsive and avoid security features, whereas if they have a positive trigger they will embrace compliance and security features. Before, system administrators can place a demand on users, a root cause analysis to investigate the real cause of the problem needs to be conducted to, understand the intrinsic values of users and what triggers defiance and behaviour.

6   Conclusion

The literature review suggest there is still a gap between system design and intended user behaviour from a security perspective and a psychology perspective. The results demonstrate that, intrinsic values that compose a user have not been fully explored nor have they been adopted in new or improved system design, therefore the risk maintains a linear position in literature and reality. The future work aim to explore these themes and hypothesize that an adoption of these key features will change behaviour.

In addition to this, most cyber security training or awareness campaigns fail to acknowledge individual differences, and how these differences affect how information is processed. Furthermore, the design of cyber security training does not measure memory retention or ways to strengthen or encourage desired behaviour, which could explain a lack of compliance even after training.

6.1 Future Work

The next level of research to address the aforementioned questions, will incorporate 300 small to medium sized enterprises (SMEs), it will begin with an initial baseline survey. The survey has two sections; the first set of questions relate to user attitude towards Information Security, while the other focuses on users general knowledge about Information Security and Risks. In the attitude survey, likert scaled will be used to gauge extreme thoughts and feelings. To maintain objective and reliable results, statements will remain neutral, peradventure there are leading positive questions, they will be matched with a negative question. This is a useful method to ensure participants are being consistent and are actually reading the questions through. The project will record what department the individual works in, for example the IT team, and this will help derive narratives about attitude and perception per department.

The survey has been designed with input from business experts and reviewed by external agency, with a rigorous regressive process to minimise bias, misunderstanding or misconception.

The second phase of research is the qualitative questions, the benefit of adopting a mixed method approach is to grasp reasoning behind answers and generate useful themes and information that is not easily classified. The users will embark on a training activity, which contextualises prominent security risks to SMEs in video based scenarios. The users finalise their activity, by completing the initial attitude and knowledge survey. The post survey means we can identify the effectiveness of the training, which is measurable against the second survey.

The data gathered from the mixed methods will enable specific analysis, to address and close certain research gaps. For example, this approach will demonstrate differences in attitudes and general knowledge from gender to gender; it will identify what age range have a better insight to Information Security, for example 18–25 year olds or 50+. Furthermore, a mixed method approach means we can see if there is a correlation between attitudes and knowledge, if there is no gap identified, we can further interrogate why users do not comply with precautionary security measures, despite having full knowledge or awareness to this need, as supposed to a blanket approach to all genders.

7   Research Validation

The initial part of the research begins with a baseline test, which is dissected into two parts. Part 1 relates to the users aptitude, it brings sheds light on the importance that SME's place on cyber security, SME's awareness of existing practicies in place, the SME's perceive cyber risk and whether they understand the effect this can have on organisational productivity. While Part 2 is the knowledge questions.

Participants will be recruited through partner networks such as Silicon South (Creative Digital cluster), Wessex Entrepreneurs, Dorset Home Care Providers, Local Charities, GP Surgeries, Industrial Park Groups, Sports and Leisure Clubs.

7.1   Data Analysis Techniques

The initial part of analysis will be an Analysis of Variance (ANOVA) [36], which captures significant differences between groups from survey data at baseline. The second part of analysis is Analysis of Covariance (ANCOVA), which blends ANOVA and regression, we aim to test interaction effects on dependent variables.

7.2   Data Anonymity

To maintain participant confidentiality, we ensure data is anonymised, which will minimise the risk of data compromisation, especially if there is no key to identify the company. In order to map trends, participants will be classified in terms of size and industry sector.

References

1. Prescott, C.: Internet users, UK - office for national statistics. Ons.gov.uk (2019). https://www.ons.gov.uk/businessindustryandtrade/itandinternetindustry/bulletins/internetusers/2019. Accessed 20 Dec 2019
2. Akers, R.L.: Rational choice, deterrence, and social learning theory in criminology: the path not taken. J. Crim. L. Criminology **81**, 653 (1990)
3. Witte, K.: Putting the fear back into fear appeals: the extended parallel process model. Commun. Monogr. **59**(4), 329–349 (1992)
4. Islam, S., Dong, W.: Human factors in software security risk management. In: Proceedings of the First International Workshop on Leadership and Management in Software Architecture, pp. 13–16. ACM (2008)
5. Tunner Jr., J.F., Day, E., Crask, M.R.: Protection motivation theory: an extension of fear appeals theory in communication. J. Bus. Res. **19**(4), 267–276 (1989)
6. Pfaffenberger, B.: The rhetoric of dread: fear, uncertainty, and doubt (FUD) in information technology marketing. Knowl. Technol. Policy **13**(3), 78–92 (2000). https://doi.org/10.1007/s12130-000-1022-x
7. Nice.org.uk: Beha Behaviour change: gener viour change: general approaches al approaches (2007). https://www.nice.org.uk/guidance/ph6/resources/behaviour-change-general-approaches-pdf-55457515717. Accessed 10 Jan 2020

8. Cranor, L.F., Garfinkel, S.: Security and Usability: Designing Secure Systems that People Can Use. O'Reilly Media Inc., Sebastopol (2005)
9. Anwar, M., He, W., Ash, I., Yuan, X., Li, L., Xu, L.: Gender difference and employees' cybersecurity behaviors. Comput. Hum. Behav. **69**, 437–443 (2017)
10. Vogel, T., Wänke, M.: Attitudes and Attitude Change, 2dn edn., April 2016
11. Martin, L.M., Matlay, H.: "blanket" approaches to promoting ICT in small firms: some lessons from the DTI ladder adoption model in the UK. Internet Res. **11**(5), 399–410 (2001)
12. Beautement, A., Becker, I., Parkin, S., Krol, K., Sasse, A.: Productive security: a scalable methodology for analysing employee security behaviours. In: Twelfth Symposium on Usable Privacy and Security (SOUPS 2016), pp. 253–270 (2016)
13. Wever, R., Van Kuijk, J., Boks, C.: User-centred design for sustainable behaviour. Int. J. Sustain. Eng. **1**(1), 9–20 (2008)
14. Pfleeger, S.L., Sasse, M.A., Furnham, A.: From weakest link to security hero: transforming staff security behavior. J. Homel. Secur. Emerg. Manage. **11**(4), 489–510 (2014)
15. Ajzen, I., Fishbein, M.: Attitudes and the attitude-behavior relation: reasoned and automatic processes. Eur. Rev. Soc. Psychol. **11**(1), 1–33 (2000)
16. Henriques, G.R.: Psychology defined. J. Clin. Psychol. **60**(12), 1207–1221 (2004)
17. Rinaldi, S.M., Peerenboom, J.P., Kelly, T.K.: Identifying, understanding, and analyzing critical infrastructure interdependencies. IEEE Control Syst. Mag. **21**(6), 11–25 (2001)
18. Abawajy, J.: User preference of cyber security awareness delivery methods. Behav. Inf. Technol. **33**(3), 237–248 (2014)
19. National Research Council, System Security Study Committee, et al.: Computers At Risk: Safe Computing in the Information Age. National Academies Press, Washington, DC (1990)
20. Dhamija, R., Tygar, J.D., Hearst, M.: Why phishing works. In: Proceedings of the SIGCHI Conference on Human Factors in Computing Systems, pp. 581–590 (2006)
21. Wilson, M., Hash, J.: SP 800–50. Building an information technology security awareness and training program (2003)
22. Grobler, M., Dlamini, Z., Ngobeni, S., Labuschagne, A.: Towards a cyber security aware rural community (2011)
23. Vaidya, R.: Cyber security breaches survey 2019. Assets.publishing.service.gov.uk (2019)
24. Kumaraguru, P., Rhee, Y., Acquisti, A., Cranor, L.F., Hong, J., Nunge, E.: Protecting people from phishing: the design and evaluation of an embedded training email system. In: Proceedings of the SIGCHI Conference on Human Factors in Computing Systems, pp. 905–914(2007)
25. Susanto, H., Almunawar, M.N.: Information security awareness within business environment: an it review. SSRN 2150821 (2012)
26. Khan, B., Alghathbar, K.S., Nabi, S.I., Khan, M.K.: Effectiveness of information security awareness methods based on psychological theories. Afr. J. Bus. Manag. **5**(26), 10862 (2011)
27. Thomas, D.R.: A general inductive approach for analyzing qualitative evaluation data. Am. J. Eval. **27**(2), 237–246 (2006)
28. Castleberry, A., Nolen, A.: Thematic analysis of qualitative research data: is it as easy as it sounds? Curr. Pharm. Teach. Learn. **10**(6), 807–815 (2018)
29. Ryan, F., Coughlan, M., Cronin, P.: Interviewing in qualitative research: the one-to-one interview. Int. J. Ther. Rehabil. **16**(6), 309–314 (2009)

30. McCambridge, J., Witton, J., Elbourne, D.R.: Systematic review of the hawthorne effect: new concepts are needed to study research participation effects. J. Clin. Epidemiol. **67**(3), 267–277 (2014)
31. Larson, K., Grudens-Schuck, N., Allen, B.L.: Methodology brief: can you call it a focus group? (2004)
32. Hesse-Biber, S.N., Leavy, P.: Handbook of Emergent Methods. Guilford Press, New York (2010)
33. Smithson, J.: Using and analysing focus groups: limitations and possibilities. Int. J. Soc. Res. Methodol. **3**(2), 103–119 (2000)
34. Karmowska, G., Marciniak, M.: Small and medium-sized enterprises in European Union (2015)
35. Smetters, D.K., Grinter, R.E.: Moving from the design of usable security technologies to the design of useful secure applications. In: Proceedings of the 2002 Workshop on New Security Paradigms, pp. 82–89 (2002)
36. Girden, E.R.: ANOVA: Repeated Measures. Number 84. Sage, London (1992)

A Framework for Privacy Policy Compliance in the Internet of Things

Constantinos Ioannou[✉]

Centre for Secure, Intelligent and Usable Systems,
University of Brighton, Brighton, UK
c.ioannou1@brighton.ac.uk

Abstract. Internet of Things (IoT) structures are pervasive, incredibly complex, heterogeneous, based on various architectures and infrastructure. IoT exposes users to a number of different privacy threats that are related to leakage of personal information and loss of service. User privacy is the most important aspect of IoT environments as user's data are transmitted among connected devices without user's intervention. Therefore, the challenges that IoT privacy and security analysts are facing is relating to having difficulties to analyse and design such complex, heterogeneous systems by guaranteeing the protection of the exchanged user data. Accordingly, tools to support and guide the analyst are needed, in order to make them to design IoT systems that are compliant with privacy policies. In this paper, preliminary results are provided for designing a tool-supported, theoretical framework, including a privacy policy language and a model for the analysis of IoT systems to enforce the protection of user data in IoT environments. In this work, the literature review is illustrated for identifying the concepts and relationships needed for such a framework, an outline our preliminary design of it and the included components.

Keywords: Internet of Things · Privacy engineering · Security engineering · Requirements engineering

1 Introduction

Internet of Things is defined as "the network of physical objects that contain embedded technology to communicate and sense or interact with their internal states or the external environment." [1]. IoT has several fields of use where it can provide really valuable services, including healthcare, transportation, infrastructure and home. Sensors and wearable devices could be used in healthcare to monitor patients and senior citizens' medical conditions, help drivers to become fully aware of driving conditions and in a home setting there are various operations to automate task such as temperature control, lighting, multi-media, window and door operations etc. It is a collection of devices attached to the Internet that

© Springer Nature Switzerland AG 2020
F. Dalpiaz et al. (Eds.): RCIS 2020, LNBIP 385, pp. 595–603, 2020.
https://doi.org/10.1007/978-3-030-50316-1_43

uses nodes (a node is a connection point that can receive, create, store or send data along distributed network routes) and controllers to collect and exchange data.

Madakam, S et al. define IoT as [2] "An open and comprehensive network of intelligent objects that has the capacity to auto-organize, share information, data and resources, reacting and acting in face of situations and changes in the environment".

Internet of Things is an emerging technology and is designed to support any device without regard to its software, hardware or even supported protocols. There are possible opportunities of attacks (also known as attack surface) as IoT expands and more devices join the network. There are many issues with IoT Devices as most of them are mass-produced and are similar in design, which means one attack can be executed in multiple systems. Additionally, many IoT Systems are poorly designed and implemented, using diverse protocols and technologies that create complex configurations.

Security scientists have found increasing weaknesses in several IoT systems which could have been avoided by taking account standard security measures throughout the development phase [3]. Throughout implementation, the action of performing security analysis, guarantees that the end product fulfils particular security standards. Applying secure practises early in the development cycle, is a method recommended by the area of requirements engineering. Requirements engineering modelling is conducted by specifying the specifications of the actors in the development process in order to achieve security requirements.

Thus, this project work is focused on a privacy framework to design and analyse IoT systems by introducing a model-driven approach. A modelling language would be developed to model an IoT system. The modelling language, will include the characteristics with which define a model of an IoT system. The system's privacy posture could be analysed depending on the model's details. The method of analysis will be formalised through a collection of algorithms. The algorithms will introduced in a software tool which supports the Framework application. Concepts defined are used to build a modelling language in the area of diagrams, to construct modelling cases of IoT systems.

The framework uses concepts from the areas of study of security and privacy requirements engineering. The concepts defined are used to build a modelling language in the context of diagrams, to construct modelling cases of IoT systems.

The rest of the paper is as follows. In Sect. 2 the Research Challenges and Questions that are derived from the literature. In Sect. 3 the Literature Review illustrates preliminary results extracted from the evaluation of existing frameworks. Finally, in Sect. 4 a proposed solution that will be implemented in the future is outlined.

2 Research Challenges and Questions

IoT applications have a range of characteristics and challenges to analysis that emerge at various levels. From creating an IoT framework to implementing it and maintaining its life cycle.

An important challenge faced with IoT is the interoperability [13], as there are heterogeneous and decentralized IoT networks for the distribution and utilization of range of informations and services. Interoperability is a characteristic of IoT system that should be articulated in a modelling language.

Equally important challenge is the identification-based connectivity that is developed between a thing and the IoT system, depending on the identification of the thing [14]. IoT applications are required to communicate to networks that provide user's credentials without their assistance. In IoT contexts, at the production phase, identifiers of a device could be given. Consequently, an identifier of an object is a resource element included in the language of modelling.

Strong-level privacy challenges relate to the linked complexity of a "thing" that leads to major security threats, including disclosure threats, authenticity, data and services dignity as well as confidentiality [15]. This drives to the result that a modelling language requires to express threats and vulnerabilities.

Likewise, manageability challenges should be tackled using formal processes at the modelling level, as IoT applications mostly of the times work automatically without human intervention [16].

IoT is unique in the fact that it incorporates traditional and robust technology with modern untested technology. The combination of developed technology with new technology leads to security and privacy concerns. Due to the unique complexities, IoT's existing solutions face the main objective of the research, which determines to what degree an engineer in IoT systems can extract security as well as privacy requirements. The prior argument could be broadened to the following questions of research:

2.1   Research Questions

- **(RQ1) Research Question 1:** What are the core aspects of privacy specification for an IoT network?
- **(RQ2) Research Question 2:** What existing Privacy Requirement Engineering (PRE) tools capture privacy concepts and are they applicable for the Internet of Things environments?
- **(RQ3) Research Question 3:** How can we coherently model IoT privacy and what are the required components of a modelling language to elicit IoT Privacy Requirements?
- **(RQ4) Research Question 4:** How can we check compliance of IoT systems with privacy policies?

Starting from **RQ1**, a comprehensive and detailed analysis of the literature was conducted. The literature review was performed to recognize IoT's unique characteristics including relevant IoT Privacy issues. Furthermore, Privacy Requirements Methodologies will be investigated towards deciding if they are applicable to IoT. This will be helpful to understand the difference between traditional Privacy Requirements Engineering practises and developers' privacy practises in the context of IoT in order to resolve **RQ2**. Accordingly, a conceptual model which will be a part of a privacy framework will be proposed in order to tackle **RQ3**. The main components of the IoT Privacy Framework will be the Terminology used to address terms which classify the concepts of the privacy framework suggested. The terminology would encourage the reasoning regarding an IoT system's privacy by creating a language between privacy engineers. The Modeling language which offers elements for constructing an IoT system model which collects the information that privacy engineer requires to conduct an IoT system's privacy analysis. The conceptual model, language semantics, and language notation will be part of the modeling process. The methodology used to create model instances of an IoT system for requirements elicitation by security engineers. The methodology will include guidelines along with limitations on how modelling instances are generated using the modeling language. Lastly, to address **RQ4** which extends RQ3 an analysis processes will be employed on models and formalized. After the formalization is done, a case study will be used to evaluate and check compliance or non-compliance of IoT systems with security and privacy policies.

3   Research Methodology

The purpose of this study is to develop a deep knowledge of the concerned area with a reference to solving these issues, therefore a design-science research methodology (DSR) [17] will be used. DSR will be applied to the problem area as it is a dynamic problem-solving paradigm. It provides a simple step-by-step approach which can be adopted in any project of information technology. This method's approach is to define particular issues as well as provide novel and practical solutions using four artifacts: frameworks, models, methods and implementations. Once a problem is identified, an artifact is developed to provide a solution. The artefact, in this case, will take the form Framework for Privacy Compliance in IoT.

4   Literature Review

A quantitative Systematic Literature Review (SLR) was carried out to establish the current progress reported in the literature on approaches (methodologies, policies, etc.) that support Internet of Things privacy-awareness [18]. To identify relevant works for this review, several selection criteria have been set. Firstly, for an article to be considered appropriate, it needed to rely on both the overall area of privacy and IoT. Given that the overall emphasis of this research is on developing of IoT system's privacy, modeling is a crucial factor to be considered. The studies found required to be under the scope of model-driven engineering and include "model-driven" methods to the design of IoT systems to be included in the study. This study avoided methods such as algebraic modelling or any other mathematical methods. Papers that were published in academic journals were obtained from freely accessible scholarly literature search engines and digital libraries such as Google Scholar, IEEE, Research Gate, SCOPUS, Springer and Science Direct. The keywords used for our searches were "internet of things privacy", "internet of things challenges", "privacy requirements engineering", "model-driven" AND "IoT Privacy", "IoT*" AND "privacy requirements engineering".

To achieve complete overview of the research area, a preliminary literature review was performed to address Research Questions 1 and 2 for identifying concepts for designing a language for privacy policy compliance.

The literature presents us with privacy frameworks which are used to obtain system privacy requirements. IoT is an area which includes specific requirements and specifications. A privacy framework should be able to fulfil IoT characteristics and requirements as mentioned in the Fig. 1, in order to be applicable for security and privacy analysis. The preliminary evaluation of the frameworks regarding the criteria is presented in Fig. 1).

Criteria	[4]	[5]	[6]	[7]	[8]	[9]	[10]	[11]
Access control	-	✓	-	✓	✓	✓	✓	✓
Anonymity	-	-	✓	-	-	-	✓	✓
Consent	-	-	-	-	-	-	✓	-
Data Disclosure	-	✓	✓	-	✓	-	-	-
Data minimization	-	-	-	✓	-	-	-	✓
Openness and transparency	-	✓	-	✓	✓	-	-	✓
Safeguard and remedies	-	✓	-	✓	✓	-	-	✓
Data Lifespan	-	-	-	-	-	-	-	-
Autonomy	-	✓	-	-	-	-	-	-
Error Handling	✓	-	-	-	-	-	-	-
Adaptive	✓	-	-	-	-	-	-	-
Run-Time Adaptation	✓	-	-	-	-	-	-	-

Fig. 1. Evaluation of frameworks

The primary motivation behind the growing interest in policy-based services, networks and security systems is to facilitate flexible adaptability of behaviour by changing policy without coding or stopping the process. This indicates that it should be feasible to dynamically alter policy rules interpreted by the decentralised entities in order to adapt their behaviour.

Policies are extracted from goals and objectives, service level agreements or trust relationships within or between entities. The refining of such conceptual policies into policies referring to specific services and then into policies that can be implemented by specific service-promoting devices is not easy and can not be automated effortless.

Nonetheless, several efforts were made from a privacy and security perspective to resolve the security and privacy concerns. Certain academic studies recognise IoT security and privacy threats and recommend potential approaches for security researchers.

In their work "A Context-Based Behavioral Language for IoT" [4], the authors, proposed the use of scenario-based programming approach and specifically the graphical language of live sequence charts (LSC). This addresses one aspect of the specification growth issue by allowing a natural break-down of the specification in alignment with the requirements. The other aspect of their solution, aiming at further simplifying and shortening the specification, is based on subjecting these scenarios to context–a key concept in IoT and autonomous robot modelling. Their modelling language must be adaptive and facilitate systematic development as the specifications are typically not known in advance and improvements would be made on an ongoing basis. Also, it should have formal semantics, allow the specification of a generic functionality and support error handling.

In this paper [5], a framework for ethical requirement elicitation eFRIEND with automated reasoning is combined. In order to provide vulnerable users with trustworthy and secure IoT in healthcare contexts, they have to implement ethics in order to meet acceptable system requirements. Their project address key principles such as accessibility, data protection, reliability, transparency, and autonomy.

Aivaloglou, Gritzalis and Skianis [6], identified a set of requirements for the development of sensing network that are aware of privacy. The suggested model was developed from an awareness based on data security standards including privacy issues. This recommendation proposes five concepts that are focused on sensor networks, the foundation for the creation of omnipresent IoT-based solutions that carry higher privacy risks.

In May 2008, a detailed privacy and security policy was published by the Center for Democracy & Technology [7] to promote health data protection. This framework is a modified version of the Common Framework published by the Markle Foundation in the Connecting for Health (Markle Foundation, 2008) initiative. The framework includes 9 concepts based on a combination of legislative action, policy and engagement from industry.

The U.S. National Health Information Technology Coordinator's Office (Local Coordinator's Office, 2008) [8] also implemented a standardized system for the digital sharing of personally identifiable information. A systematic study and evaluation of these concepts were carried out by taking into account as many differences as possible while also keeping in mind how they can be applied to electronic data. The ONC framework incorporates eight principles which act as guidance for public and private sector organizations keeping or sharing individual health-related electronic data and helping direct the implementation of health information technology by the government.

Alqassem and Svetinovic [9] published a taxonomy on the IoT's criteria for security and privacy in 2014. In an IoT smart grid case, the taxonomy provided value characteristics which were enforced. The paper provides support for further review of IoT-related vulnerabilities and threats to the expected privacy and security. The four concepts mentioned specifically address IoT's security aspects.

Recently, in the scope of disabled people, AL-mawee [10], published a survey of security and privacy concerns in IoT healthcare applications. There has been a broad range of IoT-based applications for the elderly. Such presentations described the applications ' security and privacy concerns. In addition, key approaches for such applications have been discussed extensively and notable privacy and security requirements have also been identified for the impaired.

Furthermore, IoT development recommendations have been published by Porambage et al. [11]. The recommendations proposed apply explicitly to education, smart homes, public safety and supply management to tackle privacy issues and concerns for different sectors. Moreover, the recommendations produced are focused on analysing the related pieces of technology or application-specific data security mechanisms and characteristics of the IoT network including the technical aspects and legislative regulations. While implementing an IoT privacy system, it offers nine features to be included.

5   Research Outputs and Proposed Solution

The outputs of a various framework elements could be linked to both the goals and research questions the above research study seeks to resolve (see Sect. 2.1). More precisely, with respect to the first research question, this was addressed with a review of the literature (RQ1) on both the key characteristics and criteria of an IoT device. For (RQ2) the findings of the research study are used to define the appropriate elements of the language of modelling. The language definition will be based on current techniques and frameworks for the network security. This will be done to make it easier for security engineering experts to use the language. The purpose for that is to allow current tooling and workflows to use Framework models, software, and processes.

The proposed contribution will be the theoretical approach and implementation of Internet of Things Privacy Policy Framework. This study also contributes to the increasing demand for field studies in the field of privacy. The obtained insights into developer approach for generating and analysing privacy standards could provide the privacy field with useful information. The privacy compliance product could not be incorporating with privacy techniques It also requires analysing the problem from its root which in some cases might be in the development phase. Maintaining IoT system's security and privacy is a complex task; the lack of open models from many frameworks and approaches is an important issue throughout the review of the literature and the implementation of the methodology. Although a number of frameworks and methods have been classified, the majority have no examples of models or the analysis other than the one incorporated in their publication.

This motivates the research project to contribute to the area of Internet of Things with a conceptual model for IoT, a methodology to construct privacy requirements and an extension in a security requirements framework that will incorporate privacy to reason IoT. The core aim of the project is to model requirement engineering privacy concepts relate to IoT throughout a conceptual model. To achieve the above existing model of Requirements Engineering as well as models of IoT systems will be reused. The project will contribute by incorporate and extending these models and enrich them with privacy concepts required in IoT.

The novelty of contribution of the theoretical framework and the supporting tool will incorporated with the following characteristics:

- **An Internet of Things modelling language which includes conceptual model:** a conceptual model will be designed to generate privacy requirements and privacy controls whenever the required data is received.
- **Privacy for Internet of Things native devices:** there is a huge growth in the Internet of Things as different devices connect to the IoT infrastructure. Currently privacy framework focus to secure specific applications or networks. Even large corporations privacy frameworks are only considering a specific range of devices. With Internet of Things these framework are limited, since IoT network could be populated by any type of device which also includes constraint devices such as sensors and actuators.
- **Support Privacy Analysis during development and deployment:** privacy mechanisms must be used while designing a device, and then modified as it moves to different stages of development, in order to be effective. When a product have already been released the assistance is limited. When a product is launched, has to be investigated by privacy analysts to identify the vulnerabilities. Based on the type of item there may be massively different methods of monitoring. The suggested privacy framework would be able to execute on both phases, development stage, as well as stage of deployment.

6   Conclusion and Future Directions

In this work, the steps towards the development of a privacy framework for design and analysis of IoT systems along with the intermediate findings of the project research are presented. In a preliminary way, RQ1 and RQ2 are addressed with a literature review and individuation of the necessary concepts for a privacy policy language for IoT. On the basis of the results extracted from the preliminary evaluation the design of a theoretical framework which includes a language, a model for privacy policy compliance analysis and supporting tool, is currently under development. The framework consists of various components that when applied can model an Internet of Things environment which comply with privacy requirements. The main components of such framework are the modelling language to illustrate IoT environments, modelling methodology to produce models, processes to check the model's privacy and finally to present methods to extend the privacy posture of the models. The design of the framework along with the supporting tool will be as dynamic as possible. Currently existing privacy frameworks are lacking the dynamic feature as their update cycle can be span to several years which is consider quite static. The practical implementation and the validity of the framework will be examined after its completion. The validity of the artefact will be determined by a variety of case studies [12] that will use the framework in order to mitigate privacy issues.

References

1. Voas, J.: Demystifying the Internet of Things. Computer **49**, 80–83 (2016). https://doi.org/10.1109/mc.2016.162
2. Madakam, S., Ramaswamy, R., Tripathi, S.: Internet of Things (IoT): a literature review. J. Compu. Commun. **03**, 164–173 (2015). https://doi.org/10.4236/jcc.2015.35021
3. Roy, S., Manoj, B.S.: IoT enablers and their security and privacy issues. In: Mavromoustakis, C.X., Mastorakis, G., Batalla, J.M. (eds.) Internet of Things (IoT) in 5G Mobile Technologies. MOST, vol. 8, pp. 449–482. Springer, Cham (2016). https://doi.org/10.1007/978-3-319-30913-2_19
4. Elyasaf, A., Marron, A., Sturm, A., Weiss, G.: A context-based behavioral language for IoT. In: MODELS Workshops, pp. 485–494 (2018)
5. Kammüller, F., Augusto, J.C., Jones, S.: Security and privacy requirements engineering for human centric IoT systems using eFRIEND and Isabelle. In: 2017 IEEE 15th International Conference on Software Engineering Research, Management and Applications (SERA), pp. 401–406. IEEE, June 2017
6. Aivaloglou, E., Gritzalis, S., Skianis, C.: NETp1-08: requirements and challenges in the design of privacy-aware sensor networks. In: IEEE Globecom 2006, pp. 1–5 (2006)
7. McGraw, D.: Comprehensive privacy and security: critical for health information technology. White paper, May 2008 (2008)
8. Goldstein, M.M.: Health information privacy and health information technology in the US correctional setting. Am. J. Public Health **104**(5), 803–809 (2014)
9. Alqassem, I., Svetinovic, D.: A taxonomy of security and privacy requirements for the Internet of Things (IoT). In: 2014 IEEE International Conference on Industrial Engineering and Engineering Management, Bandar Sunway, pp. 1244–1248 (2014)
10. AL-mawee, W.: Privacy and security issues in IoT healthcare applications for the disabled users a survey (2012)
11. Porambage, P., Ylianttila, M., Schmitt, C., Kumar, P., Gurtov, A., Vasilakos, A.V.: The quest for privacy in the Internet of Things (2016)
12. Piras, L., et al.: Defend architecture: a privacy by design platform for GDPR compliance. In: 16th International Conference on Trust, Privacy and Security in Digital Business (TrustBus) (2019)
13. Al Fuqaha, A., Guizani, M., Mohammadi, M., Aledhari, M., Ayyash, M.: Internet of Things: a survey on enabling technologies, protocols, and applications (2015)
14. Atzori, L., Iera, A., Morabito, G.: The Internet of Things: a survey (2010)
15. Mahmoud, R., Yousuf, T., Aloul, F., Zualkernan, I.: Internet of Things (IoT) security: current status, challenges and prospective measures, Vancouver (2010)
16. Madhura, P.M., Jain, P., Ranjith, J., Bilurkar, N.: A survey on internet of things: security and privacy issues. IJITR **3**(3), 2069–2074 (2015)
17. Wieringa, R.J.: Design Science Methodology for Information Systems and Software Engineering. Springer, Heidelberg (2014). https://doi.org/10.1007/978-3-662-43839-8
18. March, S.T., Storey, V.C.: Design science in the information systems discipline: an introduction to the special issue on design science research. MIS Q. **32**(4), 725–730 (2008)

Social-Based Physical Reconstruction Planning in Case of Natural Disaster: A Machine Learning Approach

Ghulam Mudassir$^{(\boxtimes)}$

Department of Information Engineering, Computer Science and Mathematics,
University of L'Aquila, Via Vetoio, 67100 L'Aquila, Italy
ghulam.mudassir@graduate.univaq.it
https://www.disim.univaq.it/

Abstract. Natural disasters have several adverse effects on human lives. It is challenging for the governments to tackle these events and to reconstruct damaged areas with minimal budget and time, but still guaranteeing social benefits to the affected population. This article presents an approach of decision-support system for post-disaster re-construction planning of buildings damaged by a natural disaster. The proposed framework determines a set of alternative plans which satisfy all constraints, accommodate political priorities, and guarantee social benefits for the affected population. The determined plans are then provided to public servants that select the plan to implement. The approach is generic and it can be applied to areas of any extension as long as the decision makers share the same goals. We will demonstrate the approach on the L'Aquila city destroyed by an earthquake in 2009.

Keywords: Decision-support system · Natural disaster · Social benefits · Political priority · Reconstruction planning

1 Introduction

Natural disasters[1] have impact on the surrounding environment, population, and societal future development. The produced effects are much higher if the disaster happens close to a residential area, where infrastructures and buildings can be heavily damaged [2].

Overcoming those effects, by assessing all the needs of the involved citizens, private companies and public institutions, is a critical and difficult task. The task is so difficult that the time after the disaster, called the post-disaster recovery phase, is defined by Contreras et al. [4] as a *complex multidimensional, long-term process involving planning, financing, decision-making, and reconstruction*. Moreover, the post-disaster recovery phase can be divided into four sub-phases:

---

[1] Such as, but not limited to, earthquakes, floods, and storms.

© Springer Nature Switzerland AG 2020
F. Dalpiaz et al. (Eds.): RCIS 2020, LNBIP 385, pp. 604–612, 2020.
https://doi.org/10.1007/978-3-030-50316-1_44

relief, early recovery, recovery, and *development* [9]. In the *relief* phase, as highlighted by [1,7], the priority is to save the lives of people through the deployment of search-and-rescue (SAR) task forces. The main objective during the *early recovery* and *recovery* phases is to bring back to the normality the destroyed areas [1]. To achieve this goal, a *recovery plan*, composed of all the actions that must be accomplished, is defined into the early recovery phase and ran during the recovery phase.

In the early recovery stage, rubble is removed, the roads are rehabilitated, damaged buildings are demolished, and temporary shelters begin to be removed. While, in the recovery phase, through continuing implementation of the recovery plan, essential services and urban facilities become fully functional, and the removal of temporary shelters finishes. Reconstruction and/or repair of buildings and environmental rehabilitation is prominent in the recovery phase [3]: monuments are erected to commemorate the disaster [1]; the construction of buildings, parks, and monuments gradually decreases, and rehabilitation of the environment continues [3].

One fundamental problem that needs to be effectively tackled, from the national, regional, and municipal perspective is to define a post-disaster recovery plan. The plan includes, but is not limited to, the definition of guidelines on how to re-qualify the affected areas, defines which are the most important facilities that are needed to be rebuilt at first, and describes all those actions that must take in place to get back the area to the normality.

The public decision makers face the challenging issue of defining a recovery plan that considers and balances all the involved formal and informal requirements and that guarantees the repopulating of the damaged area. On the one hand, they must consider the benefits that come from optimizing some values, e.g., the vulnerability of buildings, the budget and time required to accomplish the building plan. On the other hand, the development plans, must be implemented in accordance with the new strategies devised to drive future development also taking into account the sustainability of the made decisions. Additionally, another unconsidered aspect, that instead should be taken into account by the public decision makers, is the societal impact and relative benefits that citizens experience from the implementation of a certain recovery plan. Indeed, the societal impact and benefits are different from one plan to another, and they should be key feature to consider in all post-disaster phases.

For the aforementioned complexities, the aim of this work is to provide to public decision makers, servants and citizens a *post disaster Rebuilding Plan Provider (pd-RPP)* mechanism that helps to effectively define and evaluate alternative rebuilding plans. The provided rebuilding plans can be employed, and later on reformulated, during the early recovery, recovery, and development subphases of the post-disaster recovery phase.

A rebuilding plan is the part of the *recovery plan* dedicated to schedule the order of the buildings, or more in general of reconstruction units, that can be rebuilt/rehabilitated. A reconstruction unit can be a private or public building, and, as first implementation, we are not considering any kind of public infrastructures (e.g., highways).

In this paper, we present an innovative *post disaster Rebuilding Plan Provider (pd-RPP)* approach that takes into account the *Physical* features of the city, time and budget constraints, and embeds *Social* needs and benefits in accordance with *Political* priorities.

The approach is generic since, changing the input parameters (i.e, political priority, considered area and social benefit model), it can generate different viable plans. The generated plans can have different territorial extension under a single municipality, satisfy different political constraints and consider different social benefit models. The approach can be applied on a wider area involving several municipalities if the decision variables are shared among the decision makers. The presented approach will be the core of a decision-support system we aim to implement.

The paper is organised as follows: Sect. 2 presents research challenges and highlights our research questions. Section 3 presents the research methodology. Section 4 sketches the used machine learning approach and reports some preliminary results. The last section contains discussions and conclusions.

2   Research Challenges and Questions

Due to its complexity, the manual definition of the rebuilding planning is risky and error-prone. In literature, there are several papers that face the problem of post-disaster recovery. Opricovic et al. [8] developed a multi-criteria model (MCDM) for analysis of post-disaster planning both at the economic and engineering level. MCDM selects, among a set of alternative plans, the best one by considering eight different parameters (e.g., location, magnitude of the earthquake, risk probability and reconstruction techniques). Fuzzy multi-criteria optimization is used to convert the qualitative variables into quantitative ones. Differently from [8], our pd-RPP mechanism considers required reconstruction time, social benefits and political priorities. Moreover, [8] used Fuzzy set theory which is not suitable to deal with real cases. Instead, we use Reinforcement learning to determine plans that work better when big data are managed as in real situations that we target.

Goujon et al. [6] proposed a multi-criteria decision support model to define the priority and the evaluation of reconstruction projects taking into account the population needs. Similarly, Tavakkol et al. [10] proposed a framework for the post-disaster decision-making process about collapsed buildings, road closures, and so on. Differently from our work, both papers do not combine in the model reconstruction time, social benefits and political priorities and do not use the reinforcement learning to generate plans.

Eid et al. [5] developed an innovative decision framework by adopting agent-based approach. They have adopted short term and long term redevelopment goals by considering three-dimensional vulnerabilities of communities like social, economic, and environmental ones. For this purpose, they have used a residential agent, an economic agent, and a state disaster recovery agent. The main purpose of the last one is to evaluate the recovery plan and prioritize the objective of the recovery. In [5], time, social benefits and political priorities are not considered.

All the related works are focused on proposing reconstruction strategies without giving an exact planning. As a result, none of the reviewed approaches can give concrete support into a real-time complex scenario. The approach we propose is different from these ones since it explicitly considers the following aspects:

- *any Physical dependencies* among reconstruction units (like bridge/ flyover) that impose ordering in the building reconstruction.
- *Political priority* constraint that imposes a threshold on the plan in order to guarantee that the building plan respects the set political strategies.
- *Social benefits* that, regarding the number of people who will use any unit/ building, describe how much the plan is beneficial for the affected community.

The treatment of such aspects as well as the implementation of a solution algorithm that can be accurate and efficient in real situations, are very challenging. The research questions deriving from these challenges are:

- **RQ1:** Which is the best way to embeds the **political constraints** into the rebuilding planning model?
- **RQ2:** Which is the best way to reflects local community needs - namely, **social benefits** - and embeds them into the rebuilding planning model?
- **RQ3:** Which is the **most appropriate approach** to implement that efficiently provides high quality rebuilding plans on real case studies?
- **RQ4:** How do we **evaluate the proposed pd-RPP mechanism** on the real case study of L'Aquila city destroyed by a major earthquake in 2009?

Work Plan - The presented research project will be carried out in three years PhD program and it considers all mentioned research questions. Currently we are at the beginning of the second year. Figure 1 reports the established work plan in the form of Gantt Chart which indicates how different tasks will be accomplished.

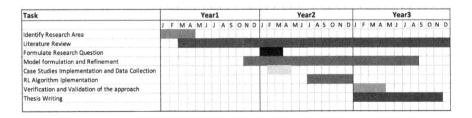

Fig. 1. Activities of the project.

3 Methodology

Figure 2 sketches the methodology we will implement for the research project. It consists of three steps. The first step, namely *Data Processing*, collects *data* about area to rebuild (such as a city) and the status of buildings. For the L'Aquila case study, we collect all the information from the municipality using the USRA (L'Ufficio Speciale per la Ricostruzione dell'Aquila) website. Such data also provides physical dependencies among buildings, their status, and how many people resides in each building. This data is then integrated with political priority. In this step, the collected data is *processed* and represented in the form of an *undirected graph* where each node is a building and the edges represent roads and streets connecting the buildings. Thanks to map representation of the city (e.g. through open street map or google maps) we are able to label the edges with distances among buildings. Where such information is not explicit in the map, it is estimated using geographical coordinates of building provided by the USRA Web GIS (Geographic Information System).

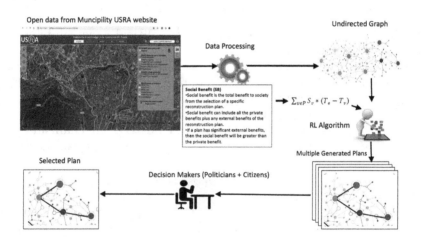

Fig. 2. Research methodology

Figure 3 describes about *physical dependencies* and *political priorities* among buildings. There are three buildings: *Building 1* is physically dependent on *Building 2* because it can be reached only through *Building 2*. Hence, *Building 1* must be reconstructed first. Moreover, political priority of *Building 1* is higher than *Building 2* that's another reason for *Building 1* to reconstruct first. Similarly *Building 3* is accessed through *Small Street* (that represents a physical dependency, namely edge *e*) from *Building 1* and *Building 2*. If *e* is damage, *e* is reconstructed first to access *Building 3*.

Using the produced graph and the definition of a function specifying the *social benefits*, the second step of Fig. 2, i.e., *RL Algorithm*, implements a reinforcement learning approach that generates a set of alternative reconstruction plans, all

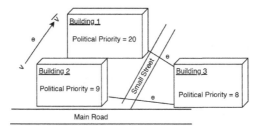

Fig. 3. Physical dependencies

satisfying budget, time, physical and political constraints. The RL Algorithm leverages on agents that, in deciding about which node to add in the plan, measures the *social benefits*, and verifies all the defined constraints.

Our definition of social benefits is inspired by the one reported in[2]. The social benefit is measured directly through local affected community and the social benefit of a plan P is defined as:

$$\sum_{v \in P} S_v * (T_e - T_v)$$

the sum of the benefit S_v gained by the reconstruction of each unit v in the plan. Indeed, the benefit starts at the time of rebuilding completion of v (i.e., T_v) and it continues until the end of the recovery phase (T_e).

At the end of second step, the generated rebuilding plans will be analysed by the *decision-makers* (politicians or affected citizens) in order to provide an evaluation that takes into account end user perspective and not only analytical measures. In final step a building plan will be selected.

4   Proposed Solution and Results

We will use reinforcement learning technique (Q-Learning algorithm) in pd-PRP mechanism because it requires minimum computation and it can be easily implemented for complex problems. Basically Q-Learning algorithm consists on *reward, action space and state space*. When agents perform action according to defined policies in any space/environment, the agents get a reward[3]. To use Q-Learning in pd-PRP mechanism, we have to modify it according to requirements. Additionally Q-Learning algorithm has to check if the priority of the whole plan (calculated as the weighted sum of the priority set by politicians on each building) is beyond a given threshold *(RQ1)*. The decision on which plan to implement will be taken by *political administrators*. The order of reconstruction (which building to reconstruct first) in any plan depends on the social benefits of every unit. If any unit has a maximum social benefit, it will be constructed first

---

[2] https://www.economicshelp.org/blog/glossary/social-benefit/.
[3] https://pathmind.com/wiki/deep-reinforcement-learning.

(RQ3). In our first implementation, the social benefit is measured as the number of people who use that building *(RQ2)*. On the other hand, if there would be any *physical dependency* among units that are part of the plan, this dependency is considered to determine the order of unit reconstruction *(first part of RQ3)*. For verification and validation of pd-PRP approach we consider L'Aquila city which was destroyed from major earthquake in 2009 *(RQ4)*. Data-sets are provided from municipality of L'Aquila and it is of sufficient quality and quantity to test our planning model.

Modeling in reinforcement learning consists of three parameters which are *Rewards* (agent receives rewards/penalties on behalf of action) *(RQ2)*, *State Space* (information for agent) *(RQ1)* and *Actions Space* (movement of an agent). Each agent takes into account all *Physical features* like *(Physical dependencies, Political priority, and Social benefits)* as Reward, State Space and Action Space as the follows:

Reward is dependent on agent actions. Some key points for the magnitude of rewards/penalties according to agent behaviour are:

- The agent gets high positive reward if considers a unit which is beneficial to the maximum number of people.
- Agent is penalized if it considers those units which are not beneficial for the people.
- Agent is slightly penalized if it considers unit which is little beneficial for the local community.

State Space defines policies for the agent to move in right direction. The policies are outlined below:

- At least 80% of the buildings should be considered from overall damage territory in every plan.
- If there is any physical dependency (bridge/flyover) among reconstruction units, this dependency must be considered in the reconstruction plan.
- Cost should be at most as the defined budget.
- Distance between rebuilt units and new planned ones should be minimum.
- Reconstruction time must be at most as the defined one.

Action Space is the set of all actions agent can take in a given state space. An action let the agent transit to a different state. In our model, action space allows the Agent to move from one unit to any other units to reconstruct available in the graph.

According to the Q-Learning algorithm, agent performs every action on behalf of defined policy in the state space and gets a reward. Once the Q-learning agent is fully trained on real data set, efficient results are obtained.

On behalf of the proposed methodology, after its implementation on a small zone in L'Aquila data, the following provisional results are expected:

R1: The proposed model is an efficient mechanism to define reconstruct plans on behalf of social benefits.

R2: Proposed framework provides a set of alternative plans which contain different order of reconstruction units.

R3: The proposed model minimizes human errors in reconstruction planning.

R4: Every plan satisfies time, budget and political priority constraints.

R5: The proposed approach has the ability to identify and consider physical dependencies among reconstruction units.

5   Conclusion

In this paper, we have proposed a generic approach of post-disaster reconstruction planning that will be the core of a decision-support system. The proposed model will help to define the reconstruction plan on behalf of the social benefits of local affected communities. Additionally, we will modify exiting Q-Learning algorithm according to requirements of our model to determine a set of alternative reconstruction plans by satisfying all posed constraints.

Acknowledgements. This PhD project is part of Terrotori Aperti project funded by Fondo Territori Lavoro e Conoscenza CGIL, CSIL and UIL.

References

1. Alexander, D.: From rubble to monument revisited: modernised perspectives on recovery from disaster. In: Post-Disaster Reconstruction: Meeting Stakeholder Interests. Firenze University Press (2006)
2. Bilau, A.A., Witt, E., Lill, I.: A framework for managing post-disaster housing reconstruction. Proc. Econ. Finance **21**(15), 313–320 (2015)
3. Brown, D., Platt, S., Bevington, J.: Disaster recovery indicators: Guidelines for monitoring and evaluation. Cambridge University Centre for Risk in the Built Environment (2010)
4. Contreras, D., Blaschke, T., Kienberger, S., Zeil, P.: Myths and realities about the recovery of L'Aquila after the earthquake. Int. J. Disaster Risk Reduct. **8**, 125–142 (2014)
5. Eid, M.S., El-Adaway, I.H.: Decision-making framework for holistic sustainable disaster recovery: agent-based approach for decreasing vulnerabilities of the associated communities. J. Infrastruct. Syst. **24**(3) (2018)
6. Goujon, B., Labreuche, C.: Use of a multi-criteria decision support tool to prioritize reconstruction projects in a post-disaster phase. In: 2nd International Conference ICT-DM 2015, pp. 200–206 (2015)
7. Kates, R., Pijawka, D.: In: Haas, J.E., Kates, R.W., Bowden, M.J. (eds.) Reconstruction Following Disaster (1977)
8. Opricovic, S., Tzeng, G.-H.: Multicriteria planning of post - earthquake sustainable reconstruction (2002)

9. United Nations Development Programme: UNDP Policy on Early Recovery (2008). Accessed Jan 2019
10. Tavakkol, S., To, H., Kim, S.H., Lynett, P., Shahabi, C.: An entropy-based framework for efficient post-disaster assessment based on crowdsourced data. In: ACM SIGSPATIAL International Workshop EM-GIS, pp. 13:1–13:8 (2016)

Explainability Design Patterns in Clinical Decision Support Systems

Mohammad Naiseh[(⊠)]

Faculty of Science and Technology, Bournemouth University, Bournemouth, UK
mnaiseh@bournemouth.ac.uk

Abstract. This paper reports on the ongoing PhD project in the field of explaining the clinical decision support systems (CDSSs) recommendations to medical practitioners. Recently, the explainability research in the medical domain has witnessed a surge of advances with a focus on two main methods: The first focuses on developing models that are explainable and transparent in its nature (e.g. rule-based algorithms). The second investigates the interpretability of the black-box models without looking at the mechanism behind it (e.g. LIME) as a post-hoc explanation. However, overlooking the human-factors and the usability aspect of the explanation introduced new risks following the system recommendations, e.g. over-trust and under-trust. Due to such limitation, there is a growing demand for usable explanations for CDSSs to enable the integration of trust calibration and informed decision-making in these systems by identifying when the recommendation is correct to follow. This research aims to develop explainability design patterns with the aim of calibrating medical practitioners trust in the CDSSs. This paper concludes the PhD methodology and literature around the research problem is also discussed.

Keywords: Explainability · Decision support systems · User-centred design · Trust

1 Context and Motivation

The development of Clinical Decision Support Systems (CDSSs) has led to a surge of interest in systems optimised not only for expected task performance and accuracy but also other critical criteria such as safety, transparency, avoiding technical debt or providing explanations. While efforts to make CDSSs transparent and explainable have been demonstrated [18,20,21], failing to calibrate user trust is one of the new errors introduced by using these tools. For example, Bussone et al. [3] studied the effect of the explanation on trust and reliance. They concluded that overlooking the human factors and user experience in the design of CDSSs explanation could lead to medical professionals over-trust the system recommendation, even when it is wrong, i.e. over-reliance. In the same way, the explanation that does not provide enough information could lead to users rejecting the suggestions, i.e. self-reliance or under-trust [13].

© Springer Nature Switzerland AG 2020
F. Dalpiaz et al. (Eds.): RCIS 2020, LNBIP 385, pp. 613–620, 2020.
https://doi.org/10.1007/978-3-030-50316-1_45

Explainability in the medical domain is defined as a set of measurable, quantifiable, and transferable attributes associated with the intelligent system that the aim to calibrate medical practitioners trust [20]. While the increasing interest in explainable clinical systems, it has become important to develop explainability design solutions that better suit the clinical decision-marking with the focus on their trust as a crucial factor. Here, the research distinguishes between the explainable model which generates the explanation and the explainable interface which makes the explanation usable and useful for the medical practitioners. This research is limited only to the explainable interface and its relevant design factors and facets to support the medical practitioners' decision-making and reduce the errors of failing to calibrate user-trust issue, i.e. under-trust and over-trust.

Among the possible ways for trust calibration (e.g. algorithmic assurances [1], automation reliability [11], personalisation [9], and explainablity [3]), this research focuses on the latter aspect of the trust calibration. This research argues that the effectiveness of the explanation design in relation to CDSSs can be itself basis or solutions to contribute to calibrate medical practitioners trust. Furthermore, this research is limited to the post-hoc explanation capabilities which refer to explanation models that are applied after model training. This PhD aims to develop HCI design patterns for post-hoc explanations in CDSSs with the aim of reducing trust calibration errors.

Qualitative research is the baseline for achieving that goal. This is due to the intense medical nature of the problem and solutions and the need for intensive input from medical practitioners. Studies including a systematic literature review, semi-structured interviews and think-aloud protocol are used to provide a conceptualisation for various aspects of explainability in clinical decision support systems. The design patterns and the explainable interface are then will be evaluated by means of two case studies (Prescribing breast cancer treatment and screening Palbociclibii Cancer treatment prescription) on IQemoi[1] prescribing system to investigate the efficiency of the produced solutions in calibrating user trust.

2   Background and Related Work

2.1   Human-Computer Interaction (HCI) and Explainability

The Human-Computer Interaction research community has identified several benefits of generating explanations by artificial intelligence agents [15]. For example, Samek et al. [17] present four social benefits aspects that are important for users interacting with intelligent systems. Interaction techniques and user feedback with explainable agents such as recommender systems and expert systems have widely studied in the literature of HCI. For example, Kuleza et al. [8] developed an explanatory debugging system that explains the decision and incorporates user feedback, which was shown to lead to better predictions, sounder

---

[1] iQemo, from iQ HealthTech, is a complete managed chemotherapy patient management and prescribing module. https://www.iqhealth.tech.

mental models and higher user satisfaction. During the development of the explainable system, the research community identifies a collection of explanation properties and requirements that are important to generate useful and usable explanations. Many of these aspects are built based on the literature of social sciences, psychology and education to mimic the human to human explanations. Sokol et al. [19] present 11 usability requirements for the explanations which are: Soundness, Completeness, Contextfullness, Interactiveness, Actionability, Chronology, Coherence, Novelty, Complexity and Personalisation. Also, the initial findings from this PhD research provide in-depth investigation about the conceptualisation of the personalisation aspect in a previous work [14]. Since the implementation of these aspects has been limited to low stake applications, these principles and findings may not translate to high stake applications where trust calibration and safety are crucial requirements. A lack of clearly defined user experience aspects that the explainable interface should be considered in high stake applications with trust-calibration is the main focus is still missing.

Additionally, the HCI research literature identifies the risks of the explainable interfaces on users decision-making and their perception of the system. These risks are likely to arise when the designers overlook the user experience factors. For instance, users may feel that the system is trying to manipulate them when the explanation does not contain enough information or consistent with their prior beliefs [6]. The ongoing research findings identify six different possible risks that could arise in the absence of user-centred approaches, which are: Overtrust, Under-trust, Refusal, Perceived loss of control, Information overload and Suspicious motivation [13]. Finally, the HCI research community argued the ability of the explainable systems to be engineered to work in a long-term and evolve during the time based on what has already explained to the end-users before [12].

2.2 HCI Design Patterns

HCI design patterns are predefined and reusable design solutions that describe and solve users' problems. Alexander [2] argued that the pattern should capture context where the pattern can be applied, the problem and its environments, and the design guidance. Designers of new systems can take benefit from the design pattern and save the efforts and resources to build usable systems. When designing the explainable system, the development process needs to consider the explainee characteristics, needs, usability aspect and safety requirements [19]. Design pattern could help the baseline for such requirements by identifying the possible design problem and make the design solution available for future practice. For instance, TELL project [5] uses the design patterns to support the understanding of the learning process that occurs within the network supported collaborative learning. To date, very little work has investigated HCI design patterns for the explainable interfaces e.g. Chromik et al. [4] present and discuss several dark design patterns that designers of the explainable interfaces should avoid it.

2.3 Trust Calibration

Existing work has investigated how users develop their trust with the intelligent systems with focusing on the factors that affect user trust in complex systems (e.g. transparency) [7,9]. Trust is a dynamic and complex psychological and sociological concept, when the trustee over-trust or under-trust the automation system could lead to critical consequences, especially in safety-critical domains. Madhavan et al. [10] defined the problem of failing to calibrate users trust as it is a failure in the system design in balancing the actual safety and the users' perceived safety. Providing explanations is meant to be one of the factors that may contribute to the problem. Users may over-trust the system when the explainable interface is not built on the user experience aspect [3]. Also, the explanation may lead to users under-trust the systems, when the explanation is perceived to have a limited quality or fitness to the user intentions and context [18]. The challenge for HCI is to define the design properties and activities for achieving the right balance between actual and perceived safety.

3 Research Aim

This research aims to develop explainability design patterns based qualitative approach to calibrate user trust in CDSSs by making the medical practitioners aware when to follow the system recommendations or not and potentially avoid under-trust and over-trust issues. The PhD contributes to the literature by helping the elicitation and customisation of the variability in the requirements and design of CDSSs interface that support medical practitioners safe and effective decision-making.

3.1 Research Questions

The research focuses on the explainbility user experience aspects and trust calibration in CDSSs by asking the following questions:

RQ1: What are the user experience aspects of explainability?
RQ2: What makes the CDSSs explainable for medical practitioners?
RQ3: What are the explainability aspects and features that may contribute to failing in calibrating user-trust?
RQ4: What explainability design features could future CDSSs have to cater to medical practitioners calibrate their trust?

4 Research Objectives and Methods

Objective 1: Conduct a Systematic Literature Review to explore the explainability user experience aspects in the literature and develop an understanding of relevant user trust calibration problem.

As a first step in achieving the goal of this research, the need to understand explainability from artificial intelligence and Human-computer interaction perspectives is important to formulate the explanation design space. The empirical literature regarding how researchers and practitioners in the field provide explanations to end-users is reviewed to provide a foundation for satisfying the research aim and also to inform the exploratory studies and the prototyping stage. The research reviews the literature concerning the explainability aspect from both Explainable Artificial Intelligence and Human-Computer Interaction perspective. In addition, trust calibration theories are reviewed with its diversity of design guidelines. The literature on decision-making in medicine is also reviewed to provide foundations to the solution and also to inform the exploratory studies.

Objective 2: An empirical investigation into the post-hoc explanation capabilities that may affect user trust in the CDSSs through series of qualitative approaches. The empirical investigation is built on the result of the first objective. This objective informs the research regarding the explanation design requirements from healthcare professionals' perspectives. Ultimately, the data collection of the qualitative approach with the healthcare professionals and the initial analysis of the results are in process with collaboration with IQ Healthcare[2] and three hospitals in the UK. To achieve this objective, several steps and methods are followed. The first study gauges the opinions of medical practitioners in relation to the functional and non-functional requirements for explainability (e.g. the framing of the explanation, the content, the delivery methods and modalities). This study uses a think-aloud protocol for the purposes of data collection to allow participants to discuss their opinions about the existing literature around explainability. The second study utilises a semi-structured interview to investigate what makes the CDSSs explainable and trustworthy for healthcare practitioners. This will help the design of the explanation in CDSSs that influence user-trust. This stage also will develop a taxonomy of these findings and their relation to trust-calibration.

Objective 3: Iterative prototyping through design sessions to build design patterns toolkit for the explainable CDSS interface that calibrate user-trust.
In this objective, the research will attempt to develop explanation design patterns for CDSSs that calibrate user trust. That means that the healthcare professionals will be better informed about the CDSSs recommendations so that the user trust is calibrated. In this stage, the consideration of participants' roles and requirements will be taken into account to help the analysis for better understanding the qualitative data. Ultimately, the researcher will attempt to find aiding design patterns that help healthcare practitioner to use the CDSS in an effective and safe way with a reduction to under-trust and over-trust errors. This

---

[2] iQ HealthTech is a software development company, with a common goal, to improve the way IT systems are used for healthcare.

objective is achieved by means of design sessions. In the design sessions, various scenarios will be shown with different interface designs. The participants will be encouraged to find better designers, so they are better informed about the CDSSs recommendations.

Objective 4: Design and conduct qualitative and quantitative user studies on the prototype to evaluate the user trust, the effectiveness of the prototype and validate the approach.

The resulting explainability design patterns for CDSSs will be tested for its trust-calibration and the effectiveness of the design. Target users are medical practitioners. Users will be asked to perform certain tasks with the developed interface. These tasks will be based on the expected functionalities of the explainable interface. Two case studies will be used in this stage i) Expert system to prescribe breast cancer chemotherapy treatment for breast cancer ii) Rule-based system for screening prescription for Palbociclib cancer treatment. IQemo prescribing system will be used to build and validate the design patterns toolkit.

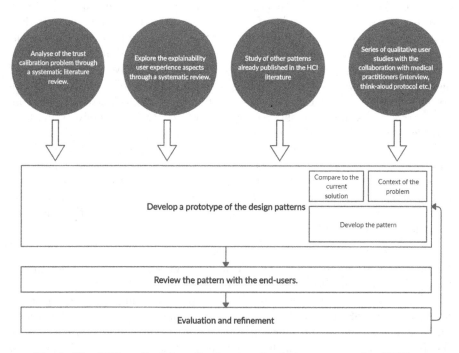

Fig. 1. The PhD methodology for forming the design patterns for CDSSs.

4.1   Research Validity

To strengthen the external validity of the research, several aspects are addressed. First, the target participants in this research are selected by a strategy combining convenience sampling and maximum variation sampling [16]. The use of this convenience sampling approach reflects the difficulty of gaining medical practitioners in this kind of research. Any possible bias traditionally related to convenience sampling tried to be mitigated by combining a maximum variation sampling so that the approached hospitals covered different characteristics regarding size, application domain, domain knowledge and practitioners experience. Second, the research has interviewed at least two practitioners per session to reduce the risk of bias and misinterpretation. Third, the participated hospitals were developing prescribing and diagnosis systems from the oncology department. It is possible that this factor may have an impact on our research findings. Therefore, it is important to highlight that the findings of this thesis might be considered more relevant to this type of expert systems (diagnosis and prescribing). However, future research is needed to validate the research findings in different application domain areas where the nature of the decision making strategy is different (e.g. dentist decision support system).

5 Conclusion and Current Progress

Driven by the increasing interest in decision support systems in the clinical settings, the understanding of potential user errors that might emerge is also essential. This paper present the ongoing PhD project that investigates explainability solutions with the aim to avoid failing to calibrate user-trust, i.e. over-trust and under-trust. Also, this paper elaborated on the status of the research problem and identified three distinct research strands in the literature that are relevant to the problem. Currently, the researcher is performing a continuous process of analysing the qualitative data that emerged from the qualitative user studies and identifying the properties of the explainability in the clinical settings. Once it has been done, the researcher will develop multiple prototypes of the design patterns and review the patterns with the potential end-users.

Acknowledgments. This work is partially funded by iQ HealthTech and Bournemouth university PGR development fund.

References

1. Aitken, M., Ahmed, N., Lawrence, D., Argrow, B., Frew, E.: Assurances and machine self-confidence for enhanced trust in autonomous systems. In: RSS 2016 Workshop on Social Trust in Autonomous Systems (2016)
2. Alexander, C.: A Pattern Language: Towns, Buildings, Construction. Oxford University Press, Oxford (1977)
3. Bussone, A., Stumpf, S., O'Sullivan, D.: The role of explanations on trust and reliance in clinical decision support systems. In: 2015 International Conference on Healthcare Informatics, pp. 160–169. IEEE (2015)
4. Chromik, M., Eiband, M., Völkel, S.T., Buschek, D.: Dark patterns of explainability, transparency, and user control for intelligent systems. In: IUI Workshops (2019)

5. WP1 Deliverable: Introducing a framework for the evaluation of network supported collaborative learning
6. Eiband, M., Buschek, D., Kremer, A., Hussmann, H.: The impact of placebic explanations on trust in intelligent systems. In: Extended Abstracts of the 2019 CHI Conference on Human Factors in Computing Systems, pp. 1–6 (2019)
7. Glass, A., McGuinness, D.L., Wolverton, M.: Toward establishing trust in adaptive agents. In: Proceedings of the 13th International Conference on Intelligent User Interfaces, pp. 227–236 (2008)
8. Kulesza, T., Burnett, M., Wong, W.K., Stumpf, S.: Principles of explanatory debugging to personalize interactive machine learning. In: Proceedings of the 20th International Conference on Intelligent User Interfaces, pp. 126–137 (2015)
9. Liu, C.: Human-machine trust interaction: a technical overview. In: Trust Modeling and Management in Digital Environments: from Social Concept to System Development: From Social Concept to System Development, p. 471 (2010)
10. Madhavan, P., Wiegmann, D.A.: Similarities and differences between human-human and human-automation trust: an integrative review. Theor. Issues Ergon. Sci. **8**(4), 277–301 (2007)
11. Merritt, S.M., Heimbaugh, H., LaChapell, J., Lee, D.: I trust it, but i don't know why: effects of implicit attitudes toward automation on trust in an automated system. Hum. Factors **55**(3), 520–534 (2013)
12. Miller, T.: Explanation in artificial intelligence: insights from the social sciences. Artif. Intell. **267**, 1–38 (2019)
13. Naiseh, M., Jiang, N., Ma, J., Ali, R.: Explainable recommendations in intelligent systems: delivery methods, modalities and risks. In: The 14th International Conference on Research Challenges in Information Science. Springer (2020)
14. Naiseh, M., Jiang, N., Ma, J., Ali, R.: Personalising explainable recommendations: literature and conceptualisation. In: WorldCist 2020 - 8th World Conference on Information Systems and Technologies. Springer (2020)
15. Nunes, I., Jannach, D.: A systematic review and taxonomy of explanations in decision support and recommender systems. User Model. User-Adap. Interact. **27**(3–5), 393–444 (2017)
16. Robinson, O.C.: Sampling in interview-based qualitative research: atheoretical and practical guide. Qual. Res. Psychol. **11**(1), 25–41 (2014)
17. Samek, W., Wiegand, T., Müller, K.R.: Explainable artificial intelligence: understanding, visualizing and interpreting deep learning models. arXiv preprint arXiv:1708.08296 (2017)
18. Schäfer, H., et al.: Towards health (aware) recommender systems. In: Proceedings of the 2017 International Conference on Digital Health, pp. 157–161 (2017)
19. Sokol, K., Flach, P.: Explainability fact sheets: a framework for systematic assessment of explainable approaches. In: Conference on Fairness, Accountability, and Transparency, FAT* 2020 (2020)
20. Tonekaboni, S., Joshi, S., McCradden, M.D., Goldenberg, A.: What clinicians want: contextualizing explainable machine learning for clinical end use. arXiv preprint arXiv:1905.05134 (2019)
21. UCLA EEE: Outlining the design space of explainable intelligent systems for medical diagnosis (2019)

Tutorials and Research Projects

Expressing Strategic Variability and Flexibility of Processes: The Map Process Modeling Approach

Rébecca Deneckère[1] and Jolita Ralyté[2(✉)]

[1] Centre de Recherche en Informatique, Université Paris 1 Panthéon Sorbonne,
90 Rue de Tolbiac, 75013 Paris, France
`rebecca.deneckere@univ-paris1.fr`
[2] Institute of Information Service Science, CUI, University of Geneva,
Battelle - bâtiment A, 7 Route de Drize, 1227 Carouge, Switzerland
`jolita.ralyte@unige.ch`

Tutorial Abstract

Typical workflow style process modelling languages have limits when designing processes at strategic level and reasoning on their variability, flexibility and adaptability. The Map [1, 2] process modelling formalism has been defined to overcome these obstacles. It offers a novel vision of process modelling, namely strategic process modeling, founded on an intention-oriented paradigm. Indeed, modeling with Map consists in focusing on what the process is intended to achieve – the intentions, and on how these intentions can be fulfilled – the strategies. Various strategies can be defined to reach an intention, allowing in this way to express the variability and flexibility in process specification and enactment. Moreover, the approach allows to deal with different levels of abstraction. Not only can operational processes be specified, but also high-level organizational intentions and strategies can be formalized and serve as decision support.

Formally, Map is a process representation system based on a nondeterministic ordering of intentions and strategies. Its graphical representation takes the form of a labelled directed graph with intentions as nodes and strategies as edges between intentions. The directed nature of the graph shows which intentions can follow which one. An intention represents an objective that can be achieved at a given point in the process. A strategy represents a specific manner to achieve an intention. A triplet <source intention, strategy, target intention> is called a section; it encapsulates a process activity, which can be executed as long as the source intention has been achieved and the strategy to attain the target intention has been selected.

Map also allows to formalize guidelines on how to progress in the process, i.e. guidelines to select the next intention, the strategy to reach this intention, and then to execute the underpinning activity. At enactment time, the order of execution of process activities is not predefined; the process is constructed dynamically considering various contextual criteria and the choices done by the

© Springer Nature Switzerland AG 2020
F. Dalpiaz et al. (Eds.): RCIS 2020, LNBIP 385, pp. 623–624, 2020.
https://doi.org/10.1007/978-3-030-50316-1

actors executing the process. Each time an intention is reached (an activity is executed), the model suggests what are the next possible intentions to achieve (the activities that can be executed at the next step). Because of the strategic nature of Map models, actors executing the process can be offered a variety of choices to perform an activity as well as to progress in the process. At each step, the Map model provides guidance to take the appropriate decision based on the current process situation (available input artefacts, valid conditions, arguments, rules, etc.). As a result, the path of the instance process is constructed dynamically. We classify Map as an intention-oriented strategic process modelling approach.

Many researchers and practitioners have been using Map for about 20 years now for modeling all kinds of processes and in different areas: method engineering [3], requirement engineering [4], decision making [5], enterprise knowledge development [6], IS engineering [1], service co-creation process [7], and so on.

The attendees of the tutorial (students, advanced researchers as well as practitioners interested in process modelling) receive a good understanding of the concept of strategic process modelling and recognize the differences of this approach from the workflow-based ones. The tutorial is highly interactive; it includes theory and practice, so at the end the attendees are able to read and construct strategic process maps.

References

1. Rolland, C., Prakash, N., Benjamen, A.: A multi-model view of process modelling. Requirements Eng. **4**(4), 169–187 (1999). https://doi.org/10.1007/s007660050018
2. Rolland, C.: Capturing system intentionality with map. In: Krogstie, J., Opdahl, A.L., Brinkkemper, S. (eds.) Conceptual Modelling in Information Systems Engineering, pp. 141–158. Springer, Heidelberg (2007). https://doi.org/10.1007/978-3-540-72677-7_9
3. Mirbel, I., Ralyté, J.: Situational method engineering: combining assembly-based and roadmap-driven approaches. Requirements Eng. **11**(1), 58–78 (2006). https://doi.org/10.1007/s00766-005-0019-0
4. Ralyté, J., Maiden, N., Rolland, C., Deneckère, R.: Applying modular method engineering to validate and extend the RESCUE requirements process. In: Delcambre, L., Kop, C., Mayr, H.C., Mylopoulos, J., Pastor, O. (eds.) ER 2005. LNCS, vol. 3716, pp. 209–224. Springer, Heidelberg (2005). https://doi.org/10.1007/11568322_14
5. Kornyshova, E., Deneckere, R.: Decision-making method family MADISE: validation within the requirements engineering domain. In: RCIS 2012. IEEE (2012). https://doi.org/10.1109/RCIS.2012.6240447
6. Barrios, J., Nurcan, S.: Model driven architectures for enterprise information systems. In: Persson, A., Stirna, J. (eds.) CAiSE 2004. LNCS, vol. 3084, pp. 3–19. Springer, Heidelberg (2004). https://doi.org/10.1007/978-3-540-25975-6_3
7. Ralyté, J.: Towards a method family supporting information services co-creation in the transdisciplinary context. Int. J. Inf. Syst. Model. Des. **4**(3), 50–75 (2013)

Data-Driven Requirements Engineering: Principles, Methods and Challenges

Xavier Franch$^{(\boxtimes)}$ (iD)

Universitat Politècnica de Catalunya, Barcelona, Spain
franch@essi.upc.edu

In the last years, we are witnessing the advent of a data-driven approach to RE. The exploitation of data coming from several sources may indeed become an extremely useful input to requirements elicitation and management but it does not come for free. Techniques such as natural language processing and machine learning are difficult to master and require high-quality data, whilst their generalization remains as a challenge. This tutorial introduces this approach, named data-driven requirements engineering (DDRE). It is structured into eight parts:

1. **Motivation**. It shows some figures and numbers making evident that RE is still challenging in software project development, and introduces the concept of DDRE following Maalej *et al.*'s seminal paper [1]. It finalizes by presenting a DDRE cycle [2] comprising several activities that are presented next.
2. **Explicit feedback**. This term denotes the feedback provided explicitly by the user. From a research point of view, it is based on the combination of natural language processing [3] and machine learning [4]. The tutorial presents a landscape of NLP techniques applied to explicit feedback gathering, with several examples taking from social networks as Twitter [5] and from App Stores [6].
3. **Implicit feedback**. This term denotes the feedback collected from the user without her involvement. It mainly comes from log files and monitoring infrastructure. The tutorial highlights the importance of context and presents the concept of contextual requirements with an example involving the application of data mining techniques over implicit feedback gathered through monitoring [7].
4. **Combining explicit and implicit feedback**. As a consolidation of the two parts above, the tutorial briefly presents the combination of both types of feedback into a single unified data source for eliciting requirements [8].
5. **Repository mining**. Whereas feedback management focuses on data gathered from system usage, repository mining [9] extracts and analyses data from software repositories as issue trackers and project management tools. The tutorial shows how quality models can help to elicit quality aspects fed by the repositories using the QUAMOCO approach [10] as running example.
6. **Decision-making**. This part of the tutorial deals with the decisional process that build on the data collected through feedback collection and repository management. Software analytics tools and dashboards are mentioned and the use of this data for software release planning is also exemplified [11].
7. **Processes**. The tutorial revisits the cycle defined in the first part [2] and provides further details on processes combining software engineering with data engineering

© Springer Nature Switzerland AG 2020
F. Dalpiaz et al. (Eds.): RCIS 2020, LNBIP 385, pp. 625–626, 2020.
https://doi.org/10.1007/978-3-030-50316-1

[12]. Some lessons learned from the use of DDRE approaches in industry are presented too [13].

8. **Conclusions and road ahead.** The tutorial summarizes the main points and presents future work both at the macro-level of DDRE as a research area inside RE [14] and the micro-level on the different techniques used in DDRE [15]. A compendium of DDRE-related resources is included also in the closing slides.

This tutorial is supported by the GENESIS project, funded by the Spanish Ministerio de Ciencia e Innovación under contract TIN2016-79269-R.

References

1. Maalej, W., Nayebi, M., Johann, T., Ruhe, G.: Toward data-driven requirements engineering. IEEE Softw. **33**(1), 48–54 (2016)
2. Guzmán, L., Oriol, M., Rodríguez, P., Franch, X., Jedlitschka, A., Oivo, M.: How can quality awareness support rapid software development? – a research preview. In: Grünbacher, P., Perini, A. (eds.) REFSQ 2017. LNCS, vol. 10153, pp. 167–173. Springer, Cham (2017). https://doi.org/10.1007/978-3-319-54045-0_12
3. Zhao, L. et al.: Natural language processing (NLP) for requirements engineering: a systematic mapping study. CoRR, abs/2004.01099 (2020)
4. El Shawi, R., Maher, M., Sakr, S.: Automated machine learning: state-of-the-art and open challenges. CoRR, abs/1906.02287 (2019)
5. Guzman, E., Alkadhi, R., Seyff, N.: A needle in a haystack: what do twitter users say about software? In: RE 2016, pp. 96–105. IEEE Computer Society (2016)
6. Maalej, W., Kurtanovic, Z., Nabil, H., Stanik, C.: On the automatic classification of app reviews. Requirements. Eng. **21**(3), 311–331 (2016). https://doi.org/10.1007/s00766-016-0251-9
7. Knauss, A., et al.: ACon: a learning-based approach to deal with uncertainty in contextual requirements at runtime. Inf. Softw. Technol. **70**, 85–99 (2016)
8. Oriol, M, et al.: FAME: supporting continuous requirements elicitation by combining user feedback and monitoring. In: RE 2018, pp. 217–227. IEEE Computer Society (2018)
9. Kagdi, H., Collard, M.L., Maletic, J.I.: A survey and taxonomy of approaches for mining software repositories in the context of software evolution. J. Softw. Evol. Process **19**(2), 77–131 (2007)
10. Wagner, S., et al.: operationalised product quality models and assessment: the Quamoco approach. Inf. Softw. Technol. **62**, 101–123 (2015)
11. Villarroel, L., Bavota, G., Russo, B., Oliveto, R., di Penta, M.: Release planning of mobile apps based on user reviews. In: ICSE 2016, pp. 14–24. IEEE Computer Society (2016)
12. Martínez-Fernández, S., et al.: Continuously assessing and improving software quality with software analytics tools: a case study. IEEE Access **7**, 68219–68239 (2019)
13. Shearer, C.: The CRISP-DM model: the new blueprint for data mining. J. Data Warehouse. **4**(5), 13–22 (2000)
14. Franch, X., et al.: Towards integrating data-driven requirements engineering into the software development process: a vision paper. In: Madhavji, N., Pasquale, L., Ferrari, A., Gnesi, S. (eds.) REFSQ 2020. LNCS, vol. 12045, pp. 135–142. Springer, Cham (2020). https://doi.org/10.1007/978-3-030-44429-7_10
15. Dalpiaz, F., Ferrari, A., Franch, X., Palomares, C.: Natural language processing for requirements engineering; the best is yet to come. IEEE Softw. **35**(5), 115–119 (2018)

Automated Machine Learning: State-of-The-Art and Open Challenges

Radwa Elshawi[✉] and Sherif Sakr

Data Systems Group, University of Tartu, Tartu, Estonia
{radwa.elshawi,sherif.sakr}@ut.ee

Abstract. Nowadays, machine learning techniques and algorithms are employed in almost every application domain (e.g., financial applications, advertising, recommendation systems, user behavior analytics). In practice, they are playing a crucial role in harnessing the power of massive amounts of data which we are currently producing every day in our digital world. In general, the process of building a high-quality machine learning model is an iterative, complex and time-consuming process that involves trying different algorithms and techniques in addition to having a good experience with effectively tuning their hyper-parameters. In particular, conducting this process efficiently requires solid knowledge and experience with the various techniques that can be employed. With the continuous and vast increase of the amount of data in our digital world, it has been acknowledged that the number of knowledgeable data scientists can not scale to address these challenges. Thus, there was a crucial need for automating the process of building good machine learning models.

In the last few years, several techniques and frameworks have been introduced to tackle the challenge of automating the process of Combined Algorithm Selection and Hyper-parameter tuning (CASH) in the machine learning domain [1]. The main aim of these techniques is to reduce the role of human in the loop and fill the gap for non-expert machine learning users by playing the role of the domain expert. In this tutorial, we aim to present a comprehensive survey for the state-of-the-art efforts in tackling the CASH problem. In addition, we highlight the research work of automating the other steps of the full complex machine learning pipeline (AutoML) from data understanding till model deployment. Furthermore, we provide a comprehensive coverage for the various tools and frameworks that have been introduced in this domain. Finally, we discuss some of the research directions and open challenges that need to be addressed in order to achieve the vision and goals of the AutoML process. This tutorial is intended to benefit researchers and system designers in the broad area of machine learning. The tutorial would benefit both designers as well as users of automated and interactive machine learning systems since a survey of the current systems and an in-depth understanding will be essential

© Springer Nature Switzerland AG 2020
F. Dalpiaz et al. (Eds.): RCIS 2020, LNBIP 385, pp. 627–629, 2020.
https://doi.org/10.1007/978-3-030-50316-1

for choosing the appropriate system as well as designing an effective system. This tutorial does not require any knowledge on automated machine learning techniques but basic understanding of machine learning pipeline is required. After attending this tutorial, the audience will have:

- An overview of the Machine learning pipeline (**10 min.**).
- A good understanding of the challenges of implementing efficient and high quality machine learning pipeline (**10 min.**).
- A comprehensive review of the state-of-the-art in the domain of automated combined algorithm selection and hyperparameter tuning (**25 min.**).
- A comprehensive review of the state-of-the-art of the centralized, distributed and interactive AutoML frameworks (**25 min.**).
- Highlights for potential research directions to improve the state-of-the-art and support the efforts towards achieving the broad vision of AutoML (**10 min.**).
- A demo of our prototype `iSmartML`[1], an interactive and user-guided framework for automated machine learning (**10 min.**).

The tutorial is timely and quite relevant for the data management and machine learning research communities due to the rapid growth in the applications of machine learning in almost every application domain. The increasing momentum for developing AutoML frameworks would enrich the discussion for potential directions to improve the usability and wide acceptance of these tools among data scientists and domain experts.

Presenters

Radwa Elshawi *Home Page*: https://bigdata.cs.ut.ee/dr-radwa-elshawi
Short Bio: Dr. Radwa El Shawi is a Senior Research Fellow in Big Data at Data Systems Group, University of Tartu, Estonia. Radwa received her PhD in Information Technology from Sydney University, Australia in 2013. She received her BSc and MSc degree in Computer Engineering from the Computer Engineering department at Arab Academy for Science and Maritime Transport, Egypt, in 2005 and 2008 respectively. Radwa El Shawi's research interest are Optimization Algorithms, Big Data and Machine Learning.

Sherif Sakr *Home Page*: http://math.ut.ee/~sakr/
Short Bio: Prof. Sherif Sakr is the Head of Data Systems Group (https://bigdata.cs.ut.ee/) at the Institute of Computer Science, University of Tartu, Estonia. He received his PhD degree in Computer and Information Science from Konstanz University, Germany in 2007. He is currently serving as the Editor-in-Chief of the Springer Encyclopedia of Big Data Technologies. Prof. Sakr's research interest is data and information management in general, particularly in big data processing systems, big data analytics and data science. Prof. Sakr has published more than 150 refereed research publications in international journals and conferences. He delivered several tutorial in various conferences including WWW'12, IC2E'14,

---

[1] https://bigdata.cs.ut.ee/ismartml/.

CAiSE'14, EDBT Summer School 2015. The 2nd ScaDS International Summer School on Big Data 2016, The 3rd Keystone Training School on Keyword search in Big Linked Data 2017, DEBS 2019, ISWC 2019 and EDBT 2020.

Reference

1. El Shawi, R., Maher, M., Sakr, S.: Automated machine learning: state-of-the-art and open challenges. CoRR, abs/1906.02287 (2019)

Managing Cyber-Physical Incidents Propagation in Health Services

Faten Atigui, Fayçal Hamdi, Fatma-Zohra Hannou[(⊠)], Nadira Lammari,
Nada Mimouni, and Samira Si-Said Cherfi

CEDRIC, Conservatoire National des Arts et Métiers (CNAM), Paris, France
{faten.atigui,faycal.hamdi,fatma-zohra.hannou,nadira.lammari,
nada.mimouni,samira.cherfi}@lecnam.net

- **Full name:** Integrated cyber-physical security of health services
- **Acronym:** SAFECARE[1]
- **Duration:** from 09-01-2018 to 08-31-2021
- **URL:** https://www.safecare-project.eu/

1 Summary of the Project

Health services are among the most critical and vulnerable cyber-physical infrastructures. The SAFECARE H2020 project aims to provide solutions that improve physical and cyber security in a seamless and cost-effective way.

1.1 Objectives

The goal of the project is to provide an integrated solution for the management of combined cyber and physical threats and incidents, their interconnections and potential cascading effects. The main objectives are:

- Risk assessment of physical and cyber threats, with respect to current EU regulatory bodies' requirements, and cost efficiency of proposed solutions.
- Improve risk prevention capacities: analysis of vulnerabilities, risk assessment and recommendations on operational active systems.
- Improve threat detection capacities: data fusion, cascading effects models
- Improve impact mitigation: manage hospital availability, inform the population, increase user awareness about incidents impacts on critical assets.
- Provide impact propagation and decision support model that describes cyber and physical assets, their vulnerabilities, incidents, and their impacts.

1.2 Expected Tangible Outputs

The SAFECARE project will produce the following main key results:

- A cyber threat detection system and a physical threat detection system
- A threat response system and a threat mitigation system
- A modular and scalable solution with standard communication protocols
- Dissemination throughout health-user community and scientific community
- Demonstration in three European hospitals

---

[1] This project has received funding from the European Union's H2020 research and innovation programme under grant agreement no. 787002.

F. Dalpiaz et al. (Eds.): RCIS 2020, LNBIP 385, pp. 630–631, 2020.
https://doi.org/10.1007/978-3-030-50316-1

2 Current Results: Impact Propagation Module

We present in this section the current work on the core module of the SAFE-CARE project that is the impact propagation and decision support model (IPM). This module relies on: (i) structural information about cyber and physical assets, their intrinsic properties and theirs structural relationships, and (ii) on knowledge about the occurred incidents and how to infer and propagate impacts. This second knowledge evolves continuously and is more dynamic than the structural knowledge. To cope with the static and dynamic knowledge and to confer more stability to the IPM module, we propose a modular ontology, called Safecare-Onto. At a high level of abstraction, the whole picture is depicted in Fig. 1.

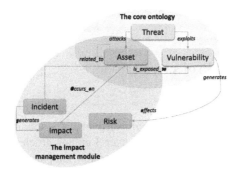

Fig. 1. The modular structure of SafecareOnto

The core ontology captures essentially the static knowledge about critical assets. It is centered on three main concepts: *Asset*, *Vulnerability*, and *Threat*.

These concepts are further refined and characterised, and their formalisation can easily be extended. This formalisation is done in such a way that it can easily be extended to meet emerging requirements. Other modules could incrementally be defined upon the core ontology. The impact management module is one of the possible extensions. It defines the concepts that are essential to the computation of impact propagation and provides indicators for assessing the severity of incidents and the likelihood of impacts. It relies on concepts such as *Incident*, *Risk* and *Impact*. Other modules could also be added as a countermeasures module.

The propagation management relies on axioms and rules that are further used to infer the impact of incidents. These rules result from several threat scenarios defined with the help of cyber and physical security experts and the collaboration of actors from European hospitals partners. A first version of a prototype that we implemented simulates impacts propagation on a near-real scenario. A reasoner is used to infer impacts propagation on assets. In this prototype, the IPM rules were expressed in terms of OWL concepts (classes, properties, individuals) using the JENA rule engine.

6.849,32 New Scientific Journal Articles Everyday: Visualize or Perish! - IViSSEM

Ana A. Baptista⬥, Pedro Branco⬥, Bruno Azevedo⬥,
Jorge Oliveira e Sá⬥, Ana C. Ribeiro$^{(\boxtimes)}$⬥,
and Mariana Curado Malta⬥

Centro ALGORITMI, University of Minho, Guimarães, Portugal
{aab,pbranco,jos}@dsi.uminho.pt,
brunomiguelam@engagelab.org, anacfrl@hotmail.com,
mariana@iscap.ipp.pt
http://ivissem.net

1 Summary of the Project

1.1 Objectives

Over 2.5 million scientific articles are published annually, totaling 6,849.32 per day in 2015; in 2018 this value was increased to over 3 million articles, totaling 8.219,18 per day [1]. Thus, finding the most relevant Research Outputs (ROs), such as articles, theses, patents, among others, is increasingly difficult due, in part, to the existing interfaces returning massive lists of results.

The project aims to develop and test a platform that incorporates social data for capturing various usage metrics to define a new metric that we call Social Scholarly Experience Metrics (SSEM) and a new visualization technique that, jointly, will support the fast access to find relevant ROs.

1.2 Expected Tangible Results

IViSSEM has four main tangible results, which are described in the following points:

1. SSEM - this is an algorithm based on weights and ponderation factors of citation-based metrics and altmetrics to be collected from web platforms. SSEM also takes into account the researchers' profiles, which includes a measure of their influence in the community [2];
2. Low-Fidelity Prototype – the main goal is to test the layout, information architecture, navigation model and visualization [3];
3. Big Open Linked Data Architecture (BOLDA) – this architecture allows the implementation of the SSEM algorithm and store all the data needed and produced in a triplestore (RDF);
4. Fully developed prototype - the main goal is the integration of the previous results to demonstrate the effectiveness of the SSEM and visualization techniques used to solve the problem.

F. Dalpiaz et al. (Eds.): RCIS 2020, LNBIP 385, pp. 632–634, 2020.
https://doi.org/10.1007/978-3-030-50316-1

1.3 Summary of Current Project Results

According to the defined objectives, the current project results are describe in the following points:

– BOLDA architecture, see Fig. 1;

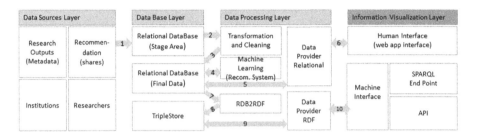

Fig. 1. IViSSEM architecture

– a low-fidelity prototype implementation to experiment some advanced information visualization algorithms, see Fig. 2.

Fig. 2. Screenshot of the low-fidelity IViSSEM prototype.

Acknowledgements. This work has been supported by IViSSEM: POCI-01-0145-FEDER-28284, and FCT – Fundação para a Ciência e Tecnologia within the R&D Units Project Scope: UIDB/00319/2020.

References

1. Johnson, R., Watkinson, A., Mabe, M.: The STM report: an overview of scientific and scholarly publishing. International Association of Scientific, Technical and Medical Publishers (2018)

2. Ribeiro, A.C., Azevedo, B., Oliveira e Sá, J., Baptista, A.A.: How to measure influence in social networks? In: 14th International Conference on Research Challenges in Information Science. Paper submitted and accepted (2020)
3. Azevedo, B., Baptista, A.A., Oliveira e Sá, J., Branco, P., Tortosa, R.: Interfaces for science: conceptualizing an interactive graphical interface. In: 7th EAI International Conference, ArtsIT, pp. 17–27 (2019). https://doi.org/10.1007/978-3-030-06134-0_3

A Model Driven Engineering Approach to Key Performance Indicators: Towards Self-service Performance Management (SS-PM Project)

Corentin Burnay[✉]

PReCISE Research Center, NADI Research Institute, University of Namur,
Namur, Belgium
corentin.burnay@unamur.be

1 Summary of the Project

Exploring and analyzing data is a key activity for any modern organization. It is an activity through which various data sources are to be identified, analyzed, transformed and aggregated in order to produce Key Performance Indicators (KPIs), necessary to inform business managers and help them make better decisions. Most existing KPIs, however, have at least two significant weaknesses; (i) they are *opaque to the business* - business managers do not really understand how they are computed - and (ii) they are *owned by the technicians* - any change request on a KPI necessarily passes by the "IT" in order to be treated. This results in KPIs that fail to receive full confidence from managers, who cannot easily assess the actual quality of an indicator exposed to them, who do not see the potential treatments that have been applied to data so as to produce the KPI, who do not grasp the full set of mathematical operations and aggregations used to compute the KPI, and who as a result may not fully trust the indicator. This also results in bottlenecks, because any update on KPIs mandatorily implies the IT. Put together, these weaknesses lead to "Decision Support System" (DSS) with poor return on investment and more critically, to business managers who do not have access to trustworthy information. The SS-PM project investigates the possibility to make the design and implementation of KPIs "self-service".

2 Summary of Expected Tangible Outputs

This proposal is at the intersection between two research areas: Requirements Engineering and Performance Management. It will focus first on the practice of identifying, modeling, analyzing and validating requirements of business managers towards KPIs. Various such models have been proposed in RE ([1, 2] or [3] are three notable examples considered in this project, among many others), but none of them focus specifically on indicators. It will also focus on Performance Management (PM), referring to practices and models used in an organization to track and improve its

4 years project - Belgian national funds/FNRS (Expected 2021–2025).

F. Dalpiaz et al. (Eds.): RCIS 2020, LNBIP 385, pp. 635–636, 2020.
https://doi.org/10.1007/978-3-030-50316-1

overall performance, by using famous PM models like the balanced scorecard [4]. Some room exists for improving the RE process of a PM system and to fix part of the problem of KPI's *transparency* and *IT-ownership*, mostly by letting users define requirements by themselves. How so? With three propositions.

A) A new modeling framework for representing KPIs: various methods exist to define KPIs. However, very few of them provide modeling support to actually formalize the KPIs and the process to produce it: which transformation? On which data? Which weights and decision rules? Why? When? This notation should be interpretable by business people, and should ease the implementation of KPIs. Most importantly, it would help business managers to have a clearer and more standard view on the KPIs; *B) A Model-Driven Engineering (MDE) framework for the computation of KPIs;* DSS systems rely heavily on the expertise of programmers (i.e., the "IT"), in charge of developing and maintaining the solution. A change in the requirements results systematically in new developments by technicians. This takes money (cost of development) and most importantly time, with a risk of bottleneck. We propose to design and implement a processor for KPIs models (from Proposition A), which code and internal functioning would depend on a business model produced by managers. This model, under the form of simple visual artifacts, would allow managers to adapt their indicators directly, without interference with analysts and technicians, and hence to reduce the cost of implementing changes to indicators. This would also favor trust in the indicators (managers know how the KPI is produced) and would ease comparison with other instances of the same indicator (comparability, fairness, etc.); *C) A new indicator processing visualization technique*: MDE as discussed in A and B does solve only part of the problem of trust in KPIs. Consumers of KPIs must have access, somehow, to the mathematical/logical process applied in order to produce it. MDE will drastically increase the trust that owners of the indicator have, but it will not help improve the trust that all consumers of that indicator need in order to make decisions. This project therefore also intends to produce a visualization tool, building on the same MDE approach as in B, that will show to KPIs consumers the process applied to compute an indicator. The visualization tool will not focus on the indicator, but on the manipulations applied to raw data that have been used to produce the indicator, with intermediary steps and values of that indicator.

References

1. Giorgini, P., Rizzi, S., Garzetti, M.: GRAnD: a goal-oriented approach to requirement analysis in data warehouses. Decis. Support Syst. **45**(1), 4–21 (2008)
2. Horkoff, J., et al.: Strategic business modeling: representation and reasoning. Softw. Syst. Model. **13**(3), 1015–1041 (2014)
3. del-Río-Ortega, A., Resinas, M., Durán, A., Bernárdez, B., Ruiz-Cortés, A., Toro, M.: Visual PPINOT: a graphical notation for process performance indicators. Business & Information Systems Engineering **61**(2), 137–161 (2017). https://doi.org/10.1007/s12599-017-0483-3
4. Kaplan, R.S., Norton, D.P.: Linking the balanced scorecard to strategy. Calif. Manag. Rev. **39**(1), 53–79 (1996)

TESTOMAT - Next Level of Test Automation

Sigrid Eldh[1], Tanja E. J. Vos[2,4(✉)], Serge Demeyer[3], Pekka Aho[4],
and Machiel van der Bijl[5]

[1] Ericsson, Stockholm, Sweden
[2] Univ. Politecnica de Valencia, Valencia, Spain
tvos@dsic.upv.es
[3] Unversity of Antwerpen, Antwerp, Belgium
[4] Open Universiteit, Heerlen, The Netherlands
[5] Axini, Amsterdam, The Netherlands
http://www.testomatproject.eu

1 Summary of the Project

Modern software teams seek for a delicate balance between two opposing forces: striving for reliability and striving for agility. In the former, teams optimise for perfection; in the latter, they optimise for ease of change. Producers of software intensive systems must deliver more features, faster without sacrificing product quality. The drive towards faster release cycles only exacerbates the problem: manual testing is not an option anymore; automating the bulk of the test load is the only way out.

Objective. The objective of TESTOMAT is to advance the state-of-the-art in test automation for software teams moving towards a more agile development process. This allows to increase the development speed without sacrificing quality. To achieve this goal, the project improves software testing tools to make them suitable for agile development. In agile development, tools should seamlessly integrate with today's continuous integration environments. By applying the state-of-the-art techniques on realistic use-cases provided by software testing teams, the TESTOMAT Project consortium pushes the state-of-the-practice in test automation to the next level.

Expected Tangible Results. The project will ultimately result in a Test Automation Improvement Model (TAIM) [1]. Inspired by similar improvement models like (CMMI, TMMI, ...) the model defines key improvement areas in test automation, with the focus on measurable and achievable improvement steps supported by tools for mutation testing, GUI testing and model-based testing that are developed or improved in the project.

2 Achievements

Mutation Testing. The TESTOMAT consortium created two mutation testing tools available under an open source license: Dextool and Timura. Dextool is

© Springer Nature Switzerland AG 2020
F. Dalpiaz et al. (Eds.): RCIS 2020, LNBIP 385, pp. 637–639, 2020.
https://doi.org/10.1007/978-3-030-50316-1

aimed at C++, mainly developped within SAAB Aeronautics[1]. Testura is aimed at C# and is mainly developped by System Verification[2].

GUI Testing. TESTAR [2][3] implements a scriptless approach for automated test case generation at the GUI level via agents that use an action selection mechanism. The TESTOMAT project has resulted in many extensions and improvements of TESTAR: extracting a state model while testing, using genetic algorithms to evolve the best action selection strategy and extending to the testing of web application using the Selenium WebDriver.

Model Based Testing. There are several partners working on Model Based Testing. Axini has a toolset AMS that supports a model-based testing for complete automation of the testing process: automatic test-case generation, execution and evaluation. The TESTOMAT project has resulted in many extensions and improvements of AMS. To name a selection: model-based testing of documentation generation engines, visualization of complex transition systems via semantic zooming, a modeling language for protocol/interface/api, an MBT course for the University of Amsterdam and the Open University. We have applied our approach and tool-set at Akka, ProRail and Achmea.

Measurable Improvements. The project defined three key-performance indicators: Test Effectiveness, Test Speed, and Product Quality. The nine use case providers in the project (SAAB, Kuveyt Türk, FFT, Alerion, Ericsson, Ponsse, AKKA, Prodevelop, Bombardier) adopted an iterative approach and measured the improvement on each of these KPIs. The results will be made publicly available at the end of the project.

Maturity Assessment. We conducted a test automation maturity survey, collecting responses of 151 practitioners coming from 101 organizations in 25 countries. We made various observations regarding the state of the practice and deduced a benchmark for assessing the test automation maturity of an agile team. The benchmark resulted in a self-assessment tool for practitioners to be released under an open source license.

Increase Technology Readiness. The project operated in between technology readiness levels 4 (validated in the lab) to 6 (prototype tested in intended environment). Several tool prototypes (both academic and industrial) have been deployed under realistic circumstances pilot projects. Several ideas have been adopted by tool vendors and consultants in the project and are ready to be incorporated in the normal offerings.

---

[1] https://github.com/joakim-brannstrom/dextool.
[2] https://github.com/Testura/Testura.Mutation.
[3] https://github.com/TESTARtool/.

References

1. Eldh, S., Andersson, K., Ermedahl, A., Wiklund, K.: Towards a test automation improvement model (TAIM). In: 2014 IEEE Seventh International Conference on Software Testing, Verication and Validation Workshops, pp. 337–342, March 2014
2. Vos, T.E.J., Kruse, P.M., Condori-Fernandez, N., Bauersfeld, S., Wegener, J.: TESTAR: tool support for test automation at the user interface level. Int. J. Inf. Syst. Model. Des. **6**(3), 46–83 (2015)

A cyberSecurity Platform for vIrtualiseD 5G cybEr Range Services (SPIDER)

Neofytos Gerosavva[1(✉)], Manos Athanatos[2],
Christoforos Ntantogian[3], Christos Xenakis[3], Cristina Costa[4],
Alberto Mozo[5], Matthias Ghering[6], and Angela Brignone[7]

[1] EIGHT BELLS, Nicosia, Cyprus
neofytos.gerosavva@8bellsresearch.com
https://spider-h2020.eu/
[2] FORTH, Heraklion, Greece
athanat@ics.forth.gr
[3] University of Piraeus (UPRC), Piraeus, Greece
{dadoyan,xenakis}@unipi.gr
[4] Fondazione Bruno Kessler (FBK), Trento, Italy
ccosta@fbk.eu
[5] Universidad Politécnica de Madrid (UPM), Madrid, Spain
a.mozo@upm.es
[6] CYBERLENS, London, UK
matthias.ghering@cyberlens.eu
[7] ERICSSON, Roma, Italy
angela.brignone@ericsson.com

1 Summary of the Project

1.1 Objectives

The vision of the H2020 funded project SPIDER (https://spider-h2020.eu/) is to deliver a next-generation, extensive, and replicable Cyber Range as a Service (CRaaS) platform for the telecommunications domain and its fifth-generation (5G). The proposed solution takes into account all relevant advancements and latest trends and capitalizes on the current state of the art offering a synthetic and sophisticated war-gaming environment. Additionally, SPIDER features integrated tools for cyber testing including advanced emulation tools, novel training methods towards active learning as well as econometric models based on real-time emulation of modern cyber-attacks. Indeed, SPIDER's basic objective is not only to train professionals in 5G security but also to provide tools able to improve the user capability of predicting the evolution of cyber-threats and to analyse the associated economic impact and cost that is brought with the attack.

Duration: 1st July 2019 – 30th June 2022 (36 months).

F. Dalpiaz et al. (Eds.): RCIS 2020, LNBIP 385, pp. 640–642, 2020.
https://doi.org/10.1007/978-3-030-50316-1

1.2   Expected Tangible Results

The main expected outputs of the project is the delivery of a cutting edge CRaaS platform able to offer to its intended users a digital gamified and serious game-based learning environment capable of training experts and non-experts. The envisioned platform represents also a serious gaming repository for sharing training material, as well as a realistic cybersecurity training infrastructure and brokerage facility for cybersecurity situation awareness, hands-on exercise experience and skills development in key cyber defence areas.

2   Summary of Current Project Results

During the first 9 months of the project, the consortium partners conducted studies towards the analysis, collection, and extraction of SPIDER user requirements that the architecture development must address. A fundamental step during this preliminary work was to define the 5G cybersecurity threat landscape, and the related SPIDER actors, to outline the possible attack scenarios which the SPIDER's training platform should address. Based on these outputs, functional requirements have been extracted and grouped by the identified SPIDER actors, assigned a priority. Finally, functional requirements were mapped to non-functional requirements. In addition, and due to the lack of real data containing attacks for training purposes, SPIDER has investigated the application of Generative Adversarial Networks to the generation of synthetic network attacks. The use case analysis led to the definition of three pilot use case scenarios, described in the following:

A. CYBERSECURITY TESTING

A1. Cybersecurity Testing of 5G-ready applications and network services
The first use case focuses on representing the end-to-end network services through their entire lifecycle, and on the orchestration of 5G ready applications and network services. The goal is to validate SPIDER in terms of its ability to support testing, performance evaluation and security assessments of new security technologies.
A2: Cybersecurity of Next Generation Mobile Core SBA
Here the objective is to develop and testing the use of new cybersecurity tools based on machine learning which simulate adversarial techniques and tactics. The main aim is to address the new risks produced by the pervasive encryption in the 5G networks Control Plane (SBA).

B. 5G SECURITY TRAINING

B1: 5G Security Training for Experts
Experts will be trained on defending to potential threats using the SPIDER platform both in team or self-paced scenarios. Also, blue and red team exercises will be implemented and tested as there is an educational gap in the already existing platforms.

B2: 5G Security Training for Non-Experts
In this scenario, non-experts in cybersecurity will be introduced to cutting edge 5G technologies and its evolving cybersecurity landscape. The goal of this use case is to validate the 5G security gamification solution in realistic scenarios and provide input to the exploitation of the solution aSter the end of the project.

C. CYBER INVESTMENT DECISION SUPPORT

The goal of this use case is to develop a decision support process integrated within the cyber range that can assist the relevant stakeholders to not only determining optimal investments to cybersecurity controls, but also in taking the necessary steps to implement them.

DECODER - DEveloper COmpanion for Documented and annotatEd code Reference

Miriam Gil, Fernando Pastor Ricos, Victoria Torres, and Tanja E. J. Vos[✉]

Universitat Politècnica de València, Valencia, Spain
{mgil,fpastor,vtorres,tvos}@pros.upv.es
http://www.decoder-project.eu

1 Summary of the Project

1.1 Objectives

The influence of software on our daily lives is continuously growing. Software is everywhere. Unfortunately, high quality software is not everywhere. Studies show that software failures exist and they have far-reaching implications in terms of money, safety and privacy. Hence, guaranteeing the quality of software throughout all the different development processes is increasingly important. However, in practice many things often go wrong during software development projects due to uninformed decisions being taken along the whole process. And these are not isolated cases, some already go as far as arguing that there are signs of a 'coming software apocalypse' [1]. Reasons for taking the wrong decisions during software development are: (1) the amount of information, and (2) the lack of proper documentation.

During a typical development process there are interactions of many stakeholders, at very different abstraction levels, and often over ambiguous and incomplete documents. This makes the integration and even more the maintenance of software systems extremely difficult and costly. The DECODER project proposes a solution to this problem having as its main objective:

Build a smart environment that could assist and help developers, analysts, reviewers and testers to improve the software development process.

The DECODER environment will give support to properly handle project knowledge derived from all different software development artefacts like: source code, specifications, informal documents, tests, etc. DECODER will provide a map through the software project intelligence fulfilling the need for instantaneous access to its documentation, abstract models, verification data and traceability matrix. This is needed to take better decisions.

This work has been developed with the financial support of the European Union's Horizon 2020 research and innovation programme under grant agreement No. 824231.

F. Dalpiaz et al. (Eds.): RCIS 2020, LNBIP 385, pp. 643–644, 2020.
https://doi.org/10.1007/978-3-030-50316-1

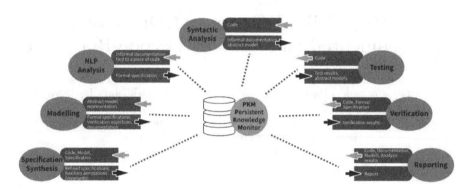

Fig. 1. The Persistent Knowledge Monitor and its surrounding tools

1.2 Expected Tangible Result

One of the core results of DECODER is the Persistent Knowledge Monitor (PKM). It will provide a "central" infrastructure to store, access, and trace all the persistent data, information and knowledge related to a given software or ecosystem. The rest of the project results are: tools for *feeding* the PKM with artefacts from different phases of the development lifecycle, tools for *querying* the PKM to obtain information to make the right decisions during different phases of the development lifecycle. The PKM will have a common communication schema to facilitate these interactions. This is depicted in Fig. 1.

2 Summary of Current Project Results

At the current status of the project, there is a first release of the PKM as a MongoDB together with a PKM API for queries, creating reports and management of users, access to artefacts or the traceability matrix. At the same time the tools for feeding and querying are being connected and different techniques are being researched for generating knowledge (see Fig. 1). A methodology has been defined for different stakeholders on how the PKM can be used to assist them in their responsibilities along the software development life-cycle. Stakeholders that are distinguished are: developers, reviewers, and maintainers. Their tasks, and the techniques they use, have been studied and the different artefacts have been mapped onto these. Finally, the pilot systems have been defined and research questions have been defined for the case studies that will evaluate the DECODER results.

Reference

1. Somers, J.: The coming software apocalypse. Atlantic **26** (2017). https://www.theatlantic.com/technology/archive/2017/09/saving-the-world-from-code/540393/

Eco/Logical Learning and Simulation Environments in Higher Education - ELSE

Christos Mettouris[1(✉)], Evangelia Vanezi[1], Alexandos Yeratziotis[1], Alba Graziano[2], and George A. Papadopoulos[1]

[1] Department of Computer Science, University of Cyprus, Nicosia, Cyprus
{mettour, evanez01, yeratziotis.alexandros, george}
@cs.ucy.ac.cy
http://www.elseproject.eu/else/
[2] Tuscia University, Viterbo, Italy
graziano@unitus.it

1 Summary of the Project

The ELSE project aims to design and disseminate a strategy and appropriate ICT tools to achieve the fundamental European goal of redesigning Higher Education, facilitating the application of Bologna principles across Europe [1, 2]. Two fundamental principles of Bologna remain unrealised: 1. Students continue to be peripheral to the process of knowledge co-construction; 2. the potential for true pedagogical innovation through new technologies that can enhance the learning experience is underexplored.

The ELSE project aims to design an innovative (ELSE) e-learning environment based on learner-centred pedagogies which can activate students' learning process through problem-solving, learning-by-doing, gamification, and digital information research. The Flipped Classroom paradigm is used where homework activities are moved from after the class to before the class, students have a first touch with the subject at home, and practice, extra material and questions are conducted later during the class. The project also aims to demonstrate to teachers that these opportunities can be realised through the application of Higher Order Thinking ICTs.

2 Summary of Current Project Results

The ELSE learning environment offers teachers with the opportunity to structure their courses using multiple Moodle activities, three of which are novel and offered by the ELSE project via three tools: EVOLI (https://evoli.altervista.org/), E-Core and E-Dash (currently not accessible online). EVOLI is a video-tagging tool that enables teachers to upload their own videos that students can access before class. Students can tag specific time points of the video to demonstrate their comprehension, which teachers may access and review. With E-Core teachers create their own game scenarios based on the course they teach. By their performance in playing the game, students demonstrate their comprehension of the specific subject. The E-Dash tool aims at harmonizing Moodle with the flipped classroom concept. Moodle needs to accommodate the innovative

© Springer Nature Switzerland AG 2020
F. Dalpiaz et al. (Eds.): RCIS 2020, LNBIP 385, pp. 645–646, 2020.
https://doi.org/10.1007/978-3-030-50316-1

activities that will be assigned to students for studying at home prior to the class. This requires the integration of new external flipped classroom tools via Moodle's LTI. With E-Core and EVOLI integrated into ELSE Moodle, teachers can provide students with links within each course's content, enabling them to use these tools. A teacher is allowed to combine the different tools within the same course and section. Consequently, students' learning data such as grades, progress and comments need to be retrieved from the external tools and stored in the Moodle course, in order for the teacher to have a complete image of the students' performance and needs. This has led to the need for the development of a comprehensive dashboard. The E-Dash tool thus offers combined and mixed learning data, including grades, comments, questions and more for each student. These data assist teachers to gain an overall picture of their students' performance, grades, and whether the students have tried the various activities or not. For a teacher, a board combining the data of all students of a specific course, and a separate personalized board for each student of the course are offered. For students, their learning data for each enrolled course are presented separately. All learning activities are categorized based on: (i) whether the activity is "mandatory", "optional" or "recommended", and (ii) whether the activity is used as "flipping", "during" (the class), or "after" (the class). By selecting an activity, teachers and students have access to a visual aggregated overview of the accomplishments, in different formats depending on the data produced by each activity/tool.

The ELSE e-learning environment was recently presented to teachers across Europe through a workshop. The aim was to collect initial feedback on design, functionality and usefulness of the tools. Regarding the E-Dash tool in particular, the feedback collection process included a large focus group session discussing aspects of the tool, and a user survey (i.e. questionnaire). The responses to the user survey (70 participants) suggest that the usefulness of the tool is evident. Due to space limitations, we will mention a few key points on the results related to visualisation of data, since this is a key aspect in monitoring and comprehending progress. Qualitative and quantitative feedback collected on this aspect further illustrate the tool's overall influence. We are currently in the process of improving this aspect by considering qualitative comments, such as: "improve visualisation", "need of an achievement bar for students", "data shown by the tool is not exhaustive" in alignment with quantitative results such as: 93% prefer mixed data (e.g. rubrics mixing quantitative and qualitative data) to better understand a student's progress in a course, and 78.6% prefer a combination of text and charts to view student data. Beyond the project scope alone, results and improvements on visualisation aspects will lead to contributions to the research, scholar and student communities in terms of designing more effective, useful and pleasing data visualisation for student self-monitoring and teacher monitoring of student progresses' within e-learning platforms.

References

Framework for the Qualifications of the European Higher Education Area (EHEA) including the Dublin descriptors (2005)

Recommendation 2008/C 111/01/CE of the European Parliament and Council of Europe, which introduces the European Qualifications Framework for lifelong learning (EQF) (2008)

IV4XR - Intelligent Verification/Validation for Extended Reality Based Systems

I. S. W. B. Prasetya[1], Rui Prada[2], Tanja E. J. Vos[3,4(✉)], Fitsum Kifetew[5],
Frank Dignum[6], Jason Lander[7], Jean-Yves Donnart[8],
Alexandre Kazmierowski[9], Joseph Davidson[10], and Fernando Pastor Ricos[3,4]

[1] Utrecht University, Utrecht, The Netherlands
[2] Inst. de Eng. de Sistemas e Computadores - Investigação e Desenv, Lisbon, Portugal
[3] Univ. Politecnica de Valencia, Valencia, Spain
tvos@dsic.upv.es
[4] Open University, Heerlen, The Netherlands
[5] Fondazione Bruno Kessler, Trento, Italy
[6] Umea University, Umeå, Sweden
[7] Gameware, Newmarket, UK
[8] Thales AVS, Paris, France
[9] Thales SIX GTS, Paris, France
[10] GoodAI, Prague, Czech Republic
http://www.iv4xr-project.eu

1 Summary of the Project

1.1 Challenges and Objectives

"Extended Reality" (XR) systems are advanced interactive systems such as Virtual Reality (VR) and Augmented Reality (AR) systems. They have emerged in various domains, ranging from entertainment, cultural heritage, to combat training and mission critical applications. As the complexity of these systems keeps increasing, testing is getting more complex too. Current toolsets do no propose XR testing technology beyond rudimentary record and replay tools that only work for simple test scenarios. The following challenges need to be addressed:

1. **Fine-grained interaction space**. XR systems more accurately reflect the real world, so they allow fine grained, almost continuous, interactions. Also, XR worlds are inhabited by independent and dynamic entities simulating the corresponding real world entities. They interact with the user as well as with each other, and often lead to emerging behavior. These result in an interaction space far larger than in traditional interactive digital products, and intractable by existing automated testing approaches.

2. **Assessing user experience (UX)**. High quality UX is very important for XR systems. If it is not smooth enough, is too boring, or too overwhelming, the users become unhappy, annoyed or can make mistakes. The latter is a serious concern for mission-critical XR applications. Since manually assessing the UX quality is very labour intensive, automation is needed. Unfortunately,

© Springer Nature Switzerland AG 2020
F. Dalpiaz et al. (Eds.): RCIS 2020, LNBIP 385, pp. 647–649, 2020.
https://doi.org/10.1007/978-3-030-50316-1

existing tools are too simplistic and lack deeper models of human emotion and cognitive capabilities to be able to judge the different emotional states that an interaction event might evoke on users. Moreover, they are not able to deal with the diversity of users nor are they able to judge the progression of the UX that is built up over time as users engage in long term interactions.

The IV4XR project aims *to build a novel verification and validation technology for XR systems based on techniques from AI to provide learning and reasoning over a virtual world.* The developed technology enables XR developers to deploy powerful test agents to automatically explore and test the correct parameters of their virtual worlds as they iteratively develop and refine them. In addition, user experience is an equally important aspect for all XR systems. We will therefore also develop socio-emotional AI to enable test agents to conduct automated assessment of the quality of user experience and parameterization by different demographic and socio economic types, such as male, female, young, and elderly.

1.2   Expected Tangible Result

1. A multi-agent framework to automate XR testing tasks featuring: reasoning agents, search algorithms to generate test coverage, automated UX assessment through a computational model of emotion, and automated learning AI. This will be provided open source.
2. A set of guidelines on how to integrate IV4XR framework and target XR systems. This will be supported by examples from the pilots that will be run during the project.
3. Studies assessing the effectiveness of the IV4XR technology.

2   Summary of Current Project Results

An initial version of the underlying multi-agent framework of IV4XR, called *Agent Programming Library* or aplib[1], has been released [1]. Aplib is inspired by the Belief-Desire-Intent(BDI) model of intelligent agents a la [2]. It features a novel layer of *tactical programming* that provides an abstract way for agent-programmers to exert imperative control on the underlying reasoning-based behavior of agents. as they search for solutions. So-called *tactics* can be defined to enable agents to strategically choose and prioritize their short term actions and plans, whereas longer term strategies are expressed as so-called *goal structure*, specifying how a goal can be realized by chosing, prioritizing, sequencing, or repeating a set of subgoals. A preliminary experiment on the viability of using this framework to automate testing tasks showed a promising result[2].

---

[1] https://iv4xr-project.github.io/aplib/.
[2] The experiment (using a configurable small 3D game) is available at https://github.com/iv4xr-project/iv4xrDemo.

References

1. Prasetya, I.S.W.B., Dastani, M., Prada, R., Vos, T.E.J., Dignum, F., Kifetew, F.: Aplib: tactical agents for testing computer games. In: To Appear in the Proceedings of the 8th International Workshop on Engineering Multi-Agent Systems (EMAS) (2020)
2. Rao, A.S.: AgentSpeak(L): BDI agents speak out in a logical computable language. In: Van de Velde, Walter, Perram, John W. (eds.) MAAMAW 1996. LNCS, vol. 1038, pp. 42–55. Springer, Heidelberg (1996). https://doi.org/10.1007/BFb0031845

Author Index

Abdennadher, Slim   529
Aho, Pekka   267, 637
Alarcón, Sofía   302
Aldhayan, Manal   157
Ali, Raian   157, 212
Amaral de Sousa, Victor   229
Andersson, Birger   129
Assar, Saïd   249
Astrova, Irina   503
Athanatos, Manos   640
Atigui, Faten   556, 630
Augenstein, Christoph   369
Azevedo, Bruno   38, 632

Bajec, Iztok Lebar   509
Bajec, Marko   509
Bampoulidis, Alexandros   515
Banerjee, Ansuman   191
Baptista, Ana Alice   38, 632
Bassiliades, Nick   58
Ben Kraiem, Ines   321
Bernard, Marc   522
Berntsson Svensson, Richard   3
Bider, Ilia   95
Biotteau, Maelle   455
Blatt, Jonas   536
Bouraga, Sarah   174
Branco, Pedro   632
Brignone, Angela   640
Bruni, Alessandro   515
Bürger, Jens   437
Burnay, Corentin   174, 635
Busch, Peter   562

Cakaloglu, Tolgahan   338
Camargo, Manuel   381
Cauz, Maxime   543
Chahim, Hatim   267
Chattopadhyay, Soumi   191
Chung, Lawrence   20
Clarinval, Antoine   229, 543

Condori Fernandez, Nelly   267
Corea, Carl   536
Costa, Cristina   640
Cyganek, Bogusław   490

Davidson, Joseph   647
de Boissezon, Xavier   455
Delfmann, Patrick   536
Demeyer, Serge   637
Deneckère, Rébecca   623
Deville, Guy   543
Dhaiouir, Samya   249
Dignum, Frank   647
Doan, Tu My   522
Donnart, Jean-Yves   647
Dumas, Bruno   543
Dumas, Marlon   381
Duran, Mehmet   267

El Bolock, Alia   529
El Rifai, Omar   455
Eldh, Sigrid   637
Elshaw, Radwa   627
Estrada-Torres, Bedilia   381

Fagbule, Omolola   585
Faulkner, Stéphane   174
Franch, Xavier   625
Franczyk, Bogdan   76, 369

Georgiadis, Apostolos   58
Gerosavva, Neofytos   640
Gharib, Mohamad   472
Ghering, Matthias   640
Ghosh, Rahul   191
Ghozzi, Faiza   321
Giachetti, Giovanni   302
Gil, Miriam   643
Giorgini, Paolo   472
Gounaris, Anastasios   58

Graziano, Alba   645
Gupta, Avantika   191

Hamdi, Fayçal   630
Hannou, Fatma-Zohra   630
Hasić, Faruk   536
Herbert, Cornelia   529

Ioannou, Constantinos   595

Jacquenet, Francois   522
Jain, Arpit   191
Janković, Marko   509
Jiang, Nan   212
Johannesson, Paul   129
Johng, Haan   20
Jugel, Dierk   145
Jureta, Ivan   174
Jürjens, Jan   437

Kapitsaki, Georgia M.   569
Kazmierowski, Alexandre   647
Kehrer, Timo   437
Kifetew, Fitsum   647
Kostova, Blagovesta   112
Kouzapas, Dimitrios   569

Lammari, Nadira   630
Lander, Jason   647
Largeron, Christine   522
Linden, Isabelle   543
Liotopoulos, Fotis   58
Lupu, Mihai   515

Ma, Jianbing   212
Malta, Mariana Curado   632
Marín, Beatriz   302
Markopoulos, Ioannis   515
McAlaney, John   157
Megdiche, Imen   455
Mettouris, Christos   645
Michailidou, Anna-Valentini   58
Mimouni, Nada   630
Möhring, Michael   145
Moretti, Gioele   285
Mozo, Alberto   640
Mudassir, Ghulam   604
Mylopoulos, John   472

Naiseh, Mohammad   157, 212, 613
Naumenko, Andrey   112
Nikolaidis, Nikodimos   58
Ntantogian, Christoforos   640

Oliveira e Sá, Jorge   38, 632

Pahikkala, Tapio   352
Papadopoulos, George A.   569, 645
Park, Grace   20
Park, Sooyong   20
Peninou, Andre   321
Philippou, Anna   569
Prada, Rui   647
Prasetya, I. S. W. B.   647

Rafiei, Majid   398
Ralyté, Jolita   623
Ravat, Franck   455
Regev, Gil   112
Ribeiro, Ana Carolina   38, 632
Ricos, Fernando Pastor   643, 647
Roman-Jimenez, Geoffrey   321
Ruiz, Marcela   285
Rychkova, Irina   112

Sakr, Sherif   627
Schmidt, Rainer   145
Schuster, Daniel   417
Seitaridis, Andreas   58
Serral, Estefanía   536, 576
Simonofski, Anthony   229
Si-Said Cherfi, Samira   556, 630
Smith, Stephen   562
Snoeck, Monique   302, 549, 576
Souibgui, Manel   556
Spielberger, Jürgen   285
Stead, Connor   562
Sugumaran, Vijayan   20
Supakkul, Sam   20
Szegedy, Christian   338

Taghavianfar, Maryam   3
Teste, Olivier   321, 455
Toliopoulos, Theodoros   58
Torres, Victoria   643

van der Aalst, Wil M. P.   398, 417
van der Bijl, Machiel   637